Sociology

Thurs Dec 20
1-3

4-6

Sociology

Social Structure and Social Conflict

Harold R. Kerbo

California Polytechnic State University

MACMILLAN PUBLISHING COMPANY

New York

FOR ELTON AND NINA

Copyright © 1989 by Macmillan Publishing Company,
a division of Macmillan, Inc.

PRINTED IN THE UNITED STATES OF AMERICA

Macmillan Publishing Company
866 Third Avenue, New York, New York 10022

Collier Macmillan Canada, Inc.

Library of Congress Cataloging-in-Publication Data
Kerbo, Harold R.
    Sociology: social structure and social conflict / Harold R.
  Kerbo.
        p.   cm.
    Includes index.
    1. Sociology.   I.   Title.
  HM51.K383   1989
  301—dc19   88-11764
  ISBN 0-02-362741-7   CIP

Printing: 2 3 4 5 6 7   Year: 9 0 1 2 3 4 5

At the end of the 1980s, it is clear that the world is in transition. The "American Century," which began its emergence in the late 1880s, is drawing to a close. Americans can no longer remain preoccupied with themselves and ignore the outside world as if this outside world were irrelevant to their own lives.

This changing world presents both a challenge and an opportunity for sociologists. In this text I have tried to confront the challenge by providing students with much more comparative information than is found in any other introduction to sociology. But I would like to emphasize the opportunity that is equally presented by the changing world. As I have visited and studied other societies I have become firmly convinced that we cannot adequately understand our own society without understanding something about social traditions different from our own. When studying other societies, we not only realize that things are not exactly the same the world over, but we are also stimulated to ask why they are not. And in asking why the behavior of people in other nations is as we find it, we can be led to question our own behavior with the same inquisitive attitude. This text contains the basic sociological concepts required in any sound sociology text: The difference is that these concepts are presented through extensive comparative examples.

A comparative perspective in sociology is almost always combined with a historical perspective. Indeed, the two are commonly said in the same breath — historical and comparative. I have given these two perspectives equal treatment. Beyond the chapters on basic concepts, every chapter will have a historical as well as a comparative section. For example, when examining race relations, class inequalities, the state, the economy, the family, and so on, we will see how these institutions and social arrangements existed in the past, how they were transformed up to the present, and how they exist in other societies.

I have a remaining note about the historical and comparative perspective of this text. Other texts usually mention comparative examples drawn from preindustrial societies. While comparative examples from preindustrial societies are useful, and they will be found in this text, an exclusive focus on such examples is misleading. Some fascinating and instructive comparisons come from France, Germany, the Soviet Union, and Japan, to name only a few. I have become especially curious about Japan and what we can learn through comparing Japanese and American societies. But, as one reviewer wrote, "By the end of the text students will have learned much about many types of societies."

I tend to favor a conflict perspective in the organization of this text; however, I emphasize that this conflict perspective is as nonideological as possible. I also believe that conflict theory, at least as it exists today, cannot explain every facet of the social world. Thus, a functional perspective and various social psychological perspectives are introduced as appropriate.

This text is divided into four parts. In Part I ("The Study of Human Societies"), the first two chapters present the basic concepts, the sociological perspective, and how we study societies. I have called Part II "The Foundations of Human Societies." The seven chapters in Part II examine basic foundations such as material and nonmaterial culture, social structure, population dynamics, socialization, social control, and social stratification. Then in Part III, I have included what I call the structural bases of inequality and conflict in human societies. The subjects of class and class conflict, race and ethnic stratification, and gender and age inequalities are, of course, obvious in their fit within Part III, as is the final chapter on group conflict and social change. I have also placed the economy and state in Part III to emphasize their impact on conflict and inequalities in human societies.

Finally, in Part IV ("Supporting Institutions"), I have included chapters on the family, religion, education, and science as "supporting institutions." The reader will find not only a functionalist treatment of these final subjects but also how these subjects can be understood from a conflict perspective.

As I sit here in my office writing this preface (the last words of this text I will write), I am trying to focus my thoughts on what I most wanted students to get out of my several years of work on this book. My obvious answer is that I hope students will gain a better understanding of the world around them, and the opportunities, frustrations, and problems presented by our social world. There are many practical and personal reasons each person can have for a better understanding of the human societies around the world. But we also have many common interests in a better understanding of the social world around us. While I favor a conflict perspective, this is not to say that I believe extensive and overt conflict must always be present. In fact, because it appears that conflict relations are deeply imbedded in the social world, we must understand this social world as much as possible in order to minimize the deadly and overt forms of conflict.

I am writing the final words of this book in Hiroshima, Japan where I am teaching for a year at Hiroshima University. In Hiroshima we live less than one mile from the "A-Bomb Dome"—the frame of a building destroyed along with more than 200,000 people in the first deadly use of nuclear weapons on August 6, 1945. This structure provides a sad symbol of why, especially today, we must learn how the underlying conflict nature of human societies must be better understood if we are to prevent more Hiroshimas and world destruction.

ACKNOWLEDGMENTS

In the long process of writing a book of this nature there are many people who give aid and sympathy to the author. I must thank my wife and daughters foremost for their understanding of the long time spent in writing this book. And again, Diane Goldman did an excellent job reading my writing and typing the manuscript, always understanding when I asked for her help on short notice. My colleagues at California Polytechnic State University have continued to provide a congenial atmosphere within which I have been able to work. Dick Shaffer, John Mckinstry, and Jim Coleman have been helpful in many ways. In a similar manner I want to thank the faculty and staff here at Hiroshima University, and especially Professor Nobuo Kawabe and Ms. Eiko Tsukamoto, for their help. In addition, I would also like to thank the following individuals who reviewed the manuscript: Thomas Feucht, Cleveland State University; John W. Fox, University of Northern Colorado; James D. Jones, East Texas State University; Kenneth J. Neubeck, University of Connecticut; Edward Ponczek, William Rainey Harper College; and Allan L. Wheeler, Morehead State University. And finally, my editor, Chris Cardone, as well as Janice Marie Johnson (production), Pat Gadban (development), and Christina Spellman and Sybille Millard (photo research) deserve thanks for their excellent work and help to an author living on the other side of the earth while this book was being completed.

                                          H.R.K.

Harold R. Kerbo is a professor of sociology at California Polytechnic State University at San Luis Obispo. During 1988 and 1989 he was also a Fulbright professor in the Division of Area Studies at Hiroshima University in Hiroshima, Japan. Professor Kerbo is also the author of *Social Stratification and Inequality: Class and Class Conflict in the United States* (McGraw-Hill, 1983) and numerous articles in sociology journals. In addition to his primary interest in social stratification, Professor Kerbo has done research and writing on the subjects of corporate power, social movements, and revolutions. In recent years he has been traveling in Japan and studying modern Japanese society from a comparative perspective as the first modern industrial society with a non-Western culture.

Brief Contents

Detailed Contents

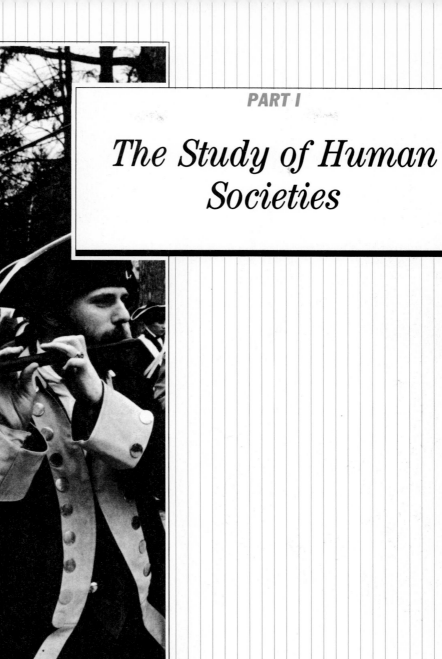

PART I

The Study of Human Societies

CHAPTER 1

The Nature of Humans and Human Society

3

The sociological imagination enables its possessor to understand the larger historical scene in terms of its meaning for the inner life and the external career of a variety of individuals. . . . The framework of modern society is sought. . . . Social science deals with problems of biography, of history, and of their intersections within social structures.
— C. Wright Mills, The Sociological Imagination

Books for introductory college courses usually begin with basic definitions, concepts, and the history of the discipline. They often tell you something about the discipline's old heroes and new accomplishments. And when there is no single dominant theoretical perspective in the discipline (which is the case in every social science today), then in the first or second chapter you are given a brief introduction to the major theories. I have found it necessary to do much the same in this book. Initially, however, the definitions and concepts are limited to the most basic. It is most important, I believe, to convince you of the seriousness and significance of the subject matter. Watching people and contemplating what they do can be highly interesting, even fun, and I hope you will find this the case. But with sociology we are also considering events that will have a major impact on your life and well-being.

Let's begin with two brief "stories" to give you an idea of the types of issues and questions considered throughout the coming chapters.

The first story involves the hopes and aspirations of a young Japanese-American girl we will call Karen Sato. Karen's great-grandparents came to California from Japan during the early 1900s. Despite extensive discrimination, Karen's great-grandparents, like many other Japanese immigrants to California, eventually developed a successful business. This eventually helped Karen's parents to move securely into the American middle class. As a "yonsei," or fourth-generation Japanese-American, Karen is as American as other girls her age with American ancestors. For the future, she wants to attend a good university and to establish herself in a profession or as a top manager.

As a middle-class girl in the United States during the 1980s, Karen has a reasonable chance of achieving these goals—a better chance than young women in America who were growing up in previous generations. We come to our first sociological

The diversity and informality of American society can be seen throughout its institutions, including the school. Compare the Japanese-American girl in this photo with the girl in the next photo. Can you imagine how their lives are different and how they are being taught to see the world? (© Elizabeth Crews/Stock, Boston)

question—why? What has happened to increase Karen's occupational life chances? Obviously, new equal rights laws have helped. But what made these laws possible? Another set of questions is related to Karen's Japanese-American heritage; although I have said that Karen is fully American, as is true of most other ethnic groups in America today, she has some lingering ethnic influences. One important characteristic of Japanese-Americans is their college attendance rate; over 60 percent of college-age Japanese-Americans attend college compared with about 50 percent for Americans of European ancestry. And this high rate of college attendance showed up soon after Japanese-Americans first came to this country in the early 1900s (Hirschman and Wong, 1986). Again, this presents an intriguing sociological question of the type we will consider again and again in the coming chapters.

Let's make these questions even more complex and I hope even more interesting with the second story. What about the other Sato family members who did not come to America in the early 1900s? Karen has a distant relative, Naoko Sato, who is a girl of Karen's age living in Tokyo today. Naoko's aspirations are very similar to Karen's, as are those of many young women in Japan today, but Naoko's life chances are quite different. As we will see in the coming chapters, Japan is an advanced industrial nation similar to the United States in many ways; but there are important differences, many pertaining to the status of women.

Though there is a relatively high rate of college attendance in Japan compared with other industrial nations, the chances for Japanese women are limited. Women make up about 45 percent of the student body in four-year colleges in the United States, but only about 22 percent in Japan. In the United States there are fewer women than men in the higher-status jobs in the professions and management, though the percentage of women in these positions is increasing. In Japan, however, the number of women in these highest-paying jobs is much lower. For example, women held about 28 percent of the administrative and managerial jobs in the United States during 1982; the figure for Japan was only 6 percent.

If Naoko's life is like that of other young women in Japan, she will probably work in a very low-paying

Some of the traditional influences of Japanese culture that will help to shape Naoko's life choices are visible in this visit to a ceremonial Japanese temple. Look closely at the differences in dress and gesture among the men and women. (© J. P. Laffont/Sygma)

office job until she marries, around the age of 25. At this time her boss is likely to pressure Naoko to leave her job to become a full-time homemaker.

Again we have many questions. Are Naoko's life chances different from Karen's "simply" because Japan is an Asian country with very different values and traditions compared with Western industrial nations? Naoko's life chances are certainly affected by these Asian traditions, but we must also ask *why* these traditions are different. However, many other important factors affect Naoko's life chances in Japan that are not simply attributable to Asian cultures. Just a relatively short distance across the East China Sea, women in the People's Republic of China make up 49 percent of the four-year college students.

Questions about the life chances of Karen and her distant relative Naoko are of the type we will ask in coming chapters. Our goal is to understand the basic features of our own society; to do so we will also examine American history and the basic nature of other societies such as Japan's. Too often in the past, American sociologists have isolated themselves within national borders and missed the opportunity for understanding American society more fully by also understanding other societies. Before we take up this task, however, let's consider one other set of questions to show the importance of our subject.

Recent figures on economic growth, productivity, and the balance of trade indicate that the United States has lost some (if not much) of its economic superiority in the world system. Many products are now produced more cheaply and efficiently in countries like Japan, Taiwan, South Korea, and West Germany. Many "smokestack" industries in the United States are turning to "rust bowls." Millions of jobs have been lost for U.S. workers, and many more are threatened.

Will the United States follow the pattern of relative economic decline like that of Holland and Great Britain, which were once leading industrial nations? And if it does, must the U.S. economic position in the world economy fall as far and as fast?

Whatever the outcome, it is clear that new industrial technology will produce big changes in the workplace and in job opportunities. In the past there was fear that new production technologies would advance so rapidly that workers would be displaced. Now, there is an additional fear that even more jobs will be lost to other nations if these new technologies do not develop rapidly enough in the United States.

The situation described for the U.S. economy may be overly pessimistic. I hope it is. But it is a possibility. If so, what is to be done? Surely we would suggest something can be done if we fully understand what is happening in the world and in our own nation. An examination of history, however, tells us that knowledge does not always result in action to prevent war or economic decline. The Dutch and the British no doubt knew they were in decline in previous centuries, but internal conflicts and disagreements prevented effective solutions. The major industrial powers knew they were drifting toward World War II in the 1930s, but miscalculations and disagreements prevented a stop to this drift (see Mosley, 1969).

Humans do have the ability to influence world events for the better. It is true that humans make history. But as one early sociologist, Karl Marx, pointed out, it is also true that humans do not always make history as they wish. This means that historical trends are not intentionally made by humans, but if humans recognize the opportunities presented by historical change, then they can make history. It is also important to recognize that solutions to many issues we face today may not exist. Or, more likely, some solutions to many issues may not be pursued because they are not acceptable to the more influential among us. Still, I believe we can assume that knowledge is preferable to ignorance. And to understand and perhaps act on the major issues of our age requires knowledge of human societies. It is the nature and patterns of interaction within human societies that most influence the major trends that affect your life. I am offering you what I believe is the best that sociology has to offer in understanding the nature of human societies. When you complete a serious study of this text, I believe you will be better able to understand the world around you and how this social world shapes your life and life chances.

In this chapter we consider the unique perspective taken by sociology and its value for understanding such forces as economic growth and decline, human conflict, and your life chances. We then examine some key questions pertaining to the basic nature of humans and human societies. Finally, I outline some divergent perspectives among social scientists and describe the basic perspective followed in this text.

THE SOCIOLOGICAL PERSPECTIVE

Because of its central importance in our subject matter, we must begin with a simple definition of human societies. The human part is obvious; our subject is societies made up of human rather than nonhuman organisms. **Society** refers to (a) habitually interacting groups of humans with (b) a common culture, (c) a common territory, and (d) relative autonomy. By referring to *habitually interacting* humans, we exclude groups of people who have not formed common, lasting patterns of behavior. If placed on a previously uninhabited island a collection of people from all over the world would not instantly constitute a society. This does not mean that all individuals within the society must interact with everyone else. It simply means that enough of them must do so to form lasting patterns of interaction. The requirement of a *common culture* further limits society to a group of people with some shared understandings. The most fundamental type of shared understanding is language. As we will see, however, many other common understandings must develop if social interaction is to be possible. Finally, by a *common territory* and *relative autonomy* we mean a group of people occupying a common geographical area with little control from an outside group or a group on a higher level.

This definition of human societies thus includes American society, British society, Soviet society, and so on. It excludes subgroups within a society like college students, Republican Party members, and the National Association of Manufacturers. These groups within a society do not alone constitute a society. They are not relatively autonomous but part of a broader collective. The requirement of "relative" autonomy, however, is stressed because many societies do experience some outside domination. For example, we recognize that Poland is dominated by the Soviet Union, and in many ways Chile is dominated by the United States. But unless this domination is perceived as complete, we can still refer to separate societies. In contrast, we can say that Alaska and Wales no longer form separate societies but are a part of the United States and Great Britain, respectively.

With our definition of human societies, we can now define **sociology** as the scientific study of human societies and human behavior in groups. We will say more about "scientific" study below, but it is useful to further specify "human behavior in groups." Sociology is not the study of individuals or individual behavior. Sociologists may consider individual behavior, but when doing so the focus is how this individual behavior is shaped by groups. A basic assumption of sociology is that human groups are more than a collection of individuals. When individuals interact over sustained periods of time, the group will develop characteristics of its own — that is, characteristics independent of individual group members. These group characteristics take on a life of their own (in a sense) and come to shape human behavior. We no longer have a mere collection of individuals but a group with rules, differing roles for members of the group, and much more. This idea will be expanded further, but the point to remember now is that the primary subject of sociology is group rather than individual behavior.

It should now be evident that the subject matter of sociology is rather broad. Because humans are extremely social animals, existing almost everywhere in groups, our subject matter includes just about everything people do. The broad nature of the subject matter of sociology is both a strength and weakness. The subject is so broad that few if any sociologists can master it all. Sociologists tend to specialize in a few subject areas — such as the family, crime and deviance, social inequality, or social change.

The broad nature of our subject matter, however, also provides some very important benefits. In contrast to more specialized disciplines like political science or economics, sociology brings a broader perspective to the study of the specific aspects of human behavior. Put another way, sociology attempts to build a general understanding of group behavior that can be applied to many aspects and areas of group behavior. Sociology's broad perspective also encourages a focus on the interrelations among diverse areas of human societies. For example, rather than studying the economy in relative isolation, sociologists are more likely to study the relations among politics, class conflicts, and the economy.

In reference to the economic and cultural issues discussed in beginning this chapter, economists of course can help us understand the U.S. economic position in the world system. Political scientists can help us understand internal and external political conflicts. Economists and political scientists do not always view their specific subject matter in isolation, but sociologists more consistently attempt to bring a wider perspective on human groups to the study of specific subjects such as economic issues. For example, we might ask how changes in the family system, the schools, and the state in the twentieth century have influenced the American economic position in the world today. The result of this wider perspective, I hope you will come to agree, is a valuable and unique understanding of human societies and major issues of today.

How Sociologists Study Societies

Two fundamental questions about the nature of sociology remain for this beginning discussion. The first asks, "How do sociologists study human societies?" The second asks, "Where do sociologists look in studying human societies?" Human behavior can be examined at different levels. The lowest level, we might say, is biological — behavior shaped by human genes. From the lowest level we can move to higher levels of generality, from small groups to the most general level of the total society. This second question pertains to the level of analysis sociologists find most fruitful in answering important questions about human societies. We begin with the question of how sociologists study human societies and save the second question for later.

Everyone, in a sense, is an amateur sociologist. We all observe human behavior. We are all interested in what people do, and why they do it. We talk about the people we know, their problems, their fortunes and misfortunes. We imagine how we would feel and what we would do in their situation. Above all, we judge people. Is this or that behavior good, bad, or simply acceptable? How should people have acted in a particular situation?

As we will see in more detail later, humans are unique in the extent to which they can reflect on themselves and others. Humans are able to reason, to think in abstract terms, to reflect on the future. A meaningless, unpredictable world is an insecure world. We do not like extensive insecurity. When it comes to human behavior we infer meaning and motives to make the behavior understandable. What all this means is that people develop "quasi theories" of human behavior, that is, theories that are not developed in an objective, scientific manner (see Hewitt and Hall, 1973). When doing so, people believe they know why humans do the things they do.

Let's consider an example. In the United States people have been concerned with the increasing amount of crime for several years. The extent of crime bothers us; we ourselves could be victims. But it also bothers us that people behave in such ways. Why can such things happen? We develop quasi theories. We remain concerned about the high crime rate, but we now believe we understand it: our criminal justice system is inadequate; people have grown selfish and inconsiderate as our moral values weaken from the influence of liberal ideas; too many people are on drugs. These explanations suggest possible solutions. Strengthen the courts; put more people in jail as examples to other lawbreakers. There is now hope that the problem of crime can be solved if only we act on these solutions. Again, the world is no longer meaningless nor quite so threatening.

These quasi theories therefore serve a very important function for us. *But how accurate are they?* How effective will the suggested solutions be? These questions must be answered with respect to how people normally go about developing or attaining their quasi theories of human behavior. For several reasons we seldom develop these quasi theories objectively.

First, our everyday world, our location in society, our experiences shape what we see and how we think. We view society and human behavior from the limited focus of the familiar. We may not understand others' options, or how their social situation has led to different behavior. In short, we usually judge what others do as if they were in positions similar to our own. As to the example of crime and punishment, if we are in a relatively comfortable position in society, if we have sufficient material rewards and self-respect, the loss of all this for a prison term would appear a strong deterrent to criminal behavior. We may easily overlook the possibility that people with less to lose may not find the prospect of prison so frightening.

Second, our quasi theories may not be accurate because we have vested interests in explaining the world in certain ways. It is always nice if what we believe furthers our material interests and social position. It is always easy to believe what we believe is best for us. For example, consider two opposing explanations of crime. One suggests that the causes of crime are related to some fundamental aspect of our society. To significantly reduce crime we must therefore change some characteristics of our society we do not want changed (such as individual freedoms or a highly unequal distribution of valued goods). Another explanation of crime focuses on the "criminal personality" and how to force criminals to conform through more punishment. It may cost us a bit more for prisons and more police, but the cost can be spread among many people. Which explanation of crime will most of us favor? Most likely it will be the second one to avoid being negatively affected by the needed social change.

Third, we will see that a fundamental characteristic of a society is a common culture. Over time, people in the same society tend to view the world in the same way, developing common assumptions about human behavior. These cultural assumptions are not necessarily right or wrong. Like quasi theories, these common cultural assumptions about human behavior have developed in response to the historical experiences and interests of most people in the society. These cultural assumptions may not be the most accurate guides to objective reality any longer, if they ever were. But they heavily influence our quasi theories of human societies and human behavior.

How, then, does sociology differ from what most people do when developing their quasi theories of human behavior? Most important, *sociology differs in the manner by which information is attained and evaluated.* As much as possible sociologists employ scientific methods in gathering the information necessary in building, amending, or rejecting their theories of human societies and human behavior.

The Nature of Science. People often think of science as a body of knowledge — physics, biology, astronomy. Most accurately, however, **science** can be defined as an objective method of gaining and evaluating information. And more than simply a set of specific tools or procedures for gaining objective information, science is fundamentally an attitude or orientation. Above all, a scientist is a skeptic, a cautious observer of the world. Nothing is accepted on faith alone but is critically examined and questioned. The goal is to gain the most objective information possible, information not shaped by our self-interests and prejudices. But science does not end with theory or a body of accumulated information. Rather, science is a continuing process of skepticism. The theories and information attained are continually reevaluated and tested. There is a fundamental difference between science and dogma. The scientist does not begin *or* end with the attitude that "this explanation is correct, now I must gather information to show others it is correct." Scientists keep an open mind, allowing new information to change their own mind about the explanation.

The true scientist will realize that I have just presented an idealized view of science. Scientists are human; they become attached to their theories and sometimes find it difficult to reject them when the evidence suggests they should. But our increase in knowledge over the past century or so has come because scientists have remained closer to this idealized view of science than people normally do.

Where Sociologists Look

Our second basic introductory question pertains to where sociologists look in attempting to explain the nature of human societies and human behavior. Given a particular social phenomenon we would like to understand, say, the increase in crime in the United States, where do we begin our search for answers? We could examine the relationship between crime and the movement of the stars and planets. We might try to correlate climate changes with crime rates. Or we might consider how some supernatural force like the ghosts of our ancestors influence crime. All these "explanations" about the causes of human events have been considered at some point in history. Some followers of astrology continue to believe there is a relationship between the stars and planets and human behavior. (I am sorry to inform astrology fans that tests of predictions by astrology have shown them to be worthless.)

In modern societies people have tended to focus on one of three levels in attempting to explain what people do. The first level pertains to biology — genetics and our biological heritage. The second level pertains to individual psychology and psycho-

---

BOX 1.1

Biological Explanations of Human Behavior: A Caution

Throughout the history of human societies biological explanations of human behavior have been about as popular as religious explanations. Observing nature and noticing that different breeds of animals had behavioral differences no doubt led our ancestors to the idea that behavioral differences in humans could be traced to biology. From that idea it is an easy step to conclude that one's own group, class, race, or sex is "biologically superior." The next step is to conclude that discrimination is right and proper because of biological differences.

Everyone is familiar with early U.S. racial views based on biology. But these early views have not been totally eliminated, and in fact they may be on the rise again. As recently as 1961, for example, a book maintaining that blacks are innately inferior was made required reading by the Louisiana State Board of Education (Simpson and Yinger, 1965, p. 28). Even more recently a "best selling" author favored by the Reagan administration has stressed that males are biologically superior to females in the workplace. Quite simply, Gilder (1981, p. 135) believes that "it is the greater aggressiveness of men, biologically determined but statistically incalculable, that accounts for much of their earnings superiority." From this idea Gilder suggests that part of the U.S. economic problem in recent years is related to an increase in the number of females in the labor force. Because of less aggressiveness in their genes, women are said to be less productive workers. This belief, of course, ignores the fact that our great economic output during World War II was made possible by a big increase in women in the labor force. And it also ignores the fact that many other nations are doing well economically with a high percentage of women in the labor force.

The history of social science has not been without theories suggesting the biological inferiority of one group or another. Most, however, were soundly refuted by anthropologist Franz Boas in the 1930s. Recent sociobiologists continue this rejection of ideas suggesting the biological inferiority or superiority of one group of humans or another. Pierre van den Berghe is most explicit on this point: "A serious examination of the biological parameters of human behavior constitutes the best antidote to racism; it clearly demonstrates the unity of the human species and the remarkable uniformity of basic forms of human behavior throughout the species" (1978, p. 21). In other words, to the extent that there are biological influences on human behavior, sociobiologists stress that these influences are common to all races.

logical development. The third level pertains to social structure and group organization. We consider each of these in turn before making the case for the primary importance of social structure in helping us answer the most important questions about human societies.

Human Biology. Humans are biological organisms. We are born; we must die; we must eat, breathe, and (at least some of us) reproduce. These characteristics we share with all biological organisms (at least on this planet). To what extent does this biological base shape and set limits on what we do? If human biology tells us no more than that people must eat, sleep, reproduce, and so on, then it will not be of much help in understanding most human activities. There is evidence that this biological base helps us understand some important aspects about human behavior, but the value of biological explanations of human behavior is a matter of debate.

In the very old "nature versus nurture" debate, sociologists have long favored the nurture side of the argument. What humans do has been explained by social environment, learning, tradition, culture. From this perspective humans are considered to enter this world as a *tabula rasa* — a blank page to be filled in by their environment. In this respect, it is believed, humans are fundamentally different from other animals, which are more captives of their genetic heritage. From this perspective we also find a more optimistic view of the human condition. If the nasty side of humans (war, crime, greed) is due to environment, then a change in environment can eliminate such nastiness.

Reacting to many social scientists' neglect of our biological heritage, a countermovement has recently developed. There is now an expanding new field called **sociobiology.** Sociobiologists reject the extreme position that humans are far different from other animals, especially our closest animal relatives. Evolution is the key to our discussion of sociobiology and the biological base of human behavior.

As first described by Charles Darwin, there is a slow process of biological evolution based on **natural selection.** The species most adapted and therefore best equipped to survive in their particular

niche in the environment pass their genes to the next generation. Those not so well adapted may not survive; this also means their genes may not survive. Over a period of about 3 billion years life has been evolving on earth. During this time of continual environmental change, random biological change resulted in some new species better able to survive, while many species became extinct. It is estimated that there may be 1,000 extinct species for every one species living today (Pfeiffer, 1977, p. 36).

Humans evolved very late in this 3-billion-year time period, with *Homo sapiens* appearing only about 500,000 years ago, and *Homo sapiens sapiens* about 40,000 years ago. But there were human-like animals called hominids much earlier, perhaps as early as 3 million years ago. We find evidence of stone tools dating back to 2.5 million years, and the use of fire about 1.3 million years ago.

A primary point of sociobiology is that to understand human behavior today, we must understand the earliest human environment. It was this early environment that shaped our biological heritage through the process of natural selection. Humans have lived in more or less settled communities with agriculture for less than 10,000 years, and in industrial societies for only 200 to 300 years. Thus, our genetic heritage was established during the hundreds of thousands of years that humans and human ancestors lived hunting and gathering existences.

As a new science, sociobiology has yet to establish many clearly accepted explanations of human behavior. And many sociobiologists have been accused of going far beyond the evidence with many of their claims. In what follows, however, we can consider some of the less controversial claims about some fundamental aspects of humans.

1. Selfishness. Are humans primarily selfish? By "selfish" we mean that humans are most concerned with their own welfare and survival — they seek to maximize their rewards and minimize pain. The response of sociobiologists to this question is a qualified yes. Without selfishness natural selection could not operate. Combined with an urge to mate and reproduce, selfishness assures that a certain set of genes is passed down from one generation to the next. If humans were not selfish they would have been less likely to survive the competition for food with other animals. In general, "animals that behave selfishly tend to have more offspring, and therefore, the genes that predispose toward selfish behavior will tend to increase their portion in succeeding generations" (van den Berghe, 1978, p. 46). But sociobiologists qualify their argument that humans are by nature selfish. I explain this qualification more fully below.

2. Conflict. Do humans have a strong biological tendency toward conflict with other humans? In many ways this question is the same as the preceding. Selfishness would most likely produce conflict over valued goods, especially if there is a scarcity of them. Again, sociobiologists agree that humans have a strong tendency for both individual and group conflict. But as we will see, this view that humans are prone to conflict is qualified. And we must also stress that conflict should not be equated with violence against other humans.

3. Cooperation and sharing. Do humans have a biological tendency for cooperation and sharing (even altruism) with other humans? Now come the qualifications. In many respects cooperation and sharing are the opposites of selfishness and conflict. And sociobiologists agree that humans do have a biological tendency for cooperation and sharing. In fact, humans are unique among the more complex animals in cooperation and sharing. No other animals share food with their own kind to the extent humans do (Leakey and Lewin, 1978, p. 133). And the extent to which humans have been willing to sacrifice their own lives for others (in ritual sacrifice and war) is unique (van den Berghe, 1978, p. 39). But there is another side to human cooperation when combined with selfishness and conflict. Humans are said to be unique in the degree to which they cooperate to exploit and dominate other humans (van den Berghe, 1978, p. 143).

The seeming contradiction between the biological drives for both selfishness and sharing is explained by sociobiologists in two ways. First, survival in natural selection refers to survival of genes, not particular individuals. This assures the survival of a species. The survival of genes at times requires sacrifice for kin, especially offspring. If this drive to sacrifice for kin did not exist, particular individuals might live longer, but their children might not. Thus, the gene pool would not survive. This tendency for sacrifice can be extended to close relations, whether kin or nonkin.

Second, as humans found they had to compete for food with other animals that were swifter and stronger than they, cooperation became necessary. As one anthropologist writes of early humans, "They would have soon become extinct if they had not observed and anticipated the movements of prey together, and together planned appropriate strategies" (Pfeiffer, 1977, p. 48). And such cooperation in hunting most likely led to sharing of food. At least in a small group (as all hunting and gathering bands must be), what is attained collectively must be shared. If it is not, the cooperative effort would cease and all would eventually starve. Again, natural selection seems to have worked against uncooperative humans.

4. Intelligence. Finally we must stress the most important biological foundation of human behavior —unique intelligence. It is estimated that about 99 percent of the genetic material of humans is similar to that of chimpanzees (Washburn, 1978). But the key difference is found in the brain. Throughout the evolution of our human ancestors there were small but very important changes in skull shape and size, indicating changes in parts of the brain. Most important for modern humans is the large size of the parts of the brain devoted to creativity, imagination, and speech.

The four biologically based characteristics of humans described above are among the most important. Sociobiologists, however, describe many others that are more controversial. For example, sex-linked differences in humans may affect behavior. But some behavior differences like male aggressiveness can be overstressed. And to the degree that size and strength differences between males and females have been important, they are less important in modern industrial societies.

Sociobiology evaluated. It is time to assess the value of biological explanations of human behavior. How much of what we do can be explained by biology? Humans are biological organisms, but when we consider most of the things humans do, the answer to this question must be "not much."

Consider the sheer variety of human behavior. Human behavior differs so widely around the world that strict biological explanations alone would force us to conclude we are looking at many different animal species, not just one. Such explanations would also force us to conclude that these many animal species can change their biological heritage by changing societies! For example, how could a strict biological explanation of human violence explain the *much* higher violent crime rate in the United States when a majority of its population have ancestors from industrial societies that today have less violent crime than the United States? (See Figure 1.1.) Was there a tendency for people with genes that cause violent behavior to come to this country, so that a less violent gene pool remained in Britain, France, Germany, Poland, and China? I certainly doubt it.

In attempting to understand human behavior and human societies, however, our biological heritage

FIGURE 1.1. Comparative homicide rates. Rate per 100,000 population means that for every 100,000 people in the society, there were so many homicides in a given year. This method allows us to compare nations with different population sizes. *(Source: U.S. Bureau of Census, Social Indicators III, 1980, p. 252.)*

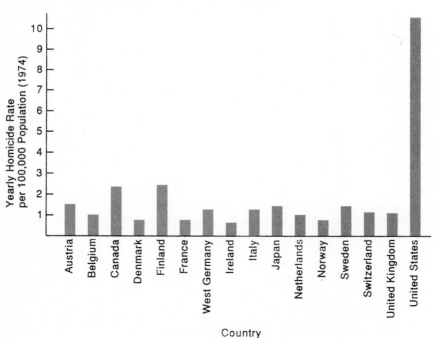

must not be forgotten. Sociobiologists have provided a few valuable insights. Three are particularly useful.

1. Humans have the capacity to be both selfish and unselfish. This leads to both conflict and cooperation. But as we will see, the exact combination of conflict and cooperation differs greatly, depending on factors other than human biology.
2. Humans have a much greater brain capacity than other animals. Many other differences follow from increased brain capacity: self-awareness; a concept of the future and, therefore, concern for security; the use of symbols, which lead to diverse outcomes like language and status competition; and most important, culture. With this biological potential for culture we can begin to understand the diversity in cooperation, conflict, technology, and beliefs that exist around the world.
3. Humans are social animals. Perhaps because of our longer infant dependency and the necessity of cooperation among early humans, we need and seek out other humans. This tendency to be social has affected our ability to create and use culture as well as the level of group conflict among humans. War is one of the most social and cooperative human endeavors. And the level of warfare in recent human history is unique in the animal world.

The Individual Level of Analysis. No other animal is close to humans in ability to reason, to think in abstract terms, and to understand the long-run consequences of behavior. No other animal develops an elaborate self-concept and orients its behavior with respect to this self-concept. And although there may be motives behind the behavior of other animals, these motives are far simpler than those of humans.

Consider a bear in the forest. This bear, no doubt, seeks food, a warm place to sleep, reproductive activity, but little else. If there is a stream nearby with easily accessible fish, plenty of unoccupied caves, and available mates, what else is there? The bear has no concern about future food shortages due to over-population, or the growing logging industry. The bear has no concern about the type of cave available.

Nor does this bear wonder whether "a bear such as I should be seen in a cave like this."

In contrast, consider the average human in modern society. This person's concept of self is important in determining the proper food (how and where it is eaten) and the proper shelter (style, size, location), among many other things. Equally important, in contrast to our hypothetical bear, this human constructs a mental image of the world. Humans seek understanding of the natural and social forces that govern the world. Security and self-interest require this. We want to know what makes things work so we can make them work to our advantage.

It is obvious that self-concepts and world views differ among humans. Thus, if these differing self-concepts and world views direct human behavior, a person interested in understanding human behavior and human societies may want to start here — that is, with individual motives and understandings that underlie social action.

Let's turn to some examples. We know that in some societies people have more children than in others. We also know that groups within a particular society differ with respect to the number of children they have. Why? This seems the proper question for a sociologist. We can establish a research project and interview people who have large families and small families. What will we find? Let's say we find that women with more children are more likely to agree that "women were put on this earth to have children, so the more, the better." We have found that differences in attitudes about the role of women and childbirth lead some women to have more children than others. Human behavior has been "grounded" (that is, located) in individual meanings and motives.

What about crime? Why do some people commit crimes while others do not? We could begin by interviewing a number of people who have committed crimes and a number of people who have not committed crimes. We could ask them questions about such things as their respect for the law, their concern for other people's well-being, and their attitudes toward work. Let's assume we find that criminals have less respect for the law and value hard work less than others. Let's also assume we find that criminals are often concerned about the welfare of others, but "know" that rich insurance companies will cover the damages suffered by their victims. Again, we have found that human behavior is guided by individual meanings and motives.

Before proceeding we must analyze what we have learned about family size and crime. Both imaginary studies present us with the same generalization: "People have values which tell them what they want . . . so, *people do things because they want to.* That is the explanation of their behavior" (Mayhew, 1980, p. 353). Many people, of course, do things they do not want to do. But as a generalization about the causes of human behavior, few would disagree with the "explanation" above. And few would disagree that this "explanation" is almost (if not totally) *worthless.* However, most people, most of the time, use similar individualistic explanations of human behavior.

We can take our analysis a bit further to see the difficulties. Let's assume we encounter significant change in family size and the crime rate. Women are having fewer children and many more criminals are found in the population. How can our "explanation" above help us? We can say that fewer women want large families and more people have no respect for the law. But why? Are more people now born with genes driving them toward smaller families and crime? With respect to crime, we could suggest that because neglected children are more crime-prone, there must be an increase in inadequate parents. But again, why?

I hope the point has been made. Our individualistic "explanations" of family size and crime are not really explanations at all. Neither tell us much about the real drop in the birth rate during the early 1970s or the rapid rise in the crime rate during the 1960s and 1970s. Most people, though, rely on these types of explanations.

None of this is to suggest that psychology has no value. Of course people have different personalities, inner conflicts, and behavioral tendencies. The reasons for these are found in differences in childhood socialization, security, caring parents, along with many other conditions.

Sociology, however, asks different questions. We want to know something about groups, group properties, group trends. Sociology, remember, is the study of human societies and human behavior in groups. Psychology may seem more relevant to our personal lives, fears, or emotions, but sociology approaches the larger issues that ultimately affect the lives, fears, and emotions of many people. The broader sociological perspective requires us to understand social structure and group properties.

Social Structure and Sociological Level of Analysis. Figure 1.2a represents the types of individualistic levels of analysis. By itself such an analysis is of little value in explaining group tendencies like crime rates, birth rates, unemployment rates, war hysteria, an increase in religious cults, to name only a few sociological-level questions. Figure 1.2b describes the sociological level of analysis.

Sociologists, however, are frequently interested in what we may call social psychology. A *sociological* social psychology will resemble the analysis outlined in Figure 1.2c. Sociologists are often concerned with the effects of social structure or groups on the individual, and then on how these individuals add up to societal-level characteristics or trends. For example, we may want to understand the development of large religious movements or religious cults. Individual psychology is, of course, involved; the people joining the new religious cults find "more meaning in their lives," "inner peace," or some other pleasing

FIGURE 1.2. Individual and structural levels of analysis.

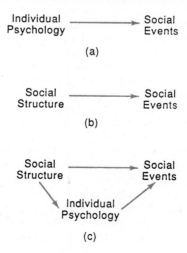

Different levels of analysis can be made of the same event. Consider the rodeo. In this photo the crowd (the group) is watching the spectacle of the rider (the individual) being thrown. They are participating in a collective activity of which he is a part. He is engaging in an individual pursuit which requires an audience. Would you gain different information by studying this event from these two perspectives? What if you added the perspective of the place of the rodeo in American Society? (© Polly Brown/Archive Pictures)

people assume that the study of suicide must be in the hands of psychologists and psychiatrists, but Durkheim began by focusing on differing *group rates* of suicide: that is, all groups may have some members who commit suicide. However, some groups like different religious groups, have much higher rates of suicide; put another way, a greater percentage of people in some groups commit suicide. Thus, suicide rates are group properties that must be studied from a sociological perspective.

Table 1.1 presents recent data on the differing rates of suicide among selected nations including the United States. The fascinating sociological question is why do these rates differ? Compared with murder rate data we have an even more intriguing question.

The rodeo is a complexly organized division of labor which includes support from corporate advertisers and an aesthetic of dress for the cowboys. The sociologist looks for these types of details to see whether they are regular (or normative) and how they change from one social scene to another. Seen together, these photos also illustrate what dramaturgical theorist Goffman refers to as the front-stage (the crowd watching the performance) and the backstage (the organization of work) of a social performance. (© Polly Brown/Archive Pictures)

psychological state. But we must move to the sociological level of analysis to understand why at one point in time many people have come to define themselves as seekers of the psychological state that religious movements seem to offer. Put another way, we must ask what common problems or experiences the *society* has presented these people that have led them to join a religious cult.

Before further defining our major concepts (such as social structure) it will be helpful to consider a couple of classic examples of our subject matter and a sociological level of analysis. An early sociological master, Émile Durkheim, has given us one of the best examples. In the late 1800s Durkheim studied a subject seemingly far removed from a sociological level of analysis — suicide. What can sociology tell us about such a personal and individual act? Most

BOX 1.2

Anorexia Nervosa and Bulimia: The Effects of Social Forces

The eating disorders anorexia nervosa and bulimia provide us with two other examples of the effects of social forces. Much like suicide, these two eating disorders are clearly rooted in individual psychological problems. But also like suicide, we can examine the characteristics of the society that help produce or inhibit these psychological problems. As Durkheim showed with the case of suicide, there are "social forces" in a society (or subgroup within that society) that broadly influence the behavior of individuals. Thus, like suicide, these eating disorders can be studied from a sociological perspective.

Anorexia nervosa is an eating disorder in which individuals so fear obesity that they literally starve themselves to death.* Bulimia is a similar eating disorder that involves eating binges followed by purging with self-induced vomiting (or sometimes heavy use of laxatives). These eating disorders have apparently been increasing rapidly in recent years, but they do not affect all groups in our society equally. Anorexia nervosa and bulimia seem to be found primarily among young (teens and early twenties) white women from relatively affluent families. Various studies estimate that somewhere between 5 and 10 percent of young affluent women in our society are afflicted with one of these disorders. One survey of the student population of a liberal arts college estimated as many as 19 percent of the female students were afflicted with bulimia to some degree. The seriousness of these eating disorders is reflected by the estimate that 10 percent of those afflicted with anorexia die, as in the case of the singer Karen Carpenter.

How can a sociological perspective help us understand these eating disorders? The information on who is most affected suggests that we must look to the social forces that particularly influence young women in our society. For example, we need to examine the social role of women and the pressure to conform to society's image of female beauty. But if this female role has stressed physical beauty for many generations, why the apparent increase in anorexia and bulimia, with some young women walking around like victims of Nazi concentration camps? The cultural ideal of physical beauty for women in our society seems to be changing. The more plump ideal of Jane Russell or

Denmark has one of the lowest murder rates but one of the highest suicide rates. The United States, by contrast, has the highest murder rate but a relatively low suicide rate. In short, Americans tend to kill themselves less but kill others much more. Why? This is a sociological question. We *must* look toward societal characteristics, not just individual psychology.

The sociological level of analysis: conclusion. It is time to conclude our answer to the question "Where do sociologists look?" in understanding human socie-

ties and human behavior. We have found that something can be learned from human biology. Humans have biological needs and a biological base that helps shape human behavior. It is highly doubtful that a particular gene for selfishness, altruism, or any other specific kind of behavior will ever be shown to exist. Nonetheless, there seems to be real human potential for these general behavior orientations. And most important, humans have a unique brain capacity; this brain capacity accounts for the great variety and complexity of human behavior found in human societies around the world. However, there

Marilyn Monroe in the 1950s has changed. Miss America winners and *Playboy* center-folds have become increasingly thinner in recent years. As one psychiatrist put it to the *Los Angeles Times,* "Every society has a way of torturing its women whether by binding their feet or sticking them into whalebone corsets that are too tight. . . . What contemporary American culture has come up with are tubular designer jeans." Not all societies "torture" women equally, and such torture is subject to change. But in contemporary America mass advertising has become an effective means of pressure. And it can be added that the cycle of binge eating then purging of bulimia may be related to our cultural contradiction shown in advertising using very thin women to push very fattening foods.

The question remains why more affluent young women are particularly susceptible to eating disorders. I have not located adequate research on the question, but there is some reasonable speculation. It may be that more affluent parents place more stress on their children to achieve "success." The mass media image of thinness is directed more toward young affluent (usually white) females. Living up to this image is viewed as one form of "success." And in a male-dominated economy, conforming to this physical image may be an important means of monetary success as well. Some young women are so afraid of not pleasing their parents with success that they take thinness to the extreme.

A more general analysis of our society has not been attempted at this point. Such an analysis will be pursued in coming chapters. For example, the broader question of why the role of women exists as it does in our society is relevant. But the main point for now is that social forces as originally described in Durkheim's study of suicide can affect even individual-level psychological behavior. These social forces are a primary subject matter of sociology.

* For useful summaries of information on the subject of eating disorders, see M. Boskind-Lodahl and J. Sirlin, "The gorging-purging syndrome," *Psychology Today,* March 1977, and the *Los Angeles Times,* July 18, 1983. I would like to thank one of my students, Lisa Zanola, for providing me with extensive sources on the subject.

is no specific gene leading humans to form demo-cratic or totalitarian political systems, nor capitalis-tic or communist economies. Human brain power allows for this variety, but our unique brains do not cause us to form particular types of social struc-tures.

Sociologists can also learn something from indi-vidual psychology. But sociologists are most con-cerned with how individuals collectively create and are affected by group properties. It is the group level, the characteristics of groups, social struc-tures, and societies that most interest sociologists.

A final note is worth emphasis; the level of analy-sis favored by sociologists is unfamiliar to most peo-ple. In our everyday experience we see human beings and deal with human motives and emotions, but we do not see social structures, nor do we think in terms of the properties of social structures. And in our particular society, our perceptions and explana-tions of human behavior are shaped by individualistic values. We are taught that people have free will and independence, and control their own destiny. (As we will see, our value system is unique in the history of human societies.) A result of this individualistic

TABLE 1.1. *Comparative suicide and homicide rates (yearly rate per 100,000 population*)*

Country	Suicide	Homicide
Austria	24.1	1.5
Belgium	14.9	1.0
Canada	12.9	2.5
Denmark	23.8	.7
Finland	25.1	2.6
France	15.4	.9
West Germany	21.0	1.2
Ireland	3.5	.7
Italy	5.8	1.1
Japan	18.1	1.3
Netherlands	9.2	.8
Norway	9.9	.6
Sweden	20.0	1.2
Switzerland	1.5	1.0
United Kingdom	7.9	1.0
United States	12.7	10.0

* Data on suicide rates are from one year in the early 1970s (1970–1975); homicide rates are for 1974.
SOURCES: Suicide rates, United Nations, *Demographic Yearbook,* 1976; Homicide rates, U.S. Bureau of Census, *Social Indicators III,* 1980, p. 252.

perspective, of course, is quasi theories of human behavior that focus on individual motives and responsibilities. A sociologist looks at crime, for example, and attempts to understand the group properties that shape a particular crime rate. Most individuals look at crime and attempt to understand why a particular person would commit crimes. These two orientations are very different and must be kept in mind throughout the coming chapters. From the sociologists' perspective, they might suggest that differing group tendencies toward crime indicate that poverty, family instability, and urban living help produce crime. The nonsociologist's response might be, "I once knew a city kid who was poor and from a broken home, who grew up to be president of a major corporation and never committed a crime." The point has been missed. Not all poor kids, living in cities, and from broken homes commit crimes. But when referring to serious street crime, more of these kids do commit crimes than

affluent kids from stable families. The sociologist wants to know why.

From the individualistic perspective it is also natural to assign blame and responsibility to particular individuals for events. To say that poverty helps cause crime seems to somehow relieve the poor of responsibility. And many criminals who happen to be poor may learn to use such explanations to justify their acts and protect their self-esteem. But to identify the social forces producing group tendencies toward certain types of behavior is not to resolve or assign blame; it is to understand human societies. The two perspectives must not be confused, though in our society they easily are.

DIVERGENT SOCIOLOGICAL PERSPECTIVES

So far you have been introduced to a general sociological perspective that most sociologists follow. But as with any scientific discipline, there are some disagreements among sociologists. In fact, sociology has more than its share of these disagreements, some of which date back to the earliest social philosophers. Many of these disagreements are quite sharp; others are less important matters of style. The broad scope and complex subject matter of sociology is no doubt responsible for these disagreements. To some degree I will take sides in these disagreements and tell you why. But all the different perspectives and theories discussed below will be of use to us in coming chapters.

Macro versus micro. The first of these divergent perspectives concerns levels of analysis. To some extent this disagreement follows our previous discussion. Although some sociologists focus on a **macro level,** others prefer a **micro level.** By a macro level we mean a more general or wider sociological perspective. For example, from a macro focus we might be interested in relations between the political system and the economy. Or at the most general level, we might be concerned with some major characteristics of the society as a whole, and the differences among societies.

Beginning with the most general level (the overall society), we can work down to major structural parts of the society (like the state, the economy, religion), to small groups, and finally to the individual. Sociologists favoring a micro orientation are more comfortable studying small groups and the individual. Remembering our previous discussion, however, you should understand that sociologists study individuals from a certain perspective; the sociological focus is the effect of the society and groups on the individual.

To some degree the macro-micro split between sociologists is simply a matter of questions asked. And many sociologists work on both levels. But at times there is disagreement over which level of analysis will provide the best answers to the same question. For example, what are the primary causes of crime? A micro-level sociologist may choose to examine how a criminal self-concept is developed through social interaction. Or a micro-level sociologist may choose to examine how criminal motivations, justifications, and techniques are learned in small groups. A macro-level sociologist, on the other hand, may choose to examine how the value system and/or group conflicts in the general society affect crime rates.

Both levels of analysis are certainly useful in understanding human societies. In coming chapters, both levels of analysis are explored. And as much as possible the levels will be linked to show how each level can help us understand something about the other. The macro level, however, will be favored. And as we will see in more detail later, the macro-level focus fits well with the historical and cross-cultural (or comparative) perspective followed in this book. For the most part, this macro level and historical-comparative focus is due to the type of questions we will examine. For example, we will consider the grand questions, such as major economic and political trends in the United States and the world, growing world inequality, the overall changes in our family structure and life-styles.

Material versus nonmaterial. The second of these divergent sociological perspectives involves the question of what sort of things most influence and shape human societies. These "things" are divided into two groups — *material* and *nonmaterial.* On one side is the stress that humans are biological organisms with basic biological needs. How humans go about meeting these needs, their technology and social relations of production, are seen as primary. For example, most people must spend most of their time working (on a job or taking care of a family at home). The conditions under which people work, the style and efficiency of their technology of work, and their return received from labor are very important aspects of their lives. Material conditions like these can shape the family system, religion, political beliefs, art, and psychological orientations, along with many other characteristics of a society and human behavior.

On the other side is the stress that nonmaterial things like values and ideas are the most important in understanding human societies. Referring to the unique power of the human brain, the view is that ideas guide human activities. The beliefs constructed in a previous age guide the action of future generations until these beliefs are rejected as outdated. For example, a set of beliefs stressing individual freedoms have shaped Western societies like the United States. In contrast, a more collectivist orientation stressing obedience and group needs has shaped Eastern societies such as China and Japan.

The material versus nonmaterial disagreement is a very complex but important issue. All sociologists agree that both material and nonmaterial factors shape human societies; disagreement lies with which are more important? And which come first? For example, a long-standing debate in sociology centers around the development of capitalism. On one side, in a sociological classic published in 1904 called *The Protestant Ethic and the Spirit of Capitalism,* Max Weber (1959) argued that new religious ideas in northern Europe led to the development of capitalism. Others, like Karl Marx, have argued that changes in technology and group conflicts over the control and distribution of goods created capitalism. Both new ideas and changes in technology and property relations were important. But which are primary? This is not just an academic debate because the future direction of capitalism is related to which side is correct. If a Protestant ethic is most important, what happens if this ethic changes? One major sociologist has argued that this ethic is changing and the future of U.S. capitalism looks bad (Bell, 1976).

In summary, the following chapters favor a macro level of analysis. The focus is on characteristics of societies and macro social structures. You will also find a slightly stronger orientation toward material rather than nonmaterial factors that influence human societies. And because we will be more concerned with societal characteristics and macro social structures, you will find a greater concern for historical and comparative methods of analysis. At the same time, none of the other approaches and perspectives will be totally neglected. But I hope that on completion of this book you will find that the combination of perspectives emphasized is most useful in understanding the most important questions facing your life, the United States, and the world more generally.

DIVERGENT THEORETICAL PERSPECTIVES

A final disagreement among sociologists must be considered as we begin our study of human societies. It has to do with theoretical perspectives. First, a few words about theory.

The social world is perhaps even more complex than the physical world. In the face of this complexity the human mind is quite limited. Humans do have more overall brain power than any other animal, but the challenge of understanding the complex social world is often overwhelming. Many factors produce the human behavior and societal characteristics we observe. With the complex nature of our task, all we can hope for is to understand the most important influences. For example, of the many factors influencing the U.S. crime rate, the best we can hope for is to understand the most important.

As with any science, sociologists have constructed general theories that help them manage some of this complexity. A general theory provides something like a map or model of society and human interaction. With a general theory our attention is directed to certain things and locations in the real society where we may find the most important answers. And the best general theory simplifies the complex social reality by focusing on the the most important factors operating in the society that provide answers to our questions.

But alas, we again find disagreements among sociologists, and for many reasons. Some of the most important disagreements are simply related to the different types of questions asked by sociologists. For now, you should be aware of the three general theoretical perspectives favored by the largest numbers of sociologists — symbolic interaction theory, functional theory, and conflict theory. And you should also be aware that none of the three is absolutely correct or incorrect. One may be more valuable than others for certain questions about human societies, and one may be more valuable in providing some answers to a greater number of questions. I believe a general conflict theory is best in helping answer more questions and more important questions about human societies. The other two general theories, however, will not be neglected, especially where they are most useful. What follows is a brief look at the three general theories.

Symbolic Interaction Theory. The first of our three general theories — **symbolic interaction theory** — is micro in orientation. Symbolic interactionism has a focus on social psychology and face-to-face interaction among people in everyday life. This theoretical orientation had its origin among many early sociologists, but especially with Max Weber and George Herbert Mead. Weber is also known (perhaps even more so) for his theories on macro social structure, as we will see in several chapters. But Weber was one of the first to stress that human societies must also be studied through an examination of the individual meanings and understandings that guide social action (a method he called *verstehen*). There are many variations of this general symbolic interactionist theory, but they will all share the following basic points.

1. People act in terms of shared meanings. With the ability to think in abstract terms, most of what humans do is in response to symbolic meaning. With few minor exceptions, other animals act only in terms of concrete objects and drives. Consider a hungry bear in the forest. This bear comes upon a camp site and smells food. The bear will cautiously check for danger, then for food. Consider a hungry human hiker in the forest who comes upon a similar camp site. We have a much more complex situation. The human will most likely consider the moral implications of stealing food, as well as how such an act will fit his or her self-image.

2. The symbolic meanings people attain come from interaction with others. We learn the meaning of such symbols as language, flags, badges, clothing styles. People also gain a symbolic meaning of the self through interaction with others. We learn what others expect of us, how they view our capabilities — in short, who we are. We come to "define the situation" through this interaction with others.

3. To understand human societies you must consider how individuals in everyday interaction maintain and reproduce shared meanings and social networks. For example, IBM continues to exist because individual actors continually come together to do its business, while all the time continuing to assume IBM exists. Using another example, we see that governments continue to exist because people assume they exist with the power and resources to back up their commands and authority. Governments, of course, do not always exist. The Czar's government in Russia fell in February 1917, not because anyone took over power (that came later), but because most people simply came to believe it could no longer exist. In the words of social interaction theorist W. I. Thomas, "situations defined as real are real in their consequences." Thus, to understand even macro social structures it is helpful to understand the micro world of social interaction as well.

There are many variations and applications of symbolic interaction theory. Among some of the most useful is *labeling theory,* which is concerned with how labels are projected onto people and how people develop self-images, then act as these self-images suggests they should act. Labeling theory is useful in helping us understand how people come to define themselves as deviant (criminal, homosexual, "crazy," etc.), then act on this deviant identity. In a similar manner this theory can help us understand how people come to accept their position in life. It can help us understand why some people excel and achieve, while others come to accept themselves as failures.

Another very useful variant of this theory is Erving Goffman's *dramaturgical theory* (see Goffman, 1959, 1967). Goffman's focus is on how people attempt to maintain favorable presentations of themselves in interaction with others. As the name implies, Goffman uses the analogy of the stage, with actors playing roles. In real life, people assume roles and try to present good "performances." They do so using various props (clothing style, body language, manner of speaking), with their behavior differing in front stage (such as a formal office setting) and backstage (at home in your room).

There are other varieties of symbolic interaction theory. *Ethnomethodology* is primarily concerned with how people make social interaction possible with many complex and unstated rules. For example, we hold many assumptions about the nature of reality and our own actions that remain unquestioned when two or more people interact (Garfinkel, 1967). If these assumptions were often questioned, other business would remain uncompleted. This and other varieties of micro-level theories will be encountered in several places in coming chapters. In most respects this type of theory does not contradict the more structural (macro) conflict theory favored in this book. In fact, in many ways the two types of theory are highly complementary — we can refer to the micro-level theories to understand the building blocks that underlie the macro social structures.

Functional Theory. What we will refer to as functional, order, or structural-functional theory is primarily a macro-level theory. **Functional theory** has a long history in the social sciences, dating back to founders like Auguste Comte (called by some the father of sociology because he first used the name, in the 1800s). Perhaps the most credit for the early development of functional theory goes to a Frenchman we mentioned earlier, Émile Durkheim. Until recently this general theory was most respected among American sociologists. Although still respected, conflict theory has emerged quite rapidly to an equally favored position. Interestingly, in contrast, functional theory has become very popular among Soviet sociologists (Collins, 1980; Yanowitch, 1977).

As a macro-level theory, functional theory begins by stressing that society must been seen as an overall *system of interrelated parts*. Much like a biological organism, the society is seen as a system with various vital parts that must make unique contributions to the survival of the overall society. The functional theorist is concerned with the *function* of various parts of the society and how they work (or do not work) together. Functional theories do not suggest particular individuals planned how these parts would work together, or even that people are aware of the general functions of their activities. Rather, societies have survived because things vital to their survival get done (intentionally or unintentionally). For example, an early functional anthropologist, Bronislaw Malinowski (1948), believed that magic or rituals intended to influence supernatural forces were vital to some early fishing as well as hunting and gathering societies. The magical rituals were not effective in controlling climate or the seas, but these rituals gave people the courage to carry on necessary tasks that were risky and dangerous.

Another major feature of functional theory is its stress on *value consensus* in societies. A major question all sociological theories must be concerned with is, "How is society possible?" How is it that some 240 million people in the United States can have social order? What prevents continuous overt conflict with everyone for himself or herself? Functional theorists answer these questions with their description of a common value system. There is social order because most people have come to learn and obey basic rules. Related to this view is the functionalists' considerable stress on values, beliefs, and ideas as the things that most shape and change the nature of societies.

Functional theory is not ignored in coming chapters, but its weak points limit its value. First, functional theory is weak when explaining social change. If, like the human body, society is an integrated system with parts working in harmony, how can there be change? Functional theorists, of course, are not ignorant of social change and do try to explain it. But they must explain change by describing *excep-*

tions to the "normally" ordered, unchanging society that functional theory envisions.

A second weakness is that functional theory tends to ignore major divisions and conflicts within the society. When society is viewed as an interrelated organism, we are led to forget divisions and conflicts of interest within the society. How can the heart and lungs have conflicting interests? And if society has conflict, it must somehow be unnatural. As we will see, conflict is far from unnatural.

A third weakness is the stress by functional theorists on value consensus. People do tend to agree on many rules and values, but often they do not agree, yet nonetheless obey. Quite often there is social order simply because people must conform to the rules to earn their daily bread. And even to the extent that we find value consensus in a society, how is this consensus brought about? Because someone has the power to create consensus on rules that primarily favor their interests? All these questions are important but tend to be neglected by functional theory.

Conflict Theory. **Conflict theory** has existed alongside functional theory since the early history of social science. Both are primarily macro-level theories attempting to explain the same social phenomena, but from opposing perspectives. The early social philosophy of Henri de Saint-Simon stressed conflict and exploitation as important aspects of the new industrial societies of the eighteenth and nineteenth centuries. Karl Marx in the mid-nineteenth century stressed the inherent conflicts of interest between workers and capitalists. Only a short time later Émile Durkheim was writing about the same new industrial societies with almost no mention of conflict. These opposing theories continue today, but with conflict theory gaining ground on functional theory in recent years in the United States.

This description of conflict theory must begin with a definition of conflict as the term is used by conflict theorists. The word *conflict* often brings to mind individuals or groups in direct overt conflict that has or could lead to violence. For example, the rebels and the government of El Salvador are en-

gaged in such conflict. But whereas this type of conflict is all too common throughout the history of human societies, it is not the only type of conflict. Conflict theorists take a very broad definition of conflict when building their theories. One definition describes conflict as "a struggle over values and claims to scarce status, power, and resources in which the aims of the opponents are to neutralize, injure, or eliminate their rivals" (Coser, 1956, p. 8). Even this definition, however, is too narrow for most conflict theorists. Only *overt* conflict is covered in Coser's definition — conflict actively pursued and recognized by two or more parties. Covert or *latent* conflict is even more important in understanding the nature of society. The conflicts of interest may not always be on the minds of all parties every day, but they are no less there. One party may in fact be working very hard to keep the conflicts of interests hidden and latent for its own advantage. Or the conflicts of interest may not be completely recognized by any party in the society. But the underlying conflicts of interest can be identified, and these conflicts can be located in the basic features of modern societies. When will these latent conflicts become overt as in the case of strikes, racial strife, revolution, and so on? What will be the outcome when these conflicts become overt? How have these conflicts remained latent? How have important group conflicts shaped the basic institutions and other fundamental aspects of a society? These are the types of questions conflict theorists find important.

As we will see, there are many varieties of conflict theory; some stress that there will always be conflict among humans, just as "survival of the fittest" always operates with living organisms (social Darwinism); others stress that there will always be major group conflicts, with a ruling class always exploiting the masses in the society (for example, the ruling elite theories of Gaetano Mosca [1939] and Vilfredo Pareto [1935]). Still others stress that conflict can be so many-sided that people are "sewn together" in overlapping conflict groups, with no major division producing extreme levels of exploitation and dominance (pluralists like Georg Simmel [1955]). And finally, others are more optimistic, believing that most conflict can eventually be elimi-

nated when the last ruling class (capitalists) is made obsolete and eliminated (Marxian theory).

The most respected conflict theories today have some common elements, despite their diversity.

1. A most obvious and fundamental common element shared by conflict theorists is a focus on the nature of conflict underlying, and built into, human societies. A history of group conflict has helped produce the social structures and social institutions in contemporary societies. And it is these inherited social structures that continue to shape the nature of present conflicts. Let's briefly consider the modern state. As we will see, bureaucracies emerged in early history as attempts by elites to control the lower classes. But with industrial societies, various forces of social change (especially economic) brought more influence to some nonelites. This new influence enabled these nonelites to force some changes in the political system. Thus, whereas the state still favors the interests of the elites in many ways, it does not do so exclusively. How the state has developed to favor differing group interests sets the stage for current group conflicts. One group wants the law or policy changed, another favors the law or policy and defends it. In this way current group conflicts are shaped by the historical development of social structures — that developed in response to the power and influence of past groups in conflict.

2. Group, rather than individual, conflicts are most important in human societies. There are, of course, individual conflicts of varying degrees whenever you find a collection of individuals. But most important for the study of human societies is how people form groups with common interests. These groups then form coalitions and come into conflict with other groups with opposing interests. The social structures a society has inherited leads to differing group interests and conflicts.

3. Society is *not* an organism (like the human body) that exists with needs of its own. Rather, society is a setting where individuals and groups come together to cooperate with some and compete

with others. It is the needs of people and the collective needs of groups of people that shape society.

4. We usually find social order and cooperation among humans. However, the social order and cooperation we find among groups in large societies is often based on some form of conflict. For example, there may be cooperation between two groups because of common interests in defeating another group. Or social order may be present because one group has the power to keep others in line through force, material incentives, or confusion (such as hiding the conflicts of interest).

5. Social change is a basic feature of human societies. Societies do not always change at the same rate, but because conflict, whether overt or latent, is fundamental to all large societies, the changing advantage of one group over others will lead to social change. For example, the conflict between workers and large factory owners and managers has produced significant social change in the past century in the United States. Wages are often higher, working hours are shorter, some dangers in the workplace have been reduced, and labor has the legal right to form unions, all in contrast to one hundred years ago. Workers and factory owners/managers are by no means equal partners in the economy, nor do they share rewards equally. But there has been social change, *and* reaction against this social change was a major feature of the Reagan Administration during the 1980s. In other words, there is an unending conflict among major groups. There are always some losses and some gains that assure a continuing process of social change.

6. A final common element of conflict theories is the focus on power and inequality and an analysis of who (or which group) is favored by the status quo. Conflict in large societies will perhaps never result in equality for all groups in that society (though some societies have achieved much less inequality and less overt conflict than others). There will always be some inequalities of power and valued goods and services. Thus, one or more groups will be favored by the status quo (present arrangements). Which group is favored by the status quo, which group has more power

and a greater share of the valued resources can tell us a lot about how various groups in the society will behave.

Abstract theories presented in brief outline are seldom exciting. However, the insights they provide when applied to major events can be quite exciting. My ultimate goal is to apply these theories to major events. But we must begin somewhere, and a basic outline of theory is that somewhere. So far the three main theories have been somewhat simplified to further your understanding of them. The complexity will come later when needed.

CHAPTER SUMMARY

Key Terms

society, 8	micro level, 20
sociology, 8	symbolic interaction
science, 10	theory, 22
sociobiology, 12	functional theory, 23
natural selection, 12	conflict theory, 24
macro level, 20	

Content

Society refers to habitually interacting groups of humans with a common culture, a common territory, and relative autonomy. Sociology is the scientific study of human societies.

All people are, in a sense, sociologists because they attempt to explain human behavior. But because our "quasi theories" of human behavior are shaped by our own interests and limited view of the social world, these quasi theories are often biased and incorrect. We must strive for an objective scientific analysis of human societies. This is a goal of sociology.

As with all animals, natural selection has resulted in biological influences on human behavior. But in comparison with other animals, the biological influences on human behavior are much more limited, primarily because of a biological development — the human brain. And whereas we can agree that natural selection has produced selfish tendencies and conflict among humans, it has also produced tendencies toward cooperation and sharing. Cooperation and sharing among some humans, however, often produce conflict directed toward other humans (the out group).

An individual level of analysis alone provides few useful insights into the nature of human societies. Even individual behavior like suicide and eating disorders can be most generally understood with reference to social forces and the characteristics of societies. It is this group level or societal level that is the focus of sociology.

Although a general sociological perspective can be identified, sociologists do favor ways and theories of breaking this down to answer specific types of questions. Your present test favors (but not exclusively) a macro perspective, a materialist view, and historical-comparative methods of analysis.

Three general theories of society are the most accepted among sociologists. Symbolic interaction theory is a social psychological-level theory focusing on symbolic meanings created in face-to-face social interactions. People then come to act in terms of these meanings of events, things, and the self. Functional theory is a macro-level theory that views societies as integrated social systems. These social systems have various parts (family, political system, economy) that function for the health of the overall society. Conflict theory is also a macro-level theory, but it views society as primarily a setting for group conflicts. Group conflicts are not always overt or violent but often latent and hidden. The major institutions in a society are both the product of past group conflicts and the major forces influencing the nature of present group conflicts. Conflict theory is most concerned with inequalities of power and valued goods, as well as social change. Of these three theories, conflict theory is favored in this book (but not exclusively).

Men make their own history, but they do not make it just as they please; they do not make it under circumstances chosen by themselves but under circumstances directly encountered, given and transmitted from the past.
— **Karl Marx,** The Eighteenth Brumaire of Louis Bonaparte

You will remember that sociology has been described as the scientific study of human societies. This attempt to adapt scientific methodologies to the investigation of human societies separates sociology from the age-old tendency merely to speculate on the human condition. Sociologists are not always successful in sticking to objective methods of gaining knowledge, but they have made progress in understanding human behavior because as social scientists, they have had at least some success in pursuing objective scientific analysis.

Given the importance of a scientific orientation, this chapter has two general and interrelated goals. First, I will describe the emergence of social science, and sociology more specifically. As we will see, the conditions allowing for the widespread development of social science are rather recent and unique in human history. Second, I will describe social science research methods in some detail. Whether you like it or not, and whether or not many people realize it, government policy and business decisions are often (if not always) shaped by social science research. The rapid spread of computer technology will further increase reliance on social science research. More and more people will be required to understand and conduct social science research. Yet much social science research is misunderstood and misused (at times, I am afraid, intentionally). In this chapter, I will try to reduce this misunderstanding and expose the misuse.

THE DEVELOPMENT OF SOCIAL SCIENCE

Although there are many, one ingredient is clearly the most crucial for the emergence and spread of social science — free inquiry. People must have at least some ability to examine and challenge old accepted explanations without fear of punishment. I suppose the strong-willed have always sought their own view of the truth at all costs. Whether or not we agree with him, Soviet writer Aleksander Solzhenitsyn, who was expelled from the Soviet Union for his beliefs, must be considered among them. But there have never been enough of these people to sustain the progress of social science in the face of strong restrictions on free inquiry. Ignorance has usually triumphed when the choice is between knowledge or personal survival.

Only rarely throughout history do we find conditions promoting free inquiry. We can locate these conditions perhaps for the first time in ancient Greece. Plato, Aristotle, and their contemporaries, who lived around 400 B.C., may not have provided many accurate theories of human societies, but they did begin asking important questions. Aristotle even established what we can call the first research institute. With the financial support of Alexander the Great, Aristotle sent perhaps a thousand men throughout the Middle East and Greece collecting information: "Nothing of the kind had ever been attempted, had even been thought of, so far as we know, before this time. Political as well as natural science began" (Wells, 1971, p. 282). But it didn't last. The support of Alexander the Great died with him and his empire. The social climate that allowed at least some free inquiry was lost.

There were a few other isolated cases of free inquiry in the ancient world. One of the most noted was around 300 B.C. at Alexandria, Egypt. A truly exciting process of intellectual expansion was achieved at the Museum of Alexandria, which was much like a university, research institute, library, and monastery for scholars combined. There was an attempt to collect copies of all the books that had ever existed. "At the outset, and for two or three generations, the Museum at Alexandria presented such a scientific constellation as even Athens at its best could not rival" (Wells, 1971, p. 317). But it lasted fewer than one hundred years. It was destroyed by people who feared the ideas allowed to emerge in its halls (Sagan, 1980).

After the Greek contributions there were a few advances in the physical sciences in the next 2,000 years or so, but almost nothing in the social sciences. In the Western world, advance even in the physical sciences were almost nonexistent. And with the fall of the Roman Empire (around A.D. 400–500), the West went into decline — the Dark Ages. Socialand political disorder prohibited intellectual advance. Recovery was slow, and even by the Renaissance (about A.D. 1500) social science had not yet emerged. The recovery of Western civilization brought rigid social order. The few people who could read and write were firmly on the side of religious and political elites. The dogmas of the elites were not to be questioned. But the stage was being set for an intellectual mobilization.

No one can cite the most important contibution to the emergence of the social sciences, beginning during the 1700s. Clearly a combination of factors created a cycle of change making free inquiry at least possible (Bendix, 1978, p. 243). A decline in power of old elites is certainly on the list of factors. As we will see in the next chapter, the old economic elites (the landed aristocracy or nobility) were losing power because of economic change. The old political elites, who usually simply served the interests of the aristocracy, went with them. Religious elites were in a somewhat similar position, but other factors were also involved in their loss of dominance.

During the Middle Ages religious elites had the task of explaining the cosmos. The relation of humans to nature, the meaning of life, the nature of humans — such questions as these were all answered with religious belief systems. And during the early Middle Ages in Europe, religion for the most part was the Roman Catholic Church. The religious dogma of the time explained why kings and landlords should be honored and obeyed, and why the Church itself should be so wealthy in the face of subsistence living for the masses. Never mind that this version of the Christian religion was difficult to support with the Bible; the masses could nct read. They were given the elite's version of the Bible.

During the Dark Ages almost no one in the West could read, but by the 1500s there was considerable improvement (Clark, 1969, p. 17; Bendix, 1978, p. 263). The invention of the printing press at this time

allowed more people to read. With respect to the Bible, many people for the first time found contradictions between Church practice and religious ideals. For this reason it is said that printing and increased literacy helped bring about the Protestant Reformation of Martin Luther in the 1500s (Thomas, 1979, p. 201). The Protestant Reformation helped eliminate the power of the Catholic Church in many European nations, and this in turn eventually eroded the power of old political and economic elites. The climate was not immediately open for all new ideas, but some free inquiry was emerging, especially in northwestern Europe, where the Catholic Church was most weakened.

Other factors were involved in what Bendix (1978) calls the "growing intellectual mobilization" of the time. Among them were new ideas from other cultures brought back to Europe with increased travel. It became more difficult to view human societies with the old, narrow vision promoted by isolation. Industrialization brought an increased need and incentive for scientific investigation in the physical sciences. An established model of scientific analysis in the physical sciences helped lay the foundation for a science of society. And industrialization also brought social disruption and other social problems. These problems (rapid urbanization, crime, poverty, a weakened family system) raised questions about the causes and possible solutions. By the late 1700s great social philosophers like Rousseau, Hobbes, Locke, and Adam Smith emerged. They began asking the sociological questions, but the questions were not yet clearly merged with a scientific mode of analysis. Social science, per se, came somewhat later, in the mid-1800s.

The Development of Sociology in Europe

A social and political climate allowing relatively free inquiry made the emergence of sociology possible, but more was needed to sustain its development. These other ingredients were finally in place by the second half of the nineteenth century in Europe. For sociology to spread there was need of career opportunities for its practitioners and new informational sources to stimulate new ideas and theory building.

The career opportunities came from increased

literacy, printing, new wealth, and a rapidly expanding educational system in Europe. The literacy, printing, and increased standard of living created a publishing industry. A career in writing became possible. "The expansion of the universities and the development of public school systems provided positions for teachers" (Collins, 1975, p. 527). It was now possible for at least a few people to make a living as social scientists.

Equally important, however, was an expanding information base that made a science of society possible. As briefly described in the preceding chapter, scientific analysis requires objective information with which to test ideas and theories. Survey research methods, opinion polls by telephone, and other popular means of gaining sociological information did not yet exist. But some of the best types of information for the development of sociological theories were increasing—historical and cross-cultural data. History as a mature field of study preceded sociology. In contrast to previous centuries, there was a much richer supply of historical information in the 1800s. Also, "various explorers and colonial administrators by now had provided a very considerable amount of comparative materials about the variety of societies existing around the world;

anthropology, although lacking much theoretical basis, had the empirical materials in hand to begin to build general statements" (Collins, 1975, p. 528). Conditions were ripe for a sound foundation for a new science of society in the second half of the 1800s. At no other time in the history of human societies do we find such possibilities.

Two individuals who can first be referred to as sociologists were Henri de Saint-Simon and Auguste Comte. As Frenchmen producing their main works in the early 1800s, they were responding to the intellectual challenges of the French Revolution. As a student of Saint-Simon, Comte came somewhat later, but he is usually referred to as the "father of sociology" primarily because he first used the term sociology (Saint-Simon's term was *science politique*). Both men argued for a positivist (that is, a natural science) approach to the study of society. Neither Saint-Simon nor Comte, however, contributed much of what today can be called sociological research. Reading their works, one gets the impression that they had much more in common with earlier social philosophers than the best sociologists of the late 1800s (see Box 2.1).

The real giants of sociology began their work around the second half of the nineteenth century.

BOX 2.1

The High Priest of Sociology

The predominance of moral philosophy over strict scientific analysis especially in the work of Auguste Comte can be seen in his model of the reformed industrial nation. In what appears very naïve and perhaps even humorous today, Comte called for a new "Positivist Society" with a new utopian "Religion of Humanity." This positivist society would be based on scientific analysis to determine what policies would be best for everyone in the society. In a central position in this positivist society would be "priests" of the religion of humanity. These priests, it is interesting to note, would be sociologists rather than theologians! Specifically, there would be "some twenty thousand priests for western Europe, presided over by a High Priest of Humanity, with his headquarters at Paris. . . . The priests should be the moral censors of the community, using the force of their opinion to keep men aware of their social duties and obligations and to warn them in case of deviation" (Barnes, 1948, pp. 100–101). The High Priest, it seems, would be Comte himself. Comte's call was for "progress through order," which today still appears on the national flag of Brazil.

And especially "by the turn of the twentieth century, the intellectual resources for establishing a serious social science were being developed" (Collins, 1975, p. 528). Many major sociologists whom you will encounter in coming chapters lived and worked in this period. To name a few, there was Ferdinand Tönnies (1855–1936), a German who helped us understand the changing nature of community; Georg Simmel (1858–1918), another German who helped us understand micro-level conflict and forms of interaction; Herbert Spencer (1820–1903), an Englishman who refined a social evolutionary perspective referred to as Social Darwinism; Vilfredo Pareto (1848–1923), an Italian who provided us with useful insights on elite dominance in modern societies. But above all others, the works of three thinkers stand out—Karl Marx, (1818–1883), Max Weber (1864–1920), and Émile Durkheim (1858–1917).

Karl Marx. The work of Karl Marx preceded that of Weber and Durkheim. And in many ways the main ideas of Weber, and to some extent Durkheim, were in response to those of Marx. Although Marx's ideas were most influential in early European social science, his influence has been increasingly felt in the United States. All of Marx's original ideas are not equally useful, but his general perspective and predictions about some aspects of advanced capitalist societies are becoming more respected by social scientists.

Karl Marx was born in Trier, Germany, in 1818. He was raised in relatively comfortable economic conditions and attended some of the best universities in Germany (McLellan, 1973; Berlin, 1963). Marx completed a doctorate of philosophy in 1841, but could not find employment in a university. He turned to journalism and edited several newspapers, first in Cologne and later in Paris. Marx's critical views of capitalism often got him in trouble as a journalist. Because of his writing in support of rebellion in the 1840s, he was first deported from Germany, then France, finally finding a permanent home in London. Marx and his family spent most of their remaining years in desperate poverty because of his inability to find steady work, although it is well known that he received support from Friederick

Karl Marx was considered a radical in the 19th century and he continues to be one of the most controversial theorists of the 20th century. The impact of his work has been global and still generates new theoretical ideas. The question is, however, how much of what is claimed as a development of Marx's thought actually is. (© Mayall, London/The Bettmann Archive)

Engels, a wealthy textile merchant. (The death of one of his children is attributed to the family's lack of money to pay for medical care.) In part because of his unemployment Marx found much time in London to research and write his most important works. He spent most of his days in the reading room of the British Museum, where he completed his three-volume *Capital* and notes for his other major work, *Grundrisse,* as well as *many* other books. It is important to recognize that Marx, in contrast to Weber and Durkheim, was both social scientist and political activist. In his role as political activist he wrote many works of political propaganda (like the *Communist Manifesto* with Friedrich Engels) and helped establish the Communist International. His goal as political activist was to help overthrow the capitalist system and establish a socialist state. In this role Marx was closer to many earlier social philosophers critical of the older feudal system of their time. But in his role as social scientist Marx also produced more cautious and objective works like *Grundrisse*. In the United States, until recently, only the activist Marx was well known. It has been relatively easy to reject these crude ideas.

This is not the place to summarize Marxian theory, but I should at least mention that it is mainly a variety of conflict theory (which is also to say not all types of conflict theory are by any means Marxian). The focus of Marxian theory is group conflict over the most important material aspects of life (land, jobs, food, and so on). This conflict is analyzed historically, with changes in the economic "substructure" considered the most important social force in history. Thus, Marxian theory is often referred to as *historical-materialism*.

Marxian theory has always been controversial—both politically and scientifically. It is controversial today primarily because of its political and economic implications. Among social scientists, beginning in Weber and Durkheim's day, Marx's ideas are controversial because of the stress on materialism and economic conflict. We will critically examine Marxian theory in coming chapters. Although it is difficult in a world increasingly polarized over Marxian ideas, my goal in future chapters will be to help you examine Marxian theory in an unbiased manner.

Max Weber. Max Weber is increasingly one of the most respected figures from the classical period of sociology. He was born in Erfurt, Germany, in 1864, and died in 1920. His life spans perhaps the most important period in the development of sociology, and he was a primary contributor to this development. Like Marx, Weber was born into a comfortable, upper-middle-class German family (Marianne Weber, 1975; Mitzman, 1969; Bendix, 1960). But

unlike Marx, Weber was an academic sociologist who rejected blending sociology with political activism. He argued for a strict separation between social science and political action. Without a "value-free" sociology, Weber believed the political debates on the left and the right could force sociologists to take sides and destroy their new academic status (Gouldner, 1973).

Much of Weber's work has been described as a debate with the "ghost" of Marx. Weber certainly agreed with Marx on the need to understand historical forces, and Weber's macro-level theories focused on power and conflict (Cohen, Hazelrigg, and Pope, 1975). However, Weber strongly rejected Marx's strictly materialistic views. One of Weber's (1958)

Max Weber investigated a broad range of social activities, including economics, law, politics, history, cities, music, religion, and the types of ideas and ethics that motivate people to succeed in life. His work on bureaucracy and types of authority is among the most important in the foundations of sociological theory. (© *Culver Pictures, Inc.*)

most respected works *(The Protestant Ethic and the Spirit of Capitalism)* attempted to show how a new Protestant belief system helped capitalism emerge. This greater stress on cultural factors in the development of capitalism is in direct opposition to Marx's more materialistic views.

Weber developed a micro-level as well as a macro-level perspective. He stressed understanding social action by considering the social meanings and motivations of individual participants in the society (a view sometimes called *verstehen*). His macro-level work, however, is often considered the most original and important in understanding the present. One of Weber's consistent themes was the growth and significance of bureaucracies (Weber, 1947; Gerth and Mills, 1946). Today we frequently hear complaints about the size, power, and inefficiency of bureaucracies. About 80 years ago Weber foresaw these future issues. He was pessimistic toward the subject because, whereas he recognized the growing necessity of bureaucratic organizations, he also recognized their inefficiency and dominance over humans. This is why he referred to these bureaucratic organizations as "iron cages" — organizations created by humans but then coming to encage humans.

Émile Durkheim. Writing at the same time as Weber, but with no direct contact, was a Frenchman, Émile Durkheim. Like Weber, but unlike Marx, Durkheim was an academic sociologist who rejected extensive political activism. Durkheim was born in Épinal, France, in 1858. He was also brought up in a respected, upper-middle-class family and held teaching positions in the best universities in his country (Lukes, 1973). Like Weber, he was a master who created and used the new sociological methodologies. And Durkheim was equally a master in using the growing cross-cultural and historical information of the time to construct sociological theory. But in contrast to Weber, Durkheim favored an order or functional theory of society. Following Comte, Durkheim viewed society as similar to a biological organism with interrelated parts. Group conflict had little place in his view of human societies (Strasser, 1976; Giddens, 1973), and his theoretical ideas are

Émile Durkheim is known for his emphasis on the "social fact" and the attempt to carefully delineate and systematically study behavior, events, attitudes, and social processes. Like Marx and Weber, he studied a broad range of topics, including religion, education, the division of labor, and social geography. (The Bettmann Archive)

less valuable than they otherwise would be because of it.

Perhaps more than Weber, Durkeim is respected for his work on research methods. Weber had much to say on the subject as well, but it was Durkheim's method of data analysis that has been the most copied. You should remember our discussion of Durkheim's (1951) book *Suicide,* published in 1899. It was especially in this book that Durkheim followed a method of using statistical information to test competing hypotheses that set the trend for future sociologists. Unfortunately, as the more internationally isolated United States began dominating sociology after World War I, Durkheim's cross-cultural orientation was less imitated. This model of social research methods was used primarily with nonhistorical American data only, and thus missed the opportunity for richer sociological explanations. As we will see below, however, sociologists today are regaining the historical and comparative orientations of the masters.

The Development of Sociology in the United States

Though sociology first emerged and spread in Europe, after World War I the United States took the lead. There are two primary reasons for the shift. First, as the United States became a leading industrial nation, it had an extensive university system to sustain the growth of sociology. Second, the United States began to dominate the study of sociology by default. The political and economic disruptions in Europe after World War I, and the rise of totalitarian governments in some European countries, created a poor environment for the free inquiry sociology requires. (A further result was the migration of many social scientists from Europe to the United States with the growing turmoil in Europe.)

When I write of a climate of free inquiry, or the freedom to pursue ideas no matter how unpopular, I am thinking in terms of degrees of this kind of freedom. There are, of course, limits to free inquiry in the United States, and these limits change from time to time. There were purges of liberal professors during the 1890s, the first "red scare" of the early 1920s, and the "McCarthy era" of the early 1950s (Goldman, 1953). There have been other, less widespread cases as well. But compared with many countries in Europe after World War I, the repression and political polarization was minor in the United States.

A brief look at U.S. history at the turn of the century is useful in understanding the development of sociology in this country. By the 1890s the United States was changing rapidly. It was still primarily a rural nation as late as 1880; for example, over 70 percent of the population lived in rural areas in 1880, whereas only a little more than one-half did by 1910. Also, by the early 1900s industry had grown rapidly. The United States moved from a primarily agrarian economy during the Civil War to a leading industrial nation by the early 1900s (Chirot, 1986). As a result of this rapid change, there was family disruption, poverty, and more visible crime. Bigger and bigger organizations were putting smaller ones out of business. Americans were less accustomed to these problems and, compared with Europe, had less of a tradition of effective government planning in dealing with them.

This extensive change and the social problems of the early 1900s brought new political movements. In the 1890s there was the Populist movement, the first massive movement in the United States calling for major reform with government action. But the Populist movement was primarily rural and directed toward the needs of small farmers (Hofstader, 1955; Goldman, 1953). Yet it led the way for the Progressive movement, beginning around 1900. The Progressive movement was a reform movement of urban, educated, and middle-class Americans. This movement sought reform of the crime, poverty, family breakdown, and other problems of urban areas. It was also a movement of the old middle-class business and professional people who felt threatened by the rapidly growing large industries, businesses, and major banks.

American sociology emerged in this context. Some of the early American sociologists were main participants in the Progressive movement, such as Edward Ross and Lester Ward. Thus, in the United States we find an inward-looking sociology with an emphasis on social problems. The Progressive movement was not a radical movement seeking basic change in the society. In one sense it was rather conservative; the traditional values of America were accepted and reform was sought in the name of these values.

The first major research university for American sociology during the early 1900s was at the University of Chicago (Mullins, 1973). The smalltown Midwestern orientation of most sociologists at the time made Chicago's urban problems seem more striking. Many studies were conducted on crime, family problems, poverty, and mental illness in Chicago. Before World War II, however, the most advanced sociology departments were located on the East Coast. The second wave of now more theoretically oriented American sociologists were found in places like Harvard and Columbia universities. General theory, and especially functional theory, became the focus of development. Particularly noteworthy were sociologists like Robert Merton and Talcott Parsons (who one day may be recognized as equaling the stature of Émile Durkheim).

The next major change for American sociology came in the 1960s. The number of sociologists and students taking sociology courses grew dramatically. There were two primary reasons for this increase. First, the "baby boom" generation entering college created greater demand for college courses in general. And the demand for social science courses increased more than for most other fields of study — evidence of interest in the social sciences. Second, during the 1960s the United States was in the middle of another major reform movement. In many ways this reform movement was similar to the Progressive movement of the early 1900s that coincided with the emergence of sociology in this country. There was renewed interest in social problems in the 1960s, and many more people, especially the young, were asking questions about the nature of society and their place in it. This, of course, brought more students to sociology courses and employed more sociologists. But the federal government also contributed to the growth of sociology with more funding opportunities for research and graduate training.

American sociology in the 1960s also changed in theoretical orientation. Functional theory remained popular, but a growing number of sociologists began turning to other theoretical perspectives. On the macro level, conflict theories grew in popularity. Perhaps a central figure in the new interest in conflict theories was C. Wright Mills. Though he died in the early 1960s, his works like *White Collar* (1953), *The Power Elite* (1956), and *The Sociological Imagination* (1959) made him highly respected in the 1960s, though these works had been heavily criticized in the 1950s for being too critical of the United States. Clearly, Mills was ahead of his time in a nation still feeling the effects of the McCarthy era.

Sociology in the 1980s. The interest in sociology has dropped since the 1960s, but interest remains substantially higher than in the 1950s, and sociology continues to hold a major position in universities. Perhaps one of the most important outcomes of the 1960s has been a recognition of the value of sociological research for government policy. Private industry as well has been employing sociologists in greater numbers. Sociology remains an academic discipline. Unlike, say, business or architecture students, sociologists are more often trained to teach and conduct basic research. As shown in Table 2.1, however, between only 1975 and 1981 there was (1) an overall increase in the number of sociologists (with Ph.D.s) and (2) a greater proportion of sociologists employed by government in nonteaching positions and private industry. When considering only those holding a B.A. or M.A. degree in sociology, the proportion working in private industry and government is much greater. One study sponsored by the American Sociological Association found 31.8 percent of those with a B.A. in sociology working in

TABLE 2.1. *Employment of sociologists holding Ph.D.s, 1975 and 1981*

Type of employer	Percent in each sector	
	1975	1981
Educational institutions	84.3	74.3
Government	5.1	7.6
Nonprofit organizations*	3.4	6.2
Business/Industry	1.2	5.0
Other	0.2	0.4
Not employed	5.7	6.5
Total	100.0	100.0
Number of sociology Ph.D.s	(7,102)	(10,612)

* This category includes hospitals and clinics.
SOURCE: Bettina Huber, "Sociological Practitioners: Their Characteristics and Role in the Profession," American Sociological Association *Footnotes* 11, No. 5 (May 1983), 6.

nonteaching positions in government or private industry (about half in each) and 27 percent of those with an M.A. in sociology working in government or private industry (again, about half in each [Huber, 1983, p. 7]).

Although increasing numbers of sociologists are in government positions, it does not necessarily mean that sociologists are shaping government policy. Sociologists tend to be researchers and consultants, providing information for establishing and evaluating government programs. Whether a program is established or continued is a political issue, it is a matter of the political process, of conflicting group interests and the power behind these interests. Sociological research may suggest that certain programs or policies can be most successful in reducing a social problem, for example, but the costs and benefits of the policy or program to powerful groups are the most important factors determining whether or not the policy or program is established. Once the direction of government policy has been determined, sociologists may conduct research to suggest how best to implement policy. Or if there are two or more acceptable policy alternatives, sociological research may help determine which is the most cost-effective and practical.

Ethical Questions. This aspect of social science has brought criticism from within the discipline. In essence, social science is often seen as working for the more affluent and powerful in helping solve what becomes a problem for them. For example, many sociologists began working in the government establishment during the 1960s. Some of these sociologists were employed to help design and administer programs to help the poor. How, you may ask, can sociology be charged with primarily helping elites when many sociologists were working in poverty programs? The response is that these sociologists were working in poverty programs because the poor were creating problems for the more affluent and powerful. There is abundant data showing that welfare programs expanded in the 1960s because the poor were rioting and the Democratic Party needed new lower-class voters (Piven and Cloward, 1971; Isaac and Kelly, 1981; Schram and Turbett, 1983). Thus, although the poverty programs of the 1960s

did help the poor in many ways, they were brought into existence because urban violence threatened the more affluent.

In a similar manner, therefore, it can be charged that social science benefits elites in the society. This charge creates serious ethical questions in a science that Weber believed should be "value-free." In some now famous cases, sociology has clearly been used to exploit and oppress lower-class groups. For example, in the 1960s "Project Camelot" was created by the U.S. military with the goal of helping keep in power Latin American governments that favor U.S. economic interests. Many sociologists were hired to do research whose basic goal was preventing lower-class groups from achieving democracy and economic change in these poor countries (Horowitz, 1967).

Comte was a dreamer when it came to his "Positivist Society" and "Religion of Humanity" (see Box 2.1). The "sociologist priests" who were to set policy for the "good of the country" would find that the country was full of different groups who saw the "good of the country" differently. It was Comte's neglect of group conflict and differing group interests that accounted for his naïve view. A totally value-free sociology is perhaps impossible. But a value-free sociology must be measured on a continuum with the extremes representing a totally value-free sociology to its opposite (a sociology that seeks not truth but to protect the interests of a particular group). Sociology can move closer to the value-free goal only with a clear recognition of differing group interests and class conflict. Only then can sociologists understand the implications of their work and how they may be led to favor particular group interests.

Sociology in the Soviet Union. We can obtain a better understanding of the nature of sociology by briefly comparing sociology in two industrial nations — the United States and the Soviet Union. The most obvious and striking lesson from this comparison is that sociology requires an atmosphere with at least some intellectual freedom.

As already described, the results of objective research may be threatening to some groups. Elites often find that things run more smoothly for them if they can control what is accepted as the truth. If such elites have the power to restrict the freedom of sociologists to reach conclusions that threaten their interests, they will usually do so.

In the Soviet Union sociology, as an academic discipline, was not even allowed to *exist* until the late 1950s (Yanowitch, 1977). Sociology was not allowed in the Peoples Republic of China until even more recently — just since the middle 1970s (*Footnotes,* 1980). The Soviet Sociological Association was formed in 1958, a few years after the death of Stalin. And by the account of two Soviet sociologists now living in the United States, Soviet sociology was tightly controlled from the first (Beliaev and Butarin, 1982). For example, the first president of the Soviet Sociological Association was the editor of *Pravda* (the official Communist Party newspaper).

Sociology was first allowed in the Soviet Union because it was believed useful for propaganda purposes. Increasingly, however, one faction of the political elite saw that sociological research could help with certain policy questions. But if it was to provide much useful information, sociology had to be allowed some freedom. Thus, some independent and objective sociological research has recently emerged in the Soviet Union, though this research is restricted to specific issues that are not threatening to elite interests. In other words, even under Gorbachev's "glosnost," or new openness policy, a Soviet version of Mill's *The Power Elite* (1956) may not be published in the Soviet Union in the near future, if ever. Such a work showing elite dominance for narrow elite interests would be viewed as antistate propaganda. However, some useful research has been published on subjects like crime, population changes, family problems, and various types of deviance. There is even a growing literature on educational opportunities, social mobility, and material inequalities. It must be pointed out, of course, that when more politically sensitive questions as these are studied, the wealth and advantages of the elites are ignored (Yanowitch, 1977).

The late emergence of at least some relatively objective sociological research in the Soviet Union suggests that sociology can be useful in industrial societies faced with increasingly complex problems. Soviet sociologists will not establish political and economic policy unless they are in high party positions, but sociological research can help with the technical implementation of policy, or deciding among policy alternatives that have the support of powerful interest groups.

SOCIAL RESEARCH METHODS

Sociological research is often a complex process. Even when conducted correctly sociological research may render ambiguous findings and more questions than answers. But it is often not conducted correctly, and its findings can be misused. Because of all this it is important to have some understanding of sociological research methods. My goal is to give you a general idea of how sociologists obtain and evaluate information about human societies. We will also examine how such information is used in constructing and testing theoretical ideas. I do not expect to make you a competent researcher with only a few pages devoted to research methods, but I do believe you will have a better idea of the process of sociological research, the quality of research you may see in the future, and how to use research information.

A Basic Research Design

A basic goal of scientific research in any discipline is to isolate cause and effect. Although the scientist may simply want to know the properties or characteristics of a substance, say, subatomic particles like quarks, this also means learning how the substance behaves under varying conditions. In short, we are still referring to cause and effect. In the case of quarks (perhaps the building blocks of all matter), their existence can be discovered only by splitting atoms in a superconducting collider. The process involves smashing particles at 20 trillion electron volts to determine if quarks are thrown off in the process. Again, we are referring to cause (smashing) and effect (quarks set free). Usually, however, we know the effect (riots, earthquakes) and are looking for the cause.

There is a basic research design that serves as the model or ideal for any science. This ideal scientific method can be called the **classical experimental design.** In its simplest form a classical experiment involves isolating a substance in a laboratory. Once isolated the characteristics or behavior of the substance can be studied by allowing interaction with another substance or a stimulus. For example, the scientist does something to the substance and the resulting change or behavior of the substance is the *effect.* If the substance is isolated with only the one additional substance or stimulus allowed, then we can be confident this additional substance or stimulus is the *cause* of any observed effect. Let me stress this point; the scientist attempts to achieve total control of all possible causes by allowing only one possible cause to be released at a time. By doing this the scientist can be certain of the cause for any observed effect.

Let's consider an example. A biologist wants to know why a particular type of plant grows larger in one part of the country than in another. There are many possible reasons — perhaps soil quality, temperature, moisture characteristics, air quality, and the list could go on. As suggested in Figure 2.1, the plants can be brought into a laboratory setting and each possible cause of larger growth brought in one at a time. More realistically, perhaps, the scientist would also check for combinations of possible causes (say, a particular type of soil with a particular quantity of water). In common terminology, the size of the plant is the **dependent variable** — the thing we want to explain, or the effect. The possible causes are **independent variables.** In general, a *variable* is any substance or condition that can have a varied state. With our example of plant growth, we have short, medium, and tall (or any measure you want) plants. Size is a variable, in this case the dependent variable. With our independent variables we can have varying quantities of sunlight, water, or carbon dioxide in the air. In some cases, of course, we might say there is no variance of a condition. To use the old saying, there is no such thing as a "little pregnant" — you either are or you are not. But in the case of such "nominal" variables we can still refer to variance at only two levels, it exists or it doesn't exist.

So far our example has implied that a scientist begins with a particular problem that needs an answer — varied plant growth. Perhaps our scientist is employed by a large agribusiness wanting to grow larger plants. The scientist is therefore involved with *applied research.* And to the extent that the scientist brings no preconceived ideas about the causes of varied plant growth, we can also say this scientist is involved with **inductive research.** With inductive research the scientist is trying to construct an explanation from observations, or the results of the experiment.

Perhaps, however, the scientist is not employed to provide specific answers to specific questions — for example, how to make plants grow larger. Perhaps the scientist wants to understand plant growth in general, molecular structure, or genetic structure. With this example we can refer to *basic research.* The goal is to construct general theories of,

Figure 2.1. Classical experimental design.

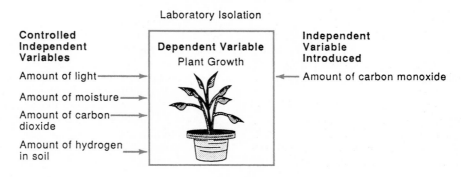

Laboratory Isolation

Controlled Independent Variables

Amount of light

Amount of moisture

Amount of carbon dioxide

Amount of hydrogen in soil

Dependent Variable
Plant Growth

Independent Variable Introduced

Amount of carbon monoxide

say, genetic structure. With an accumulation of empirical observations, through time, theories of genetic structure have been developed. The scientist's job is to test the theories through research. When working from theory and devising research to test the theory, we can refer to **deductive research,** rather than inductive research. Using another example, we observe that a theoretical physicist wants to know if the theory that quarks are the building blocks of all matter is accurate. This physicist is doing basic research rather than applied research. As with applied research, however, the classical experimental design can still be involved.

As indicated in Figure 2.2, the process of scientific research can be viewed as a cycle. In principle we may begin with either observations or theories. In reality, however, the scientist begins with some mixture of the two. If the scientist is working more from firm theory to be tested, the deductive side is involved. If the scientist is working primarily with observations and empirical generalizations, and is attempting to formulate theory, the inductive side is involved.

Beginning with the deductive side of Figure 2.2, we note that specific hypotheses must be drawn from general theories. **Hypotheses** can be described as specific predictions that can be tested. A very simple example might be, when x interacts with y, a result will be z. An example from genetic engi-

neering might be, if we remove x gene from bread mold, we will find enhanced cell growth.

The next step in the research cycle is operationalization. By **operationalization** we refer to concrete definitions and indicators of the variables suggested in a hypothesis. At times operationalization is rather straightforward. In the example above, cell growth can be easily defined and indicated. In sociological research, however, operationalization is often very complex. A sociologist may want to explain the causes of revolution, but what exactly do we mean by revolution? Do we mean only cases where rebels actually take power and produce massive social change (for example, Russia in 1917, China in 1949). Or do we mean by revolution all cases of massive political violence, whether the rebels win or not? There are many more cases of the latter, and it can make a big difference in research on the causes of revolution depending on what we refer to as revolution. **Measurement** most simply means a method of indicating amounts, degrees, or conditions of a variable. Measurement is sometimes simple to accomplish — plant height in centimeters, molecules of CO_2 per cubic inch, and so on. Sometimes it is quite difficult — measuring the weight of unseen quarks. In the social sciences measurement is seldom easy because we are dealing with complex attitudes, complex behavior, unseen social forces, and so on.

Finally, from observations made in the research process we may form empirical generalizations. These can be simply defined as generalizations from the empirical observations. For example, with a specific observation a scientist finds that when x and y combine, the result is z. Assuming the research was conducted properly, without unknown independent variables affecting the process, the empirical (observable) generalization is: whenever x and y combine, the result is always z. The empirical generalization is then compared with the existing theory (or used to produce one). If it is totally consistent with the theory, it is supported. Most likely this is only one part of the theory and thus other parts require testing. And also most likely, the findings (or empirical generalizations) are only partially consistent with the theory, or totally contradictory.

Figure 2.2. The cycle of scientific research and theory testing.

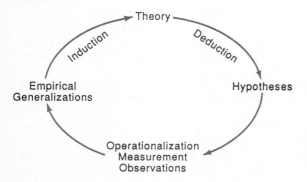

In this case the theory must be amended and further research conducted.

The Unique Problems for Social Research. I have just described the *ideal* classical experimental design and the *ideal* cycle of scientific research. In most cases, even in the physical sciences, the ideal cannot be followed completely. In the social sciences, however, the situation is often more difficult, especially in attempting to follow the classical experimental design. I first describe these problems presented in sociological research; then I describe the specific methods of research that social scientists have devised in attempting to overcome these problems.

Social scientists have at least five primary problems in attempting to follow the classical experimental design.

1. When working on a macro or structural level, the social scientist cannot bring the subject matter into a controlled laboratory setting. Something like this is possible when studying small groups, and generalizations about the more general society can be made. But there are other limitations.

2. One of the most important limitations is that the social scientist's subject matter can think or respond to manipulation. The process of being studied is of no concern to atoms and quarks. People, as well as groups of people, usually respond in some way to the process of being studied itself, as well as to the independent variables designed to affect their behavior. In other words, isolating a human in an attempt to control for the effects of other variables is itself an independent variable. Social psychologists sometimes do employ experimental research by resorting to various tricks for deception, but there are usually questions about the success of the deception, not to mention ethical concerns.

3. Another very important limitation results from the lack of control over many factors possibly influencing the behavior of humans and human societies. For a social psychologist, the behavior of an individual under study is influenced by a very complex set of current social cues and past experiences. These past experiences cannot be controlled but affect the individual's response to present stimuli. For example, how an individual responds to a given task in a laboratory may depend on childhood experiences, education level, experiences related to income level, religion, and learned sex roles, and the list goes on. Faced with this problem, the social scientist can use various techniques of statistical manipulation of data obtained in empirical research. We consider some of them below. In general all these techniques involve **post hoc research,** which means that the social scientist is trying to control (or more accurately, sort out) the effects of previous or past influences (the influence of background factors like education, religion, sex, and so on).

The sociologist working on a macro level has the same problem and uses similar techniques to counter the problem. However, a fairly large sample of cases is required for statistical sorting or controlling for previous influences, and when the unit of analysis is industrial societies, the number is limited. The problem is not insurmountable, as we will see, but certainly limiting.

4. Compared with the subject matter of the physical scientist, the subject matter of the social scientist often involves more complex multiple causation. A physical scientist studying damage to the ozone layer may be able to point to some specific independent causes. But what causes political revolution? We might conclude that some kind of severe hardship is required to motivate people to rebel. It is clear, however, that hardship alone is not enough. Simple observation tells us this much: If hardship alone produced revolution, we would find many more revolutions all over the world than we have known in the past. As we will see in a later chapter, many factors must come together to produce revolution, and to make things more complex, the mixture of factors may not be the same in every case. The social scientist is often led to seek the most important causes, rather than all the causes in the mixture.

5. Finally, there are very important ethical limitations with the classical experimental design for social science research. We simply do not want to treat humans as we might nonliving objects in research experiments.

Additional limitations related to the research cycle described in Figure 2.2 must be briefly considered. The process does work more or less as described by the cycle, but it is seldom completely followed even in the physical sciences. At this point I will focus only on the theory construction stage. The scientist is human, which means she or he grew up with many preconceptions about how the world operates. These preconceptions may or may not be correct, but they nonetheless creep into our theory construction. Einstein, for example, admitted a preconception ("God does not play dice with the world") that led him to resist probability models in physics (Clark, 1971).

Because of the subject matter, however, the social scientist is faced with more preconceptions that may influence theory construction (Strasser, 1976). All cultures provide us with preconceptions or assumptions about humans and human societies. There are very few, if any, learned preconceptions about, say, the behavior of atoms and quarks. But our culture may tell us such things as humans are by nature bad or good, that lust is sinful, individual freedom is the highest ideal, and material objects are very important or not very important. The social scientist must be cautious and continually on the lookout for the impact of these preconceptions on their theory construction.

This does *not* mean that a social scientist must be or even can be amoral (that is, lacking any moral convictions). A social scientist may deplore violence, poverty, capitalism, or communism, and favor a particular religion. And social scientists may attempt to use social science to meet the objectives of their values. *But the social scientist must still be objective in the research process.* For example, poverty will never be reduced by social research so unobjective that the causes and solutions to poverty are never adequately understood.

Varieties of Sociological Research Methods

Human societies can be studied in many ways and from many differing perspectives. Although none of the differing methods is necessarily better than the others, they all have contrasting strengths and weaknesses. Which method a sociologist uses depends on the research question, the theoretical perspective preferred, and limitations or opportunities related to the subject to be studied. Each of the methods described below employs different techniques to overcome the unique limitations of sociological research that we have described.

There is, however, an important common element in all the methods discussed below. All are concerned with data collection and analysis.

Data collection is simply the process of collecting information. The exact means of collecting information (interviews, questionnaires, content analysis, examination of historical records, and so one) depends on the research method used. But whatever method is used, the data collection must be accurate. With each method of data collection there are various techniques for checking the accuracy of data collection.

Data analysis is the activity of processing data for the meaning the data are expected to reveal. There are two basic forms of data analysis. **Descriptive analysis** and descriptive statistics present a profile of the subject. If the subject is poverty, we can present the percentage of the population living in poverty, the percentage of blacks living in poverty, and so on. **Explanatory analysis,** or causal analysis, on the other hand, attempts to show causal relations more directly. The question is more specifically, does x cause y? (See Box 2.2 for more details and the type of statistics used.)

It is important to recognize, however, that all forms of data collection and analyses do not rely equally on numbers. For example, detailed direct observations of people in everyday life (if done properly) can tell us much about human societies. Historical and cross-cultural comparative methods of analyses sometimes do not rely on statistical analyses. The types of data collection and analyses relying extensively on numbers and statistics are often called **quantitative analysis.** Methods of data collection and analysis not doing so are often called **qualitative analysis.** The terms are suggestive; quantitative relies on more cases for analysis (thus numbers can be used), whereas qualitative relies on fewer cases, but more detailed (quality) analysis of each case. In summary, the type of data analysis used depends on the questions asked and methods of research used. All can be useful, with different strengths and weaknesses.

Experiments. Despite the limitations social scientists face in following the classical experimental design, modified forms of this research method can be used. As we will see, one type involves differential treatment of research subjects for controlled comparisons in a natural setting. The most common type, however, involves bringing individuals into a laboratory setting. The individuals are asked to respond to some controlled condition or task and their reactions are recorded. Individuals may be asked to perform some task while the researcher varies the conditions under which they work on this task (see Box 2.3). The goal, of course, is to determine effects of independent variables controlled by the researcher.

The primary limitation of this type of social experiment (compared with the classical experimental design) is the experimenter's lack of control over all important variables. The environment, of course, can be controlled when isolating an atom for research, but even with an individual isolated in a laboratory the social scientist can never achieve full control over important variables. Besides the effect of being in an unfamiliar laboratory setting, the simple knowledge of being studied can influence human behavior. In an early, now famous social experiment, workers in a factory were studied to find what factors might increase production. This experiment, known as the Hawthorne study, found that the workers' awareness of being studied was the most important factor influencing production. This influence on subjects has come to be called the **Hawthorne Effect.**

But equally important, each person brings a unique set of prior experiences to the experiment, and some of these prior experiences may have important effects on how the individual reacts to the experiment. To some degree, even this limitation can be overcome. We know that a few prior experiences may be most important in influencing the type of behavior being studied (exactly which depends on the type of study). Some examples could be experiences associated with being a minority, poor, female, Catholic, and so on. Through proper sampling techniques the researcher can examine any differences in behavior by people in these categories. The conclusions of the experiment can then be adjusted for the particular subcategories of people. The researcher, however, can never control or check for all prior experiences that may affect human behavior. That is why social scientists never reach conclusions like, "When in this situation, all people have *x* reaction." Social scientists must work with *probabilities* or tendencies, because people never act exactly the same way, owing to prior experiences (and perhaps even because of genetic differences). Thus, a more likely conclusion will be something like, "When in this situation, 75 percent of the people have *x* reaction."

In the laboratory setting, of course, research is conducted with individuals or small groups. But even laboratory experiments with individual subjects can be useful for sociologists as well as psychologists. With such experiments the sociologist may be able to draw conclusions about the effects of the society or group on the individual. One striking example is the Milgram (1974) experiment described in Box 2.3. The shockingly high obedience rate of people in this study tells us some important things about social control and the potential for mass violence.

Finally, *field experiments* can be conducted with groups in more or less natural settings. This type of experiment has become increasingly popular in "evaluation research" where the effectiveness of a policy or program is tested. Remember that a primary characteristic of experiments is the examination of effects that have been induced by the researcher. In a natural setting the researcher can begin by dividing people into groups with similar characteristics. In this way the effects of many secondary independent variables can be controlled (that is, the effects of these variables can be measured and separated from the effects of primary independent variables).

Then by treating each group differently and observing the different responses, the researcher can understand the effects of how each group was treated.

One of the largest field experiments of this type

BOX 2.2

Common Statistical Terms

The standard statistics for descriptive analyses are the mean, the mode, and the median. All three present different characteristics of the population being studied. The **mean** is what most people refer to as the average. It is the total of the separate figures collected (say, family incomes), divided by the number of cases. The mean family income for four families with incomes of $10,000, $15,000, $20,000, and $30,000 is $18,750. But although useful, this statistic can be misleading, or hide other information. A mean income of $18,750 can be the result of four families all with incomes of $18,750, or of four families where three have no income and one has $75,000. The **mode** helps overcome some of these problems because it refers to the number recurring the most often. For example, family incomes of $10,000, $15,000, $15,000, and $30,000 would have a mode of $15,000. But again, this can be misleading with "skewed" distributions. Skewed distributions of numbers do not follow the "normal curve" pattern, where most figures are in the middle and fewer at either end (the "bell curve" pattern as with $1,000, $5,000, $10,000, $10,000, $15,000, $20,000). Finally, the **median** refers to the midpoint in the distribution. Incomes of $5,000, $10,000, $15,000, $20,000, and $75,000 have a median of $15,000. The median is less influenced by extreme figures (for example, the $75,000). All three of these measures of "central tendency" tell us something different and important, and all should be considered in descriptive analyses.

Although descriptive statistics can suggest causal relations, explanatory analysis is more directly concerned with showing cause and effect. For example, the more direct question may be, does *x* cause *y*? The most commonly used statistic in explanatory or causal analysis is the **correlation coefficient**. A correlation coefficient tells us the degree of association or covariance of two or more variables. For example, if *x* increases, does *y* also increase or decrease? If *x* increases by a measure of 5 and *y* also increases by a measure of 5, we have a strong positive relation. Or the same can occur

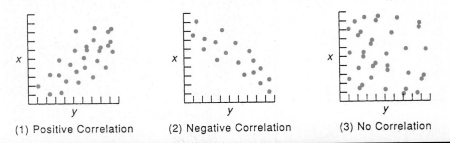

(1) Positive Correlation   (2) Negative Correlation   (3) No Correlation

was the New Jersey Income Maintenance Experiment (Kershaw and Fair, 1976; Rossi and Lyall, 1976). With this experiment part of the state was divided into districts with similar characteristics (minority group status, work opportunities); then, people in each district were offered a different type of welfare aid program if they qualified for assistance. In this manner sociologists were able to understand the value, costs, and effects of variations in public assistance programs for the poor.

in the opposite direction and show a strong negative relation (x increases by 5, whereas y decreases by 5). Two-dimensional graphs can indicate the relation between two variables x and y as shown below. The first represents a rather strong positive relation between x and y (each dot is a plot of one case on the x and y axes). The second represents a rather strong negative correlation between two variables, whereas the third indicates no correlation. Such covariance between two variables *may* show a causal relation (x causes y). But other tests are needed because the covariance may occur for other reasons (x and y may be related not because x causes y but because a third variable z causes both x and y).

A correlation coefficient is measured from $+1.0$ to -1.0. A $+1.0$ correlation is a perfect positive correlation, and -1.0 is a perfect negative correlation. A correlation of .00 shows absolutely no correlation between two variables. Normally, in sociological research with much multiple causation, a correlation of $+.50$ or $-.50$, and perhaps even .30, is an important finding. But this depends on many factors, like sample size.

Statistical techniques also allow for **multiple correlations,** which are very useful in sociological research. With many possible causes of a particular effect, we need a method that will allow us to determine which variable may be the strongest cause or only cause. For example, a person's income level may be influenced by education level, IQ, father's income and education, and years of job experience, among other things. Multiple correlation techniques help us determine which of these things are the most important in influencing income. The multiple correlation will still read from $+1.0$ to -1.0, but in this case the number will represent the strength of the correlation that remains after considering all the other possible causes together.

Finally, the **significance level** of a correlation is important because it tells us something of the confidence we can have that the correlation presented is the true relationship between two or more variables. Because of sample size and other factors we may have more or less confidence in the correlation. With the significance measure scientists are referring to the probabilities that the correlation coefficient shows an accurate relation between two or more variables. For example, a significance level of .01 indicates that there is only 1 chance in 100 that the correlation is inaccurate. Sociologists normally consider a significance level of .05 or less as acceptable. In other words, if the correlation between x and y is $+.50$ with a significance of .05, we can accept that there is a correlation between x and y. If the significance level were .30 or even .10, however, the social scientist would report no confidence that the correlation of $+.50$ is accurate.

Sociologists use many other statistical techniques that are usually more complicated but often a variation on these most common types.

In summary, sociologists may find experimental research designs useful. As in the classical experimental design, the sociologist is introducing a stimulus (a required task, threat, reward, etc.) to the subject of research, then observing a response. For several reasons, however, many (if not most) sociologists do not favor experimental designs; first, experimental designs are primarily restricted to micro-level questions. There are exceptions, and field experiments like the New Jersey Income Main-

With laboratory experiments Stanley Milgram (1974) examined the extent of obedience to authority among people who were led to believe that their own obedience would harm another person. Disguising the research as an experiment in learning behavior, Milgram told volunteers (subjects) to give electric shocks to another "subject" (the "learner") when the "learner" failed to provide the correct answer in a word-association test.

The learner was in fact part of the research team and no electric shocks were actually given. But the key is that subjects in the research (given the role of teacher) believed electric shocks were received by the learner when they pulled a switch. On a desk in front of the teacher was a series of switches labeled 15 to 450 volts (30 switches in all, with the last six marked "danger: severe shock"). The so-called teacher was asked to pull a progressively higher switch (in voltage) each time the learner gave an incorrect answer. In a major part of the research, the teacher and the learner were separated by a wall but could communicate verbally.

With the research in progress, there was a prearranged response pattern to the shocks "received" by the learner. For example, with the lower-voltage shocks there was simply an "ouch" that got louder with higher voltage (Milgram, 1974, p. 56). But at 150 volts the learner would plead, "Experimenter! That's all. Get me out of here. I told you I had heart trouble. My heart's starting to bother me now. . . ." This type of prearranged response continued through 330 volts, at which point the learner became silent, not screaming or responding to questions through the remaining voltage levers.

The main question was how many teachers would continue through all switches to 450 volts. How far would subjects go in following the orders of an authority figure (the psychologist)? After the cry of protest from the learner at 150 volts, almost none of the subjects wanted to continue shocking the learner. But they were told to do so by the authority figure.

In this variation of the research, over *60 percent* of the subjects actually followed these orders, however reluctantly, through *all the switches to 450 volts*. In another variation of the research the learner and the teacher sat next to each other. Here the teacher was required physically to place the learner's hand on the shocking device. Even in this case, 30 percent of the teachers went through all the switches to 450 volts.

Milgram's research subjects represented people from all walks of life — housewives, students, business people, and so on. Few if any of these people enjoyed hurting others. They resisted giving further shocks, but most followed orders to do so.

tenance Experiment can sometimes overcome this limitation, but there are other limitations especially with laboratory experiments. Second, attempts to control for the effects of the experimental environment itself may not always be successful. Third, the researcher often does not have extensive control over many important independent variables. Fourth, there are ethical limitations on what can or should be done to people in experiments. Some of the most noted experiments, like the Milgram obedience experiment, raise serious ethical questions. Finally, some of the most important sociological subjects cannot be studied in experiments for a variety of reasons. The complex processes of industrialization, urbanization, and revolution, for example, are difficult or impossible to simulate in an experi ment. These are among the reasons why sociologists usually favor other methods described below.

Survey Research. As in most research designs, the underlying goal of **survey research** is to uncover causal relations by controlling independent and dependent variables. A key difference between experimental research and survey research is that in the latter we are trying to uncover causal relationships that have already happened. This is why survey research is a form of post hoc research — after events. The main goal of survey research is therefore to reconstruct the causal events to examine how they developed. This goal is achieved primarily through manipulation of empirical data with statistical techniques. In understanding survey research we must start with a focus on sample selection and data manipulation.

Let me begin by being more specific about discovering relationships that have already occurred; assume we want to know why some people participated in the urban riots that occurred in the 1960s and others did not. One approach may be to question blacks in urban areas where riots occurred to understand the differences between rioters and nonrioters. The study might focus on prior events that affected rioters and nonrioters differently. Such prior events or conditions might be a history of unemployment, family trouble, level of education, and so on.

After deciding what you want to study and designing and pretesting a questionnaire, the next critical step for survey research is *sample selection*. In short, you must decide whom to interview. The first consideration is deciding on the *population* you wish to study. Are you interested in the attitudes and characteristics of all U.S. voters, all college students, all females, men in Chicago, blacks in Los Angeles, or some other group? The group you choose to study depends on generalizations you hope to make. If you want to know why women voters in the United States tended to vote against Ronald Reagan, you would need a sample of women voters in the United States. If you want to know the health characteristics of Chinese-Americans in California, you need a sample of Chinese-Americans in California. All of this should sound logical, but there

can be very critical mistakes made if the sample is not properly selected. The most famous case, I suppose, is the 1936 *Literary Digest* poll that predicted Alfred Landon would defeat Franklin Roosevelt in the presidential election. Because the sample included a disproportionate percent of Republicans, the poll was inaccurate.

The most important factor is collecting a **random sample.** If the task is to determine the outcome of a national election, the sample must reflect the general characteristics of the population to be studied — in this case, U.S. voters. A random sample means that people are selected without bias, with all people in the target population having an equal chance of being selected. In the case of the 1936 polling mistake predicting a Landon victory, the sample was drawn from telephone directories and auto registration lists. Especially during the Depression, the more affluent were more likely than the rest of the population to have telephones and automobiles. And because the more affluent are more likely to be Republicans, the sample included a greater percentage of people saying they would vote for the Republican candidate, Landon, than actually existed in the population.

It is useful to add that the size of the sample is not as important as the sample's representativeness. For example, the characteristics of the U.S. population and voting behavior can be accurately predicted (within two percentage points) with a sample of only around three thousand individuals. For the sample to be representative, it must mirror its population.

After the sample is selected and the questions are asked and recorded, the next step is data manipulation. If the survey research is for a descriptive study, data manipulation involves only tabulating percentages, means, medians, or the mode. (You may want to reexamine Box 2.2 at this point.) For example, the pollster wants to know what percent of the voters will vote for which candidate. But if the survey is for an explanatory study, data manipulation is more complex. In this case the goal is to uncover causal relationships, post hoc, as described above.

The basic principles of data manipulation for explanatory surveys are rather simple. As indicated in Table 2.2, casual relations may be *suggested* by how the data "line up." (I stress only "suggested" at this

TABLE 2.2. *Imaginary table on father's income and son's education*

		Son's education		
		Low	High	Totals*
	low	cell 1	cell 2	
		75%	25%	100%
Father's		(530)	(180)	(710)
income	high	cell 3	cell 4	
		25%	75%	100%
		(220)	(670)	(890)

* Note how this table is tabulated: We are concerned with the effect of father's income on son's education. Thus, the numbers are tabulated from left to right as indicated by 100 percent to the right. Actual numbers are often in parentheses with percentages above. This table indicates that low-income fathers tend to have low-educated sons (75 percent in this example), and high-income fathers tend to have higher-educated sons (again, 75 percent).

point.) The data manipulation involves nothing more than sorting the data into categories. And in the "old days" before high-speed computers, this was literally what was done. Now, of course, computers do roughly the same thing with more cases more rapidly. When sorting, the researcher is looking for variables that tend to go together. Perhaps we want to know if a father's income level usually influences his son's education level. As shown in Table 2.2, the cases in the imaginary study line up in cells 1 and 4. This indicates that fathers with higher incomes tend to have sons that received more education. We cannot yet say that there is something about having a more affluent father that causes his son to seek and attain more education, because many more variables need examination. But this simple relationship between fathers' income and sons' education points us in a direction for a closer look.

Especially since World War II the most popular methodology among sociologists has been survey research. Indeed, the popular image of sociological research is the door-to-door or telephone interview used in survey research. However, although survey research is very suitable for opinion polls and describing population characteristics, it has limitations

for explanatory studies. We will examine some of these limitations after considering historical and comparative methods.

Historical and Comparative Methods. As noted earlier in this chapter, sociology was born with historical and comparative methods of research. But by the twentieth century, especially in the United States, sociology lost this methodological focus and turned toward case studies and survey research. This loss of historical and comparative methods, however, is increasingly criticized, and there has been a new surge of interest and use of historical and comparative methods in the past few years (Tilly, 1981). The recent reemergence of historical and comparative methods has come in a time of the computer and new complex statistical techniques, and thus, these methodologies today are somewhat different from those of Durkheim and Weber. Weber's historical and comparative works were more "qualitative" — that is, Weber focused on only a few cases for more detailed or quality data. In other words, you will find little statistical analysis in Weber's work. Durkheim did use descriptive statistics to some extent, but his works are strikingly different from many today that are much more quantitative. The same trend, it is interesting to note, can be found among historians as well (Tilly, 1981; *Los Angeles Times,* April 23, 1981). Durkheim would probably be pleased by the new quantitative trend in comparative and historical research; Weber, on the other hand, would probably be troubled by the extensive attention to statistics (Ragin and Zaret, 1983).

Sociologists have been turning to historical and comparative methods in part because computers have expanded our ability to analyze vast amounts of data. But sociologists have also turned toward historical and comparative methods in reaction against survey research that has become overly social psychological, ignorant of history and other cultures. When computer technology first emerged in the 1950s, it allowed for rapid analysis of large quantities of information. To utilize this new technology sociologists first turned to large samples of individuals who had responded to questionnaires. Sociology became even more social psychological. But the trend is being reversed as sociologists have learned to tap large quantities of historical and cross-national data.

As with any research methodology, the goal is to control variables to uncover causal relations (Smelser, 1976). **Historical and comparative methods** are forms of post hoc research, as is survey research. Through controlled comparisons among nations or regions, the similarities as well as differences can reveal patterns that suggest causal relations. Some sociologists today prefer the detailed comparisons of just a few cases. For example, Moore (1966, 1978) and Skocpol (1979) have contributed much to our understanding of the causes and effects of major revolutions by comparing cases like the French, Russian, Chinese, and English revolutions. Others prefer to examine many nations, often generating massive amounts of statistical data for analysis. For example, in an impressive work, Paige (1975) analyzed statistics of various kinds from most agricultural regions of the world to help us understand the causes of agrarian political violence. Also, many researchers have recently conducted impressive studies on the effects of investments by multinational corporations in Third World nations (Chase-Dunn, 1975; Rubinson, 1976). Similarly, sociologists favoring historical methods have learned to manipulate large quantities of historical data to reveal the causes of events in the past and/or compare the past with the present.

Cross-cultural data for comparative studies can be gathered from many sources. Quite often the data come from official statistics published by governments and international organizations like the United Nations and Europe's Organization for Economic Cooperation and Development (OECD). These types of data have become available especially since World War II. Some comparative studies have even obtained survey research data in more than one nation for comparison (Bell and Robinson, 1980). And if the researcher is interested in nonindustrial societies, anthropologists have compiled impressive amounts of comparative data that are highly organized and easily obtainable (for example, see Murdock, 1967).

The praise for inventiveness, however, must go to many researchers seeking historical data. Some of the data come from logical sources but require vast amounts of time to compile and analyze. For example, old biographical publications (like *Who's Who*) can be researched for important information on the relations between government and economic elites (Freitag, 1975, 1983). Newspapers, especially those that are extensively indexed, can be excellent sources of data on topics like riots or attitudes of political elites (Kerbo and Shaffer, 1986). One of the most impressive examples is Tilly's (1981) many works on several countries for periods covering more than a century. Many thousands of events from news stories have been coded for computer analysis by Tilly and his researchers.

Other researchers have looked in less obvious places. For example, Thernstrom (1970) examined marriage license applications and tax records from Boston during the 1800s. At the time these records contained employment and occupational histories of families that provided valuable insight into economic opportunities in the early United States. In another example, Burrage and Corry (1981) obtained city records from London from 1328 to 1604. These records ranked occupational guilds by status for ceremonial occasions in early London. With these data the researchers were able to tell us something about how and why occupations moved up or down in prestige and influence.

Sociology began with a focus on important macro-level questions. Early sociologists wanted to understand such things as how communities changed with industrialization, the effects of state expansion, agricultural decline, and so on. The social survey research of the midtwentieth century took away this focus and stimulated more social psychological research. Recent developments in historical and comparative research, however, have allowed us to pick up the broader questions again — the ones sociologists are uniquely qualified to pursue. The major advances in statistical methods of analysis using computers came with survey research. But sociologists have learned to use many of these same techniques for historical and comparative research. And with these methods we can now better analyze societies and social structures, rather than just the psychological states of individuals.

Participant Observation. Sometimes the subject matter of interest to sociologists cannot be easily measured and assigned numerical scores. At times the subject matter cannot be understood with standard questions asked by social surveys. Many times sociologists are not even sure of the questions to ask. And in other times there will be no one recording information for later use if sociologists do not take to the "field" to observe events. Consider the example of crowd behavior.

In 1895 a leading French social theorist, Gustave Le Bon (1960), published a book called *The Crowd* in which he attempted to explain crowd behavior like bread riots and mass protests. Le Bon argued that there exists in all of us a "collective mind" inherited from lower animals. This collective mind, he believed, was especially present in nonwhites, as well as "women, children, and savages." When people are in large crowds, Le Bon believed, this collective mind is activated, producing "irrational" protest behavior. Le Bon was an aristocrat who could not understand why the lower classes were protesting in the streets below his balcony. To him their behavior was irrational. Although we have much to learn about crowd behavior, progress has been made primarily because social scientists have climbed down from the balcony to take a closer, more objective look at crowds.

The exact methods for carrying out **participant observation** vary, but the main characteristic is that the social scientist goes to the subject matter for direct, long-term observation. Such observation may involve direct participation in activities along with the people being studied, with the research subjects' knowledge that they are being studied. Examples of this are Hillery's months of observations in monasteries (Della Fave and Hillery, 1980) and Palmer's excellent studies of private detectives (1974), Paramedics (1983), and massage parlors (Bryant and Palmer, 1975). But participant observation is sometimes conducted without the knowledge of the research subjects. For example, Festinger (Festinger, Riecken, and Schachter, 1956) studied a small cult predicting the end of the

world and their own escape in flying saucers. Researchers joined the group, participating in their activities, only later revealing their research objectives.

Participant observation techniques, of course, began with anthropologists studying small cultures far different from our own. Anthropologists had no choice but to spend extensive time (months or years) in such cultures if they were to understand them. A questionnaire and survey research do no good when you don't even know the questions and how to ask them. Some sociologists, however, believe that we often assume we know too much when studying modern people, even from our own culture. They call for more *qualitative* research, in contrast to the more *quantitative* research of surveys. Much like anthropologists, sociologists have studied various groups of people in modern industrial societies using participant observation. For example, sociologists have used participant observation to study police officers, mental patients, prostitutes, CB radio club members, and medical students, to mention a few.

As may seem obvious, sociologists who favor participant observation methods also tend to favor micro-level theory. Their focus is on people in their everyday lives, what they do, and why they do it. As described in the previous chapter, micro-level theorists usually believe that the meanings people give to reality and their activities are the most critical things about the social world. Some form of direct observation of people over extended periods is seen as the best method of study by these sociologists. But again, there are limitations and weak points in participant observation. We are now prepared to compare the weak and strong points of the major types of social research methods.

Methods of Research: Summary and Comparison

Faced with many limitations in using the classical experimental design, sociologists have developed several alternative research methods. Four of the most frequently used methods have been described. Each, however, has different weaknesses as well as strengths. It will be helpful to summarize them briefly (see also Table 2.3).

TABLE 2.3. *A comparison of research methods*

Type research method	Primary characteristics	Primary level of analysis	Strength	Weakness
Experimental	1. Subjects studied in controlled lab setting	1. Micro	1. More control over variables	1. Artificial setting
	2. Comparisons of differently treated populations in field setting	2. Micro or macro	2. More control over variables	2. Time-consuming
Survey	Questionnaires given to sample of population	Primarily micro but can be macro	Many cases for analysis Conclusions generalizable	Difficult to answer macro questions Questions often superficial
Historical and comparative	Comparing data historically and/or across nations	Macro	Can answer macro-level questions	Cases often limited Good quality data scarce and limited
Participant observation	Personally observing subjects over extended time	Micro	More detailed and in-depth information	Difficult to generalize Time-consuming Researcher effects Difficult to control researcher bias

Experimental methods attempt to come closest in following the classical experimental design. There are two major varieties of experimental research; one type is conducted on individuals (or small groups) in a laboratory setting, whereas the other is conducted in a field setting by treating segments of a population differently to observe outcomes. Experiments in laboratory setting may allow for more control over some important variables (compared with other sociological research methods). Still, it is impossible to control all important variables with research on humans, and the setting itself is artificial and may affect behavior in unpredictable ways. A primary difference with field experiments is a greater ability to test macro-level questions. But although field experiments can also give the researcher more control over important variables, the research is very time-consuming and expensive. Because of the value of field experiments, however, they are increasingly used in testing alternative public programs.

Sociologists are best known for their use of survey research. Though the percentage of articles published in major sociological journals using survey research has declined rapidly in recent years, most people continue to think of door-to-door or telephone interviews when sociological research is mentioned. Survey research has two basic strengths. First, many cases (usually individuals) can be obtained for analysis. A large sample (if obtained correctly) can allow for firmer conclusions and examination of many variables. In other words, more cases usually provide a wider variety of differences (variables) that can be examined for their influence on the dependent variable. Second, if the sample is obtained properly, the findings can be generalized to a very large population. The researcher can predict the outcome of nationwide elections, or explain a widespread characteristic of the population. However, survey research has two main weaknesses. First, it is not always appropriate for macro-level questions. The researcher is measuring the opinions and characteristics of individuals, not societies per se. Second, survey research does not allow for detailed, quality questions. When studying many cases you can know less about each case. Do all people read the questions the same way? Are the opinions and characteristics more complex than can be indicated in questions for survey research? The answer to the first question is usually no, the second yes.

More sociologists are returning to the historical and comparative methods of sociology's founders. The primary strength of historical and comparative methods is that they allow sociologists to consider sociological-level (macro) questions. As more data on national, regional, or urban areas become available, more sophisticated statistical methods can be used. Still, a major limitation often continues to be limited cases. A study of highly industrialized nations may provide the researcher about 10 to 20 cases. Some survey research deals with more than 20,000 cases. Also, the quality of some data is questionable. Data collected by major industrial nations and organizations like the United Nations and the World Bank are usually reliable, but these nations and organizations have been collecting data for only a few decades. Historical data of equal richness is limited. And often these nations and organizations do not collect data that sociologists want. For example, government officials in industrial nations vary in the ways they define poverty and collect information about poverty. This makes international comparisons of the causes and effects of poverty difficult.

Finally, observational case studies like participant observation allow for more detailed and in-depth data collection than do any other method. The researcher can find out more about the subjects, what they do, what they think. But, of course, the information gathered is limited to the micro level, which is a problem for macro-level theorists. Even micro-level theorists, however, face many problems with participant observation. First, the research findings are difficult to generalize. The researcher has studied one small group; are all groups similar? Which ones are not? Second, the research is very time-consuming; the researcher must spend extensive amounts of time with the subjects. Third, the presence of a researcher can disrupt the normal behavior the researcher is interested in studying. Over an extended period of time this problem can be reduced as subjects become comfortable being observed. But this increases the time required for the research. Fourth, it is usually more difficult to replicate the research and control for researcher bias. With other research methods it is easier for another researcher to replicate the research and compare results. In this way we may judge the accuracy and objectivity of research. We all tend to see what we want to see, and objective measures of our subject matter (ratings, scores, ranks) and multiple observers can thus help increase objectivity. But both are difficult to come by with participant observation.

All the research methods discussed above have contrasting strengths and weaknesses. When possible, therefore, it is advantageous to obtain research findings from a combination of methodologies. When a hypothesis is supported by findings from several studies using different methodologies, we have more confidence in the conclusions. Often, however, sociologists are very limited in their ability to obtain data. Consider research on trends in the inequality of wealth throughout U.S. history. Experimental research, survey research, and participant observation are excluded at the outset. The best the researcher can hope for is good quality data on wealth holdings from more than one source.

Yet any methodology is only as good as the care and diligence of the social scientist conducting the research. The social scientist must be committed to seeking objective, accurate information. It is easy to "cut corners" or disregard rules of sound research when such a commitment does not exist. An open community of scholars is probably the most important safeguard against shoddy research. Ideas and research must be freely shared and criticized, for it is only in this manner that sound research can be identified.

To help maintain quality research, the discipline of sociology operates as most scientific communities. Research papers are presented at meetings for critical appraisal, and most important, research published in major sociology journals has been anonymously reviewed by several sociologists before publication is decided.

CHAPTER SUMMARY

Key Terms

classical experimental
  design, 41
dependent variable, 41
independent variable, 41
inductive research, 41
deductive research, 42
hypotheses, 42
operationalization, 42
measurement, 42
post hoc research, 43
descriptive analysis, 44
explanatory analysis, 44
quantitative analysis, 44

qualitative analysis, 44
mean, mode, median, 46
correlation coefficient,
  46
multiple correlations, 47
significance level, 47
Hawthorne Effect, 45
survey research, 49
random sample, 49
historical and compara-
  tive methods, 51
participant observation,
  52

Content

If sociology is to exist, there must be at least some free inquiry. This condition has been rare in human history, and helps us understand why sociology and other social sciences did not fully emerge until the late 1700s or 1800s.

Of the early "classical" sociologists, the three most important were Marx, Weber, and Durkheim. All three sociologists were able to build sociological theories with new historical and comparative methods of analysis.

After World War I the United States took the lead in sociological research, but here sociology became more social psychological and social problem-oriented. Only recently has American sociology become more diversified. There are now many varieties of macro and micro theories, with a wide range of methodologies.

The most basic research design is classical experimental research. But sociologists encounter several difficulties in using this research design and have developed several modified methods.

Four basic sociological research methods are social experiments, survey research, historical and comparative methods, and participant observation. Each of these four has strengths and weaknesses and, depending on the research design, can be used interdependently.

PART II

The Foundations of Human Society

CHAPTER 3

Material Culture
and the Evolution
of Human Societies

Like other kinds of progress, social progress is not linear but divergent and re-divergent. Each differentiated product gives origin to a new set of differentiated products. While spreading over the earth mankind have found environments of various characters, and in each case the social life fallen into, partly determined by the social life previously led, has been partly determined by the influences of the new environment; so that the multiplying groups have tended ever to acquire difference, now major, now minor; there have arisen genera and species of societies.

— Herbert Spencer, Evolution and Culture

There is an immense variety of human behavior. Just about any behavior considered vulgar or unacceptable in one society is considered acceptable (maybe even highly regarded) in another. One of our goals is to understand this variety, for only by understanding it can we really understand ourselves.

The first two chapters in Part II examine two somewhat opposing explanations of the variety of human behavior. The first explanation, considered in Chapter 3, favors material explanations. The second explanation, in Chapter 4, favors values, belief systems, or, more generally, nonmaterial explanations. As we will see, however, even if material factors are shown to be the most important in shaping human societies, material and nonmaterial factors are of necessity interrelated. Both are important in producing unique, but in other ways quite similar, human societies.

Culture and the Diversity of Human Societies

Humans are clearly among the most adaptable organisms ever to populate the earth. Few organisms are able to match the human ability to adapt our behavior to changes in the material environment. And what makes humans unique is their ability to adapt without genetic change. As a class, insects may be the most adaptable organisms, but their adaptability comes from overwhelming numerical advantages in reproduction. With massive numbers of offspring the chances are good that at least some insects will have a slightly altered genetic code that can provide new behavior adaptive to a nitch in the altered environment.

Humans, on the other hand, have been provided with an alternative means of adaptability — the human brain. Intelligence allows for self-correcting behavior; it provides the ability to access the future outcomes of action and to correct this action if the assessment indicates nonrewarding outcomes. In one sense this description of human adaptability may be overly optimistic. Humans have a long way to go in just matching the 135-million-year existence of dinosaurs. We may destroy ourselves with the products of this superior intelligence (for example, nuclear weapons). But even during the short time humans have existed on the earth, human ability to adapt to almost all extremes of climate around the world is quite remarkable. Humans have taken up residence in the frozen regions, in deserts, and in all climates in between. There are even prospects for long-term residence under the seas and in space. No other animal has been able to do this without significant biological changes.

The product of human intelligence that directs human behavior and allows for adaptability is generally called **culture.** We can define culture most broadly as the learned part of human behavior. Culture is the blueprint for living, or the guide to what we do that has been created and passed down over the centuries. Culture must also be divided into its material and nonmaterial elements. By **material culture** we mean all the material products of humans, including art, tools, buildings, weapons, and, more generally, all aspects of technology. By **nonmaterial culture** we mean all the nonmaterial products of humans, including beliefs, values, ideologies, religions, and language. Our focus in this chapter is on material culture, and especially on human technologies and the behavior specifically related to material technology. We consider nonmaterial culture in the next chapter, as well as the biological foundation for the development of human culture.

An Introduction to the Materialist Perspective

Despite superior intelligence, humans have a fundamental characteristic that must not be overlooked when studying human societies — *humans are biological organisms.* No matter how different we consider ourselves in comparison with other animals, we are still biological organisms. Once we recognize this obvious and basic fact, several other fundamental facts follow. (1) Like all other biological organisms, we are not self-sufficient. We depend on an environment outside ourselves for food, water, oxygen, and other basic necessities. (2) We must be active in relation to this environment — we must in some way adapt the environment to our own needs. In the simplest form, some people adapt this environment by merely clearing a space to sleep in a cave and gathering plants that grow wild in a forest. Today, of course, most of us must go much further in adapting the environment for sustaining life, but in every society at least some of the population must work at adapting the environment for human use, or support others who do so. (3) In the process of adapting the environment to human needs, humans also shape their lives in a more general manner. Extensive amounts of time, energy, and planning must be devoted to adapting the environment and attaining our material needs. Because of this, what we think, how we relate to other humans, how we treat our closest family members are all affected by what we commonly call our "work." (4) Humans around the world have faced differing material environments and developed differing methods (technologies) of adapting those environments. Thus, varied environment and historical differences in the methods of adapting the environment are major forces behind the creation of different varieties of human societies.

Let's consider an elementary example. Because men tend to be physically stronger and faster than women, they are usually required to do the hunting in simple hunting and gathering societies. When a tribe must depend heavily on meat because other kinds of food are more difficult to obtain, the good hunter is highly regarded and given more influence than others in the tribe. Thus, tribes depending on meat usually have higher levels of male dominance (Leakey and Lewin, 1977, p. 235; 1978, p. 247). Similarly, when a tribe depends heavily on meat, the male dominance usually leads to a kinship system (family system) that traces family descent through the male's ancestors (that is, a patrilineal rather than a matrilineal kinship system). Relying on Murdock's sample of "simple horticultural societies" from his massive data set on the characteristics of societies around the world, Table 3.1 indicates a negative association between percentage of subsistence obtained from hunting or herding and a matrilineal kinship system. The point is this: the environment and the level of technology (both material factors) have shaped other basic (nonmaterial) characteristics in these societies.

Simply stated, the materialist view is that the material environment and the technology created by humans to adapt this material environment to human needs are most important in shaping human societies. As roughly indicated by Figure 3.1, it is the material environment and type of technology that shapes both cultural values and societal characteristics. Cultural values, of course, refer to the nonmaterial culture (beliefs, ideologies, values, and so on). Societal characteristics simply refer to the many major attributes of a society like its family system, divorce rate, political system, level of material inequality, and so on. The materialist perspective does recognize the importance of cultural values

TABLE 3.1. *The relation between a dependence on meat and kinship system in simple horticultural societies*

Percentage of subsistence obtained from meat	Percentage of societies matrilineal	Number of cases
26 or more	13	16
16 to 25	25	28
less than 15	39	23

SOURCE: Lenski and Lenski (1982, p. 155). The original data were compiled by Murdock (1967); see Lenski and Lenski (1982, p. 454, fn 12).

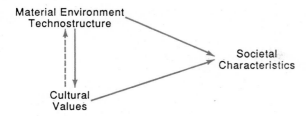

Figure 3.1. The impact of material environment and technostructure on cultural values and societal characteristics.

in shaping societal characteristics, as the dashed arrow from cultural values to societal characteristics indicates in Figure 3.1. But also indicated with the arrow from technostructure to cultural values is the assumed dominance of technostructure over cultural values.

We can return to our opening example for clarity. Why do simple societies that depend on meat have a higher degree of male dominance? The materialist position rejects the singular effect of cultural values. Rather, in view of the male's physical characteristics, this type of technology or economy makes others more dependent on strong males. This dependence is usually turned into other advantages and more rewards for males. No doubt we are likely to find beliefs and values approving male dominance in these societies, but the materialist view is that these values are shaped by the technostructure and come to provide support or approval for a condition (male dominance) that is primarily the result of technology and environment.

It is certainly possible for the values supporting male dominance to become important in shaping human societies by themselves. For example, perhaps the environment has changed so that meat is no longer very important for the tribe. Yet the tradition of male dominance may continue for some time. But the main point for the materialist view is that the tradition of male dominance had its roots in a real-life environment.

Two broad studies are useful in showing that material factors like the type of economy (or level of technology) shape much more than sex roles. In one

of the most sophisticated studies, Heise, Lenski, and Wardwell (1976) examined 51 characteristics of small societies and tribes from a sample of 330 living societies of all types. Among the 51 characteristics listed for each group were type of technology (hunting and gathering, different types of agricultural economies), family system, religion, sex inequality, and political organization. With a statistical technique that indicates which factors were related to (or caused) the biggest number of other factors, support for the materialist view was obtained. Specifically, these researchers found that a relatively small group of six technology-related factors of a group of several material and nonmaterial factors had more influence over most of the other characteristics of societies. Similar though less extensive studies also using the same type of data have reached comparable conclusions (Gouldner and Peterson, 1962).

In another study data were obtained on national characteristics rather than particular cultures. Sometimes cultures correspond to national boundaries, but often they do not. The correspondence is close for the United States, for example, but not so close in many African nations. This study, therefore, provides us with a different way of examining the materialist view. Sawyer (1967) compiled data on 236 characteristics from each of 82 nations with populations of 800,000 or more. Three factors were indicated to be the most important in influencing more of the other characteristics — national wealth, geographical size, and type of political system. Of these three, the first two are mainly indicators of technology and environment.

Furthermore, the materialist perspective implies some kind of evolutionary model of societal development. There are differing social evolutionary theories, but those favoring technology and material factors usually follow the pattern indicated in Figure 3.2. The material environment is seen as shaping human behavior by making certain adaptations to the environment more likely. The human behavior required by the environment in turn shapes nonmaterial culture (values, beliefs, etc.). Through time humans create new technologies for dealing with the environment (quite often because of further envi-

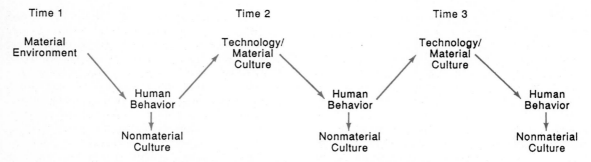

Figure 3.2. Environmental/technological influence in evolutionary perspective.

ronment changes). Then, the new technology and material culture in Time 2 shapes new forms of human behavior and nonmaterial culture as indicated in Figure 3.2. The process can be traced back to the earliest humans and forward to the present.

The process of historical change in the environment and technology (as suggested in Figure 3.2) is, no doubt, more complex. Seldom do changes occur in a nice, orderly progression. Especially today with the accelerated developments of science, technology can change more rapidly than values or attitudes. Thus, at any particular time, the values and beliefs shaped by the previous type of technology or material environment may in some ways conflict with a new technology or material environment. For example, many U.S. beliefs and values are the products of our older agrarian frontier environment and may be in conflict with the new industrial urban setting. An early American sociologist, William F. Ogburn (1964), described this condition as **cultural lag** (by "cultural" he was referring to nonmaterial culture). But despite the complexity of the process, the materialist position is that over time, and most often, social change operates as roughly described in Figure 3.2.

With these basic ideas and concepts in mind, we now turn to the social evolutionary record. We must consider the history of human societies for what this history can tell us about earlier humans, what their societies were like, and how we got where we are today. We will begin, as they say, in the beginning — or at least with this beginning as scientists believe it to be.

A HISTORY OF HUMAN SOCIETIES

According to the most accepted estimate, the universe is about 15 to 20 billion years old. The earth itself is relatively new, some 4 to 5 billion years old. Long after the earth was formed the first evidence of life appeared (3.2 to 3.4 billion years ago). Humans, of course, appear very late in natural history. Shortly after the extinction of dinosaurs (about 65 million years ago) the first primates evolved. But it was not until about 15 million years ago that an apelike creature (Ramapitheus) began what anthropologists believe was the line of development leading to *Homo sapiens.* There is evidence that our early ancestors (various pre-*Homo sapiens* hominids) began walking totally upright about 3 million years ago and made stone tools about 2.5 million years ago. *Homo sapiens* themselves emerged about 500,000 years ago, and *Homo sapiens sapiens* (the human animal that populates the world today) emerged only about 40,000 years ago (for sources of all these figures, see Leakey and Lewin, 1978, pp. 13–85; Thomas, 1979, pp. 3–7; Pfeffer, 1972, 1977). But whereas humans are very new to this earth, industrial societies as we know them are extremely recent. Even if we say that humans have been around for only 500,000 years, then approximately .0005 percent of human existence has been in industrial societies. In fact, even stable human settlements have existed for fewer than 10,000 years, or less than .02 percent of human existence.

The interesting question becomes, why did industrial societies emerge? Also, after some 500,000 years of foraging or hunting for wild plants and animals for food, why did agricultural settlements emerge about 10,000 years ago? And there are many related questions. What were humans like thousands of years ago? Did they have families as we have today? Did they kill each other as often as people do today? We do not have completely accurate answers to all these questions, but we do have some information for reasonably good answers. And the information we have helps us understand how human societies evolved over the centuries and why.

The information about early human societies that we will consider comes from two main sources. First, humans did not leave written records until many centuries after agricultural settlements emerged. But early humans did leave a rich archaeological record that helps us understand many of the characteristics of their societies. Second, many human groups today live with technologies roughly similar to those we believe were formed by early humans. For example, currently about 300,000 people live in hunting and gathering societies around the world (Leaky and Lewin, 1978, p. 95). Unless these people are extremely isolated from others with more complex technologies (a very rare situation today), it is unlikely that they live exactly as the earliest humans did. But hunting and gathering people today can be studied for clues to the characteristics of early human societies.

In this section we trace what is believed to be the development of human societies from thousands of years before agriculture through the industrial revolution some 250 years ago. We will begin with early hunting and gathering people, move to early horticultural settlements, describe agrarian empires, and conclude with the industrial revolution. Industrial societies are covered extensively in coming chapters; thus, our task at this point is to understand how we got to the industrial revolution and how preindustrial history has shaped what exists today.

Hunting and Gathering Societies

The type of society formed by the earliest humans can be called **hunting and gathering societies.**

The name refers to the means of attaining basic necessities used by these people — their technology. Quite simply, hunting and gathering technology refers to hunting animals and/or gathering edible plants found naturally in the environment. In its simplest form a hunting and gathering technology is hardly more complex than that employed by chimpanzees in the wild (see van Lawick-Goodall, 1971). Humans using a hunting and gathering technology may have a few tools like stone axes or spears, but little else. They may construct crude dwellings of sticks, mud, or animal skins, or just select a suitable cave. Most of these people probably used fire for protection and/or cooking because evidence indicates humans used fire about half a million to a million years ago (Pfeiffer, 1977, p. 53). Some hunting and gathering people use a somewhat more complex technology for hunting, with tools like traps, and bows and arrows. These represent the highest complexity in this type of society.

Outcomes of a Hunting and Gathering Technology. The type of technology used by hunting and gathering people is associated with many other social characteristics. To begin with, most of these people are nomadic or seminomadic. Without agriculture (cultivating crops), food sources in the environment are usually depleted through time, and hunting and gathering people must move on. Only those hunting and gathering tribes with a small population living in a very rich environment are not nomadic. Even when they are nomadic, however, the environment usually restricts their population size. An examination of contemporary hunting and gathering tribes shows they average only about fifty members (Murdock, 1949, p. 81), and about 90 percent are nomadic or seminomadic (Murdock, 1957; Lenski, 1966, p. 98).

Another consequence of a simple hunting and gathering technology is a minumum of material possessions. Few material goods can be transported frequently, especially when people lack animal power as do hunters and gatherers. A further implication of a hunting and gathering technology, nomadic life-style, and few material goods is material equality. Few if any tribe members are better off than others materially. What goods they do have, as well as the food obtained, is divided equally (Lenski, 1966, p. 102).

Related to material equality is general political equality. It is very difficult for a particular individual or small group to dominate others without material inequality and free time away from a daily search for food (Lenski, 1966). Extensive material inequality gives some people the means to reward others for obeying their rules, and free time allows for organization and planning to control others; both are lacking in hunting and gathering societies. Hunting and gathering societies do sometimes have informal or even formal leaders like a chief, shaman, or medicine man (Fried, 1973; Sahlins and Service, 1960), though these are part-time leaders (Lenski, 1966, p. 100). The part-time leadership status is most likely based on skill — skill in storytelling, performing rituals, predicting natural phenomena, or attaining food. Thus, leadership status in hunting and gathering societies is usually based on functional contribution.

Kinship as the Primary Subsystem. The most developed subsystem in hunting and gathering societies is the kinship system (family system). In fact, other subsystems are not needed because "kin groups perform many of the functions that are performed by schools, business firms, governmental agencies, and other specialized organizations in larger, more advanced, and more differentiated societies" (Lenski and Lenski, 1982, p. 114). Most hunting and gathering people are highly conscious of their exact kinship ties to others because the kinship system provides an important sense of identity and also operates for sharing resources, protection, and aiding those in need, among many other things.

Hunting and gathering families tend to be male-dominated and monogamous (only one spouse), though there is much variation in the extent of male dominance. I noted in beginning this chapter that dependence on meat may provide males with a highly regarded position. This advantaged position can lead to extensive male influence in other matters. For example, though most families in hunting and gathering societies are monogamous, the most influential males often practice polygyny (have more

than one mate); (Lenski and Lenski, 1982, p. 115). I should caution, however, that male dominance in most hunting and gathering societies does not mean it must exist in all other types of society. The extent of male dominance varies even in hunting and gathering societies (for example, with dependence on meat) and can certainly vary (or disappear) in very different societies.

Finally, because the family is the "all-purpose" subgroup in hunting and gathering societies, other subgroups or organizations found in more complex societies are lacking. In addition to the lack of formal government, there is no special military organization or police force — the family protects and seeks revenge for family members. Hunting and gathering societies lack a complex or organized religion. There are perhaps something similar to religious beliefs about supernatural forces and ancestor worship, but nothing systematic. Nor is there anything like a formal, distinct educational system. Essential knowledge is passed on to the young by the previous generation.

The Neolithic Revolution

It may seem incredible that humans lived with a hunting and gathering technology for hundreds of thousands of years without major change. What is really incredible, however, is that change occurred at all. Even if there was the time and energy for change, there was no real incentive. Hunting and gathering people often enjoyed better health, nutrition, and more leisure than most people with advanced technology (Sahlins, 1972). It took a significant change in the lives of early hunting and gathering people to propel them into a cycle of increasing technological change that continues to this day.

The change came for an increasing number of hunting and gathering people about 10,000 to 15,000 years ago. Most archaeologists agree that a primary stimulus for the change was a steady increase in population in many areas in the face of declining food resources (see Redman, 1978, p.88 – 112; Cohen, 1977; Harris, 1977). Population had increased before, but by this time it was more difficult to find new territory not already claimed by others. In addition, some argue that "there was less land as well as more people. Land had been decreasing ever since the height of the last ice age 20,000 or so years ago, when so much water was locked up in polar ice caps and glaciers that the ocean levels stood 250 to 500 feet lower than they stand today" (Pfeiffer, 1977, p. 69).

In what were the more populated areas of the world at the time, such as northern Africa and the Near East, the ever-increasing scarcity of food and land produced more intertribal conflicts (Pfeiffer, 1977, p. 33). We have some archaeological evidence of this increase in violent conflict. Archaeological sites dating back to the time just before agriculture show human remains with arrowheads and other stone projectiles piercing the bones (Pfeiffer, 1977, p. 246). We have no extensive evidence of organized violence against other humans before this period.

The pressure of less land and more people provided the impetus for change. We will never know with certainty exactly where and when human beings found that through settled agricultural methods more people could be fed, but current evidence seems to show that this happened in the Near East about 10,000 years ago. It is unlikely that someone suddenly discovered that plants could be cultivated — the Eureka theory. It is more likely that the knowledge was already present.

What happened was that it became necessary for more and more people to apply agricultural methods. Everyone in the tribe was required to participate in agriculture to survive. The pattern of nomadic hunting and gathering was altered for more and more people. Those who did not change did not survive in these highly populated areas. The Neolithic revolution had arrived.

Most social scientists regard the **Neolithic revolution** as the earliest, most important event in the evolution of human societies (Childe, 1952). Not only do we find a change in the technology of food production; we also find change in almost every aspect of human organization. The changes, of course, did not come as rapidly as did those during the industrial revolution. Human settlements at this time were more isolated, and transportation and communications were still undeveloped. It took about 5,000 years for agricultural methods to be established firmly with farming villages and irrigation (Pfeiffer, 1977, p. 144).

At first, people remained in small tribes, mixing farming with their old hunting and gathering ways. Their first agricultural tools were simple digging sticks. Consequently, the level of food production remained relatively low. But because of the new agricultural methods, there was at least some surplus food that freed an increasing number of people from full-time food production.

Through time, however, especially in the more populated areas like the Near East, hunting and gathering methods increasingly gave way to full-time agriculture. And our ancestors became better at it. In fact, the population increase that provided part of the stimulus for agriculture was given an even greater boost. It is estimated that during the first 8,000 years of agriculture (beginning about 10,000 years ago, remember), the total human population rose from 10 million to 300 million people (Leakey and Lewin, 1977, p. 176). Through hunting and gathering methods of food production it had taken human beings more than a million years to reach a population of 10 million. This relatively rapid population growth, itself an aspect of new agricultural methods, produced further change in human societies.

Horticultural Societies

The type of societies that first emerged with the Neolithic revolution about 10,000 years ago can be called **horticultural societies** (Lenski, 1966; Lenski and Lenski, 1982). This type of society slowly spread around the world and was the most advanced in technology until the emergence of **agrarian societies** some 5,000 years later. There were, of course, many horticultural societies in this 5,000-year period, and they were different in some important respects. But many major social changes did not come until the significantly more advanced agrarian societies around 3000 B.C.

As the name implies, horticultural societies were based on a form of agriculture; but it was a very simple agriculture. At first the tools were no more complicated than a digging stick, and later the hoe (the plow came much later). The earliest horticultural societies had no irrigation, animal power, or wheels for transportation. The first simple step into agriculture, however, led to many social transformations. Simple horticultural societies had settled communities, increased division of labor or specialization, new subsystems like religion and politics, and the emergence of warfare, inequality, and slavery.

Population and Cities. The nomadic life-style was altered in simple horticulture. Even simple agriculture requires more or less stable communities. The people must tend crops, store their harvest, and protect the fruits of their labor from thieves and nomadic invaders. There is evidence of a few very small settlements before agriculture (Harris, 1980, p. 144). In a few areas with plentiful wild cereal grains, some people could gather enough grain for survival from one growing season to the next without cultivation. But with early agriculture, communities became quite common and reached populations of a few hundred people to as many as 3,000 (Lenski, 1966, p. 120). Some of the first relatively large horticultural cities like Jericho and Catal Huyuk (in Turkey) date back to 8000 and 7000 B.C., respectively, with archaeological excavation revealing housing for 2,000 to 3,000 people (Hamblin, 1973).

With more improved horticultural methods, producing an even greater surplus in later horticultural societies, many more people could be supported within a geographical area. In Central America, for example, the Inca Empire had a population of about 4 million at its height, and the Maya civilization came close to 3 million (Steward and Faron, 1959, p. 121; von Hagen, 1961, p. 221). Cities were also able to attain much larger populations. For example, Uruk, one of the first large cities located in southern Mesopotamia about 5,000 years ago, attained a population of about 20,000 (Pfeiffer, 1977, p. 159). Later, the city of Teotihuacán, near what is now Mexico City, had a population of 125,000 (Pfeiffer, 1977, p. 369).

Specialized Subgroups. Because agriculture is usually a more efficient means of producing food than hunt-

ing and gathering, not everyone must work in the fields. Among other things this means that a more specialized division of labor develops, with some people specializing in other activities. One of the most important activities pursued was religion. Organized religious beliefs with special personnel devoted to religious ceremonies date to the period of early horticultural societies. We find all kinds of evidence of early religion with sacred symbols and monuments like England's Stonehenge. The importance of religious elites and their ability to command many people is suggested by the estimate that it took 30 million hours of human labor to construct Stonehenge (Pfeiffer, 1975, p. 95).

Table 3.2 indicates the relation between level of technology and religion using a sample of living societies. Hunting and gathering societies and simple horticultural societies are both unlikely to have even a conception of a supreme creator. But as we move to more advanced horticultural societies and agrarian societies, we find more complex religious beliefs.

TABLE 3.2. *Level of technology and religious beliefs*

Level of technology (type of society)	Percentage with type of religious* beliefs				Number and percent of societies
	A	B	C	D	
Hunting and gathering	60	29	8	2	85 (99%)
Simple horticultural	60	35	2	2	43 (99%)
Advanced horticultural	21	51	12	16	131 (100%)
Agrarian	23	6	5	67	66 (101%)

* A = no conception of a supreme creator; B = belief in a supreme creator who is inactive or not concerned with human affairs; C = belief in a supreme creator who is active in human affairs but does not offer positive support to human morality; D = belief in a supreme creator who is active and supports human morality.
SOURCE: Adapted from Lenski and Lenski (1982, p. 96). The original data were compiled by Murdock (1967); see Lenski and Lenski (1982, p. 454, fn 12).

Another subsystem to develop with early agriculture was politics. There were now more political positions with full-time occupants. These political elites were certainly more powerful than the leaders in hunting and gathering societies, but their power was still limited compared with that of later kings and pharaohs. In simple horticultural societies we typically find a leader who helps redistribute food and leads ceremonial activities (Wenke, 1980, p. 343). In later horticultural societies, however, political elites became increasingly powerful. Such societies were no longer just one family with its dominant male as the chief or headman. There came to be a ruler who appointed and dismissed a staff of aids. In addition, the political elites and religious elites were often one and the same because the semireligious nature of the political system helped rulers justify their rule. Increasingly these rulers did not function simply to distribute surplus goods or lead rituals any longer. Because of the expanded power of the ruler and his aids, the surplus was now viewed as his, and redistribution of the surplus occurred only when people obeyed his rule. As Lenski (1966, p. 168) put it, "an institution which began primarily as a functional necessity of group life became, in many advanced horticultural societies, an institution employed primarily for self-aggrandizement and exploitation."

It is also important to recognize that the growth of political power led to a state with expanded territory. Early horticulture brought settlements that were politically autonomous, but with more powerful elites and a staff to control the population, villages were often ruled by higher, more centralized political authority (Lenski and Lenski, 1982, p. 160).

Another new dimension of human societies that agriculture brought was extensive warfare. An examination of contemporary human societies makes this clear. Although warfare was rare or absent in 73 percent of the hunting and gathering societies in the sample, warfare was rare or absent in only 41 percent of the simple horticultural societies (Leavitt, 1977). Evidence for this is also found in the remains of many of the earliest cities; these early cities often had huge walls for protection. When some people are freed from the daily pursuit of food, and when some people are able to accumulate possessions and food reserves worth stealing, warfare is unfortunately not an unusual outcome.

We also find a professional military emerging with agriculture. Other changes, of course, would lead us to expect a military. First, the power of the state and political elites must be maintained; second, the geographical extension of political rule called for a military to maintain this rule; and third, the military was useful in taking accumulated goods from others and protecting what had been obtained. Following all these changes we find yet another — slavery. When people produced only enough to feed themselves and their children, slavery did not make economic sense. There was nothing to gain from owning other people. With more efficient agricultural technology, however, slavery began (Thomas, 1979, p. 39; Wells, 1971, p. 194). And with the expansion of military organization and technology as horticultural societies became more advanced, the extent of slavery became even greater. Along with other goods captured through warfare came more slaves.

The kinship system remains, in the face of all these changes, though with a few reduced functions. In the earliest horticultural settlements the kinship system continued to organize the relations of people and provide aid, a "police force," and a group identity. At first the kinship system overlapped with the new roles of political and religious elites. For example, the political leader attained that position because he (seldom she) was the head of the most respected family in the community (Lenski and Lenski, 1982, p. 153). But with later horticultural societies the kinship system came to overlap a bit less with the religious and political systems. Still, the attainment of these positions often depended on family ties.

Although the family system, as always, continued to be very important to people in more advanced horticultural societies, there was one important change — the growing economic importance of marriage. Daughters eligible for marriage came to be viewed as valuable property by their male kin. Men wanting to marry them paid a price. Approximately one-half of the hunting and gathering societies require an economic transaction with marriage;

this figure jumps to 97 percent with advanced horticultural societies (Lenski and Lenski, 1982, p. 162).

The Rise of Inequality. From a hunting and gathering technology with a low level of production, human societies began moving to a simple horticultural technology with a greater level of production. A key question pertains to how the surplus was distributed: Did inequality emerge because one group was able to control the surplus? The archaeological data and information from living human societies are quite clear; a shift from hunting and gathering technology to agriculture produces dramatic increases in the level of inequality. And the increase pertains to material inequality as well as political and social inequalities. The question can be put another way: Did the standard of living of most people improve as they moved from a hunting and gathering technology to agriculture? Emerging elites benefited from a greater surplus of material goods and gained increasing power over others. The material standard of living of the common people, however, improved very little if at all, and in many ways their life-style became more harsh and difficult. Many people were enslaved, and others were forced to work long hours for the benefit of elites. As writer H. G. Wells put it in *The Outline of History* (1971, p. 193), "There was a process of enslavement as civilization grew; the headmen and leaderly men grew in power and authority, and the common man did not keep pace with them; he fell by imperceptible degrees into a tradition of dependence and subordination." Let's briefly look at examples of the archaeological evidence (for an extensive presentation of the data from living human societies, see Lenski, 1966).

The two main types of archaeological evidence that concern us are burial practices and housing structures. With horticultural societies it became common practice to bury personal possessions with the dead (Redman, 1978, p. 197). What these burial sites show is increasing inequality with the advance of agricultural technology (Redman, 1978, p. 277). As Wenke (1980, p. 349) writes, "Some ancient cemeteries have three or four distinct classes of burials. Some types are well constructed of stone, have rich grave goods, and are centrally located,

while others are simple graves with little in them except the corpse." And it is reasonable to infer that these divisions correspond to different economic and social classes.

In addition to the burial data there are indications of growing inequality reflected in housing (Redman, 1978, p. 277; Wenke, 1980, p. 346). With advances in agriculture we find villages with many simple, common houses, but toward the center are often larger, better-constructed family dwellings. Pfeiffer (1977, p. 94–95) describes one such site in southern Jordan occupied for many generations:

. . . a 7000 B.C. occupation level is made up entirely of small houses averaging some 120 square feet, the size of a small twentieth-century bedroom. In the level immediately above a different pattern appears, representing the same settlement no more than a few generations later, the beginnings of a range of hierarchy of house sizes. The village now consisted mostly of small houses distributed around a slightly raised central area, a section reserved for houses three to four times larger than the rest, with large hearths and plastered walls and floors.

This general increase in the level of inequality and power as we move through history (until the era of industrial societies) is one of the most fundamental things to understand about human societies. The increasing level of inequality shapes many other aspects of life like the family, politics, and religion. And it provides a base condition for conflict between different groups in the society. Again and again throughout history we find conflict becoming more overt and violent. Sometimes this conflict produces change, sometimes not, but whatever the outcome, conflict is a recurring aspect of human societies to the present day.

In concluding this review of horticultural societies it is important to stress that they have not all been identical. They vary in size, the power of rulers, and aggressive military actions, among other things. And it appears that much of this variation is due to different environments. For example, horticultural societies located in rain forests in Africa are less likely to have a distinct political system, perhaps because of the greater difficulty in transportation: "A complex state presupposes the ability to move both men and goods easily and cheaply" (Lenski, 1966, p. 162). Despite their differences, however, horticultural societies all over the world, from their first appearance until today, are remarkably similar in many basic respects. And because it was the technological base that shaped these similarities, as this technological base changed, so did many characteristics of these societies.

Agrarian Societies

The most important technological change in the next stage of social evolution began about 3000 B.C. in the Middle East and North Africa — it began the age of the plow. The plow did more to change the nature of human societies all over the world than anything else since the Neolithic revolution and until industrialization. The plow, of course, did not appear all over the world at once, and there are still people today untouched by this technology. But during a period covering almost 5,000 years, the plow was the key element in the technology that shaped many aspects of human societies in countries from ancient Egypt to the very early United States. Thus, the history of agrarian societies is in many respects "partly an elaboration on the history of the plow" (Thomas, 1979, p. 88).

The reasons for the importance of the plow are quite easy to see; with more agricultural productivity the same land can feed more people, with fewer of these people required to work the land. The digging stick and hoe of earlier horticultural people was more time-consuming and did not turn the soil sufficiently. But the first plow invented by Egyptians was able to turn the soil, stirring up "those fertile elements in the soil that in semi-arid regions are liable

These scenes of urban gardening in Chicago, a North Carolina farmer plowing his field, and a sophisticated 12-row planter sowing corn in Coon Rapid, Iowa illustrate the progress made using different forms of energy and show how technological innovations, like the hoe and plow, revolutionized agriculture. The shift from human, to animal, to machine power allows a large scale of work to be done while freeing human activity for other forms of civilization building. (© Paul Sequeira/Photo Researchers, Inc.; © Arthur Tress/Photo Researchers, Inc.; © Joe Munroe/Photo Researchers, Inc.)

to sink down beyond the reach of plant roots" (Childe, 1936, p. 100). Throughout its history the plow has been improved to become an even more efficient tool, and it has been adapted to different climates. For example, the Egyptians first used a flint edge, the Romans discovered the value of iron plows, and later Europeans used horses (rather than slower oxen) after horseshoes and the horse collar were invented (Thomas, 1979, pp. 88–92). Thus, metallurgy, animal power, and the plow were all important to the new technology (Lenski, 1966, p. 190). But the key element was the plow.

Agrarian societies covered a very extensive period, with even more variation worldwide than with previous types of society (Lenski, 1966, p. 190). Despite the variation, we do find many strong similarities in these societies owing to their common technological base.

The common standard of living. It must be recognized, however, that the overall standard of living did *not* show much improvement for most people with the emergence of agrarian societies. As shown in the fascinating account of the fourteenth-century French village of Montaillou (Le Roy Ladurie, 1978), the material possessions and hard work of these people were not much different from the Egyptian masses over 4,000 years earlier, or the first horticultural people more than 9,000 years earlier. Lenski (1966, p. 271) also provides a general description of what you could expect if you were an average peasant living at about the time of these Montaillou villagers:

. . . the diet of the average peasant consisted of a little more than the following: a hunk of bread and a mug of ale in the morning; a lump of cheese and bread with perhaps an onion or two to flavor it, and more ale at noon; a thick soup of pottage followed by bread and cheese at the main meal in the evening. Meat was rare, and the ale was usually thin. Household furniture consisted of a few stools, a table, and a chest to hold the best clothes and other treasured possessions. Beds were uncommon and most peasants simply slept on earthen floors covered with straw. Other household possessions were apparently limited to cooking utensils.

As late as the eighteenth century in England it was common to find one-room hovels and houses with mud floors. And "in Russia, many houses showed scarcely any improvement on the huts of hunters of the days before 10,000 B.C." (Thomas, 1979, p. 410).

Although the material standard of living of the common people was little different, agrarian societies differed in fundamental ways when compared with horticultural societies. It is time to focus on the major characteristics of agrarian societies.

Elites. If you were moved by a time machine from horticultural to agrarian societies, you would probably find the wealth and power of elites in the latter the most striking change. From some of the earliest agrarian societies like ancient Egypt, through the Chinese and Roman empires, up to the European kingdoms just before industrialization, the wealth and power of a small group of self-perpetuating elites was astounding. Most people are familiar with the riches of Tutankhamun, who ruled Egypt from 1334 B.C. (Edwards, 1976). Such riches were quite common. And more important than the ownership of gold and castles in agrarian societies was the ownership of land, the root of all wealth in this type of society. "The King of Prussia, for example, owned nearly a third of his kingdom as late as 1750" (Thomas, 1979, p. 102). In France during the sixteenth century it is estimated that the nobility (1.5 percent of the population) owned 20 percent of the land (Soboul, 1974, p. 35). And because of inequality in land ownership, there was extensive income inequality. The king of England during the thirteenth century had an income 24,000 times greater than that of the average peasant, and the governing class in general (2 percent of the population) usually had about one-half of all the national income (Bendix, 1978, p. 7; Lenski, 1966, pp. 212, 228).

There were four main elite groups in agrarian societies. The first were economic elites who owned most of the land; the second were political elites who controlled the new state bureaucracies; the third were religious elites who controlled the new church bureaucracies; and the fourth were warlords who dominated through the new technology of war. Sometimes the four groups were one and the same, or overlapped extensively. For example, beginning with the first Japanese emperor in 660 B.C., "the

Japanese emperor was believed to be the descendant of deities and to be a deity himself" (Bendix, 1978, p. 63). In Japan the political elite and religion were merged. More commonly, however, we find four distinct elite groups, all powerful and wealthy, who usually cooperated in maintaining power over the vast majority of others in the society.

The state and political elites. The *economic elites* need little further discussion. They simply owned the land when land was vital to everyone's well-being — the masses had to depend on them for food and jobs. The state and political elites require more discussion. With hunting and gathering societies we found no state or distinct political elites. With horticultural societies we did find the emergence of a simple political hierarchy; with agrarian societies, however, the political system comes into its own. We find a state bureaucracy staffed with people to control commerce, tax, fund government projects, fight wars and rebellions, as well as control people in many other ways. It is no coincidence that major construction projects like the Egyptian pyramids began with agrarian societies. For example, the Great Pyramid (built around 3000 B.C.) weighs about 5 million tons and was constructed over a period of time that saw three pharaohs come and go (Wells, 1971, p. 146). These projects required many people freed from the land (often slaves) and a government bureaucracy for controlling the labor, planning, procurement, and financing.

Religion and religious elites. Organized religion emerged with horticultural societies. Religion emerged for many reasons, but one early outcome was political control. There is evidence that the first powerful rulers held their positions because of religious influence. But with more diversified and complex agrarian societies the religious and political systems were more often separated. The earliest temple discovered was located around Sumer (in the Middle East) and dates back to about 3500 B.C. (Thomas, 1979, p. 132). Like the earliest Egyptian temples, here the priest (or god) and ruler were sometimes one and the same.

As agrarian societies progressed through time, however, there was a secularizing trend in politics (religious and political systems became more distinct). Political and religious elites continued to work together for the most part because religious beliefs are often useful in organizing, controlling, and motivating people (Lenski and Lenski, 1982, p. 173). But there was conflict from time to time over who was the more dominant — political or religious elites. Popes were sometimes imprisoned or killed by political elites, and religious elites sometimes ordered their followers to rebel against political authorities. This uneasy relationship is nowhere better symbolized than at the crowning of Charlemagne, the first king in early Europe, by Pope Leo III (A.D. 800). Although the ceremony did not call for it, the pope placed the crown on Charlemagne's head (to the surprise of the new king). With this act the pope sought to signify what he saw as the authority of the church over the affairs of secular leaders.

Warfare and military elites. In agrarian societies military conflicts were chronic. Considering only Greece, Rome, and Western countries from 500 B.C. through industrialization, one sociologist examining the historical record found 967 "important wars" (Sorokin, 1941, p. 213). With this situation the potential influence of military elites seems obvious. For the most part, however, the military specialists *were* the political elite. That is how they maintained or gained their political power. And most of the large agrarian societies were conquest states that had grown by taking control of other societies through military campaigns (Lenski, 1966, p. 195).

Before moving to other characteristics of agrarian societies I should stress again the pervasive inequality. The time span that covers agrarian societies is great, but most of them are quite similar with respect to inequality. "The Egyptian priests of the sun might not have found themselves immediately at home at the court of the Sun King, Louis XIV [of eighteenth-century France], nor among the Inca worshippers of the sun conquered by Pizarro, but they would nevertheless have recognized . . . the absolute dominance of religion, as well as the unquestioned territorial and agricultural basis of the absolute hereditary monarchy" (Thomas, 1979, p. 43). The common people did not always accept enslavement and domination without resistance. We have historical records of riots and strikes around 494 B.C. in Rome (Wells, 1971, p. 356). The gladiator Spartacus lead a slave revolt in Rome in 73 B.C. No doubt earlier revolts occurred before recorded history. But only rarely did these revolts reduce political and material inequalities — and when they did so, the reduction was short-lived.

Population and Urbanization. The extent to which agrarian societies were conquest states brings us to the question of size. Without the improved means of travel (mainly the wheel and sail), as well as the military technology, the agrarian empires would have been unable to attain vast geographical size. To list some examples of size, the Russian Empire of Peter the Great (1689–1725) spanned 6 million square miles, and the Ottoman Empire ranged over a million and a half square miles during the 1500s, as did the empire of Alexander the Great around 300 B.C. (Lenski, 1966, pp. 194–195). And the Roman

---

BOX 3.1
Mohenjo-Daro

In 1922 a railroad employee of the British government working in India became interested in the extensive quantity of stray bricks in an area under survey not far from the Indus River, in what is now southern Pakistan. When the man started digging, what he began uncovering, though he had no idea at the time, was part of what may be the third oldest known human civilization. The remains he found were once the city of Mohenjo-Daro, part of the Harappa civilization that began about 4,500 years ago. Only cities of Egypt and Mesopotamia are believed to be older. The Harappa civilization (named after another of its cities) at its height expanded from what is now Afghanistan to much of northwestern India.

The city of Mohenjo-Daro and the people who lived there were quite remarkable in many ways. The city at one time had a population of about 40,000. Archaeologists have been startled by the "urban sophistication" and well-designed plan of this city. It has been described as the "very first 'first city' in which a 20th century visitor could have found his way around without the aid of a nature guide . . . " (Hamblin, 1973, p. 123). The streets of Mohenjo-Daro are laid out on a grid of straight parallel streets much like New York City today. The streets were built of weather-resistant fired bricks with a sewer system along the side below street level. The houses actually had running water and sit-down toilets made of brick tied to the citywide sewer system. The city also had large public baths, apparently for ritual bathing, made of bricks so tightly laid that they could hold tons of water.

The people of Mohenjo-Daro had oxcarts much like those in the area today, their own written script, and a system of weights and measures, and they were probably the first to wear cotton cloth. The size and shape of many of Mohenjo-Daro's buildings suggest the city was an important trading center.

The city was probably dominated by a privileged class of priests, though the extent and form of their rule is not yet clear. There were certainly privileged families whose homes have been uncovered. These upper-class homes "had lodgings for several servants, an interior courtyard, a fine downstairs guest room . . . , an upper story for the family's bedrooms, and . . . a well that provided fresh water for an interior plumbing system" (Hamblin, 1973, p. 152).

Empire around the first century A.D. covered northern Africa, the Middle East, southern Europe, and western Europe up to the British Isles.

Although it was military technology that brought great geographical size, the large urban population of agrarian societies was more directly related to improved agricultural methods (primarily use of the plow). "According to the best available evidence, a number of these great cities of the past attained populations of several hundred thousand" (Lenski, 1966, p. 199), and perhaps even 1 million for brief periods in later agrarian societies. Babylon had a population of about 250,000 around 430 B.C., and the population of Rome was about 650,000 around A.D. 100. One of the largest cities in an agrarian society was Peking (Beijing), with a population of 670,000 in A.D. 1500 and 1,100,000 in 1800 (Lenski and Lenski, 1982, p. 280). Conditions in these agrarian cities were sometimes bad, with crowding, filth, and disease. But many of these early large cities were cleaner, better managed, and safer than early industrial cities (Thomas, 1979, p. 410).

The Industrial Revolution

The cycle of change stimulated 10,000 years ago when humans first turned to agriculture and settled communities reached a new stage about 250 years ago — the industrial revolution was underway. There is some disagreement on exactly when it occurred and why. It is clear that it began in Europe, primarily England. But although most people place the beginning of the industrial revolution in the mid-seventeen hundreds, there is evidence of innovations leading to industrialization somewhat earlier (Wallerstein, 1974, p. 227). The more important question remains, however, as to how and why the industrial revolution began.

Compared with agrarian societies, industrial societies differed with respect to "the manufacture of goods for sale outside the neighborhood concerned, in a factory, and by a machine" (Thomas, 1979, p. 247). Trade across national or local boundaries has existed throughout history. But never before was so much of the production oriented toward trade. Also, when nonagricultural goods were pro-

duced prior to the industrial revolution, they were produced by artisans in their homes or in small shops. With the industrial revolution, workers were brought together in increasingly large factories where labor could be controlled and organized. Finally, and most important, more and more was produced by laborers using machines. And these machines were primarily driven by mechanical forms of energy. A primary outcome of all this was that more and more production in society came from machines and less and less from land. As a result, the primary means of production shifted from land to **capital.** In this context capital means the products of human labor used to produce other goods — that is, factories and machines. At this point industrialization is not the same as capitalism. There are both capitalist and communist industrial societies. Most simply, capitalist industrial societies have mostly private ownership of the means of production (factories, financial resources, and so on), whereas communist industrial societies have mostly state ownership of the means of production.

Causes of the Industrial Revolution. Of key importance for the industrial revolution were the technical innovations of many kinds. By 1500 China was probably the most advanced area with respect to technical innovations (Harris, 1980, p. 349), but there was an explosion of technical innovation in Europe beginning at about this time that helped establish the technical capabilities for industrialization. The causes of the wave of technical innovations in Europe are complex and clearly depend on a whole cycle of change going on at the time. For example, as different parts of the world became more accessible with sea travel, there was more trade; with more trade came more incentive to create and use technical innovations. Thus, the emergence of a capitalist orientation with trade helped encourage innovations and industrialization. But the increased sea travel that began this example was at least partially stimulated by new technical innovations like the compass (Lenski and Lenski, 1982, p. 236).

Additional factors were involved in creating the conditions for the industrial revolution. The printing press increased literacy, knowledge, and the spread of knowledge. These developments stimulated technical innovations. A rapid increase in money (in the form of metals like gold and silver) from overseas colonialization helped finance industrial expansion (Lenski and Lenski, 1982, p. 238). But again, the printing press and the increased money supply (because of sea travel) were themselves related to technical innovations.

What we have identified with the industrial revolution is a cyclical process of change and innovation that led to a new mode of production. It is difficult to say what is most important in the whole process because most, if not all, of the specific changes and innovations were related to others. This is where "materialists" and "nonmaterialists" take sides.

Nonmaterialists point to something like a new intellectual environment, with new ideas, as leading to change like the industrial revolution (Bendix, 1979, pp. 249–258). The nonmaterialist certainly recognizes the technical innovations leading to industrialization, though they focus on new ideas as stimulating the technical innovations. Max Weber, in his classical work, *The Protestant Ethic and the Spirit of Capitalism* (1958), made the most famous nonmaterialist case for the rise of capitalism and industrialization in Europe. In essence, Weber argued that the new Protestantism emerging in western Europe encouraged individual initiative, thrift, and the accumulation of material goods. One reason for this is that early Protestantism thought that worldly success was a sign of God's blessing and future salvation. But material success was combined with an attitude toward thrift and saving, thus leading profits to be reinvested for the further expansion of industrialization.

Weber's supporters also stress that China at about the time (or even earlier) of Europe's industrial revolution had the technical capacity for industrialization. The argument is that the Chinese did not have a value system that could lead them to use this technical knowledge for industrial expansion.

Weber's argument certainly makes sense, but it does have problems. Some sociologists have shown that capitalism, in fact, predates Protestantism (Cohen, 1980). Thus, Protestantism did not cause capitalism; it is perhaps the other way around. As for China, there are probably more important reasons

for the lack of industrialization. As is common in any agrarian society, when merchants and industrialists become strong, the rich landowners are threatened. The new "capitalist class" will attempt to change the economy and political system to favor their interests. But in the case of China, because the wealthy landlords firmly controlled the powerful state bureaucracy, they were able to use state power to hold down the merchants and industrialists. As a result, China did not industrialize.

The landlords often tried to prevent industrialization in Europe, but the clear difference between China and Europe was the strength of the state. The state in China was bigger, more bureaucratized, more powerful, and thus able to retard industrialization while wealthy landlords dominated the state. Now for a key question: why was the state stronger and more rigid in China? To answer this question we must turn to early material and environmental conditions.

When China first became an agrarian society the material environment required somewhat different agricultural methods in comparison with most of Europe. Specifically, China's agriculture required more irrigation. The independent farmer was less able to make it alone because irrigation required extensive cooperation with others, resources, and planning. To construct and maintain the irrigation projects, a state bureaucracy emerged earlier with more power compared with those in Europe. Marx has described this different form of agrarian society as an "Asian mode of production," and others have called it a "hydraulic civilization" (Wittfogel, 1957). Thus, it is argued that it was the rigid state bureaucracy controlled by wealthy landowners in China that prevented industrialization (Wallerstein, 1974, p. 58; Harris, 1980, pp. 349–352).

Industrial Societies

Much as the Neolithic revolution and the plow had done before, the shift to an industrial mode of production produced many wide-ranging changes in the characteristics of human societies. Because the subject matter of remaining chapters will primarily be aspects of industrial societies, at this point we need only briefly discuss the nature of industrial societies; the detail will be added later.

1. One of the most fundamental new characteristics of industrial societies is the nature of work for most people. No longer do we find most people employed in agriculture. We can use the United States as an example: In 1820, 72 percent of the labor force were in farm occupations. By 1880 the United States reached a 50–50 percentile split in farm versus nonfarm occupations. In 1980, slightly more than 2 percent of workers were in farm occupations (U.S. Bureau of Census, 1960, p. 72; U.S. Bureau of Census, 1981). In this respect the contrast of agrarian societies could not be sharper.

2. Corresponding to the occupational shift has been another involving urbanization. Again from the example of the United States, in 1790 about 95 percent of the population lived in rural areas. By 1900 this figure had changed to 60 percent. But by 1980, 75 percent of the population lived in metropolitan areas (U.S. Bureau of Census, 1960, p. 9; U.S. Bureau of Census, 1981). Corresponding to this shift is the growth of cities, many reaching populations far and beyond what was possible in agrarian societies. For example, New York City's population of over 16 million (including suburbs) would be impossible in any other type of human society that we know.

3. The specialization and further division of labor found in the economy of industrial societies is also reflected in the society's own subsystems (or institutions). You will remember that in hunting and gathering societies the kinship system was the all-purpose social unit. With industrial societies, however, there has been extensive subsystem or institutional specialization, with many former roles of the kinship system taken by these other institutions. For example, the political system, the legal and criminal justice systems, the educational system, and welfare systems, among others, now perform tasks once served by the family. The family system itself has changed considerably, shrinking to the core nuclear family of husband, wife, and dependent children in most industrial societies. And in some nations, even the nuclear family is threatened with a high rate of divorce and separation.

4. In the realm of political and material inequalities, we have seen a steady, sharp increase in political and material inequalities as we moved through the history of human societies. H. G. Wells's (1971, p. 193) phrase, used earlier in this Chapter, says it well with only some exaggeration: "There was a process of enslavement as civilization grew." With all industrial societies, however, the trend has been reversed. The level of both political and material inequality has been reduced, at least within industrial societies. There are some differences among industrial societies, especially with respect to political inequalities, but in all of them the standard of living for the masses in general has improved. There are certainly powerful, wealthy elites remaining in industrial societies, and we find increasing inequality on a worldwide scale. But the big change is that for the first time the common people have made significant material gains and reduced the gap between elites and masses.

5. Finally, in another respect, there has been both change and no change with industrial societies. There has been change in the *form* of group conflict with industrial societies; but there has been no change in the sense that conflict remains, even though in altered form. Differing interest groups and economic classes are in conflict, even though these groups may be historically unique. Societies are in conflict in the world, even though the details of these conflicts differ from those of the first agrarian settlements.

EVOLUTIONARY PERSPECTIVES AND SOCIAL CHANGE

Our outline of history has followed what can be called the "new evolutionary perspective" (Lenski, 1976). It will be useful to conclude this chapter with a brief discussion of the primary points of this evolutionary perspective and contrast it with other perspectives.

Since the birth of sociology, theories of social evolution and social change have been popular topics. Virtually all the early important figures in sociology developed a theory of change and social evolution. You will remember that sociology was born in the change from agrarian feudal societies to industrial societies, and the reality of extensive social disruptions due to this change led these sociologists to attempts to understand the mechanisms and direction of social change. This produced a rich variety of theories of social change, though we can identify two general types for our current purpose.

Early Evolutionary Theories. Most early sociologists developed some type of optimistic **evolutionary theory,** a view that societies will evolve (or "progress") through a series of stages, and at each stage there is progression to a "better" stage of social development. For example, Comte believed that so-

cieties progress through three stages. In the first, the society and state is directed toward conquest and a theological mentality will dominate (Barnes, 1948). The next stage leads to defensive states and a metaphysical mentality. In the final stage there would be industrial states with a scientific mentality. With this final stage there would be more rationality, less military conflict, and great material progress to improve the standard of living for all. As he wrote in the early 1800s, he believed Western societies were moving toward the third stage.

Herbert Spenser developed an evolutionary theory somewhat similar to that of Comte, at least

---

BOX 3.2

Industrialization and the Advance of Human Societies?

Back in 1609 when the Algonkian Indians discovered Henry Hudson sailing up their river, they were living off the fat of the land. They lived so well yet worked so little that the industrious Dutch considered them indolent savages and soon replaced their good life with feudalism.

Today, along the Hudson River, in a city called New York, supposedly free citizens of the wealthiest society in the history of the world work longer and harder than any Algonkian Indians ever did, race around like rats in a maze, dodging cars, trucks, buses, bicycles and each other and dance to a frenetic tempo destined to lead many to early deaths from stress and strain.

Thus has civilization bestowed its blessings on America.

Getting Americans to sit down and keep still will take a lot of undoing. For as the late anthropologist Peter Farb observed, "The fact is that high civilization is hectic," whereas "primitive hunters and collectors of wild food, like the Shoshone (who roamed the great western desert, including southeast California), are among the most leisured people on earth."

Despite the popular misconception that primitive peoples have to scratch relentlessly to eke out a miserable existence, today's hunter-gatherers, although restricted to inhospitable deserts, tropical rain forests, Arctic tundra and other inferior environments, typically work only two to three hours a day to obtain an abundant, nutritious, protein-rich diet. According to Farb, "they are among the best-fed people on earth, and also among the healthiest."

It was the advent of agriculture, and the need to intensify production to feed populations that had exceeded the natural carrying capacity of the land, that began the long, slow slide from the Garden of Eden of yore to the United States of Busyholics of today. Even so, the pace remained relaxed until relatively recently.

Throughout antiquity and the Middle Ages and right up until the Industrial Revolution about 200 years ago, most of the world continued operating on a loose timetable. The ancient Romans enjoyed 150 to 200 public holidays a year, which meant they had a

with respect to the idea of progress (Perrin, 1976; Barnes, 1948). Although Spenser's theory is complex, the driving force leading to progress was a **Social Darwinist** view of "survival of the fittest." Through conflict and competition the "better" societies would survive; those least "fit" would change or be conquered. Spenser also saw the final stage as rational, industrial societies—the type he saw emerging in the Western world at the time.

Finally, you should remember the Marxian view of evolution. Marx too saw societies as progressing through various stages to an ideal form. For Marx, the matter of progression was technological change and class conflict. With only some oversimplification, we can say his theory stressed that technological changes gave new classes advantages in conflict with other classes. Landlords dominated agricultural societies, while peasants were exploited. With industrialization the new capitalist class who owned the capital was dominant, and the working class was exploited. With further advances of technology and the enlargement of industrial firms, the working class would become a united force. They would overthrow the capitalist class and take collective ownership of industry through state control. And because Marx believed the working class was the last class to

---

day off for each day they worked. Medieval European peasants, craftsmen and nobles alike averaged 115 holidays a year—plus 52 Sundays.

The Industrial Revolution greatly lengthened the workweek, while adding monotony, mechanical discipline and the speedup of factory routine. Workweeks in the early British textile mills, as well as in the sweatshops of New York, were shocking.

The workweek in U.S. manufacturing fell dramatically from an average of 70 hours in 1850 to 38 hours in 1940, returning American production workers to the position of 13th-Century European Guild craftsmen. But there it bottomed out, averaging 39 hours last year [1982].

Meanwhile, workers' wives, who left the work force in the late 1800s and early 1900s to devote themselves to home and family, have poured back to work, undoing one of the most profound reforms of recent history and signaling a possible resumption of the historical trend toward more toil.

Although men have been retiring earlier, increased job-holding by women and youths 16 to 24 years old has escalated Americans' labor-force participation rate since 1960. According to a U.S. Bureau of Labor Statistics survey, the only major industrialized country to keep pace with the United States in putting a greater proportion of its population to work, at least in boom times, is Canada. In contrast, proportionately fewer Japanese, West Germans and Italians work now than in 1960.

One of the first social critics to identify social speedup as a major American problem was not even an American but rather was a Swedish economist named Staffan B. Linder. Back in 1970, Linder published in this country a slim but seminal study titled "The Harried Leisure Class." In it he analyzed why, as goods become more abundant, time becomes scarcer, the tempo of life grows more hectic and "people die an early death from overstrain and insufficient time instead of, as previously, from a shortage of goods. Deaths are now caused by high productivity, not low productivity."

Source: A. Kent MacDougall, "Employer's Changes Offer Hope for Harried Workers," *The Los Angeles Times,* April 19, 1983, pp. 1, 15.

be exploited, this final stage would be a communist society with no more conflict, inequality, or deprivation.

Cyclical Theories. In contrast to optimistic evolutionary theories, what I call pessimistic **cyclical theories** of social change see no such progress in human societies. In this view, change proceeds through cycles, with history roughly repeating itself, and with no real cumulative progress. For example, in the historical theories of Oswald Spengler (1932) and Arnold Toynbee (1946), civilizations emerge and prosper, as did the Roman, Greek, Egyptian, and Western industrial societies. But the advance of civilization set in force the process of decline as well. Neither of these social scientists stressed any significant cumulative progress from one civilization to the next.

Italian sociologist Vilfredo Pareto (1935) also developed a cyclical theory, though his was based on the idea of a "circulation of elites." Most simply, Pareto believed that selfish elites would always rule societies. Once in power, elites would hold this power and pass their positions on to their offspring or others like themselves as long as they could. But subsequent elites are seldom capable of governing. Thus, as one set of elites held power there would be social decline over time. When the decline reached a crisis, the old elites would be thrown out, with new elites taking power. If the new elites had the talent and ability to revitalize the society, they would remain in power — until, of course, decline began anew.

New Evolutionary Theory. It should be easy to see why grand theories of social change like these could be quite popular. If you "get it right," the theory is able to explain much of the past as well as to predict the future. Unfortunately, however, for one reason or another, these earlier theorists never really "got it right." This is *not* to say that none is useful today; they can often be used, at least in part, in answering questions about human societies. *Yes,* civilizations do rise and fall, and elites of some type usually replace others. But even though civilizations do fall,

this does not mean there will be no accumulative change or social evolution. And because elites have ruled complex societies since the first horticultural societies, it does not mean elites will always remain as dominant, as exploitative, with the masses never better off. *Yes,* societies do more or less evolve throughout human history. There are accumulative innovations in technologies and culture. But even though there is this tendency toward social evolution, it is extremely complex. There are no precise simple stages through which all societies will progress. And complex, "advanced" societies at the forefront of change (like industrial societies today) are not necessarily better. The term "better" is in many ways a value judgment — better often depends on what you value. For example, you should think carefully before deciding which group has (or had) a better life: inhabitants of New York City who live in the most technologically advanced society in history or Algonkian Indians living with a hunting and gathering technology along the banks of the Hudson River until pushed out by early New York settlers (see Box 3.2).

Because of their rigidity and blind value assumptions, theories of social evolution became unpopular. However, recent archaeological and anthropological evidence suggest that we do find a very rough social evolutionary process throughout the history of human societies. Thus, there is increasing support for "new evolutionary theories" that are less rigid and freer of blind value judgments (Lenski, 1976). This new social evolutionary perspective has guided our examination of the history of human societies in this chapter. The primary points of this new social evolutionary perspective can be listed in brief form (Lenski, 1976).

1. There is a general tendency throughout history for societies to become more complex in social organization and technology. But it is only a general tendency, with some regressions from this increasing complexity and some societies surviving quite well in older, less complex modes of technology.

2. There are no precise stages of social evolution that all societies must follow. This also means that the future for any society can never be precisely predicted.

3. There has been a general tendency toward more complex technology and social organization because societies are often in conflict for resources and growth. Those societies or civilizations with more complex technologies and social organization, in the very long run, have tended to survive, take over others, and/or serve as models that other societies copy. This is not to say this will always be the case — the most advanced in technology may some day destroy themselves and others with them.

4. The stimuli for social change are both *internal* and *external*. It seems clear that at first the stimulus for change was external — from the material environment. As we have seen, about 10,000 years ago it appears that hunting and gathering societies had to change to overcome severe resource crises. Along the way there have been many other changes by societies in response to environmental factors. And external change can also come from the social as well as material environments. Societies often adopt innovations from other societies in a process we call *diffusion*.

As for internal changes, we can identify a cycle of innovation and complexity that feeds on itself. As we saw with our history of human societies, once people are freed from the everyday necessity of producing their own subsistence, they may produce innovations in their free time. With more innovations, more people may be free to produce further innovations. New innovations themselves often lead to new innovations in technology. Thus, in a rough sense, the first horticultural innovations set the stage for the industrial revolution almost 10,000 years later.

5. Considering material versus nonmaterial innovations (that is, technology versus ideas and ideologies), I have stressed that material factors tend to lead in social change. This view should not be oversimplified or considered overly rigid. But the historical and cross-cultural evidence favors the materialist view.

6. Finally, all change must not be considered "progress" or "better." It is simply social change, even if in the direction of more complexity in social organization and technology. People survived with a simple hunting and gathering technology for tens of thousands of years. Industrial societies have been around for 250 years and their survival is by no means certain. At the present rate of resource consumption and environmental disruption, industrial societies will not come close to the record of hunting and gathering societies.

CHAPTER SUMMARY

Key Terms

culture, 61	horticultural societies, 67
material culture, 61	agrarian societies, 67
nonmaterial culture, 61	capital, 75
cultural lag, 64	evolutionary theory, 78
hunting and gathering societies, 65	Social Darwinism, 79
Neolithic revolution, 67	cyclical theories, 80

Content

This chapter began with a general description of culture and its material and nonmaterial elements. Material culture and environment was stressed as more important in shaping the nonmaterial characteristics of human societies (values, ideologies, level of inequality, and subsystems of the society like the family, religion, and politics).

We next examined the history of human societies. For tens of thousands of years humans existed with hunting and gathering technologies. But roughly 10,000 years ago humans increasingly found it necessary to pursue new horticultural technologies. The Neolithic revolution had extensive influence on many aspects of human societies.

Some 5,000 years later horticultural societies were eventually transformed to more complex and productive agrarian technologies, especially because of innovations like the plow, irrigation, animal power, and the wheel. This was the beginning of the first great civilizations — the Egyptian, Greek, and Roman empires. In these new agrarian societies we again found basic change in most other characteristics of these societies. Especially transformed were religion, the political system, warfare, and the characteristics and size of cities. And again we find more inequality and more powerful elites. But throughout the history of human societies to this point the standard of living for the common people had not yet significantly improved.

Roughly 5,000 more years again brought change, this time to industrial societies. The industrial revolution was set in motion by a cycle of technological changes leading to new ideas and values. And again basic characteristics of the society were transformed. But this time there was considerable improvement in the standard of living for the common people.

In concluding this chapter we considered general theories of social change. Both pessimistic cyclical theories and optimistic evolutionary theories were rejected for different reasons. New evolutionary theories focusing on cumulative technological change, without assumptions of progress, are able to overcome the criticisms of earlier theories of social change. It is this type of evolutionary change that has guided our outline of history.

CHAPTER 4

Culture: The Nonmaterial Foundations of Human Societies

I compare, rather, a certain number of structures which I seek where they may be found, and not elsewhere, in other words, in the kinship system, political ideology, mythology, ritual, art, code of etiquette, and — why not? — cooking. I look for common properties by examining these structures, which are all partial expressions, though especially well suited to scientific study of this entity called French, English, or any other society.
— Claude Lévi-Strauss, Postscript to "Linguistics and Anthropology"

When Europeans first encountered hunting and gathering people from such distant places as South America and Africa, they were astounded and shocked. Their basic assumption had always been that all humans were roughly similar to themselves in most respects. Some Europeans even reacted by denying that the hunting and gathering people could in fact be human.

The Europeans, of course, were not alone in their reactions. Imagine how the Native Americans who first met the Pilgrims in 1620 must have felt. To begin with, the Pilgrims were probably considered rather strange-looking with their white skin, beards, and layers of clothing. It is also quite possible these Native Americans found Europeans to have an unpleasant odor (the Pilgrims believed frequent bathing was a sin). The Wampanoag Indians, who shared all their possessions, may also have considered these Pilgrims rather greedy. And on top of all this, the Pilgrims could not even take care of themselves. The Wampanoags had to teach them how to secure enough food.

The typical image of the first Thanksgiving Day is one of refined European natives sitting down to eat with crude "savages" who probably had no table manners. However, given the view of table manners held by most Americans today, neither group would probably be considered well mannered. Until about one hundred years *after* the Pilgrims sat down with the Wampanoags, Europeans ate with their hands. They had knives for cutting, but spoons and forks were almost unknown. Neither did they have plates or individual drinking cups. Food was simply placed on the table, where diners went after it with their hands (Thomas, 1979, p. 238). (The Chinese, who ate from bowls and used chopsticks as early as 400 B.C., were probably the earliest humans to have anything like our modern "table manners.") When table manners began to be refined in the eighteenth cen-

tury, a manual on manners advised people "against noisy eating, spitting, and direct physical threats against neighbors." The table, however, was not the only place where Europeans in the Middle Ages had bad manners in the eyes of contemporary Americans. Early medieval people "had little concern with the control of impulse and apparently felt little shame. Men and women bathed together in the nude, housing accommodations allowed for little or no privacy, and bodily functions were performed in public" (Bendix, 1978, p. 232).

Rules pertaining to such things as table manners vary greatly around the world, as they have throughout history. Most of the rules that vary, of course, are far more important than table manners. All these rules are a part of the more general human product called culture.

As briefly noted earlier, **culture** can be defined as the *learned part of human behavior*. It is what we learn as a member of society; it is, in fact, what makes us human. Without culture we would be human only in a biological sense; we would not resemble humans in other respects without the existence of culture. Defined in this manner, as it was for the first time by Edward Taylor in 1971, culture includes beliefs, art, language, law, values and customs, tradition, styles, and fashions, and the list could go on and on. As you should be able to see, all these things are the products of collective human creation. Each generation must learn them to be considered members of society (Ogburn, 1937).

In the previous chapter I made the case for why the material world (including material culture created to deal with this material world) can be considered most important in shaping human behavior. Human behavior is not totally shaped by material forces, however, as even the materialist Marx recognized (Bottomore, 1973; Appelbaum, 1978; Harrington, 1976). This is especially shown in Marx's more objective works like *The Grundrisse* (1973). At times such things as ideologies, customs, and religious beliefs created by humans become primary forces in human societies. More often than not, these ideological forces themselves grew out of material conditions in the distant past. But even to the extent that material conditions shape these nonmaterial things, they usually take on a life of their own, therefore influencing much of what we do. We cannot understand human societies without extensive consideration of nonmaterial culture.

THE NATURE OF CULTURE

We should begin with a fundamental question: What makes the development of human culture possible? Related to this question is another: do nonhuman animals have culture? In part, the first question is easy to answer; it is obvious that the capacity of the human brain is behind the ability of humans to create and pass on culture. We must, however, look more closely.

The Human Brain. The brains of our early ancestors have been distinct from apelike brains for at least 3 million years (Leakey and Lewin, 1978, p. 161). But in one sense the human brain is similar to that of all other animals. What scientists speculate has occurred through the process of biological evolution is that the brain has been refined, with additional parts added along the way. Within the human brain is the core reptilian complex, which is similar to what developed with the first reptiles several hundred million years ago (Sagan, 1977, pp. 53–83). Some scientists believe that within this R-complex is the basis of aggressive behavior, territoriality, ritual, and social hierarchies. This does *not* mean that humans must always be equally aggressive and selfish, because the other parts of the brain (at least to some extent) can overpower these tendencies.

Over this R-complex within the human brain is the limbic system. This is the brain part we share with other mammals. The limbic system probably evolved along with mammals more than one hundred and fifty million years ago and apparently is a primary base for emotions of all kinds such as fear, anger, and happiness. However, none of the brain parts described here has the exclusive function of aggression or emotions. For example, the olfactory system (smell) is also located in the limbic system. But the general conditions of, say, emotions and aggression are located in these parts.

For our present purpose, the neocortex is the most important part of the brain. It is found among higher mammals like primates, and first appeared tens of millions of years ago with the higher mammals. But this neocortex has not remained unchanged; it has been further refined, especially in the past few million years as we approach humanlike hominids. The most important functions of the neocortex are thought, reason, and similar complex processes. In other words, the ability to develop human culture is found in the neocortex.

Humans are not unique in possessing a neocortex, but does this mean, therefore, that all animals with a neocortex have culture? A tentative answer at this point is, not necessarily. When considering mental ability what appears most critical is overall brain capacity, not simply brain size or structure. And the key factor in brain capacity is brain size in relation to body size. This ratio is important because the larger the body the more brain capacity is required just to control body functions, with consequently less brain capacity remaining for other functions like thought. In the ranking of brain: body ratios, humans come out on top (Jerison, 1973), with chimpanzees not far behind. A close third, however, is held by dolphins; this supports other evidence suggesting dolphins are quite intelligent animals.

Language

Although considerable brain capacity is fundamental to the development of human culture, one part of this human culture is itself most important for the further development of culture. I am referring, of course, to language—and more specifically, communication using a system of **symbolic signs.** In and of themselves symbols have no meaning. The marks I've placed on this page have no inherent meaning. They probably have no meaning to a person in, say, Tibet. The symbols

/\ ⊓ ⅃⅄ 𝘬 ⋂ — 𝘬 have no meaning to the vast majority of people reading this book (except that you probably know it is some kind of oriental writing). But the English words I have written in this book mean something to you because we have agreed and learned that they have certain meaning.

In contrast to symbolic language is communication by **natural signs.** This type of communication is quite common in the animal world but is much more limited in its capacity to convey information. Body gestures used by apes showing aggression are good examples. Chimps use natural signs very similar to some used by humans. For example, when greeting after a time of separation chimps may bow, hold hands, kiss, or pat each other. As van Lewick-Goodall (1971, pp. 247–248) concludes, "In fact, if we survey the whole range of postural and gestural communication signals of chimpanzees on the one hand and humans on the other, we find striking similarities in many instances." But the key difference, again, is that the amount of information conveyed by natural signs is very limited. Natural signs cannot communicate abstract ideas. Natural signs cannot be of much use in planning future behavior, designing buildings, or explaining complex ideas. Try explaining the meaning of democracy with natural signs. (Note that sign language which uses hand signals does not represent natural signs. Just as the spoken language we use involves symbolic signs, so does sign language.)

No one knows for sure when language first emerged. We have found remains of written language, but verbal communication through symbolic sounds or gestures almost certainly came much earlier. Examining archaeological evidence like skull capacity and tool design, Leakey and Lewin (1978, pp. 213–216) suggest that language emerged over one million years ago with some of our early ancestral hominids. (For a later estimate, see Washburn [1978].)

As for written language, it appears that the first hieroglyphic script emerged about 3500 B.C. in one of the first cities, Uruk. This script had about 1,500 separate signs, most of which are still undeciphered today. The signs that have been deciphered to date relate to business transactions, suggesting that the increasing trade of early cities created the need for written records (Thomas, 1979, pp. 33–35). Other types of writing followed relatively soon, such as poetry and perhaps a novel around 2100 B.C. (though some claim the first modern-style novel, *Tale of Genji,* was written around A.D. 1000 in Japan [Reischauer, 1977, p. 49]).

The importance of symbolic signs and language for the development and expansion of culture cannot be overstressed. In fact, even the creation of extensive, abstract thought depends on symbols. Could our earliest ancestors have thought about religion, democracy, or even planned collective activities without some form of symbolic communication? The answer, of course, is no. And even more important for the rapid expansion of culture is a written language, with which ideas can be stored, reexamined, and sharpened.

Linguistic Relativity. Language is so important for the development of culture that language both reflects what is most important to a group of people and limits and shapes their knowledge and world views. Thus, by **linguistic relativity** we mean that all languages must be seen as relative to the social setting or culture in which they are located.

By studying the language of a people, we can learn something about their overall culture. For example, Eskimos have not one word for "snow" but several because their experience has led them to make distinctions between many varieties of snow. Similarly, because of the importance of rice in their history, the Japanese have more words for rice than do Westerners. The Japanese word for uncooked rice is *kome,* whereas boiled rice is *gohan.* The word for boiled rice is even the root word in their words for breakfast, lunch, and dinner *(asagohan, hirugohan,* and *bangohan).* More complex cultural orientations can also be understood through the study of language. For example, we can understand that Sioux Indians have a different view of time because they have no words for "time," "late," or "waiting" (Hall, 1959).

One of my favorite cases of a different cultural orientation relates to the Japanese. The Japanese have a more group-oriented society than Americans, and are usually more concerned with the feelings of others. This orientation is reflected in the Japanese language. For example, the Japanese use their equivalents of our pronoun "I" much less often; to do so would appear egotistical. Also, they are usually extremely polite when interacting with others, and highly concerned with showing proper respect, especially toward people in higher positions than theirs. Many languages have polite and familiar forms of speech, with the choice of form determined by the prestige and familiarity of the person you are speaking to. The Japanese language, however, goes much further in this respect than others. Rather than a simple word change as in the polite or informal "you" in French *(vous, tu),* the Japanese often have completely different sentences! For example, if you want to ask a person of lower position whether he or she has gone somewhere, you ask, *"Mo itta ka?"* But to ask your boss the very same question you must say, *"Mo oide ni naremashita ka?"* (Christopher, 1983, p. 40). Only *"mo"* (yet) and *"ka"* (indicating a question) are the same in the two sentences; the other words selected depend on the rank or position of the person spoken to. As you might expect, the Japanese have an important custom of exchanging business cards indicating their position in the society when first meeting so they will know how to speak to one another.

The idea that language can shape and limit knowledge is controversial when taken to the extreme, as done in the Sapir-Whorf hypothesis (Sapir, 1929). When taken to such an extreme this implies that people brought up with different languages can never really understand one another or come to view the world in the same way. Although rejecting this extreme view, we can still accept the idea that language does, in fact, become a somewhat independent force in shaping how we think and what we can understand.

Humans: The Uniquely Cultural Animal?

Most of what animals do is directed by biological instincts. A bird isolated from others of its kind will build the same type of nest, follow similar migration patterns, search for food in the same way. In other words, what they do is not based on learning and therefore not guided by culture. This is in drastic contrast to humans. If we separate a human from

other humans at a very young age and the isolated individual can survive at all, he or she will have very few behavior patterns in common with humans from the parents' culture.

There are some animals, however, that possess elementary components of culture. One of the clear indications of this was observed by some primatologists studying a group of macaque monkeys on an island (Sagan, 1977, pp. 125–126). These scientists unintentionally threw grains of wheat on a sandy beach near the monkeys. The monkeys began eating the wheat with difficulty because sand was, of course, mixed with it. But one monkey happened to place the wheat in the water. Because wheat floats, it was separated from the sand. The monkey, obviously pleased with the results, repeated the washing of wheat. Other monkeys observed this behavior and eventually copied it. With subsequent observations of later generations of monkeys on this island, the scientists found that every monkey now washed food like wheat. These scientists had seen a new behavior introduced into the group of monkeys that eventually became a new element of the monkey's culture. These monkeys had learned food washing and taught it to future generations of monkeys.

Other examples come from the fascinating studies of chimpanzees in the wild by Jane Goodall (van Lewich-Goodall, 1971). Until her years of study with chimps living naturally in the forest, it was believed that humans were the only tool-making animals. But we now know that at least chimps can crudely make and use tools and teach their young to do so. For example, Goodall found her chimps could fashion a stick, carefully selected for the proper size, to probe termite mounds for the termites they love to eat. And in even more direct evidence that chimps have the capacity for culture, chimps have been taught to use sign language (see Box 4.1).

It seems clear that some other animals do have a very simple culture, and some such as chimps can even be taught to effectively use and teach sign language. So why do chimps not build bridges, construct belief systems like religion, or substantially change their primitive life-styles with new technology?

It has been estimated that chimps share about 99 percent of their genetic material with humans

This chimp, one of those studied by Jane van Lewick-Goodall, has transformed a stick into a tool. Why is the use of tools so critical to creating culture? What do you think the chimp is using the stick to do? (© James Moore/Anthro-Photo File)

(Miller, 1977). Jane van Lewick-Goodall has found that, among other things, chimps make and use tools, use many gestures similar to those of humans, share food (to some extent), use weapons, practice organized hunting, have a fear of deformed chimps, and become emotionally upset with the death of friends or kin. So why did humans have to teach chimps complex language? Why have chimps not developed anything but a very simple culture?

Despite some similarities between human and chimp brain structure, the chimp brain is simply not at the stage where extensive abstract reasoning is possible. From research data it seems that like the monkeys who learned to wash wheat, the chimp's use of tools is not an extensively planned and reasoned process. It is doubtful that the first chimp using a stick to get termites reasoned, "How can I get those damn termites? Let's try this stick." More likely, this chimp happened to be playing with a stick around a termite mound and by accident discovered the stick's value as a tool. But the chimp did have the brain capacity to realize what it learned, and teach it to others. The same can be said about chimps' use of sign language. They could not invent the language, but they could learn to use it.

ELEMENTS OF CULTURE

Having traced the biological roots of human culture, we now consider more specifically the elements of nonmaterial culture. Because culture is a very broad concept (e.g., the learned part of human behavior), it includes many diverse elements. In this section we examine some of these most important elements — specifically, norms, laws, values, mythologies, and ideologies.

Norms

One of the most fundamental, numerous, and, we might say, "everyday" elements of culture is **norms.** Norms are the general rules of behavior that people are expected to follow by other members of the culture. Norms may also be described as the standards held by a group with a common culture that define "right" and "wrong." And in contrast to abstract ideals, norms are more specific rules (e.g., "these are the accepted types of clothing for going to class"). As Homans (1950, p. 123) writes, "A norm, then, is an idea in the minds of members of a group, an idea that can be put in the form of a statement specifying what the members or other men should do, ought to do, are expected to do, under given circumstances."

Because norms are the basic operating rules of the society, you can imagine that there are literally thousands of norms. Some norms are considered very important (e.g., you are not allowed to kill others except under certain conditions), whereas other norms are not so important (e.g., do not talk with your mouth full, do not stare at people in an elevator). One early sociologist, William Graham Sumner (1906), called the former "mores" and the latter "folkways."

The more important norms (mores) are no doubt most familiar to you. But thousands of lesser norms also help make social interaction possible. We usually follow these norms and are aware of them after they are pointed out to us, but in everyday life we do not think about them. Let's consider some examples.

Imagine yourself walking down one of the main sidewalks on a college campus. Coming toward you,

BOX 4.1

Conversations With Chimpanzees

Imagine the strange feeling one must have actually "talking" with a chimpanzee. Chimps cannot actually talk verbally with humans, but they can do the next best thing—communicate through the standard sign language used by deaf humans.

The first monkey taught to communicate with humans using sign language was a chimp named Washoe (Gardner and Gardner, 1969). Washoe has learned to interact quite well with humans and some of the studies are to the point where chimps are teaching their offspring sign language.

These studies have raised the criticism that chimps like Washoe simply learn to copy gestures that have no real meaning to them. But evidence suggests this criticism is incorrect (Meddin, 1979). Washoe has learned to put words together in an order and with a meaning she has never been taught. Once, when a doll was placed in Washoe's drinking cup, she responded, "Baby in my drink." Washoe can also combine words to name objects she has never seen before. Knowing the words for water and bird, Washoe called a duck a "waterbird" on seeing it in a lake. Having never seen an orange, but knowing the word "apple" and the colors, when first seeing an orange Washoe called it an "orange apple" (Sagan, 1977, pp. 116–117).

When a *New York Times* reporter who knew sign language met another chimp (Lucy) who also knew sign language (Leakey and Lewin, 1978, pp. 201–202; Sagan, 1977, pp. 118–119), there was the following exchange:

Reporter: holding up a key, "What is this?"
    Lucy: "Key."
Reporter: holding up a comb, "What is this?"
    Lucy: "Comb." "Comb me" (which the reporter did).
Reporter: "Lucy, you want to go outside?"
    Lucy: "Outside, no. Want food; apple."

More recently, as the following news article describes, some of the chimps have been forced to take up painting to support themselves.

some half block away, is a friend going to class. What do you do in this situation? This is a relatively simple situation, but it involves many norms, and it sometimes involves fast thinking by the people involved.

Your first response to my question may be to say hello. To say hello is probably the expected behavior (i.e., the norm), but other questions follow: When do you say hello? How do you say hello? It is unlikely that you think about it, but there is a more or less standard distance at which people walking toward each other say hello (say, five or six steps, depending on terrain and crowding). Back to the beginning of

our example: you are half a block away; what happens until you reach five or six steps apart? If you watch people you will probably notice that until the proper distance is reached they look away—they look at the sidewalk, flowers, their shoes, anywhere to avoid eye contact too early. Then suddenly, when both people reach the proper distance, they look at each other on cue and say hello.

Let us continue this example. It is likely that you will simply say hello and walk on; but the "level" of greeting depends on things like how well you know the person, how much you like each other, and how

It's a real jungle in the nonprofit world, especially for five chimpanzees trying to make it without a federal handout.

The chimps are the celebrated wards of Roger Fouts, a psychology professor at Central Washington University in Ellensburg. Over the past few years, he has taught them to communicate using American Sign Language for the deaf. At least one chimp, 18-year-old Washoe, has mastered more than 60 signs.

Two years ago, the National Science Foundation decided not to renew Mr. Fout's research grant. As he understands it, the cut in funding has something to do with a shift in the study of primates, away from the pure behavioral aspect and toward applied, biomedical research. "They are cutting our friends up," says Prof. Fouts.

So the chimps, like many self-reliant Americans, learned to turn a hobby into a livelihood. They have always liked painting, and now their teacher-cum-dealer is selling their pictures at prices from $25 to $35.

The works range from the abstract to the more representational. Still lifes of fruit are favorites. Some of the chimps demonstrate strong stylistic idiosyncracies, says Prof. Fouts; one is so fond of the color black that she will cover an entire canvas with it. She herself is covered in glossy black fur.

The chimps, using sign language, have given their own works such titles as "Electric Red" and "Paint That Black." Many of them have been exhibited in art shows, where Prof. Fouts reports, most other artists have been "pretty open-minded." Sales of the paintings should generate about $3,000 a year.

However, the chimps' expenses add up to $40,000 a year, excluding donations of food and help. So Prof. Fouts has done some fund raising of his own. Last year, he went to work for Hugh Hudson, director of "Chariots of Fire," teaching human actors how to play chimps in a new movie, "Greystoke: The Legend of Tarzan, Lord of the Apes."

Prof. Fouts told the actors everything he knew about the morphology of the ape — how to gesture, how to stand, when to squeal or bare the teeth. While teaching the "chimp waddle," he encouraged them to "walk as if they had basketballs between their knees."

For his services, Prof. Fouts received $40,000. He has used the money to create an endowment, or nest egg, for the chimps, and he likes the logic of the funding. "After all," he says, "I learned everything I know about apes from them."

Source: Jane Mayer, "Their grants lost, these artists cannot afford to monkey around." *Wall Street Journal,* March 3, 1984.

long it has been since you last saw each other. If you are good friends and haven't seen each other for months, a simple hello without stopping would not do. You would be breaking a norm and perhaps damage your friendship. If you are only casual acquaintances and see each other two or three times a day walking across campus, a very warm greeting (as if you were "long lost friends") would lead people to question your motives or your sanity.

As the example above suggests, norms are not always rigid. They usually have *boundaries* (or a range of acceptable behavior). The boundaries may, for example, give you a range of acceptable clothing styles for everyday campus activities. In other words, norms usually do not say "you must do or wear exactly this." The boundaries of formality in men's clothing for students on campus may be from sports jacket and slacks (without tie) to blue jeans and T-shirt (perhaps cutoffs). A business suit and tie or holely T-shirt and bathing suit may be outside the boundaries. The exact boundaries, of course, differ somewhat from one campus to another and from one part of the country to another.

Norms, however, are also *situational.* If you are

in an a typical situation, the norms may be liberalized. For example, if a male student wears a business suit and tie to class, this may be acceptable if he explains that he has a job interview after class.

It must also be recognized that norms, especially less important ones (but others as well), are subject to change. From our example of clothing formality on campus, in the 1950s in the United States the norms were relatively more to the side of formality compared with the 1960s. The student movements and the questioning of traditional values led to more informality in clothing. During the 1980s it appears that clothing rules to some extent shifted back to more formality.

Rules, and especially important rules, require enforcement mechanisms. Norms are "backed up" with *sanctions.* Normative sanctions are both positive (rewards for compliance) and negative (punishment for noncompliance). And as you would expect, the degree of sanctions varies with the importance of the norms. Wearing a coat and tie to class without an acceptable excuse may get you disapproving looks and gossip ("who is this guy trying to impress?"); wearing nothing to class may get you a jail term.

Rules that have been formalized by the state and are backed up by formal state authority are called **laws.** In contrast to norms, laws specify types of negative sanctions and provide specific mechanisms for enforcement (e.g., police, courts).

Laws and norms often overlap, but never completely (see Figure 4.1). When there are laws against some type of behavior, the behavior is usually outside of acceptable normative boundaries as well. Killing your neighbor is a reliable example. However, even in this case the law and norms may be in conflict. In some societies norms may give approval to (even demand) killing a neighbor in response to some wrong done to the person's family. The state, however, may outlaw this type of revenge killing. Thus, law has come into conflict with accepted norms. Every society has many of these conflicts, though they are usually minor compared with revenge killing. Driving faster than 65 miles per hour on the highway is one such example in the United States.

Laws are actually relatively recent in the history of human societies, originating with the development of the state during the first agrarian empires. Before that time, and still in some places where a legitimate, formalized state is lacking, the violation of important norms was a matter for the kinship system. Dominant individuals enforced the behavior of kinship members and avenged transgression by outsiders against kinship members. But as societies became larger, more complex, and diversified, the state took over the task of defining and enforcing the more important norms through laws. Whereas before there were transgressions against individuals and families, they are now considered crimes against the state, enforceable and punishable by the state (Weber, 1947). In fact, it became a crime against the state to "take the law into your own hands."

Cultural Universals. Considering the types of rules and norms examined thus far, do we find any **cul-**

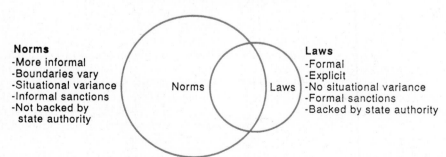

FIGURE 4.1. Norms and laws.

Norms
-More informal
-Boundaries vary
-Situational variance
-Informal sanctions
-Not backed by
 state authority

Norms   Laws

Laws
-Formal
-Explicit
-No situational variance
-Formal sanctions
-Backed by state authority

Eating provides a good example of norms and behavior. How we eat, the types of utensils we use, the manners that govern how we chew and whether we talk while eating, our relationships to the food we consume—are all normative. At your next meal, look at your eating habits. What norms govern your behavior in those situations? (left: © Marc Riboud/Magnum; bottom left: © Renee Lynn/Photo Researchers, Inc.; below: © Erika Stone/Photo Researchers, Inc.)

tural universals? That is, are there any elements of culture like norms that exist in every society? Our answers to these questions depend on how specific we want to be in our meaning of cultural universals. If we are referring to general cultural elements, then yes, there are cultural universals. Despite a diversity of specific norms, all societies do have norms of some type. For example, all societies have norms regulating such things as property rights, sexual behavior, and personal violence, among many other things.

When we move to the level of specific norms, however, we find extreme diversity. On this more specific level we find very few, if any, cultural universals. If asked to provide examples of cultural universals of this type, sociologists may think of incest taboos, which are quite widespread. With the common problem of regulating sexual behavior to reduce family conflict, through time, all societies may find incest taboos necessary. But there are many variations in how societies define incest and, thus, many variations in incest taboos. Although virtually all societies have norms against sexual relations between close biological relatives, societies vary greatly in norms against sexual relations, with more distant relatives. And even with close relatives, there have been some historical exceptions, for example, among royalty.

Culture Shock. Considering what we have learned about the need for culture as a guide to living, we would expect the absence of culture to produce extreme disorientation and psychological stress among people. What if a person is transported into a drastically different culture? There is no absence of culture, but for this person the effect is the same. The person is not familiar with the culture and does not know what to expect. Imagine yourself suddenly in a very different culture where you do not know the language, the system of money, or where to find help. You would experience a disorientation that is called **culture shock.**

To experience culture shock, however, such drastic cultural differences need not exist. More common is culture shock where a person is simply unfamiliar with the many minor norms of social interaction we normally take for granted. We want to know what is expected of us, but in this situation we do not know. We want to predict the behavior of others, but in this situation we cannot. Perhaps the expected distance between two people in conversation is different. Perhaps the people are expected to be extremely polite and take much time before getting directly to the point in conversation. Because of the *many* small, often unnoticed rules that guide our everyday behavior, people experiencing culture shock may not precisely realize the cause of their discomfort.

Values

Although norms are more or less specific rules that guide behavior, **values** are more general, abstract principles or beliefs that tend to carry strong emotional appeal. Values do not define specific behavior but limit the range of acceptable behavior or acceptable social arrangements. It is the task of norms to specify how the values apply in specific situations. Thus, it is important to keep in mind that (1) values are more general and abstract compared with norms, (2) norms are often guided by abstract values, and (3) values can be applied in more than one way in specific situations.

If you ask the average patriotic (and economically comfortable) American citizen what is most important about her or his nation, you would probably get a reply citing something like freedom, democracy, equality of opportunity, or free enterprise. (You are also likely to receive a more materialistic response citing our high standard of living, but as Americans are taught that some moral principle should be followed, free enterprise will probably be cited as the reason for our high standard of living.) All these responses can be related to our general value orientation called **individualism,** which stresses that individuals and their needs are more important than the larger group and its needs. In contrast to individualism is **collectivism,** which places greater stress on group needs. Neither collectivism nor individualism can be taken to extremes without destroying a society. But societies certainly differ in the degree to which they fall to one side or another on the individualism/collectivism continuum.

All societies have a multitude of values, with varying degrees of abstractness and importance. Some of the more important values found around the world include stress on religion, physical strength and aggression, material comfort, old age or youth, large families, equality, hereditary inequality, and so on. With such a possible mixture of value orientations, speculations on national character have always been a great pastime of professional writers and at cocktail party conversations.

Consider two separate news articles appearing the same day in the *Los Angeles Times* pertaining to the French "national character" (Dec. 19, 1983, pp. 1, 12). In one short article we were told the French "peacekeeping" troops in Lebanon were sent Christmas presents of "goose, duck and pork liver patés and a bottle each of Jurancon and Madeira wine." The U.S. Marines in Lebanon, however, were brought "140,000 giant chocolate chip cookies" by comedian Bob Hope. Exactly one month after this news article, NBC Nightly News broadcast a short segment of film comparing the daily meals of the British, Italian, French, and American troops in Lebanon. The British meals were not particularly special, but prepared much like a restaurant would prepare good meals in a standard kitchen. The Italian, and especially the French, meals were elaborately prepared and often served with a good wine. The U.S. Marines, on the other hand, had cold canned foods (the new C-rations) for lunch and warmed frozen dinners (like TV dinners) in the evening.

In the other (much longer) *Los Angeles Times* article we are told the extent to which the French value philosophy and intellectual discussion more than any other country, particularly the United States. As evidence, the article describes one of the most popular weekly television programs in France called "Apostrophes," in which a different group of four authors discuss their recent books. The program is shown for 75 minutes on prime time TV every Friday night without commercials. Following this theme of the value of intellectualism in French society, one American diplomat says, "I don't think a political leader could get ahead in this country [France] if someone mounted a whispering campaign that he was not well-read. It would be like a whispering campaign in the United States that a politician was gay."

We can, of course, point to a unique mixture of values that make up a national character. And these values may have significant outcomes for a nation. For example, the French produce and consume more wine than any other nation and they have the second highest death rate due to cirrhosis of the liver in the world (Kurian, 1979, pp. 182, 298; de Gramont, 1969, pp. 374–381). In Paris, 26 percent of hospital admissions are for alcoholism. The French greatly respect philosophers, often electing or appointing them to high public office (de Gramont, 1969). And the French produce more books per population than the United States, though not substantially more (Kurian, 1979, p. 361).

Although interesting, it is sometimes easy to exaggerate the importance of a particular national character. Limitations must be recognized when considering the values of a nation.

1. Values are *not equally accepted* by all in the society. Differences in education, economic position, religion, race, geography, along with many other differences produce varied support for particular values in a nation. There are, no doubt, many gourmets in the United States, but overall it is probably correct to say the French are more interested in *"haute cuisine"* than are Americans. And whereas the United States has had presidents who value books, philosophy, and intellectuals (e.g., John F. Kennedy), recent history shows there have been few.

2. Some values are more general and more important than others. This is to say, some values have more overall effect on the society than others. The French fascination with good food and intellectualism is less important than their values of individualism, democracy, and equality of opportunity. More of the overall nature of French society is shaped by these latter values. And with respect to these more important values, the French are closer to the United States than they are to most other nations.

3. Because the more general, important values in a nation are highly abstract, they can be interpreted differently by groups within the nation. Also, nations with the same abstract values can interpret and apply the values in a different manner. For example, although most people support the general value of equality of opportunity in the United States, those with less income tend to believe that income should be distributed much more equally than those who are more affluent (Alves and Rossi, 1978). And the actual income distribution is much closer to what the affluent prefer.

4. Although general values certainly influence what is done in a society, the unequal distribution of power among interest groups is often more important in influencing exactly what is done. Because values are abstract, as noted above, it is quite easy to interpret them in a manner that favors one's own interests. And if the group making the interpretation is very influential, their interpretation usually comes to be applied in concrete situations.

5. Important values often come into conflict with each other. And because one interest group may favor a particular value that is in conflict with another value, it again comes to a question of which group has more influence in the nation.

Two values in partial conflict in the United States are equality of opportunity and freedom. The value of equality of opportunity generally holds that everyone should have an equal chance to compete. This value does *not* favor equality per se; in fact, it favors the opposite. Inequality *resulting* from an equal opportunity to compete is favored. Freedom, of course, can be interpreted to mean that individuals should be able to pursue their own self-interests without interference by government. Now, what happens when an economic class or racial group beccomes so wealthy and influential (maybe even originally through equal competition) that it can prevent others from competing? Should this favored group be allowed the freedom to restrict equality of opportunity and discriminate against others? Which value should be given preference? Questions like these are often behind a nation's political debates.

Value Integration. Finally, we should consider **value integration.** Following the logic of sociologists who stress the importance of nonmaterial culture in society, we can say that the major values of a society will shape most aspects of that society. A nation stressing individualism should have an economic system, family system, political system, religious system, and so on compatible with individualism. Likewise, a nation stressing collectivism should have subsystems compatible with collectivism and different from those in a nation stressing individualism.

We do indeed often find this tendency toward value integration around the world. Figure 4.2 represents how the value of individualism is related to other aspects of American society. For the United States, a small nuclear family, free-enterprise capitalism, political democracy, and an individualistic type of religion like Protestantism are valued. (Countries with similar higher values like individualism do not necessarily have identical subsystems. Remember that these higher values are abstract and can be applied differently to concrete situations. For example, many countries may value political freedom but all have somewhat different political systems. Norms represent values applied to concrete situations in different manners.)

We do in fact find a tendency toward value inte-

FIGURE 4.2. Value integration in American society.

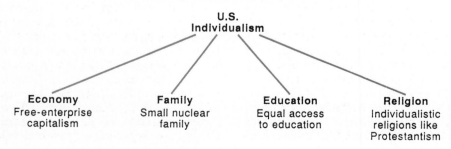

gration around the world. However, we must be cautious in trying to explain the reasons for value integration. And we must recognize that value integration may be much less in some nations.

1. Although a nation may tend to value a particular type of condition, that doesn't mean reality fits the values. Free-enterprise capitalism is certainly favored in the United States. And in many respects we meet the value more than other "capitalist" nations (Kerbo, 1983, pp. 169–171). But because of extensive corporate concentration and political influence in the economy, we are far from the pure ideal of free-enterprise capitalism.

2. As noted in discussing values, value integration does not mean that all groups equally support the same values in a society. For example, behind the Cultural Revolution (1965 to middle 1970s) in China was a virtual civil war over such things as the extent to which capitalist-type reforms in the economy should be attempted. Since Mao's death the "capitalist roaders" (those favoring some economic reforms) have won (at least for now). In the United States we find increasing calls for more government economic planning as found in Japan, but conservative political elites in the United States are unlikely to accept such change (though there is certainly government involvement in the economy in other ways).

3. We find many cases where nations have copied characteristics of other nations with seemingly incompatible value systems. And the characteristic copied has not produced extensive conflict with other characteristics of the nation.

For example, Japan has done very well in adopting capitalism, even though Japan is primarily a traditional Asian country favoring collectivism. And though many aspects of Japanese society are changing to adjust to capitalism (like the extended family system), these aspects of Japanese society are not changing to the extent many people believed they would (Morgan and Hiroshima, 1983). It must also be recognized, however, that capitalism itself has been altered to some extent to fit the cultural values of Japan.

4. Most important, value integration in a society may not only be due to the force of major values (like collectivism or individualism). Rather, value integration may be (in fact, most likely is) *caused by the force of the material environment and material culture in the society.* This can happen for two general reasons: (1) the continuing force of material conditions on the values, and (2) the continuing force of values that were originally shaped by material conditions.

In the first case we can say that the economic technology in a society shapes the values. For example, referring to Figure 4.2, we can say that the values of individualism, the nuclear family system, and so forth are integrated because they are shaped by the needs of a capitalist industrial technology. This, of course, is the materialist position, which turns the idealist position upside down.

In the second case, we must recognize that values do have an independent force and relative autonomy in the society once they have developed. These dominant values can, therefore, be a force for value integration. But the dominant values were most likely originally shaped by previous material conditions. For example, differing agricultural systems have led to value differences between East and West (or the Orient and the Occident). Although this is a rough generalization, we usually find a collectivist value orientation in Oriental nations and an individualistic one in Western nations.

Subcultures. I have stressed that not every individual and group within a society is equally supportive of each and every value or norm in that society. Some groups, in fact, are distinct enough to represent what can be called **subcultures.** Such groups live within the more general national culture, accepting perhaps most of the national values and other elements of the culture. But these groups either reject many of the dominant values and/or have many additional, unique values of their own (Gordon, 1947). There is no exact point at which we can say a group becomes a distinct subculture. Culture can refer to values and norms of groups on different levels of generality—we can refer to a broad culture like Western culture or more distinct national cultures. So even within a national culture we can make even more distinctions to identify subcultures.

Subcultures are often based on ethnic or racial differences. For example, American Indians who no longer follow their traditional culture but have not been totally integrated into the more general American culture certainly represent a distinct subculture. These Native Americans may not speak English, may have values in conflict with American materialism, and may even have some values closer to what we have described as collectivism. American Indian tribes, of course, differ with respect to their values and other distinctive characteristics (Rosenthal, 1970). But it is difficult or impossible to find Native Americans today who are not heavily influenced by the dominant American culture.

Among tribes like the Cheyenne-Arapaho living in western Oklahoma there can be found an interesting mixture of cultural elements. Visiting a powwow (as I did a few years ago) you can see American Indians dancing in traditional dress to traditional drum beats and songs. (Such powwows are usually not just shows for visitors but continue to have important ceremonial meaning for the tribe.) The powwows I have observed, however, open with the American flag leading the dance procession. Some time afterwards there may be a gift-giving ceremony, where honor comes to those people who can give away the most material possessions (rather un-American in some respects). Later, there may be the traditional dance honoring young warriors. Today, however, they usually honor a tribal member serving in the United States military, who will be asked to lead the traditional dance in military uniform. Finally, they may don "cowboy" clothing to stage an all-American rodeo. When the weekend powwow ends, the members of this tribe get back into their campers to return to whatever jobs and homes they have in the area.

A subculture is not always based on any racial or ethnic differences. A unique environment, occupation, belief system, or life-style may lead to the development of unique cultural elements. Thus, we can refer to a subculture of jazz musicians, rock musicians, intellectuals, and professional athletes. To some extent, it is useful to recognize differing economic class subcultures. The upper class, middle class, and working class often have differing tastes or preferences in such things as music, clothing, food, recreation, and so on. More important, we also find differing tendencies toward such things as child rearing methods, speech patterns, and values on education. We must be cautious not to overestimate these class differences, or stress that they come from different values when in fact they are due to different incomes. But as we will see, because of different problems, experiences, and occupations, among other things, it is useful to recognize somewhat distinct class subcultures.

Other Elements of Nonmaterial Culture. As our general definition of culture implies, there are *many* more elements of nonmaterial culture than just norms and values. Language, of course, is a very important element of culture considered earlier. But there are others that require at least brief description.

Several important elements of culture found in one form or another in every society can be grouped under the title **belief systems.** By a belief system we mean a set of beliefs or explanations of some aspect of the world (material or social) shared by a group of people. Two similar types of belief systems are **ideologies** and **mythologies.** Sometimes these two concepts are used interchangeably, but more often ideology refers to modern political or religious belief systems, whereas mythology refers to the belief systems of people in hunting and gathering or horticultural societies. Ideologies and mythologies are not necessarily correct or incorrect explanations of the real world. In fact, they are sometimes quite accurate, sometimes quite inaccurate, but often both accurate and inaccurate. Their purpose is to provide such things as meaning, security, group unity, and plans for action.

For example, all people seem very interested in questions like "Who are we?", "Where did we come from?", "How did we get here?", and so on. In response to these questions, all societies have "creation myths." There are literally thousands of these creation myths that have existed throughout the history of human societies. The early Egyptians had different religious groups, each with their own version of a creation myth. Egyptians living in the city of Memphis around 2900 B.C. believed the god Ptah created the world by his verbal commands. For some other Egyptians, the god Atum created himself, then other gods, and finally the world and all living things. This view addressed the question (however inadequately) of where the first god originated. Other Egyptians preferred a more "earthy" explanation; for them, Atum was a bisexual god who created the other gods and humans through masturbation. At about this same time the Sumerians had a significantly different creation myth. In the beginning there was Nammu, the primeval sea, the mother of all. Other gods later emerged, with rather humanlike conflicts and sexual contacts. Humans were finally created to work for the gods after the worker gods rebelled in response to overwork (Larue, 1975, pp. 28–35).

Creation myths vary in complexity, but virtually all societies have them. Modern science, of course, can tell us much about the origins of life. But science leaves many unanswered questions about the cosmos and its origins. For example, there is increasing evidence the universe as we know it was created according to the big bang theory (Sagan, 1980). But where did the original material producing the big bang originate? Some scientists believe there may have been (and will continue to be) a succession of collapses of the universe, then a big bang producing a new universe. But where and when did this all begin? In other words, when did time begin? Scientists also tell us the universe is currently expanding. But expanding into what? Does it extend forever, without end? Nothingness? What is nothingness?

The point is, even modern science cannot answer all questions about the origins of the cosmos. People find these unanswered questions mind boggling and often somehow threatening. Our insecurity leads most of us to favor some form of creation myth.

Ideologies usually involve justifications for specific actions and conditions, explanations of the social world and how it works, or other such belief systems with emotional content. Communism, capitalism, Protestantism, Catholicism, Buddhism, and so on are all ideologies. You may object to the listing of your own religious and political belief system among, say, communism or fascism. But you must recognize that all ideologies are belief systems providing orientation and directing action. And although all ideologies contain elements of fact and fiction, they differ in consistency, emotional appeal, and the mix of fact and fiction.

We can group some other elements of culture under the title "shared symbols, tastes, and styles." Every society has important **symbols** that convey meanings. These symbols can provide an extensive amount of information in a very compact manner. Consider the following: a small American flag worn in a coat lapel, a fraternity crest, a wedding ring, a cross worn around the neck, a high school letter jacket, a Cadillac. And as we have already discussed, one of the most important sets of symbols is language.

Tastes and styles also exist in every society simply because cultures generate preferences toward certain things. Americans tend to prefer certain foods and have learned that other substances are not "proper" to eat. The power of culture can be seen in your reaction to some foods highly valued in other cultures—for example, raw fish, stir-fried silkworms, oxblood, and even human flesh. "The eyeball of a sheep is a great delicacy among the Bedouin; but what induces salivation in the Arab induces nausea in the Yankee. . . . Whether we enjoy something or vomit is not a physical but a cultural response" (Plaut, 1983, p. 268). Likewise, we prefer certain styles of clothing because they give an identity that we want to convey at particular occasions. As with food, we may find it difficult to appear in public wearing clothing highly valued in another culture.

IN ORDER AND CONFLICT: THE DUAL NATURE OF CULTURE

It is time to consider our subject from a broader perspective. What are some of the general outcomes of our ability to produce and learn nonmaterial culture? As we have already seen, humans and human societies have a dual nature. We are subject to social order and cooperation as well as conflict and selfishness. Considering the fundamental importance of nonmaterial culture for human societies, we must understand that culture helps promote this duality in human societies.

Order and Adaptation

The most obvious outcome of nonmaterial culture is that it helps produce order and unity. Unlike other organisms, humans have not been biologically programmed to behave in ways that make group life possible. The clearest contrast to ourselves is found among bees. They live in a highly group-oriented society, with a division of labor and simple communication network that makes possible their group existence. But none of this behavior is cultural; it is all biological.

Consider the situation of ten unrelated people stranded on a Pacific island. Let's assume there is an equal balance of young males and females, and that they share no common culture. These people could all go their individual ways and try to survive, but this is unlikely for several reasons; people tend to desire companionship; collective efforts at survival may be more efficient; people are frightened and insecure, all of which will no doubt pull them together.

With this example we can imagine the creation of a whole new culture in a way comparable to the actual research on the macaque monkeys washing wheat considered earlier. Of course, my island example cannot represent a totally pure case of the emergence of a new culture because these ten young adults must have brought with them ten separate cultures. I could have all ten people bump their heads when jumping into lifeboats, thus losing their memory, but that's a bit taxing on the imagination.

Considering what we know about culture, we must ask, what are these people going to do? They must meet physical needs, like finding food and shelter. Given their past experience and the material conditions of the island, we would probably find some new conglomeration of old technologies brought by these people now adapted to the new material realities. We will have, in other words, a new material culture and technology.

Very early in the new collective existence of this island group, they will need to work out some means of communication. At first, natural signs will have to

do. A finger to the lips could mean quiet; a hand brought to the mouth could mean "let's eat," and so on. But very little complex information could be shared in this manner. How do you communicate "you build a fire, we will gather berries, while you build traps for wild monkeys"? Without symbolic language it could be done, but only with great difficulty, and wasted time. Thus, this group will most likely develop a symbolic language. Again, we can imagine it will be a merging of the languages brought with them to this island.

This example, I hope, has helped consolidate our previous discussion of the origins and adaptive nature of material and nonmaterial culture (also see Box 4.2). With respect to the nonmaterial elements in our imaginary island culture, we have seen the *social construction of reality* (Berger and Luckmann, 1966, who also gave me the idea of a new island culture). This means that our beliefs, ideologies, norms, and so on have been constructed by humans over the ages and handed down to us. This does not mean these beliefs were consciously created by particular individuals (though that is certainly possible). Rather, it is more likely that the beliefs have been slightly altered and expanded over the generations. Also, this does not mean these beliefs are only the product of idle speculation or imagination. They are, of course, products of the mind, but we must recognize the influence of the material environment and the technostructure in shaping the nonmaterial elements of culture as described in Chapter 3.

Cultural Diversity

With all these dimensions in mind we can now consider the roots of cultural diversity. I do not need to tell you that there is a diversity of human cultures. At this point some sociology texts attempt to shock readers with descriptions of "wild" and "strange" behavior of people in other societies. Just about anything we would consider immoral or strange (and many things we would never even think of) can be found acceptable in some society somewhere. I will not belabor the point, but I want to help you understand *why* this diversity exists.

We begin by remembering the purpose of

BOX 4.2

Missionaries and the Baby Boom in Kenya

It was the missionaries, trying to stop polygamy, who sparked Africa's population boom, Kenyans say. And although there may be wider, more complex reasons than that, it is true that the social taboos that ordered life even a few decades ago have fallen. The sexual revolution has reached Africa.

Traditionally, Kenyans say, a man didn't marry until he had been circumcised at about age 20, had killed a lion or an enemy to prove his bravery, and had acquired enough cattle and land to support a wife. By that time, he was perhaps 30, his wife perhaps 20.

Moreover, a man abstained from sex with his wife — the two didn't even live together — while she was nursing their child. And traditionally, a woman nursed for four or five years — until the youngster was old enough to help with the chores. For a woman to bear another child after her oldest had married was scandalous; so, her sex life was limited to about 20 years, and her family to four or five children.

A man of wealth and prestige might take other wives; Kenya's Agriculture Minister says his grandfather had 50. Thus, a man's family could be enormous. But a woman's family — and the birth rate is based on the number of children borne by each woman — was far smaller than today's average of eight.

Kenyans say the missionaries encouraged cohabitation in an effort to discourage polygamy — and ended up with both. One-third of Kenya's marriages still are polyga-mous, a 1978 government fertility survey found. One government minister claims 20 wives and five dozen children, and in the village of Athiru Ruujine, a schoolteacher says all his friends have two wives.

There were reasons besides the missionaries for the changes in Kenya's family structure, of course. The arrival of European settlers attracted men to paying jobs on the commercial farms and in the cities; they left their wives behind to tend the family patch. The chiefs lost their power to remote government offices, and with it their authority to uphold tribal customs.

Now the stigma attached to an unmarried mother has faded; the average first pregnancy in Kenya is at age 15, and the average age of marriage is 17. Women are nursing their infants an average 13 months and bearing them an average 33 months apart.

The change worries population planners — and many Kenyans. "We have lost our traditions; we are losing our way," says Margaret Festus, a community-health worker in Maua, a village near Mount Kenya.

In Maua Hospital's maternity ward, Hellen Kalingi, who lives on a coffee and banana farm that she works for her husband, says she is "about 30." She has just delivered her seventh child. Asked how many more she wants, she smiles and says, "As many as God will give me."

Source: Wall Street Journal, "Kenyans Say Missionaries Who Tried to Stop Polygamy Caused Baby Boom," April 11, 1983.

culture — it allows humans to adapt to their material and social environment. Thus, if the material and social environments differ for two groups of people, through time they will come to have significantly differing cultures. Let's explore this idea a bit further.

It is impossible to say exactly when human culture emerged. It was no doubt a gradual process that occurred parallel to biological evolution. Current evidence suggests that the process of biological and cultural evolution began in northern Africa. As our most recent hominid ancestors all emerged in this area, we can assume that they had roughly the same culture. (Of course, there would be some differences among tribes, but in terms of general characteristics like type of technology and quasi-religious belief systems, these tribes should have been rather similar.)

Less than 1 million years ago, archaeologists believe that many early hominids began leaving northern Africa (Pfeiffer, 1977, p. 53). These early hominids moved north into Europe and East into Asia. By 15,000 to 25,000 years ago, some *Homo sapiens* had moved from Asia to North America over the then-existing land bridge from Siberia to Alaska. Once in North America these humans moved southward through Central America into South America.

The tie between this migration and cultural diversity should be easy to understand. If culture helps humans react to their environment, and is thus very much a reflection of that environment, then we would expect cultural diversity as people dispersed around the world. (Incidentally, the same explanation can help us understand racial differences around the world.)

Cultural diversity, however, cannot be totally explained through internal (indigenous) developments. We find extensive **cultural diffusion** around the world — which means that through contact with other people some elements of foreign cultures are borrowed. For example, though Japan remained isolated until recent times more than most other nations, the Japanese began borrowing much of Chinese culture around A.D. 645 (Reischauer, 1977, p. 44). Thus, we find many similarities in Chinese and Japanese culture.

What is borrowed and retained is usually adaptable to the overall cultural and material environment of the people. Though China and Japan are culturally similar in many ways, their material environments are not identical. For example, both countries have been dependent on rice production, but rice production in China more often required large-scale organization for irrigation. In Japan, because of more rainfall and water runoff from mountains, rice was produced by small groups working together. Though both countries required group cooperation in producing food, the scale of cooperation differed significantly.

Because of this, it appears that Japan could not adjust to much of Chinese culture that developed in response to the Chinese environment. For example, early Japanese agriculture did not require a large bureaucratic state, extensive land inequality, and a belief system that supported these things. Thus, by about A.D. 900 to 1000 much of what Japan had borrowed from China had been changed or eliminated.

Still, compared with the culture of Europeans, Japan and China are much more similar to each other. In the process of human migration and cultural diversity several large groups of humans became relatively isolated from one another. These people settled in similar environments and/or experienced extensive cultural diffusion with other people in the area. Because of this we find relatively distinct *cultural areas* around the world. Two of the largest are represented by "East" and "West," also referred to as the Orient and the Occident. There are many other cultural groupings (Middle Eastern, Native American, African, etc.). All these cultural divisions are relative to how broadly or narrowly we choose to define cultural differences and similarities. Compared with all cultures in the world, Japan and China are quite similar. But comparing only Asian countries there are more clear differences.

Nonmaterial Culture and Human Conflict

Ironically, although culture helps us adapt and cooperate, it also produces the potential for extensive human conflict. We are the most violent animals on earth. No other animal kills for ideals and principles. One example of this (there are many) are the eight Crusades (A.D. 1097 to 1212) by Christian Europeans against the "infidel" Muslims in the Middle East. At the urging of the pope, the Crusaders embarked in a "mood of religious frenzy" to kill Muslims (Thomas, 1979, p. 150). "Never before in the whole history of the world had there been such a spectacle as these masses of practically leaderless people moved by an idea" (Wells, 1971, p. 563). One account of a battle during the first Crusade reads: "The slaughter was terrible; the blood of the conquered ran down the streets, until men splashed in blood as they rode. At nightfall, sobbing for excess of joy, the crusaders . . . put their blood-stained hands together in prayer" (Wells, 1971, p. 564).

Again and again throughout the history of human societies we find exploitation and mass murder based on ideals. This is not to say most cases of mass violence are based only on ideological principles. Most conflict (both overt and convert) is to some degree based on real material interests (e.g., one group gains at the expense of another). But even when material interests are at stake, people are often led to violent conflict only when moral principles are invoked as justification. To explore this further, let's briefly return to some things we have learned about the human ability to create ideas.

An important outcome of our brain power is the feeling of insecurity. Perhaps no other animal is fully aware that it will some day die (Sagan, 1977, p. 99). We also understand that what we do today can affect our long-term future. This insecurity about our future leads us to planning and activities to protect our interests, which may bring us into conflict with others trying to protect themselves and their interests. We create beliefs that "explain" to us where threat lies and what to do about it. We may then act on these beliefs by attacking others to "defend" ourselves.

Another outcome of our brain power can be an insatiable desire for more and more material wealth. No other animal can envision what to do with material goods after basic needs have been satisfied. But humans can apply symbolic meaning to things. Owning several cars will not provide us with more personal transportation — we can ride in only one at a time. They can, however, serve as symbols that indicate to others (and to ourselves) how successful and "important" we are. Thus, our ability to create symbols also creates a level of conflict greater than it otherwise would be. It creates conflict even after more than sufficient necessities are met. It helps create a highly unequal distribution of world resources, which can produce violent conflict when some people object to this extreme inequality.

Finally, without weapons humans would be rather harmless animals. We are not exceptionally strong, and we lack the dangerous natural weapons of some animals (like sharp teeth and powerful jaws). But our material culture has changed all of this. We can now make weapons so deadly they threaten the entire world.

None of this means humans are always (or must always be) such violent, conflict-prone animals. Biology cannot explain all human conflict. We have already seen the tremendous variation in the level of violence among human societies. Thus, because this biological potential for violence is common to all people, we must look to environment, social arrangements, and cultural differences that produce more or less conflict and violence.

Internal Conflict Relations. We can be more specific about how culture influences human conflict within a society and between societies. I have already noted the necessity of social order and cooperation for meeting human needs. Our values, norms, ideals, and other elements of nonmaterial culture can help us establish this order. But at the same time, we must ask *what* social order and *whose* social order. Is the social order based on the exploitation of some groups within society?

In one respect simply our ability to apply meaning to otherwise meaningless objects, conditions, or situations can help produce conflict. We can dislike others because they are somehow different from us. If we come to regard ourselves and others like us as good, then it can follow that others unlike ourselves are somehow bad. Perhaps some people are disliked because of their skin color. Perhaps other people are disliked because their occupations are considered dirty and degrading. These people may then be excluded from the main group and treated differently. Such isolation and treatment can cause anger, mistrust, and hostility leading to conflict.

Combined with this, ideals, ideologies, and the manipulation of information can make it possible to exploit others even with their acceptance of the exploitation. What other animal could be led to accept misery under the belief that it is noble to do so? What other animal would accept deprivation because it believed that by doing so it would get to a happy afterlife or be brought back in the next life in a more honored and comfortable position?

External Conflict Relations. Related to our ability to dislike others in our society because of symbolic differences is the equally strong ability to dislike people from other cultures seen by us as different. Sociologists call this important characteristic **ethnocentrism.** Simply because we have norms, values, and ideologies that tell us what is right and wrong, other people with different norms, values, and ideologies are likely to be judged wrong or even evil by us. Ethnocentrism is not inevitable; at least, it can be reduced. People can be taught to respect **cultural relativism,** which is a recognition that

Cartoons offer a powerful way of portraying conflict using imagery that exaggerates ethnic or political characteristics. Why do you think U.S. President Reagan has been represented as an octopus? What can you infer about ethnocentrism from the images of the Contras, Iran, the CIA, and Israel? (© Abe Blashkos/Impact Visuals)

other people have legitimately different values due to different needs and historical forces.

Ethnocentrism provides fertile ground for international conflicts. At times elites manipulate this ethnocentrism for their own needs (to maintain political support, economic advantage, or their own ideological zeal). For example, during the 1950s, when China was considered an enemy of the United States, information favorable to China was suppressed (Mosley, 1978). At the time, the Chinese for their part were spreading the word about the evils of the United States. When American author Edgar Snow was traveling in China during the 1960s (one of the few Americans allowed to do so), he found very distorted ethnocentric attitudes toward the United States. Once, while talking with some Chinese college students, he was asked amusingly naïve questions about the hardships for people in the United States. At one point Snow (1970, p. 253) asked these students "'Do you think you are happier than American students?' Howls of derision greeted this, laughter and exclamations of surprise." One student responded, "What an odd question! How could American students possibly be happy—slaves of American capitalism!"

Negative American ethnocentrism is often directed toward the Soviet Union. For example, we were told by an American president that the Soviets are "the focus of evil in the modern world." The Soviet government, with much greater control over information, tells their people much the same about the United States. This is not to suggest that people should not prefer their own values and way of life. Neither is it to suggest that nations do not have many real conflicts of interest that can lead to hostility. However, throughout history people have been highly susceptible to ethnocentrism and have often been willing participants in international conflict.

The history of conflict between the Soviet Union and the United States is strikingly similar to that between Oceania and Eastasia in George Orwell's *1984*. Oceania elites sponsored "Hate Weeks" to stimulate emotion against Eastasia (even shifting the hate against Eurasia to hate against Eastasia toward the end of a particular Hate Week)

to create more unity within the nation (see especially pp. 148–165).

CHAPTER SUMMARY
Key Terms

culture, 85
symbolic signs, 86
natural signs, 87
linguistic relativity, 87
norms, 89
laws, 92
cultural universals, 92
culture shock, 94
values, 94
individualism, 94

collectivism, 94
value integration, 96
subcultures, 97
belief systems, 98
ideologies, 98
mythologies, 98
symbols, 99
cultural diffusion, 102
ethnocentrism, 104
cultural relativism, 104

Content

The development of complex human culture must be traced to the evolution of the human brain. Our unique brain capacity allows for the development of ideas, language, tools, and other elements of culture. Of all these human creations, however, language is the most important, not only for communication, but also for the further expansion of culture.

Language is so important for human culture that it both reflects the important characteristics of a particular culture *and* to some extent limits and shapes what people may understand.

Humans are the only animals to create a complex symbolic language. Chimpanzees, for example, do have the brain capacity to learn a symbolic language but not to create such a language.

As culture has been defined, a few other animals, especially higher primates, are able to develop and learn elements of culture. This culture, however, is primarily limited to such things as very simple tool making.

There are many important elements of nonmaterial culture. Included among these are norms, which are the many rules that organize and guide human behavior. Values, rather than representing specific rules, are more abstract ideas and principles that have strong emotional appeal. Every society has a number of major values that usually are integrated, though often there are also conflicting values. For the most part, value integration (to the extent it exists) is due to material conditions that shaped the values.

Because humans depend on learning and culture to guide them in almost everything they do, different cultures and learning have led to an immense variety of human behavior. We can assume that most human groups were generally similar hundreds of thousands of years ago. But as human groups spread over the earth, became more isolated from one another, and faced different environments, the variety of human cultures increased.

One of the most important aspects of culture is that it allows humans to maintain social order and adapt themselves to a particular environment. However, the dual nature of human societies is also reflected in the outcomes of culture. Cultural differences help produce and enforce group conflict, and culture also helps maintain inequality and conflict within human societies.

Social Structure: Groups and Organizations

. . . The production of life, both of one's own in labor and of fresh life in procreation . . . appears as a double relationship: on the one hand, as a natural, on the other as a social relationship. By social we understand the co-operation of several individuals, no matter under what conditions, in what manner, and to what end.
— *Karl Marx, The German Ideology*

As you have already learned, our earliest human ancestors were most likely very group-oriented. In the face of tough competition from other animals, the human brain provided the competitive edge; we survived not because of superior tools or weapons, but because of the group cooperation in hunting and gathering that human intelligence allowed. Hundreds of thousands of years later we continue to find humans cooperating with each other in small groups. However, since humans took the first step toward settled agricultural communities about 10,000 years ago, the nature of this group existence has become increasingly more complex. Consider these more recent examples.

In the year 1605, the French newspaper *Mercure Français* reported:

During the summer of this year the King, who was in Paris, was warned by a certain Belin that in Limousin, Perigord, Quercy, and other nearby provinces a number of gentlemen were meeting to restore the bases of the rebellion that the late Marshal Biron and his co-conspirators had laid down. (Tilly, 1981, p. 1)

The newspaper goes on to criticize the growing rebellion that finally resulted in the assassination of Henry IV in 1610.

In the year 1765 the *South Carolina Gazette* (of Charleston, South Carolina) described a protest in which an angry crowd broke windows at the home of the local tax collector. After hanging an effigy from a 20-foot-high gallows, the newspaper says the crowd demanded

. . . that all internal duties imposed on them without the consent of their immediate, or even virtual, representation, was grievous, oppresseive, and unconstitutional, and that an extension of the powers and jurisdiction of admiralty courts in America tended to subvert one of their most darling legal rights, that of trials by juries. (Tilly, 1981, p. 98)

In the year 1974 there was widespread protest in Kanawha County, West Virginia, over school textbooks described as "dirty, anti-Christian, and anti-American" (Billings and Goldman, 1983, p. 70). The protestors closed the schools for several days and about 3,500 miners went on strike for several weeks in support of the textbook protest. The more violent protestors destroyed school property, shot at empty school buses, and dynamited the board of education office. In a *Washington Post* article (Billings and Goldman, 1983, p. 73) the protestors were described as "troubled and confused by the 'new morality,' the 'new secularism'" that they see as "blasphemous, obscene, and unpatriotic."

I expect a confused reaction from my readers at this point, but if you think about it, one fact becomes quite clear. Despite the varied nature of these protest events, ranging across some 470 years of history, there is a strong similarity. All three events involved conflict with outside authorities, which assumes that communication with that authority is necessary. The key point is this: for quite some time, as these cases suggest, we no longer find small groups operating more or less independently. The small groups certainly remain; but in addition we find larger, more complex human organizations. And as we would expect, individuals in the larger organizations often have views and interests that conflict with those of individuals in small, localized groups. But as we will also see, both large organizations and small groups are necessary in modern societies.

The two previous chapters explored two basic foundations of human societies (material and nonmaterial culture); we are ready to move to a third — groups and organizations. Some of these groups are rather concrete and within our everyday experience (groups made up of our family members, fellow workers, close friends, and so on). But what we do not see is the complex, interlocking network that these many small groups create. The pattern of this network can have a profound effect on the nature of the overall society; in fact, it is this network that creates and maintains the more general society (Blau, Beeker, and Fitzpatrick, 1984).

Imagine a society of 50 million people. No one in this society can know every one of these people, but they are all most likely linked together through many small groups with overlapping memberships. These groups are *the means through which these people form a society*. But the nature of this group network can take many forms — some groups may be more closely linked with others, some groups may even form almost isolated clusters. If this second case becomes a widespread condition, the potential for overall social unity is weaker, and major conflict is more likely.

Organizations are also formed by individuals interacting in groups. But in this case group networks are more formally organized; they have a specified structure, function, and chain of authority. Although equally concrete at their human base, organizations usually appear more abstract. What is the government? What, really, is General Motors? We can easily see parts of these complex organizations — someone from "the government" brings our mail, sends us tax forms, and so on. General Motors makes cars that many of us (though unfortunately for American workers fewer and fewer) drive. But in both of these cases there is much more to the organization than we can see in our everyday experience.

SOCIAL STRUCTURE AND INSTITUTIONS

It's time for some rather difficult concepts. My discussion here is critical for tying together many of the concepts for a more general understanding of the nature of societies (as I hope you will see). I begin with one of the most important, and perhaps most ambiguous concepts — social structure. When thinking of structure, we most often think of something like a building. There is a material form, with concrete objects placed in spatial relationships that create these kinds of structures we call buildings.

People form social structures that are no less real, though more difficult to see and impossible to touch.

Social structures are created by the relationships people form with each other. It might help to visualize social structures as the girders, or steel beams that form the basic structure of a large, modern office building. These steel beams represent the ties between individuals and groups. And like the steel beams in a building, these individual and group ties that form social structures are usually rather long-term ties. In other words, the interaction and behavior in social structures are repetitive and rather predictable. Social structures never last forever and are subject to change; but so are office buildings. With this in mind we can define **social structure** as a system of social relations among individuals within groups and among groups or categories of people in a society (Blau, 1974, 1977).

Status and Roles. Considering the place of individuals within groups and organizations, we must turn to two additional concepts. The first, **status,** is the position of a person in specific groups and organizations. (Status also refers to prestige or honor, but I will be specific when using the term in this way in later chapters.) For example, a person can hold the positions of student, club president, father, husband, son, and cook at a fast-food restaurant — all at the same time. In fact, most individuals have more status positions than these. Some are more important than others, however, in influencing many aspects of an individual's life. We can most likely learn more about a particular individual by knowing that person is a student and a mother, than by knowing that person is a member of a bowling club. A person's most important status position (or positions) is sometimes called a **master status.**

One reason that status positions are important is that each position contains norms and behavior expectations we call **roles** (see Figure 5.1). We can say simply that people "occupy" a status whereas they "play" roles (Linton, 1936). For example, when occupying the status of student you are expected to follow certain rules. As a student you also have duties and obligations, as well as rights and privileges. Students are expected to attend classes and

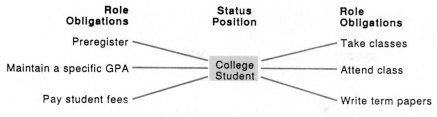

FIGURE 5.1. Status and roles.

take exams. More specific behavior expectations may vary among universities (e.g., students may be required to live on campus, dress in a certain manner, maintain a certain religious faith, and so on).

Some of the roles of one specific status may be difficult to follow at the same time. This condition is called **role strain.** For example, student athletes may have difficulty maintaining a high GPA, attending 15 hours of class per week, and reading dozens of books, while at the same time they are expected to devote many hours to athletics.

Another problem can flow from **role conflict.** In this case the role expectations of two or more positions are in conflict. For example, the role of mother may conflict with the role a career woman in a particular society. With this example we can examine the problems many women face in our own society as they feel more pressure and desire to seek occupational careers, while continuing traditional maternal activities.

Institutions. You may have noticed that with our description of roles we have begun to *merge social structures and culture.* The status positions are

aspects of actual social groups and organizations; the roles (rules of behavior, expectations, etc.) are *aspects of culture* (see Figure 5.2). One of the early founders of sociology, Georg Simmel (Wolff, 1950), made a similar distinction between the "forms" of social life (group forms and organizational structures) and the "contents" or "materials" of social life (motives, desires, norms, values, or culture more generally). The groups and organizations must be maintained with live, interacting humans. As we will see, characteristics of the social networks people form (e.g., group size, pattern of interaction ties) shape behavior (through such things as limiting options for behavior) irrespective of norms and culture. But equally important are the cultural traditions of the previous generations that continue to shape the behavior of the living through values as they interact in groups.

The merger of culture and social structure becomes even more important when we consider **institutions,** which are clusters of norms centered around important tasks in the society. Consider the family: Every society is faced with the task of training and caring for its young. Cultural traditions (i.e.,

FIGURE 5.2. The merger of social structure and culture.

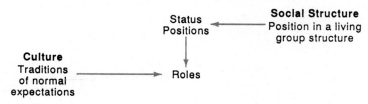

In the children's rhyme about what to be when we grow up, we learn about different options for master status — "doctor, lawyer, Indian Chief." These portraits of a businessman and a member of the Grosventre Tribe from Montana present information about status, honor, and role. For each man, list three observations about status that you can draw from the photos. (© John Running/ Photo Researchers, Inc.)

clusters of norms) that develop in response to this task guide members of the society. Thus, when we refer to *the family* we mean the family as an institution — the clustering of norms related to caring for the young (as well as the family's other functions). Specific families are, of course, living social groups that actually perform the work of caring for children. But these specific groups are then merged with culture, so to speak, in the form of "the family" as an institution with its cluster of norms and roles.

As this implies, there are several institutions in a society, each related to a particular important collective task. For example, every complex society has a cluster of norms related to important tasks like caring for children and personal needs (the family), attaining basic material necessities (the economy), setting goals and providing collective mobilization for achieving the goals (the polity), providing moral guidance and explaining the cosmos (religion), and training members of the society to perform specialized occupational tasks (education). This is not to say that separate institutions have norms for only one task (e.g., the family, religion, and education may all teach the young and provide moral guidance). And as we will see, neither is this to say that all groups in the society are equally served by these institutions (they can also further dominance and exploitation by a group).

THE MERGER OF TECHNOSTRUCTURE, CULTURE, AND SOCIAL STRUCTURE

So far we have focused on the merger of social structure and nonmaterial culture (roles, norms, etc.), but material culture also has a central position in this merger. (Remembering our description in Chapters 3 and 4 of how nonmaterial culture is shaped by material culture and the material environment should make the next step clear.) Environment and material culture enter this merger in one way by shaping basic institutions in the society. As outlined in Chapter 3, we find certain types of family institutions, religions, and political systems more likely to coexist with specific types of technology (e.g., hunting and gathering, simple horticulture, and so on). Thus, with our new concept of social structure we can see how real live groups of people are directed and shaped by

1. the overall type of technology,
2. which has also shaped the norms and roles of the status positions these people hold.

We must also clarify the place of group conflict in all of the above before turning to examples. When describing institutions as "centered around important tasks in the society" (like educating the young), we invite the danger of assuming that society represents only a unified whole. But remember that society also represents a setting for major group conflicts. Especially important are the group conflicts shaped by the type of technostructure in a society (see Chapter 3). And as we saw in Chapter 4, norms, values, and other elements of nonmaterial culture are often influenced by major group conflicts. The values favored in a particular society, and how these values are interpreted, are influenced by group power. Thus, because institutional norms and roles are a part of nonmaterial culture, these norms and roles are also shaped by the process of group conflict.

Let's consider an example. We have seen that agrarian societies with extensive warfare tend to give males more power than females. In this situation male/female roles develop that complement the unequal power relation. Men may be given total control over family property, the right to punish females for extramarital affairs, and so on. The female role develops in correspondence to the male role — she is to accept all this treatment as right and proper. It is obviously beneficial for all in the society that men and women have complementary roles so that the business of producing and raising children runs smoothly. *However,* the details of how this gets done (i.e., the exact roles) can vary so that one party is advantaged.

As the technostructure is changing in industrial societies, the most influential positions in the society no longer require physical strength. The chief executive of a major corporation, for example, does not need the strength and speed of a good warrior or hunter. Women are slowly moving into higher positions, and the male/female roles are also slowly changing. As an indication of this slow change, you should remember that women in the United States could not even vote in National elections until 1920.

Figure 5.3 presents a summary of the main points of our discussion. The upper-central position locates status positions and the roles that accompany them. Focusing first on the right side of this figure, to understand how the status *positions* developed, we must understand how concrete groups and organizations developed. As we will see, groups emerge from social interaction over extended periods of time. But also important is how the *technostructure shapes*

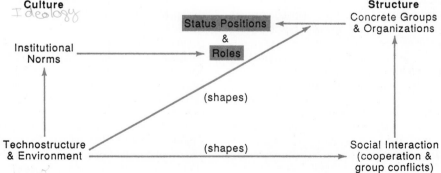

FIGURE 5.3. The technostructural and social structural base of status positions and roles.

the interaction patterns so that some people are more likely to interact with each other. In most agrarian societies, for example, peasants are more likely to interact with other peasants, and land-owners are more likely to interact with other land-owners. In industrial societies much the same happens with people in similar occupational positions (though we will see that relations in these societies are more complex). This interaction process tends to produce distinct, small groups with at least some opposing interests with other groups.

Also, large organizations are usually shaped by their type of technostructure (indicated by the line from "technostructure" to "organizations"). For example, we saw that China developed a large state organization early in its history, in contrast to Japan, because China's geography required large agricultural projects. Industrial production will result in larger economic organizations (bureaucracies) with characteristics significantly different from those in agrarian societies. These organizations will usually operate to reproduce or maintain the type of technostructure that exists, which means that status positions in these organizations will operate in a like manner. For example, in a capitalist industrial society there will be some organizational means of controlling the labor of many workers. Many managerial positions in capitalist economic organizations are devoted to this purpose; thus, we can say these positions for controlling labor help "reproduce" or maintain the capitalist technostructure over time.

On the left side of Figure 5.3 are some of the key influences on the roles followed by people in certain status positions. Roles, remember, are formed by rules and norms related to the nonmaterial culture. The nonmaterial culture, as already described, is influenced by the technostructure and environment. Again using the example of the family as an institution, we have seen how the type of family institution is influenced by the technostructure. In an agrarian society with very little geographical mobility and an economic incentive for many family members cooperating to produce food, an extended family system is likely to exist. Conversely, in an industrial society with extensive geographical and occupational mobility, an extended family system could be detrimental.

Throughout time, the nuclear family has tended to dominate in industrial societies.

Figure 5.3 is a simplified model of what happens in the real world. This is to say that the real world is more complex. As indicated in Chapters 3 and 4, nonmaterial culture does influence material culture and the technostructure. But the purpose of a model like that represented in Figure 5.3 *is* to simplify. From the many things operating in the real world, a model attempts to represent what the scientist believes are the most important processes. By "most important processes" I mean those that explain more of what happens in the world. Figure 5.3 represents much of what we have already learned about the social world, and it can help us understand many of the subjects in coming chapters.

GROUPS

We spend most of our lives in groups. We are born into a group; children form peer groups; adults form groups at work and play and to achieve any variety of goals. On the average, each person belongs to five or six groups, which is estimated to result in some 6 to 7 billion groups in the world today (Mills, 1967). So extensive is the network of groups in the United States that Milgram (1970) has estimated that, on the average, any two people picked at random can be linked through seven friendship relations. In other words, the first individual selected has a friend, who has a friend, and so on through seven people until the two randomly selected people are connected.

There are many reasons for forming groups, but whatever the utilitarian reasons, group relations apparently also serve important psychological functions. One of the most striking examples of this occurred after the 1972 Buffalo Creek flood in West Virginia, which happened when a large dam broke and totally destroyed the community of Buffalo Creek. Such disasters have occurred many times throughout history in the United States. And each time the lives of people have been severely affected in many ways. But one thing that occurred after the Buffalo Creek flood made the situation much worse. The survivors were provided with trailers for shelter, but these trailers were located in many places around the county and people were assigned to trailers in such a way that community ties were not respected. All the small group ties that had existed in the community before the flood were broken. A result was that 93 percent of the 615 survivors had various kinds of emotional disorders that lasted for an exceptionally long time compared with people with such problems after other disasters (Erikson, 1976).

Types of Groups. Before proceeding, as usual we have a few definitions. The most important definition is that for a group. A simple collection of people in one location does *not* constitute a group. If this were the case, there would be hundreds of billions of groups around the world rather than the 6 or 7 billion noted above. A **group** consists of two or more people who interact with other members of the group over an extended period of time, forming more or less ordered and lasting relationships. Shoppers in a major area of town do not constitute a group. Spectators at a sporting event or the audience at a concert do not normally represent a group. A college fraternity or sorority constitutes a group, as does a social club, a work group, and a family.

The best description for these collections of individuals who have not formed lasting group ties is a **social aggregate.** It is also useful to distinguish between a group and people who simply have some characteristic in common, whether or not the people are gathered in one location. People with common characteristics (such as all university students, people with similar levels of education, and so on) are often called a *social category,* though the term social aggregate is used equally as often.

Groups themselves can be divided into two major types—primary and secondary. **Primary groups** are small groups in which personal ties are very strong among members. There is extensive face-to-face interaction in these groups, which is a major reason primary groups are small. Another important characteristic is that primary groups tend to be all-purpose groups in the sense that they are not maintained primarily for a specific purpose. The emotional support and companionship received are most important. There are many examples of primary groups, though a family, children's peer groups, and adult friendship groups are the most common.

The members of **secondary groups** do not have strong emotional ties, and the groups are formed for more specific, limited purposes. Secondary groups can be either large or small because strong personal ties are not important. As you might expect, people in industrial societies tend to be involved in more secondary groups. But secondary groups are still groups, which means there must be some individual interaction and relationships over an extended period of time. Students attending a small college class may not constitute a secondary group at first (unless there was extensive prior contact among them), though it could soon evolve into a secondary group. This college class (or segment of it) could also evolve into a primary group if relationships grow strong enough and the function of the group expands to other activities. Most secondary groups are found where people come together for a specific task, as they do in a work setting.

Group Formation

It is likely that humans have some kind of biologically based urge to form groups. Acknowledging this, however, tells us very little. We still have questions such as why do people form certain types of groups, why do some people belong to many more groups, under what conditions are people most likely to form groups, and of what types.

With groups formed primarily for personal gratification and friendship the question is not so much why they are formed, but when they are formed, and with whom. We can begin seeking answers by considering the conditions likely to bring people together, thereby making group formation more likely. For example, such groups are more likely with people living in the same neighborhood, attending school together, working together, and so on. This aspect of group formation may sound rather simple (and it is), but it must be kept in mind when trying to explain other things about people. For example, why do people tend to marry others from similar income and educational backgrounds? One important reason is that people of similar income and educational backgrounds are more likely to come together in the same neighborhoods, schools, work groups, churches, and many other places.

Mobilization and the Free-rider Problem. The formation of what I call mobilization groups is more complex. By "mobilization groups" I mean groups intentionally formed by their members to act on some common interest or interests. (Excluded from this type are more permanent groups formed by someone else, like work groups.) Mobilization groups are obviously highly dependent on situations that create common interests.

As noted already, the technostructure and environment are strong forces producing common inter-

---

BOX 5.1

Sociograms and a Case of Hysterical Contagion

One aspect of a small group structure is the pattern of social relationships among the members of a group. In a group of ten people, for example, we will most likely find that some like each other better and associate with each other more than they do with others in the group. Social scientists can map these social relations, as indicated below. Such a figure is called a *sociogram.*

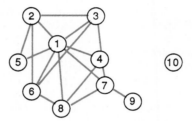

The sociogram shown here uses lines to indicate strong social relations between our ten imaginary people. These lines can represent strong friendship ties, respect, or social activity like eating lunch together. Our imaginary figure can indicate various levels of involvement in a small secondary group in a factory. Person 1 is a central member of the group, as shown by the more extensive ties to other members of the group. Person 10 is at the other extreme; this person is in the group but is a social isolate in terms of any ties to other group members. Person 9 is almost a social isolate, with only one tie to person 7. The other group members (2 through 7) are about equally involved in the group.

Sociograms like this, as well as *social network analysis* within and across groups, can tell us much about the nature of a group and intergroup ties. For example, some sociologists have used network analysis to determine the most powerful people in the United States, where they come from, and the sources of their power (Moore, 1982). Sociograms can also help us understand many aspects of group behavior like an outbreak of hysterical contagion.

Hysterical contagion involves a highly emotional fear of some mysterious force that is passed through a group resulting in symptoms of actual physical illness like nausea, rashes, headaches, and fainting (Kerckhoff and Back, 1968, pp. 23–25). If it is a true

ests. On many issues peasants have many interests in common, whereas these interests often conflict with those of landowners. Workers in a capitalist society have many interests in common that often conflict with interests of factory owners. Workers in the bottom ranks of a large bureaucracy have many common interests (Dahrendorf, 1959), as do people

in the same neighborhoods, the same religion, the same occupation, the same region of a nation, and so on.

Knowing the extent of common interests among a category of people, however, is *not* enough to accurately predict the formation of mobilization groups. To begin with, people may not even recog-

case of hysterical contagion, there is no physical cause of the illness (such as a chemical agent or biological organism), and the illness is thus psychosomatic (has a psychological cause). Many possible cases of hysterical contagion are reported each year, often involving school children. In April 1983, for example, there was a highly publicized case involving Arab schoolchildren in Israeli-occupied territory. The panic or hysteria affected 943 children and caused 394 to go to the hospital. The belief among these children was that they were being subjected to a poison gas by the Israeli military. Many scientists investigated this case and concluded that the cause was psychological (*Los Angeles Times,* April 4, 1983).

The main question with possible cases of hysterical contagion is whether or not there is an actual physical cause of the rapid outbreak of illness. In the case of the Arab schoolchildren, the illness could have been caused by some gas or chemical, though extensive study ruled out these possibilities. In a somewhat similar case, even more extensive research shows that it was, in fact, a case of hysterical contagion without a physical cause.

The case involved people working in a textile factory in the United States (Kerckhoff and Back, 1968). The hysterical belief was that a strange insect had been brought into the factory with imported fabric. Many people were sent to doctors with symptoms of nausea, rashes, and fainting. The factory was closed for several days while scientists investigated. No physical cause of the illness could be found so social scientists were employed to investigate the mysterious illness. The social scientists found clear evidence indicating hysterical contagion. For example, the people affected by the illness were found to have more stress in their lives compared with people not affected by it. Even more interesting, the outbreak of the illness was related to group social structure.

In a primary location in this factory was a woman who had fainted on previous occasions without producing anything like hysterical contagion in the group. This particular woman was a relative social isolate similar to person 10 in our sociogram. On the day the hysterical contagion began in this factory, however, a central person in the group (like person 1 in our sociogram) also fainted and said afterward that she had been bitten by an insect. This event sparked a wave of illness following the lines of influence shown in a sociogram constructed by sociologists investigating the case (Kerckhoff and Back, 1968, pp. 115–124). There was apparently no poison gas or insect randomly producing an illness but a psychological process following lines of association in the group.

nize their common interests, in which case mobilization is impossible. Such groups have been referred to as "latent interest groups," whereas those actively working toward their common interests are "manifest interest groups" (Dahrendorf, 1959). Marx (Marx and Engels, 1965) referred to these groups as "a class in itself" versus "a class for itself."

Even when a latent interest group (i.e., a group not yet mobilized) recognizes some common interests, mobilization is often difficult. For example, opinion polls show that large segments of the population oppose such things as the ownership of handguns, nuclear weapons, nuclear power plants, and deficit spending by the government. Many more examples can be found with specific issues on the local level.

A major question becomes why, if these people realize a common problem, are they not working together to solve it? There are many reasons: pessimism over chances for change, disagreement over methods of change, and lack of time or resources that could be used to create change. But one barrier to mobilization is even more common.

Let's use the example of people opposed to a nuclear power plant in their community. A majority (maybe as many as 80 percent) of area residents oppose the nuclear power plant and thus realize they have conflicting interests with the owners of the power plant. However, only 5 to 10 percent of these residents have formed a mobilization group (a manifest interest group) to stop the power plant. A common problem, but why?

As noted early in this book, we can learn a lot

Box 5.2

The Three Miles Island Nuclear Accident and the Free-Rider Effect

In March 1979 the nation's most serious nuclear power plant accident occurred near Harrisburg, Pennsylvania. The power plant came close to a meltdown, and potentially dangerous amounts of radioactive steam escaped into the atmosphere. Approximately 150,000 residents of the area were evacuated, and some stayed away for a few weeks. Following this nuclear accident there was a rapid increase in protest activity against nuclear power all over the United States. A major demonstration against nuclear power, with 200,000 people in Washington, D.C., occurred in May 1979.

As might be expected, there was a rapid increase in the number of antinuclear organizations in Pennsylvania after the Three Mile Island accident. Also as expected, there was an increase in the number of people in the Harrisburg, Pennsylvania, area with strong attitudes against nuclear power. *However,* a study by two sociologists soon after the accident found that only 6 percent of the people living in the area were actively involved in the protest (Walsh and Warland, 1983). The table below indicates the percentage of the population for and against nuclear power (restarting the power plant) in the Three Mile Island area after the accident. Also shown is the percentage of people *actively* working for or against these goals, along with those people not active (free riders).

As this table shows, the accident certainly polarized community opinion. But most interesting is the finding that only 6 percent of residents were actively involved in some kind of activity to oppose restarting the power plant (beyond signing a petition or attending a meeting). Another 1 percent became actively involved in pushing for a restart of the power plant. Among those with strong opinions against the power plant but not active, some stated reasons for lack of involvement including "lack of time," "family responsibilities," and lack of knowledge about a protest group.

about human societies by assuming that humans are selfish. Of course, humans do not *always* act selfishly, but let's see what this assumption can tell us about group mobilization. If the 5 to 10 percent of the people who are working hard (spending their time and money, getting arrested, etc.) to stop the power plant are successful, the total 75 to 80 percent will also win. In other words, by doing nothing the much larger inactive category of people will receive the same benefits without the effort. This situation, called the **free-rider problem** (Olson, 1965), has received considerable research interest by sociologists (see Box 5.2).

To overcome the free-rider problem group members must usually come up with the right mixture of personal incentives or rewards for participation and negative sanctions for nonparticipation (Oliver,

1980). For example, incentives can include special favors, prestige, free parties, free rock concerts, contact with a famous person, and standard material benefits like extra money. Examples of negative sanctions include loss of some benefit, physical threats, and actual physical violence.

Labor unions have always had difficulties with free-riders. If a union is able to win a good contract from the employer, all employees get the benefits, whether or not they have joined the union and/or the strike. Especially before labor unions had legal rights in the United States, they often had to rely on at least some physical threats to counter the physical threats from agents hired by employers against potential union members. Since attaining more legal support for their existence in the 1930s, however, unions have come to rely on positive personal in-

	Total (%)	Active (%)	Percent Free-Riders Within Each Category
Opposed to restart of TMI	49	6	(87)
In favor of restart of TMI	46	1	(98)
Undecided	5	—	—
	100	$n = 673$ people	

(*SOURCE:* Data from Walsh and Warland, 1983, p. 772).

Sociologists refer to this lack of involvement, even by people with strong attitudes for or against a situation, as the *free-rider effect*. Because such people often realize that one additional person's involvement will have little effect on the success of a protest group, and because they realize they will benefit by the success of a protest group even if they are not involved (the power plant is closed for everyone), it is often difficult to mobilize a large group of people for protest activity. Leaders of a mobilized interest group, of course, are working to get as much support and involvement as possible from the population to maximize their chances of success. Sociologists are not in agreement over the exact magnitude of the free-rider problem, but they all recognize that it is an extensive problem for interest group activists (Marwell and Ames, 1979). Because of the free-rider effect, small groups that are powerful and unified often have little to fear when even a large majority of the population is opposed to the interests of their group.

ducements. Union members may be offered "members only" pension plans, low insurance rates, counseling, and recreation.

If you consider events occurring around you now, I am sure you can see how the free-rider problem applies to many kinds of group activities. Political candidates may be trying to get more active support from party members who know they will benefit whether or not they help with the election. Revolutionaries and government authorities in Central American nations are both trying to win over peasants and workers by providing material aid and physical threats. Corporate executives in a particular industry are trying to get contributions from everyone in the industry to fight a new government policy. And the list goes on.

Not every group faces the free-rider problem equally or faces it in the same way. When people are in extensive close contact, group bonds and norms are usually stronger. In this case, research (Marwell and Ames, 1979) shows people are more likely to contribute what is considered "their fair share" simply because they believe it is morally right, whether or *not* they get direct benefits. Thus, it is doubtful that our early hunting and gathering relatives had to contend with the free-rider problem; like many other problems, this one slowly began to emerge and grow when larger groups evolved from settled agriculture.

Outcomes of Group Structure

A group may exist to produce a product, elect a candidate, praise a god, or to enjoy recreation. Simmel (Wolff, 1950) referred to these motives or group purpose as group "content." Such motives certainly affect group behavior. However, groups with common motives can differ dramatically in behavior because of differences in group structure (or what Simmel called group forms). In this section we examine some important characteristics of group structure like membership size, communication links, group boundaries, and out-group conflict.

Group Size. Consider two small groups of three people each. The similar size of the groups leads to important similarities in behavior no matter whether the groups have very different tasks (content).

To make this clear we examine the effects of group size for two-person groups, or **dyads,** versus three-person groups, or **triads.** As indicated in Figure 5.4, when we move from dyads to triads the possible interpersonal relations become much more complex. It is for this reason that dyads tend to be more stable groups. With only two members, if the group is to continue than the relation between the two must be strong and they must guard against sharp disagreements. With a triad, on the other hand, Simmel observed that "no matter how close a triad may be, there is always the occasion on which two of the three members regard the third as an intruder" (Wolff, 1950, p. 135).

Figure 5.4 suggests that several important changes occur as we move from dyad to triad. First, simply the number of possible interaction patterns increases. As shown at the center of Figure 5.4, A and B may have a relationship, as do B and C (#1). However, A and C may not have this particular relationship (say, love for tennis). In other combinations the relationship may be lacking between A and B or B and C, or the relationship may exist among all three members. I am sure you can imagine many concrete examples of these combinations; the arrows may indicate sexual relations, common interests in music, stronger friendship ties, and so on. With a dyad there is either a basic relationship (or relationships) or the group doesn't exist. With a triad there can be many more patterns, and the complexity of possibilities makes diplomacy among group members more delicate and unstable.

Even more complex can be influence relations or power relations in a triad. In a dyad either one person is dominant or there is equality of influence. But with the first example (#1) at the bottom of Figure 5.4, actor A is clearly the most dominant and actor B is the least influential. This is because A influences B and C, whereas C influences B, who influences no one. Examples #2 and #3 indicate some other possibilities of one-person dominance, though there are even other possible combinations. Example #4 indicates a situation where actors A and B are equal in

Group Size

Interaction Patterns

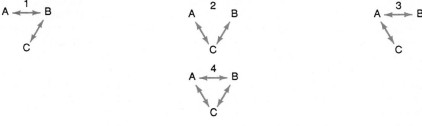

Influence Patterns

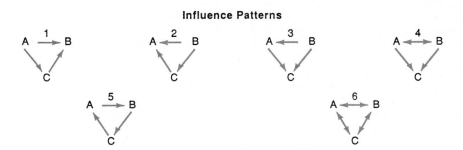

FIGURE 5.4. Dyads and triads.

power, and both dominant over C. Again, there are several combinations of a coequal power relationship.

Finally, Figure 5.4 indicates two forms of democracy (#5 and #6). The first of these is a rather interesting situation in which A influences B, who influences C, who then influences A. For instance, B may highly respect the wisdom of A and is therefore likely to follow A's suggestions. Actor C, on the other hand, respects the wisdom of B, and A most respects C. Thus, the influence is circular. Example

#6 indicates a form of democracy in which all have equal influence on each other.

Another way of approaching this is to use folk wisdom. Folk wisdom tells us "two is company and three is a crowd." Three children who are able to play together in combinations of two may produce seemingly endless conflicts when together as a triad. Folk wisdom also tells us that the biggest change for a married couple (and an unmarried couple as well) is the first child, not the second. Part of this is because the couple has learned to adapt to children by the time they have the second child. But if we simply look at the possible interaction combinations, we see that a group moving from a dyad to a triad produces a greater jump in relative complexity than a group that increases its members from three to four.

As we move to larger groups, the complexity, of course, continues to increase, but the social impact of the increase in complexity is more gradual than that produced with a move from a dyad to a triad. Still, when we approach very large groups, we reach a new plateau of complexity. When the group becomes so large that all the members cannot know each other personally, a qualitative change in the group takes place. Such things as cooperation and consensus become more difficult to achieve. The free-rider problem becomes more acute because of less face-to-face interaction enforcing a sense of moral responsibility. In short, *if the large group is to be maintained, a new means of providing social organization must be created.* This new means of organization is usually found with formal organization and bureaucracy, as is described in more detail later in this chapter.

Communication Networks. Consider the patterns of communication among a small group of four people in Figure 5.5. Several observations can be made about these different patterns. (It is worth noting

FIGURE 5.5. Communication networks (Adapted from Mayhew, 1980).

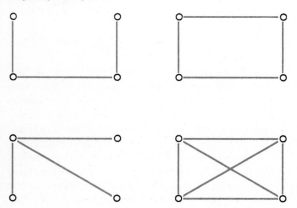

that these patterns can have similar effects on four groups or four nations, as well as a group of four individuals.) First, notice that the two groups on the left are less secure because the loss of any communication link reduces group size (Mayhew, 1980). The two groups on the right can lose a communication link but still maintain the group through other communication links.

Second, because greater access to information can lead to greater influence in the group, we find possible power inequality with the two groups on the left in Figure 5.5, but equality on the right. The most powerful and important position is found in the bottom-left group. In this case all information must flow through one position. In the upper-left group, two positions are more influential and two are dependent positions. In both groups on the right there is equality in access of information. (Keep in mind that we are referring to *positions*, or statuses, in a group, not individuals. Irrespective of individual characteristics, holding certain positions gives more or less influence.)

Third, of all four group communication structures, the quality of information exchanged is most likely best in one group — the bottom-right group. It is only in this group that everyone has information from everyone else. The accuracy of the information is more easily subject to scrutiny and multiple validation. In the other groups, if anyone provides incorrect information it is more likely passed on without correction. There is, however, a possible negative consequence of the communication pattern in the bottom-right group. Although information may be more accurately conveyed and less subject to manipulations, the process may be more time-consuming. In terms of time, the most efficient means of conveying information may be found in the authoritarian group structure (bottom-left).

We can briefly consider some concrete implications of the above. When we realize that direct communication among everyone in large groups is impossible, we begin to realize that people who are important links in the communication chain have much influence. And even though the chief executive of a corporation or nation is very powerful for many reasons, these people depend on others for most of their information. For example, the people who manage a president's appointments with other officials can be very powerful by controlling the information to and from the president.

As a final example; seating arrangements in a small group have been shown to be important to group behavior (Patterson et. al., 1979). Circular seating arrangements, which allow all individuals equal chances for communication (verbal and nonverbal), increase individual participation, decrease the time between communications, and create a feeling of greater satisfaction with the group experience. You have most likely experienced the effects of seating arrangements in a classroom situation. Even in a class with a small number of students, student participation is less when all students face the instructor at the front of the room, compared with a class where all individuals face one another in a circle.

BOX 5.3

Group Structure and Corporate Stock Prices in an Options Market

When we present basic sociological concepts like social structure, students are sometimes left with the impression that none of this really matters in the real world. Let me assure you that these sociological concepts matter a good deal; such things as group structure influence political decision making, how much you learn in a certain educational setting, and I could give many other examples. To make the point, let's consider one example in some detail.

A recent study by a sociologist who is also a vice-president of a financial consulting firm in Washington, D.C., found that group structure has an important impact on the prices of corporate stock traded in options markets (Baker, 1984). Untold millions of dollars have been made (and lost) because of a social structural effect that has only recently become understood in financial markets.

Futures markets exist for all kinds of commodities and goods of value, including corporate stock. In the last example, people speculate on the future price of corporate stock that is sold in another speculative market — the stock market. To do this people physically come together on a market floor (sometimes called the "pit") and bargin with each other to buy and sell these stock options (for themselves or for clients).

This is where the group structure effect comes in. Economists had generally assumed that the more people trading in a market, the more rational the economic decision making. Because more people are bidding for financial securities, the buyer and the seller can obtain a clearer idea of the value of what is being sold by the trend of the bids. In essence, the economic actors have more information to guide them with a larger group buying and selling.

In contrast to this assumption, Baker (1984) found that an increase in the size of the group of people trading in stock options made prices more unstable. In other words, prices can take unrealistic swings up and down. People can make and lose money more readily and corporations can be misled about their strengths, among other problems. The reason for this effect is that when a certain group size is reached on the market floor, the group begins to break up into small cliques within the larger group. Then information about what is happening in the overall trading group is lost, which produces more insecurity over decision making. People are then more subject to emotional swings in pricing stock options. But also important, in a larger group it is more difficult to detect and control people who may be trading unfairly by withholding pricing information. The characteristics of social structure, in short, can mean a lot.

Group Boundary Maintenance. All groups must have boundaries to define who belongs and who does not. But whereas all groups have them, boundaries are a dimension of group structure that varies considerably. Some groups have fairly open boundaries; they accept almost anyone as a member. Other groups seek to limit membership and are highly selective.

A group's boundaries can result from specific policies on the part of a group. Thus, the purpose of a group (or the "content" of a group, as Simmel called it) can affect the characteristics of a group's boundaries. However, a key point is that similar boundary characteristics can have the same effects on groups, no matter what type of group is involved.

The main intent of having open boundaries may be to expand membership. A political party wants more active supporters. Most religious groups (though not all, or to the same degree) seek more members, as do labor unions, the YMCA, and Girl Scouts. In these groups, given their purpose or mission, bigger is better. But relatively open boundaries can have negative effects. A fraternity usually seeks more closed boundaries, as do honor societies, many social clubs, and some professions. Outcomes of closed boundaries are usually (1) greater group prestige, (2) more group unity, (3) stronger personal relationships in the group, and (4) control of important characteristics of members. The intent of a social club is often to provide close personal relations and prestige. By making the club exclusive or highly selective, the group is trying to convey the idea that people allowed into it are the very best people. Exclusiveness, of course, can also be maintained for protection and/or power. A criminal orga-

Group boundaries are reinforced through participation in shared activities, wearing uniforms, and developing consensus regarding values. What impact does celebrating a birthday or anniversary have on group unity? Do you think these Girl Scouts will learn more about their troop from joining in celebrations? Will this create greater group loyalty? (© Roberta Hershenson/ Photo Researchers, Inc.)

nization is careful in selecting members, but so is a powerful elite organization. Other groups may simply seek close personal relations and thus limit group size for that purpose. And still other groups may be selecting members for highly skilled tasks; thus the pool of potential members is limited.

We conclude with an example of the effects of group boundaries. Small groups that have elected to maintain an isolated existence have special problems of long-term in-group unity. These groups must create strong emotional commitment to the group, otherwise in-group conflict can become extensive and members will be lost. In a very interesting look at the many communes in the United States beginning in the early 1800s, Kanter (1972) found that communes that existed for a long period of time (some over 100 years) were more concerned with boundary maintenance. Many of these communes — such as Harmony, Amana, and Zoar — were careful to select new members who were well known by old members and had similar religious, social, and educational backgrounds as those of people already in the community.

Out-Group Conflict. Another important group characteristic is out-group conflict. Some groups are highly involved with such conflict, sometimes to the point of actively seeking conflict with another out-group. In large part, variance in the degree of out-group conflict is related to a group's material and social environment. In some cases a tradition of out-group conflict has become so much a part of a group that it seems unable to exist without the conflict. One reason for this, as we will see, is that out-group conflict can have important outcomes that are often positive for some members of the group.

We begin with an elementary observation; as Sumner (1906) and Simmel (1905, 1955) pointed out, an in-group presupposes an out-group. If a group is to exist, it must have at least some boundaries, which means there must be an out-group. And as we've seen, groups differ with respect to boundary maintenance; thus, we can also expect that groups with more rigid boundaries will have more out-group conflict (the distinction between insiders and outsiders is more important to such groups).

Although in-group unity can be a cause of out-group conflict, in-group unity can also be an outcome of out-group conflict. As Sumner (1906, p. 13) put it, "Loyalty to the group, sacrifice for it, hatred and contempt for outsiders, brotherhood within, warlikeness without — all grow together, products of the same situation." But it must also be recognized that in-group unity can often be increased *after* an increase in out-group conflict. Did the Argentine government invade the British "owned" Falkland Islands for the purpose of creating more in-group loyalty in Argentina? We will probably never know for sure, but the Argentine action did enhance in-group unity — that is, until the British easily retook the islands and created even worse problems of loyalty for the Argentine government. A few months later the military government was replaced, and the former military leaders were in jail.

Out-group conflict need not involve a real enemy to have unifying effects; it is only necessary that the threat be believed. Following historical records, Erikson (1966) showed that the witch hunts in Salem, Massachusetts, in the 1600s were manipulated by religious authorities. Their purpose was to strengthen loyalty that had been reduced by increasing internal disagreements. In another case the Reverend Jim Jones was able to create such a high degree of in-group loyalty with imaginary outside threats that over 900 people committed suicide at his command (or were killed by others before they committed suicide) in Jonestown, Guyana, in 1978 (Wooden, 1981).

As might be expected, in addition to increasing in-group loyalty, out-group conflict produces more intolerance within. Groups highly dependent on out-group conflict, such as Jim Jones's Peoples Temple mentioned above, tend to lay claim to the total personality involvement of their members. Their social cohesion depends on total sharing of all aspects of group life and is reinforced by the assertion of group unity against the dissenter" (Coser, 1956, p. 103). In such groups people must highly conform or be forced out of the group.

A high degree of in-group loyalty seldom produces anything like the mass suicide in the People's Temple. And it should equally be recognized that unifying out-group conflict need not be violent. We can return to the communes studied by Kanter

(1972) for examples. The people in these communes during the early 1800s were often quite happy, nonviolent, and strongly committed to humanitarian religious values. But they had highly negative attitudes toward outsiders, which helped maintain their in-group unity. One of these groups, the Oneida community, saw outsiders as evil, though members were required to be friendly and courteous to them. But after visitors left, members had a ritualistic "scrubbing bee" to "purify" the community. In addition to this, if anyone from the Oneida community found it necessary to go into the outside world for some reason, he or she was required to attend special criticism and confession sessions before and after going outside. Similar practices were found in the other communes like Amana (Kanter, 1972, pp. 85–86). (Both Oneida and Amana were very successful economically, and after the religious communes dissolved both incorporated to commercially produce household goods.)

We conclude this section by describing a now classic small group study of the effects of out-group conflict. Known as the Robber's Cave Study (Sherif, 1966), it was conducted at an Oklahoma summer camp for 11- and 12-year-old boys. The researchers began by forming the boys into two distinct groups. Group unity was developed by such things as scheduled activities requiring group cooperation and individual group symbols (like the names "Rattlers" and "Eagles"). The researchers then brought the two groups together for various contests. In a short time they developed strong hostility toward each other, and in-group unity increased. Out-group conflict reached the point of fist fights, property destruction, and derogatory name calling.

The researchers then set out to manipulate events to reduce the level of out-group hostility. They first tried religious services stressing cooperation and love. The fights continued. Next, they introduced "superordinate goals." The water supply for the whole camp was made to "break down." The two groups were required to work together to repair the water line. The two groups were also required to pull a food supply truck that had "broken down." Through these and other events producing common interests and cooperation, the out-group conflict was finally reduced. The similarities between these groups of small boys and rival high schools, ethnic groups, and nations need no further comment.

Groups in Historical Movement

As already noted, evidence suggests that humans have always been highly social animals. Most of our time is spent with other people, which means that most of these social contacts are in groups. However, though group involvement is a consistent factor throughout the history of human existence, the nature of this group involvement, and more specifically the type of group involvement, has changed dramatically. The transition from small hunting groups to small farming groups about 10,000 years ago was very important in many ways, but it had little immediate effect on the nature of group involvement. For most people, most group contacts continued to be with small primary groups.

Some three to four hundred years ago, however, the nature of group contacts slowly began to change for more and more people. I began this chapter with some indications of this change as small local groups became more influenced by larger outside organizations. Combined with the growth of large organizations was a slow shift of the population to larger cities. Especially about 250 years ago, the number of people working in agriculture began to decline with industrialization. What this means is that people now have more and more contact or participation in secondary groups.

Gemeinschaft and Gesellschaft. Early sociologists like Marx, Weber, and Durkheim were acutely aware of the changes going on around them in the newly industrializing societies. More than any other early sociologist, however, the writings of Ferdinand Tönnies were focused on the nature of this change on group relations. In one of his major works (Tönnies, 1957) originally published in 1887, Tönnies made famous the German words describing the two types of societies resulting from this shift — gemeinschaft (Community) and gesellschaft (Society).

Gemeinschaft is a small community environment in which most people know each other rather well, family contacts are extensive, and most people live very close to their relatives (if not in the same household). A result of all this is extensive primary group contacts with people who share similar world views, values, and life-styles.

Gesellschaft is a society in which many more social contacts are through secondary groups, with people who are not well known and even strangers. This also means that the interpersonal contacts are usually less emotional and more temporary. Primary groups certainly remain important. There is not so much a decrease in primary groups as simply an increase in secondary groups.

Outcomes of the Shift to Gesellschaft. Many outcomes of the change to a gesellschaft society are evident. For example, there tends to be more value diversity and life-styles. Much of this stems from reduced surveillance by primary group members. In a very small town where everyone is known and observed by primary group members much of her or his daily life, people are less likely to experiment with new life-styles. But there is the added effect of not wanting to be different and even intolerance of people who are different.

Some outcomes of a shift to gesellschaft, however, have been exaggerated. Many early American sociologists from the Chicago School had a clear bias favoring small towns; in many ways the big city was considered bad; that is, full of evil, crime, and immoral life-styles. They believed that a reduction in close personal relationships would produce these problems, as well as others like mental illness and family breakdown.

Although these problems were certainly evident in newly industrialized cities, people have been able to adjust to the new gesellschaft existence much more than expected. One inaccuracy in the earlier theories has to do with primary groups. Primary group contacts have *not* been reduced; rather, secondary groups have simply grown (Kasarda and Janowitz, 1974). The support, emotional aid, and identity provided by primary groups remain, and people have developed new norms of social interaction to control or manage contacts with strangers (Lofland, 1973).

None of this is to say that large gesellschaft societies do not have many problems. These problems certainly exist, in some nations more than in others. The main source of inaccuracy in the old theories, however, seems to be in their overly positive view of gemeinschaft societies. In the thirteenth-century village of Montaillou, France, for example, there were many problems of crime, violence, and deviance considered more prevalent in gesellschaft-type societies (Le Roy Ladurie, 1978). And add to these problems in old gemeinschaft-type societies can be the negative effects of forced conformity, boredom, and intolerance with the ever present surveillance from primary group members can be found. Considering that rural areas and small towns today continue to have some gemeinschaft characteristics, the forced conformity, boredom, and intolerance may be reasons why mental illness is actually somewhat higher in rural areas in the United States (Fischer, 1976).

BUREAUCRATIC ORGANIZATIONS

Bureaucracy — just the name conjures up negative images of uncaring bureaucrats, "red tape," inefficiency, long waiting lines, and coldness. When we think of specific bureaucracies, we often think of government agencies, the university administration, or a big utility like the phone company. The term bureaucracy has such a negative connotation that when an organization is giving us trouble, we call it a bureaucracy; otherwise we refer to it as our university, city government, or whatever the agency represents. As we will see, bureaucratic organizations are certainly filled with problems. But for the most part, they have received a "bad press." We usually want bureaucracies to be fair in following specific procedures, then become upset when we are treated in a formal, standardized manner that impartiality requires.

In the next few pages we examine modern bureaucracies. We begin by considering the views of one person who has taught us the most about bureaucratic organizations — Max Weber. It was Weber, more than anyone else, who recognized the dual character of modern bureaucracies. While praising their efficiency, Weber also saw bureaucracy as an "iron cage." These organizations have been created for and by humans; they help us manage the collective tasks that make modern life possible. But at the same time they have come to dominate and control people, almost taking on a life of their own. Thus, the "iron cage" built by humans has come to dominate its makers.

The Characteristics of Modern Bureaucratic Organizations

Before we proceed further into our discussion of modern bureaucratic organizations, we must be specific about the characteristics of the things we are discussing. At times these definitions are necessary, and this is one of those times.

Weber (Gerth and Mills, 1946, pp. 196–198) has stressed six major characteristics of modern **bureaucratic organizations** that help us understand how they work and how they differ from what preceded them.

1. Bureaucratic organizations contain rather explicit laws, rules, or administrative regulations. These rules define the tasks of the organization, what it can do and cannot do, when and where. In other words, these are not organizations of people who can do what they please. This characteristic may seem obvious, but if so it is only because we are accustomed to these new organizations.

2. Bureaucratic organizations contain a hierarchy of offices with differing levels of authority. In Weber's words, there is an "ordered system of superordination and subordination in which there is a supervision of the lower offices by the higher ones." In other words, some people have more responsibility and influence *because of the position they fill.* These higher officials give orders to and control the work of people in lower positions. People's positions in a specific bureaucracy can be judged by how many people are above them (can give them orders) and below them (to whom they can give orders).

3. "The management of the modern office is based on written documents." Because of the formal rules and legality of the procedures, a bureaucratic organization must document what has been done, how, by whom, for whom, and so on. And practically,

when the work of the organization involves many people, they cannot all come together in face-to-face discussion. The president of a firm can seldom yell down the hall to give orders to all workers. The orders must be passed on in written form. This is not to say everything done by the organization is well documented. As noted above, we are referring to general characteristics common in all bureaucratic organizations, if not equally met in all of them. The U.S. Army, for example, is very much a bureaucratic organization. Not every order, move, or activity is documented, but most are. An old war movie may show John Wayne jumping into a jeep to pursue the enemy. What you don't see is the office clerk chasing behind calling "but where is the paper work on taking this jeep."

4. Officials holding positions in the bureaucracy are expected to have special training. Again, to people in modern societies this statement seems obvious. A glance through history, however, shows this statement has been obvious to very few people. The most accepted practice prior to the emergence of the modern bureaucracy was to staff organizations with friends, relatives, or literally the highest bidder, irrespective of training and other qualifications.

5. The activity of the bureaucracy demands the full working capacity of the officeholder. "Formerly, in all cases, the normal state of affairs was reversed: official business was discharged as a secondary activity." When it was common to assign official state positions to relatives or those who payed for the position (as in France before the Revolution of 1789), the position holder was more interested in the prestige and influence the position brought. The official duties of the office were secondary; the primary activity of the officeholder was to use the position to advance his or her business position, land holdings, and so forth.

6. Finally, Weber stressed that bureaucracy "follows general rules, which are more or less stable, more or less exhaustive, and which can be learned." Before the modern bureaucracy, the rules were often what the officeholder said they were. And likewise, the rules were subject to the whims of change related to the needs of the bureaucrat, the wealth and prestige of the subject in contact with the bureaucracy, or a change in staff.

All these characteristics represent general tendencies, or what Weber calls *ideal types*. These are models, which means that, in reality, the characteristics are not always equally accurate. Bureaucracies do not always act as they are outlined above. And as we will see, there is an informal side to bureaucracies created by the live actors who must make these things work in the face of limited resources, human characteristics, and other pressures. However, these six characteristics allow us to place the modern bureaucracy into perspective and compare it with what has existed previously.

A Short History of Bureaucratic Organizations

It is really not very difficult to see why large bureaucratic organizations developed. Going back to small gemeinschaft communities, we can consider what would happen with a threat to the community. We can assume that a common method of farming in a rural community has led to the potential destruction of fertile land. In the short run farmers can produce more with the old method of farming, but in the long run they will produce nothing if their farming methods are not changed soon. It is not unreasonable to assume that when recognizing this problem farmers will have a meeting and agree to change farming methods. After making the decision it is likely that most farmers in the area will follow it, if for no other reason than they can all observe one another's work. Probably more important, however, is the feeling of group spirit that creates a feeling of obligation to conform.

Now imagine a similar problem in a large society of thousands or millions of people. It is impossible to bring these people together to discuss the problem and decide solutions. Almost everyone must go along with the new farming method or the solution will not work. But remember the free-rider problem. In the short run the old method of farming will produce more. Thus, if many farmers go along with the new method (and produce less), there is a strong *individual* motive to go against the new method to realize great profits. But all the farmers understand this, so no one cooperates and everyone will go down to ruin. There is no means of creating agreement on, or compliance with, new needs when mutual obser-

vation and community responsibility are lacking. Bureaucratic organizations emerged, in part, to provide the necessary coordination that became increasingly impossible in gesellschaft societies.

Bureaucratic organizations, however, do not operate solely to serve collective needs or for mutual benefit of all in the society. Even if bureaucratic organizations emerged to serve the mutual needs of the society's members as a whole, *because bureaucratic organizations can provide the means of controlling people,* they have often been used to serve the selfish interests of specific groups. But whatever group needs are being served by bureaucratic organizations, once they emerge, they create a hierarchy of positions. And with such a hierarchy in the bureaucracy there are conflicts of interest between high and low ranks. Thus, for these two reasons (the means of control and the creation of unequal ranks), *bureaucratic organizations are often at the center of group conflicts in modern societies.* Let's now turn to some historical evidence.

Under Louis XIV in the eighteenth century, France had a large, centralized state organization that most sociologists refer to as a bureaucracy. The king, for the most part, was in sole control of this state. He appointed officials as he pleased, often selling official positions when he was short on cash (Soboul, 1974). But more common, when the king was short on cash he would simply decide to tax the population. Various methods of taxing were used; sometimes a region of the country was required to pay a certain lump sum, with local leaders deciding how much each person in the area was charged. Other times a tax farming system was used. This method involved selling the position of tax collector, the price being the amount of tax the king wanted to collect. Then, after buying the position, the tax collector could tax the local population to recover his money, plus whatever profit he could get away with without sparking revolt.

The French state of the eighteenth century was a bureaucracy in many ways; but its arbitrariness was not what comes to mind when Weber described the modern bureaucracy that emerged somewhat after the French Revolution of 1789.

It is hard to say when the first bureaucratic system developed; the date depends on how strictly one adheres to the main characteristics of the modern bureaucracy. But it is clear, as Weber fully recognized, that a modern-style bureaucracy did not develop at once with all the ideal-type characteristics Weber described. Rather, organizations emerged in many places around the world at different times. As we have seen, a large state developed very early in China because of the need for collective agricultural production projects. But this large state organization did not come to resemble Weber's ideal-type bureaucratic organization until around A.D. 1500, and even then not in every respect. Most interesting about this Chinese bureaucracy was its system of competitive examinations for staffing the bureaucracy. These examinations were nominally open to all groups in the society, though the affluent were about the only people with the time to learn to read and write. With this examination system an educated bureaucratic elite called mandarins was created to run the bureaucracy (Wells, 1971, pp. 205, 492–493).

Other early empires, of course, also developed large state organizations resembling bureaucracies. The Roman Empire had such a state organization. Toward the end of the Roman Empire, around A.D. 500, some 40,000 people worked for the state, not counting the army, (Thomas, 1979, p. 161). But the Roman state was not the rational, legalistic system found with the modern bureaucracy. The rules were rather arbitrary, there was extensive corruption, and the positions were often hereditary.

Today, modern industrial societies operate with huge state and corporate bureaucracies. Everyone seems to complain about the inefficiency of these bureaucracies, and there are problems; but we must realize what existed before. As for the size of the state bureaucracies, Figure 5.6 presents one method of indicating size. The federal government of the United States, including all its agencies like the military, costs the equivalent of more than 35 percent of the gross domestic product (GDP—i.e., the value of all goods and services produced inside the U.S.). But as Figure 5.6 also indicates, the U.S. state bureaucracy is actually lower in cost (in relation to the size of the economy) compared with other industrial nations. Still, the U.S. government bureaucracy is one of the largest in the world in actual size, with almost 3 million employees in 1983 (World Almanac, 1984, p. 117), compared with the high of 40,000 during the Roman Empire.

In Washington, D.C., the mile after mile of government office buildings you pass can give at least a sense of the size of the overall bureaucracy. Imagine the paperwork going on behind those walls with over 300,000 people handling millions of office memos a

FIGURE 5.6. *Comparative government spending as a percent of gross domestic product.* *(Source: U.S. Central Intelligence Agency, 1986, p. 11.)*

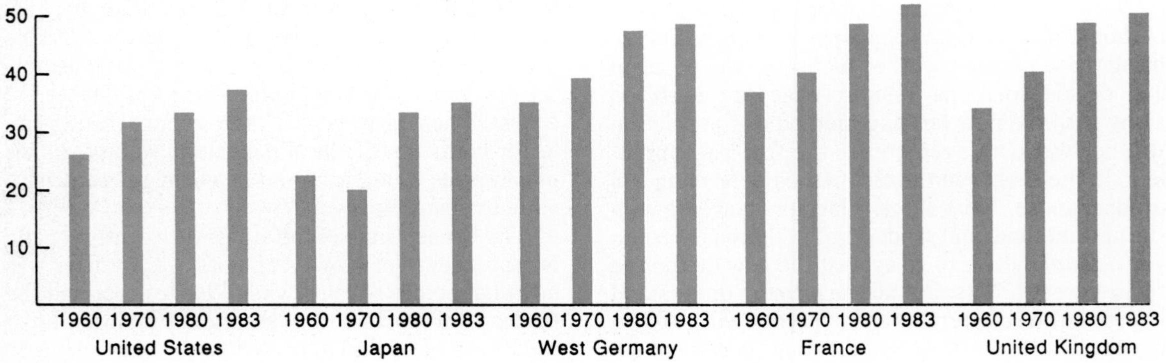

day. In the 1950s, C. Wright Mills (1956, p. 187) estimated that office workers in the Pentagon alone produced "ten tons of non-classified waste paper a day."

Before industrialization, the only true large bureaucratic organizations were state and religious institutions. Today, however, the corporate bureaucracies of such companies as AT&T, Exxon, and General Motors are among the biggest in the world. For example, the top 50 multinational corporations have combined sales larger than the gross national product of any nation in the world except the United States (Chirot, 1986). Within the United States the top 100 industrial corporations employ about 45 percent of all industrial workers.

Controlling and coordinating the work of all these people requires bureaucracy. And the people running the bureaucracy in these big corporations are growing faster than the number of workers actually producing goods and services. As indicated in Figure 5.7, the number of supervisors per 100 workers has gone up dramatically just since the 1940s in the United States. A final way to indicate the size of these corporate bureaucracies is by the number of specific, unique positions or ranks for workers in a particular company. We can use the case of Polaroid; there were 6,397 workers at Polaroid in the late 1970s placed in 2,100 *different job categories* within Polaroid's bureaucratic structure (Edwards, 1979, p. 134).

The Growth of Bureaucratic Control

We are now ready to consider *why* state and corporate bureaucracies grew when and where they did. To understand this we must recognize one of the main tasks of bureaucracy, which is to *coordinate and control people*. Remember the example of a society with thousands of farmers who must change their methods of farming. By *not* changing, as long as most others did, each *individual* farmer would substantially increase his or her profits. Thus, to assure that the change occurs at all, the people in this large society will most likely develop a bureaucracy like the Agriculture Department to monitor compliance, as well as plan and do research and other things to help maintain food production.

In this agricultural example the bureaucracy controls and coordinates people to benefit the society as a whole. But at times (1) some groups may receive more benefits than others, and (2) some groups may not benefit at all from bureaucratic control. In fact, in the second case one group may be using the bureaucracy to control other groups for its exclusive benefit. There is some recent historical research on these points.

In an interesting study, Hechter and Brustein (1980) examined information on different regions of Europe from A.D. 1200 to the development of some of the first state bureaucracies about 200 years later (though these state bureaucracies did not yet fully fit

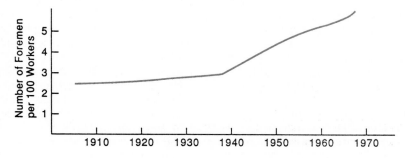

FIGURE 5.7. Number of foremen per one hundred workers in all manufacturing firms. *(Source: Edwards, 1979, p. 135.)*

Weber's ideal type). Hechter and Brustein found that state bureaucracies first developed in the regions where the old, wealthy nobility was most threatened by peasant revolts and a new class of merchants was trying to expand their economic influence. These researchers argue that because the state was run with extensive influence from the noble landowners, the state grew as a tool to control groups threatening these rulers.

In similar historical research, Antonio (1979) found that the Roman state expanded between A.D. 1 and 300 as wealth inequality became more extreme and the empire was threatened by peasant revolts. Again, the implication is that the state bureaucracy expanded as a tool of upper-class control over the lower orders.

Problems with Bureaucratic Organizations

We can end our discussion of bureaucratic organizations with brief attention to some of their most problematic characteristics. At the outset, however, we must stress that bureaucratic organizations are often far more efficient and trouble-free than people realize. The qualification "compared with what" must be kept in mind. Compared with what preceded them, many bureaucratic organizations do quite well. It is remarkable that the vast majority of mail is delivered on time, that university records offices process so many grades with so few mistakes. But bureaucratic organizations, especially certain types, do have problems, or at least present humans with problems.

One general problem Weber warned us of many decades ago: bureaucracies are very legalistic and impersonal and tend to treat people in the same manner. People do not like being treated as an impersonal object or a case. As Merton (1957) notes, we are actually ambivalent about bureaucracies. We demand that they treat everyone fairly, but then, when we are treated in such an impartial manner, we become offended.

Coupled with this is that people cannot always be categorized and treated alike. No matter how we divide them into similar categories so that procedures can be developed for efficient, standardized

processing, people show up that just don't fit in. You may respond by suggesting that procedures should be created for giving special treatment to unique cases. The suggestion is well taken though problematic. We often hear of the especially needy person whom the welfare system can't help because he or she has a unique situation that makes him or her ineligible for aid. The case gets publicity and somebody like the nation's president intervenes to make an exception in this one case. Such publicity is nice for the person helped, and usually nice for a president seeking a good image, but the general problem in the welfare system remains because it is too costly to change the system. There is the ever present chance that calls for special treatment will "catch on" with so many people making such demands that the system breaks down. We usually feel defeated by a bureaucratic official's cold logic that "if I make an exception in your case, then. . . ."

Another problem is that bureaucratic organizations can create "trained incapacities" (Merton, 1957, pp. 197–198). As noted earlier, bureaucracies rely on trained specialized personnel. But what happens when the situation changes rapidly? A highly specialized organization may have difficulty adjusting. Much has been written about the lack of flexibility in the Soviet military. For example, after the Soviets shot down a South Korean airliner over Soviet airspace in September 1983, it was revealed that Soviet pilots lack discretion; higher command on the ground has almost total control, with Soviet pilots acting much like robots. Organizational inflexibility, though, is not absolute. To some extent training and more subordinate discretion can reduce inflexibility. A recently popular novel written by a British NATO general (Sir John Hackett, *The Third World War: August 1985*) has the United States winning World War III owing to "superior technology and greater military flexibility and discretion among lower ranking personnel." Extensive bureaucratic flexibility and subordinate discretion, however, can cause other problems.

There is a growing number of bureaucratic organizations that specialize in public services that contain some special problems. Lipsky (1980) calls these organizations **street-level bureaucracies** because lower-level bureaucrats providing services to clients often (in reality) make policy through their actions. This takes more explanation.

When working with human services and human problems in "the field" and away from the eyes of supervisors, street-level bureaucrats tend to have extensive discretion and autonomy. When conflicts of interest emerge between top officials and lower staff, the lower staff can often resist orders to change. For example, an order may be given to stop handing out information on birth control and abortion; the order may or may not be followed.

An especially important aspect of street-level bureaucracies is the lack of clear measures of performance. There are street-level bureaucracies to prevent crime, educate children, treat mental illness, and so on. In all these cases there is no clear "bottom line" showing agency performance. So crime has gone down; is it due to police efforts or something else? So suicides go up; is this due to lack of effort by mental health agencies? Student test scores have been going down in recent years. Is this due to teacher incompetency? It is usually very difficult to say. Given the difficulty in measuring performance, how do you identify and fire incompetent employees? In extreme cases it can be done, but most cases are not extreme.

On the other hand, how do you identify very competent employees for praise and rewards? And even more serious, what often happens with especially good workers is that they are unintentionally punished for doing good work. When the job is done quickly, efficiently, and successfully compared with the performance of other workers, the good worker is rewarded with more work. In this case there may not be a strong incentive to do well.

Finally, with bureaucratic organizations of all types, there is a potentially more serious problem. Weber described bureaucracies as one of the most rational means to achieve large collective tasks. However, this says nothing about the *rationality or morality of the ends or goals* toward which bureaucracies are applied (Marcuse, 1971). Weber himself recognized that a bureaucracy can be "easily made to work for anybody who knows how to gain control over it" (Gerth and Mills, 1946, p. 229). Bureaucracies, remember, are mechanisms for control and organization. There is evidence that the state organization created toward the final centuries of the Roman Empire functioned well to control the lower class and prevent needed reforms as the empire crumbled (Antonio, 1979). And the efficient bureaucracies created in Bismarck's Germany continued to work efficiently in killing millions under Hitler's control.

CHAPTER SUMMARY

Key Terms

social structure, 110
status, 110
master status, 110
roles, 110
role strain, 111
role conflict, 111
institutions, 111
groups, 115
social aggregate, 115
primary groups, 115
secondary groups, 115
free-rider problem, 119
dyads, 120
triads, 120
gemeinschaft, 126
gesellschaft, 126
bureaucratic organizations, 128
street-level bureaucracies, 132

Content

Along with the technostructure and culture, social structure represents one of the basic foundations of human societies. Social structures are formed by predictable human relationships. The patterning of these relationships tie the society together and form many of its characteristics.

People occupy status positions in social structures. Though they occupy more than one status, one or a few tend to be the most important for an individual and are called a master status. While people occupy a status, they "play roles," which are the roles and norms to be followed when occupying a particular status.

Institutions are clusters of norms and roles centered around important tasks in the society. For example, the family is a key institution with roles and norms specifying the behavior expectations of family members. Other key institutions include the economy, the state, educational establishments, and religious organizations.

The major building blocks of societies can now be seen as the technostructure, culture, and social structure, which merge to create the status positions (in live groups) and roles (from nonmaterial culture) that place people within the society and guide their behavior.

Two basic types of groups are primary and secondary groups. The first type are small groups formed by people with stronger emotional ties: the second type are groups with a more limited purpose, like a work group. Groups have characteristics or forms that shape group behavior, irrespective of the purpose of the group or the personalities of individual members. Important group characteristics include size, communication network, boundaries, and out-group conflict.

With industrialization, societies have been transformed from what Tönnies called gemeinschaft to gesellschaft. In gemeinschaft societies, primary group contacts are more prevalent than secondary group contacts, which tends to produce more conformity and less tolerance of alternative values. Early sociologists, however, exaggerated the social cohesiveness and other positive aspects of gemeinschaft as well as the negative aspects of gesellschaft. But despite the exaggeration, we do find significant differences between the two types of societies.

One of the most important types of organizations in modern industrial societies are bureaucracies. According to Weber, compared with what existed previously, the rational formalized procedures of bureaucratic organizations have produced greater efficiency in accomplishing collective goals.

Bureaucratic organizations have been at the center of conflict in modern societies. On the one hand, they create internal divisions or interest groups that can form the basis for conflict. On the other hand, bureaucratic organizations are means of control and domination. A group or groups that can gain control of major bureaucratic organizations in the society can dominate other groups through these organizations.

Despite their efficiency and rationality, bureaucratic organizations present us with very important problems. For example, we are often treated in an impersonal and inflexible manner. Also, bureaucracies are rational means to goals; the goals themselves may be highly irrational or immoral (in terms of group survival).

CHAPTER 6

Population and Urbanization

135

136

Society becomes more effective in moving in concert, at the same time as each of its elements has more movements that are peculiarly its own. This solidarity resembles that observed in the higher animals. In fact each organ has its own characteristics and autonomy, yet the greater unity of the organism, the more marked the individualisation of the parts. Using this analogy, we propose to call 'organic' the solidarity that is due to the division of labor.

—*Emile Durkheim*, The Division of Labor in Society

A society, of course, cannot exist without the people who make it up. Collectively we refer to these people who are members of a society as its *population.* This population, as we will see in more detail, can have many characteristics that profoundly influence other aspects of the society. And it is obvious that these people must live somewhere. This somewhere can be in cities or farming areas, dispersed throughout the national territory or concentrated in small areas. The characteristics of the population and where people live are no less fundamental aspects of a society than material technology, culture, and other foundations.

We can briefly consider the case of Japan and the most populated urban area in the world, Tokyo. Because of Japan's recent, rapid industrialization, its population characteristics have been changing. For example, women are having fewer children and people are living much longer. As of 1984, Japan had the highest life expectancy of any nation. Because of this there will be many more older people in the future, which will change many aspects of Japan even further.

With industrialization, people in Japan have been moving to cities very rapidly. In the late 1800s, about 80 percent of the Japanese lived in rural areas; Today only 10 percent of the population is in rural areas (Fukutake, 1981, pp. 6–23). The urban crowding has caused many problems and changes in other aspects of Japanese society, such as the family system (Christopher, 1983, p. 134). One of the many little (but in total, important) changes that occurs in large cities is the pace of life. For example, some international comparisons indicate that people in the world's largest urban area, Tokyo, walk more rapidly and have more clocks than people in any other city (*Japan Times,* March 18, 1985).

With the rapid growth to almost 30 million people in the overall Tokyo urban area (including Yokohama), there is extensive crowding and planning problems. Tokyo has an excellent public transit system, but it is very crowded. Not long ago the public transit system hired workers who had only one task —to push people onto the trains so more people could be packed in. This is no longer done because, as anyone who has ridden Tokyo commuter trains between 8:00 A.M. and 9:00 A.M. will tell you, the passengers are now quite skilled in doing it themselves.

Tokyo has other problems related to crowding. In many areas outside of central Tokyo septic tanks are still used instead of sewage treatment plants. Also, Tokyo has only 1.2 square meters of park area per capita in contrast to 22.8 square meters in London and 19.2 square meters in New York City. This situation creates problems for all the people of Tokyo, but perhaps the situation is the most problematic for young adults. Young people are less likely to have cars in Tokyo than in the United States and, because of the housing shortage and very high rent, young people are forced to live with their parents until their midtwenties (when most people marry in Japan). As a consequence, young lovers have nowhere to go to be alone except in a park — but they must get there very early to reserve a park bench in a place like Tokyo's Yoyogi Park. (However, it is very safe to be in one of Tokyo's parks at night, in contrast to those in New York City.)

POPULATION

In many ways, the most important foundation of any society is its population—the people who make it up. In contrast to other foundations of a society like norms, values, and social networks, the population (or at least some of it) can be seen, touched, and experienced as physical realities. But, the social forces of population characteristics shape our lives and society in ways that are difficult to immediately experience. For example, our chances of finding stable employment, attaining education, and even becoming a victim of crime can be influenced by general characteristics of the population in our society.

The study of population characteristics and change is called **demography.** The study of population, however, can be carried out from two perspectives. On the one hand, the population itself, its characteristics, and the reasons for changes in these characteristics can be the focus of study. In this case the term demography applies best. On the other hand, we can study population characteristics (age/sex ratios, population distributions, etc.) and changes (births, deaths, migrations) with a focus on how this subject influences the society more generally (Goldscheider, 1971; Nam, 1982). This second perspective can best be called the **sociology of population.**

In the first half of this chapter we favor the sociology of population perspective. But, we must begin with an examination of population characteristics and changes, that is, the subject of demography.

Population Characteristics

One important characteristic of a population is its size — how many people are members of the society. But several other characteristics of a population can be equally important; for example, the geographical location and density of the population, its age and sex distribution, and rate of growth and geographical mobility are often very important in shaping many aspects of a society. Because of the contemporary importance of population size and growth, we will consider this subject in a separate section. And the subject of geographical location of the population will be considered in the second half of this chapter on urbanization. The other population characteristics will be considered first.

Age Distribution. The average age of a population is simply one aspect of the population. To arrive at this

figure we total the ages of all members of the society and divide by the number of people. But a more useful method of examining the age of a population is through consideration of an age distribution.

Figure 6.1 shows the varied age distributions of six societies. The age distribution of Mexico is typical of developing nations. The largest age group in Mexico is made up of children five years old or less. This characteristic reflects the higher birth rate of most Third World nations and a life expectancy that is less than that of developed nations. In other words, with a higher birth rate and with people dying at an average age that is lower compared with industrial nations, a greater percentage of the population will be children.

The age composition of the United Kingdom is more typical of advanced industrial nations. Figure 6.1 shows that a smaller percentage of the U.K. population is children and a larger percentage are over 65, as compared with Mexico. In fact, the percentage of each five-year age segment is close to all others, until the 65-and-over categories, which began tapering off.

The age distributions for industrial societies, however, are certainly not identical, and it is interesting to see some of the history of a nation represented in its age distribution. Figure 6.1 shows a bit different pattern for Japan. During the 1970s Japan had a more "Chinese lantern"-shape age distribution owing to its more recent status as an industrial nation (Weller and Bouvier, 1981, p. 244). When nations reach fully industrialized status, their birth rate drops. Japan's drop shows up just in the 15-year-or-fewer age groups. In contrast to the United Kingdom, the base is smaller and the middle is much larger in Japan.

Figure 6.1 shows another variation in the U.S. age composition. The U.S. age composition also shows a bulge toward the middle, but this bulge is primarily due to what is called the "baby boom." Following World War II (after 1945) there was a higher than typical rate of new families formed with the return of individuals involved in the war. These new families began producing children (and producing them at a higher rate than in previous years) in the late 1940s and continued childbearing into the early 1960s. Thus, we find a bulge in the 1980 age

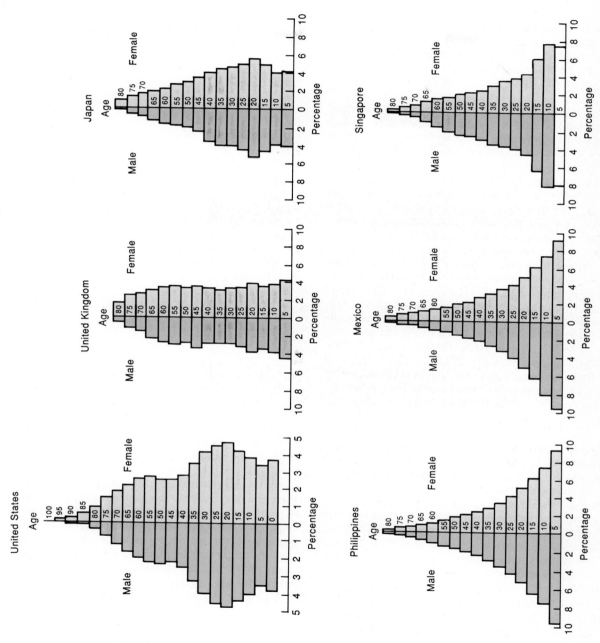

FIGURE 6.1. *Comparative age–sex population distributions.* (*United Nations, 1973, pp. 266–267*)

distribution from the 15- to 30-year-old age group. Also interesting is the smaller number of 40 to 49 year olds in 1980. This "indentation" is due to the reduced birth rate during the harsh economic conditions of the Great Depression during the 1930s.

Sex Ratios. Figure 6.1 indicates that the sex ratio (that is, the ratio of men to women in a society) does not differ greatly in these societies, but there is some difference. In the upper age categories in the industrial societies (United Kingdom, Japan, and United States) we find a significantly greater number of females. This differing sex ratio in the higher age categories is not found in less industrialized societies, which tends to indicate that improved medical care and living conditions in industrial societies has favored females more than males.

At birth there is actually a slightly greater number of males than females (about 105 males to every 100 females). This 105 : 100 ratio does vary around the world because improved medical care and a more healthy environment helps more males survive before birth and after birth (Weller and Bouvier, 1981, p. 237; U.S. Department of Health, Education and Welfare, 1975, p. 357). Males, in other words, are somewhat less likely to survive in poorer environments. Other conditions in a society, however, can make the male-female ratio vary even more widely.

Table 6.1 shows a significant difference in the sex ratio around the world (lower numbers indicate more females). Whereas there are only 86 males to every 100 females in the Soviet Union, the figure is 114 males to every 100 females in Pakistan in the mid-1970s. There are several reasons for the variance in sex ratios. As already noted, after the first year of life improved health conditions help females more than males. Another factor is warfare. The low rate of males in the Soviet Union is related to their very high casualty rate during World War II. For the Soviet age group that was in their twenties and thirties during World War II, there are only 60 males per 100 females today (Weller and Bouvier, 1981, p. 238). Finally, another factor influencing the male-female ratio is migration. Males are more likely to migrate from an area, meaning that places with extensive immigration from other areas (such as

TABLE 6.1. *Comparative sex ratios, 1975*

Country	Sex ratio (percentage of males to 100 females)
Soviet Union	86
West Germany	91
Colombia	94
Brazil	95
Czechoslovakia	95
United Kingdom	95
United States	95
Benin	96
France	96
Indonesia	97
Japan	97
Zambia	97
Argentina	100
Canada	100
Mauritania	100
New Zealand	100
Australia	101
Mexico	102
Gambia	103
Cuba	104
India	108
Pakistan	114

SOURCE: United Nations, 1977, pp. 166–201.

Alaska) will have a higher proportion of males, whereas areas with extensive out-migration will likely have a higher number of females remaining.

Migration. **Migration** occurs when people change their primary residence from one geographical area to another. As you might expect demographers consider many questions when studying migration. For example, it is important to know the rate of migration, the origin and destination of the migration, the characteristics of the individuals involved, and the reasons for the migration.

Migration can also be subdivided between *internal* and *external* migration. The former occurs within the same geographical area (such as a nation or state), whereas the latter occurs across these geographical boundaries. Most industrial societies like the United States have fairly high rates of inter-

Historically, the United States has been a country of immigrants. This photograph from 1930 shows a family disembarking at Ellis Island, an island in New York harbor where millions of European immigrants entered the U.S. The "American Dream" of upward mobility was one of the primary "pull" factors for the vast waves of European migration. (© The Bettmann Archive)

nal migration, which occurs primarily for economic reasons (e.g., for a better job or area with a lower cost of living). On the average in the United States, 1 person in 5 changes residence each year, and 1 person in 14 makes a more extensive move (a move at least farther than a normal commuting distance to a job).

Table 6.2 indicates the extent of net migration (the balance of the in- and out-migration) among a number of industrial nations. Nationally the United States has had the most net in-migration between 1950 and 1970, when looked at from a regional perspective, whereas North America and Western Europe more generally have had the highest net in-migration. As this table suggests, migration tends to flow toward countries with more favorable political and economic conditions, a pattern that can be seen even more clearly when considering less developed nations as well.

Demographers study what can be called *push* and *pull* factors influencing migration. For example, there may be very harsh economic and/or political

TABLE 6.2. *Comparative migration, 1950–1970*

Region and country	Net migration (thousands)	Region and country	Net migration (thousands)
Europe	−3,028	Northern Europe	−698
		Denmark	−32
Western Europe	+8,748	Finland	−214
Austria	−103	Ireland	−558
Belgium	−211	Norway	−10
West Germany	+4,780	Sweden	−297
France	+3,258	United Kingdom	−181
Luxembourg	+22		
Netherlands	−50	Northern America	+8,698
Switzerland	+630	Canada	+1,802
		United States	+6,896
Southern Europe	−7,301		
Greece	−651	Oceania	+1,857
Italy	−1,958	Australia	+1,712
Malta	−81	New Zealand	+145
Portugal	−1,958		
Spain	−1,377		
Yugoslavia	−1,282		
Eastern Europe	−3,777		
Bulgaria	−178		
Czechoslovakia	−174		
East Germany	−2,488		
Hungary	−161		
Poland	−526		
Romania	−250		

SOURCE: United Nations, 1974.

conditions that push people out of an area. This is the situation found in many less developed nations today that tended to be overpopulated, at least with respect to resources in the area. Quite often peasants are literally pushed out of agricultural areas by wealthy landowners who find they can make more profits through exploiting the land formerly used by the peasants. This push, called "enclosure movements," often occurs when an agricultural area first becomes tied to the world market. Enclosure movements began in European nations with early trade in the New World economic system (Wallerstein, 1974) and, as we will see in the World System chapter, they, continue today in Third World nations.

The pull factors, of course, involve the beliefs that conditions will be better in another area. I stress the word "belief" because quite often it is only a belief or rumor that better conditions exist in another area that stimulates the migration. An example of such rumors can be found in the migration of Midwestern farmers in the 1930s. The "Dust Bowl" conditions in the Midwest at the time, combined with economic depression, sent many farmers (generally called "Okies") to California with rumors of abundant agricultural employment.

One of the important political issues facing the United States today is the extent of immigration, both legal and illegal, from Mexico. The current estimate of the number of illegal immigrants in the United States ranges from 3 to 12 million persons, 90 percent of whom are Mexicans. For Mexicans migrating to the United States it is a classic case of push and pull, which also results in a classic case of class conflict over the issue of immigration in this country. In some parts of the United States there is a great demand for unskilled labor, such as the agricultural South and Southwest, and an oversupply of labor reduces wages and thus increases the profits of landowners.

Fertility and Mortality. Two primary demographic variables affecting other population characteristics

(especially population size) are birth rates and death rates. The **crude birth rate** is the number of births in a given year per 1,000 people in the society. The **crude death rate** is estimated in a similar manner (that is, the number of deaths in a given year per 1,000 people in the society). The crude birth rate in the United States has been around 15 to 16 in recent years, and the crude death rate is around 8 to 9. Table 6.3 indicates how the United States compares with other regions.

These crude rates, however, can be quite misleading in many respects and hide important information about a society. For example, it is important to know other population characteristics before we

---

BOX 6.1
Comparative Population Densities

So you think the neighborhood is getting crowded? Census Bureau geographer Alan Patera puts residential population densities into perspective. A typical U.S. suburb of single-family homes contains 5,000 to 10,000 people per square mile. Move to the center city, where the housing mix is a combination of row houses and low-rise apartments, and the density typically climbs to 25,000 to 30,000 people per square mile.

New York City has the most densely populated square mile in the U.S., a section of Manhattan's affluent Upper East Side, bounded by Central Park and the East River and 69th and 91st streets. The housing there is almost exclusively high-rise apartment buildings. The density is about 139,000 people per square mile.

But Manhattan seems positively barren compared with some crowded cities overseas. In Egypt, Cairo's densest neighborhood houses 250,000 people per square mile, mostly in low-rise tenements. In Hong Kong, in an apartment settlement east of Kai Tak airport, the density is 380,000 people per square mile. Mr. Patera says that in the Kowloon district, there are high-rise apartment neighborhoods of less than one square mile where the density reaches 430,000 people per square mile. "There may be a saturation point beyond which a higher human population density cannot be tolerated, but Hong Kong doesn't seem to have reached it yet," he says.

But the prize for crowded conditions goes to India. In 1971, in an area north of Bombay's commercial district, census takers measured a density of 453,000 people per square mile. Detailed results aren't yet available from India's 1981 census, but since Bombay's overall population grew almost 40% in that decade, it's unlikely the numbers in the crowded neighborhoods declined.

Think of it this way: Increase the population of Manhattan's Upper East Side more than three times. Then raze the high-rise apartments and replace them with two- and three-story buildings. Welcome to Bombay.

Source: "A Perspective on Population Densities," *Wall Street Journal,* May 1, 1984.

TABLE 6.3. *Comparative crude birth rates, 1980*

	Annual deaths per 1,000 population	
Africa		46
Northern Africa	42	
Western Africa	49	
Eastern Africa	48	
Middle Africa	45	
Southern Africa	37	
Asia		28
Southwest Asia	40	
Middle South Asia	37	
Southeast Asia	36	
East Asia	18	
North America		16
Latin America		34
Middle America	38	
Caribbean	28	
Tropical South America	36	
Temperate South America	24	
Europe		14
Northern Europe	13	
Western Europe	12	
Eastern Europe	18	
Southern Europe	15	
U.S.S.R.		18
Oceania		20
World		28

SOURCE: Population Reference Bureau, 1980.

can make accurate estimates of population growth. Maintaining a crude birth rate of 15 in coming decades would mean very different growth rates for Mexico in contrast to the United States. A glance back to Figure 6.1 can give you a clue as to why. If Mexico maintained a crude birth rate of 15 (it is actually higher), with so many children per population today, population growth would be much higher in the future because there will be proportionally more women of childbearing age in the future.

To account for the differing age and sex distributions when estimating future population growth, the general fertility rate, or simply **fertility rate,** is a useful estimate. The fertility rate measures the number of births per 1,000 women of childbearing age in the society. The fertility rate for the United States has been approximately 68 in recent years.

As should be clear by now, these major demographic variables like death rate, fertility rate, and migration rates are very important when estimating many other characteristics of the population. For example, a federal government commission (Commission on Population Growth and the American Future 1972) concludes the following differences in the U.S. population between 1970 and 2000 if families average three children instead of two (Weller and Bouvier, 1981, p. 73):

1. There will be an additional 51 million people by the year 2000.
2. There will be 46 percent more persons of elementary and secondary school age and 36 percent more persons of college age in the year 2000.
3. Food prices will be about 30 to 50 percent higher.
4. Expenditures for health care during the 1970–2000 interval will be $20 billion greater.

The U.S. Population: A Short History. When Christopher Columbus arrived in North America, there was an estimated 1 million people living on the continent (many of the figures in this section can be found in Petersen, 1975; Weller and Bouvier, 1981, pp. 52–72). Today there are about 240 million people living in the United States. Humans first came to this continent about 15,000 to 25,000 years ago from Asia (the exact time is in dispute [Pfeiffer, 1977]). In this long period of history before 1492, population change had been very slow, but afterward the pace substantially increased.

The first permanent settlement of European natives was at Jamestown, Virginia, in 1607. At first there were only about 100 settlers, but by 1650 there were 50,000, and by the first U.S. census in 1790 almost 4 million people lived in the United States. The population increased substantially during the nineteenth century, so that by 1900 there were 76 million people in this country. This dramatic increase in population was largely due to immigration.

About 50 million people have migrated to the United States since 1776, but the level of migration was not at a steady rate. There were about 2.5 million immigrants between 1819 (when the U.S.

Immigration and Naturalization Service began recording such information) and 1850. Between 1850 and 1900, however, there were 17 million immigrants. And in contrast to the period before 1850, when the immigrants came mostly from England, Ireland, and Germany, between 1850 and 1900 the immigrants more often came from eastern and southern Europe. The different origins of immigrants have led to ethnic divisions that remain with us today. For example, the northwest European immigrants who arrived sooner held better jobs and more political power by the time of the second wave of European immigrants, which resulted in ethnic conflicts (e.g., Irish versus Polish, West European Jews versus East European Jews; Howe, 1976).

Immigration into the United States was greatly reduced after World War I. In 1900 more than 34 percent of the population was foreign-born or born to parents who were foreign-born. By 1950, however, only 22.5 percent of the population was of "foreign stock," and only 16 percent by 1970. The origins of immigrants into the United States changed again in the twentieth century. From 1861 to 1900, 68 percent of the immigrants were from northern and western Europe and 22 percent were from southern and eastern Europe (Bouvier, Shryock, and Henderson, 1977, pp. 24–25). Between 1901 and 1930 these origins were almost reversed — 23 percent from northern and western Europe, 58 percent from southern and eastern Europe. By the 1960s immigration from Europe was shrinking, but was growing from other regions. During the first half of the 1970s, 41 percent of the immigrants were from Latin America, 32 percent from Asia, only 13 percent from southern and eastern Europe, and 7 percent from northern and western Europe. Political conflicts over immigration policies, of course, have shifted focus to Mexican and Asian immigrants and the possible economic and social impacts of these groups.

Because of the declining rate of immigration since the early 1900s, population growth in the United States is lower than it otherwise would have been. But population growth continued no less, now for other reasons. One cause was a substantial drop in the crude death rate and a corresponding increase in life expectancy. In 1900 the crude death rate in the United States was 17.2 and life expectancy at birth was only 47 years. By 1979 this had changed to a crude death rate of only 8.7 and a life expectancy at birth of 73.5 years. For a girl born in 1984, her life expectancy at birth is 78; for a boy, it is 71. When people live longer, simply put, there are more alive in the society.

The crude birth rate and fertility rate, for the most part, have also been going down since the 1800s, another factor reducing population growth. In 1850 the crude birth rate was 44.3 and women had an average of 5.5 children. By 1900 the crude birth rate was 29.8, with an average of 3.6 children per woman. These rates were even lower by 1937 (a crude birth rate of 17.4 and an average of 2.2 children per woman). But after World War II there was an interesting reversal of these downward trends.

What is referred to as the "baby boom" after World War II had several causes. For one thing, many people who had delayed starting families during the War made up for "lost time" in the late 1940s and throughout the 1950s. Thus, the decline in childbirth during the Great Depression and World War II was reversed. But in addition to more marriages and births, the average number of children per family increased after the long trend of decline. From the average of just over two children per family during the 1930s, there was an increase to almost four per family by the mid-1950s, when it again began to decline. By the 1970s this rate was below two children per family, though it has increased slightly again in the 1980s. The impact of this baby boom is certainly still with us today, and will be beyond 2050.

No one can say for certain what the future trends in the U.S. population will be. Demographers were certainly caught by surprise with the magnitude of the baby boom, for example. But because these population trends are so important for business planning and government policy, there will always be great effort made to predict population trends. The trickiest part is predicting changes in family size. The death rate declines at a rather steady and somewhat predictable rate. Few people make a decision to die earlier than they must, given the current state of medical technology. But people do change their minds about preferred family size. And only a small change in the average number of children per family can have big consequences in the future. As indicated by Table 6.4, with a family size of 2.7 the population will be 488 million in 2050, versus 231 million if average family size holds at 1.7.

Population as a Social Force

As noted already, we must recognize that the characteristics of a population (size, age distribution, and so on) have an extensive impact on many aspects of a society, almost like the material forces of technology. It is a social force not always seen, but it is no less real. Sociologists as far back as Durkheim in the late 1800s were aware of the force of population characteristics, though until recently this social force has not been adequately studied (Nam, 1982).

Effects of Age Distribution. The age distribution of a population, as already noted, can have important effects on the society. Some of them are rather obvious, whereas some are not.

Crime. Serious crime has been a major problem in the United States. The crime rate grew very rapidly in the 1960s and 1970s, while dropping only slightly in the early 1980s, only to move higher again in the late 1980s. Political leaders have been making many speeches about what should be done about the problem, and they have rushed to take credit for the crime decrease in the mid-1980s.

A few basic facts about crime are needed at this point. Most serious and violent street crimes are committed by young men. This has been a constant factor since crime statistics have been collected. So why did the number of serious crimes increase rapidly in the 1960s and 1970s? There were many reasons, but one simple reason is that there were proportionately more young men in the crime-prone age group at the time (Maxim, 1985) because the baby boom generation reached their teenage years in the 1960s and 1970s. Why did the crime rate go down in the mid-1980s? The simplest but only partial explanation is that the percent of young men in the society is down in the 1980s. A look at Figure 6.1 (or Figure 6.2) clearly shows that. No matter what politicians have done to take credit for reducing serious crime, it would have been reduced about as much had they done nothing.

Standard of living. The standard of living can be roughly estimated by the gross national product (the value of all goods and services produced) per capita. Thus, even when the economy is growing rapidly, if population is also growing rapidly the standard of living for people in the society will remain about the same. This is one of the basic problems faced by Third World nations today. For example, England and Wales had a population of about 9 million at the early stage of their industrial revolution. By the 1980s their population was about 50 million—about a sixfold increase. However, their gross national product increased about ninetyfold in the same period; thus the standard of living improved considerably (Lenski and Lenski, 1982, p. 278).

TABLE 6.4. *Varying U.S. population projections, 1977–2050*

Average family size differences	Population size (millions) 1977	Population size (millions) 2000	Percent increase (since 1977)	Population size (millions) 2050	Percent increase (since 2000)
2.7	217	282	(30)	488	(73)
2.1	217	260	(20)	316	(18)
1.7	217	246	(13)	231	(−6)

SOURCE: U.S. Bureau of Census, 1977, pp. 22–24.

Unemployment. Unemployment has been a serious and persistent problem during the 1970s and 1980s in the United States. After each recession since the 1960s the unemployment rate has gone down, but never to the rate before the recession began. By 1985 the United States was enjoying economic growth, but the unemployment rate did not dip below 7 percent until the last year of the Reagan administration. If you again consider the pattern of age distribution caused by the baby boom, *part* of the persistently high unemployment can be seen — during the 1970s and 1980s more people started looking for jobs than ever before (*Wall Street Journal,* February 25, 1985). Many economists argue that it is actually remarkable that the U.S. unemployment rate is not even higher.

But as the baby boom generation gets older, and fewer young people are entering the labor force, the unemployment rate should drop in the 1990s. In fact, many economists are predicting future labor shortages in the United States without substantial immigration.

Social Problems for Blacks. As we will see in more detail in a later chapter, compared with other groups, blacks in the United States have a higher rate of many kinds of social problems such as street crime, poverty, families breaking up, illegitimate births, and illiteracy. The causes of these problems are many and complex but in one respect quite understandable. Blacks have recently gone through an extensive internal migration in this country. About 90 percent of blacks lived in rural areas and worked in agriculture before 1900; today over 80 percent of black Americans live in cities. Most of this migration has occurred only since World War II.

Most groups that have experienced such extensive migration (such as the Irish and Chinese migration to the United States many decades ago) have experienced the same social problems in the first two or three generations after the migration. For example, one current debate involves the reasons for the lower average IQ scores for blacks compared with whites. Using historical records on the subject, Sowell (1978) has been able to show that the IQ scores for the children of recent immigrants such as Italians, Greeks, Poles, Lithuanians, French Canadians, and many others were similar to those of blacks today, and they improved in subsequent generations. In other words, population migrations often produce many negative effects in the second and third generation when the migration is forced by economic necessity.

Other Effects of the Baby Boom. The effects of the baby boom after World War II can be overstated. For example, it is doubtful that most of the low economic productivity in the 1970s was caused by the big increase in new workers. However, most people have neglected the effects of this baby boom and it is therefore worthwhile to consider some other possible effects.

Figure 6.2 projects the changing age distribution in our society into the 2030s. With this age shift in mind we can consider many changes that we face.

One of the most obvious effects will be the strain on the Social Security system and health care system when so many people reach age 65. This will be especially hard for the Social Security system because there will be relatively fewer workers paying taxes to support the system at the time.

We can also see how education will be affected by the changing age distribution. As the baby boom generation began leaving the universities in the 1970s there was an oversupply of building space and teachers. The extent of the problem in the future is not totally predictable because the rate at which young people attend universities can change, which has already happened to some extent. Even though there are fewer college-age people, the college population may not be reduced an equal amount because young people may go to college at a greater rate. Also, people who are older may return to universities or begin a college education later in life — all of which is happening.

There is also another trend so new that it has not been included in the projections shown in Figure 6.2. This new trend has been called the "baby boom echo." During the first years of childbearing age, the baby boom generation was producing children at a lower than expected rate. More recently, however, the baby boom generation has been producing chil-

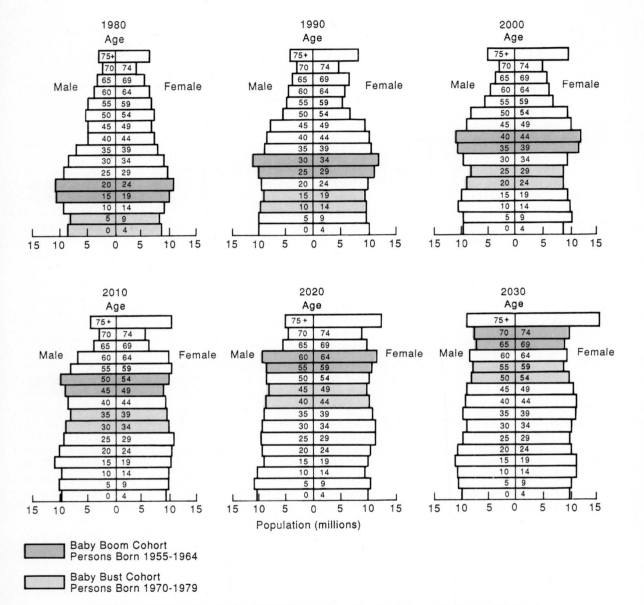

FIGURE 6.2. U.S. age–sex population distribution—projections. (U.S. Bureau of Census, 1977, p. 23)

dren at a later age and higher rate. Thus, we are beginning to see a higher number of children beginning their grade school education. Another, but smaller bulge in the age distribution will produce future effects similar to the original baby boom.

We can consider many effects of the changing age distribution that are less important, at least for most people. Because of the proportionately larger market, businesses tend to direct their products and advertisements to the baby boom generation. When this generation was in their late teens and early twenties, the recording industry was experiencing economic boom. Clothing styles have been affected as the clothing industry tries to capture the largest market. The "Pepsi Generation" shown on TV advertisements will start graying in coming years. Because of the potential market, being older will no doubt become more acceptable as the TV image makers make it so to sell their products.

Finally, many women of the baby boom generation have complained that "all of the good men are married." In one sense, there has actually been a shortage of men for women of the baby boom generation. Women still tend to marry men a few years older than themselves. A look back at Figure 6.2 indicates the problem. In 1947, for example, 3,834,000 babies were born, about an equal number of males and females, as usual. However, in 1946 there were only some 3,400,000 babies born, and in 1945 only about 2,800,000. Following tradition, the women born in 1947 would tend to marry men born in 1945. There lies the problem.

Generational Conflict. There have always been conflicts between the generations in a society, though the conflicts can certainly be greater in some time periods. There are two principal reasons for generational conflicts: On the one hand, the social conditions that shape the views and values of each generation can change; on the other hand, the generations have some differing material interests.

Studies have shown that the political, economic, and social events occurring when people are in their teenage and young adult years can have lingering effects on their values and world views for years to come (Simonton, 1976; Fendrich, 1977). The generation "coming of age" during the Great Depres-

sion of the 1930s certainly has different experiences compared with the baby boom generation coming of age in the 1960s and 1970s. To some degree these different experiences can be used to explain the "Youth Movement" in conflict with the older generation in the 1960s (Flacks, 1971). Interestingly, this process now seems to be occurring on a smaller scale in reverse. Young people coming of age in the 1980s have more conservative political and social views than their parents, a theme now found in popular TV programs and mass media news programs.

Material conflicts can arise over such questions as the cost of Social Security and education, and the chances of death in military conflicts. The older generation, which no longer has children to educate, may be more critical of their tax dollars going to education. At the same time, young workers may be critical of so much of their taxes going to support the Social Security system. This conflict, however, is not as extensive as it might be because many of these young workers have parents supported by Social Security, parents they would otherwise have to help support themselves. This is one reason why the Social Security system has such wide support. Finally, with respect to generation conflict over foreign policy, a popular antiwar poster summarized the feeling of many young people during the Vietnam War; it read, "Old soldiers never die, only young ones do."

Social and Material Influences on Population

So far we have examined the effects of population characteristics on the society; now we will briefly examine the reverse influence. Technology and other characteristics of societies can and often do have considerable effects on many aspects of population. In this section we examine some of the most important effects.

Effects of Technology and Economics. The economic effects on population growth were recognized as long ago as the middle 1800s. For example, Marx wrote that "every special historic mode of production has its own special laws of population, historically valid within its own limits" (Marx, 1906, p. 693). But neither Marx nor others during the time were fully aware of the complex manner in which economic relations shape population.

It has long been recognized that population tends to grow rapidly when there is change from an agrarian society to one with at least some industrialization. But population growth was not always consistent around the world during the early stages of industrialization. Recent studies have shown that the traditional type of labor relations (agricultural wage labor, sharecropping, or industrial wage labor) can influence the extent of population growth with early industrialization (McQuillan, 1984). For example, when old traditions required peasant-held land to be divided equally among male offspring, there was an incentive to keep population low. But when there is agricultural wage labor by landless peasants, there is incentive for more offspring. More hands in the fields mean more profits.

Other material-technological conditions have influenced population growth, such as the technology of birth control. Improved medical care, food production, and sanitation, not to mention the technology of war, have clearly affected population. The population of the world increased substantially, perhaps for the first time, after simple agriculture was established some 10,000 years ago. Quite simply, more food was produced to support a larger population.

Thomas Malthus. The first extensive theory of population change was put forth in 1798 by Thomas Malthus. We know today that the theory was mostly inaccurate, but at the time it was widely received and stimulated much discussion about the need to limit population.

The primary point made by Malthus was that although the supply of food increases in an arithmetical ratio, population does so in a geometric ratio. Thus, he believed that there would always be overpopulation (too many people for the food supply) unless population growth was held in check by some social means. And because he believed that rational means would not be followed, population would be kept in check only through famine, disease, and war.

So far, at least, Malthus has been shown incorrect. There has certainly been rapid population growth at times, especially in certain parts of the

world. But at the same time, most societies have limited their population growth. On balance, the rate of food production around the world has been greater than the population increase. For example, food production increased 30 million tons a year in the 1970s, with only 22 million tons of this increase going to the increased population per year. This is not to say we do not have overpopulation in some parts of the world, or that we will not have worldwide overpopulation in the future.

The Demographic Transition. Before the process of industrialization, world population growth was comparatively slow. But between 1650 and 1850 world population doubled, from 500 million to 1 billion; between 1850 and 1930 it doubled again to 2 billion, and between 1930 and 1980 it again doubled to 4 billion. In July 1987, the world population was more than 5 billion. Before the twentieth century this growth rate was primarily accounted for by the industrializing nations. Today, however, population growth in these industrial nations has slowed considerably, and in many cases population is actually declining. The industrial nations have gone through a process called the **demographic transition.**

As shown in Figure 6.3, the first stage of this process has both a high birth rate and a high death rate. Population does not show much growth because the two balance each other. As societies began to industrialize, however, there was a rapid increase in population. In the initial stages of industrialization there was a population increase due to a slight increase in the birth rate. When people moved to the cities and away from rural traditions, the marriage age dropped significantly, producing this upswing in the birth rate. Another reason for the increased birth rate may have been the increased economic incentive for more children; the new factories had employment for children as well as adults (McQuillan, 1984). *However,* the increase in population due to an increased birth rate was short-lived and limited. The primary reason for rapid population increase with industrialization was the substantial drop in the death rate caused by better living conditions, better sanitation, and to a very small extent (if at all) better medical care. For the most part, better medical care did not come to industrial nations until

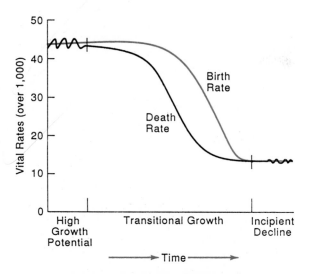

FIGURE 6.3. The demographic transition.

the twentieth century, well after their zone of transition.

Figure 6.3 shows that the rapid population growth in the zone of transition was due to the gap between the death and birth rates, which had been in balance prior to the zone of transition. But as these nations became fully industrialized, the birth rate also dropped to a point where the birth rate and death rate were again in relative balance, producing only very slow population increase, if any at all.

The reasons for decline in the birth rate are more difficult to specify, but a few factors are no doubt involved. For one thing, as people saw infant and childhood mortality drop, they no longer saw the need to have many children so that at least a few would survive into adult years to care for their aged parents. Also, in the later stages of industrialization children were no longer an economic asset, but in fact, an economic liability. They required education for a longer period and could not earn extra wages at an early age. And equally important, women often had other role options besides staying home with children.

In some European nations a lower birth rate has reached the stage in which the population is no

longer replacing itself — below what is called "zero population growth." For example, West Germany's population today is 62 million. At the current birth rate the West German population will be reduced to 20 million by the year 2100, excluding immigration changes.

This demographic transition did not happen in exactly the same way in every industrial nation (Tilly, 1978). For example, the birth rate drop came much sooner in France during the nineteenth century, even though France was somewhat behind England in industrialization. But this process of demographic transition did occur in every one of the nations in the advanced stages of industrialization.

World Population Trends

The major question pertaining to population growth at present is, will the less industrialized and underdeveloped nations go through the demographic transition as did the already developed nations? Most of the less developed nations today are in the zone of transition. Will they come out of it as previous nations have done? In other words, will it really be a zone of transition? The answer is not clear, though it is vital to the trend toward overpopulation in the world.

The world population trend since the development of early horticultural societies is shown in Figure 6.4. We see a rather startling pattern that suggests Malthus may ultimately be correct if the trend is not changed. At the time of the first agricultural societies, about 10,000 years ago, world population was around 5 to 10 million people. During the time of the Egyptian Empire, around 3000 B.C., there may have been 100 million people in the world. World population had probably increased to 250 million (a bit more than the current U.S. population) during the time of Christ, 2000 years ago, and only to 500 million in A.D. 1500. When industrialization began, world population stood at about 750 million — less than the population of either India or China today (Thomas, 1979, p. 49).

Since 1750, and especially during the twentieth century, population growth has been phenomenal. By the year 2000 we may have over 6 billion people in the world, in contrast to a population of about 5

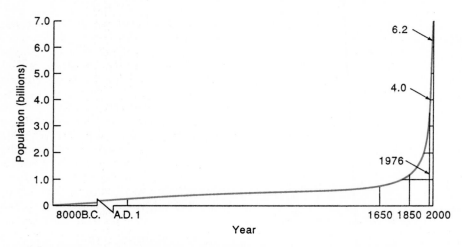

FIGURE 6.4. Historical growth of world population. *(Population Reference Bureau, 1976)*

billion today. It is quite likely that we can feed 6 billion people with current world resources; but if the current growth rate continues much beyond the year 2000, there will clearly be a crisis. At the current growth rate, in 700 years there will be one person for every square foot of the earth's land surface.

The reason that world population was kept low before industrialization was the high death rate that balanced the high birth rate. Before agriculture began 10,000 years ago, life expectancy was probably around 25 years. At the beginning of industrialization in Europe, life expectancy was not much different. Today, however, life expectancy is around 71 in Europe, 62 in Latin America, 56 in Asia, and 48 in Africa (Thomas, 1979, p. 51).

In contrast to the lower death rates in most nonindustrial societies today, the birth rate is still high (and in some cases higher). There are many reasons for the continued high birth rate. For one thing, old traditions and beliefs are hard to break, especially when religious values are involved. But equally important, the masses of people in Third World nations have not experienced the higher standard of living that creates a life-style with more diversity and choices. In advanced industrial nations people be-

come aware that more children means providing less for each of them and a lower standard of living for themselves as well.

The most pessimistic assessment is that these Third World nations today may not experience further industrialization. Unlike the already advanced nations when they were developing, the less advanced nations today have to contend with advanced nations in a world economic system. These advanced nations have economic ties to the less advanced nations that often harm the latters' potential for further growth. (We consider this situation in some detail in Chapter 13.) Thus, will these Third World nations today continue to have limited opportunities for economic growth and remain in the zone of transition with respect to their population growth rates? Such a situation is not impossible for many of the nations.

There is some slight optimism in the recent world population growth figures. According to the United Nations "State of the World Population 1984" report, for the first time since detailed figures have been kept, the rate of world population growth slowed somewhat in the previous decade — from an annual growth rate of 2.0 percent to 1.7 percent. No one knows if this rate will continue to decline slightly, but even a 1.7 percent annual increase will make the earth unlivable in a few hundred years.

I end this section by stressing that world population is not the primary cause of world hunger. The world today has plenty of food to support a population of more than 5 billion people. The problem is the unequal distribution of this food. This is a matter of unequal power and conflict among nations, and people within nations. This subject is of extreme importance and is considered in some detail in Chapter 13.

URBANIZATION

Throughout the centuries people have generally had a love/hate relationship with cities. The ambivalence of most people toward large cities no doubt reflects that the best and worst of a civilization are often concentrated in its cities. Perhaps New York City provides the best example. New York City is clearly a capital for great artistic talent of all kinds. It is the financial capital of the nation. But the people of New York City often fear for their lives in the streets and subways. New York City has one of the highest concentrations of welfare recipients and homeless people sleeping in the streets. The fancy cars of the affluent commonly pass the bag ladies and drug addicts in the streets as they take their passengers to Lincoln Center's Avery Fischer Hall to hear some of the world's best music.

In what follows we consider some of the most important aspects of cities and the process we call **urbanization** — the tendency for a greater concentration of a population in cities. At the outset we must stress that cities are important physical and social settings for human interaction. As a physical setting the city is studied from the perspective of **human ecology,** which is concerned with the relationship between the physical environment and human behavior (Schwab, 1982). The study of urbanization is also related to our previous topic — population. With the process of urbanization we must consider the location of the population, its density, and its movement toward and away from cities.

Before proceeding, however, it will be useful to consider a few definitions. One of the most necessary, of course, is the city. We can define a **city** as a physical area with a concentration of people living more or less permanently in that area who are not primarily engaged in agriculture (Hawley, 1981; Palen, 1981). The term **urban** is often used in the same sense, but this term more strictly refers to a style of life associated with cities — that is, an urban versus a rural life-style.

There are, of course, important distinctions between cities and urban territories. The U.S. Census Bureau uses a designation called a **metropolitan area** to refer to a central city and its nearby suburbs. This term is important because the political boundaries of a city do not always correspond to the interrelated concentrations of urban populations. The term metropolitan area, for example, does not refer to the political boundaries of the city of Los Angeles, but to the combined areas of cities like Long Beach, Anaheim, and so on. More specifically, the U.S. Census Bureau uses the term **Standard Metropolitan Statistical Area (SMSA)** to refer to counties with at least one city of 50,000 or more population. According to the 1980 census there are 318 SMSAs in the United States, with about 75 percent of the U.S. population living in these 318 SMSAs.

Finally, we should consider the process of urbanization. This trend began very slowly with agrarian societies, but it has occurred very rapidly with industrial societies. This trend has, of course, had an immense impact on industrial and developing societies, and as we will see, much of the impact has been negative.

The Emergence and Evolution of the City

As we have seen in a previous chapter, it was the development of early agriculture some 10,000 years ago that made human settlements slowly increase in number. The first "cities" were probably more like small villages with huts of "baked mud and baked reeds, comparable to a beaver's nest," suggested Lewis Mumford (1961). An example of such a city was Jarmo, in what is now northern Iraq, which had a population of 150 about 9,000 years ago. Later examples were Catal Huyuk in Turkey, and Jericho, now in Jordan, which had populations of maybe

2,000 about 4,000 years ago (Thomas, 1979, p. 29). What made these early "cities" possible were agricultural methods that allowed for a small concentration of people in a permanent settlement and the storage of grain that could provide food in the months after harvest. There were small villages in some preagricultural areas when fishing provided a stable source of food, but such areas were limited.

Though there were rather stable settlements in some areas like the Middle East, it must not be assumed that people all over the world turned to agriculture. Most people did not for a few thousand more years, and many of the people who did turn to agriculture remained seminomadic. Still others, in places like central Asia, practiced a method of agriculture called "slash and burn" in which a clearing was made in the forest and burned. The land was then cultivated for a few years, after which the people moved on. In places like Jericho, however, we find evidence of many generations of families living in the same city.

As agricultural methods advanced, when the plow and irrigation brought more abundant food,

civilizations and cities expanded. The first agricultural settlements were not, strictly speaking, cities because almost all the people were still involved in agriculture. But about 6,000 years ago agriculture had advanced to the extent that true cities could emerge with at least a small percentage of the population freed from the land for other occupational activities (see Figure 6.5).

One of the most remarkable things about these early cities was the rational planning and almost modern sanitation — characteristics more advanced than most cities during the early stages of industrialization. For example, ancient Babylon "showed a knowledge of the elementary principles of drainage and there were both sewers and cesspools" (Thomas, 1979, p. 211). In Assyria, there were lavatories and bathrooms much like those found in Europe today and better than those in most of the rest of the world. In another ancient city, Mycenae, there was running water through underground pipes. Rome had running water from twelve aqueducts that fed 1,352 fountains and as many as 1,000 public baths.

FIGURE 6.5. The emergence of cities in different world regions. *(Sjoberg, 1965)*

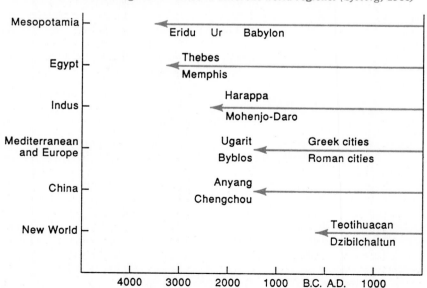

The religious and political symbolism of architecture can be seen in this sketch of Senna-cherib's Palace in ancient Mesopotamia. What image of a political elite does the structure create for you? What types of activities do you imagine took place in the open court on the palace? (© *The Bettmann Archive*)

The early cities were primarily centers for religion, commerce, and political administration. There is evidence that the first public buildings served religious functions as well as grain storage. It was in these great cities that a united political and religious elite with extensive power over others first emerged.

The population of these first great cities was quite large even by today's standards. For example, the Roman Empire contained several cities with more than 200,000 inhabitants each (Palen, 1981, p. 33), and Rome itself may have had over 1 million inhabitants about 2,000 years ago. Somewhat earlier, the Greek city-state of Athens had a population of perhaps 180,000.

V. Gordon Childe (1950) lists ten aspects of what he calls the first "urban revolution" just described:

1. Permanent settlements in dense aggregations
2. Nonagriculturalists engaging in specialized functions
3. Taxation and capital accumulation
4. Monumental public buildings
5. A ruling class
6. The technique of writing
7. The acquisition of predictive sciences—arithmetic, geometry, and astronomy
8. Artistic expression
9. Trade
10. The replacement of kinship by residence as the basis for membership in the community.

These ten characteristics were not necessarily found in every major city of the period (Palen, 1981, p. 24), but there was a tendency for the ten to be found together. For example, trade made the development of writing useful to keep records of commercial transactions, and a ruling class helped create a more centralized government (and vice versa) with taxation and monumental public buildings.

With the fall of the Roman Empire about 1,500 years ago, however, the urban advance found earlier in Europe and the Middle East declined. Large urban populations could no longer be protected and adequately supplied. People fled to rural areas and small villages that were in many ways like the small villages before the urban revolution. But with social order reestablished, the Renaissance brought a new phase of urban growth in Europe. During the period between 1100 and 1300 more new towns were founded than in any other time between the fall of the Roman Empire and industrialization. By 1363 there were about 80,000 people living in Venice; 60,000 people were living in Paris by 1192; and over 50,000 people were living in Florence and Milan in the 1300s. With increasing international trade these cities became important commercial centers, but also centers for art, technological innovation, and the spread of new ideas in general. It is obvious that the phenomenon of the Renaissance would have been impossible without these great cities.

It should be mentioned, however, that in physical characteristics these new cities of the Renaissance were primarily inferior to those of the previous age (Wells, 1971, pp. 643–644). The typical house was often poorly constructed and the city was laid out with little or no planning. Some problems, like keeping swine inside the city (and often inside the house), brought laws attempting to correct the situation. There were, of course, the great churches of Renaissance architecture, and though it is this grandeur that first comes to mind, the less grand was much more common.

During the industrial revolution the next stage of urbanization occurred, and for European cities it occurred quite dramatically. Before 1800 only in England and the Netherlands did more than 10 percent of the population live in cities. Worldwide in 1800, only 3 percent of the people lived in towns of more than 5,000 inhabitants. By 1850, however, over one-half of England's population lived in urban areas, which was the first time that happened anywhere in the world (Thomas, 1979, p. 410). By 1900 only 10 percent of the English population were involved in agriculture. And worldwide, 30 percent of the people lived in cities of 5,000 or more inhabitants by 1950, compared with 3 percent in 1800. By the year 2000, over half the world population is expected to live in urban areas.

Industrialization and urbanization are not necessarily related, however. Industry can be dispersed rather than concentrated in cities, and overpopulation can push people into cities without much industrialization. Egypt, for example, has a greater percentage of its population living in urban areas than does France, but Egypt is much less industrialized. Yet throughout Europe in the 1700s and 1800s, population increase and industrialization occurred together.

The European urbanization at the time was partially due to increased trade in agriculture. With a larger market for agricultural goods, large landowners began pushing more peasants off the land so that it could be cultivated for trade rather than to supply food for peasants. For lack of anywhere else to go, most of the peasants were pushed into cities. (Though there were peasants who stayed in the countryside and became bandits, directing their anger and criminal activities toward the wealthy, as did Robin Hood.) The prospects of some employment in new urban industry, of course, also attracted some peasants to the cities.

Although the cities of the Renaissance were not as sanitary, well planned, or of quality construction compared with the cities of the earlier empires, these conditions were far *worse* in cities during early industrialization. Waterways through cities were often polluted; rarely did people make a distinction between sewers and water mains. Thomas (1979, p. 417) writes that in England in the 1800s "ditches in cities were everywhere used as latrines. Dead animals were left to rot where they lay. The decomposing bodies of the poor in common graves stank." Visiting Venice in the 1800s, Goethe complained that rubbish and human excrement were simply pushed into piles in the street to be carried away, but carried away infrequently. With rapid growth, cities had a most serious problem with sewage. In 1850, London dealt with the problem by collecting human waste in "privy buckets" to be dumped in one of 250,000 open cesspools around the city, which of course created further problems, owing to the city's dependence on well water.

Despite the early deplorable conditions created by rapid urbanization, this new period (1700s–

1800s) has been called the "second urban revolution," the first occurring when cities first emerged with agriculture. By the late 1800s, in addition to the high degree of urbanization in England, 30 percent of Holland's population lived in cities of more than 20,000, and over 20 percent of Germans lived in cities (Hawley, 1981, p. 79).

Because the United States was a relatively new nation whose economy was still based on agriculture until the late 1800s, U.S. cities grew more slowly at first, but they grew nonetheless (see Figure 6.6). And it is interesting that urban conditions were better in the United States than in Europe at the time. For example, New York City was the first big city to assure its population an adequate supply of good water. And New York City was also envied for its well-planned layout and park and sewer systems, among other sanitation advances.

By the early 1900s in the United States the *metropolis* had emerged — a large central city representing other cities and towns grown together. But in addition to growing outward in territory, these big cities were growing upward. The first steel skyscrapers were built in Chicago in 1890 and in New York in 1894, where there were 29 by 1900. Such skyscrapers were not built in Europe until after 1945.

FIGURE 6.6. Number of U.S. urban areas, 1790–1970. *(U.S. Bureau of Census, 1975)*

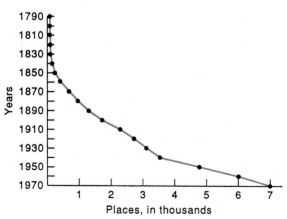

The large American cities grew with two sources of immigration. The first source came from abroad, but after the early 1900s the second source for internal migration became the more important. With increasing amounts of farm mechanization and the concentration of land ownership, especially after World War II, there was rapid movement into U.S. cities.

After 1945 another urban trend appeared in the United States — **suburbanization.** People began moving away from the central cities into smaller communities outside the main urban area. Today, over 40 percent of the U.S. population lives in suburbs, whereas slightly over 30 percent live inside large cities. Several factors have contributed to this movement to suburbs. One was the increasing problems of central cities like crime and crowding. Another factor was the movement of large factories out of central cities to areas where they had more room for expansion. One of the most important reasons was the transportation system. More people could afford an automobile, and the federal government and the states put billions of dollars into new roads and highways (with a push by oil companies and the auto industry [Blair, 1976]). Now, even people who worked in the central cities could live in the suburbs.

Community Power Structures

There has been a long tradition of community power studies by American sociologists. These studies ask such questions as "Who has power in the city?" and "Which groups are most successfully able to influence city policies to protect their interests?" On one side, "pluralist" theories argue that many interest groups have the political resources to protect their interests in U.S. cities, meaning there is a high level of democracy (Dahl, 1961). On the other side, "power elite" theories argue that one or a few groups (usually the wealthy and big business leaders) are able to dominate city politics in their own interests (Hunter, 1953).

For example, the study of community power in Atlanta, Georgia, by Floyd Hunter (1953) is one of the earliest and best-known community power studies. Hunter found that city politics in Atlanta were

This is an aerial shot of a suburb on the outskirts of Tokyo; it could, however, be an American or a European suburb. With suburbanization, people can choose private, single-family houses as opposed to the crowding of large cities. The automobile, as the major form of transportation, and a highway system linking suburbs to places of employment are critical links in this move to the country. (© *Rick Smolan/Woodfin Camp and Associates*)

dominated by a small business elite. The next famous study was conducted in New Haven, Connecticut by Robert Dahl (1961). Dahl claimed that many interest groups had power in New Haven, and thus his pluralist theory was supported. There have been many community power studies since these two, some of which support pluralist theory and some of which support power elite theory. The results of these studies, in part, differ because of differing research methods (Walton, 1976), but clearly we can say that some cities are more democratically operated than others. Although we cannot say that a

small power elite always runs a city as it pleases, reanalysis of some community power studies leads us to be more skeptical of the pluralist theory. G. William Domhoff (1978), for example, has reexamined the case of New Haven and found that a powerful business elite was able to dominate very important city projects like urban renewal.

Territorial Conflict. In a new variation of community power studies, sociologists have come to stress that cities and metropolitan areas are not undifferentiated areas, but in fact have different areas with different kinds of people and interests. There are even different kinds of suburbs, some with industry and some with only residential areas (Logan, 1976). These different territories and the people in them are often in conflict over what urban policies will be established (Logan, 1978).

In one of the most noted works on the subject, Molotch (1976) describes the city as a growth machine because of the usually constant stress on urban growth in major cities. But although this urban growth brings more profits for the wealthy, it also brings many problems like crowding, pollution, higher taxes, and a lower standard of living for other people. Molotch also argues that, more often than not, the benefit of more jobs that is stressed by elites when promoting growth does not materialize because more unemployed end up coming into the city. The key point in understanding the continued stress on urban growth in the face of so many negative outcomes, therefore, is that business elites who are pushing growth live in protected suburbs. Thus, they receive the profits of urban expansion but suffer few of the negative consequences.

Urban Ecology

Human ecology is the study of the relationship between humans and their environment. Therefore, **urban ecology** refers to the study of the relationship between humans and their urban environment (Hawley 1981, p. 9). The study of urban ecology is very broad, but two subjects have concerned sociologists most — the effect of human behavior and the physical environment on the development of cities, and the effects of the physical urban environment on humans.

Spatial Development of Cities. The spatial development of cities was the concern of the earliest urban studies by American sociologists. During the 1920s and 1930s American sociology was dominated by the University of Chicago, and it was research on the characteristics of Chicago that heavily influenced urban sociology at the time.

The form of spatial development of Chicago resembles the pattern shown in Figure 6.7 and is called **concentric zones.** In the center is the "cen-

tral business district," which contains major businesses like banks and department stores, as well as office buildings and government buildings. The next zone is the "zone in transition," which contains a mixture of business and residential areas. The residential area was once where earlier residents of the city lived, and often the earlier wealthy citizens. As the residential area aged, however, and as more and more lower-class immigrants moved to the city, this second zone became a rundown, low-cost housing area for the poor. The third area is the "zone of workers' homes," an older residential area but one that has deteriorated less than the residential area of the second zone. In the fourth circle is the "middle-class residential zone," the fifth circle is the upper-class area, and the sixth circle is the "commuter zone," where middle-class professionals live who prefer to be further away from the city.

The concentric zone pattern is a useful way to understand urban spatial development through history, but such a pattern is not universal. Often city development follows major transportation lines (railroads, highways, waterways) in its growth, which is described by *sector theory* (Hoyt, 1939). However, often a city does not have the single central downtown area that is assumed by both concentric zone and sector theory. A *multiple-nuclei theory* (Harris and Ullman, 1945) describes how a city may develop in such a manner with different areas developing around different important activities for a particular city (such as a port sector, industrial sector, or financial sector).

Although the three patterns of spatial development described above are useful, spatial development has been more diverse in major cities because many factors have affected spatial patterns (Choldin, 1985, pp. 373–382). One important variable neglected in the previous theories of urban spatial development is the nature of class conflict in the urban area. Upper classes with more influence in city government may influence urban spatial development in relation to their interests (Logan, 1978). For example, the upper classes make sure the areas of industrial development will be far from their residential neighborhoods and that the beauty of their landscape is protected. Also, when urban decay threatens their business prosperity, the more afflu-

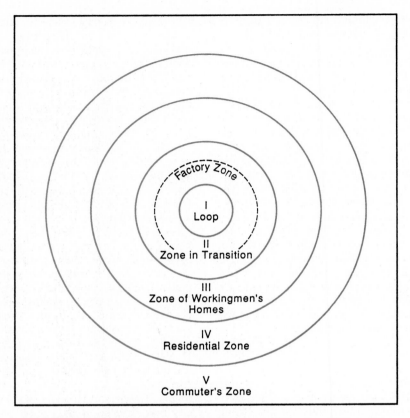

FIGURE 6.7. Burgess model of concentric zones. *(Burgess, 1925, p. 51)*

ent have forced urban renewal projects that push the poor to other parts of the city. In particular, a problem called "gentrification" has resulted in the middle classes and upper classes moving back into the central cities because of the attractiveness of urban culture, proximity to an urban workplace, and urban renewal funds. The problem results from increasing property values that price low-income families out of the housing market, and often into the streets.

Effects of Urban Environment on Human Behavior. In the tradition of human ecology we can also look at some of the effects of urban environment on human behavior. You should recall that many early sociologists believed that an urban environment was harm-

ful to humans. The extensive daily contact with strangers, the crowding, the lack of strong social ties — all considered products of urban environment — were believed to cause many problems such as mental illness and crime. Conditions like crowding, in fact, have been shown to produce various kinds of behavioral problems in nonhuman animals.

With the human animal, however, the situation is much more complex. Numerous studies of crowded urban conditions and crowded housing have not shown a consistent relationship between various mental problems and this crowding (Booth and Edwards, 1976; Choldin, 1978). And in contrast to what is often assumed, we have already seen that mental illness is actually somewhat higher in rural

Middle-class residents who reclaim central city areas and modernize old housing are the new gentry. Fresh paint and new windows are the most obvious signs of change, but what else is going on? How do you think the residents of the renovated house will fit in with those of the old building next door? (© *C. Spellman*)

areas than in cities (Choldin, 1985, p. 55). Also of note is that an urban environment alone does not seem to produce high crime. There certainly is a higher crime rate in cities than in rural areas, but this seems due to other factors often found in cities like poverty and many children without adequate family support. And one factor perhaps related to a higher crime rate in cities is that criminals are attracted to these areas because there are more potential victims (Gibbs and Maynard, 1976).

The primary reason that conditions like crowding do not always cause problems for humans, in contrast to nonhuman animals, is that our intelligence and culture have allowed us to make adjustments (Gans, 1968; Suttles, 1972). In her interesting study of personal interaction in the city, Lyn Lofland (1973) found that people can adjust to urban life's problems in many ways. For example, they learn to use appearance and the location of strangers as clues to their nature and potential behavior. These strangers have then been given an identity (at least to some extent) so that one knows how to interact with or avoid them. Also important, however, is that the number of close human relationships is not reduced by the city environment. Lofland notes that at the point of about 10,000 people, anonymity seems to take over in a city. But all that has happened is an increase in the number of strangers, not a decrease in the number of close personal relationships that seem necessary for mental health.

When we move from the broader city environment to a person's more immediate physical environment, we find more significant effects on human behavior. For example, crowding within a particular household, not simply urban crowding, has been shown to have some negative effects like mental stress (Carnahan, Grove, and Galle, 1974; Grove, Hughes, and Galle, 1979). Cultural factors are still important in explaining the effects of household crowding, however, because the Japanese have learned to live with much more household crowding than have Americans.

In addition to crowding, aspects of housing design have been found to adversely effect human behavior. For example, multiple-dwelling housing rather than single housing units are related to higher rates of juvenile delinquency (Gillis, 1974). In fact, the floor on which a family lives is related to the rate of juvenile delinquency — the higher the floor, the higher the rate of delinquency. This relationship seems to result from a lower degree of parental supervision over children when the family lives high above play areas.

In one of the most extensive works on the subject of housing design and human behavior, Newman (1972) found that the architectural design of buildings can effect such things as crime in the building and how well tenants take care of the property. For example, a housing design promoting "defensible space" is associated with less crime and property destruction. By "defensible space" Newman is referring to a sense of personal territory people may come to have; a feeling that it is their territory to be protected and taken care of. One of the primary reasons for the failure of government housing projects for low-income people is that such design aspects were not considered when constructing the low-cost housing.

Urban Problems

The process of urbanization has created many problems in all industrial societies, though in many respects the problems are now much worse in the United States than in other industrial nations. Because people in the United States tend to have a more negative view of government than in other industrial nations, or collective interests as opposed to individual interests, American cities are less likely to receive the support and resources they need to deal with their problems. Compared to people in many other industrial nations, Americans are more concerned with buying a new car for themselves, for example, than they are in paying taxes to improve schools, roads, public transportation, parks, or the urban environment, among the many things our cities need.

As John Kenneth Galbraith (1977, pp. 319–321) puts it, capitalism "is inherently incompetent in providing the things that city dwellers most urgently need." In fact, "Where capitalism is efficient, it adds to the public tasks of the city; it increases the number of automobiles that must be accommodated in and through the city, adds to the detritus that must be picked up from the streets and makes progressively more difficult the problem of keeping breathable air and sustaining a minimum tranquility of life."

Urban Infrastructure. **Urban infrastructure** is the underlying public material supports that make urban living possible — water lines, sewers, roads, bridges, and so forth. In most major American cities this infrastructure is badly in need of expansion and repair, but these needs are being neglected. In some cities water mains are so old that thousands of dollars worth of water is lost everyday. Streets and bridges are becoming dangerous, and some bridges are actually collapsing, which results in many deaths. At the same time the 8 to 10 million unemployed need work that could result in rebuilding the urban infrastructure.

As Galbraith (1969) has described, part of the problem is related to the American stress on private wealth at the expense of public needs. But urban trends have compounded the problem in recent decades. To finance infrastructure repair, cities must generate tax revenue. With the process of suburbanization, however, the people remaining in the cities are often poor, with little or no income to tax. Some large cities have tried to levy an income tax on individuals employed in the city but living elsewhere. This method of generating tax revenues has usually been voted down or challenged in the courts.

Another trend making the infrastructure decay even worse was the "tax revolt" experienced in many areas of the nation in the late 1970s. Cities and local governments usually rely heavily on property taxes for their revenue, in contrast to income taxes and sales taxes that generate most revenues for states and the federal government. Property taxes have most often been the target of tax revolts, which means city and local governments have been harmed the most. To some extent tax losses by cities have been compensated by the federal government through "revenue sharing"—federal money redistributed to cities. But in the 1980s this source of revenue has also been reduced. Thus, it is likely that the urban infrastructure in the United States will continue to deteriorate in the future.

Transportation. It is obvious that a large urban area requires an adequate system of moving people and material from one place to another. And especially with the pattern of residential suburban growth described above, there must be some means of getting people to and from work.

Automobiles are a very inefficient means of transportation in crowded urban areas. The ratio of space taken by each commuter is much higher with single-passenger auto transportation compared with any means of public transit. Yet this remains the primary means of transportation for most Americans. Since World War II the use of mass transit by Americans has actually fallen rapidly. By 1970 the number of people using mass transit was less than the number in 1910.

To some extent Americans' increasing use of automobiles as their primary means of transportation is related to values—a stress on independence. More important, however, is probably our lack of

adequate mass transit systems in most large urban areas in the United States. The Japanese living in Tokyo, for example, have a rate of auto ownership almost as high as people living in New York City or Los Angeles. People living in Tokyo, however, use their cars primarily for weekend trips. Relatively few people drive daily to work in Tokyo. No matter where a person lives in Tokyo, a commuter train line or subway is within a 15-minute walk or so and once at the train line the wait for a train is seldom longer than 10 minutes. Tokyo commuter trains are very crowded between 8:00 and 9:00 A.M. but seldom at other times, and the fare is comparatively inexpensive. In addition to all the above, given that a normal 20-minute train commute in Tokyo would take two hours by car, the Japanese heavy use of mass transit is understandable. (An additional benefit to people living in Tokyo is the rarity of injuries or deaths caused by drunken drivers. Tokyo has its share of drunks, but they have no need to drive.)

A primary reason for the comparative lack of mass transit in the United States is the political choice made after World War II to fund an extensive highway system rather than mass transit. This political policy was established under extensive lobbying by oil companies, auto companies, and tire companies (Harrington, 1976). And these companies found other means to keep Americans dependent on autos and gasoline. For example, in the 1930s Los Angeles had what was described as one of the best mass transit systems in the country. But it was closed before the end of the 1930s. A 1974 Senate antitrust investigation found that shortly before this mass transit system was closed, it was bought jointly by Chevron, General Motors, and Firestone (Sampson, 1975, p. 154). In years since, the voters in California have been given the chance to support state-funded mass transit. But in almost every case massive funding by large corporations (primarily oil companies) in support of campaigns to block mass transit has contributed to the defeat of these propositions (Whitt, 1979).

Housing Problems. Most industrial nations have experienced inadequate housing, but few of these nations have a housing problem comparable to that of the United States. There is a housing shortage in most major U.S. cities, but the problem is not just one of a lack of housing; it is also a problem of unaffordable housing.

Although it is difficult to measure precisely, an accepted estimate is that 2 million people were homeless in the United States in 1984 (*Los Angeles Times*, Feb. 17, 1985), mostly in major urban areas. For example, over 30,000 people were homeless in Los Angeles in 1984, with the same figure found for New York City in the late 1970s (*Newsweek*, March 23, 1981). During the high unemployment of 1982–1983, however, the estimate of people sleeping in the streets in New York City was as high as 50,000. Very few people can be seen sleeping in the streets of major cities in Japan, and although European nations have a problem with homelessness, it is seldom as extensive as the American problem (*Wall Street Journal*, April 25, 1983).

The housing policies of the U.S. government have, for the most part, made the housing situation worse. The tax deduction for home interest payments has helped about one-half of Americans to own their own home. But this policy has not helped the growth of low-cost housing and has in fact contributed to central city decay. The middle class and working class have been leaving the cities for suburbs where this housing is usually located. Urban renewal programs beginning in the 1960s surprisingly contributed to the housing shortage because, in contrast to stated goals, more housing was actually torn down than was built. One of the biggest failures of federal housing policy was the rapid construction of large public housing projects in the 1960s (Huffman, 1979). The housing projects were poorly constructed and designed, and too many people were crowded into small areas. Today many of these housing projects have been abandoned.

CHAPTER SUMMARY

Key Terms

Content

Much like culture and the material foundations of human societies, the characteristics of a society's population influence much about that society. Especially important population characteristics are age distribution, sex ratios, migration patterns, fertility, and mortality rates.

Like other industrialized nations, the United States has a more stable and slower population growth compared with developing nations. As the United States became an urban nation, the death rate and birth rate have been reduced. But the United States has experienced extensive immigration throughout its history, especially during the late 1800s and early 1900s.

Considering only the age distribution of a society, we can tell much about its past and future. Developing nations will have continued population growth simply because there is such a high proportion of the population currently under 15 years old. Industrial nations will have future problems in caring for older people because their population is becoming older. In the United States the "baby boom" will have continuing effects on the society.

Although population characteristics shape the nature of societies, their dominant cultural and material substructure also shapes population characteristics. One of the most important effects is the "demographic transition." In agrarian societies death rates and birth rates both tend to be high. However, as societies industrialize the death rate tends to fall, and then the birth rate tends to fall.

Thomas Malthus predicted that the world would always face overpopulation because food production could never keep up with population growth. But Malthus did not live to see the demographic transition in industrial nations. With respect to developing nations Malthus's predictions at least thus far have been more accurate. Most undeveloped nations have not gone through the demographic transition yet, though there is recently more optimism that this may happen. Because of undeveloped nations the world has been going through a period of very rapid population growth in the twentieth century.

With advanced agriculture, cities became an important feature of human societies. There were small villages before advanced agriculture, and even small fishing villages before agriculture emerged about 10,000 years ago, but the city could exist only when agriculture was advanced to the point of freeing some of the population from everyday work in the fields. With industrialization, urban areas became a dominant feature of the society. During the early 1900s, for the first time a majority of the U.S. population lived in urban areas, and today over 70 percent of Americans live in urban areas. Since the 1950s the dominant trend for American cities has been suburbanization. The affluent and middle class have been leaving the central cities to the poor and moving into suburbs.

The physical structure and spatial design of cities have important influence on human behavior. The study of the relation between the physical urban environment and human behavior is called human ecology. Early studies in urban ecology, especially at the University of Chicago, were concerned with the spatial development of cities. A "concentric zone" pattern of development was believed to be the most common. Further studies, however, have found more variation in urban spatial development, and these recent studies have also shown how class conflicts over urban land use influences the spatial development of cities.

With advanced industrial technology and an ideology stressing private wealth rather than collective needs, U.S. cities face many problems today. For example, the urban infrastructure is in serious decay, adequate mass transit is almost nonexistent (compared with other industrial nations), and many people are homeless in this nation.

CHAPTER 7

Social Psychology: Socialization, Social Interaction, and Crowds

*I have argued that the self appears in experience essentially as a "me" with the
organization of the community to which it belongs. This organization is, of course,
expressed in a particular endowment and particular social situation of the individual.*
— George Herbert Mead, Mind, Self and Society from the Standpoint of a Social Behaviorist

As we will see in some detail in Chapter 15 on gender inequality, there are considerable differences in the life chances of men and women in modern industrial societies. For example, women in the United States receive on the average less pay for the same jobs as men and are more often found in the lower-paying types of jobs. Also, women are much less likely to be promoted to higher ranks in bureaucracies that give them authority over others. The status of women is not exactly the same in all industrial societies; in some societies the status of women is better, in some, such as Japan in particular, the status of women is lower compared with that in the United States. In Japan, the pay of women compared with that of men is lower than in the United States, and women are even less likely to hold positions of authority. For example, in 1982, although 28.3 percent of the administrative and managerial positions in the United States were held by women, only 6 percent were held by women in Japan (Foreign Press Center/Japan 1985, p. 82).

College women reading this book today, however, will find that their occupational life chances have improved considerably compared with those of their mothers. There are many reasons for these improvements, including new laws, the push of the women's movement, and changed economic conditions. Also important are attitude changes about the roles of women. As we will see in Chapter 15, today many more people in this country, as well as in Japan, believe women should be treated equally with men in the workplace and that it is acceptable, even desirable, for married women to be employed. Women's views of themselves have also been changing, and these views are partially involved in the improved educational and occupational chances of women these days.

In this chapter we concern ourselves with such subjects as self-concepts and socialization (i.e., the process by which self-concepts are developed). With our example above of changing attitudes toward the role of women, we can ask why and how these attitudes are changing, and in fact how they are formed to begin with. The development of sex roles, in particular, is quite complex and begins at a very early age. For example, when one nine-year-old girl was asked by a *Los Angeles Times* reporter *(Los Angeles Times,* Sept. 10, 1987) what she wanted to be, she replied "a teacher." "But if she were a boy, she would want to be an astronaut. When it was suggested that girls could become astronauts, she replied, 'yes, but that would be too scary.'" Even at a much younger age children will tell you the "proper" dress for boys and girls, as well as such things as acceptable male versus female roles.

The primary focus of this text has been, and will be, macro sociology. In contrast to a course in psychology or even social psychology, our concern here is the basic nature of societies and their subdivisions. However, societies are made up of individuals. And though we can understand such things as male/female inequality with a focus on group structure and culture, it is useful to consider how individuals develop a self-concept, how social structures are reproduced over the generations with this process of developing a self-concept, and how human interactions in small and large groups affect the overall society and these self-concepts. These subjects and similar ones are considered in the present chapter, which generally treats the subject of social psychology.

We first consider how individuals are shaped by the society through a socialization process. Without socialization there would be no socially functioning humans to form societies. And without a socialization process leading most people, most of the time, to accept their position in the society, there would be constant overt conflict. We will next consider the process of face-to-face human interaction in small groups. Societies are made up of not just people, but people in networks of interaction. The basic nature of everyday interaction must therefore be examined at least briefly. Finally, we consider the interaction process of people in large crowds. The dynamics of crowd behavior have shaped and continue to shape societies in both negative and positive ways. In this chapter we examine the social psychology of crowd behavior such as riots, panics, fun-seeking riots, and hysterical contagion. In summary, this chapter covers social psychology from the individual to large crowds.

THE SOCIALIZATION PROCESS

As biologists and anthropologists have shown, humans are the product of millions of years of genetic evolution. We are, in other words, a product of our genes. But as we have already seen, this genetic heritage has also presented us with a unique situation compared with that of other animals. Humans cannot live by genes alone. What I mean by this is that we must *learn* how to live, how to find food and protect ourselves from the elements, among many other things that make life possible. Our unique genetic heritage has left most of human behavior open and adaptable. How we survive, how we live as well as die is primarily the product of our cultural heritage. To guide our behavior this cultural heritage must get into our heads through a process called **socialization.**

Consider the example of identical twins raised apart. In this case we have unique natural experiments showing us the importance of biology versus learning on human behavior. Studies of such twins have found that the identical genes of these twins have made them similar in many ways. For example, these twins are usually similar in temperament and athletic ability. They may also have similar talents for mathematics, music, or other arts. But depending on the degree of dissimilarity in the social environments where they were raised, twins tend to be very different in other ways. They may speak different languages, have different political and religious values, be hard-working or lazy, and, of course, have different levels of education.

What makes twins raised apart quite different are differences in the socialization process. They may

have been raised in different cultures or have had unique combinations of pieces of a common culture placed in their heads. The content and experiences of a socialization process can never be exactly the same for two individuals, and thus, even identical twins raised in the same family can never be exactly alike.

The importance of the socialization process can be seen in the few documented cases of children who have spent most of their early childhood in almost complete isolation (Curtiss, 1977). In a typical case these children have been locked in a small room with almost no human contact. Because of this lack of contact with other humans, these children are in a sense not human.

Kingsley Davis (1949) has described the case of two girls raised in isolation, both hidden because they were illegitimate. One child, Anna, had almost no human contact, and the other, Isabelle, had contact only with her deaf-mute mother. Neither girl could speak, but Anna was especially restricted in her development as a human, unable even to walk when she was discovered at six years of age. Perhaps because she had at least some human contact, however, Isabelle was able to develop into a normal child a few years after she was discovered at six years old.

Nature versus Nurture. Much of what I have written in introducing this chapter is relevant to the old nature versus nurture debate among people contemplating human society that we considered briefly in Chapter 1. On the one side (nature) it is argued that humans are mostly a product of biology. Whether we are good or bad, talented or losers, is said to be the product of the unique biology of each individual. On the other side, it is stressed that humans are born with the potential to be anything —good or bad, talented or untalented, winners or losers. A common way of expressing this view was to say that the brain is in the beginning a "tabula rasa," a blank slate that must be filled in by the culture and learning.

In the past, social scientists leaned very heavily to the nurture side of the debate. Especially early anthropologists such as Franz Boas (1859–1942) stressed the theory called **cultural determinism**, which in its extreme form maintains that almost everything we do is learned. Later, Margaret Mead, a famous anthropologist, tried to support the idea of cultural determinism through some of her studies of young people in Samoa (Mead, 1928). Sociologists as well have tended to accept the idea of cultural determinism, which can be seen especially in the work of functionalists like Talcott Parsons (1958).

More recently, however, social scientists have questioned this "overly socialized" view of humans. For example, Margaret Mead's work on young people in Samoa has been criticized (Freeman, 1983). Specifically, Margaret Mead tried to show that the stress of growing to adulthood was much more a product of our own culture and not a phenomenon found in all other cultures. She believed she found such a culture in Samoa, but subsequent studies suggest she did not.

Sociologists have also been taken to task for the "overly socialized" view of humans (Wrong, 1961). For example, some older sociological theories of mental illness claim social influences, stress, and faulty socialization are the primary or even exclusive causes of mental illness. In many cases of mental illness, we know today this extreme position is incorrect. More accurately, we can say there are a combination of social factors and a biological potential for mental illness that bring out the illness in most individuals.

And so it is with socialization. The development of a personality and the characteristics of that personality depend on a combination of biological and social factors. Still, most of what makes us functioning members of a particular society is placed in our heads through a socialization process. There is no biological predisposition to speak English rather than Hebrew, to be a good capitalist rather than a good communist, or to be a Democrat rather than a Republican. And recent evidence even suggests that exceptional talent in art and science depends more on effort, parental encouragement, and opportunities to learn than on inherent ability (Bloom, 1985). Thus, although we must recognize some elements of truth in both sides of the nature versus nurture debate, as sociologists we are more often concerned with the parts of human character that are nurtured.

The family provides the child with a frame of reference for both the family's values and the culture's. In China, where there is a strict population control policy of one child per family, young children are dressed in bright colors while adults dress in uniforms. In part, this allows children to feel that they are at the center of the culture. What other purposes do you think it serves? (© Elliot Erwin/Magnum Photos)

Developmental Theories of Socialization. There is a general recognition of biological limits, or rather timing, that must be considered in the socialization process. An infant can learn neither English nor Chinese, for example, until a certain biological stage of physical and mental development has been reached. It also seems a certain stage of physical development must be reached before moral values and self-identity can be developed.

One of the most famous individuals to investigate

these stages of cognitive development is Jean Piaget, who found four primary stages. From birth until about age two children are in what Piaget (1970) called a "sensorimotor stage" in which motor skills and their senses are developing. During this time children are also able to realize that objects still exist when they are blocked from view. In the "preoperational stage," from about age two until seven, most cognitive development is devoted to language skills, at least early in this stage. It is also during this stage, however, that important social skills develop, most importantly the ability to overcome strong egocentrism and understand the feelings of others. Next, during the "concrete operational stage," which lasts from about age 7 to 12, children develop skills of concrete logic. For example, they should come to understand that a change in the shape of an object does not mean a change in the mass or volume of the object. Finally, in the "formal operational stage," which begins about age 12, children come to think more abstractly and develop logical reasoning that allows learning beyond simple trial and error.

More recently Lawrence Kohlberg (1980) has found there seem to be important stages in the moral development of children. At first children can think only in terms of the physical consequences of misbehaving and the rewards or punishment their actions may bring. Only later are children able to understand moral principles and orient their behavior toward them, rather than thinking only in terms of the rewards or punishment of their actions.

All social scientists now recognize that there are stages of biological development in the socialization process. In other words, there are restrictions on the socialization process, though there are disagreements over the exact nature of any developmental stages. For example, there is evidence that there are historical and cultural variations in some of the stages of development (Riegel, 1979). Finally, although it is important to recognize the developmental stages in the socialization process, sociologists (in contrast to psychologists) are most concerned with the *content* of the socialization process, that is, what is placed into the heads of individuals, their development of a "self" that guides their behavior, who helps place all this into peoples' heads, and how.

Development of the "Self"

Central to the process by which people shape the future behavior and beliefs of others is in the development of **"the self,"** or self-concept. The self can be described as the image we have of ourselves, our abilities, and our character, which guides how we behave and what we do. There is evidence that humans are the only animals to fully develop such a self-concept that orients their behavior in a very broad manner. And although this development of a self begins, and is most important, at a very early age, the process of developing and changing the self never fully stops.

The importance of this self should be further considered for a moment. We all have a self-concept, a view of who we are and what we can do. This self-concept may lead us to think we are appealing to the opposite sex, good or bad at making others like us, humane and caring or tough and demanding of others, intelligent or dull, talented in one thing or another — the list goes on and on. Although at times the view we have of ourself may be an illusion, it remains important because we tend to act upon this self-concept. In other words, as W. I. Thomas put it, situations defined as real are often real in their consequences. Thus, if a person thinks he or she is appealing to the opposite sex, this person may act in such a manner. The confidence and motivation for certain actions gained through a self-concept can be very important. If the young person feels unattractive to the opposite sex, it is likely that this person will devote more time and effort in other directions — being a scholar, an artist, an athlete, or street gang member (though, of course, all these activities do not conflict with an image of being appealing to the opposite sex). And the importance of the self-concept may be seen in its effect on a person's life chances. As an example of this, I conducted a small, very modest study of the failure rate of American Indian college students (Kerbo, 1981b). In part, the high failure rate among American Indian college students seems related to their self-concept. The students who identified themselves as being more like white students had greater success in college, irrespective of percent of American Indian blood, previous high school achievement, and other background factors.

Returning to our example of people who view themselves as appealing to the opposite sex, we can ask how this self-concept is created and maintained? It is unlikely that a very unappealing person would develop such a self-concept, or at least be able to maintain it over a long period of time.

The "Looking Glass Self" and the "Me". Charles Horton Cooley (1902) recognized that the self is a social product that comes from interactions with others. Through what he called a **looking glass self** we see our actions reflected in the responses of others. We learn to play roles — and we learn what others think of our behavior through judging their reactions. Through early responses to our behavior, for example, we may come to think of ourselves as appealing to the opposite sex. Once this idea develops, the person comes to act upon it, judging the reactions of others. If the responses from the opposite sex are primarily negative, through time this self-concept will be altered. Thus, it is a looking glass self in that the self is developed through the images others have of us. And this is to say that without a society, or others who provide long-term interaction, there is no "self."

The ideas of Cooley were expanded by another American sociologist, George Herbert Mead (1934). Also important in the process of socialization, Mead pointed out, is the ability to *take roles* and anticipate what others expect of us. At first, we respond only to the expectations of *particular others,* who are immediate individuals like parents. Later, however, people develop a sense of what is expected by the *generalized other,* that is, the wider society. For example, the very young child can respond only to what the mother and/or father expects. In time, however, people come to take *roles.* They now understand the role of the college athlete, the business executive, the mother, and so on. They learn what the general society expects of people in one of these roles, and they usually behave accordingly.

Finally, Mead is also noted for the dual concepts of **the "I" and the "me."** Mead recognized that we do not simply respond to the expectations of others like robots. The *me* is the self-concept developed through social interaction and the "looking glass self." But we also maintain an *I* that allows us to analyze the role we are placed in and is more spontaneous and self-interested. Like the great psychoanalyist Freud (1930), Mead recognized there would always be a conflict between the independent self-interests of individuals and the social roles and rules created for individuals by the society.

The Self and Society. It should now be apparent that the development of the self is one of the most important social psychological links between the individual and the wider society. *Through development of the self the person is placed in the context of her or his society and learns what others expect of her or him, and the roles she or he is expected to play.* It is through the development of the self that people come to be functioning members of the society with a sense of who they are and "their purpose" in life.

Through consideration of the development of the self we can understand many other things about human behavior and society. For example, as we will see in the chapter on crime and deviance, we can in part understand the causes of crime and delinquency by considering how a criminal self-concept is developed. Also, as we will see, social control and social order can in part be understood with the development of the self. For example, a basic question in almost all societies is how to persuade people who have very little to accept a high degree of inequality in the society. What prevents people who have very few rewards from rebelling to try to change the situation? A partial answer to this question is that those on the bottom of society, or those who are rewarded much less, often accept the situation because they have developed a self-concept that leads them to believe they deserve less.

Socialization Agents

The socialization process is not something that happens in childhood and is then over. Although it is true that the most important stages of socialization occur during childhood, socialization is a lifelong process.

For this reason, the family or parents are not the only agents of socialization for individuals. In this section we consider some of the main agents of socialization and their importance.

Because the socialization process is a lifelong process, we can also see that there are different kinds of socialization. **Primary socialization** is the basic form of socialization in which language, cultural norms, basic personality, and a world view is developed. But there is also **anticipatory socialization,** which involves learning of a future role that a person will have or would like to have. For example, if a person aspires to be a professional soldier, then as a young person, the life-style, traditions, beliefs, and even the body language of professional soldiers may be learned. **Developmental socialization** is the socialization that builds on the primary socialization of a person's younger years. As an adult, new experiences and skills are added in a nonending process. Finally, **resocialization** occurs when there is a major break from what has been acquired in a person's primary and developmental socialization. Quite often this resocialization occurs in "total institutions" like prisons, military basic training, monasteries, or some other place where there is an attempt to change some basic aspects of a person's previous character. Resocialization also occurs when individuals join some cults that follow very different life-styles compared with others in the society.

Family. Although no longer as strong or as important in most modern industrial societies, the family is still the most important socialization agent, especially for young children. Many other socialization agents affect the development of children in modern societies today — schools, the mass media, and youth agencies like the Girl Scouts. But parents continue to be most important in shaping the development of

The Ecuadorian mother is nursing her child while tending her market stall. The American mother nurses her baby in the privacy of the bedroom. What do these images communicate about the values of each culture? Do you think the two societies differ in their attitudes toward breast feeding? (left: © Eugene Gordon; right: © Vinnie Fish/Photo Researchers, Inc.)

children during the most critical first years. How parents treat their children and what they teach them is influenced by how the parents themselves were raised and many characteristics of their current situation. This is why studies of occupational and educational achievement indicate that about 50 percent of what explains such achievement, or the lack of it, is related to the family background of individuals (Jencks et al., 1979).

Given the importance of the family on childhood socialization, the characteristics of the family become very important. For example, with over 50 percent of married women now in the labor force, there are questions about the effect of this on children. The evidence does not indicate that working mothers tend to create problems for their children, though much more research is needed (Bronfenbrenner, 1970). Some research has in fact indicated that the children of working mothers may have higher achievement in later life (Elkin and Handel, 1978). In the case of single-parent families (which usually represents mother and children), unfortunately, the evidence is clearer (McLanahan, 1985). This is unfortunate because of the high number of children who will live in single-parent families for at least several years of their lives (over 20 percent). This is not to say that all children living in female-headed households will have problems, or that the father's absence is the only important thing, but the children of single-parent families are more likely to become delinquent and do poorly in school.

Research also indicates that family size affects many characteristics of children, though it is not always clear how much is due to family size alone or other factors related to family size like the economic status of the family. Whichever is the cause, children from smaller families do better in school, have higher test scores, and are less likely to become delinquents (Hirschi, 1969). It is also of note that birth order affects the socialization of children. The first-born child has a slight tendency to be more independent and achieve a higher position in later life. And the only child tends to be somewhat different on some characteristics like self-centeredness, which may present a problem for China's government policy promoting single-child families if the same effects are found in China.

There are some interesting class differences in child-rearing methods, as well as cross-national differences. As we will see in more detail in the chapter on social class, middle-class parents tend to raise more independent, creative children. But most variation in child-rearing is found among different societies.

In Japan, for example, the mother-child bond is especially strong, in part because men are expected to devote more energy to their occupation. Mothers in Japan tend to spend considerable amounts of time in studying the latest advice on child-rearing in popular books and magazines, perhaps because old traditions in Japan are changing and young mothers are uncertain about how to raise their children (Fukutake, 1981; Vogel, 1971). The strong mother-child bond in Japan and the extensive time spent on the child's education by the mother may influence the low rate of most social problems among Japanese children (except suicide), as well as the greater dependency on the parents. The strong family bonds for children in Japan, however, may be related to lower social skills as young adults (Nakane, 1970), especially in interaction with the opposite sex.

In an interesting contrast to Japan, children in the Soviet Union tend to be more secure outside the family. This is perhaps due to the reported fondness for all children (not just their own) that the Soviet people seem to display (Bronfenbrenner, 1970).

Peer Group. After the importance of the family, the child's peer group is perhaps next in importance in the socialization process, and this is especially the case after the first few years of life. There is considerable evidence that the peer group is becoming more important as children in industrial societies spend more time away from their parents. As an indication of the importance of the peer group today, the education and occupational attainment studies cited above indicate that the peer group effect on attainment is a close second to family background (Sewell and Hauser, 1975).

In the early years of life, of course, the peer group is important for the play activity and "role testing" that such play activity provides in developing a self-concept (Denzin, 1975). But in addition to spontaneous play, games are important in teaching children organized social interaction, the importance of rules, and self-control (Neal, 1983).

In later childhood the peer group is most important in influencing the values, attitudes, life-style, and aspirations of young people. What parents have no doubt always known has been supported by sociological research; whom children "run around" with is quite important in influencing much of what children do.

In contrast to preindustrial societies, we find what can be called youth subcultures in industrial societies. In preindustrial societies childhood is a much shorter social status; teenagers do not have the freedom and independence from work and raising other children. In this situation children move

rapidly from the role of child to that of adult. But in our own society young people are in a social status between childhood and adulthood for an extended period of time. This social position of young people creates a youth subculture with values and a life-style often in conflict with that of their parents (see Box 7.1).

Schools. One function of the educational system is to provide technical information and other kinds of knowledge so that the young can become contributing members of the society. But schools do much more than this; there is a **hidden curriculum** that teaches obedience, respect for authority, and the dominant values of the society.

BOX 7.1

Youth Subcultures from the Soviet Union to Southeast Asia

Only recently have young people not had the responsibilities of job and marriage for an extended period of time. In the year 1900 in the United States fewer than 6 percent of the 17 year olds had finished high school, and the figure did not reach 50 percent until 1940 (Flacks, 1973, p. 10). Youth, as a social category, has been greatly extended. Now, instead of beginning a full-time job and starting a family in their teen years, young people commonly wait until their twenty's. As we will see in more detail in later chapters, a job (and type of job) and family responsibilities strongly shape a person's life-style, views of life, and other individual characteristics. Young people today, in other words, for the first time in history have been freed to develop what can be called a youth subculture. And technical advances in the mass media have greatly increased the spread of the youth subculture.

The United States is not the only country with a youth subculture that leads young people to a life-style in conflict with that of their parents, nor are other Western countries alone in this respect. In Japan — a country noted for its hard work, conformity, and parental control — the rapid spread of a youth subculture stressing hedonism, rock music, punk clothing styles, and a rejection of other values the older generation holds dear has shocked most Japanese. The youth subculture can be seen most clearly in Tokyo's Yoyogi Park, where Japanese youth come dressed in their punk style, Al Capone gangster costumes, or 1950s-era rock-and-roll black leather jackets and greasy hair. The main activity at Yoyogi Park is dancing in a circle to loud music, and of course being seen. Japan so far has only a small problem with drugs and youth crime, but these problems are increasing *(Newsweek,* Oct. 8, 1984). It is also interesting that many of the Japanese young people seen in Yoyogi Park brought their costumes from home in a sack, and changed into this clothing at the park. (And though the boys in Yoyogi Park with their black leather jackets look like tough gang members during the

Consider the example of the flag salute; five days a week throughout the school year, at about 8:30 or 9:00 in the morning, millions of children stand, place their right hand over their heart, face the flag, and recite, "I pledge allegiance to the flag of the United States of America. . . ." This is a political ritual that few if any people object to in this nation, though most would not like to have it called what it really is, political indoctrination. Most parents in this country, as in the Soviet Union, Great Britain, France, and so on, want their children to grow up as patriotic citizens, and thus they do not object to the "right" political values taught in the schools. Because parents know the influence of schools over their children, the educational system is often brought into

conflicts in the community. When there are groups with different political or religious values, each group wants the schools to teach its values, or at least not have its values rejected by teachers.

In an interesting study of the effect of U.S. education on the values of children, Cummings and Taebel (1978) asked children their opinions about the nature of capitalism. For example, young elementary school children generally believe it is unfair that only a few people own the land and factories while workers own no significant property. By the high school years, however, there is a dramatic change in this view — now most students think such wealth inequality is acceptable. The point is that because these school children are taught the dominant

---

1950s in New York, a friend of mine claims that if you bump into them they still bow and very politely say "I'm sorry.")

The Soviet Union as well has a highly developed youth subculture. And as the following description from *Time* (Feb. 27, 1984) indicates, youth subcultures all over the world are heavily influenced by young people in the United States:

At a festival in Soviet Armenia, 5,000 rock-besotted fans sway and twitch in the stands of a bicycle stadium. Onstage, half a dozen Soviet groups belt out numbers in a Berlitz of languages, including English, Italian and French. As midnight slips by, the gray-uniformed police stationed by the amplifiers glower, but the beat goes on. Suddenly a combo swings into an Elvis Presley classic, and the fans roar along, "Mah bluh svade shoos."

The craving for Western goods, and its implied materialism, is evident everywhere. Jeans and rock music are even more popular than they were a decade ago, and now those fads have filtered from the city to the countryside. A pair of brand-name denims fetches $400 on the black market in Siberia; tapes of Michael Jackson and the Police go for $54 in Moscow. Teen-agers are so fond of Adidas sneakers that a new Russian adjective has been coined: adidasovsky, meaning "terrific." A trendy girl is described as firmennaya, from firma, meaning an item with a Western brand name.

Western pursuits are copied just as eagerly. Soviet youths who have come to love pizza and disco music are now smitten with skateboarding and jogging. Among the well educated in Moscow and Leningrad, Jane Fonda is a cult figure, but not for her politics. Her popularity stems from movies and, even more surprising, from bootlegged tapes of her exercise routines.

Donning Levi's and a college T-shirt emblazoned STANFORD is not an act of political rebellion but of status seeking. For Soviet youngsters, Western products proclaim to their friends, "I can get what I want." A scarf with a designer signature adds a dash of color to what can be a gray existence. Nor are Soviet officials immune to the temptations; it is often their children who are first to sport the latest Western clothes, courtesy of a trip abroad or a state store reserved for the elite.

American political and economic ideologies, they have come to view the world differently. If a study such as this were replicated in the Soviet Union, we would almost certainly find that support for characteristics of communism has increased as children advance through their educational system.

Mass Media. Virtually every family in the United States owns a television set. The Japanese, however, hold the record for the most time spent watching television during the week—about three and one-half hours per person (Fukutake, 1981). Among other things, the extensive exposure to common images and information through the mass media in industrial societies has led to the view that we have created a **mass society.** In such societies the ideas, life-styles, and values of the people become more and more similar because the socialization of these people is dominated by a common mass media exposure.

Although it is a complex matter, studies do indicate that people's beliefs are affected by what they see on television (Comstock et al., 1978). There is general agreement that the most important effect of viewing TV comes after many years of exposure, and a few studies have explored these long-range effects of extensive TV exposure. Research by George Gerbner (*Newsweek,* Dec. 6, 1982), for ex-

---

BOX 7.2

The Mass Media and Violence

Social scientists are just starting to learn about the influence of mass media violence on actual violence in our society. The evidence is beginning to show that the influence clearly exists but operates in subtle ways. In a series of studies on the effects of mass media violence, David Phillips (1979, 1982, 1983) has found that highly publicized boxing matches on TV seem to increase the U.S. murder rate about three days after the boxing match. Phillips's most recent study was explained in the following article from the *Los Angeles Times* ("Coverage of Boxing May Trigger Murders," Aug. 10, 1983).

Mass-media coverage of heavyweight prizefights may trigger some murders, a statistical study by a sociologist at the University of California, San Diego, indicates.

The national homicide rate briefly rises by an average of 12.46% after a heavyweight championship fight, according to David P. Phillips, whose previous work has uncovered several possible links between violence in the mass media and in daily life.

This is apparently "the first systematic evidence suggesting that some homicides are indeed triggered by a type of mass-media violence," Phillips said in an article scheduled for publication today in the American Sociological Review, the official journal of the American Sociology Assn. "The evidence suggests that heavyweight prizefights stimulate fatal, aggressive behavior in some Americans."

Homicides of young blacks increase after championship fights in which blacks are beaten, and those of young whites rise after young whites are beaten, he said.

Heavily publicized prizefights tend to be followed by particularly large increases in homicides.

Still, Phillips cautioned, the findings "should be considered preliminary and tentative until the findings have been replicated by other researchers."

In a series of studies since 1974, Phillips has documented an increase in U.S. suicides and auto accidents after heavily publicized suicide stories.

In 1978 he found that highly publicized murder-suicides are followed by a significant increase in small-plane crashes with multiple deaths. He suggested that some pilots may have committed suicide by crashing their planes.

ample, shows that the long-range impact of watching TV is very extensive. This research first examined the images created by heavy exposure to TV. For about 15 years Gerbner's research team examined over 1,600 prime-time programs in detail for their content. Among other things, they found that male characters outnumbered female characters by three to one. And both male and female characters tend to be in traditional roles (e.g., few female TV characters were employed outside the home). The same stereotypes were given for the elderly and minorities, who were also very outnumbered in TV programs. Heavy TV viewers also got a distorted image of work. Most TV characters were in upper-middle-class or elite occupations; seldom were they working-class people, farmers, or small business people. And as you would expect, TV viewers got extremely heavy doses of crime and violence. During prime time, 55 percent of TV characters were involved in at least one violent confrontation per week, whereas in real life the average is far less than 1 percent.

In research to explore the effects of heavy TV exposure, Gerbner examined the views of people who were heavy TV viewers versus those who were not. Many control variables were employed in this research to try to show that the attitude differences were in fact caused by the heavy TV viewing. Some

---

Last year, Phillips reported that fictional suicides on TV soap operas tended to be followed by a spurt in the national suicide rate. . . .

Phillips has long sought to determine whether mass-media coverage of violence can trigger more violence. He chose to study prizefights because they are heavily publicized and exciting, and the winners receive large financial rewards — all factors that, in theory, might inspire violence in everyday life.

Also, he notes, media coverage treats the fights as positive rather than negative events. "No one up there is saying, Look at this guy, beating up the other guy — it's terrible." If this happened on the street, he'd be arrested," Phillips said.

Phillips based his study on all homicides committed in the United States during a six-year period, from 1973 to 1978, a period that included 18 heavyweight championship fights. Daily homicide counts after 1978 had not been compiled by federal authorities at the time of the study, he said.

He found an average increase in murders of 12.46% per prizefight.

In actual numbers, 193 more people were killed after prizefights than would have been the statistical norm during the six-year period, Phillips concluded.

The largest single increase was 32.3% after a fight between Muhammad Ali and Joe Frazier on Oct. 1, 1975, in Manila. Whereas the expected number of homicides was 82, the total was 108 — that is, 26 extra homicides.

Another fight between Ali and Joe Bugner, on July 1, 1975, was followed by a 27.8% increase in homicides.

By his reasoning, a murder "followed" a fight if it occurred within three weeks after the bout.

"The major increase [in murders] comes three days after the prizefight," Phillips noted.

Phillips did not analyze the details of any specific murder to determine if it was triggered by a prizefight.

But did coverage of prizefights actually trigger the murders? Or was some other factor responsible? Phillips tried to find out.

For example, he wondered if gambling associated with prizefights could have led to the increased murder rate.

This was unlikely, he concluded, because the murder rate does not rise significantly after the Super Bowl, another well-publicized event connected with gambling.

findings are remarkable. About twice as many TV viewers were afraid of crime in their area. Following the low number of elderly on TV, heavy TV viewers were likely to believe that the number of elderly in our society is actually being heavily reduced, whereas it is growing rapidly. In many other responses like these, it was found that light TV viewers have a more realistic and accurate picture of life in the United States. Television, in other words, seems to be an important socialization agent, and unfortunately a socialization agent that today often distorts reality (see Box 7.2).

There are, of course, many other socialization agents in modern societies because any social group or organization that creates extensive ties for the individual can operate as a socialization agent. The process of secondary socialization is carried on in a person's work group and any important voluntary organization. And if a person comes to be a voluntary or involuntary member of a total institution (the military, a prison, a monastery, or a mental hospital), these organizations provide secondary socialization, or more likely resocialization. But overall, the socialization agents described above tend to be the most important.

A Conflict Perspective on the Socialization Process

It is usually assumed that the socialization process is for the good of all in the society. It creates people who can fit into the society, cooperate with others, accept the values and norms of the society — in other words, it creates stability and makes society possible. This is the view of the socialization process stressed by functional theorists, and this view cannot be rejected. But we can also learn much about the socialization process from a conflict perspective.

As already noted, we can ask what type of social order and who's social order is promoted by the socialization process. For example, the socialization process has been involved throughout history as a tool in class conflict. A primary goal of socialization is often to get people in low positions in the society to accept that low position — to make them feel they deserve that low position.

Considered from a micro level of analysis, the primary socialization process can also be understood through conflict assumptions. Parents, for example, can be considered the authority in much the same way the ruling class in a nation is the dominant authority, and children represent the subordinate class in this minisystem of political authority. Much like the ruling class, parents try to make their children conform to *their own* behavior expectations and values. This is very similar to the process by which a state tries to create political legitimacy.

Considering it in this fashion, we can begin to see that the process of socialization in the family is influenced by the resources that parents may have to enforce compliance. (1) When the resources of parents (or parent) are reduced in comparison with the resources of children, the socialization process can break down. Also, (2), parents in different positions in the society will have more or fewer resources (and different types of resources) and thus, there will be different patterns of socialization in the society. This is especially so among parents in different economic or class positions in the society. Consider the following differences.

Control of children through greater use of physical punishment tends to make boys more aggressive to outsiders, more authoritarian, and more ethnocentric, and makes "fear of punishment rather than internalization of moral standards" a greater influence on behavior throughout life (Collins, 1975, p. 266). Because the lower classes in our society tend to have fewer other resources (e.g., material rewards) with which to socialize their children, they are more likely to use physical punishment. Thus, we do find that lower-class children differ in some ways from middle-class and upper-class children — and subsequently differ in their adult years as well. The greater resources of more affluent parents give them greater options in the socialization process. More affluent parents may use material rewards to influence children's behavior. Also, parents who have more time, perhaps because the mother does not have to seek employment, can use many resources to control children.

Similarly, "control by shaming or ridicule produces strong self-control, especially over one's public demeanor and emotional expressiveness, and an emphasis on conforming externally to the group's expectations" (Collins, 1975, p. 267). But this method of control requires a high degree of surveillance that only parents with the resource of time or crowded living conditions may have. Social control by shaming or ridicule has been a primary form of socialization in many Asian countries, especially Japan, in part because of crowded conditions in the single household allowing greater surveillance over children (Nakane, 1970). But it is also clear that value differences, like the high value placed on conformity, lead to this type of socialization method in most Asian countries.

Following this line of reasoning we can understand why children from poor female-headed households have a higher than average rate of delinquency. Because there is only one parent the resources of time, and energy and an alliance with another adult for socializing children are less. Also, because the family is poor there are few resources to control children through material rewards, and the family will likely live in a crowded urban area, making surveillance of children difficult (e.g., the children are often out in the streets). Finally, the size of the child must be recognized as a resource in childhood socialization. With large, young sons the single mother can be overpowered, and a young delinquent is likely to be aware of the mother's inability to use the final means of social control over him — physical force.

The main point of this conflict perspective is that in human interactions there will often be differing interests among the two or more individuals. In the family, children frequently have interests in conflict with their parents (for example, taking the car for the evening). The greater the resources of the parents in socializing and controlling their children, the more likely are the children to grow up with the behavior and values the parents wish.

SOCIAL INTERACTION

We are ready to make the transition from socialization, which involves social interaction, to a focus on social interaction itself, in all situations. As already pointed out, society is made up of individuals who form networks of interactions. We can learn many things about the nature of societies by looking at the macro level only. But even from the macro perspective it is useful to touch base, so to speak, with the micro level of human interaction as we have in this chapter.

In a strict sense macro structures in the society, say, the government, are abstractions. The physical structure of government exists as buildings, equipment, written documents, and the people who are doing the work of government. Most important, however, a macro structure like the government is made up of combinations of "micro events" or chains of human interactions as people do the work of government and interact with citizens (Collins, 1981). The government as an abstract reality with a power over people exists because people assume it exists. For example, the people who work for the Internal Revenue Service assume they represent the government's interests as they go about their work of collecting taxes, and the tax payers assume they might get caught if they are not careful when cheating on their income tax return. Thus, in the minds of both parties, the government exists and has influence over their behavior. Under unique situations, however, these assumptions may change and the government can, in fact, cease to exist, as it did in Russia during the first stage of the February Revolution in 1917 (Skocpol, 1979). That year, a minor protest event occurred and the army didn't follow the tsar's orders to stop the protest. The crowds in the streets developed a new assumption that the government could no longer control them, and the assumption came to be shared by government authorities. The redefinition of the situation by both parties meant that, in a sense, the government no longer existed.

We must, of course, look at other factors that influence the assumptions people have about the existence of their government. In Russia these other factors were the government's growing inability to continue the war with Germany, protect its people, and assure basic necessities. This set in motion chains of "conversation rituals" that led people to redefine the government in a network of conversations all over the country. Then, one incident brought all the conversations about the fall of the government in Russia to a focus, and the government fell.

This means that, though we can work on a macro level to understand the nature of society, it is important at least to recognize how the micro processes of human interaction help make the social structures come to life. In this section we first consider the influence of interaction and groups on human behavior, then examine theories that help us understand human interaction.

The Power of the Group

As we have already seen, most of what people do is done with other humans. What we now need to consider is the influence that people have on the behavior and the beliefs of one another. As we will see, in the process of social interaction the behavior, views, and other characteristics of humans are certainly altered.

We can begin by considering again Stanley Milgram's (1974) experiment on obedience to authority. You will remember that Milgram was able to induce 60 percent of the research subjects to give what they thought was an electric shock of 450 volts to a person they already believed was in danger of being severely harmed by the experiment. In other variations of the experiment Milgram introduced other actors into the research setting to examine their effects on obedience. In one variation he included two authority figures instead of just one, and in another variation he introduced two other people who the "teacher" (the research subject giving the shock) believed were also "teachers" for the experiment.

These additional individuals significantly affected the results of the research. When two authority figures were in disagreement about continuing the electric shocks, none of the research subjects gave shocks at the 450-volt level, in contrast to more than 60 percent who did so when only a single authority

figure ordered them to do so. Most interesting at this point is the effect of two "peers" who were secretly told to defy the authority figure. In this case, when the "teacher" had allies for defying authority, the obedience rate fell from over 60 percent to only 10 percent.

Many other studies have also concluded that people have a powerful influence on the behavior and perceptions of one another. In one of the earliest and most noted experiments of this kind, Asch (1952) asked a person to judge the length of lines drawn on a card. But before the person gave an answer several other people were secretly told to verbally give an obviously incorrect judgment of the length. After hearing these other judgments, 74 percent of the subjects agreed with the wrong answers at least once. With further questioning, it was found that some of the subjects were actually unaware they were wrong in their perceptions of the length of the line, whereas others knew the group's estimate was wrong but conformed to it so as not to appear "different."

Experiments like these suggest the degree to which people will conform to a group, even when they do not agree with the group's behavior or opinions. If the group becomes involved in deviant or violent behavior, for example, people sometimes go along with it even though they disapprove.

Group Decision Making. Because most important decisions in complex societies are made by committees, we must understand how these decisions are reached, how they can be manipulated, and how to improve the quality of the decision making process. The jobs of millions can be affected by decisions made in the corporate boardroom; the lives of many more can be affected by the decisions made in a president's cabinet.

There are two important aspects of committee decision making that should concern us, and both are interrelated. One common principle is involved; in the presence of others, people can be convinced of things they would not accept if alone. Thus, if a group has made a wrong decision, though it may be clear to most people outside the group that the decision is wrong, the group may be able to counter outside criticism with its own mutual support. On their own, people find it difficult to maintain an opinion with which everyone else disagrees. But when a group as a whole has made an incorrect decision, they provide their own social support system, leading them to stick to their original decision. An economic depression may be getting worse, but we hear that prosperity is around the corner; a war may be lost, but we hear that victory is at hand. This phenomenon has been referred to as "groupthink" by Janis (1972).

A related phenomenon is called the "risky shift." Again, according to the principle that people can maintain attitudes with group support they could not maintain alone, people can also shift to extreme attitudes they would not hold without group support. The risky shift phenomenon does not occur with all groups, and we now have some evidence that cultural values play a role in producing a risky shift. Hong (1978) has found that a risky shift is more likely to occur in group decisions among Americans than Chinese. Hong's interpretation is that bold risky action is more respected in American culture, whereas more cautious, calculated action is respected among the Chinese. Thus, in groups the Chinese are likely to make even more cautious decisions than are Americans.

There are other significant cultural differences in group decision-making processes, and one has received particular attention in recent years. The Japanese are much more likely to work for group consensus by means of collective decision making. In contrast to people in Western cultures, especially the United States, the Japanese feel uncomfortable about allowing one person to make most decisions without extensive input by all involved. This method of making decisions (called *"nemawashi,"* or "root-binding") takes more time but has the positive outcome of creating more agreement and cooperation (Christopher, 1983). Recent research in the United States indicates that wider involvement in group decision making increases membership commitment and cooperation (Knoke, 1981). Also, even if the decision-making process is less democratic, an increase in communication about the decisions that

have been made can help produce more agreement and cooperation.

Interaction in Everyday Life

Having considered the social roles people are given by their society and the development of the self, we can now examine one of the most useful social psychological theories of everyday interaction. This theory is useful because it can help you understand much of what you and other people do in everyday social interaction.

The master of this perspective on everyday interaction was Erving Goffman, whose books on the subject are highly interesting and readable (Goffman, 1959, 1961, 1963a, 1967, 1971). Goffman's perspective is often called by the awkward term **dramaturgical theory,** but the term should be easy to remember because it refers to human interaction as a stage production or drama. Goffman took quite literally the lines from Shakespeare's *As You Like It,* which begins, "All the world's a stage, And all men and women merely players."

Role Performance. As we saw in Chapter 4, people come to accept roles like teacher, student, wife, athlete, minister, business executive, and so on. Once given these roles, Goffman stressed how people and others around them are concerned with **role performance.** We judge ourselves and are judged by others in terms of how well we perform in the roles we are given or have adopted. A good performance gains us status or respect with ourselves and our audience — the people with whom we interact and who are observing our role performances.

Following this logic we can then see how people become concerned with **impression management** — controlling the impressions others have of us to enhance our role performance. Goffman asks not so much what is the "true" self, but rather, what type of image a person is most capable of giving to others through impression management.

Impression management is a complicated task because each role taken by an individual has many expectations and images associated with it. For example, a role like "campus playboy" involves many images, activities, and other characteristics that must be performed well if the person is to be judged a competent campus playboy. The clothing style must be correct, for an improper style of shirt or shoes may dramatically stand out to others who know the role, and the incompetent person will lose status. Quite often body language is involved in role performances. People who are judged especially good at a certain role may be very good at the proper walk, way of holding the head, or moving their arms. For example, some people claim to be able to distinguish a career military person by the way he or she walks. Speech patterns are also often important for good role performance. It may simply be the style of speech or knowledge of a special terminology. For example, I have always found it interesting that proper role performance requires that social scientists use the German pronunciation of Max Weber's name, (the German "v" sound for the "w"). Also, acceptance into the British upper class, among other things, requires the proper accent. And acceptance as a competent computer specialist today requires what seems an ever increasing list of special terminology.

Every role has many subtle but important images, styles, behavior patterns, and tasks that must be performed well to be accepted as a competent role player. This is especially true with an audience who knows the role expectations well.

What makes all of this more complex is that people play multiple roles. In addition to being mother and wife, a woman may be a teacher or business executive, political activist in the community, and/or religious leader. Each of these roles has expectations that are usually complex and often subtle. It can become difficult to perform well before a knowledgeable audience, and many of the separate role expectations and images can be in conflict. The problems of multiple roles are not always great because we usually have multiple audiences as well. To one audience we are husband and father, to another audience a business manager, to still another audience perhaps a "playboy" business manager. We can therefore give separate, distinct performances before each of the separate audiences. However, problems often occur when two or more separate

audiences come together. Impression management becomes very difficult in the face of conflicting images given to these audiences in the past.

It is also useful to recognize that performances are not always solo. As in the theater, teams work together to present a good performance. Examples of performance teams include husband and wife trying to present a favorable image to people outside the family, a division within a company trying to create a favorable image to company executives, and a college fraternity trying to impress new students. Similar to actors in a stage production, these performance teams may rehearse their lines and performances. But the reality of a collective performance may be simply recognized by these actors in everyday life without conscious coordination of activities. For example, while in the presence of important guests, children may behave improperly. One parent may simply give the other a look that says "do something with those kids." The parents, in other words, are working together to present a favorable image of the family.

Finally, we may consider Goffman's useful analogy of the *front stage* and *backstage* in everyday interactions. There are often special places in which role performances are carried out—this would be the front stage. The backstage includes those areas the actors hope the audience will not see. The backstage is where actors can relax from the efforts of maintaining proper impression management before an audience.

Depending on the role performed, the front stage may require important stage props, without which the correct image may not be created and the performance is therefore discredited. For example, a physician must have an acceptable waiting room for patients. A waiting room that appears shabby and unclean, without the proper chairs, potted plants, and magazines, can lead to an image problem. In the course of participating in research on veterinarians a few years ago, my colleagues and I found an interesting distinction between small animal veterinarians and large animal veterinarians. Veterinarians who specialize in treating large animals tend to work with farmers, who are concerned less with the office props than with economic results. However, small animal veterinarians cater to the pet owners in urban areas who tend to see a veterinarian as a medical doctor who treats animals. Therefore, these veterinarians have found that their practice is enhanced if their front stage office gives some resemblance to that of a doctor for humans. In the backstage, however, where pet owners seldom go, any resemblance to the work area of doctors for humans dramatically ends.

Most other performance teams have a front stage and a backstage. In the average home, for example, there is a room where important guests are entertained (front stage) and a place like the bedroom or den where only close friends or relatives are invited (backstage). In the front stage, the furniture is better, the pictures and books on the coffee table are "proper" for the image of the family, and more effort is given to keeping things neat and orderly. Other places where a backstage-front stage separation is clearly evident are restaurants, most retail stores, government agencies, and massage parlors (Bryant and Palmer, 1975).

There are, of course, degrees of closeness between people. With some people we know well there is less concern with impression management. We know they know us well, have seen many performances, and know we are competent. A slip in the performance creates less concern. But there are others we find very important to impress for various reasons. Thus, there is more formality and greater effort in the performance. One indicator of the closeness of the relationship between two individuals, for example, is whether or not either is allowed into the other's backstage.

In one sense, Goffman's dramaturgical perspective fits well with a micro conflict perspective (Collins, 1975). We find performance teams or individual actors trying to manipulate others through creating and maintaining the proper impression. The audience may be aware of this and is therefore on guard to catch slips in the performance. And if for no other reward, the impression management is important in maintaining a favorable self-image, which can be a very important reward in and of itself. On the audience's part, the watch for a slip in the performance may reduce the status of the performer and thereby improve the status of the audience — "that person is not as skilled in that role as I."

COLLECTIVE BEHAVIOR

Thus far we have considered social interaction only between two individuals, among individuals in small groups, and interaction heavily guided by norms or role expectations. But there is also social interaction among people in very large groups where traditional norms guiding behavior are less specific or even absent.

In May 1985, for example, the fans at an international soccer match in Brussels, Belgium, rioted, killing 38 people and injuring over 300. Before a soccer match between an Italian and a British team began, British fans were taunting Italian fans, which led to some fighting. Very soon the fighting spread to several hundred fans, with the British primarily leading the attack. Although not often so destructive, riots like these are quite common in Europe and Latin America. And, of course, similar behavior is found in other events in the United States, such as rock concerts.

The general subject in which sociologists study crowd behavior is called **collective behavior,** which refers to group behavior that is relatively unplanned and spontaneous. Most behavior in groups is highly regulated by norms or rules — the extreme case being behavior in formal organizations or bureaucracies where the expected behavior of individuals is explicitly described. In contrast, a good example of collective behavior is behavior during or shortly after a major natural disaster (Weller and Quarantelli, 1973). In this situation new groups of people are often formed in which members must act but there are no rules of action.

There is a good deal of controversy among sociologists about what type of group behavior should be included in the subject of collective behavior (Miller, 1985; Quarantelli and Weller, 1974). There is agreement that unstructured crowd behavior such as panics, riots, hysterical contagion, and disaster behavior should be included in the field of collective behavior, but until recently the group behavior we call social movements was always included within the subject matter of collective behavior. **Social movements** are more organized and long-lasting groups trying to create or resist social change in the society (such as the Civil Rights Movement). Thus, because of the relatively more organized nature of social movements, many sociologists argue they must be considered as a different kind of group behavior.

Early Views of Crowds. Most early social scientists wrote about crowds with many negative biases and even strong fears. In the work of Gustave Le Bon (1895), for example, crowd behavior was believed to be the result of a dominance of the "collective mind" over the "civilized mind." Although normally repressed in "civilized" societies, the collective mind could be brought out when people gathered in large crowds, thus making these people "irrational" and dangerous. This "collective mind" was believed to be inherited from our "primitive" ancestors, and according to Le Bon, more likely found in "women, children, and savages." These "lower orders" were therefore seen as more likely to participate in crowd behavior like riots. Le Bon also believed that the crowd was primarily destructive, especially when the lower classes were involved in it.

Like most scholars of his time, Le Bon was a member of the upper classes. He saw the world through the eyes of the upper classes, and unlike today, there was little effort directed toward understanding the behavior and position of people in the lower classes. Because of this upper-class bias, Le Bon's ideas are often called the "aristocratic view" of crowds.

In contrast to the theories of earlier social scientists, however, contemporary studies of crowd behavior like demonstrations and riots indicate that crowds are not often irrational and guided only by destructive emotional urges (Couch, 1968).

In fact, angry crowds often operate with a sense of "elementary natural justice" that has a logic that can be understood, even if one does not agree with the behavior of the crowd. For example, in the bread riots of eighteenth-century France, crowds did in fact break into bakeries and take bread, but they usually left what they believed was a just payment for the bread (Rudé, 1964). In the urban riots during the 1960s in the United States, rioters did not often burn and loot every store in the ghetto area. Rather, they were more likely to burn and loot white-owned stores where they believed the store owner had

been taking advantage of the poor. One may not agree with such crowd behavior, but the crowd's sense of rationality must be recognized. Riots, in other words, are not simply caused by crazy, irrational people on a destructive rampage. This is not to say, however, that all crowd behavior is rational. What we must guard against are assumptions that consider all crowds as somehow irrational and "bad."

Le Bon's views of the crowd were not totally useless. He did see that a feeling of power in numbers could make people bolder in a crowd and that there could be a circular emotional reaction within a crowd that heightened excitement among people. This later view of "collective excitement" through a "circular emotional reaction" was used by one of the early American sociologists writing about the crowd, Herbert Blumer (1939). A "circular emotional reaction" is said to occur when one person's excitement creates a reaction of excitement in another person, which in turn is passed back to the first person to create more excitement in this person, and so on. Although useful in understanding how excitement can spread, the idea must not be carried too far. If this emotional reaction were so simple, we would all become uncontrollable once anyone in a crowd became excited, which is obviously not the case.

Theories of Collective Behavior

We are now ready to consider some recent theories and research that can help us understand such behavior as riots at soccer matches and other forms of collective behavior. The type of theory found in the work of Blumer described above can be called **contagion theory.** The focus of this theory is the "emotional circular reaction" said to occur, making the emotion contagious, somewhat like a disease. Although this type of theory is not without value, we will consider four recent theories that are more useful.

Emergent Norm Theory. The basic premise of **emergent norm theory** is that new norms emerge within the context of a crowd that redefine what is expected of people (Turner and Killian, 1972). In other words, in answer to the question, "why do people do things in crowds they otherwise may not do?," emergent norm theory explains it is because new norms emerge or old ones are temporarily redefined that guide the behavior. For example, during a campus "panty raid" it becomes "ok" to break into the girls' dorm or destroy campus property because the crowd has collectively redefined previous norms.

As we know, norms are social products and are created by people in a society through a long process of historical development. Thus, because norms are social products they can at times be recreated or redefined by a group. At times, a crowd can represent the group that, at least temporarily, produces collective agreement on redefining norms previously inhibiting such behavior. And again this can be understood in reference to the power of the group over individual behavior, even over individual thinking and perception.

Rational Calculus Theory. A **rational calculus theory** of crowd behavior agrees that people are often influenced by the group into doing things they would not otherwise do, but for different reasons. According to this theory, changes in the risk versus rewards of involvement in crowd action are more important in motivating participation than any change in norms (Berk, 1974). A "risk/reward ratio" is used in analyzing the outbreak of crowd behavior. If the risk of getting caught and punished for the behavior is high, whereas any reward for participation is low, the crowd behavior is not likely. However, if something changes to make the risk very low and/or the rewards very high, then crowd behavior is more likely.

Considering first the risk factor, the power of numbers mentioned about 100 years ago by Le Bon can be important. As a crowd grows in size it may overwhelm the social control authorities. Individuals in the crowd feel they cannot be caught and punished by the police, so their participation is more likely. On the reward side, a belief may emerge that important changes may be achieved by attacking some group, or that many material goods can be taken in a riot, making the riot more likely. On a college campus, a "fun-seeking riot" may break out when something causes a crowd to emerge in an atmosphere of "partying." The size of the crowd is likely to overwhelm the campus police.

In comparing emergent norm theory with rational calculus theory, we find that the latter does not focus on norms or rules. This theory simply assumes that individuals in crowds make more or less rational decisions about their risk versus rewards.

Convergence Theory. Although convergence theory may not contradict the above, the stress of this theory is on what brings like-minded people together, forming a crowd. In other words, there can be a riot at a soccer match because people who like to fight are commonly attracted to soccer matches. The focus of this theory is therefore the process by which people with similar characteristics are pulled together to form a crowd (Miller, 1985).

The vast majority of more than 300 black urban riots in the United States between 1964 and 1968 began in the evening and during summer months (Salert and Sprague, 1980). During this time young people were out of school, unemployed, and often in the streets because of the summer heat. These riots occurred in urban areas where poor and already angry minorities could easily converge in one place when some special event occurred. In England, soccer matches attract young males who favor a "macho" image of aggressiveness. And in a setting of high unemployment that gives more freedom, and international matches that bring out nationalism, soccer riots are possible.

These theories are not necessarily contradictory. Each focuses on a set of factors that can be useful in understanding crowd behavior. But before we summarize them, there is a final, more complex theory to consider.

Value-Added Theory. Smelser (1962) describes five stages in the development of collective behavior, each of which adds a new value (so to speak), making the outbreak of collective behavior more likely. Thus, the theory is often called **value-added theory.**

The first stage is called *structural conduciveness.* The factors at this stage do not help cause the collective behavior as much as simply make it possible to occur. For example, to have a riot there must be many people who can interact with one another at one point in time and space. A prison riot cannot occur if all prisoners are locked in individual cells. Also, if a panic is to occur people must believe that escape from some threat is possible, but not certain. A fire in a crowded theater with only a few exits can produce a panic; a fire in an almost empty theater where exit is quite simple produces no panic. I again note that most urban riots have occurred in crowded ghetto areas when many people are out in the streets.

The second factor is called *structural strain.* At this point Smelser presents a functional theory of what has created social strain in the society that led many people to feel some type of anger, discontent, or fear. The basic assumption is that only people feeling some type of discontent will participate in collective behavior events. Although most sociologists generally accept this assumption, there are major points of disagreement with Smelser's theory at this point. (1) There are many variations of discontent theory that attempt to explain the anger or fear leading to collective behavior. This qualification presents no problem for the value-added scheme itself because any of the particular discontent theories can be used at stage two in the scheme. (2) Other theorists, however, argue that fear or anger (although usually found among collective behavior participants) is not one of the most important causes of collective behavior (McCarthy and Zald, 1977). They argue that many, perhaps most, angry or frightened people do not participate in collective behavior; thus other factors are more important in the development of collective behavior. The research findings on this point are mixed (Muller, 1985; Kerbo, 1982; Kerbo and Shaffer, 1986), but certainly we can say that at least many types of collective behavior require us to study the causes and pattern of strain or discontent to understand the collective behavior. Finally, (3) there are some types of collective behavior, such as "fun-seeking riots," where it is difficult to locate an underlying feeling of fear or discontent. The behavior of British rioters at a soccer match may be understood in reference to

the frustrations of unemployment leading to an angry attack on a substitute target. But it is more difficult to explain a fun-seeking riot after a campus beer party with reference to some underlying discontent.

The third stage involves a *generalized belief.* This means that people must have some explanation of the source of their fear or anger and what could be done about it before some type of collective behavior is possible. No matter how angry people become, if they do not understand the source of their troubles, there is no target for attack and no prescribed action for change. With angry people, however, an "explanation" for their anger and what or who can be attacked, whether or not correct, is likely to develop rapidly. This is one reason minority groups (Jews, blacks) in a society may be attacked in times of frustration for the general population. They make easy, often powerless scapegoats. However, as often as scapegoating occurs, we must not assume that all people in collective behavior events are always acting in an irrational manner, as the more powerful people who become targets of crowd action try to make people believe.

The next stage requires a *precipitating event* or precipitating factors. With all of the factors above in existence, there must be some event that focuses the attention of the crowd on their common anger or the possibility of collective behavior. In the case of a riot or hostile outburst, the precipitating event can be described as the spark that sets off the explosion. In the Watts riot of August 1965 in Los Angeles, the precipitating event was an attempted arrest of a carload of black residents. During the attempted arrest a crowd had gathered to witness what was believed to be more police brutality.

Finally, *mobilization* of the crowd is necessary. Often the mobilization comes at almost the same time as the precipitating event, but there can be a significant delay. Mobilization primarily requires that some leader or leaders show the way or become guides for action. These leaders may not recognize themselves as such, or they may explicitly try to direct the crowd. Often a leader may emerge simply because he or she is in a better position to be seen or heard by the crowd. For example, we can assume that the mobilization beginning the Watts riot oc-curred when the first person threw a brick through a police car window, leading others to take similar action.

Understanding the development of collective be-havior also requires examination of *social control.* Smelser notes that social control agents can inter-vene in each of the five steps of the value-added scheme to prevent the collective behavior. For example, a prison riot can be prevented by isolating inmates — eliminating structural conduciveness. Social control could also be directed toward the source of structural strain, thus reducing the anger or fear. Or social control could be used to manipulate generalized beliefs, confusing people to prevent their action or proving more accurate information showing that the original generalized belief is inac-curate. Finally, social control can attempt to prevent a precipitating event from occurring and/or leaders from mobilizing action.

Smelser's theory organizes many of the ideas contained in other theories and orders them chrono-logically. For this reason, his theory provides a sim-ple tool that can be used to understand many collective behavior events one may encounter in the daily newspapers.

CHAPTER SUMMARY

Key Terms

socialization, 170
cultural determinism, 171
the self, 172
looking glass self, 173
the "I" and "me," 173
primary socialization, 174
anticipatory socialization, 174
developmental socialization, 174
resocialization, 174
hidden curriculum, 176

mass society, 178
dramaturgical theory, 183
role performance, 183
impression management, 183
collective behavior, 185
social movements, 185
contagion theory, 186
emergent norm theory, 186
rational calculus theory, 187
value-added theory, 187

Content

Humans are biological organisms with much of their behavior influenced by biology. With the human animal, however, most behavior is guided by culture and learning. A socialization process is therefore required to shape individuals so that they can fit into a particular culture and society.

A key element of this socialization process is the development of a self. Through interaction with others we come to see ourselves as others see us, thus leading to a socially acquired self-concept. We see ourselves as intelligent, popular, athletic, ugly, and so on because of the creation of this "looking glass self."

There are many agents of socialization in modern societies. One of the most important, is the family, where we have the most social contact and social contact in the most important early years. A per-son's peer group is also an important socialization agent, especially in modern societies that have a youth subculture. But also important in modern soci-eties are the mass media because of the widespread contact people have with TV, movies, and the printed page.

The socialization process must also be considered from a conflict perspective. During childhood social-ization, for example, there is often conflict between parents and children over what is acceptable behav-ior, with parents having varying power resources to influence their children. The resources parents have (or lack) for socializing their children help us under-stand the different outcomes in childhood social-ization. The socialization process helps maintain in-equality and dominance in the wider society. Those people on the bottom of society are often made to feel they deserve no better through the influence of the socialization process; thus they are kept at the bottom and social order is promoted.

In our examination of social interaction we first considered the power of groups over individuals. Our behavior toward others, including our ability to harm others as well as our perceptions and decision making, are heavily influenced by the group situation.

To understand everyday social interaction we considered Goffman's dramaturgical theory. This theory focuses on the performance of roles before others considered to be the audience. An important part of our everyday social interaction involves impression management so as to give others (and ourselves) favorable images of ourselves to enhance our position or status within the group.

We considered the social psychological dynamics of crowd behavior. Although the statement can be carried too far, people sometimes do behave differently in large crowds, and such behavior must be recognized as possibly constructive as well as destructive to the society. Several theories of crowd behavior were considered, concluding with Smelser's value-added theory, which organizes much of what we know about the causes of crowd behavior into a time sequence process.

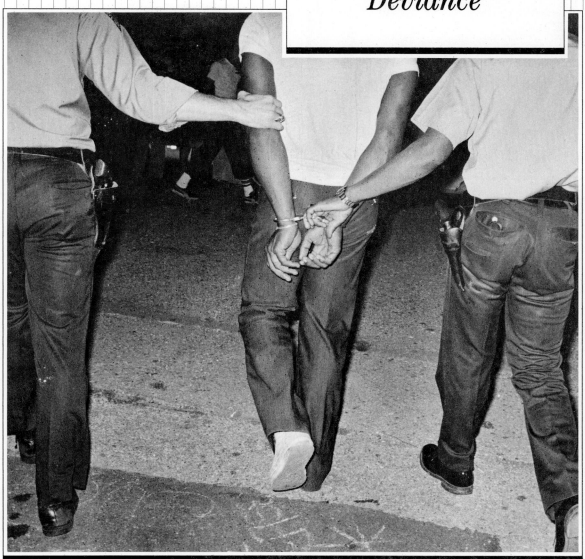

CHAPTER 8

Social Control and Deviance

In fact, the shift from a criminality of blood to a criminality of fraud forms part of a whole complex mechanism, embracing the development of production, the increase of wealth, a higher juridical and moral value placed on property relations, stricter methods of surveillance, a tighter partitioning of the population, more efficient techniques of locating and obtaining information: the shift in legal practices is correlative with an extension and a refinement of punitive practices.
—Michel Foucault, Discipline and Punishment: The Birth of the Prison

Every society must provide at least a minimum level of social order. People must be able to leave their homes without much concern about death in the streets and feel at least some security about the property and family they left at home. In our daily routines, we must be able to predict with at least some accuracy how other people will behave, the rules to be followed, and the rules to be broken. Without such predictability and security the daily process of meeting human needs becomes very difficult, and a spiral of overt conflict and social disorder will emerge, as it has time and again throughout history as societies disintegrate into revolution or civil war.

Consider just one aspect of post-World War I Germany that established fertile ground for Hitler's movement; between 1914 and 1923 the total inflation rate in Germany was 1,422,900,000 percent! Many factors contribute to inflation, but one factor is a lack of predictability or faith in the future social order. Without faith in future stability, people buy as much as possible, as soon as possible, which pushes up prices. Investors within the country and without withdraw investments, reducing economic stability and producing a devalued currency, as happened in South Africa in 1985 with increasing political violence.

The current situation in Lebanon represents a case of extreme social disorder (see Box 8.1). The term "Lebanon Syndrome" is in fact often used today as a general description of extensive social breakdown. Lebanon's crime rate, for example, is perhaps the highest in the world (37,384 crimes per 100,000 population, compared with 4,890 in the United States in the mid-1970s [Kurian, 1979,

p. 337), and for a time in recent years there were as many as 100 rival political and religious groups with 53 different military factions actually fighting each other in civil war. In the 1940s a new independent government in Lebanon was created after colonial rule by the British and French. But by the early 1970s the compromises once held together by a central government broke down and social disintegration followed.

As the case of Lebanon indicates, social order does not come automatically. There must be mechanisms to create and maintain it, some of which we have already considered in the socialization process. But there are many other social controls to be examined in this chapter.

It must be stressed, however, that stability and social order do not mean an absence of social conflict. It often means that the social conflict has been repressed or held underground, at least for a time. When we say there is social order, we must also ask "whose social order?" For as we will see more clearly in the following chapters, some groups in the society usually benefit from the status quo more than others, which is to say the current social order favors their interests. When a particular social order breaks down, as it has in Lebanon, different groups will work to create a new social order, but one that favors *their* interests.

To say that social order is never complete is to say there will always be at least some departure from the norms. In fact, when there are norms and laws in a society (as there are in all societies), there must be some deviance or at least a threat of deviance; otherwise there is no need for norms and laws. This can be stated even more strongly by say-

---

BOX 8.1

National Disintegration: The Example of Lebanon

Lebanon, before it began to disintegrate into warring clans in the mid-1970s, had been a small paradise of a country. With its glorious green mountains, dotted with rich Christian, Muslim, and Druze villages descending to the azure blue of the Mediterranean, it had worked out a special social compact among its sectarian members.

By the 1980s it had become hell in a small place. Its hatreds imploded. Christians killed Muslims without quarter. Muslims killed Christians with a ferocity unknown since the Crusades. Druze and Palestinians entered the dark fray, until at any one time there were as many as 53 "irregular" armies fighting in Lebanon. Indeed, the "Lebanon syndrome" became the metaphor for irregular warfare and purposeless killing in our times.

What had happened here? The tragedy was played out in four stages. First, the country had been held together by a 1943 pact hammered out between the country's traditionally warring sects and clans which gave each side a part of the power. For 35 years it worked beautifully. Second, the balance began to unravel — at first, only underneath the surface — when the Muslim birthrate in the late '60s began to surpass that of the Christian population. Third, the change in the balance of internal power was known by everyone, but no one said anything about it for fear of upset or upheaval. Fourth, the explosion came in 1970 and 1971, when the Palestinians thrown out of Jordan in the war with King Hussein poured into Lebanon, thus destroying whatever was left of the crucially important population balance. At that point, the country was doomed.

When I returned to Beirut in the spring of 1977, I wanted to know what the war had been like — really like, inside. "What is striking here," a member of the French

---

ing that if a society has no apparent deviants at one time, *some will be found*. I explain this statement more fully in the second part of this chapter.

SOCIAL CONTROL

In the earliest human societies social control was the exclusive task of the kinship system. The dominant family member, often a dominant male, would enforce social control within the family. Or in more democratic kinship systems, social control was enforced collectively against deviant members. The kinship system also had the task of enforcing social control externally. If a family member was injured by someone from the outside, other members of the family were responsible for avenging the wrong.

As societies became more complex, separate institutions for the maintenance of social control emerged. Transgressions against individuals or families came to be defined as crimes against the state and were dealt with through a criminal justice system and a police force. In fact, it became illegal to "take the law into your own hands." Other institutions with at least some responsibility for social control in the society also emerged, including the educational system, occupational and economic organizations, and religion. The educational system works to enforce social order by convincing children they must follow rules and cooperate with others. Occupational organizations discipline their members, and economic bureaucracies have many means of creating an orderly work force, as we have already seen. And religion usually operates to maintain social order through its stress on socially defined (or elite-defined) moral standards.

architectural team that was then trying to redesign the city said, standing in the midst of this perverse devastation and shaking his head, "is that it is as if there were a willful and deliberate effort to destroy."

Umayam Yaktin, one of a group then studying the "Lebanon syndrome" for the American University of Beirut, told me, "Both sides wanted to kill innocent people. All the hospitals were hit — from all sides. I could go into Freud — that people were born with innate aggressive impulses — but I think it's more than that."

What the world was seeing, actually, was a totally new kind of war. Once the various sides saw that no group could win, at any cost, each side began to bomb its own people, to hit its own neighbourhoods with artillery, and to bomb theatres in which its own people were watching movies. The American general Andrew Goodpaster told me this was "irrational warfare."

Whatever title one wanted to give it, it was not really war; it was the breakdown of war. And it catapulted the foreign correspondent — as well as all the other "in-between people," like diplomats, businessmen, missionaries, Red Cross people — into a new kind of danger that we thought was impossible in "modern" times.

In these dark new wars, there were no borders. There were no recognized civilians — indeed, the "civilians" became the deliberate targets. There were no respected neutrals. Red Cross trucks and hospitals were deliberately hit, instead of being protected. Children fought and were killed, without second thoughts.

Source: Georgie Anne Geyer, "The Menace of Global Anarchy," *Britannica Book of the Year* (Chicago: University of Chicago Press, 1985), pp. 12–13.

Methods of Social Control

Durkheim (1966, pp. 68–69) once wrote:

Imagine a society of saints, a perfect cloister of exemplary individuals. Crimes, properly so called, will there "be unknown," but faults which appear venial to the layman will create there the same scandal that the ordinary offense does in ordinary consciousnesses. If, then, this society has the power to judge and punish, it will define these acts as criminal and will treat them as such.

The point of Durkheim's statement is that all societies will have deviance; no matter how trivial the deviance may appear in a society that highly values the rules that have been broken. Thus, the question of whether or not a society has deviance is meaningless; rather, we ask how much and what kind of deviance exist. In a similar manner, we need not ask if a society employs some means of social control to induce conformity; rather, we ask what means of social control will be used, and who benefits. With respect to the latter we must ask, is the social control used to exploit one group (an ethnic minority, the lower class, etc.) or is the social control used to induce a minimum level of social order necessary for the well-being of all in the society? Quite often these two questions are difficult to answer. Those who are exploiting another group (such as the white rulers of South Africa) will always claim their use of force is for the common good.

External Means of Social Control. Although the distinction is sometimes difficult to make, we can generally divide methods of social control into external means and internal means. External means are some inducement or force, whereas internal means rely on a person's acceptance of rules and values. With

Tokyo police are well known in their neighborhoods. What is the impact of a visible and familiar police presence on crime and deviance? What does the presence of a policeman on the street mean to you? Do you know your neighborhood police officer? (© Hires/Gamma-Liaison)

external means of social control the person is conforming to achieve some reward or avoid punishment. With internal means of social control people conform because they believe it is right and proper to do so; in other words, "moral" constraint is operating.

Force. Throughout history some form of overt force or threat of force has been employed as a means of social control, especially since the emergence of stable agricultural communities. However, force or the threat of it as a means of social control is often

expensive and inefficient in many situations. For example, force requires surveillance or territorial control; otherwise those experiencing it may simply escape or organize resistance (Collins, 1975, p. 313). Also, the use of force requires extensive resources: weapons and personnel to operate the weapons, which are both resources that could be used for other means. Finally, force or its threat cannot be used to control people needed to perform tasks that require initiative and creativeness, and who must work independently. Prisoners can be induced to dig ditches at gunpoint, but other means of compliance will be necessary if these prisoners are to create adequate computer programs.

Even though overt force may not be the primary means of social control in industrial societies, it continues to be used against some groups, and it remains a means of control when all else fails. For the control of the domestic population, this means of force is concentrated in the police, or the **criminal justice system** more generally (including the courts and prison system, as well as the police). Looking at Table 8.1, we find that Western industrial societies (and Japan) have police forces of similar size, but other aspects of their criminal justice systems do differ significantly. For example, Japan's police force is well known for its efficiency, though it

TABLE 8.1. *Number of people in the population for every police officer — comparative figures, 1980*

Nation	Population per police officer
Austria	466
Belgium	586
Canada	358
France	485
Italy	286
Japan	556
Netherlands	553
Poland	350
Portugal	654
United Kingdom	400
United States	459

SOURCE: Constructed from *Britannica World Data Annual* (1985, pp. 940–944).

is also known for its power to invade civil liberties that are somewhat more protected by the American criminal justice system (see Box 8.2).

Despite more formal legal rights with respect to police restrictions, however, the United States has a larger prison population (per population size) than any other major Western industrial nation. In fact, the United States has more people in prison (as a percent of population) than any other major industrial nation except the Soviet Union. The continuing need to use force to maintain social control among some segments of the population is shown in the relationship between police force size and level of inequality in U.S. cities. The greater the level of income inequality in a city, the larger its police force as a percent of the population (Jacobs, 1979). This indicates that higher inequality generates more conflict between the more affluent and the poor (Blau and Blau, 1982), and the police force grows in an attempt to suppress this conflict, which can come in the form of lower-class crime. The relationship between inequality and conflict is also indicated by cross-national figures showing that higher inequality within a nation is related to high levels of political violence (Muller, 1985).

Material rewards. With the abundance of material goods produced in industrial societies, social control

Prison overcrowding in New York City is so extreme that this floating troop barracks has been refitted as a jail. The barge, "The Bibby Venture," serves as a 196-bed detention center.
(© UPI/Bettmann Newsphotos)

BOX 8.2

Crime and the Criminal Justice System in Japan

With Japan having one of the world's lowest crime rates, the country's police and prosecutors have been praised by criminologists, emulated by foreign countries and held in high esteem by the Japanese public.

Police catch 60 percent of all violators of Japan's criminal law — including 88 percent of violent criminals and 97 percent of killers. Of suspects taken to trial in 1981, 99.88 percent were convicted, thanks in large part to the fact that 89 percent of them signed confessions during interrogations by police and prosecutors.

But now doubts have been raised about the Japanese "super-cop" image. And attention is being focused on a authoritarian-like aspect of Japan's post-World War II democracy that has previously drawn little notice from either foreigners or Japanese.

The controversy centers on the fact that in interrogation rooms at Japanese police stations, suspects are isolated and without protection.

Officially, police can detain suspects for three days before they must go through what has become a mere formality of obtaining a judge's consent for two additional 10-day detentions. Usually, the total 23-day period enables police and prosecutors to extract confessions in interrogating sessions that, even the police acknowledge, normally last 10 to 12 hours a day.

But if even 23 days is not enough, police can — and do — rearrest suspects on a series of separate charges, thus stacking up detention periods during which continual interrogations are conducted, and question suspects about crimes not specified in the arrest warrants.

Although police are not often accused of physical brutality, as was common before the American occupation reforms after World War II, people who have endured lengthy interrogation periods have charged that authorities use mild forms of physical abuse and frequent psychological trickery. Police deny such charges.

Nearly all defendants who confess during interrogations but later claim innocence say it was the sheer length of the interrogation sessions that induced them to confess, according to Futaba Igarashi, a lawyer working with the Japan Federation of Bar Assns. on prisoner detention issues.

through material rewards becomes a greater possibility. If one group within the society is able to dominate the supply of material goods, this group can achieve great power over others by distributing these material rewards to those who obey their rules. Powerful dictators in less industrial societies often use a combination of material rewards and force to maintain their power. The ruling group's control over material rewards allows then to buy the support of a group that will then help protect the ruling group with force. In industrial societies, however, material goods are so abundant that most of

the population may be controlled through material rewards, bypassing the need for overt force, though of course this force is still likely to be used more often against those at the bottom of society.

Marx predicted that the working class in industrial capitalist nations would become more revolutionary through time. Many sociologists now recognize that Marx may not have been accurate in this view, in part, because he did not realize the extent to which the working class could be influenced by material rewards and consumerism (Aronowitz, 1974; Marcuse, 1964). Capitalist societies have been suc-

Interrogation, according to Seki, the detective official, usually is conducted for up to 12 hours a day, beginning at 9 A.M. and "ending at 7 or 8 P.M., or at the latest, 9 P.M."

There are no trials by jury in Japan and, until last year, judges apparently paid scant attention to the postwar constitution that forbids admission as evidence of confessions "made . . . after prolonged arrest or detention." They also had ignored a constitutional ban against convicting defendants "in cases where the only proof against him was his own confession."

Police retain a high level of public trust, because of their long record of efficiency in solving crimes and winning convictions.

Police also have won esteem partly from their efforts to be polite, even accommodating, to citizens. Illegal parking by deliverymen, salesmen, and customers that occurs day after day in front of small shops, for example, is overlooked — even when it causes massive traffic jams — so as not to inconvenience shopkeepers.

Neighborhood patrolmen get to know the people on their beat, sometimes offering advice on relations between husbands and wives and employment opportunities for children, Kokichi Shimoinaba, superintendent of the Tokyo Metropolitan Police, told foreign correspondents at a lunch here.

They also provide excellent service when asked to do so. Patrol cars respond, on average, within five minutes to calls for help anywhere in Tokyo. Occasionally, a patrol car will arrive while a citizen is still on the phone asking for help, Shimoinaba said.

Police are given a degree of authority most Americans would not tolerate because "Japanese people's consciousness of human rights is very low — a remnant of the prewar respect for authority," said Masahiro Hinamoto, chairman of a liaison committee of citizens' movements supporting defendants and convicts believed to have been framed by police.

Opinion polls confirm the immense trust placed in law enforcement authorities, Hinamoto admitted. Asked "Who protects human rights the most?", people responding to polls here rank the courts first and the police second.

Source: Sam Jameson, "Super-Cops of Japan; The Glow Fades," *Los Angeles Times*, Sept. 6, 1984.

cessful in creating a strong desire for material consumption through mass advertising, which sets the stage for this form of social control. When workers must follow the orders of those who control the jobs, and when workers must have the jobs to pay for the consumer goods they strongly desire, social control is made more simple.

Information control. Generally, ignorance is an effective means of social control. Nothing will be done by a group whose interests are being violated if that group is unaware of the situation. One of the basic rules of large organizations, including government agencies and corporations, is to provide as little information to the public as possible (Schattschneider, 1960). In an interesting case study of this, Molotch and Lester (1975) found that a major tactic of an oil company responsible for a major oil spill was to let out only as much information as necessary about its negligence, and to do so gradually, thus minimizing the effects of this information on the public. A similar pattern was found in the Nixon White House with their attempts to minimize the damage of the Watergate scandal.

Related to the control of information are attempts to influence opinion through making information supporting your interest group as widely known as possible. The wealthy are by no means the only people trying to manipulate information in their favor, but the wealthy have more resources with which to manipulate information. For example, advertising is not only an attempt to sell a product; it is also used to enhance the image of corporations (Miliband, 1969). We continually hear how oil companies are helping us by finding oil with "inadequate" profits, how chemical companies are giving us better lives, how safe all their products are, and so on. The more affluent in our society have also formed many organizations that specifically try to shape public opinion. The Council on Foreign Relations and the Committee for Economic Development are two such organizations funded by the U.S. upper class that are involved in public opinion influence (Domhoff, 1979; Shoup and Minter, 1977).

Government agencies have also been involved in secret attempts to influence public opinion, at times with clearly false information. For example, the CIA has secretly helped publish well over 1,000 books in recent years and at one time even established a dummy news service (Forum World Features) to provide news stories (sometimes false) to the world press (Mintz and Cohen, 1976, p. 238; Marchetti and Marks, 1974, pp. 156–181). There is also evidence that more than 400 American journalists have worked with the CIA from such publishers as the *New York Times*, CBS, and Time Inc. *(New York Times,* Sept. 12, 1977).

Finally, in considering the control of information we must consider the mass media, especially the printed media and TV, which carry the news. In the United States, the mass media are not censored as in many, perhaps most countries. But this is *not* to say that the mass media are not biased in their news coverage. First, television networks are highly dependent on the wealthy for their existence. On the one hand the major banks control considerable amounts of stock in the three major TV networks (U.S. Senate Committee on Governmental Affairs, 1980), and on the other hand the TV networks are very dependent on major corporations for advertis-

ing revenues. None of this means that the TV news is censored by major corporations, but the TV networks know they must be cautious in what they say.

It must also be recognized that the television programs most people see have an additional influence on shaping world views and information. Studies have shown that TV programs strongly support (and we can say reflect) the traditional way of thinking in the society (Gitlin, 1979; Sallach, 1974; Vidmar and Rokeach, 1974). There is no simple conspiracy to influence the mass media in this way. The process of image making is best viewed as circular. Mass media elites do have some influence over what we see and believe, but both wealthy and average people influence what the media elites present. I have already noted how the wealthy have influence; the average people have collective influence because the mass media must sell, and if the public doesn't buy, the media go out of business.

Let's consider a brief example. In the 1950s, Secretary of State John Foster Dulles reportedly withheld some information favorable to the new mainland Chinese government because he wanted to keep the Cold War going by showing only the negative side of China (Mosley, 1978). Given the political mood of the country at the time it was easy for political elites to keep the public misinformed about China — most of the public *wanted* to hate the Communist Chinese.

Finally, let's consider how a particular world view held by newspeople and the general population can lead to biased news reporting. In September 1983 the Soviet Union shot down a South Korean airliner, killing over 200 people. There are still many unanswered questions about what the airliner was doing over Soviet territory for more than two hours before it was shot down. But it is interesting that the day after the airliner was shot down, I watched Canadian TV commentators discuss the possibility that it was on some spy mission for the United States. In the United States, however, TV and newspapers gave almost no attention to such a possibility. Then, in the summer of 1984, a respected British magazine, the *Economist,* published a story that presented information strongly suggesting the South Korean airliner was in fact on a U.S. spy mission. Since that time two books have been published in the United States that also suggest this possibility (Dallin, 1985; Clubb, 1985). After the *Economist* story the issue was again front-page news—all over the world—but not in the United States. If the *Economist* story of a spy mission was reported at all in U.S. newspapers, it was well hidden behind other stories. Was the CIA telling newspeople not to print such stories? I think the most likely explanation of the behavior of U.S. journalists is that, like the American people, they couldn't believe such a story, or more accurately, didn't want to believe it, even in the face of evidence supporting it.

A more recent example involves the shooting down of an Iranian airliner in July of 1988 by the U.S. Navy, killing more than 290 civilians. As might be expected, over 80 percent of the American people said that the United States should not be blamed for this tragedy only two days after the event, and before any detailed investigation could be made (*New York Times,* July 5, 1988). It is quite possible that the American people were correct in their view; the point, however, is how quickly this positive view of the U.S. action was formed.

Internal Means of Social Control. As the example above indicates, what I am calling the internal means of social control is extremely important in understanding the overall process of social control. By the *internal means of social control* I am referring to the attitudes, values, and self-images people have developed that make them follow the rules, but at times also allow them to be easily manipulated and controlled by others. We can ask why people are so often ready to believe individuals in high positions, accept their unequal share of rewards, and are thus so easily controlled at times. Internal control, if successful, is most efficient and inexpensive. There is no need for surveillance, guns and prisons, or even extensive rewards to buy loyalty if internal control is extensive.

Internal control, of course, depends primarily on the socialization process examined in the previous chapter. But we can separate from this socialization process its content—what people come to believe

and how they view themselves. In this respect we can examine ideologies, rituals, and self-evaluations.

Ideologies. The belief systems that guide people's behavior and order the information they receive about the world can be called *ideologies*. These ideologies can be political, economic, religious, and usually a combination of all of these beliefs.

With respect to religious ideologies, Marx called religion the "opiate of the masses" because he stressed the tendency for religion to make people accept their position in life ("Give unto Ceasar") rather than try to change it. We must agree that this has often been the case, though certainly not always. As we will see in the next chapter, one of the most unequal, oppressive societies (to those at the bottom) was remarkably stable through a long period of history because of the Hindu religion. But we must also recognize that there are counterexamples, like the religious base of the black civil rights movements in the United States and South Africa, and church-sponsored reform in Central America.

Because of the importance of ideologies in leading people to support elites and counterideologies leading to the rejection of elites, the struggle for minds is often intense. We have already seen how the wealthy and government officials try to manipulate ideas. It is also important to note that various groups try to monitor what is taught in schools, for they recognize the importance of the struggle for minds. Most universities have trustees or directors who come from major corporations and the upper class (Smith, 1974; Dye, 1979; Kerbo, 1983, pp. 389–390; Useem, 1984). These trustees do not often censor what is taught in the classroom, but there are limits that are enforced from time to time.

Collective rituals. All societies have developed what can be called *collective rituals* that celebrate some important value or aspect of their society, most often religious and/or political heroes or values. Examples include celebration of the founding of a nation, the birth date of a political or religious leader, and so on. These emotional collective rituals can make the group and its values seem more important and even transcendental or god-given rather than simply human made. If something is considered simply created by humans, then it can be recreated and changed. But if something is made to appear part of inevitable law or made by a god, then it is worthier of strong respect (Collins, 1975, p. 153). Furthermore, the strong emotional support shown by others in collective rituals reinforces an individual's commitment.

It is understandable that through collective rituals people emphasize their commonality, that is, the social values, institutions, and social relationships they have in common. This means that the values, institutions, and social arrangements that exist, for whatever historical reasons, are given support and strengthened through collective rituals. Because of this, elites in the society seek to control collective rituals because through these rituals their position in the society comes to be associated with important traditions. Their power, therefore, can be more firmly established. And if the power and privileges of elites are threatened or weakened, a call for support through traditional rituals can be a means of reasserting the positions of elites.

Collective rituals also may involve emphasizing some outside threat, real or manufactured. One of the most soundly supported sociological ideas is that out-group conflict tends to produce in-group solidarity (Coser, 1967). Thus, the more powerful in the society can use the perceived threat as the basis for collective rituals that can strengthen their power in the society. In a classic study of this, Erikson (1966) found that the Salem witch hunts of the later 1600s were a means of strengthening the power of old religious elites. Likewise, in some capitalist societies, communism is as useful as the devil is for highly religious societies, and communist elites find "capitalist imperialists" of equal value.

Self-evaluations. A potential source of overt conflict and disorder in all societies is the unequal distribution of rewards and positions. Those on the bottom, with few rewards, become a potential source of disorder if they reject their low position. Following what we have already seen about the socialization process and the development of a self-concept, we can understand how people's self-evaluation can be constructed so that they come to view themselves as deserving a high or low position in the society, and thus do not threaten social order (Della Fave, 1980).

As we have already seen, beginning with our earliest socialization experiences we develop a self-image. When children reach school age the self-concept and self-evaluation are developed further by a wider social circle. But it is in adult years that this self-evaluation comes to be related to our high or low position in society (Rosenberg and Pearlin, 1978). The key to all this is that those toward the bottom of society usually come to have a lower self-evaluation and are thus more likely to accept their low position.

One of the most important sources of feedback in the self-evaluation process during adulthood is a person's employment. People's relation to authority, how they are treated by the boss and co-workers, contributes to their self-evaluation. Although those in lower positions usually receive more negative feedback about their worth, those in higher positions usually receive more positive feedback, and there are often many people below them ready to give praise.

Limits of Social Control. The extent to which social control is successfully employed in most societies can be rather frightening. You may remember that in the Milgram (1974) study discussed in earlier chapters, 60 percent of the research subjects followed orders to give what they believed was a 450-volt shock to a person already screaming in pain. Even 30 percent of the research subjects went so far as physically forcing the person's hand on the shock plate so the person could receive the 450 volts of electricity. None of the people in the research liked giving the 450-volt shock, and this shows even more clearly the power of authorities in inducing compliance to their orders. As Milgram pointed out in this study, we must learn the mechanisms that induce such compliance to authority if we are to understand how the German people allowed the execution of 6 million Jews, plus millions of other people. Although most of the German population during World War II did not know exactly what was happening in the extermination camps (Hughes, 1962), most of them did have some idea of what was happening, and thousands of Germans had to do the actual work of killing.

Turning to another example, we must realize that throughout history people have willingly obeyed the authorities who selected them for human sacrifice. In modern warfare we sometimes find a similar situation. For example, in just one battle during World War I, 145,000 French and British troops died taking only six miles of French territory. On just *one day* of battle on July 1, 1916, over 19,000 British soldiers were killed. But the soldiers on both sides marched on to battle the next day when ordered to do so.

We must recognize however, that social control and obedience are seldom complete. Sometimes soldiers do throw down their guns and refuse certain death, as they finally did in 1917 in Russia toward the end of World War I. Sometimes people selected for human sacrifice went kicking and screaming to their death. Less dramatically, millions of people in our society defy the authorities and break the norms, laws, and minor rules. This points up the existence of deviance, our subject for the remainder of this chapter.

DEVIANCE

We can define **deviance** as breaking the rules or norms of a society, either through behavior or beliefs that are prohibited or by failing to do what is required by the norms. Deviance ranges from the very serious (murder) to the very minor (perhaps talking in class). But once we leave these general characteristics of what is called deviance, the subject becomes much more complex. A distinction between what is and is not deviance, and what is minor or serious deviance, can vary from society to society, from one time period to another, and even from one context to another in the same society. And as we will also see, what is considered deviant in a society often depends on power and influence — the ability to label something or someone as deviant or prevent that label from being applied to someone else.

When raising the subject of deviance, the questions that most often come to mind are "what is wrong with those people?" and "why do they do those things?" These questions are legitimate ones for sociological analysis, but there are other, and from a sociological perspective, even more important questions. To fully understand the nature of deviance we must not only ask questions about the deviant person but we must also ask about the nature of society. Why are some things considered deviant in one society and not in another? And why do societies even seem to *need* deviants to such an extent that a society may even seek out deviants when there seem to be too few? These are some of the more sociologically interesting questions we will examine before considering deviants themselves and a particular kind of deviance we call crime.

Deviance and Society

Society, as we have seen, requires social organization, culture, and norms guiding behavior. This means there are rules, and thus, a high probability there is deviance because rules will be broken. At this point, however, two primary points should be stressed. First, the nature of deviance, especially serious deviance, is defined by a society in terms of what is most valued in that society. If it is a highly religious society, some of the most serious deviance in that society centers around the violation of religious norms. Second, because people have egos, which means they generally prefer to feel good about themselves, to boost this, some people will always be considered different, of low respect, and probably deviant. In essence, this means that if people are to know they are "good people" there must be some "bad people." In other words, there must be social differences. How else do you know there are good people if there are no bad people? Sociologically, and at present, the first point is the more interesting, but both points tell us there will be deviance in every society. Even more is implied; societies and individuals will seek out deviants.

The Need for Deviants. All societies have norms that vary in importance. But seldom is it explicitly stated that some norms are much more important than others, and the importance of particular norms in a society certainly changes. Thus, there must be mechanisms to show people which norms are the most important at the time. This information is primarily conveyed through the punishment of deviants. It then becomes clear that these laws and norms are the ones that should not be broken. At times this may create problems for authorities when an insufficient number of deviants is found, but the problem is not inconsiderable because innocent people can often be labeled deviant in most societies.

An example of the above is the changing and selective rate of enforcement of the English Poor Laws in the 1600s. These laws prohibited giving charity to "able-bodied workers" with the intent of insuring a sufficient supply of hungry workers who would work for low wages. But the Poor Laws were enforced very strictly at times and not at all at other times. Interestingly, historical research has found that the Poor Laws were most likely enforced during times of mass plagues when the supply of workers was sometimes reduced by more than one-third (Hartjen, 1974). The conclusion is that it was in such times of labor shortage that the Poor Laws were most needed to prevent giving aid to people who could work and to keep as many people as possible working at low wages. Thus, to keep aid from going to the poor at least a few people had to be punished under these poor laws as examples.

As noted earlier, elites can often increase their power by making it appear as if some kind of threat to the society exists. In this case, if the elites have at least some support in the general society, a perceived threat can increase support for elites. This effect is often found during war, but it can also be created through a belief that deviants within the society pose a serious threat to everyone.

We have already considered Erikson's (1966) famous study of the Boston "witch hunts." The phenomenon we call "witch hunts," of course, is not restricted to cases of "witches" but is found throughout history when elites use some imaginary or exaggerated threat to increase their control over the population. Stalin, for example, used this tactic many times (Ulam, 1973), and similarities can be found in the "red scares" of the 1920s and early 1950s in the United States.

In an interesting empirical examination of witch hunts, Inverarity (1976) studied lynchings in Louisiana during the late 1800s. Lynchings are attacks on a minority population by a dominant group that considers the people attacked a threat, much like "witches" were considered a threat in Boston during the 1600s. Between 1890 and 1918, Inverarity found considerable variation in the number of lynchings, with generally higher rates during the 1890s. Inverarity suspected that these lynchings had something to do with the Populist movement that was gaining strength in the South during this time. The Populist movement was a reform movement especially seeking economic reforms to help white farmers, but it was also mildly opposed to racism. The Populist movement posed a threat to the social order of strongly racist Southern whites. Much like the people suspected of being witches in Boston, blacks in Louisiana were lynched to emphasize a threat to social order. Among the evidence used by Inverarity to support Erikson's (1966) theory that witch hunts are attempts to reestablish authority and social order are data on the relationship between the number of lynchings and election periods in the 1890s. As can be seen in Figure 8.1, the number of lynchings increased significantly during the elections of 1892, 1894, and 1896, when Populist candidates were winning office in Louisiana.

I conclude with a final example of a society's apparent need for deviants. The Japanese have one of the most homogeneous societies in the world. About 99 percent of the population are fully Japanese in terms of birth, race, and culture. The 1 percent who are not Japanese are primarily Korean and Chinese in origin. And though these non-Japanese Asian people were born in Japan and educated as Japanese, the citizenship laws continue to make it quite difficult for them to become Japanese citizens. To non-Asian gaijin (foreigners), these non-Japanese Asians are identical to the Japanese, but to the Japanese they are still outsiders and often considered deviant.

Given Japan's extremely homogenous population, one might think this small number of foreign Asians are the only outgroup of deviants that can be

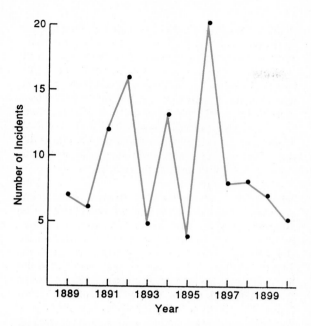

FIGURE 8.1. Lynchings and elections in Louisiana, 1889–1900. (Source: Inverarity, 1976, p. 267.)

located. But there is another deviant group within the Japanese society called Eta or Burakumin who number between 2 and 3 million and are considered despicable deviants to be looked down on by the in-group (Christopher, 1983). These Burakumin, however, are extremely difficult to identify, just as the "witches" were difficult to identify for the Puritans in seventeenth-century Salem. The Japanese nevertheless make a great effort to check the family backgrounds of possible marriage partners and potential employees to assure there has been no Burakumin among the person's relatives.

The Selection Process. When considering the subject of deviant individuals it is quite natural that people focus on the individual characteristics of deviants. Furthermore, people tend to generalize the characteristics of deviant individuals; that is, if a person is found to be deviant in one characteristic or have

committed one type of deviant act, people tend to assume the person is deviant in many respects. After interacting with prisoners in a typical state prison, however, most people find it strange that most prisoners look and act "so normal." And people tend to be especially shocked when told that the "nice young men" who were tour guides are in prison for murder.

Who is and who is not considered a deviant is a complex process that often depends on the characteristics of the society as much as, or sometimes more than, the characteristics of individuals. And deviance can seldom be generalized to more than one or very few characteristics of an individual.

Who is and who is not identified and treated as a deviant by the society is related to many factors (Higgins and Butler, 1982). It is important that the factors involved in the selection process be understood because most people who have committed deviant acts do *not* become known as deviant by the general society and thus are not treated as such. In the eyes of their society, in other words, they are not deviants.

One of the most important elements in the deviant selection process is *power* and *influence*. This means that some people use power to hide their deviance and if detected are able to prevent the information from becoming public. Official statistics on many types of deviant behavior show higher rates of deviance for the lower classes. In some cases like street crime, it does appear that the lower classes have higher rates of deviance. But in most cases the higher rate of deviance among the lower classes shown in official statistics is more a reflection of relative powerlessness among the lower classes than actually higher deviance. The alcoholic who can afford only a small apartment in a crowded area is more likely to cause trouble and have his or her deviance detected; the more affluent can more easily hide their alcoholism behind their own walls. The less affluent man who beats his wife and children is more likely to have his deviance detected by social workers and others who pry into their lives; the more affluent have more privacy. The less affluent criminal must steal in a manner that is more easily detected; the more affluent criminal may have access to corporate account numbers and computers so as to steal in a less detectable manner.

Related to the above is the extent to which the deviance causes trouble for other people. If the deviance does not disrupt the lives of others, it is less likely treated as official deviance by the police, courts, or other agencies. For example, the person seeking a prostitute on the street is more likely to be arrested than the person who uses a more expensive prostitution service by telephone. The person who is begging in the streets is more likely to be seen as deviant than the idle rich who live off of the work of others. The mentally ill person who is disrupting traffic is more likely to be treated as a deviant by the public than is the mentally ill person taken care of behind closed doors.

Crime

When most people think of deviance, criminal behavior first comes to mind. **Crime,** however, is a specific type of deviance that can be defined as an intentional act in violation of a law. This definition, sometimes called a "legal definition" of crime, is not the only one, but it is the most used definition. A primary weak point in this definition of crime is that we are letting the political system and the people who have the most influence in the political system define crime for us. For example, whereas in Guatemala it is not necessarily against the law for the government to use torture against people suspected of opposing the government, it is against the law to publish material critical of the government. In the United States it is against the law to put poison in someone's drink, whereas until a few years ago, it was not illegal to dump chemical wastes in areas where it would surely seep into a city's drinking water.

Legal codes specifying crimes date back to about 2270 B.C. in Babylonia. But most societies did not formalize legal codes until much later. Around 2,000 years later the Roman legal codes were formalized, which much later influenced the development of English Common Law after A.D. 1066, which in turn influenced the U.S. legal system.

Legal codes developed for several reasons. As the state emerged there was an attempt to control random individual vengeance against people seen as victimizing others. Also, as societies became more complex, with more problems, and more people in contact with one another, there was a need to regulate conflicts and promote social order by defining what can and cannot be done. We must always keep in mind, however, that laws are formed by the state in response to political pressure (Hartjen, 1974). Thus, laws are designed to provide a social order that is favorable to those with most power to influence the establishment of these laws.

Types of Crime. Crime is a very broad subject. There are many types of crime and we must be specific about the type of crime being discussed. Crime can be divided into many categories, but I have found the following categories most useful — traditional crime, organized crime, white-collar crime, and political crime (Haskell and Yablonsky, 1974).

Traditional crime (or we can call it "street crime") is the type traditionally recognized by all societies as crime. Included are such crimes as murder, rape, robbery, and so forth. Not all societies

Bernhard Goetz shot four youths on a subway train in New York; he claimed they were going to rob him. Even though he was sentenced to six months in jail for gun possession, he is shown here honored by the Federation of New York State Rifle and Pistol Clubs. Do you think vigilantism is justified? (© NY Daily News)

define each of these crimes in exactly the same way, but they all see these transgressions against individuals or property as crime in one way or another. One reason that all societies recognize these acts as crime is that anyone can visualize herself or himself as a victim.

Organized crime often involves the same illegal acts as traditional crime, but as the name implies the crimes committed are supported by a criminal organization. Organized crime involves a hierarchical organization of people with varying ranks of authority in the organization. There is also the use of threats and bribes to cover the criminal activities, which, in contrast to traditional crime, can be done because of the persistent, organized manner of this criminal activity.

Organized crime can exist on many levels. There are many cases of small-scale organized crime in only local areas. Indeed, a recent trend has been a movement among traditional criminals to organize themselves. This trend has occurred extensively among former prisoners in the state of California, for example. The organizations were formed in the prisons and then maintained inside and outside of the prisons as some convicts were released. Another recent example is the "Hells Angels" motorcycle club, which has apparently turned to organized criminal activities.

What first comes to mind with organized crime, however, are the big, powerful criminal organizations called by the names Mafia or Cosa Nostra. Movies like *The Godfather* and *The Valachi Papers* (based on a book about an organized crime member's life) have made these powerful criminal organizations well known. These criminal organizations account for billions of dollars in crime and are actually even well known by the police and federal law enforcement agencies. Congressional investigations have uncovered what these organized crime families do, who they are, and where they live. But these people continue to operate, which indicates the skill of their organization, their ability to hide their illegal activities with legal front operations, and the effectiveness of bribes and threats.

White-collar crime involves crime committed by a person in the course of his or her otherwise legitimate occupational activities (Sutherland, 1961;

Coleman, 1985). Included are crimes like violations of antitrust laws, misrepresentation in advertising, infringements on patents or copyrights, and violations of labor laws. These crimes are clearly the most costly of all types of crime in terms of property loss. And we are increasingly aware of violent white-collar crime (Coleman, 1985). Examples of violent white-collar crime are businesses that dump chemical wastes in an area they know will harm people and the production of consumer goods in a manner known to be dangerous for consumers when it would be more costly to produce the goods safely. Coleman (1985, pp. 39–46) has provided a long list of recent examples of violent white-collar crimes similar to these, as well as violent white-collar crimes that involve violations of laws designed to assure a safe environment for workers. There is plenty of evidence that these white-collar crimes persist because government agencies that are supposed to prevent them are sometimes more sympathetic to the industry they oversee than they are to citizens. Officials of these government agencies often have ties to industries they are to watch or may expect to get well-paying jobs in the industry after government service if they do not anger top executives in these industries.

Finally, **political crime** can be defined as crimes committed with the intent to produce or resist change in the general society. Political criminals may be doing some of the same things as traditional criminals, like robbing banks, kidnapping, and murder, but the crimes committed by political criminals are intended to benefit the wider society or at least a large group seen as exploited or threatened. In other words, the true political criminal is motivated by ideology, not personal material gain. It is difficult to determine what is really in the mind of the political criminal, but actions do tend to indicate what is political crime and what is not. Stalin, the Soviet leader who sat down with Franklin Roosevelt and Winston Churchill during World War II, was involved in bank robberies before the Russian Revolution of 1917. But Stalin did not use the money gained in this way to obtain a high material standard of living for himself at the time. Rather, he sent the money to Lenin, who was in hiding in Switzerland, so that Lenin could finance revolutionary activities.

We can use another example; the Cosa Nostra and revolutionaries (or counterrevolutionaries) in Central America may be involved in similar activities. The Cosa Nostra, however, cares only about enriching itself, whereas the revolutionaries are working to benefit a wider group in their societies like peasants and workers. You may not agree that the actions of revolutionaries will actually help people, but the difference between political criminals and traditional or organized criminals should not be confused.

Let's consider examples of why the two should not be confused. The traditional criminal seeks personal gain. If achieving this personal gain is made risky through the possibility of being caught and punished, it is possible to deter the criminal activities of traditional criminals. If he or she ends up with a long prison sentence, this criminal loses. This is not necessarily the case with political criminals. They do not primarily seek personal material gain, so if they end up in jail they can organize and recruit revolutionaries from prison. And even the possibility of death may not deter exceptionally committed revolutionaries. The goal of revolutionary change may be achieved if they become martyrs; thus they may be ready to drive a truck full of explosives to destroy a political target and themselves.

Who is and who is not a political criminal, however, is again subject to the power of definition. Throughout history and around the world today we often find governments that are trying to prevent social change by actually committing more crimes than the people seeking social change. Governments tend to have more resources to make the public think they are taking only legal action while their opponents are the "real" criminals. And on top of this, many government leaders who themselves came to power through revolution (e.g., in the Soviet Union, Cuba, Israel, France, and the United States) were once seen as political criminals. One person's "freedom fighter" may be another person's vicious criminal.

Crime Rates. This discussion of crime rates is limited to traditional crime. Other crimes, like white-collar crimes, which are in fact more costly, will be neglected. Unfortunately we do not have adequate measures of other types of crime for several reasons. A primary reason is the greater difficulty in detecting white-collar crimes. However, there is also a class bias in the criminal justice system that leads to less concern with white-collar crime committed by the more influential in our society (Coleman, 1985; Hagan and Parker, 1985).

Our principle measures of serious traditional crime in the United States come from statistics compiled by the FBI in their annual *Uniform Crime Report*. These reports began in the 1930s, though the early methods of collecting these data were questionable at best. The *Uniform Crime Reports* contain crimes *reported to the police* and, thus, have been shown to underestimate the true crime rate. More recently (since the early 1970s) the crime rate has also been measured more reliably through *National Crime Surveys* that are conducted like other standard social surveys.

The crimes selected to indicate the trends in crime (what you see reported periodically in the newspaper) are what the FBI calls the seven serious crimes (though an eighth — arson — has recently been added but not stressed as an indicator). The seven serious crimes include murder, rape, robbery, aggravated assault, burglary, larceny-theft, and auto theft. (Robbery involves taking something from someone personally, burglary involves breaking into private property to steal, and larceny-theft involves taking property from a place of public access.) The first four of these crimes are classified as violent crimes because they involve the use or threat of violence, whereas the latter three are property crimes.

Table 8.2 indicates the crime rate for 1986 in the United States. Included in this table are the actual number of crimes estimated to have occurred in 1986 and the rate of these crimes per 100,000 population. This latter figure is necessary if we are to compare changes in the crime rate across time periods with varied population size. Table 8.2 also shows the usual comparison of violent and property crime rates.

One of the most important questions examined by these crime statistics is the change in the level of crime from year to year. Table 8.2 shows that serious crime has increased in the United States in the

TABLE 8.2. *Index crime rates, 1977–1986*

Population*	Crime index total**	Violent crime‡‡	Property crime‡‡	Murder and non-negligent manslaughter	Forcible rape	Robbery	Aggravated assault	Burglary	Larceny-theft	Motor vehicle theft
Number of offenses:										
1977-216,332,000	10,984,500	1,029,580	9,955,000	19,120	63,500	412,610	534,350	3,071,500	5,905,700	977,700
1978-218,059,000	11,209,000	1,085,550	10,123,400	19,560	67,610	426,930	571,460	3,128,300	5,991,000	1,004,100
1979-220,099,000	12,249,500	1,208,030	11,041,500	21,460	76,390	480,700	629,480	3,327,700	6,601,000	1,112,800
1980-225,349,264	13,408,300	1,344,520	12,063,700	23,040	82,990	565,840	672,650	3,795,200	7,136,900	1,131,700
1981-229,146,000	13,423,800	1,361,820	12,061,900	22,520	82,500	592,910	663,900	3,779,700	7,194,400	1,087,800
1982-231,534,000	12,974,400	1,322,390	11,652,000	21,010	78,770	553,130	669,480	3,447,100	7,142,500	1,062,400
1983-233,981,000	12,108,600	1,258,090	10,850,500	19,310	78,920	506,570	653,290	3,129,900	6,712,800	1,007,900
1984-236,158,000	11,881,800	1,273,280	10,608,500	18,690	84,230	485,010	685,350	2,984,400	6,591,900	1,032,200
1985-238,740,000	12,430,400	1,327,770	11,102,600	18,980	87,670	497,870	723,250	3,073,300	6,926,400	1,102,900
1986-241,077,000	13,210,800	1,488,140	11,722,700	20,610	90,430	542,780	834,320	3,241,400	7,257,200	1,224,100
Percent change; number of offenses:										
1986/1985	+6.3	+12.1	+5.6	+8.6	+3.2	+9.0	+15.4	+5.5	+4.8	+11.0
1986/1982	+1.8	+12.5	+.6	-1.9	+14.8	-1.9	+24.6	-6.0	+1.6	+15.2
1986/1977	+20.3	+44.5	+17.8	+7.8	+42.4	+31.5	+56.1	+5.5	+22.9	+25.2
Rate per 100,000 inhabitants:										
1977	5,077.6	475.9	4,601.7	8.8	29.4	190.7	247.0	1,419.8	2,729.9	451.9
1978	5,140.3	497.8	4,642.5	9.0	31.0	195.8	262.1	1,434.6	2,747.4	460.5
1979	5,565.5	548.9	5,016.6	9.7	34.7	218.4	286.0	1,511.9	2,999.1	505.6
1980	5,950.0	596.6	5,353.3	10.2	36.8	251.1	298.5	1,684.1	3,167.0	502.2
1981	5,858.2	594.3	5,263.9	9.8	36.0	258.7	289.7	1,649.5	3,139.7	474.7
1982	5,603.6	571.1	5,032.5	9.1	34.0	238.9	289.2	1,488.8	3,084.8	458.8
1983	5,175.0	537.7	4,637.4	8.3	33.7	216.5	279.2	1,337.7	2,868.9	430.8
1984	5,031.3	539.2	4,492.1	7.9	35.7	205.4	290.2	1,263.7	2,791.3	437.1
1985	5,206.7	556.2	4,650.5	7.9	36.7	208.5	302.9	1,287.3	2,901.2	462.0
1986	5,479.9	617.3	4,862.6	8.6	37.5	225.1	346.1	1,344.6	3,010.3	507.8
Percent change; rate per 100,000 inhabitants:										
1986/1985	+5.2	+11.0	+4.6	+8.9	+2.2	+8.0	+14.3	+4.5	+3.8	+9.9
1986/1982	-2.2	+8.1	-3.4	-5.5	+10.3	-5.8	+19.7	-9.7	-2.4	+10.7
1986/1977	+7.9	+29.7	+5.7	-2.3	+27.6	+18.0	+40.1	-5.3	+10.3	+12.4

* Populations are Bureau of the Census provisional estimates as of July 1, except April 1, 1980, preliminary census counts, and are subject to change.
** Because of rounding, the offenses may not add to totals.
‡‡ Violent crimes are offenses of murder, forcible rape, robbery, and aggravated assault. Property crimes are offenses of burglary, larceny-theft, and motor vehicle theft. Data are not included for the property crime of arson.
All rates were calculated on the offenses before rounding.
SOURCE: U.S. Department of Justice (1987).

past ten years, and there has been a large increase in violent crime in this time period. However, compared with the level of crime 20 to 25 years ago, and the dramatic increase in that time period, the recent small increases in the crime rate are clearly very small indeed.

Figure 8.2 gives us a longer perspective on the U.S. crime rate. Although it must be kept in mind that the earlier crime figures were much less accurate, there is wide agreement that the crime trend has been roughly that indicated in Figure 8.2. When we see the trend of crime presented in this figure, we logically move to the question of why. What happened in this country to produce such a pattern? Many theories are designed to answer this question, most of which are examined in the next section. But before we can fully understand traditional crime, we must consider the characteristics of people committing these crimes.

As seen in Table 8.3, traditional criminals are overwhelmingly male and young. In fact, it is said that one of the best solutions to crime is aging, not prisons. We also see in this table that whites commit most crimes but that blacks had a higher arrest rate (that is, given their population size) for traditional crime. There are two primary reasons for this; blacks have a much higher rate of poverty compared with whites, and poverty is related to serious crime (Thornberry and Farnworth, 1982). Also, the fig-

FIGURE 8.2. Total index crimes per 100,000 population, U.S., 1933–1980. (Sources: Constructed from "The Challenge of Crime in a Free Society," 1967, pp. 22–23; U.S. Department of Justice, 1983, p. 348.)

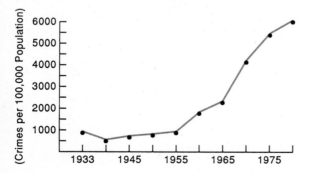

ures in Table 8.3 represent *arrest rates*, not actual rates of committing crimes. There is evidence that the poor and minorities are more likely arrested for crimes compared with middle-class whites.

We should consider murderers and the murder rate separately because it presents an interesting contrast to the other crimes. Most murders are committed by relatives or close friends of the victim; hence murder is much less likely to be a premeditated crime. The typical pattern is an argument in which someone picks up a gun or knife and attacks the other person well known to the attacker. This reason seems to make clear that *effective* gun control would reduce the murder rate — the aggression and anger would not necessarily diminish, but the means of killing would be less efficient without guns. But it would have to be truly effective gun control if it were to reduce the murder rate. The Japanese, for example, believe it is strange that the United States allows such freedom to buy guns, and gun control is strongly and effectively enforced in Japan. However, the Japanese do not have a frontier mythology praising guns and thus no strong desire to buy guns. And we must realize that Japanese gun control laws are nationwide and that the Japanese have more control over their national borders than does the United States.

Having considered the information on the characteristics of criminals, we can now return to our question about the pattern of crime increase shown in Figure 8.2. With the knowledge that most traditional criminals are young males, we should remember the demographic patterns described in Chapter 6. Because of the "baby boom" generation, there were more crime-prone people in the 1960s and 1970s as a percent of the population — that is, young males. This demographic shift helps us understand part of the crime pattern between 1950 and 1985, but only part (Maxim, 1985). Crime did rise rapidly in the 1960s and 1970s as the changing age distribution would suggest, then slowly began to drop in the mid-1980s, but not as much as expected, and the crime rate again regained its upward trend in the second half of the 1980s. Another demographic pattern also helps us understand part of the crime pattern — single-parent families and the divorce rate. As we will see, the rate of female-headed fami-

TABLE 8.3. *Characteristics of persons arrested for serious crime, 1984*

Characteristic	Percent of total arrests for FBI index crimes
Age	
16 years old or less	12.9
17–29	54.5
30 and over	32.4
Sex	
males	83.3
females	16.7

Crime	Whites (%)	Blacks (%)	Native Americans (%)	Asians (%)
All crimes	73.4	24.9	1.0	.6
Murder	53.7	44.9	.7	.7
Rape	52.8	46.0	.7	.5
Robbery	37.5	61.5	.4	.6
Assault	60.5	38.1	.8	.5
Burglary	70.2	28.5	.8	.5
Larceny-theft	67.6	30.3	1.1	.9
Vehicle-theft	68.1	30.2	.9	.7
Arson	77.6	20.9	.8	.6

SOURCE: U.S. Department of Justice (1985).

lies and divorce rates follow the crime rate rather closely in this time period. Thus, though the percentage of young males was less in the 1980s, because of other social problems their rate of committing crimes was higher. But again, other factors are involved in the causes of crime and deviance in general.

Explanations of Crime and Deviance

As you can guess, people have always been interested in the causes of deviance. Whenever people see behavior that is considered improper or vulgar, something that a "normal" person wouldn't do, there are questions that must have answers if the world is to continue to be perceived as an orderly place. And as you can also guess, the answers have usually been directed to something about the character of individuals considered deviant. These quasi theories of deviance that people devise generally begin with some examination of criminal motives, which people find understandable, even if despica-

ble. For example, "The person wanted money, was too lazy or uneducated to get it through employment, so the person robbed a liquor store." Or, "The person has a weak character and thus developed alcoholism." Thus, we do not agree with what the deviant person has done, but it has been made understandable by quasi theories.

There are, of course, situations and behavior that people simply cannot understand through examining individual motives. For these situations we have a *residual category* to place things that do not seem to fit elsewhere—"crazy." This is why sociologists sometimes refer to mental illness as **residual deviance.** Authorities like the police must categorize deviants for processing. Cases that cannot be categorized as easily as street crime, family violence, sexual deviance, drunk and disorderly, and so on create problems in handling as well as explanation. Thus, the residual category "crazy" is convenient for the authorities as well—they simply call the local mental hospital.

Social scientists also began with explanations of

deviance by focusing on the characteristics of individuals — in fact, biological characteristics. But as discussed earlier in this text, it is clear that we must generally focus on factors outside the individual if we are to understand major kinds of deviance like crime, alcoholism, and even mental illness. The characteristics of individuals may be involved in producing such deviance, *but the deviance cannot be fully understood without examination of wider social conditions.* For example, without consideration of wider social conditions we would be left with explaining the rapid increase in traditional crime in the 1960s and 1970s with a focus on something such as criminal personalities. But this tells us almost nothing; why were there more individuals with personalities leading them to commit crimes?

In what follows we will consider some of the theories of deviance and crime. The causes of deviance and crime are complex and numerous and the theories that follow attempt only to pick out what may be the most important causes of crime and deviance. This is also to say that all the theories discussed below are helpful in explaining crime and deviance (with the exception of most biological theories), but the question is, which are the most helpful?

Biological Theories of Deviance. One of the first biological theories of deviance was put forth by Lombroso (1911), who believed that body characteristics such as body shape and facial features were related to criminal behavior. Since that time other criminologists have published similar theories (Sheldon, 1940), but none of the theories suggesting a relationship between body characteristics and crime has been supported by research.

More recently it has been argued that the XYY chromosome pattern in men is related to crime (Owen, 1972). Normally males have an XY chromosome pattern that determines their sex, but a small percentage of men have an extra Y chromosome. Studies have shown that the percentage of men with the XYY chromosome pattern is somewhat higher among prisoners than the general population. Thus, it can be argued that the XYY chromosome pattern affects men in such a way that they are *slightly* more

prone to crime (such as less able to control their temper). We can accept this biological factor as having a possible effect on crime; however, we must be cautious in accepting this theory because (1) it can account for only a very small part of crime, and (2) factors outside the individual are still the most important in leading XYY chromosome males to commit crime. As to the second point, most XYY chromosome males do not commit crimes. As to the first point, with this biological theory we *cannot* explain broad social trends or major social problems like crime. Again, as we have already seen, the U.S. crime rate went up very rapidly in 1960s and 1970s. How are we to explain this with a biological theory? Did nuclear testing lead to chromosome damage so that more XYY chromosome males were born? Or were some cosmic rays involved? No, we must look to sociological trends rather than biology.

With some types of deviance, we must recognize that there can be a biological cause. One example is mental illness. But even in this case the biological cause of mental illness is often overestimated. And we must also recognize there is likely to be an interaction between the social environment and biology. No doubt some people are more genetically prone to some types of mental illness. If the mental illness is to materialize, however, the person prone to it must have something like stress in the social environment. Thus, if we are to understand differing rates of mental illness at different time periods, and in different groups of people, we must see how social environments differ.

Social Stress and Anomie. Sociologists have most often looked to factors like social stress, anomie, culture, learning, and the social psychological process of developing a self-identity when explaining deviance. We begin with the social stress and anomie theories.

Social stress means that some condition exists that creates frustration or psychological stress for individuals, which can then lead to some form of deviance. In particular, it can be argued that conditions of poverty or high inequality can lead to crime, mental illness, or other forms of deviance like alcoholism. Sociologists have debated the extent to which poverty and a low class position are related to higher rates of street crime. The trend of the research findings is that people from a lower-class background *are* more likely to commit traditional kinds of crimes (Thornberry and Farnworth, 1982). But we must be careful to note that poverty per se is not necessarily associated with high rates of deviance; otherwise we would find the world's highest rates of crime in countries like China and India. One aspect of poverty that is more important is the level of inequality in a society, not just poverty. When the level of inequality is high, there can be (1) more conflict between people at the top and bottom of the society leading to crime, and (2) more frustration and anger among those at the bottom leading to crime. Recent studies have shown more violent crime in nations with higher levels of material inequality (Messner, 1982) and more violent crime in U.S. cities with higher levels of material inequality (Blau and Blau, 1982).

Other forms of stress can also be related to deviance. Family conflict, pressure experienced at work, and failure in some important activity are among other situations that can produce stress, anger, and frustration. For example, failure in school is one factor that can contribute to delinquent behavior. Mann (1981) has found that failure in school produces low self-esteem and that young people may turn to delinquent behavior to increase their self-esteem in the eyes of a select peer group of other delinquents.

Another example of this can be found in Japan. Compared with that of the United States, the Japanese crime rate is almost insignificant. (An interesting example of this occurred with a national outcry in the summer of 1984 when a policeman was killed in Tokyo. News commentators in Tokyo were wondering if Japan was getting as bad as the United States because it was the fifth policeman killed in Tokyo — *since 1945!)* But Japan does have an increasing problem with delinquency, especially among middle-class young people. As we will see in the chapter on education, the educational system in Japan creates a high degree of stress on teenagers, which is clearly related to a high suicide rate. In addition, because educational success in Japan is

very important for success in later life, young people who fail school become alienated from the society in general and seek other means of self-esteem, often through deviant behavior.

Finally, a discussion of various kinds of stress leading to deviance must include anomie. **Anomie** means normlessness or a contradiction between norms or between norms and actual conditions in a society. In the 1890s, Durkheim (1951) was the first to show that anomie can lead to deviance, and Merton (1968) later expanded the concept and applied it to the United States.

The most important form of anomie that can lead to deviance is a condition wherein (1) the society places great stress on success, but (2) does not provide adequate means for achieving this success among some segments of the population. The segment of the population that has come to value high success but has little means of achieving it will be prone to anger, stress, and perhaps using illegal means to attain material success.

More than most societies, the United States stresses material success. *And* it is stressed that everyone, no matter how poor, should strive for material success because "there is equality of opportunity." As we will see in more detail in the next chapter, however, the United States has perhaps the highest level of inequality among industrial nations, and no more equality of opportunity than others. Thus, as indicated in Figure 8.3, although the material aspirations are high for all in the society, there is a big gap between what many people aspire to and their means to achieve these goals. It is the large gap, not poverty per se, that can produce a tendency toward crime. This is in contrast to a different kind of society, say, a feudal agrarian society, in which there is high inequality but low expectations among those on the bottom. In such a society a poor blacksmith's son may aspire to becoming a good blacksmith rather than a wealthy merchant. The son's aspirations are realistic, and when attained they will lead to less alienation and anger.

Control Theories. Whereas strain theories focus on what motivates the individual to become deviant through anger or a rejection of the rules, control

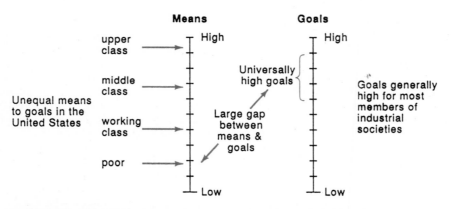

FIGURE 8.3. Universally high goals with unequal means in the United States.

theories focus on why some people are less attached to, or bonded to, the society to begin with. The individuals are then, in a sense, more free to break the society's rules.

Hirschi (1969), for example, argues that individuals are bonded to the society in the following ways. (1) People are usually bonded to the society through *attachments* to other individuals like parents and teachers. (2) Bonding also comes through *involvements* in the traditional society through such activities as work, going to school, and participating in other community activities. (3) People are bonded to the society through commitments and support of the *values* in the society. The bond to society created in the above ways will work to prevent a person from becoming deviant.

Delinquents, therefore, are more likely to be young people who lack strong emotional ties to parents or teachers, who do not have strong ties to the society through school activities and employment, and who have few personal commitments to and less respect for the values of the society. There is some research support for this type of theory (Krohn and Massey, 1980), but it seems less able to explain more serious forms of deviance — the kind of deviance that requires a stronger motivation.

Culture and Learning. Although some theories of deviance focus on some kind of deprivation or stressful condition motivating individuals to participate in deviant behavior, other theories focus on subcultural values and learning the deviant behavior.

A brief beginning example can be the effects of violence seen on television. There is now evidence that television violence can lead children to behave in a more violent manner (Phillips, 1982b). This suggests that children are learning that violence is acceptable and a means of achieving goals or expressing anger. But the relationship between the mass media and deviant behavior is quite complex. Let's take another example of deviance; when we compare nations we find no relationship between pornographic literature and sexual deviance like child molestation and rape. Nudity and pornography are much more restricted in the United States than in most other industrial nations, but our rates of sexual deviance are still high. Japan again provides an interesting contrast. Nudity is found in magazines and advertising much more often in Japan than in the United States. Along the streets of Tokyo can be found vending machines with pornographic magazines. But teenagers in Japan are much less sexually active than in the United States.

One of the most respected theories of deviance that focuses on learning is **differential association theory** (Southerland, 1949). The main point of this theory is that deviant behavior must be learned in interaction with people who are already deviant.

The extent of the interaction is important, because the greater the interaction with others who are deviant in contrast to nondeviants, the more likely is a person to become deviant. Also important is what the person has a chance to learn. Both the techniques of deviant behavior plus the rationale and motives for deviant activity must be learned. For example, few people could begin on their own and become successful burglars. How do you go about this activity without being caught? And what do you do with the stolen property? You must learn where to safely sell it.

Differential association theory can help us understand why certain types of deviant activity like delinquency are higher in some areas and how even previously well-behaved teenagers can become involved in crime (Jensen, 1972). But the theory neglects how some people become motivated to participate in deviant behavior and how family disruption can lead to improper socialization of young people leading to deviance.

Finally, some theories suggest that different subcultural values may be at the heart of some kinds of deviance. People from the dominant culture may look down on those with these different values and label them as deviant. A classic case of this is one in which a Navaho Indian was locked in a mental hospital and thought to be psychotic because of his more traditional passive life-style and inability to speak English well (Jewell, 1952).

In a variation of this subcultural theme, Walter Miller (1958) suggests that *lower-class subculture* is responsible for more delinquency among the less affluent in our society. According to Miller, a lower-class subculture, more than the broader U.S. culture, stresses "being tough," "getting in trouble" as a positive trait, and "conning" or outwitting people. These subcultural values bring the lower class into conflict with official agencies (police, schools, workplace) dominated by the middle class.

Theories like Miller's may have some value, but they are highly criticized today. To begin with, it is questionable that these subcultural values are extensive among the lower classes. And perhaps more important, when considering all types of crime, some studies indicate there is not more crime among the lower classes (Tittle, Villemez, and Smith, 1978), or at least not more crime of a less serious nature among the young born in the lower classes (Thornberry and Farnworth, 1982).

Labeling Theory. One of the most popular theories of deviance in recent years has been labeling theory. With many types of deviance, **labeling theory** is very useful in helping us understand how people may in fact come to see themselves as deviant.

Labeling theory works on a social psychological level, though it begins with the assumption that something about the wider society results in some people being selected and treated as deviant. Primarily, however, the theory builds on the work of social psychologists like George Herbert Mead who, as we saw in the previous chapter, explained how people develop a "self" that guides their behavior.

Labeling theorists point out that most people have committed deviant acts. Only a few people, however, come to actually think of themselves as deviants *and* get extensively involved in deviant behavior. The first kind of deviant act can be called **primary deviance,** whereas the deviance of people who have come to view themselves as deviant is called **secondary deviance** (Lemert, 1972). The task for labeling theory is to explain how one is transformed into the other.

Several specific theories outline the labeling process leading to secondary deviance, but I have always favored the one by Matza (1969) as the most useful and complete. Matza's theory considers seven stages in the labeling process.

1. The Ban: Being Bedeviled. To begin with, to have deviance some act or characteristic of people must be banned or seen as deviant. But in addition, there are usually stereotypes and exaggerations about what "these deviant people" are like. The actual first step for the deviant, of course, is committing the deviant act — "being bedeviled."

2. Transparency. After committing the deviant act people usually feel guilty and very sensitive about what they have done. They feel "transparent," as if people could see through them and know what they had done. The feeling is somewhat like that of a child who somehow feels his or her mother

How can you use labeling theory to explain the differences in appearance among these girls? Do you think any of them sees herself as deviant? Why? Do you see any of them as deviant? Why? (top left:© Eugene Gordon/Photo Researchers, Inc.; top right: © Richard Friedman/Photo Researchers, Inc.; left: © Kenneth Murray/ Photo Researchers, Inc.)

always knows when he or she has been bad. This sensitivity makes the individual wonder whether or not he or she does in fact fit the common stereotypes of people who have committed that type of deviant act. These feelings set the stage for the next step in the process.

3. Apprehension: Being Selected. Now, of all the people who have happened to commit deviant acts, the person has been selected — that is, caught. Other people now begin reacting to this person in a different manner.

4. Being Cast. In very subtle ways people begin treating the individual differently, who picks up on this. This new treatment, through time, can begin making the individual come to think he or she is in fact a fully deviant person. In other words, the individual is coming to develop a deviant self-concept. Matza gives an example of this subtle shift in treatment: Before being apprehended, people walk by, see Johnny playing baseball, and think, "there is Johnny playing baseball." Now, however, after the boy has been caught in a deviant act such as robbery, these people walk by Johnny doing the same thing and think, "There is Johnny behaving himself."

5. Exclusion. As people come to view the apprehended person differently, this person comes to be excluded from the everyday world of "normals." Needing companionship and psychological support, the person often must seek the company of other deviants, which further leads to their exclusion from "normals," and further labeling.

6. Display of Authority. When individuals are apprehended in a serious deviant act, they face a display of authority to signify the seriousness of the act. They may go before the court, be sent to a lecture by a top company official, face a board of inquiry, and so on. Although it is intended that through the display of authority they and others who may be potential deviants now see the seriousness of their act and will not do it again, the individuals involved may react differently; they may think, "I must really be a bad person if they are going through all of this display."

7. Building an Identity. In this final stage the individual has been labeled a deviant by others and is now interacting with other deviants, forming a more complete identity of herself or himself as a deviant.

A final note can be added to the display of authority. At this point we usually find the use of **degradation ceremonies** to shape identities or control people. By degradation ceremonies sociologists refer to ceremonies or rituals (formal or informal) in which people are humbled and depersonalized to show the power of the organization over them, and to show they no longer can have the self-identity they once had. Examples of this are the body searches and other degradations on entering a prison or basic training in the military (Goffman, 1961; Garfinkel, 1956). People labeled deviant are likely to experience degradation ceremonies when coming into contact with the police and the courts.

And these degradation ceremonies are likely to reinforce a deviant identity.

Labeling theory helps us understand much about the social psychological process that leads a person to become a secondary rather than a primary deviant. There is agreement among sociologists, however, that labeling theory cannot help us understand the motives or stress that leads some people to become deviants. In other words, it does not tell us who becomes a primary deviant (at least for serious deviance) to begin with. It helps us understand what happens after such individuals are caught, but not why they committed their first act. Other theories attempt to answer this question.

Conflict Theories of Deviance. Conflict theories of deviance can include many of the elements of the theories discussed above. As noted in earlier chapters, however, conflict theories begin with the basic point that there are groups with different interests, values, and power in the society. Who gets labeled deviant, what types of acts are considered deviant, and the motivation to break the rules, among other things, cannot be fully understood without reference to group conflict in the society.

For example, acts committed by the relatively powerless that create problems for the more powerful are more likely to be against the law and these laws are more likely to be enforced. Vagrants sleeping in the streets are often jailed, whereas college students sleeping on the beaches and parks of resort towns during spring break are tolerated. Until quite recently, workers who met to form self-help organizations were often arrested for conspiracy, yet corporate leaders could legally maintain strong organizations protecting their collective interests. Studies show that the poor and minorities are more often arrested and given longer prison terms compared with the more affluent who commit the same types of crime (Quinney, 1977). And the types of crime receiving more police and court attention follow this pattern; traditional street crimes, more often committed by the poor and minorities, are given much more attention than corporate crime, which is vastly more costly to society (Coleman, 1985).

Conflict theorists also stress that laws are made by the more affluent in society, and the institutions that enforce the laws (police and courts) are highly influenced by the more affluent. Thus, the whole criminal justice system is biased against the less affluent. As an eighteenth-century French philosopher put it, both the rich and the poor are prohibited from sleeping under bridges. The point is that the rich do not need to sleep under bridges, and other behavior of the more affluent that may cause someone problems (like destroying low-cost apartments) is less likely to be made illegal.

There have been several attempts by conflict theorists to combine basic conflict principles with several other theories of crime and deviance. In one of the best theories of this type, Colvin and Pauly (1983) begin with a basic characteristic of corporate capitalism that leads to different types of occupational control and motivations for people in different class positions. The upper class and top managers of corporations feel much more attachment to the organizations they work for and the society in general; thus these people are motivated by the goals and aims of the corporate organization itself. If the corporation grows and produces profits, they win because they own and/or control the corporation. People in lower management positions or professional positions tend to be motivated more by direct rewards. People in the lowest working-class positions, however, tend to be controlled in a more authoritarian manner in a capitalist society. These workers are less likely to be given more pay for better work and instead get an hourly wage. They are simply told to follow orders or get fired. In addition to this, these low-ranked workers are given very little voice in how things are done; again, they are simply told to obey orders. This type of worker control creates more alienation among workers, who are then less likely to identify with the corporation and its goals. These workers are therefore more likely to break the rules when they feel they can get away with doing so.

You are probably wondering what all this has to do with youth crime. Colvin and Pauly discuss research showing that the way parents socialize their children is influenced by the parents' work experience. For the working class this means that children

tend to be socialized in a more authoritarian manner. This, in turn, leads working-class children to be more alienated from their parents, schools, and society in general. And this makes working-class children more likely to break the law and become delinquents.

This conflict theory begins with the basic class conflicts in capitalist society, then adds other theories of deviance to show why delinquency is higher among the lower classes. But the causes of deviance are many and complex, and therefore any particular theory will be incomplete for all kinds of deviance and across time and cultures. We must recognize that capitalist societies are not the only ones with delinquents. Also, not all capitalist societies have the same rate of delinquency. Japan provides a good example of this because it is a capitalist society with *much* less crime and delinquency, and its delinquency is found more in the middle class. We have already considered why Japan has a higher rate of delinquency in its middle class than in its working class, but let's see what conflict principles can help us understand Japan's lower crime rate in general.

One of the most important differences between Japan and the United States is the homogeneity of Japan's population in contrast to our many diverse racial and ethnic groups. Thus, there is a greater potential in the United States for intergroup conflicts—whether based on race, ethnicity, religion, or class—that can produce a high potential for crime. There are two main reasons for this. (1) When groups are greatly divided, and outgroup members become dehumanized to some extent, it is easier to harm these outgroup members through violent crime and property crime. Milgram's (1965) experiments on obedience when given orders to shock victims indicated this; the further removed the victim, the easier it is to harm her or him. (2) With extensive in-group versus out-group divisions in a society, material and political inequalities are likely to overlap with these in-group/out-group divisions. This highly visible form of inequality leads to more anger among the less advantaged outgroup, which can then provide a motivation for crime. The point of the above, of course, is that with a much more homogeneous population these factors apply much less in Japan.

Finally, one of the greatest strengths of a conflict theory of crime is the simple point that high inequality is quite likely to generate conflict in a society, and that one way the conflict often materializes is through crime. We need to know more about crime, because high inequality does not produce the same level of crime in every society. However, empirical research using city and international comparisons do show a strong tendency for high inequality to produce more crime (Blau and Blau, 1982). A comparison of Japan the the United States alone is useful; as we will see in more detail in the next chapter, among all capitalist industrial nations, Japan has the lowest level of material inequality, and the United States has the highest level (with the possible exception of France).

Solutions to Crime

We conclude this chapter with a brief discussion of solutions to crime. This country has gone through many shifts in its views about what can and should be done about crime. Suggested "solutions" range from "getting tougher" with criminals by hiring more police and giving longer prison sentences and more executions to solutions such as rehabilitation of criminals and reducing the underlying social conditions like poverty that help breed crime. These are all variations of suggested solutions between these extremes. The research and generally failed attempts to reduce crime, however, seem to point to a pessimistic conclusion—the things that *can* be done in attempting to reduce crime do not work very well, whereas the things that *cannot* be done easily to reduce crime would be most effective.

We can get "tougher with criminals" as is being done in the political climate of the 1980s. The number of people in prison in the United States jumped over 11 percent in just one year—1982. Between 1975 and 1985 the rate of incarceration doubled. Nationwide, in 1985 there were about as many people in prison as lived in San Francisco (678,000). As a percent of population, the United States has perhaps the largest prison population of any major nation except South Africa and the Soviet Union. Some people have recently argued that the big increase in

sending people to prison has reduced our crime rate slightly in the 1980s, but it is only a slight reduction (and a very expensive one at that). There is evidence, however, that a high prison rate does not reduce crime (Hurst, 1983).

A more efficient police force could perhaps help reduce crime, and there is some evidence of that with Japan's police force. An efficient police force does not necessarily mean that civil liberties would be violated, but the police do violate some civil liberties in Japan and in many other nations that we would not accept under our constitution and values of freedom and individualism (see Box 8.3). And it should be noted that in the United States approximately 6,000 people are wrongfully convicted of serious crimes each year, with about 100 innocent people convicted of murder in this century, 13 of whom were actually executed (*Los Angeles Times,* March 17, 1985).

It seems clear that the most effective way to reduce crime would be to change some of the underlying social conditions producing it. A recent study found that guaranteeing jobs to men coming out of prison significantly reduced their rate of returning to prison—much more so than guaranteeing a welfare check (Berk et al., 1980). Thus, we could reduce the crime rate by guaranteeing jobs to men leaving prison. The problem is that the United States has had high unemployment for many years. Under these conditions very few politicians are willing to sponsor legislation to guarantee jobs to prisoners and not other people who are unemployed.

Other factors help produce crime. Poverty, of course, is one. It is very likely that reducing poverty now would reduce the crime rate for the next generation. But if we are to reduce poverty, many people would have to pay higher taxes for welfare and higher prices for things like food that depend on low-wage labor. Racial and ethnic divisions along with discrimination contribute to crime, as does the high rate of fatherless children. But again, we are unwilling or unable to change these things in a simple manner.

The situation is not totally hopeless, but the things we can do help in only a small way. For example, the preschool program for poor children called Headstart has been shown to reduce crime at least

BOX 8.3

Crime and the Criminal Justic System in Saudi Arabia

At high noon last Nov. 4 [1983], as thousands of worshipers — their prayers ended — poured out of Jamia Mosque, a black police van carrying a man and woman drove into the empty parking lot outside and stopped next to a piece of cardboard that had been placed on the pavement.

Ali Fakieh and Mouvira Sabie stepped from the van, blindfolded with their arms bound behind them. They walked on wobbly legs toward the piece of cardboard and the man who waited there — a muscular former slave of Ethiopian descent who carried a three-foot-long, double-edged sword. The former slave would earn about $350 that day for severing each of their heads. . . .

Fifteen years ago, when they were in their twenties, they had robbed and killed a man. But the victim's eldest son had not reached the age of consent and thus was not in position to approve the death sentence — or offer forgiveness, which under Islamic law would have earned them their freedom. So, they had waited in prison for the young man to grow up and make his choice. Now, the eldest son had become an adult and he had decided: They would die. . . .

Saudi Arabia is the world's only country whose legal system is based entirely on the Sharia, the body of Islamic law. The Saudis have no constitution. The Sharia is a system of checks and balances, compassion and harshness. Little understood or studied in the West, its punishments — public beheadings, amputations and floggings — are often dismissed as nothing less than medieval barbarity.

To this criticism, the Saudis have a quick response: The tough penalties are a deterrent that have made Saudi Arabia probably the most crime-free country in the world on a per capita basis. "If there is a safer place anywhere, I don't know of it," said the well-traveled minister of trade, Suleiman Selim.

According to government statistics, there are only 14,220 major and minor crimes — including consumption of alcohol and adultery — committed during 1982 in Saudi Arabia, a country of 7 million. In comparison, Los Angeles County, also with a population of 7 million and with fewer actions considered crimes, recorded 159,662 arrests for felony crimes during 1982. Misdemeanor arrests in 1982 totaled 339,837, and there were 1,415 murders committed.

The most common crime in Saudi Arabia was theft, accounting for 30 percent of the total, followed by alcohol consumption, 22 percent, and burglary, 20 percent. The Saudi figures included 97 premeditated murders and 31 suicides. Foreign workers were responsible for 39 percent of the offenses, the Interior Ministry said.

"The implementation of the Sharia has gotton a bad press in the West because it runs counter to our trends of thought," said Frank Vogel, an American lawyer and Fulbright scholar who is studying Islamic law for a doctorate. "We treat morality and behavior as an individual matter. The Saudis treat them as social matters that are the responsibility of the entire society."

"Why is the Sharia effective? Because there's basically no crime in Saudi Arabia. In the United States, how many women are raped each year? How many people are killed? How many billions of dollars are spent on burglar alarms and anti-crime devices? So here they cut off a few hands of guilty people and avoid these horrors. Can you really say that makes them barbaric and us civilized?"

No one has proved conclusively, though, that there is a direct relationship between Saudi Arabia's harsh penalties and low crime rate, just as it remains unproven that the use of the death penalty in the United States deters capital offenses.

Critics offer some other possible explanations: Saudi Arabia is a country where most people are rich and no one is poor, its people are religious and moral and they believe the Koran, the Islamic holy book, when it says one should not drink, steal or commit adultery. The Saudis — members of the predominant Sunni branch of Islam — are also a tribal people with communal bonds, a society that believes in the sanctity of the family and the inviolability of the home.

Sharia translates in Arabic as the road to a watering place, hence the path of God. It differs fundamentally from Western law in that it is not, in theory, man-made; it is divine, based on Allah's revelations to the Prophet Mohammed in the 7th Century and on Mohammed's sayings. Since Sharia is not case law, judges are not bound by precedent or the decisions of higher courts.

Under the Saudi system, anyone suspected of a crime is usually arrested immediately and required to make a statement without a lawyer being present. Investigations are carried out by the Ministry of Justice, which recommends to the provincial governor whether to prosecute. During the inquiry, suspects remain in prison, jammed into cells where 60 or more people may be held. Unlike in the United States, however, little violence occurs in Saudi prisons.

Judges in Saudi Arabia are recruited by the Justice Ministry from the top law school graduates and are widely respected for their incorruptibility. They alone decide guilt or innocence and punishment. Their courts are generally closed to all but the accused's family, and no counsel is present at the proceedings. There is no jury, no bail, no writ of habeas corpus. Under Islamic law, suspects can be held for months, even years, while investigations are under way.

Despite this, many Western observers are impressed with the general fairness of the system and the discretion used in meting out punishment. All sentences must be personally approved by the king, and no more than about a dozen executions a year are carried out here. A guilty verdict is rendered only if there is a confession or there are two male witnesses to the crime. If there is the slightest doubt, judges reduce the charge to a lesser offense.

Anyone found to have falsely accused a chaste woman of adultery is given 100 lashes, 20 more than one gets for consuming alcoholic beverages. Whippings — administered in public, as is all punishment — are designed to humiliate, not maim. The victim remains clothed, his skin is not to be broken and the flogger swings a supple, cane-like stick with only the lower part of his arm.

Punishment, as in most societies, is based on retaliation — or as the Koran says, "a soul for a soul, an eye for an eye, a nose for a nose, and ear for an ear, a tooth for a tooth . . . " — and on fear. Amputations, the Koran says, "will be a disgrace for them in this world, whilst in the next a terrible punishment awaits them."

However, any criminal can be cleared if the family of his victim offers forgiveness — the Koran promises great rewards for this act of charity — or if the family agrees to accept compensation. The cost of buying out of a murder conviction averages about $40,000, according to Western sources.

Other Islamic countries — among them Egypt, Iran, Kuwait, Pakistan, Yemen and Afghanistan — have tried to graft various aspects of the Sharia to their existing legal systems, but none uses Islamic law purely and exclusively, as does Saudi Arabia.

Source: David Lamb, "For Saudis, Religion and Law Are One," *Los Angeles Times,* Jan. 10, 1984.

somewhat when these children become young adults. Also, organizing neighborhoods to watch out for crime in the area may help reduce crime.

But what has not yet been effective is to try to change young adults from their criminal ways after years of poverty and neglect. The underlying conditions that produce these people must be changed to reduce the future supply of criminals. Currently we have the reverse of a "supply-side social problems policy"—we do not try to reduce the supply as much as simply lock it (young offenders) up after the abundant supply of criminals has already been created.

CHAPTER SUMMARY

Key Terms

criminal justice system, 196
deviance, 203
crime, 206
traditional crime, 206
organized crime, 207
white-collar crime, 207
political crime, 207
residual deviance, 211

anomie, 213
differential association theory, 214
labeling theory, 215
primary deviance, 215
secondary deviance, 215
degradation ceremonies, 217

Content

All societies require social organization and social order if life for the large number of people making up the society is to be possible. But societies are made up of people and groups whose individual and group interests are sometimes (or often) in conflict with the interests of other groups or the society more generally. Thus, all societies use various means of social control to maintain social order in the face of these conflicts. We do not ask whether or not a society employs means of social control, but what are the means of social control employed and in whose interests (the society's more generally or some subgroup within it).

The methods of social control can be divided into external versus internal means. External means of social control include force, material rewards, and information control. Internal means include internalized ideologies and belief systems, collective rituals, and self-evaluations through a socialization process.

Just as all societies must employ various means of social control to maintain social order, all societies have deviance. No society is ever totally successful in controlling deviance, nor would a society want to be so successful. We have seen how, in fact, societies need some deviance to define their normative boundaries. And equally important, elites often emphasize the threat of deviants (real or imagined) to enhance their own power over others in the society.

From the perspective stressed in this chapter, it is more important to understand the nature of societies (norms, values, type of social organization) in understanding deviance than to understand the characteristics of individual deviants. It is also important to understand the process by which deviants are selected and labeled as such. Not all individuals who have committed deviant acts are actually perceived as deviants. The position of people in the society, their influence, and whom they disturb by their deviance are all important in determining whether or not they are actually selected and treated as deviant.

Crime is a specific type of deviance that involves breaking laws established by the political system. For this reason the nature of crime must be examined within the context of power and the political process. The four major categories of crime are traditional crime, organized crime, white-collar crime, and political crime.

The extent of traditional crime in the United States is measured by the FBI through crimes reported to police and social surveys. There has been a rapid increase in crime in the United States during the 1960s and 1970s, with only a slight decline during the 1980s.

Sociologists disagree about the most important causes of crime and deviance. Several theories, each of which stress a different aspect of the causes of crime, were examined. These theories are categorized as biological theories, social stress theories, control theories, culture and learning theories, labeling theories, and conflict theories.

We briefly explored some of the possible solutions to crime in the United States. Research indicates ways in which crime can be reduced, but unfortunately the "solutions" that are possible to employ and do not harm powerful interests in the society are solutions that are not very effective.

CHAPTER 9

Systems of Social Stratification

Class is a system for limiting freedom: it limits the freedom of the powerful in dealing with other people, because the strong are constricted within the circle of action that maintains their power; class constricts the weak more obviously in that they must obey commands. What happens to the dignity men see in themselves and in each other, when their freedom is checked by class?

— Richard Sennett and Jonathan Cobb, The Hidden Injuries of Class

We have come to one of the most explosive questions in human societies — who gets what, and why? How are we to divide and distribute all the goods, services, and other things people value? Throughout history it is quite probable that more people have been killed over this question than for any other reason.

Consider the conflict in Northern Ireland today: The violent conflict there is between Protestants and Catholics. A young Catholic boy growing up in Northern Ireland today, we can call him Michael O'Leary, will probably learn to hate Protestants just as Protestant boys will learn to hate Catholics. And if the hate and frustration become strong enough, and if Michael has an opportunity to join the Irish Republican Army, he may do so, in which case he may begin to kill Protestants. But will Michael come to kill Protestants primarily because of their religion? The answer is clearly **no.** The killing is over the question of who gets what, and why. And it is a question that goes back a few centuries in Northern Ireland.

By the 1600s, England had become a Protestant nation (in part because in the early 1500s Henry VIII had a problem with the Pope over all of Henry's wives — but that is another story). Under the leadership of Cromwell in the 1640s, England invaded Ireland, which, as today, was a Catholic country. After invading Ireland, Cromwell took the best property in Northern Ireland and gave it to his military officers and others from England who would settle in Northern Ireland (Fraser, 1974). Thus, it is from this legacy that Michael O'Leary is more likely to have low wages and be unemployed when he grows up compared with Protestant boys his age in Northern Ireland. This is to say that religious hatred overlaps the more concrete hatred related to the question of who gets what, and why. The Irish Republican Army would like to change the government, which is still supported by the British Army, that maintains laws helping to continue the advantages of Protestants (former invaders) in Northern Ireland today.

Let's consider examples closer to home. In societies like ours people never seem bored with the similar theme of who gets ahead and how. We flock to movies about people who achieve success through determination in athletics, dancing, or marriage to a rising military officer. The most popular television shows in the 1980s have been about the life-styles of the wealthy. We buy books telling us how to get ahead through intimidating others, dressing right, investing in real estate, getting right with God, or getting right with our psyche.

All these themes and questions pertain to the subject matter of this chapter — social stratification. Like material culture, nonmaterial culture, and social structure, social stratification is a fundamental part of all societies. In this chapter we explore such things as the nature of social stratification, theories of social stratification, and the different kinds of stratification systems that have existed throughout history. Details about our own system of social stratification come in a later chapter. As we will see in the present chapter, the nature of our economy and political system are very important in understanding our particular system of social stratification. Thus, on leaving this chapter we will consider these subjects before returning to our own particular system of social stratification for a closer look.

THE NATURE OF SOCIAL STRATIFICATION

All animals have a method of deciding the question of who gets what and why, involving either hierarchy or territoriality, or a combination of the two (van den Berghe, 1974). Animals that exist in solitary family units, such as predatory birds and cats, tend to possess a strong sense or urge toward territoriality. What is in their territory is theirs and they will defend it. More social animals like wild dogs and higher primates are likely to possess a system of hierarchy within the group. One, or perhaps a few, in the group are dominant, with the right to lay claim to more than an equal share of whatever is valued. For example, chimps living in the wild establish a hierarchy with the top position attained by a male who is able to intimidate others most successfully (van Lawick-Goodall, 1972). Once this intimidation has been accomplished, the system of ranking and method of distribution has been established. Overt conflict over the question of who gets what has been settled — at least for a time. Before long, a new challenger will emerge, and if successful, will change the system of ranking. But at least for a time every chimp knows who is on top so that daily living can continue without consistent conflict.

Humans, of course, cannot be compared with other animals in all respects. With social stratification, two general differences are most important. On the one hand, unlike other animals, humans often have *both* hierarchy and territoriality. Human societies usually have a system that ranks people within the society and a system of dividing territory. This unique characteristic may suggest that humans can be especially possessive, selfish, and conflict-prone. But on the other hand, humans also have an immense variety of systems of social stratification. For example, human conditions vary from almost total equality to the other extreme of very high inequality — a level of inequality *much* higher than is found among any other animals. As described in previous chapters, an obvious implication of this second point is that humans are much less programmed by a biological heritage than are other animals. When considering human stratification systems, we must look for underlying social conditions, not simply those related to biology or individual psychology, that produce the variety of stratification systems.

With this subject of human societies, try to free yourself from preconceived ideas about who should get what and why, and consider the possibilities. We could say that everyone in the society gets an equal share of what is highly valued. In one sense this

seems fair; but will it be accepted by all in the society? If we are referring to anything other than small hunting and gathering societies, this solution will most likely not be accepted. Some will argue, rightly or wrongly, that for some reason they deserve more than others. Maybe they believe they have worked harder, are more talented, have contributed more to the society, or for some other reason deserve more. Other people will most likely counter these claims with some of their own.

In the face of this disagreement a system of rules will emerge defining and "justifying" who gets what and why. As we will see, people in certain positions in the society have the means and opportunities to successfully demand more rewards. Thus, we must *understand the underlying characteristics of the society to understand social stratification*. We may refer to these underlying characteristics as the "objective rules" shaping social stratification. In addition to these objective rules, however, are ideological rules and justifications. Although never accepted by all in the society, during periods of social stability, these rules are usually accepted by most people. And to the degree the rules have been accepted, the system of stratification has defined who gets what and why, reducing overt conflict over this explosive question — at least for a time. As history shows us, the objective rules as well as the justifications behind a particular system of social stratification are subject to change, again bringing open conflict over who gets what and why. When such overt conflict becomes widespread, we occasionally find that a new stratification system emerges.

The main point of the above is that social stratification can best be understood in reference to *group conflict*. A system of social stratification is based on social conditions that allow some groups to demand and receive more than an equal share of valued things. Other groups who are getting less than an equal share, or at least receive less than they believe they should, will be in conflict with the more privileged groups. *Overt conflict* will not always exist, however, because a system of social stratification will often be able to justify the inequality, make it appear inevitable, or give people the hope they may improve their own rank in the system through individual effort. But as history shows, the underlying conflict over who gets what and why is never totally eliminated.

You may have never thought of our own stratification system in the general way I have just described. In fact, given American values of individualism you may even find it troubling to consider how people rank others in our society. But when we consider evidence from history and other societies today, even from nonhuman societies, you may begin to see our own society in a different way. Whether or not you like what you see, whether or not you believe the system should be changed, I hope you will agree that we must understand what exists as best we can.

Some Basic Concepts. Social stratification is more than simply an unequal distribution of valued goods, services, honor, or positions in the society — what we can call **social inequality.** By **social stratification** we mean a *system* of social relationships and rules that leads to an unequal distribution of valued goods, services, honor, and positions (Kerbo, 1983, p. 11). The unequal distribution, in other words, is not random or haphazard but is rather orderly and systematic (there is a logic or system of rules behind the distribution process).

When a social stratification system is established (we sometimes say "institutionalized"), people have come to expect that individuals and groups with certain positions in the stratification system will be able to demand more influence and respect and accumulate a greater share of goods and services. Such systematic inequality may or may not be accepted equally by a majority in the society, but it is recognized as the way things are. As noted earlier, systems of social stratification commonly contain normative rules and justifications that "explain" why rewards are distributed in an unequal manner and why people are placed in certain positions in the system. High levels of inequality often need justifying ideologies that obscure the real causes of inequality.

For example, consider a society in which the lowest-ranking people are extremely poor. In addition to being materially poor, these people are considered unclean and disgusting by others in the society. This lowly group may not eat in the same place as higher-ranking people and must either hide or bow with their face in the dirt when higher-ranking people pass them on the street. Further, when a person is born into a family of this low rank, he or she has no chance of working out of this low position.

The situation I have just described is roughly similar to the position held by untouchables in ancient India. Remarkably, historical records show almost no revolts by untouchables over the centuries, at least until quite recent times (Moore, 1978, p. 62). This high level of acceptance by untouchables is in large part due to a religious belief system. The Hindu religion supports the belief that souls are reborn after death — reincarnation. Most important is the belief that individuals are reborn in a higher or lower position in the society, depending on how well they followed the rules and duties of their position in the previous life. Thus, untouchables are people who have broken the most important rules in their previous life. This is one reason why untouchables are held in such low esteem. But it is important to see that this belief system works to control untouchables because they do not want to remain untouchables in their "next" life! So for this life they will bear the insults, dirty work, and wretched conditions as is expected of them. In short, the stratification system has been justified and stabilized by a belief system that "explains" who gets what, and why.

All systems of social stratification, of course, do not resemble the caste system of India. Stratification systems differ in many ways, most importantly with respect to a few major criteria. First, people may be placed in ranks in the stratification system through ascription or achievement. **Ascription** means that people are placed in ranks because of criteria they cannot influence, such as rank of their parents at birth, sex, race, or religious heritage. **Achievement** means that people can have some control over their placement. For example, if they follow certain rules they may be able to work up to a higher position, or fall to a lower position if they are unable to do so. In reality, most stratification systems contain a mixture of ascription and achievement rules. As we will see, the caste system of India falls toward the ascription extreme, whereas most industrial societies have more achievement-ori-

Societies with stratification based on achievement offer more mobility than those based on ascribed status such as race or sex. In both the United States and West Germany, women have begun to assume positions in industries traditionally thought of as male—the construction industry is a good example. Can you think of occupations or professions where ascribed status continues to dominate? (top: © Will McIntyre/Photo Researchers, Inc.; bottom: © George Fischer/Photo Researchers, Inc.)

ented rules of placement (though ascription is certainly not absent).

Another dimension of social stratification that varies from one society to another is the degree of **social mobility** up and down the ranks. We can refer to social mobility in a person's own lifetime (intragenerational mobility) or the mobility that may occur from a parent's position to the position attained by the adult offspring (intergenerational mobility). A stratification system that stresses achievement criteria over ascription will likely have more social mobility. As we will see, however, the exact amount of social mobility varies widely even among societies that have some achievement oriented rules of placement.

Systems of social stratification also differ in terms of the primary factor or factors determining a person's location or rank in the system. Marx believed that a person's relationship to the means of production was the most important criterion in determining position in society. Those who owned land in agrarian societies, or industrial capital in industrial societies, were on top in the stratification system, whereas those who owned very little and depended on others for their livelihood were on the bottom. Marx, we can say, stressed one form of economic relation as important in ranking people.

Some fifty years after Marx developed his theories, Max Weber introduced his highly respected **multidimensional view of stratification.** Weber (Gerth and Mills, 1946) agreed with Marx in part that economic factors were often important in determining class, but Weber added two others called status and power (or party).

By **status-honor** Weber meant prestige or respect that comes from living up to certain values and ideas—thus, status-honor is more an element of life-style. By **party** or **power** Weber meant the ability to influence others through organization, as in a political party or control in a bureaucracy. But Weber also saw **class** or economic factors as important in two ways. In addition to the ownership versus nonownership of the means of production stressed by Marx, Weber stressed economic skill level. Even if a person owned nothing, a special economic skill could bring that person a higher wage and more secure job than a person with no ownership and no special skill.

Weber recognized that these primary dimensions of stratification are usually interrelated, though not always. If a person is high in status, he or she is usually high in class and power as well. But especially in times of change in a society, these three dimensions can become unconnected, with people, for example, high in class not always high in status. And finally, Weber also recognized that one of these dimensions can be the leading factor in a particular stratification system; that is, in one society class may be more important than in another, and high placement in the class dimension can bring a person high position in status and power as well. In other societies status or power may be the key dimension. Thus, systems of social stratification can differ with respect to which of these dimensions—class, status, or power—is the most important for ranking people.

Types of Stratification Systems

When we look around the world, and throughout history, we find an immense variety of stratification systems. If we compare these systems in detail, we find that no two stratification systems are exactly alike. But on a more general level it is important to recognize that only a few basic types of stratification systems have existed. We now examine these major types of stratification systems in terms of the criteria and dimensions outlined above.

Primitive Communal Systems. The first humans, and most people living in hunting and gathering societies today, have a form of stratification that can be referred to as **primitive communalism.** Compared with all other stratification systems, however, it is rather difficult to see that these societies have a stratification system at all. Their level of material inequality is nonexistent to low, which means that they need no complex rules defining who gets what and why. Most commonly, all goods, especially food, are divided equally. These societies may have leaders, but the leaders are seldom very powerful. If they cannot lead or serve some special function for the tribe, they are replaced.

About the only important dimension of stratification in these types of societies is status-honor. The most skilled in finding food, organizing the tribe, or passing on wisdom may receive more status-honor. This higher standing with respect to status-honor may result in some material rewards and a bit more

influence. We have already seen that adult male hunters are favored in hunting and gathering tribes with a high dependence on meat for food. However, it must also be remembered that there are very few material goods to produce inequality. Status-honor, on the other hand, is not necessarily a scarce commodity and can therefore be unequally distributed (Lenski, 1966).

We will probably never know the extent of variation among hunting and gathering tribes before the first horticultural societies about 10,000 years ago, but with contemporary hunting and gathering societies we do know there are some differences in social stratification. These differences, however, tend to be minor and center around the degree of influence held by the tribal leader (Fried, 1973; Sahlins and Service, 1960).

To summarize, in terms of major characteristics of stratification systems, the ranks in primitive communal societies are open, placement is made through achievement, status-honor is the primary form of inequality, but the overall level of inequality is very low (see Table 9.1). This is true because no one is able to dominate others within the tribe to any great extent. If the son of the best hunter, for example, is not the best hunter when he grows up, he will not retain the status of his father. As we will see, this is in vast contrast to most other types of stratification systems.

Slavery. One of the most persistent forms of social stratification throughout history has been **slavery.** The main characteristics of this form of stratification include (1) the economic ownership of other humans, and thus the predominant form of inequality is economic; (2) generally closed ranks; (3) ascription as the main form of placement; and (4) a relatively high level of inequality among people in slave societies.

I must caution, however, that we find extensive variance among slave societies with respect to these characteristics. Also, not every society with any slavery can be called a slave society because slavery may not be the main form of stratification. For example, the United States was not primarily a slave society before the Civil War. Through much of the Roman Empire, Egyptian Empire, and Greek city-

TABLE 9.1. *Characteristics of major types of stratification systems*

Type of stratification system	Ranks	Placement	Primary basis of rank inequality	Relative level of material inequality
1. Primitive communal	Open	Achievement	Status-honor	Low
2. Slave system	Generally closed	Ascription, but not always	Economic	High
3. Caste system	Closed	Ascription	Status-honor	High
4. Estate, feudal system	Primarily closed	Primarily ascription	Economic	High
5. Asian system	Primarily closed	Ascription, but some achievement	Power, state, position	High
6. Class system	Primarily open	Mix of ascription and achievement	Economic and bureaucratic power	Medium

states, however, slavery did tend to dominate. In the case of the Roman Empire, about one-fourth of the population may have been slaves (MacMullen, 1974).

When we speak of slavery, most people in the United States tend to think about the U.S. form of slavery. Slavery in the United States, however, was untypical in many respects. A primary difference is that, unlike in the U.S., slavery throughout history has usually not corresponded with a rigid racist belief system.

Though the position of slave has often been a closed position based on ascription, there is also much variance in this respect. In some societies a person could be held as a slave for only a limited period of time. In other societies, a slave could work overtime, saving money to buy freedom. And in a few ancient societies, slaves were sometimes highly rewarded and even placed in positions of high influence. Some wealthy and powerful slave owners have felt that slaves could be controlled and trusted with power more than nonslaves who might legitimately aspire to an even higher position and threaten the position of the slave owner. For example, during one period of the Ottoman Empire centered in Turkey, "all of the high officials of state were selected from the ranks of youths taken from Christian families,

made slaves to the sultan, trained for military or civil careers, and converted to Islam" (Lenski, 1966, p. 287).

Throughout history there have been three major ways of falling into slavery—birth, capture, and debt. The hereditary form of ascription into slavery was primary in the United States (after the first generation of slaves brought from Africa), but not throughout world history. Most common has been slavery through capture, as found in the early empires like those of Rome and Egypt. Somewhat less common was slavery through falling into debt.

Material inequality in slave societies was quite high, even excluding the common condition of poverty among slaves. If workers had to compete with slave labor, wages would no doubt be low. But we can also expect that slave owners were generally able to attain more wealth and income compared with nonslave owners. In the Roman Empire, for example, elites (with senator status) had income and wealth more than 250,000 times that of the average laborer (Dunean-Jones, 1974; Antonio, 1979).

Caste System. Most important among the distinguishing characteristics of a **caste system** are its almost complete ascriptive placement and rigidly closed ranks. There is seldom if ever any social mobility; the rank in which you were born, that is, the rank of your parents, is where you stay. Also very important is the extent to which status-honor is stressed as the primary dimension of inequality in a caste system. People are high or low in the stratification system because of the prestige of their group, their "purity" in terms of religious values, their race, or the prestige of their inherited occupation. There is certainly unequal wealth and power in a caste system, but if it is a true caste system then the traditional status ranks are more important than wealth and power. For example, in a caste system, a lower-status person could acquire a large amount of money, but it would hardly affect the individual's rank; she or he would still be seen as unfit to associate with upper-caste people.

A caste system has existed in its extreme form in only a few places, most notably in India. The roots of the Indian caste system can be traced to the conquest of the area by Aryan invaders about 4,000 years ago (Pfeiffer, 1977). As these invaders settled into the new area, they held positions of dominance through military force and economic control. The caste system of status ranks and Hinduism supporting this system came later (Thapar, 1966). Thus, the system of stratification in India has a material base in military force and economic dominance. However, once the caste system of status ranks was developed to support the material dominance, it took on a life of its own. This caste system began breaking down only with British rule in the 1800s and was made illegal with Indian independence after World War II. However, the tradition of caste in India remains a powerful force.

In the Indian caste system there are four main divisions or castes (varnas), with brahmans (priests) and kshatriyas (a warrior caste) on top. These top positions are held by the descendants of the early Aryan invaders. In addition to the four main castes there are many subcastes (jatis), with much local variation based on occupational specialization (Dumont, 1970). But not everyone in the population occupies a particular caste or subcaste. There are a large number of "outcastes," or untouchables, who lack a formal status rank; thus they are on the very bottom of the stratification system.

One of the most remarkable aspects of the Indian caste system are the complex and numerous rules pertaining to rituals and ranking (see Box 9.1). Different caste members must eat only certain foods and in certain specified ways and places, have only certain occupations, bathe in the proper manner, touch and greet other caste members in a specified way, and so on. These rules and rituals in total help determine the status or caste ranks; that is, one caste is higher than another because of their "purity" in relation to these practices. Also remarkable, however, is the almost total lack of social mobility and closure of ranks. The caste of birth is where one stays — caste intermarriage or change in later life is (or was) very rare in India.

At least some characteristics of caste can be found outside India, and it is common to hear any form of inequality based on ascription referred to as a caste ranking. For example, race and sexual inequalities are often referred to as caste divisions, and so is the ascriptive status maintained by old upper-class families in countries like the United States. But there has been controversy over the extent to which race and sex divisions constitute caste divisions. To begin with, race and sex inequalities in modern societies are nowhere near the level of closure found in ancient India. Minority group members in modern societies are seldom totally barred from marriage to other groups or totally excluded from some occupations. But most important, two other things are lacking with race and sex divisions today: (1) these divisions are less supported by a complex belief system like the Hindu religion, and (2) the lower-status groups do not usually accept their lower position to the degree found in the old Indian caste system. We conclude by noting that there are at least some caste characteristics in race and sex ascription in modern societies like the United States. And for the same two reasons described above, a caste system in its complete sense does not exist even in South Africa today.

Estate System. Although the caste system is found in its most complete form in India, the estate system (or feudal system) was most completely found in Europe during the Middle Ages. This **feudal or estate system** is a stratification system based on

BOX 9.1

*Purity Versus Impurity:
The Indian Caste System*

One of the most remarkable and complex forms of social stratification began developing over 3,000 years ago in India. Westerners, with their views of individualism and personal dignity, find this system of ranking almost incomprehensible. But this system has been one of the most stable and accepted (by its members) in the history of human societies.

Because of the multitude of rules and caste divisions, I cannot hope to adequately describe this stratification system, and I therefore encourage interested readers to consult Dumont (1970). But I can give you a sense of some of the basic elements of the Indian caste system.

The key to caste ranking in the status hierarchy is purity versus impurity with respect to prescribed practices and characteristics of a group. There is a *long* list of these practices and characteristics that also are ranked in importance, though this ranking varies among differing castes. This means that the rank of one caste relative to another can sometimes be determined only after a lengthy comparison of the purity rules each caste must follow. And because the rules vary by region of the country, no one is sure how many castes there are in India. (There are well over 100 castes.) The castes were often associated with particular occupations or functions of groups, but this is not always the case, and the original occupational specification often no longer applies.

The complexity in this system can be understood by considering some of the purity rules. The following kinds of contact with someone from a lower (or less pure) caste are ranked in the order to which they are to be avoided: serving you boiled food, serving you fried food, touching your brass utensils, smoking from your pipe (but not the same mouthpiece), touching you, and touching your children. But even this ranking of closeness of contact has many exceptions with specific situations and the specific caste members who are in contact. For example, a caste member who washes clothing does

land ownership, with extensive ascription and very low rates of social mobility between ranks.

Three broad ranks or divisions tend to be primary in estate systems: the first estate (the priestly class), the second estate (the land-holding nobility or aristocracy), and the third estate (or commoners, which includes everyone else). Religion played an important part in the estate system, as the makeup of the first estate indicates. But religion, which was primarily the Catholic religion in the European estate system, was never as central as the Hindu religion in the Indian caste system. More important in the estate system was the state's legal sanction of the divisions.

There is a controversy over whether the estate

system was based primarily on military power or economic dominance (Heller, 1969). Marx stressed the importance of economic control through land ownership, whereby one group owned the major means of production (land) and others lived at their mercy. Bloch (1961) disputes the economic view by describing the origins of feudalism in military power held by some families during Europe's early Middle Ages. I will enter this debate at this time (before Chapter 11 on the state) only by suggesting that in the early European age of feudalism the military power aspect was more important, whereas economic and political forms of control increased in importance later.

During the early period of feudalism in Europe

not pollute the house of higher-caste members when normally entering the house to pick up dirty clothing. However, when this person brings clothing and fabric for weddings, the house is polluted and must be ritually cleaned (Dumont, 1970, pp. 133–134).

I noted above that serving food is considered a very important form of contact. But the rules pertaining to the touching of food by someone from another caste are quite varied. For example, there are no rules prohibiting acceptance of raw food from a lower-caste person. Contamination by touching becomes progressively more serious for food that is fried and food that is boiled. It is not just the food itself, however, but the container in which it is cooked and where it is cooked and eaten that is also important. An earthen pot touched by a very low-caste person must be replaced, but the same situation with a bronze pot requires only ritual washing.

I have described only a small number of the many rules of purity in the Indian caste system. And whereas we can sympathize with untouchables who clearly had a harsh position in this caste system, consider also the situation of high-caste members. The higher the position in the caste system, the more one must be concerned with becoming polluted by others. The highest brahmans were especially sheltered when eating and for this reason often ate alone. "Any unforeseen contact, not only with a low caste man (sometimes going as far as his shadow) or an animal, but even with someone from the house (woman, child, man who is not purified for eating) would make the food unfit for consumption" (Dumont, 1970, pp. 138–139).

This caste system in India has been breaking down ever since the British occupation in the 1800s. Today the system is illegal. But a culture shaped by thousands of years of existence will not be eliminated in a mere 100 years. If you watch the mass media closely, it will not take long for you to catch reports of new cases of violent conflict in India between people in caste positions rejecting and supporting the new laws against caste discrimination.

the continent was filled with overlapping and fragmented areas of authority. A system of small landholding had emerged with the decline of the Roman Empire after about A.D. 500. People fled the urban areas and sought survival and protection on small agricultural estates. Thus, land was dominated primarily by rather independent noble kinship groups, but with shifting alliances to other noble families in an area. As these ties between noble families became more extensive, increasingly dominant noble families emerged, forming kingdoms. Later, after about A.D. 1200, state political systems grew to further institutionalize the authority of the more dominant nobility (Hechter and Brustein, 1980), making possible the powerful royal families.

There was extensive ascription and little mobility in the estate system, but neither was as extreme as a caste system. People were broadly restricted to the estate position of their birth. However, the especially talented peasant could attain high positions in the state, as a knight in the military, or in a religious order. Even the most talented peasant, though, was unlikely to move into the nobility or higher clergy.

We leave the estate system by stressing that it did exist in many agricultural societies around the world, though the European form stands out as the typical example. To some degree, Japan's early agricultural history shows evidence of a similar feudal or estate system with a nobility, a warrior estate (shogun), and peasants (Bendix, 1979). By the 1600s, however, the Tokugawa dynasty established rigid ranks based on status very similar to a caste system, with even a group of "outcastes" called Eta.

Asian Systems. Although the agricultural stratification systems in the East and West differed in many ways from the start, the differences became more apparent as the West slowly turned to estate systems after the fall of the Western Roman Empire. Most important in the estate or feudal system was agricultural production by wealthy, independent landowning families. Only later were these merged under the control of kings and a state organization, but even then small-group production remained.

In Asia, the development of the **Asian system** (or Asiatic mode of production) was related to agricultural production that required extensive irrigation. Because irrigation required a higher form of social organization, even though land was at times common property, something like a state elite emerged to plan and control common projects like irrigation systems. Through time, in places like

Before industrialization, Japan had a rigid stratification system similar to both the feudal and caste systems. These historic photos of an Ainu tribesman and a Samurai warrior provide valuable information about the cultural worlds of Japan's old stratification system. The Ainu were an aboriginal people living close to the land. The Samurai warrior is dressed in formal military attire, illustrating the importance of force in maintaining the old social order before industrialization.

China, this state elite grew to dominate the society. Thus, unlike the estate system, in the Asian system of stratification there was the early development of an elite based on political position in addition to land ownership (Mandel, 1971; Krader, 1975).

With the example of China we find a hereditary ruling class much like the European nobility. But land ownership was less important to this Chinese elite than was state control. Because of the importance of the state organization, a unique class of *mandarins* actually ran the state. An important qualifying characteristic for mandarins was the ability to read and write — a difficult accomplishment with the Chinese language. Mandarins were required to pass written exams before attaining their positions; in a sense this was the first civil service exam.

Because the position of mandarin was based on achievement, we therefore find some chance of mobility in the Chinese system. Such mobility was very limited, however, because few but the wealthy and children of mandarins had the time and help to master the Chinese language.

Not all Asian countries had an Asian stratification system as it is described here. For example, as noted in an earlier chapter, Japan's early system of agriculture did not require large state-run irrigation projects. Thus, the state elite was not so important in the early history of Japan. Although there were important differences, as noted above, Japan's early stratification system (before the Tokugawa period) was more similar to Europe's feudal system than to China's Asian system (Halliday, 1975; Reischauer, 1977).

Class System. The final major type of stratification system in human societies is the **class system.** In contrast to all other systems except primitive communal societies, we find much more social mobility and achievement-oriented placement in a class system. There is certainly a hierarchy of ranks in this system (called classes), but these class ranks are more open, though to varying degrees. As we will see, in the United States there tends to be rather extensive social mobility among people in the middle ranks in a class system, whereas there is less mobility at the top and bottom class ranks.

In a class system the primary dimensions of stratification are economic — ownership of property and skill level in the economic productive system. Class systems are found in industrial societies; thus the most important form of ownership is capital or industrial production facilities (factories) rather than land. Because such ownership continues to be subject to extensive inheritance, class ranks are not completely open or based on achievement. However, because occupational skill depends on training and education, the relatively higher degree of achievement and mobility found in class systems is located in this characteristic (though there continue to be limits to achievement, as we will see).

In the more advanced class systems, where industrial production has become more complex and a state has expanded, bureaucratic position also becomes a primary source of inequality. With a hierarchy of bureaucratic ranks we find inequality. A high position in a bureaucracy in either the private sector or government can bring a higher income, among other rewards.

Unlike the more rigid stratification systems of caste and estate, the ranks or classes within a class system are less clearly delineated. As we will see in more detail with our own class system, because a complex set of factors influences class position, and because some of these factors involve continuous grades, we cannot always specify exactly where the boundaries of one class stop and another begin. But we can identify general class rankings that have very important consequences for the people located in these class positions.

The broadest class divisions are **upper class, middle class,** and **working class.** The upper class is made up of the wealthiest families who own huge amounts of capital. (Capital can be defined as property or wealth used to produce more wealth.) The middle class (or white-collar or nonmanual workers) is made up of people who work in more skilled, nonmanual occupations. The working class (or blue-collar or manual workers) is made up of skilled to unskilled manual workers. Manual labor means physical rather than mental labor.

The complexity of our class system requires refinement of class divisions and more explanation later. But even this very broad, three-level class division is useful in understanding differences in family income, life-styles, health, family relations, child-rearing methods, and many other differences among people.

A final word on communist, socialist, or "class-less" societies is in order. Capitalist industrial societies do have stratification systems that differ from those of communist or socialist societies. But though communist industrial societies claim to be classless, they do have stratification systems quite similar to our own class system in many (but no means all) respects. As we will see in more detail below, with only some alterations, we can use the basic characteristics of a class system to describe stratification in communist industrial societies.

A HISTORY OF INEQUALITY

As you have no doubt noticed, my description of stratification systems has implied change through history. At this point we are ready to consider why this change has occurred. By doing so we can also better understand how and why our own stratification system emerged, as well as your own life chances in this stratification system.

The description below follows the work and ideas of many social scientists whose theories differ widely. But these theorists, like Marx and more recently Lenski (1966), do agree that broad historical change in stratification systems has been primarily based on material or technological changes. In other words, how people go about producing their basic necessities, the technology they use, and who owns and controls the means of production are important factors shaping the rest of the society, including the level of inequality and type of stratification system. Thus, when this material base changes, there will be other changes in the society and in stratification systems more specifically.

Lenski's Evolutionary Perspective

After an extensive examination of the history of human societies, Lenski (1966) concludes that the level of inequality and general type of stratification system in a society is related to (1) *the level of tech-*

nology, and (2) *the level of economic surplus in that society.* These two factors are usually related; the higher the level of technology in a society, the greater the surplus production. By level of technology Lenski is referring to the complexity and productivity of the society's means of producing goods. For example, the plow and irrigation represent more complex technology than a digging stick. Throughout history there has been a trend toward more complex technology.

In Lenski's view, the level of technology is most important in effecting stratification and inequality because of the surplus of goods that can usually be produced with a more complex technology. With a surplus of goods produced, some people are freed from everyday work to devote their time to other activities. The activities pursued often lead to controlling other people (e.g., through political organization, military organization, and/or religious activity). But more important, when a surplus of goods is produced, a person or group gaining control of the surplus can use it to buy the loyalty of others or support an army to control others.

Considering the history of human societies, do we find that inequality has increased with the steady increase in the level of technology and the level of surplus? In general, historical, archaeological, and anthropological data show that this is in fact the case, at least until recent history.

As we have already seen, the first human societies were based on a hunting and gathering technology. This very simple technology produced very little if any surplus, and as Lenski predicts, these societies tend to have very little inequality and social stratification (primitive communalism).

With the Neolithic Revolution about 10,000 years ago we find the first settlements based on a simple horticultural technology. The digging stick and hoe did not produce an extensive amount of surplus food, but the surplus was enough to free some people from work in the fields. We find the first significant levels of inequality and the first powerful elites attaining their positions through ascription.

Further advances in agricultural technology resulted in more inequality, with the biggest jump appearing with agrarian societies about 4,000 to 5,000 years ago. More complex systems of social stratification were also emerging. Slave systems were among the first, but soon we find Asian systems, feudal systems, and a few caste systems.

In these stratification systems the power and riches of a few elites were immense compared with the holdings of the common people. Pharaohs, kings, and queens could command large armies, build castles, and rest reasonably well with the knowledge that their offspring could inherit it all. As for some examples of income and wealth inequality during this time, income of the elite (senators) in Constantinople around A.D. 350 was 24,000 times that of the average peasant — 120,000 pieces of gold versus 5 pieces of gold (Thomas, 1979, p. 300). The king of England in the thirteenth century also had an income about 24,000 times that of the average peasant (Lenski, 1966, p. 212). In France during the sixteenth century it is estimated that the nobility — about 1.5 percent of the population — owned about 20 percent of the land (Soboul 1974, p. 35). Overall, Lenski estimates that in agrarian societies between 3000 B.C. to A.D. 1700, the ruling classes (2 percent of the population) usually received about 50 percent of all income.

The next major change in the level of technology and surplus occurred about 250 years ago with industrialization. With new machine power the surplus production of all kinds of goods was starting. And with this new technology we find the emergence of a new type of stratification system — the class system. For the first time since simple agriculture appeared about 10,000 years ago, however, *we find a reduction in the overall level of material inequality within human societies.* This has occurred, as shown in Figure 9.1, not because the standard of living and wealth of elites has declined, but because the standard of living and income of the common people has increased substantially.

The major question before us at this point is why, after a trend toward greater inequality for almost 10,000 years, we find reduced inequality with class systems and industrialization. In the past, an increase in technology and a greater surplus nearly always produced more inequality. Why did the even greater increase in technology and surplus with industrialization not have the same effect? We can easily rule out the answer that the rich finally decided they were being unfair and greedy, and thus decided to give more to the lower classes. Such an event on a wide scale has never occurred. Rather, there are several other answers to these questions, with the following among the most important (Lenski 1966, pp. 313–318).

1. With a much more complex technology elites have found themselves in a position of ignorance about much of it. This is because no individual or even small group of individuals can possess the knowledge needed to run the vast industrial enterprise. Thus, elites have had to make concessions to their authority for the sake of efficiency, and these concessions have resulted in greater rewards for nonelites. Elites in the economy *do* have extensive

FIGURE 9.1. The progression of inequality in human societies.

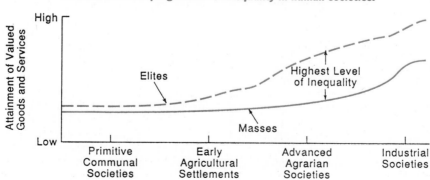

influence today, but they have delegated some influence on technical details.

2. Allowing the lower classes more of the economic surplus has increased productivity. This is partly because a lower class that is less hostile because of increasing personal benefits from work is less likely to strike, stage slowdowns, or indulge in industrial sabotage. Also, with a rapidly expanding industrial output, if wages were kept on a subsistence level there would be no market for increases in industrial goods. In short, with a general population having no money to buy goods above the basic necessities of life, increased profits for elites would be difficult to obtain.

3. Also important is the reduced rate of population growth in industrial societies, especially for the lower classes. In previous societies, as production increased, so did the population. With the population growing at a rate that closely equaled the increase in production, there was only enough produced to support this growing population without reducing the proportion going to elites. But with production increasing along with a more stable population, there is much more to divide among both the elites and the masses.

4. The first point noted that the increasing complexity of industry forced elites into a greater reliance on technical experts. But throughout the industrial system much more knowledge and skill is required. A large class of poor, ignorant peasants would not be useful in today's industrial society. Again, concessions must be made to insure a more skilled work force.

5. The spread of a more egalitarian ideology and democratic political systems has generally followed industrialization and revolution. In large part, this is because the new class of merchants that replaced the powerful agrarian nobility at the end of feudalism did so only with the help of the masses. In order to insure the support of the masses in these revolutions, it was necessary to make democratic political concessions. And with at least some voice in the new industrial state, the general population has been able to push for other concessions toward greater equality.

6. With increasing international conflict and the development of total war, elites could not afford to lose the allegiance of a large segment of the population. To place one's life in jeopardy for a nation requires a belief that the nation is worth fighting for. Slaves may go to battle, but they may also flee if the chance arises.

Inequality in industrial societies like our own continues to be quite high. Consider that even excluding the super rich, the range between the high and lower incomes in the United States is around 300 to 1 (Lenski, 1978). Or consider the distribution of wealth; although the richest 0.5 percent of the people in the United States own over 20 percent of the wealth, the poorest 20 percent own about 0.2 percent. These figures are less than the 24,000-to-1 income ratio between kings and peasants in thirteenth-century England, but we are nowhere near equality in present industrial societies.

Lenski's theory provides a general perspective helping us understand the broad trends in inequality throughout history. But we have more questions concerning the nature of social stratification. To see how some sociologists have tried to answer these questions, we turn to other theories of social stratification.

THEORIES OF SOCIAL STRATIFICATION

Throughout history people have shown interest in the question of why some are rich while others are poor. "Some of the earliest records of thought on this subject are found in the writings of the early Hebrew prophets who lived approximately 800 years before Christ. In the writings of such men as Amos, Micah, and Isaiah we find repeated denunciations of the rich and powerful members of society" (Lenski, 1966, p. 3). Aristotle as well had much to say about inequality, but for him there was no criticism of this "natural condition" (Dahrendorf, 1968, p. 153).

Unfortunately, since these early times the debate over the nature of social stratification has been influenced by people's political values and economic interests. The more affluent tend to think the type of social stratification in their society is good and necessary and therefore should not be changed. Those who are less affluent or are more sympathetic toward the poor tend to be more critical. With such an emotional question it is often difficult to follow methods of unbiased theory building and testing.

Contemporary social scientists continue to disagree on the causes and nature of social stratification, sometimes because of more or less hidden social values. In what follows we will examine some of these theories, then conclude with a general conflict theory that I believe is more useful and less burdened with value bias.

Marxian Evolutionary Theory

In many respects Marx would have agreed with Lenski's description above of the history of social stratification — but not in every respect. Marx's theory has been generally referred to as **historical-materialism** (Kerbo 1983, pp. 100–109). Such a description is not totally accurate, for Marx did not stress that *only* material forces shape history. However, it is useful to begin with this historical-materialist perspective in understanding the Marxian view of social stratification.

The materialist side of Marxian theory stresses that material, especially economic, forces are the most important in shaping society. These underlying material forces are often called the **substructure.** Within the substructure are the **means of production** and **relations of production** (Marx, 1971; Marx and Engels, 1965; Giddens, 1973). The means of production are primarily types of technology (as we have followed with Lenski's view). They can be hunting and gathering, some form of agriculture, or industrial. The relations of production refer are the human relations in the production process — who controls the work, who owns the land or factories, who determines the way in which workers are organized to produce, and so on.

To complete this simple outline we must now see that the **superstructure** in Marxian theory includes all other aspects of the society — the family system, political system, religion, and so on. Putting all this together, we find that the substructure with its economic base shapes the superstructure as indicated in Figure 9.2. The kind of family system in a society, the form of religion, the type of political

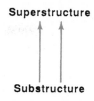

Family System, Political System, etc.

Superstructure

Substructure

Means of Production,
Relations of Production

FIGURE 9.2. The Marxian model of society.

system, among other things, are shaped (not totally determined) by the economic substructure.

Now we can consider the historical part of historical materialism. As the substructure of the society changed, Marx believed the superstructure of society would be led to change. Basically this is because the substructure and the superstructure must be in rough alignment with each other if the society is to survive; that is, if the family system or the political system operate in a manner that makes economic production difficult, the society will be threatened.

Bringing this all to bear on the subject of social stratification, we note that given the importance of the substructure, those who own and/or control the means of production in the society will be dominant in the stratification system. In hunting and gathering societies no one can really own or control the means of production, so there is general equality. However, with settled communities and agriculture the history of social stratification and inequality really begins.

The people who own the most land in agricultural societies or control the necessary tools for growing crops (such as irrigation) dominate others in the society. And through their economic dominance these upper-class groups were able to control or dominate the political systems. They made sure the state controlled peasants and others who may challenge upper-class dominance.

With industrialization we have a new substructure. The new means of production is machine technology; and in the new relations of production, wealthy factory owners emerge — the new upper class. The changing substructure would at first produce deep conflict between the old upper class (aristocracy), which still dominated the state, and the new upper class (called capitalists or the bourgeoisie). There were revolutions all over Europe in the 1600s to 1800s as the two groups (with various allies) were in conflict over control of the state. Toward the late 1800s most conflict of this nature was over, though it would continue in some form or another (as always) between the upper class and those below.

In capitalist industrial societies we have an upper class (capitalists) that dominates the substructure and a working class that must depend on the upper class for jobs and basic necessities. Marx recognized other class positions, but these are the two he stressed. As these capitalist societies advanced, Marx believed that more and more people would end up workers, and fewer and fewer capitalists would own and control the wealth.

In the last stages of capitalism we would have **monopoly capitalism** and another change in the substructure. The means of production are basically the same (industrial technology) but the relations of production have changed. There are very few people who own capital, but many, many workers in large factories *collectively* produce the products; that is, there is *collective production* but concentrated *private ownership*. Marx believed this situation would give workers potential power, eventually allowing them to eliminate capitalists and achieve collective ownership *and* collective production. This would bring a communist society with much less inequality, class dominance, and class conflict. No one would be in a class below workers (who would be in control) to dominate and exploit.

Critique of Marxian Theory. My summary of Marxian theory has been extremely brief and in some ways oversimplistic. But I hope it has given you a general sense of a Marxian view of social stratification. With this perspective we can understand something of how and why social stratification evolved over the centuries, but unfortunately we find this perspective somewhat less useful in understanding recent changes in social stratification. Although making many accurate predictions about future trends in

capitalist societies, Marx failed to foresee a few very important developments.

1. Marx failed to completely recognize the growth of the middle class in advanced capitalist societies. His belief was that the capitalist class would grow smaller and the working class would rapidly expand. Some Marxian theorists today have redefined the working class to include white-collar workers, and thus Marxian predictions seem more accurate (Wright, 1978). But the fact remains that a white-collar labor force has grown to include about one-half of all the employed population in industrial societies. This new middle class has some characteristics in common with the working class (blue-collar workers), such as lack of ownership and a work process they cannot control. This new middle class also differs in several respects, however, such as education level, closeness to management, and more job prestige, which have precluded a more united front among all workers (Aronowitz, 1974). This division has reduced the power of workers in their conflict with capitalists.

2. Marx accurately described the growth of an *industrial reserve army* of workers that would be out of work in times of recession to save corporate profits. This increasing industrial reserve army has had some effect on keeping wages lower than they otherwise would be as workers compete for jobs. In most capitalist societies so far, however, there has not been increasing economic hardship for most workers. In fact, higher incomes and consumerism have made most workers much less critical of capitalism than Marx had predicted.

3. One reason Marx did not foresee the growth of the middle class is that he did not foresee the growth of bureaucratic organizations that provide the base for many new middle-class occupations. Marx did not recognize how the bureaucratic corporate structure would also create a new elite of corporate managers that sometimes replace the old capitalist families in power.

4. Finally, Marx did not predict the growth of the state. For two reasons this has produced trends Marx did not foresee. (1) The state has helped smooth some of the rough spots of capitalism. This state has provided welfare benefits to many in the industrial reserve army and perhaps prevented some lower-class rebellion. The economic swings of boom and recession have also been controlled, at least to some extent, by state action and planning. So far the economic crisis leading to communism has not occurred. (However, some recent Marxists have predicted this welfare state will finally create a physical crisis in capitalism, leading to socialism [Wright, 1978; Piven and Cloward, 1982]. We consider this view in the next chapter.) (2) Marx neglected the extent to which bureaucratic position in the state could create another very important dimension of social stratification. And he neglected how this bureaucratic state position could lead to a new class that could dominate others much like the capitalist class had in the earliest capitalist societies. Because of this new class it is quite clear that if Marx were alive today, he would not claim the Soviet Union as the utopia he believed would emerge.

Although Marx did understand that group conflict was both a cause and a result of social stratification, he failed to see the full extent of such conflict. Economic conflict tends to be important in most societies, but conflict is more diverse. In this respect Weber's already discussed multidimensional view adding especially bureaucratic power as a base of conflict is a useful complement to Marx, as many new Marxists recognize (Wright, 1978, 1979; Harrington, 1976; Piven and Cloward, 1982).

Functional Theories of Social Stratification

In clear contradiction to Marxian conflict theory is functional theory. As you will remember, functional theory tends to focus on social order, value consensus, and a holistic view of society. If a widespread behavior or condition exists in a society, the first reaction of a functionalist is to ask what need it serves for the society. In other words, in contrast to the Marxian view, which asks why a privileged class is able to dominate and continue taking advantage of others, the functional view asks how the system benefits the overall society and its people.

In what is still one of the clearest statements of the functional view of social stratification, Davis and Moore (1945) argued that social stratification and

inequality place the most talented people in the most important positions in society. Because most people in our society would probably more or less agree with this theory, and because the theory can be highly misleading, it is important to consider it in some detail. I examine the theory through five basic points, with the example of two occupations — physician and garbage collector (Tumin, 1953).

1. The Davis and Moore theory begins with the assumption that some positions are more important than others and require special skills. The question of the functional importance of an occupation is difficult to show, as you can see if you imagine what would happen to a large city that has a strike by both doctors *and* garbage collectors for an extended period. The absence of either group would do severe damage to the people of the city. But a key factor in functional theory is the further assumption that the occupation of physician requires special skills in contrast to that of a garbage collector.

2. Only a few people in the society have the talent and can be trained for the most important positions. Thus, it is assumed that only a few people can be successfully trained as physicians, whereas most physically healthy people can be trained as garbage collectors.

3. Davis and Moore argue that the conversion of talents into skills requires a long training period and sacrifice by those receiving the training. Physicians must go through much personal sacrifice to be trained for their profession, in striking contrast to garbage collectors and their training, if any.

4. To induce the people with talent to make the sacrifice while receiving the necessary training, their future position must carry high rewards. For example, struggling medical students must know that they will be highly rewarded for current sacrifice. Because just about anybody who needs a job can qualify to be a garbage collector, and no long training period is needed, the job does not need to carry a high reward to attract occupants.

5. Thus, social stratification and unequal occupational rewards are beneficial to all because the best people are attracted to the most important jobs.

At face value the Davis and Moore theory of stratification appears a simple but valid explanation of social stratification, especially in industrial societies. In a major sense it is a labor market model analyzing the supply and demand of labor as it relates to rewards for labor. But as we will see, the theory is open to criticism on this point, as well as on many other points. We begin to see one problem immediately when we consider the pay scale for some garbage collectors. Although certainly not higher than physicians, in some cities the pay scale for garbage collectors (now often called "sanitary technicians") has increased dramatically.

Other functionalists take a broader view of the causes of social stratification by focusing on the dominant values in a society. Because all human societies have value systems, these theorists argue that social stratification will exist when some groups or individuals are better able to live up to these values (Parsons, 1964, 1970). Thus, these people will receive more status-honor or prestige, which will then bring more material rewards and power (or influence). Most sociologists agree that differences in class (economic factors), status, and power are behind systems of social stratification. Functional theorists like Davis and Moore, and Parsons, however, believe that status-honor and occupational prestige are the most important factors in producing stratification, in contrast to conflict theorists, who view economic variables (class) and/or power variables as primary and causes of the amount of status one receives (Figure 9.3).

Occupational Prestige. To the degree that people view the society and occupational structure in a way suggested by functional theory, we would expect them to rank the prestige of occupations in terms of

the level of skill and training required, as well as functional importance for the society.

Since 1947 sociologists have asked several national samples of the U.S. population to rank a standard list of occupations in terms of prestige (North and Hatt, 1947; Hodge, Siegel, and Rossi, 1964, 1966). The 1964 ranking is listed in Table 9.2. In all the U.S. studies there has been a strong consistency in the overall average rankings for each occupation. Also, similar studies have been done in a number of other industrial nations with similar results (Hodge, Treiman, and Rossi, 1966; Treiman, 1977).

As can be seen in Table 9.2, U.S. Supreme Court justice was on top in 1963, followed closely by physician, nuclear physicist, and scientist. The occupations of shoe shiner, street sweeper, and garbage collector are at the bottom. This ranking appears consistent with the predictions of the Davis and Moore theory, but we must consider why people rank occupations the way they do and the extent of class consensus on ranking.

Whereas people do consider the importance of an occupation for the society when ranking the prestige of occupations, recent studies indicate that the rewards and wealth of people in the occupation ranked are more important (Hope, 1982; Burrage and Curry, 1981). Thus, if it can be shown that the wealth and rewards of an occupation are due to factors other than a scarcity of talent and the social value of that occupation, then the Davis and Moore theory must be questioned. As we consider below, this is in fact the case.

Also, recent studies have shown more disagreement on occupational prestige rankings than previously realized, especially across classes. Most important is that factors like racial background, occupation, and education influence the agreement rate in occupational prestige ranking studies (Guppy and Goyder, 1984). The highest agreement is found among people with more education and higher-paying jobs.

We do find rather remarkable agreement, through time and across societies, on the prestige of occupations. But there is less agreement than previously believed, and the reasons for the agreement are diverse. It is not so much the honor of contributing to the society that leads to a high rank as it is the

FIGURE 9.3. A conflict theory view of the relationship among class, status, and power in modern industrial societies.

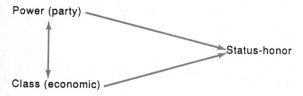

TABLE 9.2. *Occupational prestige ranking in the United States*

Occupation	Score
U.S. Supreme Court justice	94
Physician	93
Nuclear physicist	92
Scientist	92
Government scientist	91
State governor	91
Cabinet member in the federal government	90
U.S. representative in Congress	90
College professor	90
Chemist	89
Diplomat in the U.S. Foreign Service	89
Lawyer	89
Architect	88
County judge	88
Dentist	88
Mayor of a large city	87
Member of the board of directors of a large corporation	87
Minister	87
Psychologist	87
Airline pilot	86
Civil engineer	86
Head of a department in a state government	86
Priest	86
Banker	85
Biologist	85
Sociologist	83
Instructor in public schools	82
Captain in the regular army	82
Accountant for a large business	81
Public school teacher	81
Building contractor	80
Owner of a factory that employs about 100 people	80
Artist who paints pictures that are exhibited in galleries	78
Author of novels	78
Economist	78
Musician in a symphony orchestra	78
Official of an international labor union	77
County agricultural agent	76
Electrician	76
Railroad engineer	76
Owner-operator of a printing shop	75
Trained machinist	75
Farm owner and operator	74
Undertaker	74
Welfare worker for a city government	74

Occupation	Score
Newspaper columnist	73
Policeman	72
Reporter on a daily newspaper	71
Bookkeeper	70
Radio announcer	70
Insurance agent	69
Tenant farmer—one who owns livestock and machinery and manages the farm	69
Carpenter	68
Local official of a labor union	67
Manager of a small store in a city	67
Mail carrier	66
Railroad conductor	66
Traveling salesman for a wholesale concern	66
Plumber	65
Automobile repairman	64
Barber	63
Machine operator in a factory	63
Owner-operator of a lunch stand	63
Playground director	63
Corporal in the regular army	62
Garage mechanic	62
Truck driver	59
Fisherman who owns his own boat	58
Clerk in a store	56
Milk-route man	56
Streetcar motorman	56
Lumberjack	55
Restaurant cook	55
Singer in a nightclub	54
Filling station attendant	51
Coal miner	50
Dock worker	50
Night watchman	50
Railroad section hand	50
Restaurant waiter	49
Taxi driver	49
Bartender	48
Farmhand	48
Janitor	48
Clothes presser in a laundry	45
Soda-fountain clerk	44
Sharecropper—one who owns no livestock or equipment and does not manage farm	42
Garbage collector	39
Street sweeper	36
Shoe shiner	34

SOURCE: Hodge, Siegel, and Rossi (1964).

Professional baseball players, like Ron Darling, are among the best paid workers in American society. According to The Sporting News, there are ten $2-million men in the major leagues and 72 in the millionaires' club. Ron Darling of the Mets earns $1 million. What are the relationships among reward, prestige, and honor in the case of professional baseball? (© *AP/Wide World Photos*)

income and influence tied to the occupation. As we will see, many sociologists believe these factors are best explained by a type of conflict theory.

Critiques of Functional Theories. General sociological theories, as noted in earlier chapters, are difficult to test. A general theory, however, can help generate

more specific ideas or hypotheses about a phenomenon (such as social stratification) that can then be tested. The failure to find empirical support for specific hypotheses does not necessarily lead to the rejection of a general theory. On the other hand, repeated empirical evidence may accumulate that, on balance, tends to favor one or another general theory. A functional theory of social stratification cannot be totally rejected and does help us understand something of the subject matter. But for modern societies a type of conflict theory seems more useful. Let's first consider some of the research related to functional theory.

In one attempt to test the value of functional theory, Abrahamson (1973) examined the average wages of several occupations in the United States from 1939 to 1967. The prediction was that the wages of military-related occupations would increase (in relation to occupations not related to defense) during wartime. This test attempts to examine the Davis and Moore idea that the most important occupations for society will receive the higher rewards. The findings of this study, however, were mixed. The military-related occupations did tend to have higher pay during periods of war, but the trend was not consistent, and there were problems in defining war-related occupations (e.g., are auto workers producing for the defense effort? [Leavy 1974]). Other information also indicates, in contradiction to functional theory, that the pay of higher military officers actually increases more in peacetime (Vanfossen and Rhodes, 1974).

In another study, Abrahamson (1979) found that the relative importance of different positions on major league baseball teams and the scarcity of talent to fill them are related to the average pay of these positions, as the Davis and Moore theory would predict. As with the previous study, however, a conflict theorist can interpret this to mean pay is higher because scarcity and importance of a position lead to power in wage demands. And a further problem comes with the recognition that the income of major league baseball players (as well as football players) has increased extensively in recent years with the appearance of player organizations (similar to labor unions), suggesting that power-related factors are the most important.

Finally, in a study designed to separate how income is affected by (1) the functional importance of an occupation, (2) the influence or power of people in the occupation, and (3) the performance of people in an occupation, Broom and Cushing (1977) examined the incomes of corporate executives. First, they found that executive salaries were higher in companies producing such things as tobacco, cosmetics, and soft drinks, and salaries were lower in companies producing food, steel, medicine, and clothing. The implication is that the importance of the product produced by a company may not be related to executive income in that company. Second, the success of top executives in producing corporate profits and corporate growth were *not* related to executive income. Rather, they found that executive pay is related to the power of the executive with respect to the board of directors and stockholders (Allen, 1981) — more power and influence means more income. This finding is quite contrary to the predictions of the Davis and Moore functional theory.

A common criticism of the Davis and Moore functional theory is that it assumes a free labor market that does not often exist. Various organizations of workers and professionals (like labor unions and the American Medical Association) operate to control wages and competition. If there was more free competition, in fact, we would probably have less income inequality today (Collins, 1975), because high pay would attract more competition from job seekers. With so many applications for the job (demand), wage levels would be driven down. In low-paying jobs, fewer applicants would be attracted, thus requiring an increase in wages to attract applications.

We know that there is seldom a perfectly free market. But the Davis and Moore counterargument would be that there are "natural" limits on talent. For example, is there a strict limitation on the number of people with the talent to complete medical school? There is some limitation, but many more people could be good doctors than are admitted to, or can afford, medical school. Rather, the high pay of doctors is related more to price controls and professional organization than to the limits of talent (Jenkins, 1981; Berlant, 1975; Larson, 1977). This helps us understand why there are higher doctor fees in areas with an oversupply of doctors. In contrast to a supply and demand effect, doctors tend to raise fees to make up for fewer patients.

This critique of functional theory concludes with a more general look at the idea that values or ideals are the primary factors producing social stratification and inequality. Because we all have values and preferences, we tend to evaluate things, conditions, and people. This means that we often rank people with respect to how they live up to our values. If this evaluation process is at the heart of social stratification, then it can be argued that people become wealthy and powerful because they are given high esteem by others in the society.

Numerous studies of small societies, or rather isolated groups, generally support the idea that value preferences lead to status inequality. For example, from an extensive study of monasteries across the United States, Della Fave and Hillery (1980) found that monks in these monasteries are ranked by their peers almost exclusively in terms of status-honor. Formal positions of influence (like abbot), material possessions, or family background were of little importance compared with a life-style that matched important religious values.

Other studies of Israeli kibbutzim (Rosenfeld, 1951; Spiro, 1970) have found much the same. These small, collective communities were established in the early stages of the state of Israel by East European Jews motivated by strong religious and social values. In most of these kibbutzim (at least in their early existence) there was strict material and political equality. However, people were ranked by their peers in terms of how well they lived by the values of the group. To illustrate this point, in one group studied by Spiro (1970) some boys were observed discussing their fathers' occupations. This particular group valued hard physical labor as leading to the ideal life. One boy bragged about his father's hard work in the fields. Another boy, whose father was a teacher, bragged about how well his father swept the floor at his school.

Given the human capacity to think, develop symbolic meaning, and thus have value preferences, we can agree with functional theorists that all societies have systems of ranking based on values and lifestyle. We have found this in hunting and gathering societies as well as in our own. But with the exception of small, highly unified groups like monks in a monastery, a stratification system based *primarily* on status-honor is rare. The Indian caste system is a unique exception, but even in this case the inequality based on military and economic control preceded the caste divisions based on status-honor.

There are several reasons why status divisions are usually not primary in large, complex societies. First, in such societies there is extensive value diversity. There may be an overall value system, but groups will vary as to their interpretation and application of the values. This makes a comprehensive stratification system based on these values at best difficult. Second, given this value diversity, groups with greater power or economic dominance will be in a position to impose their interpretation of the values on other groups. Thus, to the extent that status ranks are important in complex societies, such ranks are not exclusively based on an independent value system. Third, in large, impersonal societies, it becomes difficult to judge others with respect to their life-style. This is one reason people in modern societies are usually concerned with displaying symbols of status-honor (e.g., proper dress, official titles, a fashionable office). Status-honor is important, but those with greater power or economic resources are better able to manipulate status symbols and what others know about themselves to create the image of a highly valued life-style. Again, the status ranking is a secondary factor.

Conflict Theories of Social Stratification

There are several varieties of conflict theory. Some conflict theorists, like Marx, stress ownership of the means of production as the primary factor behind social stratification. Others, like Weber, stress economic skill level as well as ownership. And still others (Dahrendorf, 1959; as well as Weber) stress bureaucratic power as important or primary. But behind all these theories is the assumption that human conflict is an ever-present factor when the distribution of valued resources is involved. By conflict they do not imply that humans are always fighting over resources. Indeed, the conflict is often covert or hidden. However, with the question of who

gets what and why, we must recognize there are extensive conflicts of interest in a society. Social forces like ownership, economic skills, and bureaucratic and organizational power give some groups the advantage in the process of conflict over the question of who gets what.

In this section I offer you what I consider to be a useful merger of several varieties of conflict theories. This merger should help you better understand our own system of social stratification.

1. From Marxian theory we may agree that economic conflicts are among the most important, especially in capitalist societies. But we may question the degree to which ownership of the means of production continues to be the principal or only line between conflicting classes today. In addition, we may question the Marxian view of the possibility of completely eliminating conflicts of interest in some future ideal society. Conflicts can certainly be reduced, but even if this is the case with economic conflicts, other forms of conflict will surface.

2. From Weber we can accept the view that conflicts in modern societies are often mediated through, or are created by, bureaucratic organizations. But we must recognize that some bureaucratic organizations are more important battlegrounds than others in the conflict over who gets what and why.

3. We can even accept some aspects of functional theory. We can accept that status distinctions are important, but not that these status distinctions are determined by a common value system unaffected by inequalities of power in large, complex societies. We can accept the functional assumption that there is an occupational structure based on skill level that influences the distribution of rewards, but not that this occupational structure simply serves the needs of society, unaffected by inequalities of power. A supply-and-demand relation does explain some of the distribution of rewards within this occupational structure, but it is supply and demand in a marketplace that is not always free. Those with power can influence the supply as well as the demand to serve their interests.

Figure 9.4 illustrates the process of social stratification, beginning with individual interests that lead to the formulation of group interests. As sociolo-

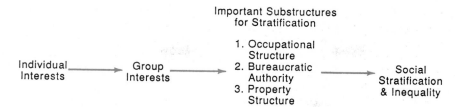

FIGURE 9.4. The process of social stratification in capitalist industrial societies.

gists, we are concerned with how groups are formed that have similar group interests that then lead to group conflicts of interest. Depending on the particular level of technology, historical and cultural influences, the international environment, and other factors that I will include in the influence of social structure, these group interests are created and contested within one or more substructures in the society. Within one society the property class structure in a Marxian sense may be primary, whereas in another the political structure may be primary. But we also find that at times more than one may be of prime significance and that these structures are usually in some way interrelated and influence each other. I have excluded other substructures from Figure 9.4 — religious, military, or status — that may at times be important in smaller or less industrialized societies.

Finally, Figure 9.4 suggests that the conflicts shaped by these substructures influence the general nature of the stratification system in each society and ultimately the distribution of rewards. How inequalities are maintained and justified, who is on top and for what reasons, the openness of the stratification system — in short, the overall nature of the stratification system — are influenced by these substructures and their degree of importance.

Within the substructure box in Figure 9.4, I have included three structures that recent research has indicated to be of primary importance in our own stratification system. The *property structure* refers to ownership of significant capital. We live in a capitalist society, which means that extensive ownership of capital (corporate stock, mineral resources, etc.) can bring other rewards and influence other aspects of society. The *political or bureaucratic*

structure refers to the growing importance of the bureaucratic state and bureaucratic corporations in our society. A high position in one of these powerful bureaucracies can bring abundant rewards. Finally, the *occupational structure* refers to skill levels or ranks in our modern industrial economy. Generally, the more skill people have (sometimes referred to as human capital), the higher the wages they can successfully demand. The other two structures, however, prevent any simple correlation between skill level and wages. For example, a monopolistic trade association or unions can increase wages above what skill level will bring. But this is to say that all three structures can have influence on one another.

One way to interpret Figure 9.4 is by considering how each of the three substructures in the society determines the question of who gets what and why. Recent research has indicated that all three substructures are important in influencing the distribution of income. Robinson and Kelley (1979) studied the influence of property ownership, bureaucratic authority position, and occupational skill level with national samples from the United States and Great Britain. They found all three factors about equally important in explaining a person's income level. Similar studies focusing on one or more of these three substructures have reached comparable conclusions (Kalleberg and Griffin, 1980; Wright, 1978; Wright and Perrone, 1977).

Table 9.3 analyzes the position of a particular group in the stratification system and the outcome in competition over rewards for the group. Let's say group A is high in occupational skill level but low in property ownership. And let's also say this group is not highly organized as an economic interest group (like a trade union) nor politically (through a voting

TABLE 9.3. *Example of group positions in occupational, authority, and property structures*

	Occupational structure	Bureaucratic authority/power	Property structure
Group A	high	low	low
Group B	high	high	low

block or lobby), and is thus low in bureaucratic or organizational power. The rewards of group A may be above average but not especially high because the group has a good position in only the occupational structure. Another group, group B, may be equal to group A, except that group B is highly organized through a professional association. This professional association may be used to control competition in the marketplace and/or gain political influence for legal protection, both of which could bring group B more rewards compared with the rewards for group A.

It should now be clear that Figure 9.4 and Table 9.3 have combined the importance of (1) the occupational structure as stressed by functionalists and conflict theorists like Weber, (2) the bureaucratic authority structure as stressed by Weber, and (3) the ownership of the means of production (property structure) as stressed by Marx as well as Weber. The three substructures (within the substructure box of Figure 9.4) are more specific to our own type of society. For example, in a communist society the property structure would be missing with the elimination of private ownership of the major means of production. In a highly religious society like Iran today, position in the religious authority structure would be very important in competition for valued goods and services. In an agrarian society the occupational structure would be much less important. In a caste system we would need to add consideration of a status dimension.

CLASS SYSTEMS

A system of social stratification implies that people are ranked or layered like strata of rock. Such is the case with class systems. *However,* with the emergence of class systems, for the first time in history the ranks were no longer clear-cut; there were no sharp dividing lines between different classes. In a caste system, for example, people were precisely located within a distinct caste that had clear boundaries separating its members from others. One reason class divisions are less distinct is that movement from one class position to another is possible. But other characteristics of a class system are more important in producing these fuzzy class boundaries.

Class Divisions

As implied above, class location is affected by three interrelated substructures. A person's position in each of these three substructures is not always consistent — that is, a person may be low in one but midlevel in another. But also, two of these substructures (occupational skill level and bureaucratic positions) contain rather continuous grades or ranks. In other words, there are many steps or ranks from bottom to top, making it difficult to show clearly where one rank stops and another begins.

Despite the complexity, we do find that it is useful to locate some rough class categories in our present class system. People in these class positions tend to have much in common, though the commonality can be taken too far. Table 9.4 lists some rather standard class categories in relation to the three substructures outlined above.

The *upper class* in the United States contains the super rich. The most important criterion for upper-class location is extensive property ownership. Such property ownership usually brings high authority in corporate bureaucratic organizations through a top corporate position. Also, with great family wealth,

TABLE 9.4. *The convergence of occupational, bureaucratic, and property divisions on class categories*

Class categories	Percent of population	Positions in three main types of substructures		
		Occupation level	Bureaucratic authority	Property relation
Upper class	0.5	high	high	owner
Corporate class	0.5	high	high	nonowner
Middle class	42.0	high to midlevel	midlevel	nonowner
Working class	42.0	midlevel to low	low	nonowner
Lower class	15.0	low	low	nonowner

most people obtain extensive education and other experience that gives them high occupational skills. They are quite often trained as lawyers and business managers. But extensive wealth is the key to upper-class location. To some extent it is useful to divide this upper class into the old rich with more prestige and the new rich with less prestige, as we will see in Chapter 12.

In the past sociologists have not always considered as a separate class the category I call the **corporate class.** One reason for this, as will be seen, is that the corporate class is somewhat recent in origin. With the growth of corporate bureaucracies we now find a powerful group of interrelated corporate managers who control or help run the biggest corporations in the world. This group does not own sufficient amounts of corporate stock to say they control a corporation through ownership, but they may nevertheless have corporate control through their top management positions. The existence of this corporate class as distinct from the upper class, however, is a controversial issue among social scientists (Kerbo and Della Fave, 1983, 1984; Niemonan, 1984).

As we move to the *middle class,* occupational skill level is more important. Members of the middle class tend to be college-educated and hold white-collar or nonmanual jobs. They do not usually perform physical or manual labor but do "paper work" in an office or work with people by teaching, managing, selling, and so on. If these people work in large bureaucracies, they tend to be in the middle ranks of authority. It is often useful to refer to an *upper middle class* and a *lower middle class.* The upper middle class generally includes professional people (doctors, lawyers, accountants, managers, etc.) who have postgraduate college training. The lower middle class includes people in less professionalized and less skilled white-collar jobs, like secretaries, sales clerks, and low bureaucrats.

The *working class* includes those who work in manual occupations, doing physical labor to build a product or run machines. They tend to be high school graduates, perhaps with some college, but this varies to some extent. Also referred to as blue-collar workers, this class can be divided into *skilled and unskilled blue-collar workers.* Those with higher skills (electricians, carpenters, etc.) tend to have better-paying, more secure jobs. Those with no important skill can be easily replaced on the job, and thus find it more difficult to gain a high wage. However, although blue-collar workers in general are usually low in bureaucratic authority, union organization may bring more bureaucratic influence and a higher wage.

The *lower class* primarily contains those we consider poor in our society—roughly 15 percent of the population today. These people, if they are employed, tend to have very unskilled jobs in industries where employment is very insecure. Most of the male heads of lower-class families tend to be unemployed a good deal of the time. However, the lower class also contains many female-headed households where the mother finds it difficult to obtain employ-

This cover of the New York Daily News announces the story of 1987's "Black Monday," the October Stock Market crash. Class divisions in the United States assume stability in property relations and ways of accruing wealth. A volatile stock market can wreak havoc and create panic, as the headline proclaims. Some investors lost as much as one-third to one-half of their wealth as a result of the market's drop. Which social groups do you imagine will be the most vulnerable to this type of downward mobility? (© Eugene Gordon)

ment because of her young children and sex discrimination.

It is worth stressing again that these class categories are rough approximations. With the complex class system and economy we have today, no classification is without problems. Some Marxists argue

that we should consider only two or three main classes (capitalists and/or managers versus the workers they employ). However, although this classification presents fewer problems in locating people in distinct positions, it oversimplifies, leading us to miss some important distinctions among people.

After we have had an opportunity to consider our economic system and political system in the next two chapters, we will return to these class categories and the many implications for the people in them. At this point, however, it is useful to compare nations with class systems.

A Comparative View of Class Systems

If the underlying structure producing class stratification is roughly the same in two or more nations, then we would expect these nations to display some broad similarities in other respects. Of course, no two nations will be exactly alike. But if the stratification system is an important force shaping other characteristics of a society, we should find many similarities in nations with class systems. In this section we explore some of these similarities and differences.

Income Inequality. If a stratification system sets limits on income inequality, nations with a class system should have roughly similar income distributions. Figure 9.5 shows this is roughly the case. This table was constructed by estimating the percentage of the total income in a nation that goes to equal population segments. In other words, for the bottom 20 percent of the U.S. population, we begin with the poorest families and work up until we have included 20 percent of the population. Then we total the income of this bottom 20 percent of the population to see what share of the total national income they have. This procedure continues through each 20 percent segment of the population. For the United States we find that the bottom 20 percent of the people receive less than 5 percent of total income, whereas the top 20 percent receive about 45 percent of the income.

Cross-national estimates of income inequality must be considered as rough estimates, but when we consider the very high levels of inequality in preindustrial societies, the nations included in Figure 9.5

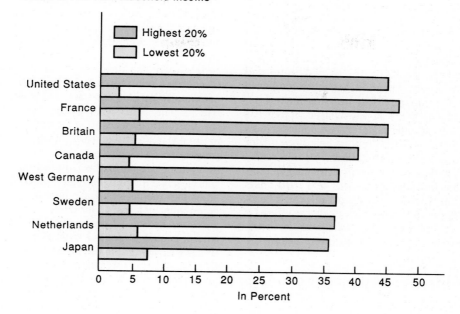

Share of Pre-Tax Household Income

The Ratio Between
Highest and Lowest 20%

FIGURE 9.5. Comparative pre-tax income inequality in the major noncommunist industrial nations based on figures for various years in the late 1970s and early 1980s. *(Source: Based on data from the World Bank and MacDougall, 1984.)*

all have much less income inequality. However, there are differences; if we look at the top 20 percent and bottom 20 percent groups in each nation in Figure 9.5, we find the most inequality in France and the United States, with the least in Japan. It is interesting that during the 1960s the United States had only an average level of income inequality compared with these other nations. But growing income inequality in recent years in the United States has changed this. In coming chapters we consider how political and economic differences help account for income differences in these nations.

Figure 9.5 does not consider after-tax income, though studies indicate taxes have *very little* effect on the income distributions reported here (Tufts, 1978). Neither does Figure 9.5 include the effects of major welfare programs. But again, welfare payments have only a small effect on these income distributions.

Income Inequality in Communist Societies. Communist nations claim to be "classless" societies without a capitalist class exploiting the working class as in present capitalist societies. Table 9.5 presents income inequality data from East European Communist nations for 10 percent population segments.

Two generalizations can be made from Table 9.5: (1) These communist nations do have less income inequality than do most capitalist nations; however, (2) the communist nations are nowhere near equality.

It should also be pointed out that the material standard of living tends to be lower in most of these communist nations compared with Western industrial nations. Thus, a 5 percent share of income for the bottom 10 percent of people in one of these nations may mean a material standard of living comparable to an .8 percent share for the bottom 10 percent of people in the United States. But again, this is very difficult to estimate because some necessities like medical care are basically free of cost in communist nations. (The United States is the *only* industrial nation where medical care is not almost free of cost to patients.) What is most important at this point, though, is the income inequality relative to others in the particular nation.

We can briefly consider why we find this different pattern of income inequality between capitalist and communist nations. It is helpful to consider first what helps generate income inequality in class systems. As noted above, studies have shown occupational skill level, bureaucratic authority position, and

TABLE 9.5. *Income inequality in east European communist nations and the United States, by income tenths and top 5 percent*

Country	Percentage of total income held by*										
	Bottom 10%	10– 20%	20– 30%	30– 40%	40– 50%	50– 60%	60– 70%	70– 80%	80– 90%	Top 10%	Top 5%
United States	0.8	3.5	4.9	6.2	7.5	8.9	10.6	12.9	16.4	28.3	17.9
Bulgaria	4.9	6.4	7.3	8.0	8.8	9.7	10.6	11.9	13.6	18.8	10.9
Czechoslovakia	5.4	6.5	7.4	8.1	8.9	9.8	10.8	12.0	13.7	17.4	9.6
East Germany	4.1	6.6	7.6	8.5	9.4	10.2	11.0	12.2	13.5	16.9	9.4
Hungary	4.9	6.4	7.2	8.1	8.8	9.8	10.8	12.0	13.7	18.3	10.4
Poland	4.3	5.5	6.4	7.2	8.2	9.3	10.7	12.3	14.9	21.2	12.2
Yugoslavia	4.5	6.0	6.7	7.6	8.4	9.4	10.4	11.9	14.0	21.1	12.7

*Data are from national surveys for the latest available year in the 1960s. Also, data are based on worker income except for East Germany and the United States, where they are based on household income. Although the differences between worker and household income inequality are very slight, the difference underestimates income inequality in the United States and East Germany.

SOURCE: Table constructed from data presented in Jain (1975).

property ownership all contribute to producing income inequality in the United States. With this in mind we can understand why communist nations are not vastly different in income inequality compared with capitalist nations — those nations included in Figure 9.5 and Table 9.5 are all industrial nations. Because they are industrial nations they must have roughly similar occupational structures. A high-level job skill and more education brings more income in the Soviet Union, just as it does in the United States (Yanowitch, 1977; Matthews, 1978).

We also find bureaucratic authority structures in all these nations. But though there are more power inequalities with these state bureaucracies in communist nations, they produce similar patterns in income inequality compared with capitalist nations.

Finally, we come to the major difference producing less income inequality in communist nations — the property structure. Again, studies indicate that significant property ownership contributes to a high income. Thus, because private ownership of the means of production has been almost eliminated in the communist nations listed in Table 9.5, we would expect them to have less income inequality.

In the Soviet Union we certainly find an elite with a standard of living considerably above that of the average citizen (see Box 9.2). In the United States, the elite or upper class maintains its position through ownership or control of the major means of production. In the Soviet Union, the elite maintains its position through control of the state and party bureaucracy — which controls the means of production.

Comparative Rates of Social Mobility. Another important characteristic of class systems is the possibility of movement from one class to another — social mobility. In no other type of stratification system has social mobility been extensive, or achievement (in contrast to ascription) a primary method of class placement. However, we must not overestimate the extent of social mobility or achievement in class systems. Given other types of stratification systems, our rate of social mobility looks very extensive; given the desires of those low in the class system, social mobility may look very limited. We examine the rates of social mobility for people in different

places in our own stratification system in a later chapter. For now we are concerned with general rates of mobility in class systems.

We begin by examining a question considered by many people in the past century or so: Is the United States the "land of opportunity?" Do people of low social origins have a better chance of moving up the class ladder in this country than in any other country? Table 9.6 indicates the answer to this question is basically no; the United States is not significantly

TABLE 9.6. *Comparative circulatory mobility in fifteen industrial nations*

Rank	Country	Circulation rate*
1	Norway	.415
2	Australia	.394
3	Bulgaria	.389
4	West Germany	.380
5	United States	.369
6	Japan	.365
7	Yugoslavia	.364
8	Finland	.356
9	Hungary	.337
10	Denmark	.318
11	France	.312
12	Italy	.303
13	Spain	.298
14	Sweden	.298
15	Belgium	.292

*The circulation rate is estimated by making the nations comparable with respect to the occupational distribution of origins (Hazelrigg and Garnier, 1976, p. 501). Circulation mobility refers to the total amount of upward and downward social mobility in the society, discounting the mobility influenced by changes in the occupational structure. In other words, nation A may have more upward mobility than nation B, but only because nation A has more economic growth with new jobs at the top of the occupational ranks. Thus, this upward mobility is not necessarily due to moving up or down the occupational ranks because of merit. The circulation mobility figure then is a better measure of equality of opportunity because it discounts mobility due only to occupational structure changes.
SOURCE: Table constructed from data presented in Hazelrigg and Garnier (1976, p. 503).

BOX 9.2

The Soviet Elite and Marxian Theory

Like the capitalist superpowers they condemn, the Soviets have their privileged elite too. And although the Soviet elite is not as rich as our own, their life-style is far above that of the average Soviet citizen.

Private property is not extensive in the Soviet Union. However, although housing is very limited in the Soviet Union, the top party and state elite have large houses in the main urban areas, as well as vacation homes in the countryside. Autos are also quite limited in the Soviet Union, but the elite have all they need, plus a chauffeur to drive them. Many consumer items as well as high-quality food items are very expensive or nonexistent for the average Soviet citizen. The elite, however, have special stores that stock plenty of the valued items at low prices. As the figures on Soviet income indicate below, the bureaucratic and party elite have incomes considerably above those of the average worker. Originally (under Lenin) the highest wage was set at only 150 percent of the average worker's wage, but this was raised considerably and even the income figures below are misleading because some of the Soviet elite are allowed incomes from two jobs at the same time.

Finally, the Soviet elite is becoming increasingly self-perpetuating. The sons and daughters of the elite go to better schools, receive special education, and have personal connections making it more likely they will obtain the best jobs in their adult lives (Matthews, 1978; Kerbo, 1983, pp. 403–428).

Elite position in the Soviet Union is found primarily in the upper officials of the Communist Party and state bureaucracy. In contrast to the United States, the highest elite status comes not through fabulous wealth and ownership of the means of production but through control of the bureaucracy, which controls the means of production (along with the military and police). Most important for the elite in the Soviet stratification system is a top position in the bureaucratic authority structure, rather than in the property structure.

Extensive elite privilege in the Soviet Union did not always exist to the degree it does today. The original elite, such as Lenin (Payne, 1964) and Mao in China (Terell, 1982), had humble life-styles and were clearly motivated by idealistic and humanistic concerns (no doubt, along with strong egos seeking fame and power as well). In the first years of the Soviet Union, Lenin pushed through many laws restricting elite privilege. But though these restrictions continue to have some effects, for the most part they have been eliminated or eroded.

Marx was never able to convincingly resolve the problem of how a "temporary"

different from several other industrial nations and does not even have the highest rate of mobility.

Comparisons of social mobility rates, however, are quite complex and can be done in many ways. Table 9.6 presents data on "circulation rates," the amount of social mobility both up and down, after controlling for the different shapes of the occupa-

tional structures (e.g., some nations may have more jobs in higher or lower positions).

Comparisons can also be made by simply considering what percentage of people born in the working class move into the middle class. In this respect some earlier studies have shown the United States was highest compared with eight other capitalist

Monthly income of selected Soviet elites

Position	Monthly income in rubles
Average factory worker	130
Party officials	
General secretary	900
Secretary of Central Committee	700–800
First secretary of a union republic	600
Assistant to member of Politburo	425
Industry managers	
coal	400
nonferrous	325–375
ferrous	300–375
chemical	290–330
oil and gas	290–300
Military officers	
Major general	600
Colonel	500
Lieutenant colonel	400
Others	
Director of research institute	500–700
Professor, chief researcher	325–525
Assistant professor	300–350
First secretary of union of composers	800

SOURCE: Matthews (1978, pp. 23–24).

dictatorship of the proletariat would not become self-serving and permanent. Marx correctly recognized that when an old upper class is overthrown by revolution, a powerful new state elite will usually be needed to restore social order and prevent the old upper class from returning to power. (The American Revolution was not a "true" revolution in that a distant colonial power was eliminated in a country that already had a system of more or less democratic self-government at the time.) The problem is that the members of this dictatorship of the proletariat may decide they rather enjoy all that power, along with the privileges they can obtain.

nations (Lenski, 1966, p. 411), though most of these countries were *very* close to the United States (with about 30 percent of working-class sons moving into the middle class). Other studies have indicated there is a bit more ascription at the top and bottom of the U.S. class system, meaning if you are born at the top or bottom you are somewhat more likely to stay

there in the United States (Miller, 1960; Fox and Miller, 1965).

Considering the above studies of social mobility, we find that all class systems have such mobility, but it is somewhat varied among these nations. There are several reasons for the national differences in mobility rates (such as more political democracy, more economic growth [Tyree, Semyonov, and Hodge, 1979; Grusky and Hauser, 1984]). But at this point I want to stress that compared with nonindustrial societies, the mobility rates of these industrial societies appear rather similar.

CONCLUSION

The nature of a country's system of social stratification has profound effects on many characteristics of the country and its people. Thus, it is fitting to end Part II of this book (*The Foundations of Human Societies*) with the present chapter. In future chapters we consider the widespread effects of our own class system in more detail. Before we do so, however, we must consider the first two chapters of Part III.

As we have seen, our own statification system is primarily shaped by three main substructures in the society. As we will see in later chapters, there are also castelike elements in our stratification system when considering race and sex inequalities. But the occupational structure, the bureaucratic authority structures, and the property structure continue to be primary, even in the cases of race and sex inequality.

Two of these structures are part of the economy; the other is related in part to the political system. Thus, it is helpful to move to the next two chapters on the economy and political system before returning to our study of class systems of social stratification. The economy and political systems are subjects of extreme importance by themselves; they are not simply subareas of social stratification. But these subjects do influence the stratification system, and vice versa, and must be considered together as well as separately.

CHAPTER SUMMARY

Key Terms

Content

Social stratification is a system of social relationships and rules that lead to an unequal distribution of valued goods, services, honor, and positions in the society. Social stratification thus helps answer one of the most explosive questions in human societies —who gets what, and why? When a stratification system has been established and is basically supported by the society, this system will reduce the level of overt conflict over this question. But because we can assume that most people in a society would prefer higher positions and more rewards, and because we assume those people on top in the society would prefer to stay there, there is always potential conflict within a stratification system.

Social stratification systems differ with respect to placing people in ranks through rules of ascription or achievement. With few exceptions, such as extreme ascription in the Indian caste system, most societies have a mixture of ascriptive and achievement rules. Societies with greater reliance on achievement
rules have a greater amount of social mobility—movement up and down ranks in the hierarchy.

Max Weber contributed extensively to our knowledge of social stratification with his multidimensional view. Unlike Marx, who stressed only the ownership and relations of production in creating class divisions, Weber stressed three dimensions—class, status, and party (power).

Throughout history we find only a few basic types of stratification systems. Although no two systems are exactly alike, several have broad similarities: primitive communal systems, slave societies, caste systems, feudal or estate systems, Asian systems, and class systems.

The level of inequality in human societies has varied considerably throughout history. Lenski (1966) describes how this inequality is related to (1) the level of technology, and (2) the level of surplus in a society. Societies with the lowest level of technology and surplus (hunting and gathering societies) had very little inequality. But as agricultural techniques became more advanced, there was more and more inequality, until we reach industrial societies. With the new class systems, high technology places nonelites in a better position to attain a greater share of the surplus production.

There have always been differing views on the nature of social stratification, with some of these views found today in different theories of social stratification. Marxian theory focuses on the economic substructure that determines who owns and controls the means of production in explaining social stratification. Functional theory stresses the need for inequality to induce the most talented people to fill the most important positions in the society. Also, functional theorists argue that unequal status-honor will always exist because of the human tendency to rank people in terms of their values.

This text stresses a conflict theory of social stratification combining components of other conflict theories. In the process of social stratification three substructures are the most important in categorizing people in our society — the occupational structure, bureaucratic authority structure, and property structure. Our society has an upper class, a middle class, a working class, and a lower class with differing positions in these three substructures.

Class systems have roughly similar levels of income inequality and social mobility. Communist societies have less income inequality than do Western industrial societies, but not drastically less. Because communist societies are industrial societies with an occupational structure and bureaucratic authority structures, they have extensive income inequality. The income inequality of communist societies is less than ours primarily because they have eliminated private ownership of the means of production — the property structure.

PART III

The Structural Bases of Inequality and Conflict

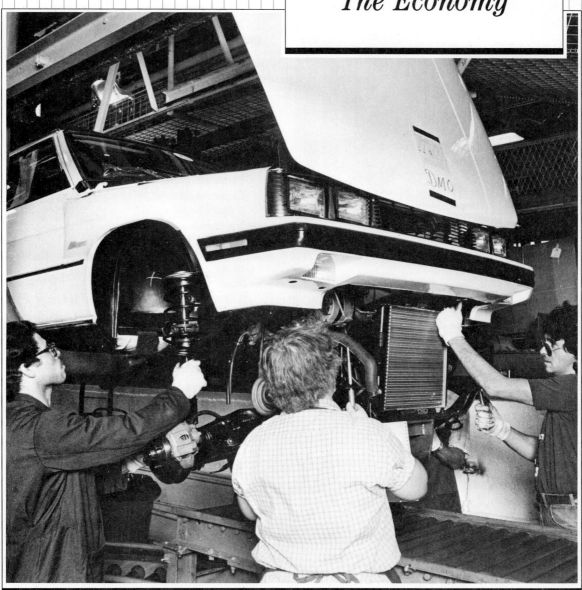

CHAPTER 10

The Economy

263

CHAPTER 10 OUTLINE

. . . It is one of the fundamental characteristics of an individualistic capitalistic economy that it is rationalized on the basis of rigorous calculation, directed with foresight and caution toward the economic success which is sought in sharp contrast to the hand-to-mouth existence of the peasant, and to the privileged traditionalism of the guild craftsman and of the adventurer's capitalism, oriented to the exploitation of political opportunities and irrational speculation.

— Max Weber, The Protestant Ethic and the Spirit of Capitalism

After a long period of remarkable economic health since World War II, the U.S. economy fell into serious trouble in the 1970s. By the early 1980s the United States was experiencing the worst economic conditions since the Great Depression of the 1930s. And although there was some improvement by the mid-1980s, there are increasingly dangerous trends in the economy. Many economists agree that the relative economic improvement experienced by some people in the mid-1980s has been achieved through government policies that can further harm the economy in coming years (policies resulting in a huge government deficit and a worsening balance of foreign trade).

Consider some of the economic statistics. In 1970 the United States had the highest **gross national product (GNP)** per capita in the world. (GNP is simply the annual value of all goods and services produced in a society. GNP is often considered in terms of the size of the population — GNP per capita — so as to roughly indicate a material standard of living that can be compared internationally.) By 1978 the United States ranked only fifth in GNP per capita, though by the middle 1980s it had regained the top position. During the 1960s the unemployment rate averaged about 5 percent. The average unemployment rate for the second half of the 1970s was over 7 percent, reaching 10.8 percent in 1983. The inflation rate was no better; it reached 12 percent in 1975 and 13 percent again by 1980, coming down only with massive unemployment in 1983. The average rate of economic growth was only 0.1 percent between 1974 and 1978, compared with 3.2 percent for Japan, and 3.0 percent for West Germany and France (Blumberg, 1980; Thurow, 1980; *1984 World Almanac)*. By 1985 the U.S. economic growth rate was still only 2.3 percent

compared with 4.6 percent for Japan (U.S. Central Intelligence Agency, 1986, p.24).

The human impact of these abstract figures must be recognized. The average **real income** of Americans was lower by the early 1980s than it was in 1965. (Real income is the actual buying power of the income, after considering inflation and taxes.) Traditionally, the U.S. population has enjoyed the highest rate of home ownership of any large industrial nation. The rate of U.S. home ownership, however, has dropped dramatically. In 1980 only 20 percent of new families could afford their own home in America. And in 1979, 30,000 people were actually homeless in New York City alone (and remember, this was before the big 1983 recession). By 1987 several estimates indicated the number of homeless people in major cities such as New York and Los Angeles was even higher.

Finally, the human misery of unemployment may seem obvious, but it involves more than a reduced material standard of living. It has been estimated that each additional 1 percent of unemployment in the United States produces as many as 37,000 deaths due to suicide, family violence, and poor health. There is also evidence that unemployment contributes to child abuse and mental illness (Bluestone and Harrison, 1982; Riegle, 1982).

I think you can understand how vital these issues are to you and your future. What kind of job will you be able to find? Will you be able to afford a home if you desire to own one? What will the standard of living be for you and other Americans in 10 or 20 years? Our knowledge (or lack of knowledge) of these economic problems may strongly influence your future well-being.

Many reasons for America's economic problems have been put forth. For example, some people claim that high taxes and government involvement in the economy have caused economic problems. Others claim that powerful unions, high welfare benefits, and a less dedicated work force have caused our economic problems. All these explanations, however, are simplistic, and some clearly incorrect.

The primary purpose of this chapter is to provide you with a general understanding of economic systems. In an economics text, of course, you will learn about the details of supply and demand, how the banking system operates, and so on. Here our purpose is somewhat different. We must recognize that economic systems are interrelated with other systems in a society — that is, the economy is part of the overall social structure. We cannot fully understand the economy and economic problems without also considering the political system, cultural values, and class conflicts, among other aspects of the society. Sociology can help provide this wider understanding, and as we will see, our current economic problems *must* be understood in this manner. Many sociologists have recently contributed ideas toward solving these economic problems (for example, Bowles et al., 1983; Etzioni, 1984; Blumberg, 1980), and many economists as well are beginning to see that the wider society and class conflicts must be recognized when speculating on the causes and solutions to our economic problems (for example, see Thurow, 1980).

We begin this chapter with some basic concepts and sociological perspectives on economic systems. Following this we consider other subjects like a comparative history of the U.S. economy. Toward the end of the chapter we reconsider some of the causes of our current economic problems in light of what we have learned. But even at that point I will indicate that our understanding of the U.S. economy requires an even wider understanding of trends in the world economic system, which will be pursued in a later chapter.

THE NATURE OF THE ECONOMY

The **economy** is the system by which humans go about producing, attaining, and distributing goods and services — the material necessities of life as well as the luxuries. In an earlier chapter we considered how the mode of production (that is, the economy in a broad sense) is one of the most important foundations of a society. We have seen how a hunting and gathering technology shaped many aspects of the lives of hunting and gathering people. We have also seen how many aspects of society changed when simple agriculture was adopted. Finally, we have briefly considered how many changes occurred in societies with industrialization. In this chapter our focus is on industrial societies and their economic substructure.

It is also important to remember, however, that all aspects of a society are not simply determined by its economic system. If that were the case, all industrial societies would be much more similar than they are today. For example, although the United States and Japan are both large industrial societies, they continue to be different in many ways. This also means that other characteristics of a society can influence the nature of a nation's economy. Thus, we must consider the interrelationships among an economic system and other parts of a society.

Economic systems, especially the more complex ones, create subdivisions within the society. In a most general sense, industrial societies have a highly developed **division of labor.** This means that people have come to perform very distinct economic roles within the society. Put another way, there are many different work tasks, or occupational positions — each of which is more or less interrelated. For example, some people grow the wheat, some construct the tractors, others bake bread, and still others transport and sell the bread.

One of the most important economic divisions is found with the differing types of occupations people have in an economic system. *Occupation* means the kind of work people normally perform. And although "the kind of work" people perform can be defined very narrowly, sociologists have found it useful to make the broad distinctions shown in Table 10.1.

We can divide occupations into nonmanual (white-collar), manual (blue-collar), and farm labor. Nonmanual includes occupations within which people work with ideas and other people, rather than doing heavy physical labor as in manual and farm occupa-

TABLE 10.1. *Occupational distribution of civilian labor force, 1900–1980 (%)*

Occupation	1900	1920	1940	1960	1980
Professionals	4	5	7	11	15
Managers	6	7	7	11	11
Sales	5	5	7	6	6
Clerical	3	8	10	15	18
Total white-collar	18	25	31	43	50
Crafts	11	13	13	13	13
Operatives	13	16	18	18	15
Laborers	12	12	9	5	5
Service	9	8	12	12	14
Farmers*	38	27	17	8	3
Total blue-collar	83	76	68	56	50

* Because some farmers own extensive farm property, it is somewhat misleading to place all farmers among blue-collar workers. However, as all farmers accounted for only 3 percent of the civilian labor force in 1980, the overall conclusions of this table are not altered.

SOURCE: U.S. Bureau of the Census, *Historical Statistics of the United States, Colonial Times to 1970,* p. 139; U.S. Bureau of Labor Statistics, *Handbook of Labor Statistics,* 1981, Table 7, p. 20.

tions. But finer distinctions are useful within the nonmanual and manual occupations in reference to the level of skill required for the job.

In upper nonmanual occupations we include the more skilled jobs of doctor, lawyer, accountant, business manager, and so on. In the lower nonmanual occupations we include the less skilled nonmanual jobs like salesclerk, secretary, bookkeeper, and so on. Then in the upper manual positions we include the occupations that require greater skill in performing the physical labor (electrician, plumber, heavy equipment operator).

As indicated in Table 10.1, the nature of the occupational structure has been changing in the long run as industrial societies become more advanced. More jobs requiring greater skills are being created, though less skilled jobs are not actually being reduced. In the past decade, although many "high-tech" jobs have been created, the number of low skilled service jobs (like serving fast food) has increased at a more rapid rate. The changing nature of our occupational structure, however, is more complex than suggested in Table 10.1. Machines have

also made many previously higher skilled jobs less complex and more like unskilled occupations. For example, some types of office work have become less complex, with machines breaking down work tasks so that office workers are performing simple repetitive tasks much like unskilled manual workers on an assembly line (Spenner, 1979). As we will see in Chapter 12, these changes in the U.S. occupational structure have been contributing to increasing income inequality in the 1980s.

Another aspect of the division of labor in industrial societies is the creation of different economic sectors. Three economic sectors are based on types of industry and their function. **Primary industries** are involved in attaining or producing natural resources or raw materials. Mining, agriculture, and the lumber industries are examples. **Secondary industries** shape these raw materials into manufactured goods. The auto, electronics, and appliance industries are examples. **Tertiary industries** provide services such as selling goods, taking care of money, educating the young, providing health care, and so on.

The assembly-line form of production represented one of the breakthroughs in the development of secondary industries, especially the auto industry. Developed by Henry Ford, he used it in the production of the Model T, shown here. The method allowed efficient mass production, lowering the cost of the cars and enabling more people to buy them. A related effect was that, with private ownership of cars, more people had geographic mobility. This meant they could move to the industrial jobs that were opening up in the first half of the twentieth century. (© *The Bettmann Archive*)

With the advance of industrialization people became further divided in economic function along the lines of these industrial sectors. Before industrialization, for example, a furniture maker was likely to obtain his own lumber, manufacture that furniture, then attempt to market the finished product. Seldom are we able to find such individuals today. As indicated in Table 10.2, there has been a steady shift away from primary industries with the advance of industrialization and the growth of secondary industries. The more recent dramatic shift has been the decline of secondary industries in the United States and the growth of tertiary industries and occupations. The United States in the 1970s experienced a rapid decline in its secondary industries, especially in the Northeast and upper Midwest. This led to the term "rust bowl," used in reference to those industries that are closing their operations (like the steel and auto industries). The rapid increase in tertiary industries has helped provide jobs for some displaced

TABLE 10.2. *Historical trends in the distribution of jobs in primary, secondary, and tertiary industries, 1900–1975**

	Percent of labor force in		
	Primary	Secondary	Tertiary
1900	37.6	35.8	26.6
1940	18.5	36.7	44.7
1950	12.1	40.3	47.5
1960	8.1	36.3	55.6
1970	5.5	34.3	60.4
1975	4.5	33.4	62.1

workers, but there continues to be serious concern about insufficient job replacement and the extent to which people can be retrained for these jobs.

Types of Economic Systems

We have already considered many types of economic systems, from hunting and gathering to industrial, when classifying societies in terms of the technical means of production. In this chapter we are primarily concerned with industrial societies. We must now consider the important differences among the economic systems of these societies.

Following Marx, among other social scientists, we classify economic systems by their technical means of production as well as their relations of production. Marx (1906) included both these characteristics in what he called the overall **mode of production** in a society. As we saw in Chapter 9, the technical means of production simply refers to the type of technology used for production, and all industrial societies are roughly similar in this respect. However, industrial societies differ greatly with respect to the relations of production. Among important aspects of the relations of production are 1) the relationships among workers shaped by the technical methods of production used (for example, whether they must work in large groups or alone), 2) the dominance-submission relationships between workers and authorities, and 3) the ownership of

capital and the distribution of profits from the economic activity (Giddens, 1973, pp. 85–88). With these distinctions in mind we examine capitalist, communist, and democratic socialist economic systems.

Capitalism. We define **capitalism** as an economic system in which the means of production (factories, railroads, banks, and so on) are for the most part privately owned and operated for private profit. It is also assumed that conditions of free competition will exist, but such an assumption is not a defining characteristic of capitalism. In most advanced capitalist societies today, many industries are highly concentrated; only a few large firms do most of the business in that type of industry. When such concentration exists, as we will see, the ideal conditions for free competition in capitalism are often compromised, with competition severely reduced or even eliminated in extreme cases. As described in Chapter 9,

The relations of production in highly automated workplaces, increasingly involve workers interacting with "smart" machinery or technology. In this photo, Japanese steel workers are conferring in the control center of their plant. Historical photos would show far more heavy machinery and would be more labor intensive; in contrast, this photo is "postindustrial." The critical role of telecommunications is demonstrated by the bank of phones. (© Abbas/Magnum)

the term monopoly capitalism is often used to describe societies with an economy dominated by a few very large companies.

Because the means of production are primarily owned and controlled by private individuals, workers often have little influence or control over the production process. This can vary extensively among capitalist societies; however, most capitalist societies in Europe have much more worker influence in the production process compared with corporations in the United States (Isaak, 1980; Heller and Willatt, 1975). Such worker influence is often achieved through unions and worker representation on boards of directors, which in most European nations is usually required by law.

The definition of capitalism above must be considered as an ideal type; actual economic systems vary with respect to these characteristics. Table 10.3 compares Western capitalist societies in terms of the degree of private versus government ownership of some basic industries. As can be seen, the United States is unique in the degree of private

ownership of these basic industries (though Japan is close). In most European nations the national governments have acquired extensive stock ownership of major industries (but seldom much more than 50 percent ownership of particular corporations). As you might think, this provides the national government with extensive influence over these companies in particular, and the overall economy more generally. But contrary to what you might think, there is no relationship between government stock control in a company and the economic performance of the company (Thurow, 1980). The extreme nature of the capitalist ideology in the United States has misled us on this point.

Table 10.4 shows that capitalist nations also vary with respect to worker protection, rights, and benefits in major corporations. Again, we find the United States unique among major capitalist nations. The U.S. government has been much less involved in guaranteeing worker rights and benefits, though there have been some increases in this type of government action recently. But American workers still

TABLE 10.3. *Cross-national comparison of government ownership of basic industry (%)*

	Australia	Austria	Belgium	Britain	Canada	France	W. Germany	Italy	Japan†	Mexico	Netherlands	Spain	Sweden	Switzerland	USA
Telecommunications	100*	100	100	100	25	100	100	100	100	100	100	50	100	100	0
Electricity	100	100	25	100	100	100	75	75	0	100	75	0	50	100	25
Gas	100	100	25	100	0	100	50	100	0	100	75	75	100	100	0
Oil production	0	100	NA	25	0	NA	25	NA	NA	100	NA	NA	NA	NA	0
Coal	0	100	0	100	0	100	50	NA	0	100	NA	50	NA	NA	0
Railroads	100	100	100	100	75	100	100	100	75	100	100	100	100	100	25
Airlines	75	100	100	75	75	75	100	100	25	50	75	100	50	25	0
Auto industry	0	100	0	50	0	50	25	25	0	25	50	0	0	0	0
Steel	0	100	50	75	0	75	0	75	0	75	25	50	75	0	0
Shipbuilding	NA	NA	0	100	0	0	25	75	0	100	0	75	75	NA	0

Adapted from *The Economist*, Dec. 30, 1978.

* The approximate percent of the industry which is controlled by the government in each nation.

NA = not applicable or neglible production.

† As of 1989, the Japanese government control of railroads was eliminated with the privatization of Japan National Railroad, and the Japanese government control of telecommunications was reduced with the sale of NT&T.

TABLE 10.4. *The rights of workers in large corporations in major capitalist societies*

Rights	West Germany	France	Japan	United Kingdom	Netherlands	Sweden	United States
Average period of notice for shutdown	2–6 months by law	1–3 months by law	1 month by law; 6 months by custom	3 months by law	2–6 months by law	6 months + by law	None
Worker representation in management	1/3 to 1/2 of board members from workers	Consultation with workers' council on decisions affecting work rules	No law, but 2/3 of companies have board members who are active in unions	None	Consultation with workers' council on all major management decisions	2 members on board; consultation on all major management decisions	None
Paid leaves for sickness (not including disability insurance)	6 weeks full pay and 4 weeks 75% pay	50% of earnings up to 36 months after brief waiting period	80% of wages indefinitely	Average 50% for 6 months	80% of pay for 1 year	6 months at full pay	None
maternity or paternity	6 months after birth and 6 weeks before birth with monthly allowance and guarantee against dismissal	4 months at 90% pay with monthly nursing allowance and guarantee against dismissal	No law, but 3 months paid leave is widely adhered to	6 weeks at 90% salary	3 months full pay	9 months full pay shared between parents	None
Employee rights on employer insolvency	First priority is 68% average pay for 1 year to all workers	Guaranteed income maintenance allowances varying by age and seniority	Full wage for 2 years; 80% of 3 months' salary guaranteed by the state	Guaranteed 1 weekday for every year of service	80% of all wages for 6 months guaranteed, then 75% for additional time to a maximum of 2 years	90% of wages for 6 months to 2 years	None

SOURCE: Adapted from Ira C. Magaziner and Robert B. Reich, *Minding America's Business* (New York: Law & Business, Inc./Harcourt, Brace, Jovanovich, 1982), p. 144.

have much less protection and legal rights in a corporation than in any other advanced industrial nation (Thurow, 1980, pp. 7–10).

Communism. Though the terms "communism" and "socialism" are sometimes used interchangeably, **communism** more precisely means an industrial society in which the state has taken almost total control of the economy. There is no longer private ownership of the major means of production; rather, the state owns and operates all industries.

Marx believed that this situation would lead to worker control and ownership because workers would control the state. With worker control would come better working conditions, a more motivated work force, and more material equality. But as we have seen in the previous chapter, this aspect of communism has not been achieved anywhere. Although the state has eliminated private ownership in countries like the Soviet Union, the authority relations in the work place have not been substantially altered compared with many capitalist nations. This is primarily because the state is dominated by a bureaucratic-political elite, rather than by workers as Marx envisioned.

A communist society such as the Soviet Union, however, is also an industrial society. The Soviet Union has an occupational structure much like that of any capitalist industrial society. The Soviet economy requires scientists, engineers, accountants, office clerks, and other occupations and jobs that are found in the United States. Related to this is an educational system that trains such people, if not directly for a specific job, at least in providing the general intellectual skills to learn the job skills.

In Marxian theory, communism is only a transition stage to socialism. (I must note that at times Marx reversed the meaning of communism and socialism.) Whereas the state must remain strong, dictatorial, and control the economy under a communist system, after the lingering influences of the revolution and capitalism are eliminated, a socialist society is predicted.

Democratic Socialism. **Democratic socialism** usually describes an economy that has much less private ownership of the means of production compared with capitalism. Unlike communism, however, the term "democratic" implies that most people in the society are able to influence the economic bureaucracies, usually through a more democratic political system that has extensive ownership in the economy. Commonly, in this type of economic system workers have various kinds of influence in their particular companies through such things as worker councils and representatives in high positions in the company.

As I have said, each nation's economy does not fit into one simple category like communism, capitalism, or democratic socialism. More than almost all other industrial nations, however, the United States fits the capitalism category, and the Soviet Union fits the communism category. Many of the industrial nations in Western Europe (such as Austria, West Germany, Sweden) come closer to the democratic socialist description than the capitalist description.

Another mixture of these economic systems can be mentioned in closing this discussion. Some East European communist nations (and to some extent China and, to a small degree, even the Soviet Union) have been moving toward what can be called **market socialism**, in which the state continues to own almost all the important means of production but has allowed more local decision making and market forces to determine what is produced and how it is produced. "Market forces" refers to the supply and demand, or free-market concepts in capitalist theory.

Capitalist Economic Theory

The basic theoretical ideas behind capitalism can be stated quite simply. Economic growth and prosperity are seen as best achieved through private individuals freely competing in the marketplace to produce and sell goods and services. Those who produce superior goods more cheaply and efficiently will see their firms grow to produce even more and better goods, while interior firms will go out of business. The most noted capitalist theorist, Adam Smith, who wrote *The Wealth of Nations* in 1776, called this the "hidden hand of the marketplace." The role of the political system in this ideal image of capitalism is to remain uninvolved in the economic system.

To understand how these ideas of Adam Smith and others developed, we must for a moment consider the historical period. Industrial technology was emerging in the 1700s, but the political and economic systems of Europe continued to operate under rules and policies that evolved under feudalism. There was economic dominance by old, wealthy elites and thus little free competition in the "marketplace." The state, which was primarily controlled by the feudal elites, was heavily involved in influencing economic activity. Thus, social scientists like Adam Smith were reacting against the old social structures that were impeding economic growth.

It is often forgotten today, however, that Adam Smith did not trust big business any more than the government. On this subject, Smith (1950, vol. I, p. 144) wrote, "People of the same trade seldom meet together, even for merriment and diversion, but the conversation ends in a conspiracy against the public, or in some contrivance to raise prices." And neither did Adam Smith favor large corporations, commonly called "joint stock companies" at the time. He saw the stockholders as unable to understand what is best for the company, and corporate directors as inefficient: " . . . being the managers rather of other people's money than of their own, it cannot well be expected that they should watch over it with the same anxious vigilance with which the partners in a private copartnery frequently watch over their own" (Smith, 1950, vol. II, p. 264).

Marx, among many others, later stressed what were seen as serious flaws in the logic of Adam Smith. Even if political influence favoring the economic interests of the wealthy can be eliminated at the outset, through time some capitalist firms will grow larger and larger, with more and more power to eliminate competition. This is one outcome of what Marx described as monopoly capitalism. Without rational economic planning, it was also argued that many other problems would occur with capitalism (such as overproduction, exploitation of workers, and wide swings in economic cycles). This is why Marx predicted a crisis for capitalism that would lead to the emergence of communism.

With some of these problems in mind, another set of economic theories became popular at a time when many capitalist nations were experiencing crisis in the 1930s. The most famous economist at the time, John Maynard Keynes, argued that the state did in fact have an important role in a capitalist economy. It was the job of the state to assure business competition by preventing monopolies, and to regulate the economy through government spending and taxing to smooth out the wide cycles of rapid economic expansion then depression. These ideas of Keynes, **Keynesian economics,** strongly guided President Franklin Roosevelt's New Deal economic policies during the Great Depression of the 1930s (Schlesinger, 1959).

Most recently, the battle of economic ideas and policies follows the old debate, with the slightly new idea of "supply-side economics" taking an anti-Keynes position. The view that the state has an important regulating role in the economy is rejected by supply-siders (Gilder, 1980). Citing these ideas, the Reagan administration claimed it would reduce the role of government. However, the recession of the early 1980s was reduced by the Reagan administration "the old-fashioned way" — with Keynesian economics. With increases in government spending and reduced taxes for the more affluent, massive deficit spending by the government stimulated economic recovery.

We consider the current debate over supply-side economics later, but we should end this section with a brief look at the economic performance of communist nations. The capitalist theories of Adam Smith would, of course, predict that a communist system with economic planning and no private economic competition could not produce a healthy economy. No communist economy today has a material standard of living approaching that of leading Western capitalist (or democratic socialist) nations. But the Soviet Union has emerged from a weak economic power before their Revolution of 1917 to become an economic power after World War II. As can be seen in Table 10.5, the Soviet Union has the second largest economy in the world today (though some figures suggest Japan may have recently gained the number two position). Many people in the United States dismiss the Soviet economy as backward and inefficient while stressing the danger of Soviet military power. A backward, inefficient economy does not produce and sustain a powerful modern military.

TABLE 10.5. *Comparative GNP, 1985*

	GNP in billions of dollars
United States	3,988.5
Soviet Union	2,062.2
Japan	1,328.6
West Germany	623.2
France	510.3
United Kingdom	443.2
Italy	357.8
Canada	331.3
Spain	169.3
Australia	153.0
Netherlands	124.2
Sweden	100.0

SOURCE: U.S. Central Intelligence Agency (1986).

The forced industrialization policies of Stalin before World War II in the Soviet Union produced severe hardships on the Soviet people (Ulam, 1973). (By "forced industrialization" we mean hard work demanded with a low level of economic reward to workers. Rather than high wages and plentiful consumer items, the policy is to save and reinvest, and to produce more machines for economic growth instead of consumer goods.) But whether or not we like it, a communist system is an alternative to capitalism that has produced economic growth, if not a high standard of living.

COMPARATIVE-HISTORICAL VIEW OF INDUSTRIALIZATION: ISSUES AND TRENDS

We have already seen how the nature of a society's economy shapes many characteristics of that society. At this point, we can be more specific in describing important characteristics and trends in modern industrial societies that shape our lives today.

American Economic Development

While many nations in Europe were rapidly industrializing in the early 1800s, the United States was still primarily an agrarian nation. Only 15 percent of the people in the United States in the 1850s lived in what the Census Bureau defines as urban areas. Only 36 percent of the total American labor force were classified as having nonfarm jobs. During the late 1800s, however, this began to change quite rapidly. By 1900, 40 percent of the population lived in urban areas, and 62 percent of workers had nonfarm jobs (U.S. Bureau of Census, 1960). What took place in that 50-year period can only be called a transformation. Not only do we find changes in the workplace and residence patterns, we also find changes in labor conflict, politics, family size, education level, and U.S. international relations, among many other things.

The U.S. Civil War was, in part, a conflict between an already industrializing North and a South that was holding to an agrarian economy. This economic split resulted in differing political-economic interests that were resolved in favor of the North after the Civil War, producing more rapid economic growth. Also important to recognize, however,

This photo captures well the heroic image of the age of American industrialization. Taken in 1930, by the internationally known photographer Lewis W. Hine, it captures both the power of the machine and the small but central role that the worker must play in relation to it. (© International Museum of Photography at George Eastman House, Rochester, N.Y.)

were changes in the world economic system. Because of reduced economic growth in Europe, many European (and especially British) financial corporations were investing money in the expanding U.S. economy, thus providing needed capital for even more U.S. economic expansion.

During the late 1800s many of America's large corporations and wealthy families emerged. Standard Oil created the wealth of the Rockefellers during this period, the Carnegie family made their fortune in steel, and the house of Morgan expanded its fortune in the financial industry, to list only a few examples.

Such fortune, of course, was not spread evenly throughout the population. There was extensive conflict between labor and the new capitalists, resulting in many bloody strikes. During this time unions were not protected by law, and capitalists could, and often did, fire any worker who tried to form a union. As some unions emerged, there was often violence directed toward labor by agents of the large corporations. A recession in 1873 brought even more labor conflict in the railroad industry; and during one major strike, the Chicago Haymarket incident led to more deaths among strikers and police in 1886; and there was also extensive hardship and conflict in rural areas, leading to the Populist movement of the 1890s. Finally, before the end of the nineteenth century, came the highest rate of unemployment that the U.S. labor force had experienced (18.4 percent in 1894).

The Great Depression.

No one can write about U.S. economic history without devoting considerable attention to the 1930s. The economic crisis was so great, and the changes produced were so broad, that many aspects of American society were influenced. At the high point of the Depression in 1933, 24.9 percent of the labor force were out of work. But even those who kept their jobs found wages cut by one-third on average (Piven and Cloward, 1971). There were studies showing increasing problems like poor nutrition and lack of other necessities among millions of people (Garraty, 1978, pp. 174–177).

The first major response to the Depression was an increase in rioting and protest by the unemployed in 1930 (Kerbo and Shaffer, 1986); the next major response was the election of Franklin D. Roosevelt in 1932. For the first time in a major way the federal government became involved in economic regulation with Roosevelt's New Deal. The laissez-faire economic views of Adam Smith were pushed aside by the newly accepted Keynesian economics.

During Roosevelt's time in office there were many new restrictions placed on banks and nonfinancial corporations in an attempt to eliminate some of the practices believed to have caused the Depression. Extensive government aid and regulatory activity was also directed toward agriculture. Because of this it can be said with only some exaggeration that agriculture is almost a socialized industry today (if by socialized we mean extensive government–private industry cooperation and planning). Equally important, there were many new laws after 1934 that helped guarantee labor rights in collective bargaining and union organization (Schlesinger, 1957, 1959, 1960).

Post-World War II Economic Trends.

With Europe and Japan devastated by World War II, the United States emerged as even more dominant in the world economy. The United States led all other nations in industrial production, foreign trade, and new technology, while unemployment and inflation remained relatively low throughout most of the 1950s and 1960s. During the 1970s, however, America's economic dominance began eroding at a surprisingly rapid rate. The United States continues to have the world's largest economy (measured in terms of GNP), but for a period of time in recent years lost its leading position in terms of GNP per capita. As can be seen in Table 10.6, the United States ranked very badly with respect to several key indicators of economic performance. And as noted in beginning this chapter, conditions of unemployment and inflation created extensive problems. By 1983, with the exception of inflation, these economic indicators were either unimproved or had worsened.

Since 1984 there has been some improvement in the U.S. economy, but many problems like a large foreign trade imbalance and huge federal budget deficits continue to indicate a troubled economy in the future.

TABLE 10.6. *Annual growth in GNP per worker and productivity in major industrialized countries, 1970s*

	% Increase GNP 1973–1979	Average % increase in productivity 1972–1977
Japan	3.4	3.5
West Germany	3.2	3.5
France	2.7	3.1
Italy	1.6	1.0
Canada	0.4	0.8
United Kingdom	0.3	1.2
United States	0.1	0.6

SOURCES: Economic Report of the President 1980, p. 85, Joint Economic Report 1979, p. 58.

As you might expect, there are many "explanations" for U.S. economic problems since the early 1970s. Some causes are easy to see. During the 1970s Europe and Japan were able to fully recover from the destruction of World War II with some new factories and technology more advanced than found in the United States. However, many of the reasons for the relative decline of the U.S. economy are complex and require more discussion.

Structural Trends in Capitalist Economic Systems

The American economy today, as well as the economies of other capitalist nations, is in many ways dramatically different from 100 years ago. The old image of an economy with individual entrepreneur capitalists facing one another in tough competition for survival must be altered in many respects. No one, of course, expects time to stand still without the evolution of social structures, and many of the changes seen today were predicted by Marx and other social scientists more than 100 years ago. For various reasons, however, many of these changes are not fully recognized by most people even today, or in many cases are ignored. To some extent, as we will see, conflicting class interests with respect to these changes lead some people to cover or ignore their significance.

Corporate Concentration. In Adam Smith's original image of the ideal capitalist economy there would be many small, individually owned firms competing for profits. In the United States today there are thousands of these small capitalist firms. But one of the most important trends in all capitalist societies is the extent to which economic activity is dominated by huge corporations. For example, of all industrial corporations in the United States today, just 100 corporations account for over 55 percent of all industrial corporate assets. As recently as 1950, the largest 100 industrial corporations accounted for only 39 percent of these corporate assets (Dye, 1983, p. 20).

As Table 10.7 shows, in 1980 the 50 largest industrial corporations in the United States controlled over 40 percent of all industrial corporate assets. This list of corporations is headed by Exxon (Standard Oil of New Jersey), which in 1980 held $49.5 billion in assets.

Even more concentration is found among commercial banks. Of 14,738 banks in the United States in 1980, just 50 banks controlled over 60 percent of all banking assets (Dye, 1980, p. 24). And as shown in Table 10.8, the top 25 banks alone control over 50 percent of banking assets. Considering the overall importance of financial corporations in the economy today, the top ten banks, and especially the six large banks in New York City, are truly powerful firms.

Other types of corporations show as much or more concentration. In 1980 there were 1,890 life insurance corporations in the United States, but only ten of these controlled over 50 percent of the total assets (Dye, 1980, p. 25).

Although the United States has some of the biggest corporations in the world, the United States is not the only industrial nation with extensive corporate concentration. In West Germany the 50 largest industrial corporations account for more than 40 percent of all production (Isaak, 1980). Much the same can be found in the United Kingdom (Stanworth and Giddens, 1975), France (Suleiman, 1978), Japan, and other Western industrial nations.

TABLE 10.7. *The 50 largest industrial corporations in the United States, 1980*

Rank	Corporation	Assets ($ billions)	Cumulative percent*
1	Exxon	49.5	4.0
2	General Motors	32.2	6.6
3	Mobil	27.5	8.8
4	International Business Machines	24.5	10.8
5	Ford Motor	23.5	12.7
6	Texaco	23.0	14.9
7	Standard Oil of California	18.1	16.4
8	Gulf Oil	17.3	17.8
9	Standard Oil (Ind.)	17.1	19.2
10	General Electric	16.6	20.5
11	Shell Oil	16.1	21.8
12	Intl. Telephone & Telegraph	15.1	23.0
13	Atlantic Richfield	13.9	24.1
14	Tenneco	11.6	25.1
15	U.S. Steel	11.0	25.9
16	Dow Chemical	10.3	26.8
17	Conoco	9.3	27.5
18	Standard Oil (Ohio)	9.2	28.3
19	E.I. du Pont de Nemours	8.9	29.0
20	Union Carbide	8.8	29.7
21	Phillips Petroleum	8.5	30.4
22	Eastman Kodak	7.6	31.0
23	Sun	7.5	31.6
24	Western Electric	7.1	32.2
25	Westinghouse Electric	6.8	32.7
26	Chrysler	6.7	33.2
27	Xerox	6.6	33.8
28	United Technologies	6.4	34.3
29	R.J. Reynolds	6.4	34.8
30	Philip Morris	6.4	35.3
31	Getty Oil	6.0	35.8
32	Union Oil of California	6.0	36.3
33	RCA	6.0	36.8
34	Procter & Gamble	5.7	37.2
35	Occidental Petroleum	5.6	37.7
36	Monsanto	5.5	38.1
37	Caterpillar Tractor	5.4	38.6
38	Goodyear	5.4	39.0
39	International Harvester	5.2	39.4
40	Bethlehem Steel	5.2	39.8
41	Gulf & Western	5.2	40.3
42	Union Pacific	5.1	40.7
43	Weyerhaeuser	4.9	41.1
44	Amerada Hess	4.9	41.5

Cont.

TABLE 10.7. *The 50 largest industrial corporations in the United States, 1980* Continued

Rank	Corporation	Assets ($ billions)	Cumulative percent*
45	Boeing	4.9	41.9
46	International Paper	4.8	42.2
47	Cities Service	4.8	42.6
48	Aluminum Co. of America	4.7	43.0
49	Minnesota Mining & Manufacturing	4.6	43.4
50	Marathon Oil	4.3	43.7

* Cumulative percent refers to the percentage of all the industrial assets held by the corporations from a certain rank and above. For example, the top 10 industrial corporations controlled 20.5 percent of all industrial assets in 1980.
SOURCE: Thomas Dye (1983, p. 210).

TABLE 10.8. *The 25 largest commercial banks in the United States, 1980*

1980 Rank	Corporation	Assets ($ billions)	Cumulative percent
1	BankAmerica Corporation (San Francisco)	108.3	7.5
2	Citicorp (New York)	106.32	14.9
3	Chase Manhattan Corporation (New York)	64.7	19.4
4	Manufacturers Hanover Corp. (New York)	47.7	22.7
5	J.P. Morgan & Co. (New York)	43.5	25.8
6	Chemical New York Corporation	39.4	28.5
7	Continental Illinois Corp. (Chicago)	35.8	31.0
8	Bankers Trust New York	31.0	33.2
9	First Chicago Corporation	30.1	35.3
10	Western Bancorp. (Los Angeles)	29.7	37.3
11	Security Pacific Corp. (Los Angeles)	24.9	39.0
12	Wells Fargo & Co. (San Francisco)	20.6	40.5
13	Irving Bank Corporation (New York)	16.7	41.6
14	Crocker National Corp. (San Francisco)	16.1	42.8
15	Marine Midland Banks (Buffalo)	15.7	43.9
16	First National Boston Corporation	13.8	44.8
17	Mellon National Corporation (Pittsburgh)	13.5	45.8
18	Northwest Bancorp. (Minneapolis)	12.4	46.6
19	First Bank System (Minneapolis)	12.1	47.5
20	First International Bancshares (Dallas)	11.5	48.3
21	Republic of Texas Corp. (Dallas)	10.8	49.0
22	National Detroit Corporation	9.5	49.7
23	First City Bancorp. of Texas (Houston)	9.5	50.3
24	Texas Commerce Bancshares (Houston)	9.3	51.0
25	Bank of New York Co.	9.0	51.6

SOURCE: Thomas Dye (1983, p. 24).

Moreover, it is estimated that today between 200 and 300 industrial corporations account for about 80 percent of all productive assets in the noncommunist world (Barnet and Muller, 1980, p. 381).

We must briefly consider the highly complex subject of corporate concentration. First, many argue that when corporations become very large they are able to reduce competition, legally and illegally. Second, because of the resources available to these firms, they can have extensive political power. Because they are so large they would severely disrupt the whole economy if they went out of business. As in the case of Chrysler in 1979 and Continental Illinois Bank in 1984, because of the economic reality today the federal government is basically required to step in to prevent the corporate giants from failing. In the classical capitalism of Adam Smith, as we have

seen, such government intervention does not promote business health because inefficient companies are saved. Finally, it can be argued that large bureaucratic corporations are less innovative, less flexible, and less likely to expand into new technologies, thus harming the overall productivity of the economy (Thurow, 1980).

Corporate Ownership and Control. One hundred years ago it was seldom difficult to determine who owned and controlled the largest corporations—most companies were primarily owned by individual wealthy families who took active control of them. Such a determination is usually very difficult today.

Corporations are "joint-stock" companies, which means that many people own parts of the company through their ownership of stock in the

As corporations become multinational and more diversified, their headquarters become important symbols of the corporation's relationship to society and the future. What does the architecture of the building shown here say about this corporation? Does this message corroborate or contradict what you know of corporate elites and interlocking directorates? (© Gale Zucker/Stock, Boston)

company. In some cases one family may own more than 50 percent of the stock issued by a company and, thus, the family owns a majority interest in the company. With ownership of a majority of the stock, this family would then control that company — that is, make the important decisions about running the company.

It will be useful at this point to briefly describe how decisions are made in a corporation, and by whom. As indicated in Figure 10.1, top executive officers (president, vice-presidents, etc.) make the day-to-day decisions of running the corporation. But these officers must answer to the board of directors, who meet about once a month to approve major policies. These directors are voted into office by the stockholders of the corporation and are supposed to represent the stockholders' interests. A key point of this is that with common stock, one share of stock brings one vote, and 1 million shares of stock bring 1 million votes. Thus, it is important to examine the distribution of stock in a company to determine who has the most power in a particular company.

Studies indicate that most very large companies are no longer exclusively controlled by individual families. There are certainly exceptions, such as the Ford family's control of about 40 percent of the stock in Ford Motor Company. A Senate study of the

FIGURE 10.1. *Authority positions in the modern corporations*

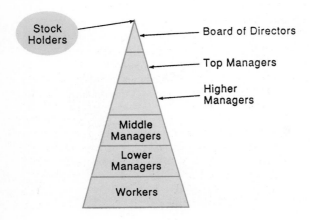

122 largest corporations of various types, however, found only 13 of these corporations clearly controlled by one family (U.S. Senate, 1978a; Kerbo and Della Fave, 1983).

Because of this increasing lack of clear family control in most large corporations, a popular theory emerged as early as the 1930s suggesting that most big corporations are now controlled by their top managers, even though these managers do not have much stock ownership themselves (Berle and Means, 1932; Burnham, 1941). However, it now appears that this "managerial control" thesis was overly simplified. There continues to be stock voter influence by companies and individuals from outside the company that the managers of each company must consider when making decisions about the company.

Though particular families do not control extensive stock in many large companies today, "institutional investors" do control huge amounts of stock. Institutional investors are financial corporations that manage money for other large organizations, such as union pension funds. In most cases institutional investors control the stock votes, a key to power in the company (U.S. Senate, 1978a). In the Senate study of 122 large corporations mentioned earlier, just 20 institutional investors held most of the top stock voting positions in these companies (Kerbo and Della Fave, 1983).

Prominent among these institutional investors are large banks. But because these banks are also corporations with stockholders, it is interesting to consider *their* major stock voters. Among the largest banks in the United States, the most important stock voters are *other banks.* As can be seen in Table 10.9, we find a pattern in which the large banks have *potential* influence over one another. This influence is only potential because the amount of stock controlled by the banks is usually relatively small. Also, within each bank a separate trust department manages the stock. This trust department is supposed to think only of the best interests of the other concerns involved (i.e., the corporation whose stock it controls and the pension funds or others who actually own the stock) when it uses the stock votes to influence other corporations. For example, the bank

Table 10.9. *Stock-voting positions in top 5 banks held by other top banks*

Rank of bank by bank assets	Name	Stock-voting rank held in the bank by other top banks*	Percentage of total stock votes held by other banks
1	BankAmerica Corp.	1 Morgan Bank	2.88
		2 Citibank	2.47
		4 First National, Chicago	1.08
2	Citibank	1 Morgan Bank	3.26
		2 First National, Boston	2.65
		3 Harris Trust & Savings	1.59
3	Chase Manhattan Corp.	1 Rockefeller Family	1.85
4	Manufacturers Hanover	1 Morgan Bank	3.88
		3 Hartford Nat'l Bank	1.09
		4 Bankers Trust	
5	Morgan Bank (J.P. Morgan & Co.)	1 Citibank	2.63
		2 Chase Manhattan	1.43
		3 Manufacturers Hanover	1.42
		4 Bankers Trust	1.10

* List of stock-voting positions held by other banks only; for example, stock voter number 3 in BankAmerica Corp. is not a bank and thus is not listed. The exception is that the Rockefeller family is listed as No. 1 stock voter in Chase Manhattan Corp.
SOURCE: U.S. Senate Committee on Governmental Affairs *(Voting Rights in Major Corporations,* 1978a:260).

should not use its stock votes to promote the merger of two companies when this would only increase the profits of the bank and not help stockholders of the company. At the very least, however, we must conclude that these banks create ties that bring them together on many issues.

The major corporations in the United States are brought together in many other ways as well. One important means of corporate linkage is **interlocking directorates** (Mintz and Schwartz, 1981, 1985). This is a situation in which a person on the board of directors of one company is simultaneously on the board of directors of one or more other companies. Thus, these companies are linked because one or more people are making key decisions about two or more companies at the same time. Direct interlocking directorates between or among two or more competing corporations (say, GM and Ford) are now illegal. But these direct interlocks are very extensive among large corporations not so obviously in direct product or service competition. And even among companies in direct competition, there are often very extensive *indirect interlocking directorates,* which are formed when two or more directors from different corporations come together on the board of directors of a third corporation (see Figure 10.2). For example, a director from GM and a director from Ford could both sit on the board of directors at Morgan Bank. In this case two competing firms (GM and Ford) are brought together in a

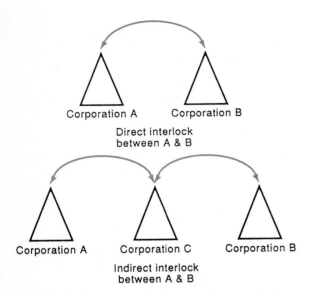

FIGURE 10.2. Direct and indirect interlocking directorates

tions in the group of 130. Figure 10.3 shows the extent of indirect interlocks among competing firms, in this case commercial banks. Each of the lines in this figure indicates a tie through shared director positions.

Corporate Concentration and the Corporate Class. At this point it is useful to consider some outcomes of the combined trends in economic concentration (corporate size, ownership-control, and interlocks). The evidence suggests a massive network of interrelations shared by the largest corporations in this country. These corporations share top personnel and stock control influence, and they have many business interests in common (Kerbo and Della Fave, 1983). These companies are certainly in competition at times, but it is not the level of individual firm competition that Adam Smith originally had in mind. *What must be understood is a modern corpo-*

situation where ideas, economic plans and philosophies, and political strategies can be shared (Mintz and Schwartz, 1985).

Table 10.10 presents some data on the extent of direct interlocks among the nation's top 250 corporations. The average number of interlocks was found to vary by type and size of corporation, but all these companies have rather extensive interlocks, especially the larger corporations and financial institutions.

In another Senate study of 130 top corporations in the United States, we also find evidence of *extensive* corporate interlocks (U.S. Senate, 1978b). These corporations were indirectly or directly interlocked with an average of 62 other companies in the group of 130 corporations. To convey the significance of these interlocks, Table 10.11 presents the companies among the largest 130 companies directly interlocked with just one corporation, Morgan Bank.

The study by the U.S. Senate also examined indirect interlocks. Just 13 of these corporations had 5,547 indirect interlocks with the other corpora-

TABLE 10.10. *Studies of interlocking directorates and sample findings*

Study	Findings
Allen's study (1970 data)*	
Average interlocks of corporations	10.41
Average interlocks of financial institutions	16.92
Average interlocks of industrial corporations	9.62
Average interlocks of nonindustrial corporations	7.41
Dooley's study (1965 data)*	
Average interlocks of corporations	9.9
Average interlocks of financial institutions	15.2
Average interlocks of industrial corporations	9.1
Average interlocks of nonindustrial corporations	8.6
Average interlocks to size of corporation	
less than $0.5 billion assets	6.0
$1.0 to $1.4 billion assets	6.8
$1.5 to $1.9 billion assets	9.2
$3.0 to $3.9 billion assets	16.4
$5.0 and over billion assets	23.7

* Top 200 nonfinancial and top 50 financial corporations (boards of directors).
SOURCE: Kerbo and Della Fave (1979:12).

TABLE 10.11. *Direct interlocking directorates from Morgan Bank directors to other top corporations, 1976*

Corporation*	Number of direct interlocks
Aetna Life	1
Bethlehem Steel	2
Burlington Northern	1
Continental Corporation	1
Du Pont de Nemours	1
Eastman Kodak	1
Federated Department Stores	1
Ford Motor Company	1
General Electric	3
General Motors	3
International Business Machines (IBM)	1
John Hancock Life	1
Metropolitan Life	1
Missouri Pacific Corporation	1
New York Life Insurance	1
Procter and Gamble	1
Prudential Insurance	1
Santa Fe Industries	1
Sears, Roebuck	1
Southern Railway	1
Union Carbide	1
Western Electric	1
Total direct interlocks	27

* Morgan Bank has *many* other direct interlocks. Included here are only the interlocks among the 130 major companies in the 1978 senate study.
SOURCE: U.S. Senate Committee on Governmental Affairs *(Interlocking Directorates Among the Major U.S. Corporations, 1978b:935–936).*

rate structure that creates an environment in which large corporations often work together and share many common interests.

For example, why did a group of 16 large commercial banks (led by Morgan Bank) come together to loan about $4.5 billion to the failing Continental Illinois Bank (the nation's sixth largest bank) in 1984 (see the *Wall Street Journal,* May 16, 1984)? This kind of corporate behavior seems puzzling in the ideal capitalist world of Adam Smith. These other large banks should be cheering when a competitor goes under, not pooling their resources to prevent the bankruptcy! However, given the type of ties among these banks, this corporate "altruism" is a bit more understandable. And these large corporations come together in many other ways when they find common interests, especially common political interests.

There are, of course, human actors behind these corporate bureaucratic ties. Primarily these human actors can be located in the mass of interlocking directorates described above. Overall, then, we can refer to a *corporate class* of affluent individuals who are high officials in major corporations in America (Kerbo, 1983). But within this corporate class there is an even smaller group that has been referred to as the "inner group" of the corporate class (Useem, 1978, 1974; Zeitlin, 1974). Most corporate managers and directors have only one or two corporate positions. However, it is this inner group that accounts for most interlocking directorates. It is this small group of 2,000 or so individuals who come together, share information, organize political activities for common corporate interests, and generally tie these large corporations together. Studies have shown that these inner group members (individuals with three or more corporate positions) are also more likely than other corporate officials to have ties with community, education, charity, and political organizations (Useem, 1979, 1981, 1984). Through these outside ties this corporate elite is able to influence the community and other organizations to further the interests of their corporations.

A Dual Economy. When tracing the history of the American economy since the Civil War, we noted the rapid growth of major corporations, but there is another side to the story. This economic growth and concentration has been uneven around the nation and among industries. Although large corporations have come to dominate some industries (automobiles, defense), in other industries firms tend to be smaller, with more competition and less profits. Thus, there is a **dual economy** in advanced societies today. We can call the industries dominated by large corporations **core industries** and those industries without large corporate dominance

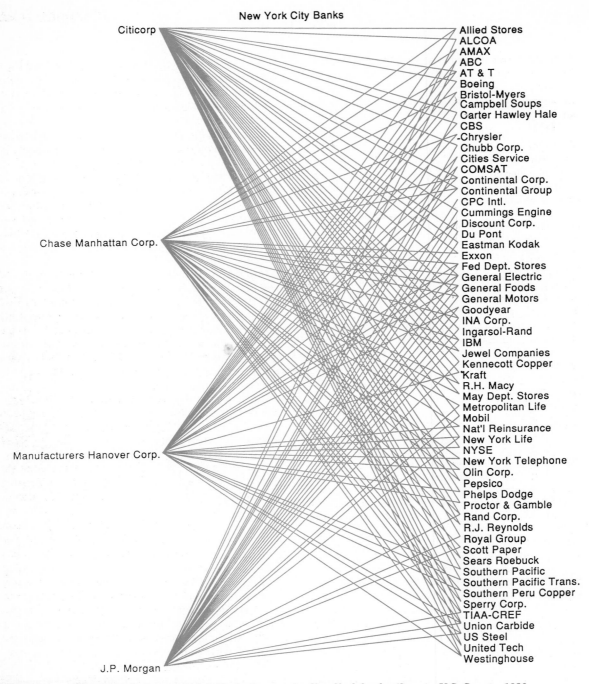

New York City Banks

Citicorp

Chase Manhattan Corp.

Manufacturers Hanover Corp.

J.P. Morgan

Allied Stores
ALCOA
AMAX
ABC
AT & T
Boeing
Bristol-Myers
Campbell Soups
Carter Hawley Hale
CBS
Chrysler
Chubb Corp.
Cities Service
COMSAT
Continental Corp.
Continental Group
CPC Intl.
Cummings Engine
Discount Corp.
Du Pont
Eastman Kodak
Exxon
Fed Dept. Stores
General Electric
General Foods
General Motors
Goodyear
INA Corp.
Ingarsol-Rand
IBM
Jewel Companies
Kennecott Copper
Kraft
R.H. Macy
May Dept. Stores
Metropolitan Life
Mobil
Nat'l Reinsurance
New York Life
NYSE
New York Telephone
Olin Corp.
Pepsico
Phelps Dodge
Proctor & Gamble
Rand Corp.
R.J. Reynolds
Royal Group
Scott Paper
Sears Roebuck
Southern Pacific
Southern Pacific Trans.
Southern Peru Copper
Sperry Corp.
TIAA-CREF
Union Carbide
US Steel
United Tech
Westinghouse

FIGURE 10.3. Corporate interlocks from major New York banks *(Source: U.S. Senate, 1980, p. 35)*

periphery industries. Although there is some disagreement on the core versus periphery placement of industries (Tolbert, Horan, and Beck, 1980; Zucker and Rosenstein, 1981), Table 10.12 gives a general idea of industry location.

Core industries tend to have less competition, higher profits, more stable corporate growth, more unionization, higher wages, and fewer layoffs for workers (Edwards, 1979; Beck, Horan, and Tolbert, 1978; Tolbert, Horan, and Beck, 1980). This tends to fit a pattern: Because a few large corporations tend to dominate the industry, there is reduced competition; because there is less competition, profits tend to be higher; because profits are higher, these companies can have more stable growth and allow higher pay for workers; because the firms are larger, workers find it easier to form unions that help keep wages higher; and because of unions and more stable corporate growth, workers' jobs are more secure. The reverse tends to obtain in periphery industries.

There are other important outcomes of the dual economy for workers. Several studies have found more upward mobility among workers in core industries (Tolbert, 1982, 1983). In part this is because larger firms have more ranks in the bureaucracy within which workers can climb (Baron and Bielby,

TABLE 10.12. *Industry location within a dual economy — select examples*

Core industries	Periphery industries
Mining (metal and coal)	Agriculture
Metal industries	Textiles
Electrical machinery	Retail trade
Transportation equipment	Repair services
Petroleum	Entertainment
Rubber	Restaurants
Airlines	Hotels
Railroads	Food stores
Utilities	Auto sales
Auto production	Service stations
Commercial Banks	Real estate

SOURCES: Adapted from Tolbert, Horan, and Beck (1980); Zucker and Rosenstein (1981).

1984). Other studies have found that race and sex income inequalities exist partially because minorities and women are more likely to be employed in periphery rather than core industries (Parcel, 1979).

The United States is certainly not the only nation with a dual economy and uneven development. Japan, for example, seems to have an even wider split between core and periphery firms with respect to the criteria listed above (Christopher, 1983, pp. 267–287). We can reasonably predict that this trend of a dual economy in the United States will continue to influence our society in many ways, some of which are considered below.

Multinational Corporations. Another important trend in our economy is the increase of **multinational corporations.** We define these as corporations that have extensive investments and trade in more than one nation. Multinational firms have existed since the early stages of industrialization, with one of the earliest examples being the British East India Company, which came to dominate much of India by the 1800s.

The increasing importance of multinational corporations today can be understood with reference to their size and growth. The yearly sales of the top 50 multinationals is now larger than the total GNP of any nation except the United States (Chirot, 1986). Of particular importance in the world are U.S. multinationals. Before World War II there was relatively little direct foreign investment by American multinationals. But by 1965, U.S. multinationals accounted for 60 percent of world foreign investment (Kodelski, 1972). And in 1974, 70 percent of U.S. foreign capital investment in developing nations was in Latin America.

Many of the largest U.S. corporations are highly dependent on foreign investments for profits. For example, one of America's largest industrial corporations, Exxon, receives about two-thirds of its profits from overseas business. Generally the same is true for many other major corporations like Standard Oil of California, IBM, and Gulf Oil.

The impact of this multinational trend in the U.S. economy is felt in many ways. In a positive respect we find improved world trade. However, this multi-

---

At the center of corporate power in the United States (and the world) are large commercial banks. With the ties created by interlocking directorates, stock votes, and debt control over other corporations, several studies have found large U.S. banks to be at the hub of a corporate network (Sonquest and Koening, 1975; Allen, 1977; Mariolis, 1975; Mintz and Schwartz, 1981, 1985). These banks have extensive ties to many corporations and appear to be in a central position within this overall corporate network. And the ties of these big banks do not stop with other corporations. The top officers of these banks are also heavily involved in government, international organizations, voluntary and welfare organizations, local communities, as well as higher education in the form of university directors (Ratcliff, Gallagher, and Ratcliff, 1979; Useem, 1979, 1983).

On top of the hierarchy of U.S. banks in 1984 was Citicorp (the parent company of New York's Citibank, which in recent years has been the largest U.S. bank.

In 1984, Daniel Hertzberg (1984) of the *Wall Street Journal* had the following comments on the power of this bank:

> Entering the giant bank holding company's headquarters at 399 Park Ave., "You realize you are at one of the vortexes of power in the world," a former Citicorp executive says. "It's like an aircraft carrier reving up to 30 knots. The place shakes."
>
> That may be a bit overstated—but not much. Walter B. Wriston, Citicorp's chairman and chief executive, recently boasted that Citicorp does business with one out of every seven U.S. households. Its $141.8 billion in assets at March 31 led the industry by a wide margin; its $860 million in 1983 net income was nearly twice that of any other U.S. bank holding company. It owns Citibank, hundreds of lending offices, and savings and loan associations in three states. It is the nation's biggest bank-credit-card issuer. It is the world's biggest private foreign lender, and nearly half of its 63,000 employees work outside the U.S., in 94 countries.

We can further understand the influence of this bank (along with the other top New York City banks) by considering its director ties. The 27 directors of Citicorp are also directors of many other companies, of which the following is only a partial list (U.S. Senate, 1978b, pp. 413–426):

Beatrice Foods Co.
NCR Corp.
AT&T
Ford Motor Co.

Bethlehem Steel
U.S. Steel
Gillette Co.
Macy and Co.

---

national trend has many negative effects. For example, millions of jobs have been lost to U.S. workers because of direct multinational investments in other nations (Blumberg, 1980). Especially in labor-intensive industries that require many workers, companies have been moving to other nations where wages are much lower. This has also kept the wages of U.S. workers lower than they otherwise would

be because of international competition among workers. And although this foreign investment has led to some improvement in the economy of other nations, it has harmed our own economy because of the loss of jobs and capital; many recipient countries of this U.S. investment have actually had their economies harmed as well (Chase-Dunn, 1975; Bornschier, Chase-Dunn, and Rubinson, 1978).

General Motors
Kraftco Corp.
Pepsico Inc.
Ingersoll-Rand Co.
Metropolitan Life
Aetna Life
Mutual Life Insurance
Equitable Life Assurance
New York Life Insurance
Standard Oil of California
Mobil Corp.
Dow Corning Corp.
Procter and Gamble
DuPont

CBS
NBC
Exxon
United Technologies
Eastman Kodak
Kennecott Copper
IBM
Xerox Corp
General Electric
Westinghouse Electric
Boeing Co.
J.C. Penney
Sears, Roebuck

Furthermore, the Citibank Trust department is among the top five stock voters in the following corporations (U.S. Senate, 1978a, pp. 267–268; again, this is only a partial list):

Atlantic Richfield
Texaco Inc.
Continental Oil Co.
Exxon Corp.
Phillips Petroleum Co.
Caterpiller Tractor
Eastman Kodak
Duke Power Co.
General Electric
GT&E
Coca-Cola Co.
Burlington Northern

First Bank System
Morgan Bank
Bankamerica Corp.
First Chicago Corp.
J.C. Penney
Sears, Roebuck
Federated Department Stores
K Mart Corp.
Southern Pacific
American Express
Du Pont

Internationally, many nations are heavily indebted to Citicorp. For example, the four largest South American nations owe Citicorp over $10 billion. Also, as noted above, Citicorp has financial operations in 94 other nations around the world.

Advancing Technology. When most people think about trends in the economy today they probably think about high-tech industries. There are famous cases of new advances in computers and microchips where, so far, the United States leads the world. We hear predictions by politicians that high-tech industries are the wave of the future and these industries will save our economy from the rapid decline experienced in the old industrial sector of our economy. Such predictions are most likely exaggerated.

The U.S. economy is going through a major shift. Our old industrial sectors (such as auto and steel production) have rapidly lost ground in world competition. While many other nations, especially Japan, have been introducing new technologies in these industries, the United States has done so less often.

One result has been called the "rust bowl" — the closing down of industries similar to the agricultural disaster called the "dust bowl" of the 1930s, which threw many farmers off their land.

To save many American jobs our old industries must become more high-tech and we must expand new high-tech industries. Even if this occurs, however, though some jobs will be saved, there will still be a net reduction in jobs. In other words, by "going high-tech" we may still be able to sell many cars around the world, thus saving some jobs. But compared with a few years ago, the cars will still be produced by fewer workers. Many jobs lost in basic industries during the severe recession of the early 1980s will never be regained (*Time,* May 30, 1983, pp. 62 – 70).

New jobs have been created by high-tech industries like computers. But of these new jobs created in the past ten years, only about 10 percent have been in high-tech fields; most have been in other industries like fast foods (Drucker, 1984). The United States has been doing surprisingly well in creating new jobs in the past ten years. As we saw in our discussion of demography, there were predictions of severe economic problems when the "baby boom" generation began seeking jobs in the 1970s. To be sure, there were not enough jobs to meet the demands of new workers in the 1970s, but it could have been worse.

However, questions are in order about our ability to expand the "low-tech" or service jobs indefinitely to cover the job losses in the old industrial sectors. But even if this is the case, our discussion of the dual economy must be remembered. The new low-tech and service jobs are mostly in periphery industries where jobs are less secure, often part time, and pay less.

An End to U.S. Economic Dominance: Some Causes

Although it is accurate to say that the United States is losing economic dominance, we should not imagine approaching economic catastrophe in this country. The U.S. economy is not so much declining as it is growing more slowly than the economies of some other nations. And the picture is complex when we consider that some U.S. industries are doing well in the world market, while others are doing poorly. Overall, however, we do find that the U.S. economy no longer has the dominant position it once had in the world. In this section we bring together some of the trends just considered to briefly examine some of the reasons for the relative decline of the U.S. economy.

Supply-side Economics. The supply-side theory or **supply-side economics** became popular in the late 1970s among a group of politicians, academics, and "new right" intellectuals and became attached to the presidential campaign of Ronald Reagan. The basic points of this theory are the following:

1. In recent decades political and economic leaders in the United States have been more concerned with the distribution and marketing of goods and services than with the supply or more efficient production of them. Thus, the supply-side view stresses increased production and productivity. (Productivity refers to how efficiently goods and services are produced.) In other words, it is argued that we need more industrial production capacity (more factories) and more efficient industrial technology.

2. A primary reason for an erosion of U.S. productive capacity has been government policy. Government regulation of private industry is said to have resulted in barriers to capital investment (building more and better factories) and reduced productivity of labor. The latter includes such things as government requirements for a safer working environment.

Government tax policies, however, are seen as most harmful to U.S. economic output and productivity. It is claimed that taxes on corporations and the wealthy are so high that they reduce the incentive for investment. If so much will be taken by the government in taxes with further economic investment, then individuals do not have sufficient incentives to make such investment. The now famous Laffer curve (Laffer and Seymour, 1979) is related to this argument, but it also considers the question of government revenues.

As Figure 10.4 suggests, as tax rates go up, government revenues increase, but only to a certain point. Once tax rates become too "high," then further investment and economic effort is reduced. The economy becomes weak, resulting in even reduced government revenues despite higher tax rates because there is less income and profits to tax. This situation is represented in the curve pattern in the upper portion of Figure 10.4.

3. The suggested solution to U.S. economic decline is, of course, less government regulation and involvement in the economy, plus reduced taxes. It is most important to reduce tax rates for corporations and the wealthy, however, because these are the people who have the money to invest if sufficient incentives exist.

4. The arguments above are also usually combined with an argument favoring cuts in welfare programs. Proponents argue that welfare budget cuts can help the economy in two ways: (1) Welfare budget cuts will reduce government spending that should go along with tax cuts; (2) but more important, welfare benefits are seen as so extensive that they reduce the work effort of many people in the society, and provide other workers with more influence to demand higher wages because they can quit their jobs and go on welfare if the wages offered are low.

A major point of supply-side economics is that increased wages have cut into corporate profits and the incomes of the wealthy. Along with the reduction in their profits and income due to taxes, this reduces capital investments (for greater production) even more. Thus, again the supply-side of the economy has been harmed, this time because of higher wages due to welfare benefits.

5. The supply-side view has a "trickle-down" dimension that is believed to take care of the less affluent. With more money in the hands of the rich, more investments will be made that create jobs for the poor.

A Critique of Supply-side Economics. Now we consider major criticisms of the supply-side view.

1. There is little argument that U.S. productivity has been in a sorry state. Everyone agrees that we need more efficient industrial technology.

2. The problem, however, is not necessarily government regulation. The U.S. government is less involved in regulating industrial activity than any government in Europe or Japan (Thurow, 1980). This is not to say some government regulations are not bad for the economy, but overall, there is less government regulation in the United States than in other countries, and many charge that this is part of the problem. Japan, for example, has a powerful government agency (Ministry of International Trade and Industry—MITI) that helps in planning and coordinating corporate activity for the long-range benefit of the overall economy (Reischauer, 1977, p. 192; Christopher, 1983, p. 230). This is not the only reason for Japanese economic success, but many economists agree it is an important factor.

As for U.S. tax policies, U.S. citizens pay less income tax than the citizens of most other industrial nations. The average taxpayer in the United States pays between 15 percent and 20 percent of his or her income in taxes. The figure for Japan is about 10 percent, but for industrial nations like West Germany, Sweden, the Netherlands, and Austria, the figure is over 25 percent. Of 17 major industrial nations, the United States ranks 13th in income taxes paid by the average citizen (Organization for Economic Cooperation and Development, 1980).

FIGURE 10.4. Laffer curve: the theoretical relationship between tax rates and government tax revenues

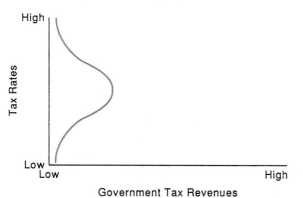

More important for the supply-side argument, however, is the tax rate of the wealthy and corporations. The actual percentage of tax revenues going to the federal government from corporations has dropped substantially since 1960 (see Table 10.13). And as shown in Table 10.14, the income going to the 20 percent of the most wealthy Americans is reduced only slightly after income taxes. The same is generally true for other industrial nations.

As for the most wealthy in a society, the highest tax rate is found in Japan. The top income tax bracket in the United States is only about 30 percent (reduced from 70 percent during the Reagan presidency). With all the deductions and loopholes, the 70 percent rate for the most wealthy in the United States before the Reagan administration's tax changes was seldom approached, and most of the wealthy had a real tax rate close to that of the average American. In Japan, however, incomes much higher than $100,000 a year are meaningless — the government takes about 70 percent of personal income above that figure. And the incomes of top corporate executives are much lower in Japan than in the United States (Reischauer, 1977, p. 160; Christopher, 1983, p. 247). In 1983, for example, the ratio between the income of the top Japanese auto executives and the average Japanese auto worker was 7 to 1. That figure for the United States auto industry was 37 to 1 (*Wall Street Journal*, April 18, 1984).

3. The problem with the U.S. economy is not that the rich need more money. But even if the rich are made richer through more tax breaks, there is no guarantee under Reagan's supply-side economics that the money will be reinvested for economic expansion in this country. As we have already seen, multinational investments outside the United States continue to take jobs from Americans.

4. The United States spends less on welfare as a percent of national income than almost any other industrial nation (see Table 10.15). Some countries (for example, West Germany) spending more for social welfare have done very well economically in the past 10 to 20 years, while other countries (for example, the United Kingdom) spending more for social welfare than the United States have done poorly. Japan spends much less for social welfare, but with a 1.5 percent poverty rate compared with that of the U.S. rate of about 14 percent, this is understandable. Overall, therefore, we find no consistent relationship between welfare spending and the economic performance of a nation.

5. Economic expansion is usually preferable to economic stagnation. An expanding economy means that jobs are created and unemployment is reduced. However, there is no simple relationship among economic growth, unemployment, poverty, and inequality. New jobs may be created but we must ask how many, what kind, and how much will they pay.

During the 1920s, corporations and the wealthy

TABLE 10.13. *Internal revenue collections by selected sources, 1960–1983*

Source of revenue	Percentage of total			
	1960	1970	1980	1983
Individual income taxes	49.0	55.4	54.9	55.7
Employment taxes	12.2	19.1	24.7	27.7
Old-age and disability insurance	(11.1)	(18.2)	(23.6)	(26.5)
Unemployment insurance	(0.4)	(0.4)	(0.6)	(0.7)
Corporation income taxes	24.2	17.9	13.9	9.8
Estate and gift taxes	1.8	1.9	1.3	1.0
Excise taxes	12.9	8.1	4.7	5.7

SOURCE: U.S. Bureau of the Census, 1985. *Statistical Abstract of the United States,* table 506, p. 315.

TABLE 10.14. *Pretax and posttax distribution of income, highest fifth of households (%)*

	Pretax share of top 20%	Posttax share of top 20%	Difference
Australia	38.9	38.8	0.1
Canada	43.3	41.0	2.3
France	47.0	46.9	0.1
Germany	46.8	46.1	0.7
Japan	42.5	41.0	1.5
Netherlands	45.8	42.9	2.9
Norway	40.9	37.3	3.6
Sweden	40.5	37.0	3.5
United Kingdom	40.3	38.7	1.6
United States	44.8	42.9	1.9

SOURCE: Tufte (1978).

were given more favorable government treatment (e.g., tax cuts) and there was business expansion. But like the 1980s, there was also a significant increase in the level of income inequality. The "trickle down," if there was any, did not allow the lower class to keep pace with the economic gains of the wealthy.

A recent study by Treas (1983) that examined the trickle-down effect more directly found that many groups of poor and unemployed in the United States have *not* been helped by economic expansion in recent history. In fact, white males who were unemployed have been the only ones experiencing significant improvement in their economic standing with economic growth after a recession. Minority men and women, and white women (especially women heads of household) have *not* felt the trickle-down effect.

There are several reasons for the findings above. First, with economic expansion in recent years many of the new jobs created have been in high-technology industries and professional services. The long-term unemployed do not have the skills to fill these jobs. Second, economic growth does not always mean new jobs will be created. The economic expansion can be limited to capital-intensive industries, that is, industries that produce goods using mostly machines rather than human labor. Both of these factors have been happening in the United

States, reducing any trickle down to the poor. The U.S. economic upturn in the mid-1980s shows this quite clearly. In spite of this economic growth, the level of income inequality increased significantly and the rate of poverty actually went up for many categories of Americans. (This income inequality and poverty rate is examined in more detail in Chapter 12.)

Some Causes of Economic Decline. We have already seen how the U.S. corporate structure has moved toward concentration and huge corporate conglomerates. It can be argued that because of reduced competition at home for the most concentrated industries, and because there was little competition overseas between 1945 and 1970 owing to World War II, American corporations became fat and lazy. When they were suddenly hit with foreign competition in the 1970s they were not prepared to compete. They had not been forced to keep up with new technology and management techniques. The politi-

TABLE 10.15. *Transfer payments as a percent of national income in 15 noncommunist, industrial nations*

Rank	Country	Transfer payments as percentage of national income
1	Netherlands	29.01
2	France	24.17
3	Norway	21.88
4	Sweden	21.54
5	Italy	19.90
6	Belgium	19.54
7	West Germany	18.59
8	Denmark	17.49
9	Austria	17.31
10	Switzerland	14.17
11	United Kingdom	13.40
12	Canada	12.85
13	United States	11.88
14	Australia	9.65
15	Japan	6.95

SOURCE: Constructed from data supplied by Nutter (1978, pp. 58–75). Data are for either 1973 or 1974.

cal influence of these corporate elites made it possible for them to gain political protection in the form of regulation, which further reduced their competitiveness.

Most new jobs, new products, and new innovative technology in recent years in the United States have come from small businesses (*Wall Street Journal,* February 5, 1982). Big corporations need not necessarily be indifferent and uninnovative, as shown by many corporations in Japan. But there is no agency like MITI prodding U.S. corporations, nor are U.S. corporate executives tied to their corporations for life, as is the case in Japan.

Another reason that long-range economic planning is more likely in Japan is due to the nature of corporate financing. In the United States, if corporations want to finance new operations, they are likely to do so through selling corporate stock. These stockholders are then most likely to be concerned with yearly stock dividends (profits paid to stockholders). In Japan, corporate expansion is more likely to be financed through bank loans (often regulated by the government). The banks are more concerned with corporate health several years from the time of the loan to assure it will be repaid (Reischauer, 1977, p. 190; Christopher, 1983, pp. 250–254). Rather than pay out profits to stockholders, Japanese corporations are more likely to reinvest their profits for further growth (Abegglen and Stalk, 1985).

It can also be charged that when corporations become large, powerful, and accountable to no strong outside interest group, the future of the U.S. economy can be jeopardized. If more profits are to be made in other countries, if wages and taxes are lower, if there is no regulation to protect workers and consumers in other countries, then these large multinationals can flee the United States. Many have been doing this in recent years, eliminating millions of jobs in this nation (Blumberg, 1980, p. 129). Much the same thing happened when the British economy began to decline in the late 1800s and British capital began flowing to the United States (Chirot, 1986).

In a similar manner, the turn of the twentieth-century American economist Thorstein Veblen described what he called "the penalty for taking the lead" to explain why economic trends never allow one country to remain dominant in the world economy for an extended period of time. Once a nation experiences economic growth, has established new technology, built its factories, and begins to settle into its comfortable new position in the world economy, it has already begun to lose its top position. The nations that are behind copy the new technology, but they also add to it. These nations then build new factories that are more modern and productive and soon overtake the previous leading nations. This is one reason why the United States moved to the top in the early 1900s and why it is losing that position today.

Another factor often cited as related to U.S. economic decline is military spending (Kennedy, 1987). We often hear that military spending creates jobs, and putting people to work helps the economy. In the short run this is true, at least to some extent, as was shown with President Reagan's extensive military spending increases in the 1980s. However, over the long run studies indicate that military spending (rather than spending and investment for nonmilitary goods) actually harms the economy (Szymanski, 1973; Devine, 1983), for several reasons. First, military production tends to be more capital-intensive, meaning fewer workers are needed than when the same amount of investment is made for nonmilitary production. Second, when a tank, fighter plane, or nuclear missile is built, the hardware has no productive use. The production of trucks, airliners, trains, and other machines add to our economic growth. Third, the research and development of a nation preoccupied with an arms race takes away research and development funds from nonmilitary production. For example, since World War II most research and development in electronics in the United States has gone to military technology. The figure in Japan is 5 percent (Blumberg, 1980, pp. 144–145). The United States produces military equipment that is probably the best in the world — and even exports some of this military equipment. In the meantime, the Japanese have taken over the world market in radios, TVs, stereos, video tape recorders, and on and on through a long list of other consumer electronics goods.

Some readers may respond, "If we know that

these things are happening that harm our economy, why don't we correct them?" For example, if we know the historical pattern has been that the corporations of a nation on top economically soon begin making investments elsewhere, why don't we prevent it? And if we know that a concentration of economic power in some industries results in less productivity, why don't we do something about it? What must be recognized in answering these questions is that knowledge does not always produce effective action. To produce the necessary change means that some interest groups will make gains while others will have economic losses.

THE NATURE OF WORK

For most people in the world, few things are more important than the type of work they do, or the work done by others in the household. As we will see, the several hours a day most people spend at their jobs shape many aspects of their lives. The material aspects are the most obvious; the kind of job people have and how much it pays influences their life chances and standard of living. But other influences are equally important; our world views and our family relations, among many other things, are shaped by our work. In this final section we consider this everyday aspect of the economy that the average person must face.

The Meaning of Work

What we think of as "work" is unique in the history of human societies. Unlike in industrial societies today, for most of history there was no real separation between home activities and work activities. In other words, the work was not performed outside the home. For example, the twelfth-century French peasant took care of the family garden and livestock (if any), repaired fences, and did household repairs as a normal day's activity (LeRoy Ladurie, 1978).

Throughout history social philosophers have had differing views on humans and the nature of work. Because we are biological organisms and have basic needs that must be met, most people must work or have others work for them. For this reason Marx believed that there must be some inherent need for work within us, and more specifically work of a particular kind. Marx believed humans have a need to produce and have a positive identification with the products of their labor (Marx, 1964, pp. 124–125). When the conditions of labor remove the identity with work, the result is unfulfillment and what he called alienation.

C. Wright Mills (1953, p. 215) had a different assumption about the meaning of work, but he arrived at a similar conclusion about the contemporary conditions of work for most workers: "Neither love nor hatred of work is inherent in man, or inherent in any given line of work. For work has no intrinsic meaning." The meaning of work given most people in our society today comes from an old ideology placing value on the work of the independent artisan and free professional. Few people today are able to do that type of work, but rather work as cogs in a factory or office assembly line. They are seldom able to take pride in a finished product they themselves have created. For this reason, Mills also believed that most people today are alienated from their work, while holding joy only in their free time. In Mills's (1953, p. 237) descriptive words, "Each day men sell little pieces of themselves in order to try to buy them back each night and weekend with the coin of 'fun.'"

From a very different sociologist we find a somewhat similar view. Daniel Bell (1976) believes that capitalism itself is undermining the value of work in the nation. In his view, our industrial system grew because people valued hard work and craftsmanship. However, the success of capitalism in producing goods that must be sold has led to advertising that stresses leisure activities and consumption, not work. "On the one hand, the business corporation wants an individual to work hard, pursue a career, accept delayed gratification — to be, in the crude sense, an organization man. And yet, in its products and its advertisements, the corporation promotes pleasure, instant joy, relaxing and letting go" (Bell, 1976, pp. 71–72). The result in Bell's view is not only alienated workers but also the weakening of industrial capitalism.

BOX 10.2

*Relations in the
Japanese Workplace*

Much has been written about the management style and harmonious work relations in the Japanese corporation. There are, indeed, some striking differences when we compare Japanese and American attitudes toward work. The Japanese strongly identify with their companies and are extremely loyal and hardworking. To the Japanese the company you work for is more important than the occupation a person has with that corporation. For example, one would be more impressed that someone works for Sony than knowing the person is a lawyer.

In Tokyo the commuter trains and subways are crammed with people going to work around 8:00 A.M. Monday through Saturday. (Most workers work a half day on Saturday and sometimes on Sunday.) Then, it is not until 8:00 P.M. to 10:00 P.M. that most of these workers finally return home. There is an effort by the government to increase Japanese workers' vacation time, but the primary problem is that the average worker does not take all the vacation time currently offered. For men especially, most of their world is centered around their work and co-workers.

For example, one survey of U.S. and Japanese workers found the following differences on how these workers view their company (Cole, 1979, p. 237):

	Workers in	
I think of my company as:	**United States (%)**	**Japan (%)**
1. The central concern in my life and of greater importance than my personal life.	1	9
2. A part of my life at least equal in importance to my personal life.	22	57
3. A place for me to work with management, during work hours, to accomplish mutual goals.	54	26
4. Strictly a place to work and entirely separate from my personal life.	25	8

One reason for the strong worker loyalty in Japan is that their culture leads the Japanese to prefer working in a cooperative group setting (Nakane, 1970). However, management styles in Japanese corporations contribute to these cooperative relations. Managers take more care in seeking out the views of their workers. There is much less income inequality between managers and their workers, a situation often creating resentment between workers and managers in the United States (Christopher, 1983, p. 247). One outcome of all this is that the number of strikes in Japan are about 30 percent of the number in the United States (Reischauer, 1977).

But contrary to the popular U.S. image of working conditions in Japan, all is not utopia. For example, the life-time guarantee of employment we hear much about is limited. First, only about 30 percent of workers are in such jobs in Japan, in large corporations (Christopher, 1983). Second, "life-time" usually means only to 55 or 60 years of age, even though most workers must work until they are past 65. Until recently this posed only a small problem because these workers from large corporations could easily find jobs with smaller companies needing their skills. But this situation is changing. The unemployment rate for men over 55 is now 4.3 percent, compared with a 2.7 percent rate for all workers (Jameson, 1984).

Worker Alienation. There have been many detailed studies of the lives of individual workers and their attitudes toward work (for example, Terkel, 1972; Sennett and Cobb, 1973; Lasson, 1971; Pfeffer, 1979). Most of these studies have stressed the alienation that most lower-middle-class and working-class people feel in their work. The major exception has been a study by LeMasters (1975) that focused on skilled blue-collar workers who work in the tradition of the old artisan.

The subject of worker alienation or dissatisfaction with work, however, is complex. It is sometimes easy for a researcher who has experienced the work of a professional to see a higher level of dissatisfaction among lower-skilled workers than in fact exists. And the subject of worker satisfaction has more than one dimension.

The more objective and methodologically sound research suggests that worker dissatisfaction is higher the lower we go in the job ranks (Jencks et al., 1972, pp. 247–252). But work satisfaction-dissatisfaction has two distinct dimensions. The first relates to the *control of the work process* itself. When workers have more voice in how their work is performed, they have more job satisfaction (Kalleberg and Griffin, 1980; Kohn, 1976). The second relates to the *complexity of the job* and the amount of skill required. When workers have more complex tasks to accomplish, tasks that are not repetitive and simple, the work satisfaction is greater (Kalleberg and Griffin, 1980).

The kind of work that led to the rapid expansion of industrial economies, that is, work on an assembly line, is the very type of work that results in most worker dissatisfaction. More recently, however, white-collar jobs have also been changing. Sales jobs and office jobs, among many others, have been broken up in assembly line fashion. For example, in the past, a secretary would type, take dictation, file reports, answer the phone, arrange meetings, and handle many other tasks. But with the introduction of new automation equipment in the office, each of these tasks may be assigned to a different person, who does only one of these tasks all day.

There have been attempts to reverse the trend toward ever more assembly line work. In Sweden, for example, Volvos have been successfully produced by small work groups, with individuals performing many tasks and even exchanging tasks (Heller and Willatt, 1975). But most large corporations have not gone this far in attempts to reduce work dissatisfaction.

CHAPTER SUMMARY

Key Terms

gross national product (GNP), 265
real income, 265
economy, 266
division of labor, 266
primary industries, 267
secondary industries, 267
tertiary industries, 267
mode of production, 269
capitalism, 269
communism, 272
democratic socialism, 272

market socialism, 272
Keynesian economics, 273
corporation, 279
interlocking directorates, 281
dual economy, 283
core industries, 283
periphery industries, 285
multinational corporations, 285
supply-side economics, 288

Content

The economy is the system by which humans go about producing, attaining, and distributing goods and services. Although there are many types of economic systems, the present chapter has focused on industrial economic systems. The type of economy a society has shapes many other aspects of the society, and thus, industrial societies have many common characteristics. But industrial societies are not exactly alike and noneconomic factors shape the nature of a society as well.

All industrial societies have an extensive and complex division of labor. We also find differing industrial sectors such as primary, secondary, and tertiary industries.

Whereas all industrial societies have similar technical means of production (that is, industrial technology), they may differ with respect to the relations of production. Industrial societies can generally be divided into capitalist, communist, and democratic socialist with respect to the extent of private ownership of basic industry and government involvement in the economy.

The United States began industrializing rapidly in the late 1800s, and by the second decade of the 1900s it emerged as the dominant industrial nation. The Great Depression of the 1930s, however, produced a severe setback for U.S. industrial expansion, but also brought extensive reform under President Franklin Roosevelt's New Deal. After World War II the United States emerged as an even more dominant economic power, but by the late 1970s there was relative economic decline. The decades of the 1970s and 1980s have brought many economic problems because of the changed U.S. economic position in the world economy.

Throughout this period of U.S. economic expansion we find several important economic trends common to other industrial nations. First, there has been increasing economic concentration with huge corporations coming to dominate many industrial sectors. Second, most of these large corporations are no longer primarily owned and controlled by a single wealthy family. Rather, a powerful network of corporate elites (a corporate class) has come to dominate the overall economy with their multiple positions in several corporations and other organizations. Third, we also find a dual economy where core industries are dominated by the corporate giants, whereas periphery industries are made up of smaller business firms. Fourth, large corporations are becoming increasingly multinational. And finally, although there is advancing technology, the high-tech trend is accompanied by an even bigger low-tech trend of low-skilled service jobs.

A popular explanation of the U.S. economic decline in the 1980s (supply-side economics) argues that taxes, government spending, and welfare programs are the primary factors harming U.S. economic strength. Historical and comparative data, however, raise many questions about the validity of this explanation. Other factors like corporate concentration without accountability and coordination, the recovery of European and Japanese industry, and the usual "penalty for taking the lead" are among the more valid explanations of the relative economic decline in the United States.

The nature of the work people do is among the most important factors shaping their lives. The way people raise their children, how they view the world, and how they participate in the world outside of work are among the things influenced by the way people spend their hours at work. There is also evidence that the type of work most people do is increasingly seen as alienating and unsatisfying.

CHAPTER 11

The State

NATURE OF THE STATE
Types of Authority
Types of Rule
Theories of the State
Functional Theory
Conflict Theories
The State as Redistributive Institution
Emergence of the Modern State
The Modern State and Class Conflict
The Emergence of Democracy
Political Economy
Change from Early Laissez-faire
Means of Government Economic Influence
Political Cycles in the Economy

CLASS CONFLICT AND THE STATE
The Upper Classes and the State
Campaign Contributions
Congressional Lobbying
President's Cabinet
Policy-formation Process
Who Rules?
Nonelites and the State
Unions and Political Influence
Outcomes of Class Conflict
The State Against Capitalism?

CHAPTER SUMMARY

There are two methods of diminishing the force of authority in a nation. The first is to weaken the supreme power in its very principle, by forbidding or preventing society from acting in its own defense under certain circumstances. To weaken authority in this manner is the European way of establishing freedom.

The second manner of diminishing the influence of authority does not consist in stripping society of some of its rights, nor in paralyzing its efforts, but in distributing the exercise of its powers among the various hands and in multiplying functionaries, to each of whom is given the degree of power necessary for him to perform his duty. There may be nations whom this distribution of social powers might lead to anarchy, but in itself it is not anarchical. The authority thus divided is, indeed, rendered less irresistible and less perilous, but it is not destroyed.

—Alexis de Tocqueville, **Democracy in America**

When we follow the progression of history, no recent development is more startling or dramatic than how the state is viewed by the general population in our society. Without looking back we simply cannot comprehend the revolutionary ideas we have today. Were we to describe our view of the state's role to a peasant living in twelfth-century France, or anywhere else during that time, we would probably be considered insane. And if we confronted the rulers of those societies with such views, we would most likely lose our heads quite soon.

Since humans formed anything like large, settled societies thousands of years ago it has been only in the last 200 to 300 years that a view we call political democracy was widely recognized. Before this time the general population knew who had political influence, and they knew it was not found with them. The state belonged to (I mean actually belonged to) and was run by a ruling aristocratic family. The state did not "serve the people" unless the ruler decided that it would do so in some way. If the ruler decided to build a pyramid as a monument to himself (or sometimes herself), then it was ordered. No matter that hundreds would die building it — the people must obey. There was no committee of representatives to decide if the project was worthwhile, expensive, in the best interests of "the people," or any other "crazy notions" as these. The phrase "the people" is today used to justify almost every political action; that phrase had no meaning to rulers more than 300 years ago (Bendix, 1978).

None of the above implies (1) that the masses never had political influence in preindustrial socie-

ties, or (2) that the masses today actually have extensive political influence. Both situations, as we will see, are incorrect. But there has been a striking trend in recent history toward the acceptance of democratic ideas, and to some degree the practice of these ideas.

In this chapter we first examine the nature of the state. We then explore the historical development of the state as we move to our main task of considering the state and its place in modern industrial societies around the world.

NATURE OF THE STATE

As we all know, the modern state has taken on many tasks; the criminal justice system, the military, the educational system, and the welfare system among many other systems are all run by the state. The state, or at least some level of government, maintains our highways and parks, attempts to assure airline safety and the safety of drugs and consumer goods, and the list could go on. But of all the activities of the state, and of all the varieties of states around the world and throughout history, one characteristic of the state is unique and important. The **state** is the organization that *dominates the means of force* in the society (Weber, 1946).

Consider for a moment the importance of this monopoly on physical force held by the modern state. In the final analysis, when two or more parties are in conflict, with neither side willing to bend to the wishes of the other, physical coercion is the remaining means to resolve the dispute. For example, if factory workers occupy a factory because of a wage dispute, and there is absolutely no hope of compromise, the final solution is force. Either the workers must be forced to leave or the owner must be forced to increase wages. The two sides may try to use their own means of force on each other as they have done many times in the history of industrial societies; the workers pick up clubs or other weapons and the owner brings in hired agents. But remember that in modern societies the state dominates the means of force; state forces (if united) can overpower either side — the workers or the owner's agents. Thus, it becomes extremely critical in a labor dispute to know on which side the state's forces will intervene. It is for this reason that the state is one of the most important organizations in modern societies. Whoever controls the state, or at least has the most influence in the state, also has influence in how the state's means of force will be employed.

In addition to dominating the means of force in the society, some sociologists, particularly functionalists, have stressed that the state is also the institution that attempts to *set common goals* and *organize efforts toward achieving these goals* in the society (Parsons, 1951). As an institution, functionalists suggest that the state is a subsystem of the society that works to maintain the well-being of the society in general, and the common interests of all members of the society. However, although the state often works for the common interests of people in a society, this is not always the case.

Throughout history we find that the state's activities (including its monopoly on force) have been used for the narrow interests of one group and against the interests of other groups. Such is also the case in modern, relatively democratic societies as we have already seen and will consider further. The state operates to *maintain social order in the society,* by use of force if necessary. But we must also ask whose order, and for what purpose. For this reason a description of the state as "setting common goals" and "organizing efforts toward achieving these goals" is too limiting.

When considering the nature of the state, a subject related to our discussion above must be considered — power. The elusive phenomenon called power is a key element in the political domain. Groups seeking to influence the state use power, and the state uses power to accomplish specified goals. A group with power can influence the state to use its power to achieve the goals of this group.

Power, however, is a rather broad concept and comes in many forms (Wrong, 1980). Max Weber (1946) considered **power** as the ability to induce others to do as you wish, even when these other people find it against their interests to do as you wish. The phenomenon of power is found in every aspect of life. But today the state is the focal point of most group conflicts, with all groups employing their means of influence over the state so that the state will help them achieve goals that are resisted by one or more other groups.

When saying that power resides in the state it is common to add that the state holds *legitimate* power. Most people in the society generally accept the right of the state to wield such power. However, qualifications such as "most people" and "generally accept" are rather important because not everyone in the society must believe the state is legitimate, or has a legitimate right to monopolize power as it does. For example, many people may agree that a state does not have the right to force citizens into the military or to pay taxes. Thus the *degree* of legitimacy held by a state is important in helping us understand the stability of that state. The waves of political violence and revolution throughout history must be examined in part by considering how state legitimacy has been reduced or eliminated. But like power, we will see that the phenomenon of legitimacy is complex and often difficult to directly estimate.

Types of Authority. Another way of describing state legitimacy is by referring to **authority.** The state that has the legitimate right to use force has the authority to use this force. Force, of course, can be used by many individuals or groups. An armed robber uses force, as does an organized crime family. Both groups may take your money, as does the state through taxation. But the difference is that the state is more likely to be considered as having the authority to take your money.

The Queen of England is the contemporary monarch who is most often thought of in the context of traditional authority. This photo, taken at her coronation in 1953, conveys some of the pomp and splendor that surround the monarchy. The Queen rules based on her hereditary birthright. Her oldest son will succeed her. (© UPI/Bettmann)

The old master on the subject of authority was, again, Max Weber (1946). Through his historical-comparative sociology Weber identified three general types of authority. The most common form of authority throughout history has been what Weber called **traditional authority.** Most rulers have held their authority because of old accepted customs. Usually these customs involved family inheritance of the kingship. Frequently combined with this custom was some reference to religious sanction for the ruling family. The monarchies in feudal Europe, the emperor during the Roman Empire, and the pharaohs in ancient Egypt provide good examples of traditional authority.

These rulers held power because they controlled the army. But we must ask what made the army loyal and what made most of the population follow the ruler's commands most of the time. The threat of force is still important in maintaining obedience, but also important were the customs and reverence given to the ruler and his or her state that led people to willingly obey.

Although once most common, traditional authority has given way to legal-rational authority in most parts of the world. With **legal-rational authority** power is made legitimate through reference to a system of rules and procedures defining the legitimate use of authority. There are written rules defining how positions of authority in the state are occupied and the rights and duties to be maintained by officeholders. These written rules are often contained in a document such as a constitution. Every state based on legal-rational authority, however, is not necessarily a democratic form of government. For example, the Soviet state is based on legal-rational authority.

A third general type of authority Weber referred to was **charismatic authority.** This type of authority is based on what people regard to be the exceptional qualities of a particular individual. Mao Tse-tung was a charismatic leader, as were Adolph Hitler, Ayatollah Khomeini, and Jesus Christ. We commonly hear that a highly respected leader like John Kennedy or Pierre Trudeau (the former prime minister of Canada) have charisma, and no doubt they have an element of that attractive personality in the eyes of their admirers. However, in the case of charismatic authority, the power of the person is based primarily on charisma, as was the case when Khomeini took power in Iran in 1979. No law said he was the ruler of that country, though such a law was written after he took power. John Kennedy, on the other hand, held power because of his *position* in the legal-rational authority structure, even though he had a charismatic personality.

As Weber tells us, however, this last form of authority is unstable. It dies with the charismatic leader, and quite often before. For this reason charismatic authority turns into one of the other forms of

Legal–rational authority involves the use of a system of rules and procedures to define how leaders are selected. Ronald Reagan is shown being sworn in for his second term of office by Chief Justice Warren Berger of the United States Supreme Court in the Rotunda of the Capitol. Both Berger and the Rotunda are highly symbolic and lend authority to the ceremony. The electoral process determines who will rule in the United States. (© Sygma)

authority after the revolution cools. And most often today the change is toward legal-rational authority.

In closing this discussion of types of authority, two further points should be clarified. First, the three types outlined above are what Weber called "ideal types," meaning they are simply ideal descriptions that do not fit concrete cases in every respect. In reality there may be elements of these three types of authority in a given society, though societies tend to fall closer to one of the three ideal types.

Second, because all three of these are called types of "authority," there is the implication of legitimacy in the rule. But governments can hold power for extensive periods of time without legitimacy given to the government by most people in the society. For such a government to stay in power there must be extensive use of force or threat of force as we find in Chile, Poland, and South Africa. In the long run the extensive use of force is expensive and inefficient, but governments can at times continue to operate for long periods without extensive legitimacy (Skocpol, 1979, p. 25).

Types of Rule. The state can differ with respect to the types of rule as well as the types of authority. When considering types of rule, we are concerned with who has power in the state and how they get and

Here, Adolph Hitler is seen addressing SS troops in the 1936 May Day celebration in Berlin. Speakers with charismatic power can hold the attention of large crowds. They create a social world in which followers blindly obey. Hitler's Germany, an example of a fascist society, violated the precepts of democratic pluralism and offered the world a lesson in the dangers of charismatic leadership using force to maintain the power of an elite. (© UPI/Bettmann)

hold such power. There are three general types of rule: autocracy, totalitarianism, and democracy.

Autocracy refers to a state with one individual or family in almost total control. The kingdoms during the 1600s in Europe or the imperial state in Japan during the same period provide good examples of autocratic rule. Often, however, there is some competition for power and compromise among a few dominant individuals or families, in which case we find an **oligarchy.** Quite often through the history of preindustrial societies there was movement back and forth between oligarchy and autocracy (Bendix, 1978). At one point in history a king or emperor would clearly dominate, whereas at another point the ruler must recognize the extensive influence of local aristocratic families in different places in the kingdom, producing oligarchy. Again, the feudal systems in Europe and Japan provide good examples of this movement between autocracy and oligarchy.

Totalitarian rule refers to a state in which one

group of political elites holds dominant power. Although there is much overlap between the terms autocracy, oligarchy, and totalitarian forms of rule, the term totalitarian is used more often to refer to the rule by a dominant group in an industrial or industrializing society. There are two major forms of totalitarian systems: communism and fascism. In a totalitarian **communist** society, rule is maintained by a bureaucratic political elite without private ownership of the major means of production. In a **fascist** society rule is maintained by a bureaucratic political elite strongly tied to or supported by the capitalist class in that society. A good example of communist totalitarian rule is the Soviet Union, Nazi Germany and Chile under military dictatorship after 1973 provide good examples of fascist rule.

Political elites are never in total control and must at least appease other influential groups in the society. In the case of fascism, political elites must keep wealthy capitalists happy, whereas in communist societies political elites must appease the middle and working classes.

With **democracy,** procedures pertaining to how individuals attain office and perform the duties of their office are designed to assure a much wider distribution of political influence in the society. Such a form of rule usually means that government representatives are chosen by people in the society. The stipulation of more or less equal political influence is important to stress, however, because as we will see, there are degrees of democracy. As with all the forms of rule described here, we are considering what Weber (1949) referred to as ideal types. We find no "perfect" cases of autocracy, totalitarianism, or democracy, only cases that tend toward one type more than other types.

Theories of the State

With different sociological theories there are differing views on the primary nature of the state. Each view of the state contains at least some elements of reality, though it can be argued that some theories further our understanding more than others. We begin with the functional view of the state for what it has to offer.

Functional Theory. Remembering the functional theory in general, you know that functional theorists view societies as similar to biological organisms. As with biological organisms, functionalists assume that a society has subsystems (like organs in the body) that perform important tasks for the overall survival of the society. These subsystems are called *institutions,* and the state is considered to be one of the primary institutions. A major task of the state as an institution is to set goals for the society and organize activities to accomplish the goals (Parsons, 1951). For example, if it is determined that an inside or outside threat exists, the state has the task of coordinating activities toward eliminating the threat.

Originally the family was the basic institution in less complex societies. In these societies the head or dominant figures in the family or clan served as the ruler or ruling council. But as societies became larger and more complex, specialized institutions developed to take over the increasingly complex tasks once performed by the family. The head of the family could no longer adequately take care of economic, spiritual, and political activities in combination.

A key view of functionalists is that the state typically operates for the needs of the overall society. Functionalists, of course, recognize conflicts of interests within the society, but the state exists in part to resolve these conflicts for the good of the whole. And like conflict theorists, they recognize that power and force will at times be used by the state. But functionalists stress that such force is legitimate and is usually employed to protect the wider interests of the society. For example, a particularly long, costly industrial strike may be forcefully resolved by state officials to maintain the overall economic health of the nation.

Conflict Theories. Although there are several varieties of conflict theory, conflict theorists agree that the state is both a battleground for conflicting interest groups and a means of maintaining or attaining advantages over other interest groups. The state is the battleground simply because it is such an important means of influence in the society. Ultimately, as noted above, the state monopolizes the final means of influence, physical force. Thus, conflicting interest groups attempt to gain influence over this state.

It is for this reason that the state is seldom an impartial force, working only for the good of the overall society. In fact, conflict theorists recognize that what is "good for the overall society" is seldom clearly known. The groups with most influence in the state work to get the state to act in their own interests while maintaining that such state action is, in fact, "really" in the interests of the entire society. Again, using the example of state action to end an industrial strike, conflict theorists would look for how this state action actually helped the interests of one group at the expense of other groups.

Marx considered economic conflicts as primary within a society and saw the state as dominated by the group with the most economic power. In a capitalist society this group is the bourgeoisie (or capitalists). The state was therefore seen as an institution that worked to maintain the interests of capitalists. Carrying this view to its conclusion, Marx believed the state would ultimately "wither away" in the future communist society, because he believed equality could be achieved and class conflicts could be eliminated. Because he saw the state as simply a tool for class dominance, the state would no longer have a purpose with the elimination of economic conflicts.

Weber, on the other hand, had a much broader view of the nature of conflict and conflict groups within a society. Thus, Weber recognized that the state would be a focal point for many competing interest groups. Most sociologists agree that Weber's view of the state and its place in society was far superior to Marx's. In fact, many Marxian scholars now combine the work of Marx and Weber when trying to understand the state (for example, Wright, 1978; Harrington, 1976).

The State as Redistributive Institution. From the conflict positions generally, one quite useful characteristic of the state can be outlined here. It does not tell us all we need to know about the state, but it helps us analyze many political events with greater understanding.

Much of politics involves taking resources from people and providing resources and services to people. In short, the state takes from people and gives to people. As such, the state is a **redistributive institution.** It takes from some in the form of taxes and service (e.g., military service). It gives in many forms—police and military protection, park and highway maintenance, subsidies to many groups like farmers, corporations, and welfare recipients. As we have already seen, virtually everyone in modern industrial societies receives government benefits in some form.

The key point about this process of give and take, however, is that some groups get more than others, and some groups must give more than others. From the perspective of simple self-interests, interest groups try to assure that the state takes as little from them as possible while getting as much from the state as possible. This process is normally called "politics."

Viewing the state as a redistributive institution we are able to see the importance of power in determining state policies and action. As Weber came close to saying, politics is the employment of power in the political arena to achieve interest group goals. What gets done, whose interests are best served, who has to give up the least is determined by relative power arrangements.

But power politics is a *dynamic process.* One or a few groups may be more dominant and win advantages from the state quite often. Such advantage, however, is never assured because few groups are totally powerless. There are many means of influence; thus although some groups hold little of one type of influence (like money) they may have more of another type of influence (like votes or many people united). Equally important, shifting coalitions of classes or interest groups may change the balance of power from time to time. We can certainly find some groups that win most often, or are able to assure that their losses are small and temporary if losses must be taken at times. But again we stress that the conflict behind the state redistribution process is in fact a process—an ongoing struggle.

Emergence of the Modern State

As noted previously, the state as a distinct institution in society dates to early agriculture or advanced horticultural societies some 6,000 years ago (Lenski, 1966). There is evidence of the first written laws about 4,000 years ago, and soon after that we find the famous Law of Hammurabi around 1750 B.C. But what can be called the modern state as a clearly separate institution with extensive control and a clear monopoly over the means of force emerged only about 400 years ago. In Europe before this time, for example, there were about 500 independent political territories. But by 1900, after most modern states had emerged some 200 to 300 years earlier, the number of independent political territories was reduced to about 25 (Tilly, 1975, p. 15).

The Modern State and Class Conflict. A major question that has always faced social scientists pertains to the location and timing of the growth of the modern state. What was happening in Europe in the 1600s to account for the emergence of these modern states?

In a recent historical analysis of Europe in the Middle Ages, Hechter and Brustein (1980) argue that the modern state emerged in response to the changing pattern of *class conflict* at the time. During the Middle Ages in Europe there was a two-pronged threat to the upper class. By the fourteenth century peasant revolts were perhaps more widespread throughout Europe than at any other period. At the same time in the cities, however, a wealthy merchant class began challenging the power of the old nobility. In response to both challenges, the nobility united to support the growth of new state systems with the power to maintain their positions of privilege.

The key to Hechter and Brustein's argument are data showing that the modern state grew in the feudal zones in Europe where threats to the privileges of the nobility were experienced most sharply. With the development of these states across the face of Europe a rigid system of inequality was again strengthened, but only for a time. By the 1700s we find considerable upheaval and change with the beginning of industrialization and democracy.

The Emergence of Democracy. Democracy came into existence many centuries ago. In ancient Greece, for example, there was an extensive system of direct

democracy: "All power was vested in the open-air meetings of all male citizens held on the Pnyx. Probably 45,000 were entitled to attend" (Thomas, 1979, p. 157). Of that number about 4,000 people customarily attended, from which a council of 500 was selected by lot to make decisions on important matters of the city-state. Small hunting and gathering tribes, as we have already seen, were also democratic in practice, but needed no formal institutions to carry out this democracy. However, since humans established settled communities about 10,000 years ago, only in isolated times and places in history do we find anything close to a democratic political system.

In recent history, however, there has been a trend toward democracy all over the world (Bendix, 1978). Social scientists often stress different conditions that may have spread democracy, like increased levels of education and literacy, and the spread of new ideas helped along by the printing press. But though many specific factors are associated with an increase in democracy, changes in the class structure and the economy with industrialization are the primary underlying conditions producing democracy.

Whether or not industrialization leads to democracy, fascism, or communism depends in the beginning on the relative power of the major economic classes (landed aristocracy, capitalists, urban workers, and peasants). The groundbreaking work on this subject was done by Barrington Moore, Jr. (1966) but has been carried on by others such as Skocpol (1979). To oversimplify somewhat, Figure 11.1 presents the basic findings from these historical studies.

1. If the landed aristocracy remain strong in the society but are forced to change in the face of international economic competition, there is likely to be industrialization without democracy. This is because no other group or class is able to push for democracy, and the old upper class prefers to control the state as it had in the past. The best example of this is Japan after the Meiji reforms of the 1860s until the end of World War II. Japan established some formal democratic procedures with the Meiji restoration, but a stable democracy could not take root until after the old *Zaibatsu* ruling families lost power after World War II (Halliday, 1975).

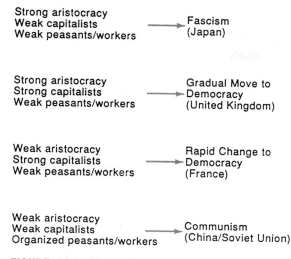

Strong aristocracy
Weak capitalists ——→ Fascism
Weak peasants/workers (Japan)

Strong aristocracy
Strong capitalists ——→ Gradual Move to Democracy
Weak peasants/workers (United Kingdom)

Weak aristocracy
Strong capitalists ——→ Rapid Change to Democracy
Weak peasants/workers (France)

Weak aristocracy
Weak capitalists ——→ Communism
Organized peasants/workers (China/Soviet Union)

FIGURE 11.1. Class structure and the development of democracy

2. When both the landed aristocracy and the newly emerging capitalists are strong, there tends to be gradual compromises leading to democracy. The best example of this is England.

3. When the landed aristocracy becomes weak very rapidly, with the existence of a strong capitalist class, there tends to be revolutionary change to democracy. The best example of this is France with the Revolution of 1789.

4. When the landed aristocracy becomes weak but a strong capitalist class has not developed, economic crisis with foreign competition has led to communism. This is especially so when there is at least some organization among urban workers or peasants. The case of some worker organization with a weak aristocracy and weak capitalist class is exemplified by Russia after the Revolution of 1917. In a similar position, but with a more independent peasantry, we find China after their revolution of 1949. If no class segment has extensive power, a new class of independent political elites can develop as in Russia and China. Such a political elite can serve their own interests more than the interests of other classes that lack power to pressure for those interests.

When changes in the economic structure lead to a new balance of power, political changes are likely. Democracy would not have emerged without the growing power of a capitalist class. But we must ask why a powerful capitalist class would favor democracy because it may seem capitalists would prefer a state that could be more easily controlled by one dominant class. Several things can be cited in answering this question. In the face of new political ideas spreading among the lower classes, the promise of democracy would give the new capitalist class the lower-class support it needed to overthrow an old state dominated by the aristocracy. And with their recent experiences of political abuses by the feudal state, all classes feared a condition in which only one group had control of the state.

It is important to recognize, however, that the dominant group in capitalist industrial societies (the owners of major capital) tends to find that political democracy in some form favors their interests. Although they lack total dominance, they can often influence this political system more than other groups or classes because of such things as their ability to organize politically, their network of communications, and the importance of money in gaining office and influencing politicians. (We consider these factors in more detail below.) But at the same time the capitalist class is not so directly a part of the state. Thus, it is relieved of some responsibility for state actions (Collins, 1975, p. 396).

Since the emergence of democracy there have been other economic and class changes that have tended to strengthen democratic institutions. Though the capitalist class found it was able to dominate states based on democratic principles in the early stages of industrialization, further industrialization made this more difficult. The expanding urban working class and the new middle class created groups of people who are more educated and politically active. These people have often had the capacity to press for the preservation of democratic practices and at times even the expansion of democracy. Comparative studies have shown that all over the world, an expanded middle class usually leads to greater degrees of democracy for example, through making more people eligible to vote (Rubinson and Quinlan 1977; Hewitt, 1977).

In concluding this discussion we note that there are degrees of democracy. Though the masses in a society are able to influence the state through voting, the upper classes may have much more influence on the state through other means. It has been said that capitalists tend to favor relatively democratic states because they can usually influence these states more than other groups can. However, there is a chance that a highly organized working class can come to dominate the state and push for political policies unfavorable to capitalists. We consider this possibility in the final section of the chapter. But for now it can be said that in this situation the capitalist class may support the reduction of democracy or even a fascist state, as was done in Chile in 1973, and Japan and Germany before World War II.

Political Economy

In modern industrial societies such as our own it can be very misleading to analyze the political and economic systems separately. These two institutions are so extensively interrelated that the term **political-economy,** which emphasizes this interrelationship, is a more accurate description than the two terms used separately. In this section we consider the extent of this interrelation and how it developed.

Change from Early Laissez-faire. The state has never been totally isolated from the economy. No matter how much it is denied, state policies have always influenced economic activities. During the 1800s in the United States, for example, government often intervened in labor disputes on the side of capitalists against labor. Because the state was usually on the side of the wealthy, political elites tried to hide the real interrelationship between the state and the economy (Piven and Cloward, 1982). The curves in Figure 11.2 indicate the extent to which people often considered the government as uninvolved in economic issues. When unemployment or inflation become high today, it is endlessly discussed by political elites who are pressured to take government action on these problems. But as we find in Figure

11.2, before the 1920s political elites remained mute on the subject of unemployment even when it reached very high levels. Political elites indeed talked about the need for tariffs to help shore up corporate profits before the 1920s (and especially during the mid-1890s), but the fate of the unemployed was largely ignored (Kerbo and Shaffer, 1986). Compared with today, the government was held less responsible for economic conditions.

Although the state has influenced the economy from the beginning of capitalism and industrialization, the extent of that influence was less in the early stages. During this time thinkers like Adam Smith, as we have seen, called for a *laissez-faire* approach by the state — meaning the state should have minimal involvement in economic matters. Such calls for a laissez-faire state arose in reaction to the heavy involvement of the state in the economy as societies were making the transition from agriculture to industrialization. At that time it was clear that state involvement was hurting economic development by protecting old economic interest groups.

As industrialization progressed, however, it became more evident that the state could not remain isolated from economic activity, and various interest groups began calling for state action to help their interests. In the 1890s the Populist movement became the first large protest movement in the United States to call for government action in the economy, in this case to help farmers (Hofstader, 1955). In the early 1900s it was small business people and the old middle class that called for protection against the increasing dominance of major corporations. It was during this Progressive Era that many of the government regulatory agencies were established. Finally, as indicated in Figure 11.2, unemployment became a political issue as early as the 1920s, when labor began more active pressure for government protection.

It was the economic crisis of the 1930s, however, that finally brought widespread calls for government involvement in the economy. Traditional economists were shifting to the Keynesian view that the state does have an important role in the economy, especially in times of economic crisis. And Marxian

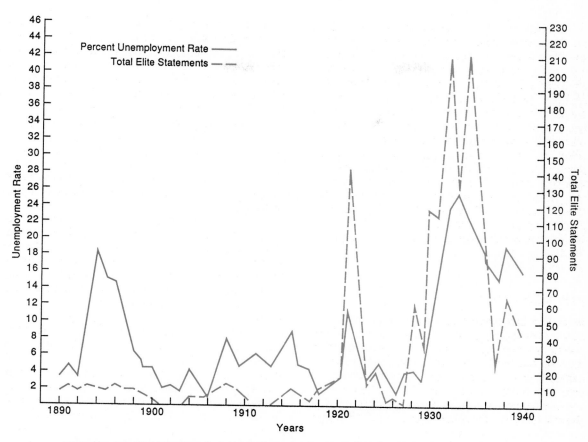

FIGURE 11.2. The public response of political elites to unemployment, 1890–1940. Total elite statements *refers to the annual number of statements about unemployment by elites reported in the* New York Times. *(Source: Kerbo and Shaffer, 1986.)*

scholars as well were beginning to revise the Marxian idea that capitalism would fall anytime soon as they saw the newly recognized ability of the state to forestall economic collapse.

Once the door was opened with the idea that the state can and should influence the economy, many interest groups then shifted their economic grievances to the state. All kinds of economic issues became politicized, so that we now have various policies for helping farmers, homeowners, truckers, bankers, factory workers, and so on.

Means of Government Economic Influence. The means of government influence in the economy are about as varied as the economic interest groups protected by government policies. But a few means of influence are most important.

One of the mcst significant means of government involvement in the economy is *government spending*. In recent years the federal government spends about $1 trillion annually on goods and services. What goods and services are bought and from whom has a major impact. Table 11.1 indicates that this

TABLE 11.1. *U.S. government expenditures as a percentage of national income, 1929–1976*

Year	Total government expenditures per national income (%)
1929	12.12
1935	23.70
1940	23.12
1945	51.33
1950	25.82
1955	29.86
1960	33.11
1965	33.19
1970	39.07
1976	41.90

SOURCE: Nutter (1978, p. 74). The original data are from U.S. Department of Commerce, *The National Income and Product Accounts of the United States* (Washington D.C., 1977).

level of government spending as a percent of national income has increased substantially since the 1930s, when economic issues were first highly politicized. Every year as the federal budget is being written there is a mad rush by various interest groups to influence it.

The next important means of government influence in the economy is *taxing policies*. If all interest groups were taxed in a like manner (say, a 15 percent tax on all income and profits), the tax system would be fairly neutral with respect to the economic interests of various groups. But the government does not follow such a taxing policy, though it has come somewhat closer to doing so with the 1986 income tax reform law. With the idea of helping certain sectors of the economy, some tax breaks are still given to affect economic behavior — inducing investment in some industries but not others through the selective use of tax breaks.

One of the most rapidly increasing means of government influence are laws and government regulations. For example, drug companies are required to show evidence their products are safe and effective, companies must sometimes assure a safe work environment for employees, stockbrokers cannot hide vital information potentially affecting stock prices,

to cite a few examples. Many people feel that the United States has one of the most regulated economies in the world. But although government regulation has certainly increased in this country, as noted in Chapter 10, we actually have one of the *least* regulated economies in the world (Thurow, 1980). It must be added, however, that the amount of regulation is not as important as its intent and effectiveness.

Many other forms of government involvement in the economy include the Federal Reserve System's regulation of the money supply and interest rates, tariffs on imported goods, and direct subsidies to many industries.

This is not to say that the U.S. government totally dominates the economy nor that when government influences the economy it does so intelligently or effectively. But government does have extensive influence over the economy, and for this reason economic issues are increasingly politicized today.

Political Cycles in the Economy. There are certain years in which political elites would like to influence some aspects of the economy for their own interests. These years, of course, are election years. During nonelection years political elites are more likely to consider the interests of the wealthy and other powerful interest groups, but during election years the successful politician cannot neglect the matter of votes. Thus, whereas in nonelection years it may pay to pass legislation favoring a powerful industry that will provide campaign contributions in the future, when election time approaches the politician must consider economic factors that affect how much money average voters have in their pocket. As studies indicate, one of the most powerful influences on how people vote in national elections is the state of the economy (Tufte, 1978, pp. 108–123).

The manipulation of the economy by national political elites during election years has produced *political cycles*. To consider how these political cycles operate in the economy, we must first consider the importance of four different time periods. The *first* time period includes nonelection years; the *second* includes "off-year elections," when only some politicians in Congress are up for reelection; the *third* includes presidential election years when some poli-

As Tufte (1978) has shown, various economic conditions in the society tend to be most favorable during election years, especially when a president is running for reelection. He also notes (half seriously) that the best way for a president to win reelection is to allow the economy to deteriorate the first two or three years of the first term in office. This is because (1) there is more room for improvement the fourth year when the economy has been bad the three previous years, and (2) voters tend to think about the condition of the economy the current year and the direction of the economic indicators that year (up or down). If the economy was bad in previous years, the trends are more likely to be up in the election year.

The 1984 presidential election provides an excellent example of the economic manipulation by political elites to win reelection. President Reagan won reelection in 1984 with one of the biggest margins in history. He won all states except Mondale's home state of Minnesota, in spite of the fact that during Reagan's first years in office the United States experienced the worst economic recession since the Great Depression of the 1930s.

A look at the figures below clearly shows what happened. In part, because of the recession of the early 1980s, inflation was quickly brought down. But after an unemployment rate of almost 11 percent in 1982, the 7.5 percent unemployment in 1984 didn't look so bad — even though it was at that level when Reagan took office. And tax cuts made most people feel that they had more money, even though the big tax cuts went only to the wealthy.

It is unlikely that the Reagan administration purposely harmed the economy to win reelection in 1984, but it is clear that economic manipulations were used to stimulate the economy as the 1984 election grew near.

Unemployment Rate and Inflation Rate, 1980-1984

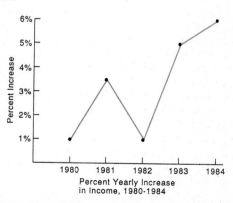

Percent Yearly Increase in Income, 1980-1984

ticians in Congress are up for reelection but the current president is not running for reelection; and the *fourth* includes years when a current president is running for reelection. As we move from the first group of years to the fourth we find that (1) more political elites are concerned with reelection, and (2) the elections thus become more important. The main difference between the third and fourth group of years is that the most powerful political elite, the president, is up for reelection in the fourth group of years.

A fascinating study by Tufte (1978) shows how politicians influence the economy to further their chances of reelection. Tufte has found that in most cases indicators of economic health are weakest in the first group of years described above (nonelection years) and strongest in the fourth group of years (when the president is running for reelection). For example, between 1959 and 1976, GNP growth averaged 4 percent in election years, but only 2.1 percent in nonelection years. Real disposable income averaged a 3.3 percent increase in years when the president was running for reelection, but only 1.7 percent in all other years.

There is no simple relationship among economic indicators, however, for several reasons. Two important reasons are that (1) some economic conditions tend to be inversely related, and (2) politicians from different parties have different constituencies. For example, inflation and unemployment tend to be inversely related. Thus, it is often difficult to achieve both low inflation and low unemployment in the same year. But despite this difficulty, between 1946 and 1976 *both* inflation and unemployment moved downward compared with previous years in 50 percent of the presidential election years compared with only 9 percent of the nonpresidential election years (Tafte, 1978, p. 22). For the overall average rates of unemployment and inflation, however, unemployment tends to be lower when a Democratic president is in office during an election year, whereas inflation tends to be lower when a Republican president is in office during an election year. The reason is that unemployment tends to harm most the interests of the less affluent, whereas inflation is of greater concern to the more affluent. (This is not to say inflation hurts the affluent the most, only that the working class is concerned with having a job first and how much their wages will buy second). Because Democrats have relied the most on the votes of the less affluent, they are more likely to bring down unemployment during election years, whereas Republicans are more likely to bring down inflation given their traditionally more affluent supporters.

Politicians are not always as successful in influencing the economy as they would like. For example, economic problems clearly contributed to President Carter's loss in 1980. Also, the economic influence held by politicians is often *short term*. They may be able to influence the economy in the next year, but not several years in advance. In fact, the short-term economic manipulations by politicians often harm the economy in subsequent years. The things done to win elections, such as increased government deficits, often cause economic problems the next year.

CLASS CONFLICT AND THE STATE

As should already be clear, different interest groups often have conflicting political interests. Class interests are not always in conflict, of course. For example, it may be in the interests of all in a particular society to reduce crime, improve medical technology, and maintain safe highways. But even with these examples there are usually class conflicts over how the goals are to be achieved. Are safe highways to be maintained through general income tax revenues, property taxes, or special user fees? Economic interest groups will be affected differently by these methods of raising government revenues.

Let's consider another example of conflicting interests. As noted in the previous section, there tends to be an inverse relation between unemployment and inflation—when unemployment is high, inflation is low, and vice versa. This inverse relationship is known as the *Phillips Curve* (Phillips, 1958). This relation is in part due to the fact that when more people are unemployed, there are fewer people with money to buy consumer items. Another reason for the inverse relationship is that when unemployment is high, workers must be more cautious in making higher wage demands with so many unemployed workers ready to take their jobs. The issue of unemployment versus inflation is often at the center of class conflict because governments in industrial societies have often worked to reduce inflation by following economic policies known to increase unemployment.

Another major issue that often divides the working class and the more affluent involves welfare spending. The more affluent are less likely to support welfare because they are less likely to need it and do not want to be taxed to pay for it. The working class, however, are more likely to need welfare sometime in their lives, and are somewhat more willing to be taxed for it as a type of insurance program against unemployment and disability. But there is another, less recognized reason why the working class may support welfare. As noted earlier, high unemployment tends to reduce wage demands. Welfare support, however, can make the unemployed somewhat less desperate to take the first job offered, no matter what the pay. Wages, therefore, may be kept higher than they otherwise would be with high unemployment when welfare support exists.

There are many other conflicting interests among the various economic classes in industrial societies. For example, the working class would prefer that multinational corporations not be allowed to move jobs overseas. The working class is also more interested in government regulations enforcing safe working conditions even though these regulations may reduce corporate profits. But even among the corporate elite we find conflicts of interest. For example, corporate directors with more foreign investments may favor government policies that help their interests at the expense of corporate directors without substantial foreign investment.

The main point is this: different classes and interest groups have conflicting interests in state policies. Some classes or interest groups are more powerful than others and are thus more likely to assure that the state follows policies favorable to their interests. But few groups are without any

means of influencing the state in a relatively democratic society.

The Upper Classes and the State

When there is at least some degree of democracy, *votes* are of importance in influencing state action and policy. The periodic trial by voting puts new people in office and keeps politicians already in office from openly straying far from what their constituents would find acceptable. But although we should not underestimate the importance of votes, neither should we overestimate their importance. Voters are often misled and manipulated in an age of slick mass media political campaigns. And because one vote means very little in a major election, such things as the degree to which interest groups are united in voting for a particular candidate become critical.

For these reasons, other means of political influence are of considerable importance. Four general means of influence are the most effective: *money, organization, attaining a government position,* and *control over information.* Money can be used to influence government policy in many ways — some legal, some illegal. But two means of influence that money allows tend to be the most important — campaign contributions and lobbying. The goal of campaign contributions is to place people in office favorable to one's interests so that when in office they will take care of those interests. The goal of lobbying is to influence political figures already in office.

Campaign Contributions. Since the campaign reform laws after the Watergate scandal leading to President Richard Nixon's resignation, individuals and groups must comply with new rules when contributing money to political candidates. In most respects, however, the campaign reform laws did not change the power of money and those who have it; only the rules that must be followed were changed.

A key component of the campaign reform laws requires a formally organized **political action committee** (PAC) if groups and individuals are to contribute money to election campaigns. These

PACs are restricted to a $5,000 contribution per candidate per year. However, there is no restriction on the number of PACs contributing to any single candidate. Since the passage of these new campaign laws, the number of PACs has grown rapidly. By 1980 there were 1,585 PACs sponsored by corporations, trade groups, and medical associations (Domhoff, 1983, p. 125), which contributed $36 million to congressional candidates in 1980. For Senate candidates alone all PACs contributed over $22 million in 1980. By 1984 this figure had increased to over $28 million.

Congressional Lobbying. If the interests of the wealthy are not insured by their campaign contributions, they can bring another force into action. Lobbying organizations in Washington have been referred to as the "fourth branch of government" (after the executive, legislative, and judicial branches) because of the number of people employed by these organizations in Washington and their power. This "fourth branch of government," of course, is not designed to answer to the general population or serve their interests. These are the organizations of the so-called special interests.

The basic job of a lobbyist is to make friends among congressional leaders, provide them with favors like trips, small gifts, and parties, and give them information favoring their employers' interests and needs. All this requires a large staff and lots of money.

President's Cabinet. Many people in politics are millionaires, but a large number of these became millionaires *after* starting a career in politics. Special investment opportunities supplied by wealthy individuals seeking a politician's support can create millionaire status. For example, Ronald Reagan entered California politics in the 1960s without much wealth. But through the help of wealthy friends who have remained his most influential supporters, real estate deals were transacted that made Reagan quite wealthy (Domhoff, 1983, pp. 123–124).

The very wealthy and the corporate elite seldom run for political office. Doing so means devoting extensive time and effort to politics and away from running the corporate world and/or maintaining their private wealth. But there is one place where the wealthy can attain powerful political positions for a limited time, then return to the corporate world. This place is the President's cabinet, and the United States is unique in this respect. Whereas in most other industrial nations people who run major government bureaucracies are career politicians or bureaucrats (Putnam, 1976), in the United States these people come from outside of government. They commonly remain as head of the government agency for only a few years, then return to their primary careers. It is therefore important to consider where these cabinet members come from and the loyalties and interests they bring to the President's cabinet.

Two sociologists, Mintz (1975) and Freitag (1975), undertook the massive job of examining the backgrounds of all cabinet members who served between 1897 and 1973. Mintz found that 66 percent of all cabinet members were from the upper class before obtaining their cabinet position. There has not been much difference between Republican administrations (71 percent of their cabinet from the upper class) and Democrats (60 percent from the upper class). Freitag focused on the corporate ties of cabinet members between 1897 and 1973 and found that 76 percent of these cabinet members either came directly from a major corporate position to the president's cabinet and/or left the cabinet for a top corporate position. In 54 percent of the cases cabinet members went both ways — going to the cabinet from a corporate position and leaving the cabinet to go back to a corporate position. Table 11.2 indicates that all presidents have selected a majority of their cabinet members with these corporate ties.

Policy-formation Process. Of the various means of upper-class and corporate political influence, the type least recognized by the general public is the policy-formation process (Domhoff, 1979, pp. 61–128; Dye, 1983). Many scholars believe, in the long run, that this means of political influence is perhaps one of the most important.

There are formal government committees where policy is made; the President's cabinet is one of the most important. But ideas and policy options are

Table 11.2. *Corporate ties to Presidential Cabinets, 1897–1973*

Administration	Interlocked with business	Unknown lawyers (possible interlocks)	Not interlocked with business	Total
McKinley (R), 1897–1901	60.0	26.7	13.3	100.0 (19)
T. Roosevelt (R), 1901–1909	80.0	20.0	0.0	100.0 (15)
Taft (R), 1909–1913	75.0	25.0	0.0	100.0 (8)
Wilson (D), 1913–1921	73.7	21.0	5.3	100.0 (19)
Harding (R), 1921–1923	66.7	8.3	25.0	100.0 (12)
Coolidge (R), 1923–1929	77.8	11.1	11.1	100.0 (9)
Hoover (R), 1929–1933	63.6	18.2	18.2	100.0 (11)
F. Roosevelt (D), 1933–1945	65.2	17.4	17.4	100.0 (23)
Truman (D), 1945–1953	72.7	13.6	13.6	99.9 (22)
Eisenhower (R), 1953–1961	85.7	0.0	14.3	100.0 (21)
Kennedy (D), 1961–1963	76.9	0.0	23.1	100.0 (13)
Johnson (D), 1963–1969	85.7	0.0	14.3	100.0 (14)
Nixon (R), 1969–1973	95.7	0.0	4.3	100.0 (23)

Percent of Cabinet members

SOURCE: Freitag (1975, p. 142).

often developed in other places, and decided and implemented only in formal government committees.

Many of the ideas and policy options are generated in universities and private research organizations with corporate and upper-class foundation financial support. Once these ideas have been generated there are policy-planning groups in which corporate elites come together to discuss policy, and publish and disseminate the policy options. Most important among the policy-planning groups are groups organized by corporate elites like the Council on Foreign Relations (CFR), Trilateral Commission, and Committee for Economic Development (CED). Studies have shown that many ideas that eventually became government policy were first discussed in these organizations (Dye, 1978; Shoup, 1975; Collins, 1977).

Another link in this policy-formation process are the upper-class social clubs. Although not formed specifically to generate and influence policy as are the organizations described above, these social clubs bring the elite from many corporations together at one time where government policy is discussed in formal meetings (Domhoff, 1974). At one two-week summer retreat held by the Bohemian Club, for example, there was at least one director from 40 of the top 50 industrial corporations, 20 of the top 25 banks, and 12 of the top 25 life insurance companies (Domhoff, 1974, p. 31). And along with these corporate members are political elites who are invited guests or members of the club. At the Bohemian Club studied by Domhoff, the political members or visitors include many people who have or had top government positions: Ronald Reagan, Richard Nixon, Gerald Ford, George Bush, Henry Kissinger, Caspar Weinberger, William French Smith, and George Schultz.

These various upper-class and corporate organizations sponsor or recommend individuals for top government positions, especially for positions in the president's cabinet. In fact, it is to these corporate and upper-class organizations that newly elected presidents often turn to find cabinet members. And with these individuals come the ideas generated by the policy-formation process. In an interesting, typical example of this, President Carter selected most of his cabinet from the Trilateral Commission (Dye, 1978; Burch, 1980, p. 317).

Who Rules? The United States is not unique with respect to political influence held by the upper classes. If we examine the relationship between the upper classes and the state in U.S. history, we find the means of extensive upper-class political influence has existed for many decades (Burch, 1980). But sociologists disagree over the extent of this upper-class political power and the importance of the means of upper-class political power described above.

On the one hand there is disagreement between sociologists called *pluralists* and *power elite theorists*. Pluralists maintain that, though the upper classes have political power, so do many other groups. Pluralists see a "plurality" of interest groups, all with extensive means of influencing the state (Dahl, 1982; Polsby, 1980). Thus, to pluralists there is pluralist democracy in the state, with many interest groups that must learn to compromise and cooperate; no one group has extensive political dominance over others.

The power elite case was first made most strongly by C. Wright Mills in the 1950s. In *The Power Elite* (1956), he outlined how the upper class and corporate elite could influence the state through such means as lobby organizations, influencing elections, and holding office in the President's cabinet. Mills considered the power elite to consist of top personnel from major corporations, important political offices, and the military, with extensive interrelations among the three groups. C. Wright Mills called them the power elite because of their positions in powerful bureaucracies, and no other groups were seen with sufficient influence to counter the dominance of the power elite.

Much of the work started by Mills has been carried on by G. William Domhoff (1970, 1974, 1979, 1983), and with the help of Domhoff and other researchers a form of this power elite view has gained much support in the social sciences. Although most sociologists today would not consider military personnel as equal with top corporate directors in the power elite, the research data produced since the 1950s makes it difficult to reject Mills's view.

Recently, however, there has been criticism of the power elite position on two accounts. First, some social scientists maintain that the state in a capitalist society *must* work for the wealthy and corporate elites, even if these elites do not have the specific means of influence outlined above (Poulantzas, 1968; Skocpol, 1980). These social scientists argue that the state must work for the interests of the wealthy even if the wealthy do not actively try to influence the state. This is because the state in a capitalist society survives only if the capitalist economy operates efficiently. If this economy operates without crisis, then the political elites can be more secure in their positions because people have jobs and a means of achieving at least some economic security. But when the capitalist economy operates efficiently, it also means the upper class and corporate elite will maintain their economic power and prosperity.

This view, called "structuralist" by some, even argues that the state must have some autonomy from the upper class and corporate elite. When the state has some autonomy, it can rise above the conflicts that sometimes exist among corporate elites themselves to follow government policies that help the long-range interests of the upper class and the corporate elites.

The second line of criticism directed toward the power elite position is that the lower classes (or masses in general) have been considered powerless. Rather, it is argued, other classes in the society do have some means of power, and because of this there is a dynamic and changing political struggle to influence state policy (Whitt, 1979). Social scientists following this second line of criticism do not go as far as pluralists, for they continue to maintain that the upper class and the corporate elite have far greater political power than others in the society. They simply argue that nonelites do have some political influence that the elites must contend with from time to time.

Nonelites and the State

Of the means of influence in a modern democratic state, nonelites are most favored with respect to votes. The elites, however powerful, are by definition in the minority. Thus, when there is at least some democracy in the society, collectively the nonelites have some influence because they account for more votes. But there are several limits to the influence of votes of nonelites.

First, even when everyone can vote in the society there tends to be less voter participation as we move down the class ranks, especially in the United States (see Figure 11.3). Several reasons are often cited to explain this pattern. For example, the lower classes feel more political alienation (Orum, 1978). They are less likely to feel they have any influence and often do not bother to vote. Another reason for less voter participation, especially in the United States, is that there is no strong government attempt to increase voter participation. In all other Western democracies citizens are either required by law to vote or at least required to register to vote (Philips and Blackman, 1975).

Second, as more people are coming to recognize, elections have come to be personality contests in

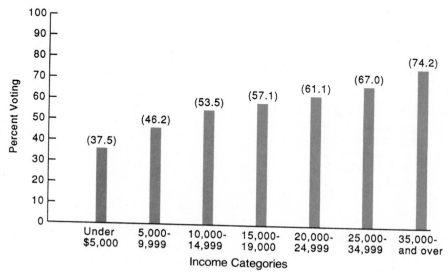

FIGURE 11.3. Voting participation by income, 1984. *(Source: U.S. Bureau of Census, Current Population Reports, P-20, Voting and Registration in the Election of November 1984, 1986, p. 7.)*

which real issues are minimized by the candidates. The candidates must please as many voters as possible, so promises are made to many interest groups that cannot be fulfilled when elected. The attempt to use the media to create images of candidates often misleads and manipulates voters. And as we have seen, when already in office, politicians can influence conditions in the economy in election years.

Third, voters in the United States are divided on many issues, often making it difficult to bring together a united voting block. For example, industrial workers may not be able to unite with service workers and white-collar workers on many issues. Voters are also divided by racial, religious, life-style, military, and regional issues among many others. Thus, though two workers may have a common economic interest in voting for a particular candidate, these workers may also be concerned with different issues related to the state's involvement in religion or civil rights. Political candidates are able to emphasize these noneconomic issues to divide voters. With voters divided, elites are better able to maintain their most important economic interests.

Having considered some limitations of votes, it must be stressed that votes *are* still important. And there is some evidence that the political influence of nonelites in the United States has been increasing in part because of voting (Piven and Cloward, 1982). Compared with 200 years ago a much greater percentage of the population can vote today. Specifically, now blacks, women, and people without extensive property can vote. Other factors, such as the direct popular election of U.S. Senators, has increased voter influence. (Before 1913 U.S. Senators were selected by state legislators.) Moreover, recent years have brought new civil rights and voting rights laws that are having a substantial impact on the number of minorities elected to office. The critical question, of course, remains, do all of those who are eligible vote?

The presidential election of 1988 has generated several grass roots campaigns to focus on issues of poverty, the economy, and social justice. Reverend Jesse Jackson's campaign offers an example of coalition building among different voting blocks, including those organized according to race. At the center of the campaign was an emphasis on the importance of voting as a means of influencing policy and programs. (© *Impact Visuals*)

Unions and Political Influence. Another important development in this century has led to more political influence by the working class — the growth of labor unions. The less affluent have traditionally lacked the financial resources for this means of political influence. However, when labor unions were given some legal right to exist in the 1930s, there was rapid growth in the number of labor unions and their membership. Although this growth has stopped in recent years (and has actually declined), broad-based unions have helped the working class pool their resources for political influence. For example, there were 1,585 corporate and trade political action committees (PACs) in 1980. In that same year there were 240 labor PACs that contributed a total of $13 million to candidates in 1980 (Domhoff, 1983, p. 125). In contrast to 80 years ago, many more politicians find it in their interest to listen to labor organizations when running for office and after

winning office when labor-sponsored lobbyists come around.

Even before labor unions became stronger in the 1930s, however, the working class was not totally powerless, though their resources for political influence were much more limited. One of the few means of political influence besides votes for a group with no wealth is street protests. Throughout history the lower classes have commonly taken their grievances to the streets when the political system was unresponsive to their needs.

In this regard it is interesting that the working class in the United States were more likely to participate in political strikes to influence elections before World War II (Snyder, 1975; Shaffer and Kerbo, 1983). But since World War II, that is, since labor unions have achieved legal recognition, strikes are not more likely during election periods. Now labor unions focus their political activities on campaign

FIGURE 11.4. Working-class political influence and comparative unemployment rates. *(Source: Tufte, 1978, p. 93.)*

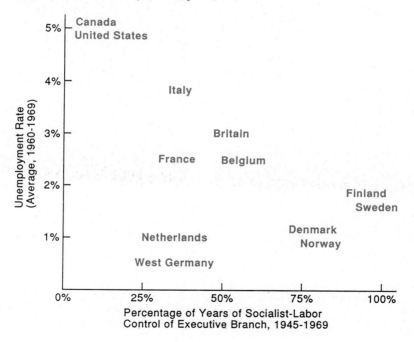

contributions and lobbying. Labor has been brought into the formal system of political influence.

Outcomes of Class Conflict. If the means of political influence held by nonelites have any effect at all, we should be able to measure them. Using comparative data, we begin by considering the effects of working-class success in backing political candidates.

The working class in capitalist societies are usually more concerned about unemployment than inflation. As we have seen, the two conditions usually move in opposite directions — rarely do we find both low inflation and low unemployment in advanced capitalist societies. Thus, in the trade-off between the two conditions, in which direction will government policy move? As Figure 11.4 indicates, there is less unemployment in societies where working-class political parties (labor or socialist) have controlled the government for a period of time since World War

II. Likewise, Figure 11.5 indicates these societies with working-class political parties in power have tended to have slightly higher inflation. And continuing to indicate this trend favoring working-class interests, Figure 11.6 shows income inequality tends to be less in these societies with working-class political parties in power.

The differences in the level of inflation and unemployment among these nations are not great. In Chapter 9 we also saw that the level of income inequality among these nations is not great. Other factors like level of industrialization strongly shape such things as income inequality. However, as indicated by the comparative data above and as several studies have indicated, within limits the state can influence the level of unemployment, inflation, and income inequality (Hewitt, 1977; Rubinson and Quinlan, 1977). It then becomes important to influence the state so the state will follow policies favor-

FIGURE 11.5. Working-class political influence and comparative inflation rates. *(Source: Tufte, 1978, p. 93.)*

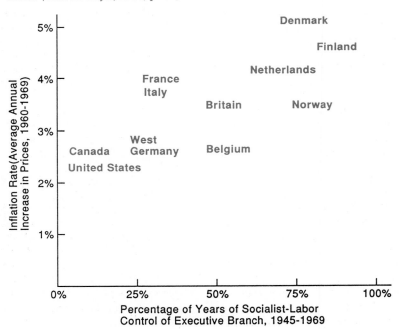

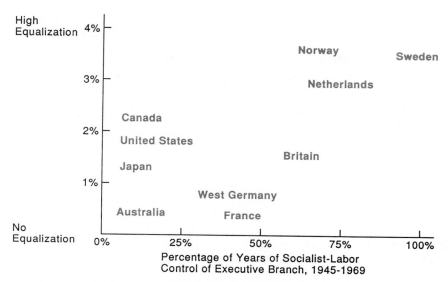

FIGURE 11.6. Working-class political influence and comparative income inequality. *(Source: Tufte, 1978, p. 96.)*

able to one's interest group. In this regard two nations with the highest degree of income inequality today (the United States and France, in contrast to the older data in Figure 11.6) have the most extensive movement of elites back and forth from top government positions to top corporate positions (Suleiman, 1978, p. 227). This interrelationship between corporate and political elites has perhaps made it more difficult for nonelites to push for policies that would favor their interests, such as policies producing less income inequality.

The State Against Capitalism? As outlined above, the working class, minorities, and the less affluent in general have made some significant gains in political influence in the past several years. Another way to put it is that there has been an increase in the level of democracy in the United States. Some social scientists have recently argued that a more democratic state in the United States may work against the capitalist economic system and the interests of the wealthy (O'Connor, 1973; Wright, 1978; Piven and Cloward, 1982). For this reason, these social scien-

tists argue that the upper class and corporate elites under the Reagan administration pushed for reducing the level of lower-class influence in the state and the benefits and protection for the lower class provided by the state. To understand this view we must first review the nature of the capitalist economic system.

Traditionally, capitalists have owned the jobs and labor has been relatively powerless in forcing capitalists to meet their various demands. Now, however, we come to the idea of increasing political democracy. The state is the only institution with the means of strongly influencing the economic sector and capitalists particularly. Thus, if the state becomes more democratic, this state can be used by labor to press for changes in the economic system. In Marxist terminology, the state can operate to reduce the level of exploitation of labor by capitalists. Because the capitalist system requires a sufficient level of exploitation, the whole capitalist economic system may be threatened by a democratic state that comes to serve working-class interests.

Another view maintains that an expanded state would protect the interests of capitalists. As became evident during the economic crisis of the 1930s, the state was needed to organize and regulate some economic activities to keep the capitalist economy healthy. There was also the problem of the expanding industrial reserve army described earlier. Who would keep these people alive so they could be useful workers in the future? The welfare state took over this function. The earlier pattern was that the welfare state expanded when the poor and unemployed became rebellious, only to be cut back later to make the unemployed desperate for any job (Piven and Cloward, 1971). The unemployed were kept alive, but still hungry for a job.

The new perspective, therefore, is that with an increasingly democratic state, the welfare benefits will continue to expand to the point where workers are protected (Piven and Cloward, 1982). With protection from hunger, wages can be pushed higher by workers less likely to fear unemployment if they do not accept just any job and by workers also less fearful of a long strike. The higher wages cut into the profits of capitalists, and so do the taxes to pay for the welfare benefits.

This new view of the state held by some social scientists (Wright, 1978; Piven and Cloward, 1982) is in many ways close to what can be called "Reaganomics"; that is, the state is seen as too large and as harming economic health in many ways. However, the two views differ in suggested solutions. The Reaganomics view is that the state should be changed back to an earlier form that did not hamper economic health. But the view held by the social scientists mentioned above is that the economy could be made more democratic to fit with the increasingly democratic state.

Whether or not we accept either of the views outlined above, we must agree that one aspect of increasing democracy is *increasing demands on the state*. In the past, only the more affluent were able to make so many successful demands that the state protect their interests. Now demands are made on the state by the working class, the poor, minorities, women, the disabled, middle-class homeowners, people living in deteriorating and dangerous urban areas, and so on. With increased political activity by all these groups, and with politicians in need of votes, the state tries to meet many of these demands.

Several problems have resulted from these increasing demands. One of the potentially most dan-

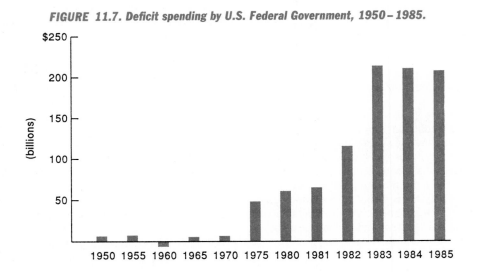

FIGURE 11.7. Deficit spending by U.S. Federal Government, 1950–1985.

gerous is huge government deficits. With so many people demanding the state provide them with benefits and services, and with so many people demanding that the state not raise *their* taxes to pay for these benefits, the result is huge government deficits. As shown in Figure 11.7, federal government deficits have increased dramatically in the past couple of decades. This pattern of government deficits is found in most democratic societies. At the current rate it will not be long before a majority of the federal budget will be devoted to paying only the interest payments on the money the government has borrowed over the years to pay for the deficits.

Another major problem may be the immobility or lack of consistency in the state. Many, if not most, of the demands made on the state are conflicting demands; that is, if one demand is met another demand cannot be adequately met. Often, however, government tries to meet both demands, and this results in conflicting policies that reduce state effectiveness in meeting either demand. To use a current example, the federal government in recent years has followed a policy to reduce cancer through discouraging tobacco consumption and supporting medical research. At the same time, it provides millions of dollars to help tobacco farmers continue to produce their crops. Examples like this can be found in almost every government policy. One group wants protection and aid, while another group does not. Often, government agencies try to appease both interest groups and effective policy in either direction is hampered.

Another important result of increasing demands has been referred to as a ''crisis of confidence'' in political leadership. The percentage of the population expressing ''a great deal of confidence'' in leaders in the executive branch fell from 41 percent in 1966 to 24 percent in 1981. The confidence rating fell even more for congressional leaders — from 42 percent to 16 percent (Lipset and Schneider, 1983). But people continue to feel highly favorably toward the U.S. form of government. In other words, the increasing problems of the state are blamed on bad politicians, not the state institution itself. There may certainly have been plenty of incompetent or corrupt politicians in recent years, but placing blame at this level only ignores some important structural changes in the state because of increasing demands that are in conflict.

CHAPTER SUMMARY

Key Terms

state, 299
power, 300
authority, 300
traditional authority, 301
legal-rational authority, 301
charismatic authority, 301
autocracy, 303
oligarchy, 303
totalitarian rule, 303
communist society, 304
fascist society, 304
democracy, 304
redistributive institution, 305
political economy, 308
political action committee, 313

Content

The state is the organization that dominates the means of force in the society. One of the primary functions of the state is to maintain social order, though the state does not always maintain social order for the best interests of all in the society. Groups having more influence over the state are usually able to assure that the state maintains a social order that is most beneficial to their interests. However, everyone in the society has some common interests, and the state helps set common goals and organize efforts toward achieving these goals, as functional theory suggests.

One of the most important concepts when analyzing the state is power. We must consider how various interest groups use their power to influence what the state does, and we must consider how the state uses power to induce compliance to its laws and regulations.

When the population recognizes the right of an organization or person to have power over others, such power is called legitimate. Three main types of authority are found throughout history. Traditional authority is based on accepted customs, legal-rational authority is based on formalized rules seen as fair and impartial, and charismatic authority is based on the belief in exceptional qualities of an individual.

There are different forms of rule, or the distribution of state power. In an autocracy one individual rules, whereas in an oligarchy a small number of individuals or families share power. A totalitarian form of government is one in which a small elite group rules and has extensive control over others in the society. If totalitarian rule is based on or supports capitalist elites, it is called fascism. If totalitarian rule is "in the name of the masses" and restricts private ownership, it is called communism. Democracy is a system of government in which the means of influencing state actions are more widely distributed — commonly through some form of political representative chosen in elections.

From a general conflict perspective, the state often operates as a redistributive institution. It takes from some groups and gives to others. Politics is the process by which interest groups try to assure that the state takes less from them while they receive maximum benefits from the state.

The modern state as an independent institution, separate from a ruling family and with broad functions in the society, is a rather recent development. This modern state emerged in Europe some 300 to 400 years ago when there was disruption due to increased class conflict. The old aristocracy at first tried to use this expanded state to protect their interests, but as this old ruling class fell the modern state emerged with some autonomy in the society.

Democracy began to emerge when classes opposed to the aristocracy cooperated in overthrowing it and compromised on the form of government to be established in place of aristocratic rule. Democracy has also been a useful political system for protecting the interests of wealthy elites, especially in early stages of industrialization. But democratic procedures have expanded with the growth of the middle class as an influential group in the society.

With the expanded state in modern societies the term political economy applies to a greater degree. The state influences the economic system in many ways and we now find political cycles in the economy. Changes in important economic conditions, such as unemployment and inflation, are to some degree related to economic manipulations by political elites during election years.

Because the modern state is able to influence the well-being of people, there is a dynamic process of class conflict behind state policies. Each class and interest group wants to influence what the state does. Whereas the upper classes have extensive means of influence (such as money to influence elections), other classes and interest groups are not totally lacking in the means of political influence. Even the working class has made political gains in this century.

Comparative data indicate that a state that has had a labor or socialist party in power for an extensive period of time is likely to have a lower rate of unemployment, less inequality, and somewhat higher inflation. This is because a state that is more influenced by the working class will have economic policies that are more protective of working-class interests. These differing outcomes of state policies follow our description of a process of class conflict behind state actions.

Among the poor, genius may stay buried behind the mask of the most implacable stupidity, for if genius can have no issue in a man's life, he must conceal it, and protect it, reserve it for his seed, or his blessing, or, all else gone, for his curse. No wonder we live with dread in our heart, and the nicest of the middle class still padlock their doors against the curse.
— **Norman Mailer, "Why Are We in New York?"**

During the early 1800s many Europeans considered the United States to be a radical new nation. After an extensive visit to the United States in the 1830s, French social scientist Alexis de Tocqueville (1969, p. 6) wrote, "No novelty in the United States struck me more vividly during my stay there than the equality of conditions." Going even further, de Tocqueville (1969, p. 56) wrote, "Men there are nearer equality in wealth and mental endowments . . . than in any other country of the world or in any other age of recorded history."

In many respects de Tocqueville's view of America was accurate. As we have already seen, the level of inequality in human societies had dropped with the new industrializing nations. And in the United States in particular, there was no strong tradition of feudal inequality that in Europe would hang on for many decades. France had its revolution for "equality, fraternity and liberty" in 1789, soon after revolution in the United States. But the tradition of aristocratic privilege in France was hard to break.

In another sense, however, de Tocqueville's remarks were misleading. Inequality was still great in the United States; it only looked small in the eyes of a European accustomed to extremely high levels of inequality. The early founders of the United States were quite wealthy, and the new government they helped establish protected that wealth (Morgan, 1956). Men without property could not vote, and neither, of course, could women and slaves.

Neither did the absence of a feudal tradition in America prevent the wealthy from trying to establish something very much like a nobility. Soon after the revolution, the Founding Fathers considered whether the presidency should be hereditary. (They also debated the proper title for the president, with suggestions such as "High Highness the President of the United States," "His Serene Highness the President of the United States," or, as Washington himself suggested, "High Mightiness" [Amory

(1960, p. 61)]. Exclusive social clubs like the Society of Cincinnati and First Families of Virginia were established to distinguish this new American upper class from "commoners." By the late 1800s a more extensive upper class of wealthy families had developed with names like Morgan, Vanderbilt, Carnegie, and Rockefeller (Baltzell, 1958).

In previous chapters we examined the overall nature of a class system of social stratification, as well as its economic and political base. We have yet to examine the degree and variety of inequality in a class system; neither have we considered the many other outcomes of class position. One particular class (the upper class) needs additional consideration, and the poor have not been considered at all. Finally, we need to know more about the patterns of social mobility among the class positions and what accounts for this movement or the lack of it. These are the primary subjects of the present chapter.

DIMENSIONS OF CLASS INEQUALITY

Not everything in the United States is distributed unequally through the class system. The rural poor of Texas get clean air that the rich in Beverly Hills are sometimes denied. The poor living in the mountains of Appalachia have a spectacular view that the rich in New York City must travel to see. However, with a few exceptions such as these, almost everything else of value is unequally distributed throughout the class system.

Material Inequalities

As has been true throughout history, at least since the development of early horticultural societies, material inequalities have been among the most important types of inequalities. In the United States today, as we would expect, people in the lower classes are less likely to own a car or various kinds of consumer goods (washing machines, dryers, dishwashers, etc., see U.S. Bureau of Census [1974, Table 649]). More important perhaps is housing inequality. Although about half of families in the United States own homes today, that figure is dropping. Since the late 1970s only about one quarter of new families can afford to buy a home (Blumberg, 1980, pp. 200–214). Even adequate rental property is beyond many Americans. For example, almost 10 percent of Americans still lack some or all of the basic plumbing facilities in their housing (U.S. Bureau of Census 1980, Table 3–9).

With respect to all basic necessities (food, energy, shelter, and medical care), there is evidence that 20 percent of American families cannot afford adequate amounts of all these basic necessities at the same time (Blumberg, 1980, pp. 182–183). These families face decisions such as whether to eat, heat their homes, or pay medical bills.

Income Inequality. In Chapter 9 we considered how income inequality in the United States compared with inequality in other industrial societies (remember that the United States has comparatively high income inequality, with much less than average income going to the bottom 20 percent of the people). At present we need to examine more recent income data and consider these data historically.

Table 12.1 indicates the degree of income inequality in the United States since World War II. There was a *slight* trend toward a reduced income share for the top 20 percent and top 5 percent of the population between World War II and 1980. But in this period gains in income shares were restricted to the 20 percent of the population just below the most wealthy 20 percent. Since 1980, however, there has been a new trend. Because of high unemployment, welfare payment reductions, changes in the ratio of well-paying versus low-paying jobs, and the first Reagan tax law changes, the rich have been getting richer and the poor have been getting poorer. This trend can be clearly seen when comparing changes in **real income** for 20-percentile income groups between 1979 and 1984 (see Figure 12.1). ("Real income" means how much money people have to spend after inflation and taxes.)

Other data indicate that the distribution of income in the United States has been quite stable going back much further, except during the 1930s

TABLE 12.1. *Percentage of aggregate family income by income fifths and top 5 percent, 1945–1985*

Year	Lowest fifth	Second fifth	Third fifth	Fourth fifth	Highest fifth	Top 5 percent
1985	4.6	10.9	16.9	24.2	43.5	16.7
1980	5.1	11.6	17.5	24.3	41.6	15.3
1975	5.4	11.8	17.6	24.1	41.1	15.5
1970	5.4	12.2	17.6	23.8	40.9	15.6
1965	5.2	12.2	17.8	23.9	40.9	15.5
1960	4.8	12.2	17.8	24.0	41.3	15.9
1955	4.8	12.3	17.8	23.7	41.3	16.4
1950	4.5	12.0	17.4	23.4	42.7	17.3
1945	5.0	11.9	17.0	23.1	43.0	17.5

SOURCE: U.S. Bureau of the Census, 1986. *Current Population Reports,* 1985:11, Table 4; U.S. Bureau of the Census. 1980. *Current Population Reports,* "Money Income of Families and Persons in the United States: 1979," series P–60, no. 123, Table L; U.S. Bureau of the Census, 1981. *Current Population Reports,* "Money Income and Poverty Status of Families and Persons in the United States: 1980," series P–60, no. 127, Table 5.

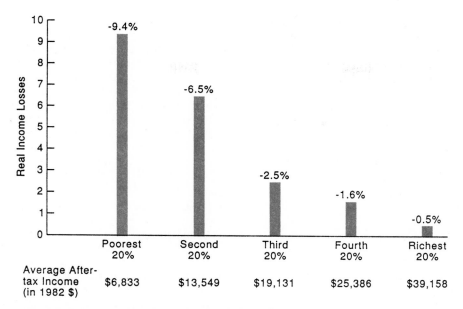

FIGURE 12.1. Percentage losses in real income by 20 percentile income groups, 1979–1984. (Source: Urban Institute.)

and 1940s, when income inequality was reduced somewhat because of depression-era reforms and full employment during World War II (Turner and Starnes, 1976, p. 51).

The figures in Table 12.1 do not reflect the effects of taxing policies on the distribution of income. When posttax income is considered, however, the income distribution is altered only slightly. For example, the income share of the top 20 percent is reduced by only 1.9 percent and the income share of the bottom 20 percent of families is increased only 0.7 percent when the effects of income taxes are considered (U.S. Bureau of Census, 1976, p. 477). This means that the income tax system in the United States is only slightly progressive, and continues to be so after the important tax law changes became fully effective in 1988.

Wealth Inequality. Another important type of material inequality is found with the distribution of wealth. In contrast to income, **wealth** represents accumulated assets. For most people this wealth is in the form of personal belongings, a home, and/or a car. Wealth inequality is a very important form of inequality because (1) great wealth usually brings high income and influence, (2) great wealth can be inherited more readily than income.

Data pertaining to wealth inequality are not collected every year, but what we have clearly shows that wealth is much more unequally distributed than income. Table 12.2 indicates that in 1962 the top fifth of the population held about 76.9 percent of all wealth, in contrast to their 41.3 percent share of total U.S. income. The bottom fifth of the population had only 0.2 percent of the wealth.

Another important question pertains to the source of wealth for the top wealth holders in the United States. As indicated in Table 12.3, in 1972 both the top 1 percent and the top 0.5 percent of the population (in terms of wealth) held a greater portion of their assets in corporate stock. In fact, the top 0.5 percent of the population held 49.3 percent of all personally owned corporate stock in the United States. As we have already seen, ownership of cor-

TABLE 12.2. *The distribution of wealth and income by family fifths, 1962*

Family fifths	Percentage of total wealth	Percentage of total income
Highest fifth	76.9	41.3
Fourth fifth	15.5	24.0
Middle fifth	6.2	17.6
Second fifth	2.1	12.1
Lowest fifth	0.2	5.0
	100.0	100.0

SOURCES: Office of Management and Budget, *Social Indicators,* 1973:164; U.S. Bureau of the Census, *Current Population Reports,* 1980:63, U.S. Bureau of the Census, 1980. *Current Population Reports,* "Money Income of Families and Persons in the United States: 1978," series P–60, no. 123, Table L.

porate stock is important because such ownership can bring significant economic power.

Finally, we have the question of where the great wealth of the top 0.5 percent of the population originated. In most cases, as Michael Kinsley's analysis of America's 400 most wealthy people in 1983 indicates (Box 12.1), it comes the old-fashion way — it's inherited. Table 12.4 presents the class backgrounds of the super-richest in the United States in four periods beginning with 1900. There was room at the top in 1900, but this is less true today. Over 80 percent of the very wealthy in 1970 were from upper-class origins — indicating they inherited most of their wealth or at least were given a substantial headstart over everyone else.

Nonmaterial Inequalities

In addition to these important types of material inequalities, there are many kinds of nonmaterial inequalities. Some of these are rather difficult to measure precisely, such as self-respect and happiness. But studies indicate these nontangibles are in fact unequally distributed by class. For example, Bradburn and Caplovitz (1965) discovered that those higher in the class system were more likely to report being happy. Similarly, Andrews and Withey (1976) have shown that there is a positive relationship between social class and a general sense of well-being (the higher the class position, the greater

TABLE 12.3. *Top wealth holders by type of wealth, 1972*

Assets	Value of gross assets held by (billions of dollars)		Percentage held by	
	Top 1%	Top 0.5%	Top 1%	Top 0.5%
Total assets	1,046.9	822.4	24.1%	18.9%
Real estate	225.0	150.9	15.1	10.1
Corporate stock	491.7	429.3	56.5	49.3
Bonds	94.8	82.5	60.0	52.2
Cash	101.2	63.6	13.5	8.5
Debt instruments	40.8	30.3	52.7	39.1
Life insurance	10.0	6.2	7.0	4.3
Trusts	89.4	80.3	89.9	80.8
Miscellaneous	83.3	59.5	9.8	6.8
Liabilities	131.0	100.7	16.2	12.5
Net worth	915.9	721.7	25.9	20.4

SOURCE: U.S. Bureau of the Census. 1980. *Statistical Abstract of the United States,* Table 786, p. 471.

TABLE 12.4. *Social origins of the super rich, 1900–1970 (%)*

Social origin	1900	1925	1950	1970
Upper class	39	56	68	82
Middle class	20	30	20	10
Lower class	39	12	9	4
Not classified	2	2	3	4

SOURCE: Thomas Dye, 1979, p. 200. The estimates for 1900 to 1950 are from C. Wright Mills (1956, pp. 104–105). These data pertain to the richest 60 to 90 individuals in each period.

TABLE 12.6. *Days of disability by family income of patient*

	Days of disability per person		
Annual family income	**1970**	**1975**	**1978**
Under $5,000	23.3	32.4	35.7
$ 5,000–$9,999	12.8	20.2	24.2
$10,000–$14,999	11.5	14.4	15.8
$15,000 and over	10.9	12.4	13.7

SOURCE: U.S. Bureau of the Census, 1980. *Social Indicators III,* Table 2–16, p. 101.

the sense of well-being). The important condition of self-worth or self-esteem has been found positively related to social class among adults (Rosenberg and Pearlin, 1978). Affluence, of course, does not insure happiness, but all things considered, the more affluent tend to be happier just about any way happiness is measured.

Other nonmaterial inequalities, many of which are tied to a state of happiness, are more easily measured. Consider physical health. In general, people toward the bottom of the stratification system are sick more often, remain sick longer, and die at a younger age than people higher in the stratification system. As indicated in Table 12.5, income level is strongly related to the prevalence of chronic diseases. And as Table 12.6 indicates, income level is

equally related to the average length of disability. Finally, we can simply ask people to assess the state of their health. When doing so we find that about 32 percent of the population with family incomes under $5,000 a year (1976 dollars) say their health is excellent, whereas about 60 percent of those with incomes of $15,000 or more say their health is excellent (U.S. Bureau of Census, 1980, p. 98).

One form of class inequality is life itself. But not all of this inequality in life expectancy is due to physical illness. Those lower in the class system are more likely to be murdered, and in fact murder is the leading cause of death among young black males living in poverty. As Table 12.7 shows, people lower in the stratification system (lower income) are more

TABLE 12.5. *Prevalence of selected chronic diseases by annual income*

	Prevalence per 1,000 persons			
Annual income	**Heart disease (1972)**	**Diabetes (1973)**	**Anemia (1973)**	**Arthritis (1976)**
Under $3,000	111.4	45.0	27.5	218.6
$ 3,000–4,999	78.0	35.9	22.0	
$ 5,000–6,999	54.5	23.8	17.1	135.1
$ 7,000–9,999	39.9	17.3	14.3	
$10,000–14,999	32.8	14.4	12.3	91.0
$15,000 or more	35.2	12.9	10.2	79.3

SOURCE: U.S. Bureau of the Census, 1980. *Social Indicators III,* Table 2–17, p. 101.

BOX 12.1

The Old-fashioned Way to Wealth — Inheritance

Numerous country-club verities have been celebrated and enshrined in public policy during the Reagan years. The most cherished of these concern the role of rich people. Two truths in particular were being suppressed by envious partisans in the liberal media until the rich and their own partisans burst out of the locker rooms and onto the streets.

First, it's darned hard to get rich. It requires grit, stamina, creativity, and daring. Second, the rich contribute more to the economy than they take out, so the more they flourish, the better it is for the country. "That is the function of the rich," explained George Gilder in his 1981 book, *Wealth and Poverty:* "fostering opportunities for the classes below them in the continuing drama of the creation of wealth and progress." The scales have fallen from Congress's eyes. It has rushed to aid the rich by cutting their taxes and inheritance duties.

It's true enough that prosperity is good for everyone, not just the rich. It's even true that a properly functioning capitalist economy should encourage people to try to get rich. But it doesn't follow that all the rich in our real-life economy deserve their wealth, either in the sense of having acquired it in ways that contribute to general prosperity. And it also doesn't follow that indiscriminate coddling of the rich is sensible government policy. You have to ask which of these geese really lay golden eggs.

The nation's fattest geese are on display in the current *Forbes* magazine, in its second annual compilation of the 400 richest people in America. Each is worth more than $125 million, including Malcolm S. Forbes, the magazine's owner and editor, who crows in an editorial: "The 400, individually and in toto, are living proof that the system works." If he means by this that "the system" has given 400 people the virtually unlimited ability to sate their material desires, he's right. If he means that we're all better off as a result, the answer is more complicated. If he means that the "Forbes 400" vindicates the Horatio Alger legend of orphaned bootblacks climbing to the top on spunk, spittle, and a smile, he should have done some subtraction, as I have.

First, let's subtract those who made their money the old-fashioned way — being born into it. Forbes reports that 134 of the 400 "inherited great wealth," but by my count it's more like 204 — more than half. We may disagree about the meaning of the word *great*. My count doesn't even include people who inherited money and then infused it with new entrepreneurial energy, such as Fred Smith, who took $3.2 million of his father's money and turned it into Federal Express, or Malcolm Forbes himself, who revived a profitable but moribund magazine.

Of the 196 remaining super-rich, about 45 got there through the ownership of gas, oil, and real estate. Once again I'm not counting active real-estate developers such as Gerald Hines (who built much of downtown Houston), or various oil barons who took big risks and suffered dry holes before hitting a gusher. These 45 are people with John Jacob Astor's philosophy: "Hold onto the land. Let udders improve." Getting rich by simply owning natural resources may be a matter of luck or even a matter of skill, but it adds nothing to the commonwealth.

So we're down to 151 of the Forbes 400 who seem to have arrived there by approximate dint of their own efforts. Of these, at least 22 are almost purely "paper entrepreneurs" — wheeler-dealers who got rich buying and selling companies and bits of companies while contributing little or nothing to the actual creation of goods and services (and jobs). Most of the 400 owe at least some of their wealth to this kind of activity. It is not socially useless: Corporate predators and deal-makers in their ghoulish way keep markets efficient and managements alert. But they're hardly the better mousetrap-makers of myth.

Another 14 of the top 400 fortunes are based largely on the existence of big government. Daniel K. Ludwig, listed as the country's third richest man, made his first billion mostly by building ships for the Navy. The Bechtels, senior and junior, got there with a construction firm specializing in government-sized projects such as dams, nuclear power plants, and airports. These government activities may be money well spent, but you cannot offer the fortunes that they created as evidence that money is better left in private hands. The other 11 government-based fortunes come from ownership of radio and TV licenses, fantastically valuable commodities that the government insanely gives away to a lucky few.

Eliminating all these categories (and eight fortunes that I couldn't place), I count 107 of the Forbes 400 — about one of four — who acquired their money in roughly the way Ronald Reagan, George Gilder, and Malcolm Forbes like to imagine. Even among these, almost half had a considerable headstart, like Forbes. Also like Forbes, almost all have been helped by government policies. Forbes has profited from years of low postage rates for magazines, subsidized by first-class mail users. Most of his high-visibility, extravagant life-style is tax-deductible as a "business expense." Such policies may be wise or not, but keep them in mind the next time a rich friend carries on about the burden of welfare.

Fifty-nine of the 400 — barely one of eight — seem really to have built their fortunes from scratch. They include some genuine Horatio Alger stories, such as Kyupin Hwang, a Korean immigrant who arrived here 15 years ago with $50, founded a computer company, and is now worth $575 million. They also include anyone I could find who started with no more than an upper-middle-class upbringing, a good education, and a few thousand dollars. (They even include a few like Bob Guccione, founder of Penthouse, who got rich by inflaming and satisfying desires that most conservatives would rather see repressed.) These happy few do deserve to enjoy their good fortune.

Source: Michael Kinsley, "Few of the Rich Really Earned Their Status," *Los Angeles Times,* Oct. 10, 1983.

TABLE 12.7. *Crime victims by family income, 1980*

Type of crime	Family income					
	Under $3,000	$3,000 to $7,499	$7,500 to $9,999	$10,000 to $14,999	$15,000 to $24,999	$25,000 or more
	(rate per 100,000 persons)					
Rape						
white	271	128	137	111	41	56
nonwhite	340	217	0	99	0	0
Robbery						
white	1,448	843	557	543	443	457
nonwhite	1,161	1,648	1,398	931	952	528
Assault						
white	4,761	2,705	2,576	2,265	2,389	2,312
nonwhite	3,450	2,550	2,424	2,686	2,467	1,824

SOURCE: U.S. Department of Justice, Sourcebook of Criminal Justice Statistics, 1982, p. 318.

likely to be victims of other kinds of serious crime as well. Class position is also related to loss of life in war. In both the Korean and Vietnam wars a higher proportion of combat deaths involved lower-class men (Mayer and Hoult, 1955; Zeitlin, Lutterman, and Russel, 1973).

Of course, other types of inequality are related to class position. For example, those in higher class positions are able to provide their children with a better education. Lawbreakers from different class positions are often treated differently by the criminal justice system. Job satisfaction and a safe working environment are related to class position, and so on. Class position provides people with more or less influence in the society, and this influence is likely to be used to effect the distribution of whatever scarce good, service, or condition is highly valued in the society.

CLASS SUBCULTURES AND LIFE-STYLES

The United States is a nation of people from many racial, ethnic, religious, and other backgrounds. Such variety becomes most clear when placed in contrast to other industrial nations—especially Japan. As would be expected, this variety of backgrounds in the United States has produced people with different world views, values, and life-styles. And added to this variety are different class subcultures and life-styles.

Life-style includes tastes, preferences, and general manner of living that are more superficial and not necessarily related to important outcomes or value differences. Many of these life-style differences can be usually traced to experiences related to class position. It will be useful first to consider some of these.

You are probably aware of class differences in the type of music people prefer. Although many variables affect musical tastes (such as region of the country), the working class generally favor country music more than does the upper middle class. And there are differences in country music so that some types have a cross-class appeal. But what we might call the "hard core" or traditional country music is more popular with the working class. This kind of music tends to stress everyday working-class problems of family stability, unemployment, relations on the job, male strength and aggression—themes that working-class people may find more important in their experience.

Other class differences not only stem from contrasting class experiences but also help maintain class boundaries. For example, one study found that people are usually able to identify the class position of an individual speaking on a tape recording (Ellis, 1967).

Close observation can also reveal many other subtle class differences in things like body language, clothing, and hair styles. Most important, these style differences can lead to differential treatment by others. Studies of class speech patterns have found that people rate unseen higher-class people as more credible and likable (Harms, 1961; Ellis, 1967). These differences, no doubt, lead to different evaluations by employers, teachers, police officers, and others in a position to influence a person's life.

Upper-class Subcultures

We have already considered the political and economic power of those at the top of the stratification system. At this point we will view the upper class from the perspective of an interrelated network of families with a distinctive life-style and world view shaped by their common experience and position in the nation (Baltzell, 1958).

Remember that we are referring to a very small elite group of people in the upper class. Represent-

ing somewhere between 1 to 3 percent of the population (sociologists disagree on the exact number), these people are among the most wealthy in the nation. However, historically in the United States there has been a split between two groups of wealthy people. Some refer to these two groups as the upper upper class and lower upper class, or simply the old rich and the new rich.

At the very top of our class system we find that a status-honor dimension has been of some importance as a ranking mechanism. The importance of status-honor for the upper class is related to two basic conditions (1) Once great wealth has been obtained, additional money loses much of its value as an indicator of importance and high rank. If the family wishes to further distinguish itself, another means must be sought. (2) New wealth is always being made, even if at a slower pace compared with some periods in our earlier history. Are these new rich equal to the established wealthy families in the social hierarchy? The older rich families tend to think not. But if they are not equal, then how is the lower status of the new rich signified? In agrarian societies there was always the more ascriptive position of royalty — the aristocracy. A blood line tied to nobility would always serve as the final ranking distinc-

What inferences about class subcultures can you draw from these photos of elderly women? The woman in the car, Rose Kennedy, is the matriarch of a powerful and wealthy political family. The seated woman is a resident of a nursing home in Washington, D.C. What types of options do wealth and influence create for those who are facing a very dependent period of their lives? (© Michael Abramson, © Martha Tabor/Impact Visuals)

 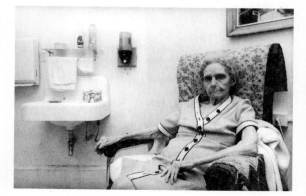

tion. The United States, of course, has never had a true nobility.

The super rich in America who have held their fortunes for several generations have drawn status distinctions around themselves to keep the new rich at a distance. What becomes important is a life-style, a respect for "high culture," that the new rich will often find difficult to acquire. The new rich are considered crude and rather uncivilized. They are the loud Texas millionaires or the Hollywood types who "crudely" display their wealth with conspicuous consumption.

Traditionally there have been a set of upper-class organizations and associations that shape this "cultured" life-style but that also operate as symbols of upper-class membership (see especially Domhoff, 1970, 1983; and Baltzell, 1958, 1964). These begin at an early age with exclusive prep schools, then include the "proper" universities and clubs within these universities. In adult life there are exclusive social clubs for men, the "proper" charity organizations for women, and blue books like the *Social Register* that are lists of "acceptable" upper-class families.

Values that stress the past lead this upper class of old wealth to emphasize their successful ancestors and family traditions. The emphasis on "higher culture" leads this upper class to appreciation of art, literature, the theater, and other intellectual pursuits. The new rich, on the other hand, tend to be self-made millionaires who stress "rugged individualism" and "toughness."

Contrasting images like these have led Dye (1983) to use the semiserious labels "Eastern Establishment" and "Sunbelt Cowboys" to describe the old rich and new rich. These labels refer to the "home territory" of the old rich versus the new rich, as well as the origins of their wealth. The old wealth tends to be based on the old industrial and financial institutions in the Northeast, whereas the new wealth tends to be based on oil, real estate, and new industries in the Southwest and West.

Taking this subcultural contrast a bit further, Dye (1983, p. 230) lists several divergent preferences that he imagines may exist between the old upper class and the new rich. For example, although

the old rich may prefer the music of Leonard Bernstein, the new rich prefer Lawrence Welk. The book by David Halberstam, *The Best and the Brightest,* was suggested as a favorite of the old rich in the 1970s, with George Gilder's *Wealth and Poverty* a favorite of the new rich. As for comedians and actors, Dye suggests Woody Allen and Alan Alda for the old rich, in contrast to Bob Hope and Clint Eastwood (following the death of John Wayne) for the new rich. Finally, as for food, Dye suggests quiche lorraine for the old rich and charcoal steak for the new rich. We may question some of Dye's examples, but I believe they are useful in indicating the contrasting subcultures.

Upper-class subcultures involve more than simply superficial life-style differences. (1) The experiences behind the subcultural differences lead to differing political views. The old upper class tend to be more moderate to liberal in their political views, whereas the new rich tend to be much more conservative (as these labels are applied today). Both groups favor economic and foreign policies that protect the wealthy, but there are differences over how best to accomplish this goal. We therefore find political swings when a presidential administration comes into office with the backing of one upper-class faction versus the other faction. (2) The lines drawn around the old rich have tended to unify them as a class and organize them into a more effective political force. The common world view and network of social ties formed during prep school, college, then continued with social clubs and corporate interlocks have, at least in the past, given the old upper class an advantage over the new rich in political as well as economic competition.

There is evidence that the distinction between the old rich and the new rich is being reduced, partially because of the increasing power of bureaucratic corporate elites (a "corporate class"). But also important is the decline of the Eastern industrial base that helped to keep the old rich in their position (even though the financial dominance of New York City banks continues to support many of the old rich). The dominance of the new rich (especially from the West and Southwest) in the Republican Party during the 1980s is an indication of the decline of the old rich. With their decline, the status-honor distinction between the old rich and the new rich may also decline in importance.

Middle-class and Working-class Subcultures

Just as different life experiences have produced some different subcultural values and life-styles between the old rich and the new rich, we find some subcultural and life-style differences among the middle class and the working class. These differences can be overemphasized, but at times they are important in affecting life chances. Also, it is important to recognize that we are referring only to tendencies with these differences. There is clearly much overlap between the middle class and the working class with respect to the orientations that follow.

Family Roles. Although there are fewer differences in middle-class and working-class family roles today, there continue to be some general differences (Matras, 1984, pp. 147–148). The middle-class family tends to have fewer ties to an extended family, for example. In contrast to the working class, they are less likely to live near their relatives. One reason for this middle-class difference is greater geographical mobility due to occupational demands.

Perhaps a more important difference involves husband and wife roles. The working-class family tends to be more patriarchal—the male is usually dominant and concerned with maintaining the traditional male-female role divisions. The male in the middle-class family tends to accept somewhat more sex role equality. For example, the middle-class wife has more responsibility in family decision making, is more likely to be respected as a career worker as well as a mother, and is given some help with household chores and child care.

In addition to being less male-centered, the middle-class family also tends to be less adult-centered. Children are given more attention and there is a bit more concern that children are given experiences that will provide future educational benefits (Kohn, 1969). Because of the importance of child-rearing methods, it is worth further consideration in the next section.

Again, it is easy to overstate class differences in family patterns. The working class especially has more diversity. It has even been suggested that we can divide working-class families into "modern" and "traditional" families, with the modern family pattern very close if not identical to the middle-class family pattern (Matras, 1984, p. 148).

Childhood Socialization. Childhood socialization patterns tend to be among the most important class subcultural differences. These differences have a large impact on the future of children and in large measure help maintain class boundaries. To some degree working-class children are raised to be working-class adults, while middle-class children are raised to be middle-class adults.

In general, research indicates that middle-class children experience child-rearing methods that stress initiative, self-reliance, an emphasis on ideas and people, achievement of higher occupation, and more deferred gratification. Working-class socialization tends to stress external conformity to rules, less self-reliance and creativity, and working with things rather than ideas (Kohn, 1969). Several studies support this view of child-rearing differences in this country (Wright and Wright, 1976) and in other countries (Pearlin, 1971; Olsen, 1973).

It is not suggested that working-class parents have less concern for their children or are harder on their children. Nor are working-class parents less concerned about their children's future. Studies indicate that parents in the middle class are concerned with high occupational attainment for their children, whereas working-class parents are concerned with their children's well-being without reference to occupational level per se (Keller and Zavalloni, 1964; Turner, 1970).

We conclude with a suggestion as to why these differences exist. In the example of differing concerns for children's self-reliance and conformity, studies indicate that parents' work experiences are the most important factors in producing these differences. Working-class parents are lower in authority on the job and have occupations that require more conformity to external rules. This experience is reflected in how they raise their children. In an interesting study examining this child-rearing characteristic using data from 122 cultures, it was found that greater supervision over parents in important aspects of life (such as work) tends to produce a greater stress on conformity in their children (Ellis, Lee, and Peterson, 1978). These findings conform to the general sociological principle that the underlying technological-material environment shapes much of human behavior.

Class Subcultures: A Summary. There are other important class differences in life-styles and subcultural values. Conflicting class interests result in differing political party support by class. In this country the lower classes are a bit more likely to vote Democratic and the higher classes are more likely to vote Republican (Knoke and Hout, 1974;

Vanneman, 1980; Szymanski, 1978). Also very important, and in this case more pronounced in the United States, there are clear differences in voter participation by class; people higher in the class system are more likely to vote in elections.

One should not overestimate these class differences. One reason is that in some respects the middle class and the working class are becoming more similar in some ways. Some of the working class are becoming more similar to the middle class in part because of increasing wage gains made possible by unionization. This **embourgeoisement** thesis (the root word is *bourgeoisie,* meaning "middle class") focuses on increasing similarities in consumption patterns and other characteristics related to standard of living.

In other ways, however, the middle class is be-

In this Nissan automobile plant in Tennessee, workers are part of a team known as a quality work circle. This method of production is the opposite of the assembly line, where work is broken down into component tasks. What type of class culture do you think is produced by team work? Is this a means of democratizing the workplace? (© William Strode)

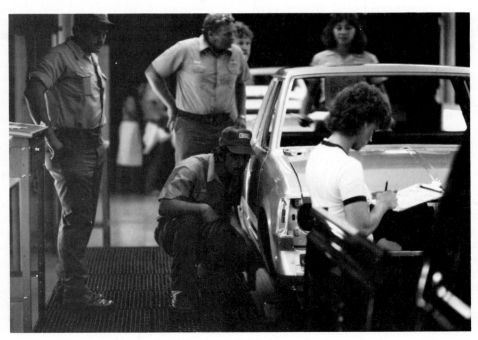

coming more like the working class. The **proletarianization** thesis focuses on the working conditions of the middle class that are often becoming more like assembly-line factory work. In offices, for example, the middle class are often becoming more controlled by machines, which produce more alienation and less job satisfaction.

Overall, however, differences between the middle class and the working class continue in many areas of life. It is very unlikely that the underlying experiences of people in these two classes will become so similar that these differences will be totally erased.

SOCIAL MOBILITY AND THE ATTAINMENT PROCESS

It will be useful to begin this section with some examples. Consider the situation of two young individuals born at opposite ends of the stratification system in the United States — one from a very rich family and another from a poor family. If you were asked to predict which of these individuals would end up toward the top of the stratification system in his or her adult life, you would most likely pick the one from the wealthy family. Such a prediction is not a sure bet, but the odds are much better than any you will get in Las Vegas. What this indicates is that *ascriptive* factors factors are still important in our stratification system.

This example is not quite so simple. All the sons and daughters of the rich do not stay rich, and some of the sons and daughters of working-class parents move into top positions in the class system. Several questions emerge. *How many* from the rich fall and how many from the working class move up? When there is movement from the top and bottom, generally *how far* up or down do people move? And perhaps the most difficult kind of question, *why* do some people move up or down in the stratification system while others remain in their class of birth? Do we find that individual characteristics like intelligence, hard work, and motivation are the most important? And if so, to what degree are these characteristics shaped by advantages or disadvantages in the social environment rather than by inherent qualities of the individual?

Given the value of "equality of opportunity" in our society and the high aspirations of most people in our society, the question of "who gets ahead" is especially important. We pride ourselves in the belief that ours is a nation where people with talent and motivation can get ahead. But as we have seen, the United States has a long way to go in meeting this ideal of equality of opportunity.

Patterns of Social Mobility

There are several ways to examine social mobility. We can look at the movement from a worker's first job to the job held at the end of the working life — **intragenerational mobility.** Or we can examine the class or occupational position of parents in contrast to the class or occupational position of their adult offspring — **intergenerational mobility.** In addition, we can examine mobility in relation to different indicators or aspects of class position, such as occupational skill level, bureaucratic authority position, or property ownership. However, most of the extensive mobility studies have focused on intergenerational mobility with respect to the occupational position attained by males.

We must begin consideration of these studies with Blau and Duncan's (1967) pioneering work. Blau and Duncan examined a large sample of the U.S. population (20,000 people) with the aid of the U.S. Bureau of Census. Nothing on that magnitude had been done before in any nation. It is, therefore, interesting to note that most of what we know about social mobility patterns has come with, and since, Blau and Duncan's famous work.

Table 12.8 contains data from the original Blau and Duncan study (the data collected in 1962) and combines it with 1973 data from a massive study by Featherman and Hauser (1978) to update the 1962 data. Table 12.8 may look rather confusing at first glance, but it is really quite simple. To begin, this is known as an *outflow mobility table.* This means that we are considering occupational positions of sons in comparison with their fathers' occupational position (that is where these sons began life). Reading down

TABLE 12.8. *Outflow mobility from father's (or other family head's) broad occupation group to son's current occupation group, 1962 and 1973*

Father's occupation	Son's current occupation (%)					
	Upper middle class	Lower middle class	Upper working class	Lower working class	Farm	Total
1962 (n = 10,550)						
Upper middle class	56.8	16.7	11.5	13.8	1.2	100
Lower middle class	43.1	23.7	14.6	17.0	1.7	100
Upper working class	24.7	17.0	28.3	28.8	1.2	100
Lower working class	17.9	14.8	21.9	43.4	1.9	100
Farm	10.3	12.3	19.3	35.9	22.2	100
Total	24.5	15.9	20.2	31.7	7.7	100
1973 (n = 20,850)						
Upper middle class	59.4	11.4	12.8	15.5	0.9	100
Lower middle class	45.1	16.6	16.4	20.7	1.2	100
Upper working class	30.9	12.2	27.7	28.1	1.2	100
Lower working class	22.9	12.1	23.9	40.1	1.0	100
Farm	16.4	9.0	22.0	37.1	14.5	100
Total	31.2	11.8	21.9	31.0	4.1	100

SOURCE: Featherman and Hauser (1978, 89). The samples include American men in the experienced civilian labor force aged twenty-one to sixty-four.

the first column in Table 12.8, we find the occupational position of the father. Across the top is the occupational position of sons. The totals run across the columns; thus the 100 percent totals are at the far right column.

Some examples within the table should be helpful. At the top left in the 1973 data we find that 59.4 percent of the sons born to fathers in upper-middle-class occupations were able to attain upper-middle-class occupations. (This can be considered occupational inheritance, even though the table indicates only that these sons attained occupations of similar rank, not the exact same occupation.) Then,

as we move across the top of the table, we see that 11.4 percent of the sons of upper-middle-class fathers moved down to the lower middle class and so on.

Toward the bottom right of Table 12.8 (again with the 1973 data) we find that 40.1 percent of the sons of lower-working-class fathers stayed in that type of occupation. Moving to the left we find that 23.9 percent of sons of lower-working-class fathers moved up to the upper middle class, 12.1 percent of these sons moved to the lower middle class, and 22.9 percent moved to the upper middle class. (Note that farm workers represented a very small percentage of the labor force in 1973, 4.1 percent, and are not discussed in this analysis.)

Several generalizations about the patterns of social mobility in the United States can be made in relation to Table 12.8 and similar studies.

1. Social mobility is more restricted at the top and bottom of the stratification system. The percent staying at the top (59.4 percent in 1973) and the percent staying at the bottom (40.1 percent) are higher than the percent retaining their father's occupational level in between these extremes. Actually we are excluding the real extremes in the class system with the data in Table 12.8. The upper class is too small to show up in the table; neither does the table accurately measure the poorest group in America. We have other information indicating that social mobility out of the very top and bottom is even more restricted than the near top and bottom in Table 12.8 (Kerbo, 1983, pp. 338–340). Toward the middle positions in the class system there is rather extensive mobility.

2. The mobility that does exist tends to be more upward than downward. This is a preferable situation for most people that has so far existed in most industrial nations in most time periods. This pattern of more upward than downward mobility is primarily due to two factors: (1) usually more jobs are being created at the top as industrial societies advance, and (2) people higher in the class system tend to have smaller families, thus passing on top positions to fewer sons. This upward mobility due to changes in the occupational system is called **structural mobility.** Both of these tendencies help create more room at the top. The pattern of more upward mobility helps produce acceptance of class inequality among the lower classes. As long as there is hope that they or their children can be upwardly mobile, the lower classes are more likely to accept present class inequalities. There is, however, a dangerous trend noted in our chapter on the economy—middle-income jobs, especially the better-paying blue-collar jobs, have been reduced while low-paying service jobs have increased. At the same time, the better-paying jobs in high-tech industries have grown only slightly. Thus, in the next ten years we will likely find the mobility data showing less upward and more downward mobility in the United States.

3. When social mobility does occur, either up or down, it is most likely to be short-range mobility; that is, when people are mobile they are likely to move only one rank up or down. This is not to say more long-range mobility is absent; Table 12.8 indicates that a good deal of long-range mobility does exist, especially into the upper middle class in the 1973 data.

4. Comparing the 1973 data with the 1962 data, we find very similar mobility patterns. In fact, though we have less complete data before 1962, there is good evidence that social mobility patterns have been rather similar throughout this century (Rogoff, 1953; Tully, Jackson, and Curtis, 1970).

5. The mobility patterns we have considered are mainly for white males. Thus, the data are not descriptive of the whole United States. In later chapters we will find that the mobility patterns for blacks and women are not identical to those of men.

The Attainment Process

In the research described above the question was primarily what exists, not why it exists. We need to know *why* some people are mobile and others are not. We have seen that the position of a father in the occupational structure influences a son's chances, but we have yet to consider why this is so. Is it because of more or less money to pursue higher education? Is it because of greater or lesser aspirations and motivation? In this section we consider these very important questions.

There are generally two schools of thought on these questions of why social mobility does or does not occur. One school focuses on individual characteristics or "human capital" (that is, the talent, motivation, and skills a person has obtained). This view studies what is called the **status attainment process**—the process whereby individuals compete to attain high occupational status. The second school of thought focuses on structural conditions *in the society* that promote more or less mobility, (called an *allocation process*) for people in certain positions in the society. The emphasis here is on the characteristics of the society that promote more or less mobility, not on the characteristics of individuals.

The Status Attainment Process. The research by Blau and Duncan (1967) not only established the direction of mobility research, it also set the direction for research on the status attainment process. With new statistical methods to specify the most important factors influencing high or low occupational attainment, Blau and Duncan found that education had the strongest effect on occupational attainment. A father's education and occupational level have a strong effect on the son's occupational attainment, but this is primarily because the father's education and occupation affect the son's education. As shown in Figure 12.2, education is a mediating factor between family background and occupational attainment.

Since Blau and Duncan's pioneering work, several other sociologists have refined the status attainment model. In what has become known as the *Wisconsin model,* several social psychological variables along with mental ability were added to the process (Sewell, Haller, and Ohlendorf, 1970; Sewell and Hauser, 1975).

As indicated in Figure 12.2, it is now recognized that other variables come between parent's educa-

tion/occupation and son's occupation. The Wisconsin model suggests that parent's position in the class system affects the son's significant others (that is, the son's peer group and others with extensive personal contact). The significant others (along with the parents) influence the son's educational and occupational aspirations (that is, what the son is motivated to achieve). These aspirations then influence the amount of education attained, and education in turn influences occupation level attained. As shown at the bottom of the model, the son's mental ability is important in influencing academic performance, which then influences the selection of significant others to some extent. But academic performance influences aspirations and educational attainment only weakly. However, it is also important to recognize that in many ways parents are able to affect the mental ability of their offspring as they are developing.

Let's put the above in perspective with a human example. We consider a person who has become a chemical engineer. Most likely, this person came from a middle-class to upper-middle-class family. Because of where the parents lived and where this person went to school, he or she had a peer group of

FIGURE 12.2. Status attainment models.

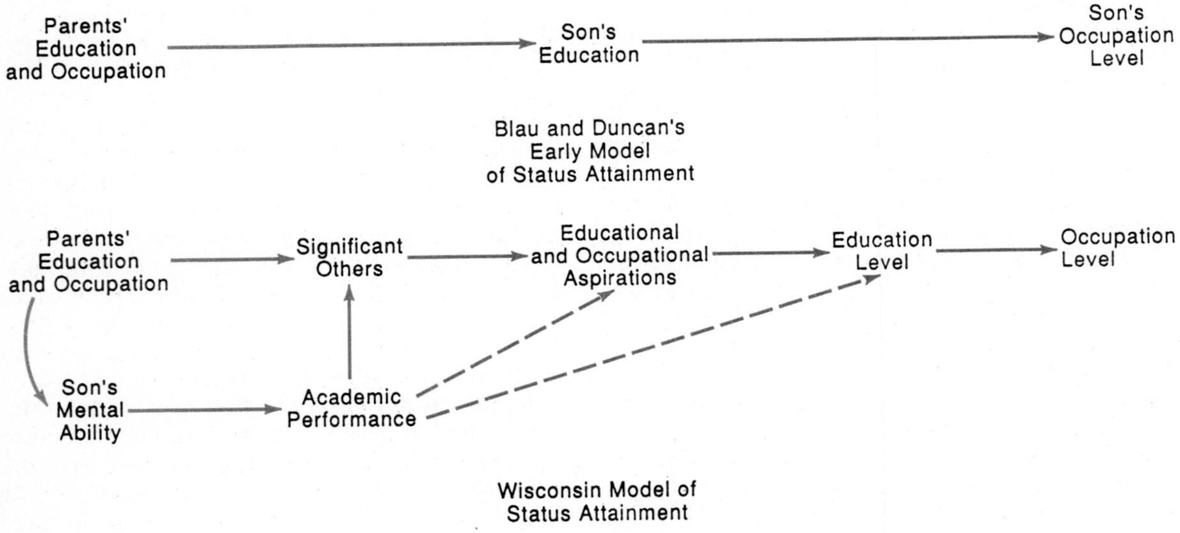

friends who expected to attend college. The parents' concern that their son or daughter do well in school contributed to mental ability and also the selection of significant others. All of this, then, led to college completion (with a major in chemical engineering) and, thus, the high level of occupational attainment.

Status attainment models indicate that *both* achievement and ascriptive factors are important in influencing where people are placed in the stratification system. For example, achievement factors like aspirations and academic performance strongly influence where people end up. But aspirations and educational performance are also heavily influenced by family class background. Research that has reanalyzed the data from several studies of the attainment process concludes that about 50 percent of what determines where people end up in the class system is related to family background. Jencks (1979, p. 82) concludes from this study that "if we define 'equal opportunity' as a situation in which sons born into different families have the same chances of success, our data show that America comes nowhere near achieving it." In other words, in the process of getting ahead, those with parents already ahead have the edge.

The Allocation Process. Research on the status attainment process has helped us understand much about what influences where people are placed in the class system. However, there are some important weaknesses in this line of research.

1. Even with the many variables measured in the research (and only the major variables were described above), they have been able to explain only a small amount of what accounts for occupational attainment. Much of what influences why some people attain higher positions and some people do not has yet to be specified with this research (Jencks et al., 1972). Roughly, of all the effects on occupational attainment, the status attainment models have explained only about half.

2. Research is now beginning to indicate that the Wisconsin model may not apply to every group in the society. Different regions of the country, types of industries, and different levels of economic development may produce different processes of attain-

ing class positions (Grusky, 1983; Mare, 1981; Stolzenberg, 1978).

3. What the above implies is an even more important criticism, that the status attainment research has *considered only individual characteristics* (for example, human capital) as affecting who gets ahead (Lord and Falk, 1980; Horan, 1978). But much research has now shown important structural effects on who gets ahead and who does not.

These studies specifying how social structure influences the achievement process are important for two reasons. First, because of the inability of status attainment models to explain much of why people get ahead, these structural studies contribute additional knowledge on this question. Second, they indicate that the view that an individual is "relatively free to move within the social system, his attainments being determined by what he chooses to do and how well he does it" is very misleading (Kerckhoff, 1976). We must recognize there is a complex social structure that restricts or increases people's options, and the process of attainment is therefore not just a matter of human capital.

For these reasons an *allocation perspective* has become a popular counter to the standard status attainment perspective. This allocation perspective recognizes (1) that there is a macro social structure that strongly determines the opportunities people may have, and (2) that classes are often in conflict over the allocation process.

We consider the first point with an example. Let's assume two brothers with equal "human capital" (education, occupational skill, motivation, etc.) leave home to seek their fortune. After receiving an MBA, one brother begins work with a large corporation producing aircraft engines in California. This brother performs his job well and is promoted through the ranks of the company, ending his career as a vice president. The second brother begins work with a small retailing firm in Michigan after receiving a master's degree in marketing. A couple of years after he joins the firm, the 1981–1982 recession hits the industrial Northeast. The retail firm where he is employed is never able to show extensive profits or growth after the recession. Ten years later the firm is acquired by a large national retail firm. This second brother reaches retirement years as a regional manager of the firm's chain of department stores in a midwestern district. The first brother retires as a vice president of a major corporation where he had a salary of $300,000 a year, not including bonuses, stock options, and the like. The second brother retires as a district manager of a large retail corporation with a salary of $55,000 a year.

To what degree can the status attainment perspective help us understand the occupational careers of these two brothers? Because their family backgrounds and human capital are virtually the same, the status attainment perspective is of limited help. And this example is not untypical because research has shown that siblings more often than not have widely differing occupational attainments in their lives (Jencks et al., 1972). We must understand that the life chances of these two brothers were shaped by structural conditions largely beyond their control. Specifically, one brother was advantaged because of the size of the company that employed him, regional differences in economic growth and expansion of the defense industry.

Several studies have shown these types of macro structural conditions have an important impact on the occupational chances of individuals. For example, the dual economy we considered in our economics chapter has an impact. People employed in the core industries have greater mobility chances, and human capital (education level and so on) will help them more than people employed in periphery (or secondary) firms (Tolbert, 1982, 1983; Jacobs, 1983). People employed in larger firms have more mobility chances because these firms have more levels in which people can rise (Stolzenberg, 1978). People with a lower-class background may have more opportunities to advance in a region of the country that is just beginning economic growth rather than in a region that began its economic growth long ago (Grusky, 1983). In short, to a large degree *positions are allocated to people in terms of the needs and characteristics of the corporate economy at the place and time people seek employment.*

The second major point of the allocation perspective is that class conflict over who gets the better positions is very much in evidence. The status attainment perspective considers only individual-level competition over who gets ahead. People compete through acquiring more human capital. But the allocation perspective recognizes that different groups would like to see the rules of the "attainment game" altered. For example, how much importance should be given to achievement tests in awarding jobs? How much importance should be given to years of education, type of education, years of experience, and so on? And equally important, there are usually many informal or hidden rules that influence who gets ahead. The main point is that different groups are advantaged with respect to some of these rules but not others. Thus, groups are in conflict over which rules should be used in the attainment process.

Because education is related to occupational attainment, much of the class conflict centers on the place of education. We examine this subject in more detail later, but here we consider a few examples. There is an interesting situation of educational inflation; a few decades ago a high school education would get you a solid, middle-class occupation. Today that same occupation requires a college education. One explanation of this change is that as the level of education increased in the society, the jobs dominated by the middle class were redefined to require a college degree. This redefinition helped middle-class sons and daughters because now working-class children usually finish high school and middle-class children are more likely to finish college (Collins, 1971, 1979). Other research has found that children with middle-class life-styles are more likely to be selected and sponsored for educational success by public school officials (DiMaggio, 1982). This suggests that these people believe students who are more like themselves are more capable. In other words, there is conflict over images and life-styles, with students from the middle class (especially upper middle class) favored in competition for educational achievement.

When it is said there is class conflict over the allocation of jobs, we are not suggesting overt class war. But there are conflicting interests over achievement criteria because some rules favor one class over another. And even when individuals from lower-class backgrounds are able to move into higher-class positions, it can be called **sponsored mobility** (Domhoff, 1970, 1983); that is, recruitment is selective to ensure that those brought into the top positions will be supportive of the class inequalities and privilege attached to top positions. Put another way, we would expect to find few top officers recruited to General Motors who are in favor of extensive income equality in the United States, restrictions on corporate class power, and greater labor union influence in the corporate boardrooms.

POVERTY

It is time to examine the bottom of the class system — poverty. We have seen that the percentage of the population at the bottom of the stratification system has been reduced as we moved from agrarian to industrial societies. But though reduced in numbers, the existence of poverty has certainly not been eliminated, and it is probably correct to say that the poor will always be with us, if by this we mean that someone must always be at the bottom. The questions, however, are (1) how many people will be down there, and (2) how far down will they be in comparison with the rest of the population? The gap between the average person's standard of living in the United States and that of the poor has been growing in recent decades, and a larger percentage of our population lives in poverty than in almost any other industrial nation (George and Lawson, 1980).

The Extent of Poverty in America

The number of people considered poor in the United States is a highly political question. Political elites wish to improve their image by showing how things have improved under their leadership — that is, figures that may indicate that poverty has increased or remained high are not welcome. Because of the political nature of the question, we are fortunate to have a government bureaucracy, the Census Bureau, that is able to collect more or less objective information on the extent of poverty. There certainly has been political pressure on the Census Bureau to change the way unemployment and poverty are measured. And the Census Bureau has made some changes in the way it measures unemployment

over the years to make unemployment appear lower (Leggett and Gioglio, 1978). Recently the bureau has been under pressure to redefine how income is figured when assessing the extent of poverty. As a result of this pressure we are now given two sets of poverty figures, as we will see below. However, though the poverty figures we have are to some degree manipulated for political reasons, at least we know how this is done and can still use these figures to understand the extent of poverty from one period to another.

The Poverty Line. In this country the extent of poverty is measured by what is called a *poverty line.* This poverty line is basically an **economic definition of poverty;** it attempts to estimate how much it costs a family of a certain size to obtain basic necessities. When the costs of basic necessities are estimated, the costs refer to the cheapest items that will keep people in good health (at least in the short term). For example, when considering the cost of food it is assumed that the poor will eat cheaper foods like beans, potatoes, and rice — what is called an emergency diet. The current poverty line assumes that the poor will spend about 50 cents per meal per person (Blumberg, 1980, p. 94).

Considering the cost of all basic necessities, the 1986 poverty line was established at $11,203 a year for a family of four people. This poverty line has been measured in roughly the same way since 1959; thus we can obtain a fairly accurate picture of the trends in the rate of poverty since that time. In 1986 the percent of the population living in poverty was 13.6 percent, or about 32.4 million people. As you can see in Figure 12.3, the rate of poverty in America shows a rather interesting pattern. It was reduced substantially between 1959 and 1970, then stabilized through the 1970s at around 11 to 12 percent of the population. Beginning in 1980, however, the poverty line shot up to the 15 percent level by 1982. We will consider why these changes in the poverty rate occurred after we consider criticisms of the poverty line.

Criticisms of the Poverty Line. There are criticisms of the standard poverty line from both conservatives and liberals in the United States. As you might ex-

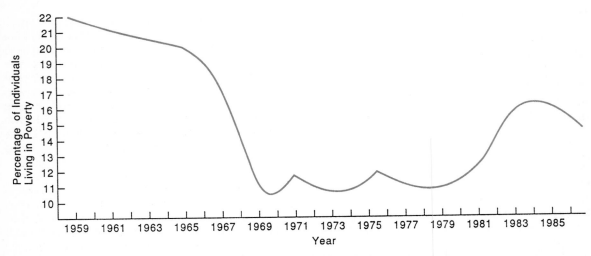

FIGURE 12.3. Trends in the poverty rate in the United States, 1959–1986. *(Source: U.S. Bureau of Census,* Money Income and Poverty Status of Families and Persons in the U.S.: 1986, Current Population Reports, *1987.)*

pect, the liberal argument is that the poverty line is drawn too low and actually much more than 13.6 percent of the population is poor in this country. Conservatives, on the other hand, believe the poverty line is drawn too high and actually much less than 13.6 percent of the population is poor.

A major point of the liberal criticism is that the level of basic necessities considered when determining the poverty line is too low. For example, the 50 cents per meal per person is believed to be less than adequate. The economists who originally developed this poverty line described their estimate of food costs as an emergency diet, one that would keep people alive but not very healthy in the long run (Miller, 1971, p. 119).

Another criticism is that the poverty line is not an adequate measure of the **relative nature of poverty.** It is not just important to know how many basic necessities people can buy, but also how their standard of living compares with that of the average person in the society. In this relative sense, the poor today are much poorer than they were two decades ago. This is because the poverty line has not been raised with the cost of living as rapidly as the aver-

age income in America has increased (*Focus,* 1984, p. 1; Blumberg, 1980).

The conservative argument is not so much that the poverty line itself is determined inaccurately, but that the measures of income used by the Bureau of Census should be expanded. With the standard Census definition, all cash income is considered when placing a family above or below the poverty line. Cash income includes all money from any source — a job, investments, rent, royalties, welfare payments, pension benefits, and so on. However, since the 1960s there has been more government welfare aid in the form of income-in-kind benefits such as food stamps and health care (Medicaid). Thus, the argument is that the value of these kinds of aid should be added to a family's cash income when determining the rate of poverty.

As we can see from Table 12.9, the rate of poverty is lower when considering income-in-kind as well as cash income. For example, in 1982 the standard income definition (Census definition) showed poverty rate at 15.0 percent, whereas the adjusted income definition showed poverty at 8.8 percent of the population.

TABLE 12.9. *Trends in the rate of poverty with three different definitions of income, 1965–1982 (%)*

Year	Census income*	Adjusted income**	Pretransfer income†
1965	15.6	12.1	21.3
1968	12.8	9.9	18.2
1972	11.9	6.2	19.2
1974	11.6	7.2	20.3
1976	11.8	6.7	21.0
1978	11.4	n/a	20.2
1979	11.7	6.1	20.5
1980	13.0	n/a	21.9
1981	14.0	n/a	23.1
1982	15.0	8.8	24.0
Percent change			
1965–1978	−26.9	−49.6	− .2
1978–1982	+31.6	+44.3	+18.8

* Includes income from all private sector sources (such as employment income, royalties, investments) as well as government cash transfer payments (such as Social Security and Welfare benefits).
** Includes all income sources in Census Income column, plus the value of income-in-kind transfer payments.
† Includes only private sector cash income sources (such as employment income, royalties, investments income).
SOURCE: Adapted from *Focus,* 1984, p. 2.

There are, however, several problems with establishing the value of income-in-kind benefits and using this to estimate the rate of poverty. For example, how do we value the medical benefits from the Medicaid program for the poor? Do we determine how often the poor are ill and get low-cost medical care? Or do we attempt to determine what they would pay for medical care without the Medicaid program? There is the additional problem that all the poor do not receive equal benefits from the income-in-kind aid program. Finally, if we are going to include income-in-kind in the income measure, we should be consistent and subtract taxes paid by the poor. Currently, this is not done even though families with income about equal to the poverty line pay about 10 percent of their income to taxes (*Focus,* 1984).

Trends in the Rate of Poverty. We now come to an interesting question about the trend in poverty since 1959. Why did the poverty rate drop between 1959 and 1970, then increase since 1980? This pattern cannot be explained primarily by the rate of unemployment or inflation in the two and a half decades since 1959. Overall the rate of unemployment was rising as poverty was going down from 1959 to 1980. And inflation was most extensive in the 1970s when the rate of poverty stabilized.

We can return to Table 12.9 for data answering our questions. I have explained the definition of census income and adjusted income (including income-in-kind). Also included in this table is "pretransfer" income — cash income that does not include income from welfare aid. When we look down the pretransfer column from 1965 to 1980, we find a rather steady rate of poverty at around 20 percent of the population (with a jump to 24 percent with the major recession of 1981–1982). But when we look down the other two columns measuring poverty, we find a steady decrease in the poverty rate until 1980–1982. Why has the poverty rate gone down in these two columns compared with the last column? Quite simply, because welfare benefits were increased, not because the poor got jobs or higher-paying jobs. Why did the rate of poverty go up after 1980?

As Table 12.9 indicates, and as other detailed research shows (*Focus,* 1984), poverty increased in the 1980s, in part because of the welfare cuts of the Reagan administration. Equally important, as a group the poor became poorer in the 1980s. This is indicated by a 7 percent increase in the number of people below 75 percent of the poverty line (*Focus,* 1984, p. 7).

It is true that unemployment was up during the Reagan years in office. However, the rate of unemployment was up during other periods during the 1970s without significant jumps in the rate of poverty because welfare benefits were more likely to protect the unemployed and underemployed. Between 1978 and 1982 the number of people in poverty increased by 31.6 percent, considering cash income from welfare and job income (column 2 in Table 12.9), whereas poverty increased by 44.3 percent considering the adjusted income column.

There was a larger jump in poverty with the adjusted income column most likely because the income-in-kind welfare programs were cut more extensively during Reagan's term of office.

The Causes of Poverty

As with the question of how much poverty exists, attempts to explain the causes of poverty arouse many ideologically sensitive issues. In a country like the United States with strong values of individualism and equality of opportunity, the poor are often blamed for their condition, as national polls have indicated (Feagin, 1975). Considering what I hope you have already learned about the relationship between human behavior and broader social forces, you should see that an explanation of poverty that simply blames the poor is very naive. Even if the poor were different from others in important ways, we cannot assume their "differentness" has caused their poverty. In fact, the causal direction is probably reversed, with poverty producing any individual differences in the poor compared with other people.

Again we raise questions of social forces in the society that shape human behavior considered in earlier chapters.

The Distribution of Poverty. Table 12.10 clearly indicates that poverty is not equally distributed in the United States. In contrast to the 15 percent poverty rate for the total U.S. population in 1982, many other groups had much higher rates of poverty. Especially important is the high rate of poverty among minorities, children, and female-headed households. In fact, the most rapidly growing poverty rate is found among female-headed households. In 1979 the poverty rate among female-headed households was 34.9 percent, compared with the 1982 rate of 40.6 percent just four years later. Currently, about one-half of all the poor in the United States live in these female-headed households. This condition has led to the term the **feminization of poverty.**

Another characteristic of the poor that is surprising to most people is their work involvement. About half of the heads of households of poor families are employed (U.S. Bureau of Census, 1983). If we excluded the female heads of households with young

TABLE 12.10. *Selected characteristics of persons below the poverty level: 1982 and 1979*

	Poverty rate		
Characteristic	1982 (%)	1979 (%)	Percentage point difference
All persons	15.0	11.7	+3.3
All families	13.6	10.2	+3.4
Related children under 18 years	21.3	16.0	+5.3
In families with female householder, no husband present	40.6	34.9	+5.7
In all other families	9.1	6.3	+2.8
Unrelated individuals	23.1	21.9	+1.2
Under 65 years	15.0	11.3	+3.7
65 years and over	14.6	15.2	−0.6
In metropolitan areas	13.7	10.7	+3.0
In central cities	19.9	15.7	+4.2
Outside central cities	9.3	7.2	+2.1
In nonmetropolitan areas	17.8	13.8	+4.0

SOURCE: Adapted from *Focus,* 1984, p. 4.

children, this figure would be even higher. The problem for these poor families is that their jobs are not secure and pay a very low wage. For example, the head of a four-person family could work 40 hours a week, 52 weeks a year, at minimum wage, and still be below the poverty line.

It is also important to mention the rate of movement in and out of poverty. In contrast to common beliefs, most of the poor are not poor for life. Several studies have shown that only about one-half of the poor are in poverty every year of, say, a five- to ten-year period (Coe, 1978; Hill, 1981). Similarly, studies have shown that most of the children of poor families are not poor in their adult years (Evanson, 1981). *However,* when the poor are able to escape poverty, they *do not move very far above the poverty line.*

These figures showing movement out of poverty can be considered in two ways. On the more positive side, many poor people do have the chance to escape poverty, if not by very far. But on the negative side the figures also indicate that *many more people than 15 percent of the population experience poverty* over an extended period of time. For example, over a ten-year period, while the rate of poverty remains about 15 percent, this 15 percent figure does not represent exactly the same people each year. In a given year, some of the poor are moving a bit above the poverty line while others who previously were not much above poverty are now moving down into poverty. About *24 percent* of all the people in the United States have lived in poverty at least one year in the past ten years (Hill, 1981).

There are many other important characteristics of the poor that I mention only briefly. Most poor people have a strong motivation to work, even when faced with the situation where welfare gives them about as much money if they stop working (*Focus,* 1984, p. 4). This was clearly shown in 1982 when the Reagan welfare cuts (involving work incentives) presented many of the working poor with a situation in which they could receive about as much money from welfare as they were making on their job, but only if they quit their job. To the surprise of most people in the United States, most of these people kept their jobs and rejected welfare.

This photo shows one of the welfare hotels where the public assistance agency of New York City, the Human Resources Administration, houses homeless recipients of welfare. Many of the residents are living in filth and conditions of overcrowding at a cost of more than $100 per night per room. Some work or participate in workfare programs. How can individuals escape the culture of poverty in such living conditions? Is part of the answer adequate public housing? (© Kirk Condyles/Impact Visuals)

There is a subgroup of the poor who do fit many of the negative stereotypes. Sometimes referred to as the **underclass,** or hard-core poor, this group is likely to have behavioral problems, long-term or multigenerational poverty, a high involvement in crime, along with many other negative characteristics. Marx referred to this group as the "lumpenproletariat." However, this underclass is estimated to account for only 15 to 20 percent of those people classified as poor in the United States (Auletta, 1983)—less than 3 percent of the population.

Theories of Poverty. We are now ready to consider some of the primary theories designed to explain the causes of poverty. Specifically, we will briefly examine the culture of poverty theory, the situational theory, and structural-conflict theory. In comparing these theories of poverty a key point is this: If we want to explain why *most* people are poor, we need to understand how the more general system of social stratification operates to distribute rewards unequally. The poor are poor because they are at the bottom in this system.

Until recently, the most respected theory of poverty fit model A in Figure 12.4. Made famous by Oscar Lewis (1959, 1966), this **culture of poverty** theory contains three basic points. First, it recognizes that economic conditions (no jobs, low pay, etc.) are at the root of poverty, at least originally (thus, the dashed arrow). Second, as the result of long-term poverty, the poor adjust to their condition by developing a subculture with unique values and life-styles. Third, this subculture then produces people with individual characteristics that make it difficult for the poor to become nonpoor.

For example, it is said that the poor in this subculture of poverty will develop a "present time ori-

FIGURE 12.4. Theories of the causes of poverty.

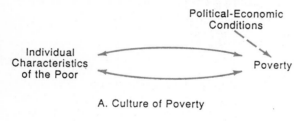

A. Culture of Poverty

B. Situational View

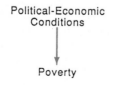

C. Structural-Conflict View

entation" that helps them cope with their poverty by "living one day at a time," not worrying about the future, and taking advantage of any chance to be happy or find pleasure at the present time. People with this value orientation would not be expected to work for improving their future standing by sacrificing in the present (e.g., seeking more education, job skills, saving money). Thus, people with this value orientation would be expected to remain poor even if opportunities to improve their position existed.

As you can probably see, this culture of poverty theory fits the general negative view of the poor held by most people in our society, with the exception that this theory recognizes the roots of poverty must be traced to economic conditions. And because, as we have already seen, most of the poor do not fit this negative stereotype, the culture of poverty theory must be rejected. Most of the poor want more education and jobs, and in fact those able to do so are looking for work or are employed. However, what can be called the underclass, that 15 to 20 percent of the poor with behavioral problems, can be understood with the culture of poverty theory. They are often the victims of generations of poverty or other social problems that leave them with psychological damage contributing to their long-term poverty.

The **situational view of poverty** shown in model B of Figure 12.4 is a rather limited theory designed to counter the culture of poverty theory rather than explain the causes of poverty in general. The main point of the situational view of poverty is that (1) to the degree the poor are different in behavior, (2) they are different only because of their immediate problems associated with living in poverty, and (3) not because of any deeply held values (Rodman, 1963; Della Fave, 1974). Thus, the situational view argues that poverty can be reduced by creating more jobs, better-paying jobs, and more educational opportunities. The problem, in other words, lies with the characteristics of the society and not with the characteristics of the poor themselves. As shown in model B, there is no causal arrow coming back from the characteristics of the poor to poverty.

Finally, a **structural-conflict view** is concerned almost exclusively with the political-economic conditions in the society that help produce and perpetuate poverty rather than the individual characteristics of the poor (see model C in Figure 12.4). This theoretical perspective is not designed to explain the individual characteristics of people in poverty. The theoretical perspective is called "structural" because it is concerned with macro-level aspects of the society. It is called a "conflict" perspective because it argues that the distribution of rewards is based on a process of conflict in the stratification system. The poor are poor because they are the losers in this process of conflict.

Many structural conditions contribute to poverty in our society, but the following are among the most important in this theoretical perspective.

1. The occupational system helps determine class position and the distribution of rewards in industrial societies. Changes in this occupational system have led to what economists call "structural unemployment" — poverty. For example, many of the poor in the United States today are former agricultural workers or their sons and daughters. Especially since World War II, farm mechanization has rapidly reduced the need for these workers. With no other job skills they remain unemployed or in the lowest-paying jobs. Other jobs are also being eliminated, as we saw in the economics chapter.

2. A structural feature of capitalist industrial societies that often helps produce and perpetuate poverty is related to the necessity of "business cycles." No one has yet found a way of preventing the cycle of economic expansion, then recession in a capitalist economy. Unemployment, therefore, often increases in times of a business downturn, then falls in times of business expansion, especially in this nation. But it is important to recognize that the cycles of unemployment are not simply unintended outcomes of these business cycles. A business expansion that lasts "too long" often brings inflation; an increase in unemployment usually brings less inflation. (As we saw in the previous chapter, the negative relationship between unemployment and inflation is known as the Phillips Curve [Phillips, 1958; Piven and Cloward, 1982, pp. 22 – 44].) Thus, unemployment is often consciously produced by government policy to control inflation.

The relation between business cycles and unem-

ployment rates is not inevitable. In Japan, for example, this is much less the case. Corporations in Japan do everything possible to keep their workers employed. Both corporate executives and workers feel greater responsibility toward one another (Nakane, 1970), which is both a cause and an outcome of the Japanese corporate attitude toward protecting workers' jobs.

3. In a similar manner poverty is related to the existence of what Marx called the **industrial reserve army.** This pool of unemployed or underemployed people is functional for the profit stability of the more affluent in the society. The industrial reserve army consists of those people on the bottom of the occupational structure who can be laid off to protect corporate profits in times of economic stagnation, then rehired when needed for increased profits in times of economic expansion. But this industrial reserve army also keeps wages lower. If worker wage demands become "too high," then employers can simply refuse higher pay and turn to this large pool of unemployed for new workers.

4. Other economic changes that contribute to poverty have already been considered in the economics chapter. For example, the loss of jobs with multinational corporate investment abroad certainly helps contribute to poverty in this nation. Also, the uneven economic development and the dual economy in the nation help explain some of the poverty due to low wages and less secure employment in periphery industries.

5. Changes in the U.S. family and economic discrimination against women have important effects on poverty. The biggest increase in poverty in recent years has been with female-headed households. A continuation of the high U.S. divorce rate and more women either unemployed or in the lowest-paying jobs, will surely bring more poverty.

Class Conflict and Welfare Expansion

It is readily apparent that the poor in America lack many resources to influence others. They have no money for campaign contributions or lobby organizations, they are less likely to vote than other groups, and they are often unemployed; thus a traditional strike would be impossible or ineffective in bringing influence. Why then has a welfare system developed in this country to provide some of the poor with some protection?

The welfare system in the United States developed primarily in the 1930s during the Great Depression. Before this time there were local welfare programs that lacked many resources and could not serve many of those in need (Piven and Cloward, 1971). A few state welfare programs developed in the early 1900s, but a relatively broad-based welfare system came in with the Social Security Act of 1935.

The next major period in the history of U.S. welfare came in the 1960s. During this decade many new aid programs were established and most of the old aid programs expanded. For example, between 1950 and 1960, one of the main welfare programs, Aid for Families with Dependent Children (AFDC), increased the number of recipients by 17 percent. But during the 1960s the welfare program increased

by 225 percent (Piven and Cloward, 1971, p. 341). What happened?

Let's consider one answer, that increased need is responsible for welfare expansion. As Figure 12.5 indicates, this answer will not fit. If we use unemployment as an indicator of need, we find that need was certainly up in the 1930s, but it doesn't fit elsewhere. During the 1890s in the United States, unemployment was as high as 19 percent, and during the 1960s, unemployment was low. In neither case does this fit a pattern of increased aid only during times of increased need.

Extensive research now shows that welfare during the post-World War II period increased with rebellion by the poor (Isaac and Kelly, 1981; Betz, 1974; Schram and Turbett, 1983; Jennings, 1983). Other evidence indicates the welfare system expanded in the 1930s and not before for the same reason (Piven and Cloward, 1971; Shaffer and Kerbo, 1983). As shown in Figure 12.5, as protest

FIGURE 12.5. Relationship between unemployment, protest, and welfare expansion. *(Source: Adapted from Shaffer and Kerbo, 1983.)*

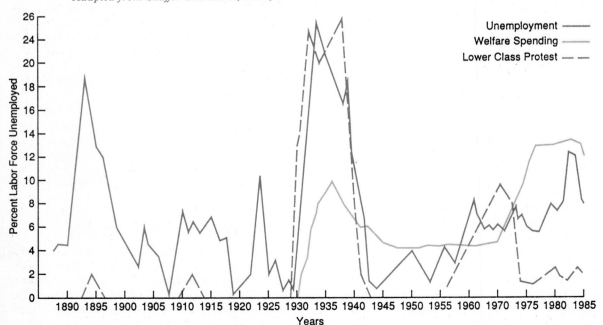

and rioting increased in the 1930s and 1960s, so did welfare. As noted above, the poor do not have many means of influence, but they do have some like protest.

Unlike the 1930s, however, welfare spending did not soon go down in the later 1960s or 1970s. There were finally some reductions in the 1980s under Reagan, but a 10 percent cut in the number of people receiving money from the AFDC program is not much compared with the 225 percent increase in the 1960s. One explanation for this altered pattern in the ups and downs of welfare is related to the growing power of labor unions. Since the 1930s labor unions have had legal support in the United States. But especially since the 1960s labor unions have achieved more influence in the political system. And they have used this influence to support an expanded welfare system. Such an expanded welfare system is important to the working class as a cushion against unemployment (Piven and Cloward, 1982).

Thus, unlike in the past, the welfare system does not only respond to riots by the poor. Through more traditional political means, labor organizations have been able to maintain pressure for a welfare system that has not been cut back as drastically in the 1980s as in the past.

CHAPTER SUMMARY

KEY TERMS

real income, 328
wealth, 329
embourgeoisement, 338
proletarianization, 339
intragenerational mobility, 339
intergenerational mobility, 339
structural mobility, 340
status attainment process, 340
sponsored mobility, 344

economic definition of poverty, 345
relative nature of poverty, 346
feminization of poverty, 348
underclass, 349
culture of poverty, 350
situational view of poverty, 350
structural-conflict view, 350
industrial reserve army, 351

Content

Of all the inequalities in capitalist industrial societies, income inequality is one of the most important. In the United States the level of inequality has been extensive and rather stable for at least several decades. Wealth inequality is in some ways even more important because great wealth brings other forms of influence and because wealth is more easily inherited. Although the top 20 percent of the people in the United States receive about 41 percent of the income, the top 20 percent of the population (in terms of wealth) hold over 76 percent of the wealth.

Many other forms of inequality are also extensive in industrial societies, though often difficult to measure as precisely as income and wealth. In fact, almost anything people value is usually distributed unequally through the class system.

Because a person's class position presents situations, problems, and other experiences that are not always shared with people in other class positions, we find unique class subcultures and life-styles in industrial societies. Some of these subcultural differences have little importance, but others operate in subtle ways to maintain class barriers, reducing the acceptance of lower-class individuals who try to move into a higher-class position. Important class subcultural differences can be found in family roles, childhood socialization, sociability and community participation, and religious beliefs.

Historically, there have also been important class subcultural differences between the old wealthy families in the United States and the new rich. There is some evidence that these differences between the old rich and the new rich are being reduced, but there continue to be some important differences.

One of the most important subjects in the study of social stratification is social mobility and the attainment process. As in most industrial societies, there is rather extensive social mobility toward the center of the stratification system in the United States. Also, because of economic change and growth, there has been slightly more upward than downward social mobility. When we look to opposite ends of the stratification system, however, the rate of social mobility is much less. People at the top are very likely to pass their advantages to their offspring, whereas people at the bottom find that their children are likely to inherit their low position.

There are two conflicting schools of thought on the subject of class attainment, or why people move up or down in the stratification system. Some sociologists focus on what is called a *status attainment process* that gives greater recognition to the characteristics of individuals in this process. Educational attainment, of course, is a key in this process. But many social psychological variables influence how family background affects educational attainment. Although these studies have shown that achievement opportunities do exist in the United States, about 50 percent of the influence on class attainment comes from family background (showing evidence of continued ascriptive influence in the class system).

In contrast to the above, many sociologists stress that an *allocation process* is more important in understanding class placement. There are many structural conditions in the society that influence a person's life chances, influences that individuals are unable to control. Changes in the economy, international competition, the type of firm where people work, among many other variables not related to individual characteristics, shape the process that allocates positions to people.

Although the level of income inequality has remained rather stable in the United States, at least until the 1980s, there have been significant changes in the rate of poverty. From 1959 the percentage of Americans living in poverty dropped from around 22 percent to 11 percent in the 1970s. However, this poverty rate again increased to over 15 percent by 1982, dropping only slightly afterward. High unemployment and reductions in welfare spending have contributed to this increase in poverty.

Poverty is not equally distributed to all groups in the society. Minorities and especially people living in female-headed households are the most likely to be poor in the United States. The rapid increase in poverty among female-headed households in recent years (called the feminization of poverty) has led to the situation where about 50 percent of the poor today live in such households.

There are three main theories of the causes of poverty — culture of poverty theory, situational theory, and structural-conflict theory. Structural-conflict theory, which focuses on political-economic factors and class conflict, is increasingly supported when considering the causes of poverty.

El gran sabo

Coca-Cola

With Latin America currently mired in a serious debt crisis and seemingly chronic inflation, with Africa suffering increasingly frequent droughts and famines, and with the highly populated parts of South Asia experiencing economic stagnation, the prospects for the rest of the century appear to indicate that, if anything, the gap between the rich and the poor will grow even faster.

— Daniel Chirot, Social Change in the Modern Era

Americans, in general, tend to know less about other nations or international events than do people of other industrial nations. Most people in the United States, of course, know their government is often in conflict with the Soviet Union, though they do not always know exactly why. For example, less than 30 percent of the U.S. adult population can identify which side the U.S. government favors in political conflicts in Central American countries. Such lack of knowledge can be tragic when the population is easily led into war or economic policies that harm their interests.

Part of this ignorance is no doubt due to our isolation and past self-sufficiency compared with other peoples. The figures in Table 13.1 show both a cause and effect of this lack of international knowledge. From a sample of 29 newspapers around the world ranked in terms of world news coverage (as a percent of all news) we do not find a single U.S. newspaper until we get down to the *New York Times*, ranked 22nd. The other two U.S. newspapers on the list (*Los Angeles Times* and *St. Louis Post-Dispatch*) are ranked last. And it is not just the rank — consider the percentage of foreign news coverage. Although the *New York Times* has about 14 percent world news coverage, *LeMonde* of France has over 48 percent and the *London Times* has 40 percent.

Although the American population was more isolated at one time, the situation is changing quite rapidly. We buy more and more products from other countries, and other countries are buying more of our products. Other countries, however, are buying far less from the United States than we buy from them. In 1986 the U.S. trade deficit reached over $160 billion — an all-time record. The situation may have improved slightly in 1988 because of the large fall in the value of the dollar against the other major world currencies, but about $160 billion continues to leave the United States every year.

There are many reasons why this trade imbalance exists, but one reason can be found in our lack of knowledge of other countries. Unlike the Japanese, for example, American business people do not have adequate knowledge of how to do business in foreign nations. Japan is now one of the most important economic partners of the United States. *All* Japanese young people must pass tough English language exams to enter a Japanese college. In the United States it was estimated that in the 1970s only 500 American professors *in the whole nation* could speak any Japanese (Reischauer, 1977, p. 381).

To make this situation worse, there is a world system outside U.S. borders that is rapidly changing in many ways that will produce problems for the United States. For one thing, there is a very large gap between the standard of living in rich nations and poor nations. This gap is increasing, producing an unstable situation in much of the world. Millions of people are starving to death in Africa. After Americans view gruesome pictures of mass starvation on television, they become deeply troubled and send aid to the starving. But it is always too little, too late. Because of our ignorance of how the world economic system operates, we tend to believe this aid is all that is needed. In fact, as we will see, this aid seldom helps very much, and in some cases it actually harms the long-term economic chances of poor people in Third World nations.

My goal in this chapter is to present you with a basic understanding of what can be called a world system. We begin by considering the major characteristics of this world system, then briefly consider

TABLE 13.1. *Foreign news coverages in selected newspapers around the world*

Rank	Newspaper	Nation	Percent of foreign news of total news space
1	South China Morning Post	Hong Kong	60.8
2	LeMonde	France	48.5
3	Times	Britain	40.1
4	Nation	Thailand	39.2
5	Nan Yang	Malaysia	38.1
6	Sin Chew Jit Poh	Singapore	37.0
7	Straits Times	Singapore	35.2
8	Australian	Australia	3.4
9	Age	Australia	29.8
10	Times of India	India	29.6
11	Asahi Shimbun	Japan	28.7
12	Renmin Ribao	China	27.5
13	Sing Tao Jih Pao	Hong Kong	26.6
14	Kompas	Indonesia	25.1
15	Pusan Ilbo	South Korea	24.5
16	Donga Ilbo	South Korea	21.6
17	Harapan	Indonesia	21.1
18	Utisan Melayu	Malaysia	20.3
19	Daily Mirror	Britain	19.1
20	Provençal	France	18.0
21	Bulletin Today	Philippines	14.6
22	New York Times	United States	14.1
23	Nishinihon Shimbun	Japan	14.0
24	Kochi Shimbun	Japan	13.9
25	Daily Express	Philippines	13.8
26	Wen Hui Pao	China	13.6
27	Thai Rath	Thailand	11.6
28	Los Angeles Times	United States	9.0
29	St. Louis Post-Dispatch	United States	7.5

SOURCE: Japan Times (October 17, 1984).

its historical development. From this we turn to the place of rich nations in this world system, and then to the poor nations.

Finally, some things you will read in this chapter may bother you. The United States is a very generous nation—helping the poor in other countries, taking in refugees, and so forth. But if you follow international events at all you may be puzzled to see that a large part of the outside world holds much contempt for the United States. They are more likely than American citizens to see some of the negative side of American international relations. This negative side is also presented in this chapter.

CHARACTERISTICS OF THE WORLD SYSTEM

We can no longer fully understand any modern society without considering its place within the world system. As we will see, diverse things such as economic growth, urbanization, and population trends are influenced by a country's position in the world system.

When referring to a **world system**, we are concerned with a set of relationships among nations, much as we are concerned with a set of relationships among groups of people in a society that can be called a social system (Wallerstein, 1974, 1980; Chirot, 1986). Like the relationships with groups in a society, these relationships we find among nations and world regions can be observed, are rather long-lasting, and have important outcomes. If you remember our discussion of sociograms, you can get a similar image with respect to the world system. The nations in this world system are tied together economically in many ways and have political, military, and even cultural links. Some nations in this system have more ties to others and more influence over others, just as some people do within a group. There are, of course, differences between a social system and a world system. For example, we find no worldwide political authority and the people do not share a common culture. But despite these differences, we will see many common characteristics between a social system within one nation and the world system.

More than anything else, at the base of the modern world system are *economic relations*. As the modern world system developed, major nations were reaching out to form economic ties with other nations. Much like economic relations among groups within a nation, we find that nations within this world system have differing economic roles. Some nations tend to specialize in certain economic activities, some nations in others. And like a domestic economic system, some nations are more dominant within the world system. In several respects, therefore, the world system is like an international stratification system, with nations in different "class positions" in this international stratification system. Some nations control more of the wealth and have extensive power over other nations; some nations have little control of the means of production in the world (even within their own territory) and are very dependent on other nations for basic necessities.

It is also important to recognize there is a *dynamic process of conflict* within this world system, much like class conflict within a nation. Nations in a disadvantaged position in the world system would like to change their position. And nations on top of the international "class system" are usually trying to gain further advantage as well as keep what they have. All this means there is a dynamic process of international conflict that can lead to change.

Considering nations as the unit of analysis in this world system can be misleading. It must not be assumed that all people within a nation have common interests. Some groups would like to continue the status quo of the nation within the world system; other groups find the status quo much to their disadvantage and would like to change their nation's position. Therefore, group differences within a nation must also be kept in mind to understand the conflict within the world system and within each nation.

Positions in the World System. **Core nations** are those most advantaged in the world system. These nations have extensive economic diversity — their economy is not centered around one or a few types of industries, but many. Core nations also have a more complex occupational structure with a relatively highly skilled labor force. In addition, core nations have strong, complex state institutions that help manage economic affairs internally and externally. Finally, core nations have many means of influence over noncore nations but are themselves relatively independent of outside control (Chirot, 1977, p. 9). (See Table 13.2 for examples of these nations.)

Similar to the lower class or working class within a particular country's stratification system are the **periphery nations** (or Third World Nations). Among the periphery nations we find those least economically diversified. Their primary economic activity tends to center around the extraction and export of raw materials. Because of very low wages in periphery nations, however, many multinational corporations move production there to use unskilled labor. There is commonly a wide division between wealthy elites and the poor masses, which also means a high level of income inequality. These nations have relatively weak state institutions, which are unable to control much of what happens within

TABLE 13.2. *Examples of core, semiperiphery, and periphery nations in the world system**

Core	Semiperiphery	Periphery
United States	Venezuela	Chad
United Kingdom	Argentina	Uganda
Canada	South Korea	Morocco
Netherlands	Ireland	Panama
Belgium	Finland	Bolivia
France	Saudi Arabia	Paraguay
Spain	Taiwan	Chile
West Germany	India	Haiti
Austria	Pakistan	Dominican Republic
Italy	Philippines	El Salvador
Japan		Nicaragua
		Thailand

* This table is a representative listing of nations in the structural positions in the world system. For a more complete list of 118 nations, see Snyder and Kick (1979, p. 1110). The partial list of nations in Table 13.2 is from Snyder and Kick's study using trade relations, military interventions, and diplomatic and treaty ties as indicators of world system positions.

and without the nation. Many periphery nations are police states, but a dominating military is not necessarily evidence of a strong state. On the contrary, it is often a weak state that must rely heavily on the military or secret police to maintain social order.

Semiperiphery nations represent those midway between core and periphery nations. These nations are moving toward industrialization and economic diversity but remain significantly behind core nations. Semiperiphery nations can also be considered midway between the core and periphery with respect to state strength, a complex occupational structure, national wealth, and income inequality.

As noted above, at the heart of the world system is a world economy. The core nations (through their major corporations) primarily own and control the major means of production in the world and perform the higher-level production tasks—they are more high-tech. The periphery nations own very little of the world's means of production (even when these are located in periphery nations) and often provide the less skilled labor for core nations. Thus, like a

class system within a nation, positions in the world system result in an unequal distribution of rewards and resources. Chirot (1977, p. 176) lists five important benefits accruing to core nations from their domination of the periphery: (1) access to a large quantity of raw materials, (2) cheap labor, (3) enormous profits from direct capital investments, (4) a market for exports, and (5) skilled professional labor through migration from the noncore.

The overall relationships among nations in the world system are indicated in Figure 13.1. Using a sample of 118 nations, Snyder and Kick (1979) examined the economic, military, diplomatic, and treaty ties among nations in the world system. They found that (1) there are many more links from core nations to all others, (2) periphery nations are almost exclusively tied to the core nations, and (3) the semiperiphery nations have extensive ties to the core and other semiperiphery nations, but not periphery nations.

A History of the Modern World System

It should be noted in beginning this section that Wallerstein (1974) argues that there have been only two types of world systems in existence. The first type has existed in several periods of history as what he calls a **world empire**. Although never covering such a large area of the world as today's *world economic system* (using Wallerstein's term), these world empires did include major parts of the world —for example, the Roman Empire, the Near Eastern empire of Alexander the Great, and the Egyptian and Babylonian empires much earlier.

The major distinction between world empire and a world system is that in the former a main goal is political, as well as economic, domination (Wallerstein, 1974, p. 60). As Chirot (1977, p. 20) puts it, "In classical empires, a political elite, as opposed to a business elite, dominated policy. This elite was composed of soldiers, glory-seeking emperors, and learned but antibusiness religious officials." Core elites in the modern world economy, by contrast, are economic elites concerned with economic *profit* rather than complete territorial control. A dominated country in the world economy is not usually

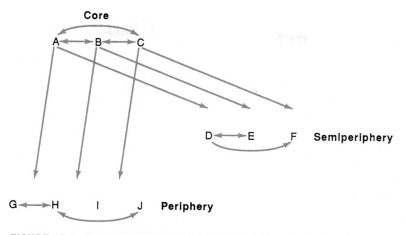

FIGURE 13.1. Outline of relationships between core, semiperiphery, and periphery in the world system. Arrows indicate Snyder and Kick's (1979) findings that (1) the core nations are tied extensively to each other, as well as the semiperiphery and periphery; (2) the semiperiphery are tied to the core and to some degree each other, but only very weakly tied to the periphery; and (3) the periphery have extensive ties only to the core, with few ties to the semiperiphery or each other.

controlled in every detail by core elites, occupied by a foreign army, or forced to pay taxes to the dominant country. All of this is rather inefficient in terms of the main goal, which is to extract profits for dominant core elites.

The distinction between world empire and world economy is also important in understanding the *development* of the world economic system. When conditions became ripe for a world economic system about 1450, Spain and Portugal took the lead in establishing economic ties to periphery nations. They were the first to explore the world for new territories and establish extensive overseas colonies. But Spain and Portugal soon lost their early lead and never became dominant core nations as did England, the Netherlands, and the United States in later centuries. Primarily this was because the latter nations learned a lesson that Spain and Portugal did not; it becomes too expensive to dominate many countries politically and militarily around the world (Wallerstein, 1974, pp. 157–179; Chirot, 1977, pp. 18–20). In short, Spain and Portugal overextended

their empire building and lost their position to the growing economic dominance and more efficient expansion of England and the Netherlands.

Although there has always been a group of core nations, not just one, at times there has been one core nation with clear economic dominance in the world system. A simultaneous lead in three economic rankings over an extended period of time can bring this clear dominance (Wallerstein, 1980). First, *productivity* dominance is important. The nation with productivity dominance can produce products of higher quality and at a lower price compared with other nations. Second, productivity dominance can lead to *trade* dominance. In this situation the balance of trade favors the dominant nation because more nations are buying the products of the dominant nation than it is buying from them. Third, trade dominance can lead to *financial* dominance. With a favorable balance of trade, more money is coming into the nation than is going out. The bankers of the dominant nation tend to become the bankers of the world, with financial resources to lend other nations

Unlike the Dutch, the Spanish colonizers were concerned with more than economic gain only. During the colonial period, Spanish missionaries in California made great efforts to influence local Indian cultures through religion and education. (© Culver Pictures, Inc.)

at favorable terms. When a nation achieves these three forms of economic dominance, *military* dominance is also likely. With a stronger economic base, and with interests tied to a world status quo worth protecting, the dominant core nation tends to build a strong military.

In the history of this modern world system there have been only three brief periods in which one core nation has come to dominate, with each period lasting less than 100 years. After Spain and Portugal failed to dominate, the Netherlands was the first core nation to do so by the 1600s. The Dutch achieved this dominance especially with efficient ship building, which also helped bring an economic lead through selling more products to other nations and providing a fleet of ships to allow them an advantage in the race for colonies (Wallerstein, 1974, 1980).

By becoming the dominant core nation, however, the Dutch set in motion a process that led to their relative economic decline. First, other nations were able to copy the new Dutch technology. With newer production equipment and knowledge of what worked and did not work for the Dutch, other industrializing nations began to challenge Dutch economic dominance, particularly England and France. The productivity edge held by the Dutch also declined with the rise in their standard of living, owing to their dominant core status. This relatively high standard of living pushed up production costs, making Dutch products somewhat less competitive (Wallerstein, 1980, pp. 268–269).

With loss of productivity dominance, the Dutch trade dominance was lost. And with trade dominance gone, financial dominance eroded. But although the Dutch continued to hold financial power,

THE WORLD SYSTEM: INEQUALITY AND CONFLICT • 363

their bankers, seeking profitable investments, went outside the country to a greater degree than in the past. With other industrial nations rising, Dutch bankers saw more profit potential in these other nations, and a flow of investment capital moved especially to England. This outflow of investment capital further eroded the Dutch economic position even though it helped the profits of Dutch bankers.

We should turn from the core nations for a moment to consider what was happening in the rest of the world system. In this early phase, the world system included only a few nations and territories, but the number was expanding rapidly. The Dutch, English, and French (along with some less powerful nations like Spain and Portugal) were moving through the world to obtain new territories for economic exploitation. Especially areas in the New World were brought into this world system as colonies and periphery nations. Core nations fought wars with the native populations in these new areas, as well as with one another, to assure hegemony (meaning control and dominance) in these parts of the world. After hegemony in an area was achieved, the core nation took the natural resources and often changed the old agricultural system to fit its own needs. Plantations were established, for example, to provide sugar and other products that core nations found profitable.

Returning now to the core, we note that the Dutch were losing their dominance by the late 1600s. With their relative decline, conflict within the core increased. There had always been wars among core nations, but now (1) the power of the Dutch to enforce world order was reduced, and (2) other nations were fighting for advantage to take the lead once held by the Dutch. The two main nations in this conflict were England and France. The Dutch had often fought the British, but by the early 1700s they were allies. It was Dutch financial investment that helped the English advance with productivity and trade, and it was Dutch military support that helped the English subdue the French. At the end of the Hundred Years War in 1763 the English finally attained the clear core dominance once held by the Dutch (Wallerstein, 1980, p. 245).

With British dominance there was again relative stability in the world system during the late 1700s and early 1800s. It was especially a time of British expansion all over the world, with many colonies in Asia and the New World. But following the earlier pattern of the Dutch, the British also began a relative economic decline. And like the Dutch, the overextended colonial system placed a strain on the British military, the cost of which also contributed to economic decline.

During the late 1800s and early 1900s we again find destabilization in the world system with the decline of Britain as the major core power. As in the early 1700s there was again extensive core conflict. This time the British and French were allies, with Germany providing the new threat. Germany started its process of colonialism late and lacked extensive influence around the world. For this reason the German elites were hungry for periphery areas to exploit economically. It was the German attempt at expansion that sparked World War I, which was not settled until after World War II in 1945 (Chirot, 1986).

The primary new element in World War II was Japanese expansion. Like Germany, Japan started its industrialization and colonialism late — after the Meiji Restoration in the 1860s. In the early 1900s the Japanese found much of the world and especially Asia, which they wanted, already taken by the European powers. After increasing American pressure attempting to slow Japanese expansion, the Japanese struck at Pearl Harbor in 1941.

The final new ingredient to the core conflict of the early 1900s was the United States. As we have already seen in an earlier chapter, during the late 1800s the United States economy was expanding rapidly. And as the British economy was experiencing relative decline, British bankers were investing heavily in the United States. As shown in Table 13.3, the United States had already gained the lead in world production by 1900 and had clear economic leadership by 1929.

After World War II the United States was even more the dominant core nation because much of Europe and Japan were destroyed by war. Over half of all the world's industrial output came from the United States, and the U.S. military could be found

TABLE 13.3. *Core portions of world manufacturing output (%)*

	1900	1913	1929
United States	30	36	43
United Kingdom	20	14	9
Germany	17	16	11
France	7	6	7
Total	74	72	70

SOURCE: Chirot (1977, p. 97).

all over the world protecting the interests of U.S. corporations. Most of the regions and people in the world had been brought into the world system by the mid-twentieth century, and most of these regions were dominated by the victorious allies of World War II.

History of the World System: A Summary. Before we focus on the postwar period, we will assess and summarize the history of the world system. We have seen how this modern world system developed during the period 1500–1700. There was economic and military competition among the industrializing nations in Europe at home and for new territories. Between the 1500s and the present, most of the regions of the world were brought into this world system through economic ties to core nations. Thus far, however, we have focused on the core nations. We have seen three core nations at different times rise to a dominant position — the Netherlands, England, and the United States. Productivity leadership, trade dominance, and financial dominance helped place these nations on top, whereas erosion of these economic conditions finally led to the relative decline of the Netherlands and England (we consider the United States in the next section).

Much like the process of class conflict within a nation, there is conflict among nations with differing ranks in the world "stratification" system (Kerbo, 1983, pp. 429–434). This process of international "class" conflict has set in motion trends that have led to a core dominance by the United States. But

this is a dynamic process subject to change, both for the United States and for previous core leaders.

Core Competition and the United States in the Second Half of the Twentieth Century

The trends of 400 years and the examples of two previously dominant core nations do not point to an inevitable path that the United States must follow. There are new variables in the world system, like the current nuclear stalemate. But the historical pattern we have just examined can help us understand much of what is happening in the world system today and lead us to speculate about the future. We begin with the economic competition, then turn to the military conflicts and periphery nations.

Current Economic Trends. One of the biggest questions for us is, will the United States follow the pattern of relative economic decline experienced by the British and Dutch before us? Some of the economic statistics, unfortunately, indicate that such a relative decline is well underway. We are talking about a "relative" economic decline, which means that other nations catch up with the dominant core nation. The nation does not fall from core status into the semiperiphery, but the relative decline does mean a loss of jobs and perhaps a reduction in the standard of living for many in the society. Let's consider the evidence on this relative economic decline.

You will remember that the first factor described as important in gaining or losing dominant core status is economic productivity and innovation. The relative standing of U.S. productivity has been falling since the early 1970s (Blumberg, 1980). Table 13.4 shows that through the 1970s a number of nations had more productivity growth than the United States. But though there is some evidence that the United States is still ahead in overall productivity — only the growth is slower (Miller and Tomaskovic-Devey, 1983, p. 53) — the trend for the United States is not good.

We began this chapter by noting the tremendous U.S. trade deficit. This trade deficit has been growing steadily worse since the 1970s. Although the balance of trade was in the negative $60-billion

TABLE 13.4. *Comparative productivity growth, 1970–1979 (base productivity in 1967 = 100)**

	1970	1975	1979
United States	104.5	118.2	129.2
Canada	114.7	133.3	156.3
France	121.2	150.7	156.3
West Germany	116.1	151.3	189.9
Japan	146.5	174.6	183.8
United Kingdom	108.8	124.2	230.5

SOURCE: *Statistical Abstract of the United States, 1980*, Table 1591, p. 913.

* Note that the base year of productivity in 1967 is set at 100 for every nation. Then each following year's productivity is compared with this base year. Thus, for the United States the 104.5 productivity figure in 1970 showed a slight increase over the 100 level for the 1967 base year.

range in 1983, it ended 1984 at over $120 billion in the red, and remained in the $150-to $160-billion range in 1988.

There is agreement that the United States continues to hold financial influence in the world economy. However, just since 1985 the big New York banks have lost their dominant position in world finance. Of the ten largest banks in the world as of 1988, seven were Japanese, and the four largest, led by Dai-ichi Kangyo, were all Japanese. However, most important for the present and future economic position of the United States is the matter of where capital investments are going. Between 1950 and 1980, direct foreign investment by U.S. corporations increased from $12 billion to $192 billion, and the largest U.S. bank (Citicorp.) received over 80 percent of its profits from foreign operations by the end of the 1970s (Bluestone and Harrison, 1982, p. 42).

This is to say that so far the U.S. economic pattern looks similar to that followed by the Dutch and the British as they lost core dominance. Countries like France, West Germany, and especially Japan have copied U.S. economic innovations and carried them a step further as they were rebuilding from World War II. They now provide stiff economic competition for the United States. In the face of this growth abroad, U.S. investments are going to places like West Germany and Japan, as Dutch investments

went to England, and English investments went to the United States in the late 1800s. What noted American economist Thorstein Veblen (1939) called "the penalty of taking the lead" to describe the British economic decline in the 1800s may be used to describe the United States situation today.

Anyone can speculate on which country, if any, may gain core dominance in the future. The Japanese are always mentioned as a possibility, given their rapid rate of economic growth. And as past patterns show, the next core leader was sponsored (in a sense) by the previous core leader. It is clear that Japan is becoming the closest U.S. economic ally.

We come now, however, to a controversial part of world system theory — where to place the Soviets. Some social scientists claim the Soviet Union does not have an important place in the world economic system but rather an alternative system of communist nations, whereas others claim that even though the Soviets are a communist nation, they act like the capitalist nations when it comes to seeking international economic advantage. (On this disagreement see Chirot [1977, pp. 229–232]; Steiber [1979]; Wallerstein [1974, p. 351]). But for whatever reason, it is clear that like previous core nations the Soviet Union is seeking to gain advantage in the world through pulling semiperiphery and periphery nations to its side.

International Core Conflict. Each time a dominant core nation was in decline, it opened up international conflict when other core nations attempted to gain influence over periphery and semiperiphery nations previously held by the declining nation. Such competition was at the root of World Wars I and II, for example.

Since World War II it seems that this conflict is recurring between the U.S.-bloc and the Soviet-bloc nations. The first big move was made by the Soviets after World War II when they began taking East European semiperiphery nations lost to Germany. Since that time the U.S. bloc and the Soviet bloc have been in competition for territory all over the world in what resembles a worldwide chess game. Both sides want to use these less powerful nations for their own economic and political purposes.

But there is an important new element in this current core competition for the periphery — a nuclear stalemate. The British and French had direct military conflict when competing for dominance in the 1700s, as did the United States and the German bloc in World Wars I and II. The U.S. and Soviet blocs, however, have thus far not met in direct military conflict, but there has been military conflict in the form of small wars in Korea, Vietnam, and other places around the world.

The typical pattern goes something like this: If the government of a periphery nation is on the side of the United States, then the Soviets support the revolutionaries in that country in hopes of taking the country from the U.S. orbit; if, however, the government of the nation is on the side of the Soviets, then the United States helps the revolutionaries. For example, the current government of El Salvador favors the United States; thus the Soviets back the revolutionaries. The current government of Nicaragua is now on the side of the Soviets, so the United States backs the counterrevolutionaries, and so it goes through a long list of conflicts around the world. As indicated in Figure 13.2, however, because the United States and its allies represent the previous core leaders, more world regions are in their hands. The Soviets are the "new guys" at the game and must try to take territory from the previous leaders, as did Germany and Japan earlier in this century. The Soviets, therefore, are more often on the side of revolutionaries around the world. At present, and since World War II, the U.S. bloc has held the advantage and therefore favor the status quo in world alignments.

There is disagreement over the extent to which core nations need to exploit periphery nations to maintain a strong economy in the core (Wallerstein, 1974; Chirot, 1977). But whether or not the core needs to dominate the periphery, core nations seem to believe they do and work hard to keep or attain these periphery nations.

For their part, the noncore nations are caught in the middle. They are forced to the side of the Soviets or to the side of the United States if they are to survive. Periphery nations that try to be independent are considered "up for grabs" by core nations. And in addition to the warfare that destroys periph-

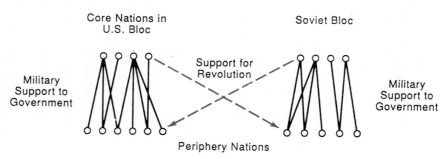

FIGURE 13.2. *United States and Soviet bloc competition for periphery nations in the world system.*

ery nations caught in the superpower conflict, other problems result from being pulled too closely to a core superpower.

THE THIRD WORLD

As core nations in the world system have been expanding their productive capacities and their territory, and fighting one another over the past three to four centuries, conditions in what is known as the Third World or periphery have also been changing. The direction of the change has usually been harmful to the masses in these nations. Conditions in many Third World Nations have been growing worse, whereas the standard of living in core nations has been improving considerably. ("Third World" is the term used to identify the 135 or so poor, underdeveloped nations, with the Western bloc and Soviet bloc representing the first and second group of nations. I generally use the term "periphery nation" interchangeably with Third World nation.)

The major capitalist industrial nations account for about 20 percent of the world's population but receive about 66 percent of the income. The bottom 30 percent of the world population receives 3 percent of world income, whereas the bottom 50 percent of the people receive only 13 percent of the income. In the United States the per capita GNP is a bit over $16,000. In 45 nations around the world, however, the per capita GNP is less than $300. In even some of the "most affluent" of these periphery or semiperiphery nations such as Brazil, over 60 percent of the population is undernourished (MacDougall, 1984).

Not only is the wealth and income gap between rich and poor nations increasing, the gap between rich and poor within these periphery nations is increasing. Again using the example of Brazil, we note that between 1960 and 1980 the most affluent 10 percent of the population increased their income share from 40 percent to 48 percent. In Mexico, where the richest one-fifth of the people had an average income 10 times that of the poorest one-fifth in 1950, the gap had grown to 20 to 1 by 1977 (MacDougall, 1984). In nations where land is so important for economic survival, in Latin America

10 percent of the farmers own about 90 percent of all farmland. Figure 13.3 indicates the general level of household income inequality between the richest 10 percent and the lowest 40 percent of the population in nine noncore nations. This unequal distribution of income and land in these nations is not being reduced, but is in fact growing wider.

In the second half of this chapter we will turn from core nations to the periphery and semiperiphery. As already noted, and as empirical research will show us below, a nation's position in the modern world system has a profound impact on many characteristics of that nation. For example, El Salvador, Nicaragua, and Bolivia are different from Uganda, Morocco, Chad, and Thailand in many ways, but because these nations are all periphery nations linked to core nations in the world system, they also

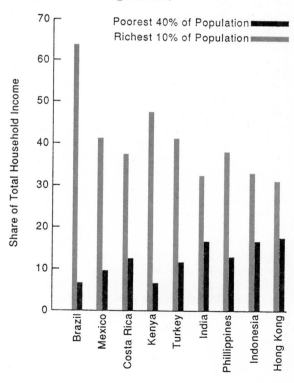

FIGURE 13.3. *Comparative Third World income inequality.* (*Source: MacDougall, 1984.*)

have many common characteristics and political-economic forces with which they must contend.

Characteristics of Periphery Nations. We have already described periphery nations as those with less diversified and less developed economies. To explain more fully, a lack of economic diversity means the economy is based on only a few productive activities, quite often only in the extraction of raw materials or agriculture. For example, one-half of the work force may be involved in producing sugar, mining copper, or harvesting coffee. Very often these economic activities are controlled — and the land, mines, or factories are owned — by multinational corporations from core nations. The case of Chile is instructive: U.S. corporations control 80 percent of copper production, which is Chile's most important industry for foreign trade (Petras and Morley, 1975).

Another characteristic of periphery nations, therefore, is the extensive ties they have to core nations. The ties come in many forms but are usually economic. Periphery nations are commonly in debt to banks in the core, they must trade with the core, and there is extensive direct investment by multinational corporations in periphery nations. When combined with the fact that periphery nations depend on the world market for trade in just a few moneymaking products, this puts periphery nations in a dependent relationship with core nations.

Because of extensive ties to multinationals, there is commonly a small, wealthy elite in these periphery nations who owe their position to these multinational corporations. Thus, this small elite usually maintains control of the state to protect their economic interests and those of the multinational corporations. The states in these periphery nations can be described as weak because they are unable to protect the interests of the population as a whole. This is also to say that periphery nations are unlikely to have democratic political institutions.

These periphery nations often have many problems like rapid population growth, rapid urbanization, high unemployment, extensive crime and political violence, a high rate of infant mortality, malnutrition, and so on. Many of these problems stem from the lack of economic development. However, there is quite often a major difference between just being underdeveloped and being underdeveloped while also extensively tied to the core. In the second case, as we will see, these problems are often worse.

Outcomes of Periphery Status

As noted above, holding a position of periphery rank has profound effects on a nation. We are ready to consider these effects in more detail, beginning with the most important economic effects. But before we do so it will be useful to consider the type of research that has been done that shows these effects of periphery status.

Until the past 10 to 15 years, we had much less knowledge of the effects of periphery status in the world system. There was much theoretical speculation and many case studies showing harmful effects, but we needed more general information. Using new statistical methods we now have more information, though much is left to learn. In general, what recent research has done is compare nations much as we do individuals to understand differences. This comparative research involves obtaining detailed information on a sample of 50 to 100 or more periphery nations. Some of these nations have less economic growth than others, for example, so we try to find what seems to be associated with having less economic growth. If we are lucky, we may find a statistical relationship between some variable x (say, the amount of foreign economic investment) and less economic growth. Thus, we find that nations with x characteristic usually have less economic growth. This also means that not *all* nations with x characteristic will have less economic growth — there are exceptions. The exceptions are often important to understand, but what we are most concerned with are the general tendencies, that is, the usual effects of periphery status.

Periphery Status and Economic Development. One of the most important outcomes of periphery status is economic growth, or rather the lack of it. This is most important because economic development is what these nations need most. Their populations often do not have enough food because they lack jobs or land. Many other problems (like rapid urbanization, crime, illiteracy) stem from the lack of economic activity.

It was once assumed that core nations were providing tremendous aid for future economic growth in periphery nations when there is investment and loans coming from the core to the periphery. However, we now know such is not usually the case.

Looking at the already developed nations, we do see a pattern of economic development that Rostow (1960) called the *stages of economic growth.* Beginning with the preindustrial stage, the developed nations went through steps where initial industrialization caused extensive dislocation and poverty, but with further investment and economic growth they overcame these problems. Thus, it was assumed that though things are now difficult in Third World nations, further aid and investment would help them proceed through the growth stages as did the present advanced industrial nations. But we now realize there is a basic flaw in such reasoning — when the currently industrialized nations were in the early stages of growth 200 or more years ago, *there were no core nations already more advanced than they.*

Many studies have consistently shown that most periphery nations that have extensive aid and investment from the core have *less long-term economic growth* (Chase-Dunn, 1975; Bornschier, Chase-Dunn, and Rubinson, 1978; Snyder and Kick, 1979; Stokes and Jaffee, 1982; Nolan, 1983). There is, of course, some economic growth in the short term — fewer than five years — because of the aid and investment coming from the core. But the longer-term prospects for growth are actually harmed by the kinds of outside aid and investment these nations have received. This seems puzzling, so let's consider it further.

Although there are many reasons for these harmful economic effects, two reasons seem the most important. The first involves a problem of *structural distortion* in the economy. For example, in a more normal economic process some natural resource, human or nonhuman, leads to a chain of economic activity. We can use the case of a core nation with extensive copper deposits. Mining the copper provides jobs and profits. The copper is then refined into metal, again providing some people with jobs and profits. The metal is then used by another firm to make a consumer product, again providing jobs and profits. Finally, the product is sold by a retail firm, again providing jobs and profits. From the mining process to the retail sales of the product, there is a chain of jobs and profits providing economic growth.

Now consider what may happen when the copper is mined in a periphery nation with extensive ties to the core. The copper may be mined by native workers, but the ore or metal is shipped to core nations where the remainder of the economic chain is completed. The additional jobs and profits from the chain of economic activities are lost to the periphery nation — they go to the core. Economic growth is harmed in the periphery nation (Chase-Dunn, 1975).

The second factor harming economic growth is related to political and economic power. When periphery nations are heavily tied to multinational corporations from the core, a small, wealthy elite develops in the periphery nation that depends on multinational corporations. This elite makes sure multinational corporations are happy with the relationship. The multinationals are allowed extensive tax breaks, they are allowed to take most of the profits out of the country, and wages to domestic workers are kept low. All this is likely to keep multinational corporations in the periphery nation and, consequently, the small elite wealthy. But long-term economic growth is harmed. Profits go to the core and the very low wages paid to workers leaves them with no buying power to stimulate the economy.

Another way of putting it is that income inequality, when overly extensive, harms economic growth (Myrdal, 1970, pp. 50–54). Several studies have also found that periphery nations with extensive economic ties to the core have *greater income inequality* (Rubinson, 1976; Chase-Dunn, 1975; Bornschier and Ballmer-Cao, 1979; Evans and Timberlake, 1980; Nolan, 1983; Fiala, 1983). For one reason, core corporations are attracted to periphery nations with low wages. However, a number of things can happen because the multinationals are there, which keeps wages low and the wealth of elites high. For example, to keep the multinationals in the country political elites suppress any union activity that might increase wages. Also, the agricultural areas are usually disrupted, which forces a flood of landless peasants into the cities in search of jobs. The surplus labor keeps wages low.

Rapid Urbanization and Agricultural Disruption. Another likely result of extensive ties to the core is rapid urbanization. When many economic ties are formed with core nations, there is an exaggerated growth rate in the periphery urban areas (Kentor, 1981). This rapid urbanization produces many problems, such as homeless families, unsanitary conditions, crime, as well as more poverty and unemployment. Both a "push" and "pull" help produce this rapid urbanization.

The push results from peasants being thrown out of agricultural areas. Landowners also develop ties

Bangkok, Thailand, like most big cities in peripheral societies, shows the effects of rapid urbanization in its housing patterns. As poor migrants flood cities, shanty towns grow up alongside modern, high-rise and high-cost housing. (© Bernard Pierre Wolff/Photo Researchers, Inc.)

to core nations and the world market in periphery nations dominated by the core. This has two common effects: the landowners change crops and engage in mechanized farming. With traditional agriculture in periphery nations production was for local consumption and there was plenty of land and workers to meet the demand. But when the landowner goes to the world market, greater profits can often be made by growing another crop (say, soybeans rather than black beans) and by using as much land and mechanization as possible. Formerly it didn't make sense to mechanize and use all the land for cash crops — only so much could be sold anyway. Now peasants are pushed out of jobs by new machines and pushed off of land they were farming to feed their families because landowners now need the land for greater profits.

The "pull" effect comes from the lure of jobs and income in the cities. Many if not most peasants moving to the cities have no choice; they have been pushed off the land. But others find the rural existence hard and unrewarding compared with life in the cities for friends or relatives who have been lucky to find jobs there.

Political Repression and Less Democracy. It is not difficult to understand that core domination of periphery nations helps produce political repression. When this domination also produces less economic growth, more inequality, rapid urbanization, among other problems, if the country is not to explode with demands for higher wages and jobs there must be a police state to maintain social order (Timberlake and Williams, 1984).

Part of the relationship between multinational ties and less democracy, however, comes from the corporate view that investments are more secure in periphery nations with a military dictatorship (Bollen and Jones, 1982). The military dictatorship is more likely to prevent change leading to higher taxes and even lost property to the corporation if a revolutionary movement or liberal political movement were successful.

Core Intervention to Prevent Change. With so many negative consequences for periphery nations extensively tied to core nations, we must wonder why these periphery nations do not change the relationship. There is often, in fact, much pressure for change from the periphery population. Two factors work against such change.

First, a small group of elites often control the economy and government in periphery nations. This elite finds the relation to the core very profitable for themselves, if not for the majority in their nation. This elite uses economic power and, most importantly, political power to bring out the police and military to prevent other groups from trying to produce change.

The political balance between core and peripheral societies is influenced by many subtle factors, including ideology and religion. This photo marks the first visit (in 1988) of an American Roman Catholic cardinal, John O'Connor of New York, to Fidel Castro, Cuban revolutionary and head of state since the Cuban Revolution in 1959. Why do you think an anticommunist priest would want to visit a head of state whose alliances are within the communist world and who many consider to be a dictator? (© AP/ Wide World Photos)

Second, if it appears that a periphery nation is moving "too far" away from the relationship it has had with the core, the core nation often takes action to prevent such change. Throughout the history of this world system the dominant core nations have taken the lead in maintaining it with military action. The United States has taken this role, especially since World War II.

As can be seen in Table 13.5, the United States has been quick to take military action in Latin American countries that establish policies considered unfavorable by U.S. political elites or threaten U.S. corporate policy. In a study sponsored by the Pentagon, it was found that the United States military was involved in a "show of force" in other nations, (for example, sending the navy within striking distance or building up troops in the area) a total of 215 times between 1945 and 1978 (*Washington Post*, January 3, 1979). The only other nation close to the United States in such activity was the Soviet Union, with 115 cases of military display since 1945.

But this study also showed that overt military threats by the United States are decreasing, whereas such activity by the Soviet Union is increasing. There was an average of 13.4 per year during Kennedy's presidency, 9.7 during Johnson's presidency, and 5 or fewer per year during the Nixon and Ford years. For whatever reason (counterpressure by the Soviet Union, lack of success, a counterproductive image, or the Vietnam disaster for United States foreign policy), it seems that the threat and use of overt military action to prevent periphery challenge (although certainly still options) are being reduced. But the covert action approach remains.

Covert actions are secret operations to achieve political and/or economic objectives. Included in such actions are assassination of political figures seen as a threat to core interests, bribes to periphery politicians or other people who may further core interests, " secret" military aid to counter revolutionaries as in Nicaragua, helping to stage coups, propaganda, rigged elections, and all kinds of "dirty tricks" that are limited only by the imagination. (Examples include plans by the CIA in the 1960s to "hurt Castro's public image" by giving him LSD before a major speech and secretly "dusting" Castro

TABLE 13.5. *Partial list of U.S. military interventions in Latin American nations, 1850–1965*

Year(s)	Nation	Year(s)	Nation
1852–3	Argentina	1912	Cuba
1853–4	Nicaragua	1912–25	Nicaragua
1855	Uruguay	1914	Haiti
1856	Panama	1914	Dominican Republic
1858	Uruguay	1915–34	Haiti
1865	Colombia	1916–24	Dominican Republic
1867	Nicaragua	1919	Honduras
1868	Uruguay	1920	Guatemala
1869–71	Dominican Republic	1924–5	Honduras
1890	Argentina	1926–33	Nicaragua
1891	Chile	1965	Dominican Republic
1894	Nicaragua		
1896	Nicaragua		
1898	Nicaragua		
1899	Nicaragua		
1903	Honduras		
1903	Dominican Republic		
1903	Panama		
1904	Dominican Republic		
1907	Honduras		
1907	Nicaragua		
1910	Nicaragua		
1910	Honduras		

SOURCE: Table constructed from data in L. Cordon Crovitz, "Presidents Have a History of Unilateral Moves," *Wall Street Journal,* Jan. 15, 1987, p. 24.

with a chemical to make his beard fall out. These and more "tricks" were actually considered by the CIA; see U.S. Senate Select Committee [1975a, p. 72]).

When these types of covert action are successful, they can achieve political and economic objectives at much less expense with respect to military resources, lives lost, and world opinion. Only recently the extensive use of covert actions by the United States against noncore nations like Cuba, Chile, Iran, the Congo (now Zaïre), the Dominican Republic, and Vietnam became widely known through the release of government documents and congressional investigations (U.S. Senate Select Committee, 1975a; 1975b). And, of course, the Reagan administration, as illustrated by Oliver North's exploits, returned to these programs of covert action in many places in the world.

The objectives of covert action can be quite varied, but they generally fall into three main categories. First, and no doubt most common, covert action can be directed toward suppressing opposition groups attempting to change governments in the periphery supportive of core interests. Second, covert action can be directed more specifically toward supporting periphery governments favorable to core interests. The distinction between the first and second is often difficult to make, but with the second we mean action like the spread of propaganda that helps the friendly government. Third, and more complex, are actions directed toward disrupting an unfavorable periphery government so as to place in power a more favorable government — one that is anticommunist, procore, and receptive to more multinational investment and trade.

Because of the importance of complex covert action by the core to disrupt new governments in the periphery unfavorable to core interests, it is worth considering in more detail. We can use the case of Chile to show (1) what the extent of dependence of many periphery nations is, and (2) how the core is able to make sure these periphery nations *remain* economically dependent on core interests. (For more detail on United States activity in the Chile coup, see Kerbo [1978]).

The Case of Chile. The increasing political violence in Chile during 1970–1973 preceding the military coup in September 1973 has been chosen for several reasons to emphasize core dominance of the periphery. One of the most basic is that we have more information pertaining to this recent case. Because of the political debate in the United States at the time and the subsequent investigations (U.S. Senate Select Committee, 1975a; 1975b), and because of the Allende government's willingness to help with research in that country (Zeitlin et al., 1974), much is now known about the political and economic conditions leading up to the political violence in Chile that helped bring about the 1973 military coup.

Also, for two other reasons Chile is probably one of the best cases to illustrate the arguments above. As many have noted (for example, Zeitlin et al., 1974; Petras and Morley, 1975; Goldberg, 1975), Chile had one of the strongest traditions of democracy in the Third World. We suggest that a foreign power will as a result have a more difficult time in helping to create and exploit conditions leading to a rejection of that constitutional government.

In addition, Chile provides an example of a country highly dependent on outside economic actors. For example, before Allende (the socialist president) took office, Chile had the second highest foreign debt in the world. In terms of foreign aid, "Between 1961 and 1970, Chile was the largest recipient of any country in Latin America, on a per capita basis, of U.S. Alliance for Progress loans, approximately $1.3 to $1.4 billion" (U.S. Senate Select Committee, 1975b, p. 32).

As Petras and Morley's (1975, pp. 8–9) research shows: "U.S. direct private investment in Chile in 1970 stood at $1.1 billion, out of a total estimated

foreign investment of $1.672 billion." Most U.S. corporate investment in Chile was in the mining and smelting sector (over 50 percent). "However, U.S. and foreign corporations controlled almost all of the most dynamic and critical areas of the economy by the end of 1970." The foreign-controlled industry included machinery and equipment (50 percent); iron, steel, and metal products (60 percent); petroleum products and distribution (over 50 percent); industrial and other chemicals (60 percent); rubber products (45 percent); automotive assembly (100 percent); radio and television (nearly 100 percent); and advertising (90 percent). "Furthermore, U.S. corporations controlled 80 percent of the production of Chile's only important foreign exchange earner — copper."

Chile's internal class structure fits closely that of a highly dependent country on the periphery with a small but powerful and united upper class with strong ties to private interests in core societies. (For detailed figures on this class structure, see Zeitlin et al. [1974, 1976]).

Chile, by 1970, although industrialized by Third World standards, was dominated economically by core nations. It was a country in which outside interests, mainly from the United States, could apply pressures that had the potential of seriously disrupting the economy and basic social structure. Rather than simply sending support for one side in the conflict after it had broken out, these foreign interests had the potential to exacerbate chronic economic imbalances already existing due to its periphery status, as well as help create new ones that could lead to serious political violence. The only thing lacking in Chile before 1970 was the motivation for outside interests to apply these pressures. With a newly elected Marxist president, one who moved toward policies viewed as highly unfavorable by these foreign interests (U.S. Senate Select Committee, 1975b, pp. 44–45), that motivation soon materialized.

After a coup supported by the United States failed to prevent Allende from assuming office in 1970 (U.S. Senate Select Committee, 1975b, p. 2), the efforts, mainly from the U.S. government and private industry, were directed toward two goals: to disrupt the economy and then aid segments within the country mobilized and mobilizing to oppose Allende's government.

Several actions were taken by multinationals and the U.S. government that helped disrupt the Chilean economy.

1. The various types of foreign aid coming from the United States before Allende took office were cut back severely (Sanford, 1976, pp. 147–148; U.S. Senate Select Committee, 1975b, pp. 33–35).

2. Short-term credits to Chile from U.S. commercial banks were virtually cut off.

3. Funds from the World Bank and the Inter-American Development Bank were cut.

4. Multinationals such as ITT worked with other multinationals and the U.S. government to organize these pressures (U.S. Senate Select Committee, 1975b, pp. 13–14; Sampson, 1973, p. 283).

5. Supplies necessary for Chile's industry were withheld, such as parts for their primarily U.S.-made machinery.

6. Pressure was applied to other countries to prevent them from trading with Chile (Farnsworth et al., 1976, p. 362; Petras and Morley, 1975, p. 111).

The measures above contributed to limiting industrial output in Chile severely by 1972. And in Goldberg's (1975, pp. 109–110) words: "The United States' credit blockage aroused intense consumer dissatisfaction which the opposition parties succeeded in mobilizing against the government. . . . Producers whose imports were also curtailed joined newly deprived consumers in protest strikes and demonstrations against the government."

The next step for foreign powers working within Chile was fairly simple—to provide support for old and newly emerging protest groups (U.S. Senate Select Committee, 1975b, pp. 29–30). In this regard, the CIA was authorized to spend $8 million between 1970 and 1973, $3 million of this spent in 1973 alone (U.S. Senate Select Committee, 1975b, p. 1). It is interesting to note that although all other aid to Chile from the United States was cut, the aid going specifically to the Chilean military was maintained at a high level (U.S. Senate Select Committee, 1975b, pp. 37–39). In line with this the U.S. military also attempted to cultivate stronger personal ties with the Chilean military (U.S. Senate

Select Committee, 1975b, p. 28) in an attempt to make it known that the United States would not look unfavorably on a coup.

The result was the coup of September 1973 that killed President Allende and thousands more (Sanford, 1976). A military dictatorship took power that reopened Chile to economic investment and trade from the core, and reestablished wealthy Chilean elites tied to core interests. The U.S. government more than restored the aid and loans that it had cut or eliminated when Allende took office in 1970 (Petras and Morley, 1975, p. 141), and top U.S. banks extended huge loans that further increased Chilean debt (Letelier and Moffitt, 1980). Chile was welcomed back to its place in the world economic system. By 1987, however, Chile's economy was in much worse condition than during Allende's first year in office during 1971.

The Potential for Third World Development

The problems of Third World nations today are many. Rapid population growth, limited economic opportunities, political violence, and urban crowding are just some. Solutions to these complex problems are very difficult to find, but in many respects any solutions will have to involve economic development. Nations that are already developed had many of the same problems faced by periphery nations today, though the problems were less severe. However, as we have already noted, core nations today were able to develop economically without the interference of already existing core nations.

The influence on periphery nations today by core nations cannot explain all Third World problems. In contrast to core nations when they were developing, the periphery nations today have fewer natural resources, a greater population problem, and often unfavorable climatic conditions (Myrdal, 1970). But core ties often compound the problems of periphery nations.

Opting Out of the World System. Many in periphery nations today believe that to begin economic development they must "opt out of the world system," meaning they must break extensive ties to the core

BOX 13.1

Soviet Repression of Poland, Unique in the World System?

In the late 1970s and early 1980s an independent labor movement called Solidarity was gaining extensive popular support among the Polish people. Lech Walesa won the Nobel Peace prize in 1983 for his leadership of this movement. Solidarity became so popular in Poland that it actually won many government concessions and was finally recognized as a legal organization. Many government officials were clearly sympathetic to Solidarity and this labor union was "allowed" to carry out a series of strikes designed to improve conditions for workers. "Allowed" to strike means that, in contrast to the usual pattern in a communist country, strikers were not simply thrown in jail.

By the early 1980s it became apparent that many people in the Solidarity movement were openly anti-Soviet. In public debates at Solidarity meetings, "radicals" called for Poland to move further away from Soviet ideology and influence, while "moderates" warned that change could not come too fast. Walesa was in the middle, trying to maintain unity and prevent Solidarity from becoming too anti-Soviet for fear the Soviets would invade the country or force the Polish government to crush Solidarity.

The Soviets finally did "have enough." After several weeks of rumors that Soviet tanks on the Polish border were not there just for war games but to invade Poland, the Polish government (now controlled by a top general) took swift action. In a highly organized move, the Polish military cut off all communications among cities and in one night arrested almost all the Solidarity leadership. The next morning all Polish government officials sympathetic to Solidarity were gone and Solidarity was outlawed. The action was clearly forced by the Soviet Union, which was denounced by all Western nations, and even conservative Western politicians opposed to much union activity in their own countries.

The suppression of attempted social change in East European communist countries is not new. Hungary was invaded by the Soviets in 1956 for this reason, and so was Czechoslovakia in 1968. The East European communist nations have been heavily dominated by the Soviet Union since World War II, when the Soviets refused to pull their armies back after the war or reentered the countries to support communist leaders taking office. These East European communist countries are often called Soviet "satellites" and are very similar to periphery and semiperiphery nations tied to Western core nations. As can be seen in Table 13.5, the United States has often been ready to prevent Latin American countries from making changes unfavorable to the United States (or at least to people with influence in the United States). Most often the action taken by the U.S. military or the CIA was against a democratically elected government. The cases of Soviet forced suppression of Solidarity in Poland and the U.S.-backed military takeover in Chile in 1973 are quite similar in many respects (except that thousands were killed in Chile and only a few killed in Poland). In both cases we find a country, dominated by a core superpower, attempting to reduce the outside domination. Americans, of course, do not like to consider that actions taken by their own government are similar to actions taken by the Soviet Union. But in many ways the comparisons are strongly similar and recognized by people all over the world, if not by Americans.

(Chirot, 1986). Breaking these ties may not be the only solution, and such a break is difficult to attain, as the case of Chile illustrates. But some cases suggest such a break can be beneficial for long-term development.

One of the newest additions to the core is Japan. Only about 100 years ago Japan was a feudal agrarian society with no industrialization to match that found in the West. Today, as we have seen, Japan has the second-largest economy in the world. Why did Japan reach industrial status? Why not China, India, Korea, or any other less developed nation? Economist Milton Friedman (Friedman and Friedman, 1980, pp. 49–52) criticizes India for its lack of development because India has more scientists, foreign investment, and foreign aid than Japan did when developing. But this, of course, is the key problem that Friedman does not recognize. Comparing China, India, Korea, and other undeveloped nations 100 years ago, we find only one that was not colonized by core nations — Japan.

Another instructive case is China. This country is now going through many economic and political changes that look promising for economic development. And one important change is that China, since the late 1970s, has been inviting multinational corporations back into the country. Will the increased core ties hurt China's development potential? At this point we need a brief look at the history of China in the twentieth century.

By 1900 China was dominated by Western core nations that had divided it into their own spheres of influence. China's cheap labor and resources profited these core nations with little benefit going to the Chinese. In 1911 China began a long process of revolution that did not end until Mao's victory in 1949. The nation was closed by the new communist government, and before the end of the 1950s even the Soviets had been expelled. Between 1948 and the middle 1970s, China went through many internal struggles and changes before reentering the world of international exchange. But when China did reopen after Mao's death, the state was in a much different order. Rather than being told by European core nations what to do, China is now in a position of strength. Multinational corporations have been asked to reenter China, but on terms that will bene-

Not only are foreign multinationals investing in China, but the Chinese are spearheading development initiatives in Third World peripheral countries. In this photo, a Costa Rican factory worker makes bamboo furniture under the direction of Chinese technical experts. (© Eugene Gordon)

fit the Chinese people. The Chinese government demands that Chinese workers be paid fair wages, investments by multinationals are regulated by the government, and profits leaving the country are limited, to list only a few restrictions. Multinational corporations are returning to China, and even competing for the opportunity.

The primary point is this: Japan was never dominated by outside powers before development, and China, like the United States under British domination, could only hope for economic development after exploitative core ties were cut and a strong state was able to develop.

Finally, we briefly consider the example of the Soviet Union. Before the Russian Revolution of 1917, Russia was far behind the other European powers economically. As a semiperiphery country, Russia was dominated by the multinational corporations of Western Europe (Skocpol, 1979; Crankshaw, 1976). But after the Revolution of 1917 these economic ties were cut and Stalin put the nation through forced industrialization, reducing unnecessary consumption to invest for future industrial expansion. The Soviet population paid a heavy price, but the Soviet Union now has the third largest GNP in the world.

Many periphery nations today look to examples such as these. This is one reason why the potential for revolution is so great in Third World nations. It is easy for a materially comfortable population in a country like the United States to condemn communist dictatorships and the forced industrialization policies of Stalin. However, hungry masses in periphery nations may see things differently.

But whereas Japan, China, and the Soviet Union may provide success stories for Third World nations, there are many failures. Countries like Mozambique, North Korea, Vietnam, Cambodia, and to some extent Cuba have had very little economic success thus far (Lenski, 1978). Cuba has produced extensive improvements in education, medical care, housing, and nutrition for the Cuban population, but the economy continues to be maintained through Soviet aid.

There are many reasons for these development problems in periphery nations that have attempted the communist model of development. Many have tribal conflicts that cannot be resolved; often their economy is harmed by the boycotts of Western core nations; and often they have bad management and few natural resources to work with. But the superpower conflicts are also part of the problem. If a nation "opts out" of domination by a Western core nation, to survive it must turn to the Soviets for support and perhaps new exploitive relations. In Cuba, Nicaragua, Angola, China, Vietnam, Korea, and Algeria, among several nations including even the Soviet Union, Western core nations have tried to overthrow new governments soon after their respective revolution. Now these nations look at the example of Chile, which tried to make extensive changes without seeking Soviet military aid. To prevent counterrevolution and a reversal of change achieved through revolution, periphery nations often turn to the Soviets for help but end up returning to exploitation by the other side in the superpower conflict.

Agricultural Reform and Reduced Inequality. Whether or not periphery nations opt out of the world system, some basic reforms will be necessary if economic growth can be achieved. These periphery nations are primarily agrarian societies and their economic improvement must begin in agriculture. The changes that have come with core contact, however, have worsened their agricultural situation. People have been pushed off the land, machines have taken agricultural jobs, and crops are now often sold on the world market and no longer go to feed the local population. Although there is extensive hunger in periphery nations, these nations overall are in fact net exporters of food (meaning they export more on the world market than they import to feed their people).

One "solution," called the "green revolution," has not succeeded (Myrdal, 1970). This approach involves aid from core nations to supply more chemical fertilizers, pesticides, and farm mechanization to drastically increase crop yields. Even if yields are increased, however, they often go to the world market to feed core populations and profit periphery elites. Peasants lose both jobs because of farm mechanization and food for local consumption.

Recent studies have indicated that a more equal distribution of land would be the best approach to agricultural problems. Currently, in Latin America for example, about 10 percent of the people own 90 percent of the land. But a United Nations study indicates that an equal distribution of land would increase farm production by as much as 80 percent (MacDougall, 1984). In addition to increased farm production there would be more periphery farm jobs as well as profits and wages going to more people, which could stimulate economic development through consumer spending. Some of the periphery nations with extensive economic growth, such as Taiwan, have achieved this growth in part through a more equal distribution of land (Barrett and Whyte, 1982).

Not only would less inequality in land help periphery economic development, but less inequality in general may help. Myrdal (1970, pp. 54–55) lists three reasons for this:

1. With so much wealth in the hands of a few it is often wasted in conspicuous consumption and the purchase of imported products. The extensive import of foreign goods, although less expensive at first, harms domestic economic growth and job creation (also see Chirot, 1977, p. 205).

2. When much of the population suffers from malnutrition, illiteracy, and other problems related to gross inequality the capacity of the people for productive labor is diminished.

3. Extensive inequality produces hostility and a climate of conflict and disorder in the nation, which also harms economic growth.

Although most people agree that the reforms above in periphery nations would help economic growth, these reforms are not likely to happen. Quite simply this is because the needed reforms would cut into the wealth and profits of the small elite that is in power. With this in mind many social scientists suggest that periphery nations must have a "hard state" to carry out the needed reforms (Myrdal, 1970, pp. 208–222; Chirot, 1977, p. 207). This means a state that is able to induce economic policies leading to long-term economic gains for the whole population at the expense of short-term profits going mostly to the rich. However, such "hard states" will be resisted by the wealthy elite, and if their policies look too much like socialism, they will be overthrown by military action (overt or covert) from core nations.

CHAPTER SUMMARY

Key Terms

world system, 359
core nations, 359
periphery nations, 359
semiperiphery nations, 360
world empire, 360

Content

We can no longer understand most major events within a nation without some consideration of the position of that nation in the modern world system. The modern world system is formed by the economic, military, and political ties among nations, creating a network of nations much like the networks of groups within a nation. Economic relations are primary ties binding nations. There is increasingly a worldwide economic division of labor. And also like the division of labor within a nation, something like an international class system is formed, with some nations having extensive power over others owing to their top position in the international economic system.

Core nations are the dominant nations within the world system. They are able to control much of the world's wealth and means of production, much like the upper class within a nation. Core nations tend to specialize in more high-technology production and have highly diversified economies. Core nations also have strong states that are able to maintain social order and prevent foreign intervention within the nation, while at the same time manipulating other nations for the benefit of elites within the core nation.

Periphery nations are the weak nations within the world system. They are poor and their economies are highly dependent on a few economic activities like supplying raw materials or cheap labor to core nations. Many aspects of periphery nations are shaped by elites in the core nations. Semiperiphery nations are in a middle position between the core and periphery in terms of criteria such as economic diversity and development.

The modern world system slowly emerged around the 1500s, when European nations began exploring the world and dividing territories among themselves. There is a dynamic process of conflict within this world system in which core nations are in conflict with one another to exploit noncore nations, and noncore nations are in conflict with the core.

Throughout the history of this world system there have been only brief periods in which one core nation held a leading position among other core nations. The Dutch were first to attain dominance, followed by the British, and finally the United States. Each time a dominant core nation has declined in power, a destabilized world system has produced increased military conflict.

Like the previous dominant core nations, the United States gained dominant status in the twentieth century through productivity, trade, and financial dominance. Like the other dominant core nations the United States has taken the role of military guardian of its core allies. But also like the previous dominant core nations, the United States shows signs of relative economic decline after a few decades of clear dominance.

Periphery nations experience many negative consequences because of their weak periphery status in the world system. Most damaging is the reduced potential for long-term economic growth when a periphery nation becomes extensively tied to core nations. Unlike the already developed nations when they were developing, the periphery nations today are subjected to core nations that take from them profits and resources needed for periphery development. Other consequences of core dominance in periphery nations are higher levels of income inequality, less democracy, rapid urbanization, and agricultural disruption.

If periphery nations are able to overcome many of their problems through economic development, it may be necessary to reduce ties to the core by "opting out" of the world system. Also needed is reduced inequality and land redistribution. However, the current level of periphery ties to the core are highly profitable to core elites and elites within periphery nations; this leads both groups of elites to fight against many of the reforms needed to help the masses in periphery nations through long-term economic development.

CHAPTER 14

Race and Ethnic Stratification

I have a dream.

—*Dr. Martin Luther King, Jr.*

We are often told this is a nation of immigrants, but unless you experience the much lower racial and ethnic mixture of most other countries, it is easy to ignore the importance of the subject for the United States. Consider an extreme example; standing before a college class for the first time in Tokyo, I was struck by the contrast to an American college class. *All* my students had black hair, dark eyes, and other physical characteristics of Asians. Only 1 percent of the people in Japan are not native Japanese, and much less than 1 percent are non-Asians. If the names are written in alphabetical characters (not Chinese characters) calling roll in a Japanese classroom is rather simple. On the first day of class in American universities, calling the roll can often create embarrassment. I was unsure how to pronounce Bustamante, Maksoudian, Mieliwocki, Pustejovsky, or Kjeldsen. In Japan, however, students always have Japanese names. Although the Japanese language is extremely difficult for Westerners in most respects, the pronunciation is always consistent. (For example, え with the "e" sound is always the same whether found in Meika, Eiko, and so on.)

Before proceeding I should provide a brief definition for two key terms. **Race** is a category of people who, through centuries of interbreeding, have developed some roughly similar physical features like skin color. These people have come to be defined by themselves and by others as belonging to the same race. An **ethnic group,** on the other hand, refers to a group that is relatively similar in cultural background. Several distinct ethnic groups may be considered racially identical. For example, although most Europeans are similar in racial characteristics, they represent diverse cultural groupings. Among U. S. citizens are ethnic groups like Polish-Americans, German-Americans, Japanese-Americans, and Chinese-Americans. Finally, the terms **minority group** and **majority group** indicate power relations and dominance, *not* population size. Thus, blacks in South Africa are the minority group and whites the majority group even though whites account for less than 15 percent of the population.

As we have seen in earlier chapters, the structure of groups, group networks, and forms of group interaction in a society are very important in shaping some of its basic characteristics. The racial and ethnic mixtures in a society have strong effects on these group networks and interactions. If, for example, a society is made up of two or more racial and/or ethnic groups, and if these groups have some mutual hostilities, then the social networks in the society will not be well integrated. Other issues will come to be divided along the lines of the disjointed social network: access to occupations, political influence, distribution of property. There is, therefore, a heightened potential for overt conflict in the society, as well as a waste of talent and resources in the conflict.

The possible negative aspects of race and ethnic diversity should not overshadow the possible benefits as well. Throughout its history the United States has received talented individuals, and the labor needed to build the country has come from racial and ethnic groups all over the world. One reason American science is the best in the world is because of immigrants like Albert Einstein who fled Germany in the 1930s. Currently the U. S. share of Nobel prizes in science far exceeds that of any other nation, in part because of the continued movement of top scientists to the United States. But equally important, waves of immigrants came to the United States during times when railroads had to be built and expanding industries needed labor. These lower-status immigrants supplied the cheap labor to be exploited by the more wealthy in the nation. The second and third generations from this exploited labor, however, have often provided talented individuals who could move into higher-skilled positions created by the expanding economy.

The primary problem for a racially and ethnically diverse nation like the United States is to learn to use the benefits of this diversity while minimizing the exploitation and overt conflict. The present chapter examines important topics pertaining to race and ethnic relations. We begin with a look at the history of race and ethnic relations throughout the world, and in the United States in particular. From this base of historical and comparative information, we consider the sociological patterns of race and ethnic relations and the causes of racism and racial discrimination. Finally, we examine the relationship between race and class divisions, as well as the programs (and prospects) for reduced racial inequality.

A HISTORY OF RACE AND ETHNIC RELATIONS

It was once believed that different races of humans descended from different ancestors. This belief was especially popular among racists because it could be used to support ideas of racial superiority and inferiority. The best evidence today, however, suggests that all humans descended from common ancestors. Racial differences like skin color seem to have developed rather recently in the history of humans.

From common ancestors, humans began to move around the world about less than a million years ago. As these humans adjusted to new environments, there were a few superficial biological changes. For example, fair-skinned people lived in cool environments, black-skinned people lived in the hot environment of Africa, and yellow-skinned people were found in the Asian tropics.

Races. Today it is almost impossible to locate any "pure" races of people, if this was ever possible. For many years scientists have tried to establish a logical classification of racial types through such characteristics as skin color, head shape, and facial features. Agreement on a precise classification has all but been abandoned. There are, of course, tendencies for orientals, blacks, and caucasions to have certain common characteristics like skin color and facial features, but the mixture within each broad racial category defies precise classification. All male and female *Homo sapiens sapiens* can interbreed, unlike different species like dogs and cats. Thus, even if "pure" races ever existed, the centuries of interbreeding has made racial categories very diverse (Marger, 1985, pp. 11–12). The racial division of Caucasoid, Mongoloid, and Negroid may be some-

what useful but is still rather arbitrary. For example, where would we place East Indians — people with dark skin but caucasian features?

When considering race, the most important aspect is *social*. Racial differences are important primarily because (1) cultural differences are often associated with race, and more important, (2) race has been *socially defined as important*. Thus, with a sociological analysis of race, we are not so much concerned with the accuracy of people's ideas about race as we are with the social, political, and economic consequences of these ideas (Beteille, 1969). People's beliefs about race can lead to what we have described as a self-fulfilling prophecy. People are often treated differently because of their socially defined race, and this different treatment has real consequences.

The History of Racism. **Racism** is a belief system defining groups of people as either superior or inferior owing to biological characteristics believed to be associated with race. Racism has sometimes been an important force in history and, of course, millions of people have been killed because of racist beliefs. The attempt to extinguish a whole race of people through systematic extermination, called **genocide,** has occurred many times.

Extensive racism in a society is rather recent in human history, however, and the spread of racism just a few hundred years ago tells us something of its causes. People have come into conflict with and developed hatreds toward other people throughout human history. As we have already seen, people tend to form a strong sense of in-group and out-group, with beliefs about the superiority of the in-group usually associated with these group divisions. We have also found a common tendency toward ethnocentrism in human societies, again with beliefs that "people of our own kind are better." Until recently, however, these beliefs of in-group superiority were not associated with racial differences.

There is some evidence that the ancient Hindu caste system in India was originally associated with racial divisions, but the basis of the caste divisions were established in religious, not racist beliefs (Dumont, 1970). There is also some weak evidence that racism existed more than 2,000 years ago in the

It is said that one of the most striking characteristics of Japanese society is its racial homogeneity. How does that compare with our society? Are there racially homogeneous communities in the United States? Does it matter if a community is homogeneous by choice rather than by coercion? (© Martine Franck/Magnum)

Middle East because of a few passages in the Bible. At one point in the Bible, for example, a person refers to shame because his skin is dark (Solomon, 1:5–6). But such minor reference can hardly be convincing when none of the Middle Eastern countries has ever developed a racial caste system or a system of racist beliefs. The most extensive and systematic racist beliefs have developed in countries having European origins and developed only in the past few hundred years (Van den Berghe, 1967).

When Europeans first came into more extensive, direct contact with dark-skinned people in the late fifteenth century, systematic racist beliefs had not yet developed. But racism was soon to develop, especially in England, the Netherlands, and the colonial societies these countries established. The Spanish were somewhat less likely to accept racism, and today less racism is found in Latin American countries compared with countries with British and Dutch roots. Although racism can be found, much the same can be said of France and its territories. The British colonies, especially the United States and Australia, and the Dutch and British territory later to become South Africa, along with the later German racism, have led the world in racist ideologies.

Other European countries and their territories have *not* been free of racism. It must also be stressed that racism developed extensively only after these Europeans began systematic exploitation of other peoples through colonization and slavery. This suggests that racism is somehow related to conflict and exploitation between groups, a suggestion that is pursued more fully later in this chapter.

Industrialization, White Dominance, and Racism. When Europeans began exploring the world during the fifteenth and sixteenth centuries, they believed they were "superior" to other peoples in the sense of technology and moral values. The Europeans had the new warships and guns, as well as many other material goods and the scientific knowledge made possible by the new enlightenment in Europe. It was easy for some people to make the next assumption that such technological superiority was due to racial differences. And it is to some extent still possible for some whites to view the continued dominance held by nations with a majority white population in the twentieth century to claim support for their racist beliefs.

There are, of course, at least two major flaws in this reasoning for white superiority: (1) whites have certainly not always been the most advanced in science and technology, and (2) the reasons for the technological advance of European nations in recent centuries have nothing to do with race.

An elementary understanding of history easily indicates the first point. With the decline of the Roman Empire around A.D. 500 there was certainly more technological advance among darker-skinned people in the Middle East, and there was the rise of an Islamic Empire. At about the same time, China was more advanced in science and technology than was Europe, and Mongol tribes under the leadership of Attila the Hun (and later Genghis Khan) conquered most of Asia, the Middle East, and much of what is now the Soviet Union. Racist beliefs, however, include only bits of information seemingly supportive of racism, while ignoring the remaining historical information.

As for the second point, we have already discussed the process of industrialization and European dominance with the new world system. From those discussions it can be understood that the rise of the West during the period shortly before industrialization had nothing to do with race. Whites were simply in a position where geography made the process of industrialization most likely. We have seen how geography and agricultural methods favored political systems that made industrialization more likely. An individualistic and rationalistic culture, shaped by geographic and economic conditions in Europe, also helped the rise of the West. Along with these factors mentioned in earlier chapters, Chirot (1984) has recently listed many others that favored European advancement: a climate that produced a favorable ratio of humans to work animals, and even the black death during A.D. 1000 to 1500, which kept the land, animal, and human ratios favorable for economic growth.

Thus, although the rise of the West had nothing to do with race per se, it did create a climate for racism as whites began moving about the world dominating other people.

The American History of Race and Ethnic Relations

American history is a history of race and ethnic relations. Table 14.1 shows that the United States is a diverse nation made up of many racial and ethnic groups. These racial and ethnic groups entered the United States at different times producing successive waves of change and conflict.

The First Europeans and American Indians. The first contacts between Europeans and Native Americans were rather positive. Christopher Columbus wrote of Native Americans as "generous" people who "show as much lovingness as though they would give their hearts." He also believed the Native Americans had "very subtle wit" and "gave marvelous good account" of themselves in navigating the seas (Hraba, 1979, p. 210). And, of course, all Americans have heard how the Wampanoag Indians saved the first Pilgrims from starvation (though they would probably have second thoughts about their helpful ways today — see Box 14.1). The first century of European settlement of North America was primarily one of accommodation between Native

TABLE 14.1. *Population by selected ancestry group and region, 1980*

Ancestry group	Number (1,000)	Percent distribution, by region				Ancestry group	Number (1,000)	Percent distribution, by region			
		Northeast	Midwest	South	West			Northeast	Midwest	South	West
European:*						Other — Con.					
English	49,598	16	23	40	21	African††	204	33	19	33	15
German	49,224	19	41	22	18	Chinese	894	25	9	12	55
Irish	40,166	24	26	32	18	Filipino	795	10	11	11	68
French**	12,892	26	27	27	19	Japanese	791	7	8	9	77
Italian	12,184	57	16	13	14	Korean	377	18	18	20	43
Scottish	10,049	19	23	35	24	Asian Indian	312	35	23	23	19
Polish	8,228	41	38	11	10	Vietnamese	215	9	14	33	44
Dutch	6,304	18	35	26	20	Jamaican	253	70	6	18	5
Swedish	4,345	15	43	12	31	Haitian	90	72	4	21	2
Norwegian	3,454	7	55	7	31	Mexican	7,693	1	9	35	55
Russian†	2,781	48	17	16	19	Spanish/Hispanic††	2,687	23	8	26	43
Czech‡	1,892	18	49	18	15	Puerto Rican	1,444	73	11	8	7
Hungarian	1,777	39	33	13	14	Cuban	598	24	4	63	9
Welsh	1,665	25	27	22	27	Dominican	171	91	1	6	2
Danish	1,518	9	38	10	43	Colombian	156	54	7	26	13
Portuguese	1,024	50	3	6	41	Spaniard	95	36	6	36	22
Other:						Ecuadoran	88	64	7	11	18
Lebanese	295	31	27	26	16	Salvadoran	85	13	3	9	75
Armenian	213	39	14	5	42	Hawaiian	202	2	3	6	89
Iranian	123	17	15	26	42	American Indian	6,716	9	24	44	24
Syrian	107	47	20	18	15	French Canadian	780	47	23	13	17
Arab/Arabian††	93	19	29	21	30	Canadian	456	42	19	15	23
Afro-American	20,965	17	22	53	9						

* Excludes Spaniard. ** Excludes French Basque. † Represents persons who reported as "Russian," "Great Russian," "Georgian," and other related European or Asian groups. Excludes Ukrainian, Ruthenian, Belorussian and some other distinct ethnic groups. See source for further information. ‡ Includes persons who reported as "Czech," "Bohemian," and "Moravian," as well as the general response of "Czechoslovakian." †† Represents a general type of response which may encompass several ancestry groups.

SOURCE: U.S. Bureau of the Census, *1980 Census of Population, Supplementary Report*, series PC80–S1–10.

BOX 14.1

The Fate of the Native Americans Who Saved the Pilgrims

The honored guest at the feast we think of as the first Thanksgiving was Massasoit, the great Wampanoag chief who taught the Pilgrims how to survive in the new land.

These days, it is the Wampanoag tribe that is struggling to survive. Here in Plimoth Plantation, a reconstruction of a Pilgrim village, an olive-skinned man who calls himself Nanepashemet is teaching his fellow Wampanoags about their past. It is a sign of the Wampanoag's troubled times, though, that Nanepashemet (who also answers to the name Tony Pollard) learned the tribal past from white men — historians and anthropologists, one of them even a Mayflower descendant.

This Thanksgiving, 363 years after the Pilgrims set foot in America, the Wampanoags say they have little to be thankful for. There are only about 2,500 of them, and many are poor, unemployed school dropouts. Some of the lucky ones hold jobs at Plimoth Plantation, where they are paid the minimum wage to act like Wampanoags for the tourists.

Some Wampanoags became bitter. "If I was there (in 1620), the Pilgrims wouldn't have gotten off the boat," exclaims Daisy Moore, a Wampanoag who hasn't picked out an Indian name yet. She and some others plan to mark this Thanksgiving as a day of mourning at the statue of Massasoit near Plymouth Harbor. Erected by the Improved Order of Red Men — then a drinking club for white men — in 1921, three years before Indians could vote, the bronze statue looms over the little cracked boulder called Plymouth Rock.

But for most of history, it was the white man who loomed over the Wampanoags. At first, they and the Pilgrims lived in relative peace, bound together in a military alliance against the Narragansetts. But the cultures were worlds apart. Wampanoags smeared themselves with bear grease, strolled about half-naked and believed in sharing land. The Pilgrims hardly smelled better (frequent bathing was a sin), but they believed in lots of clothes and in property boundaries.

As more settlers arrived — by 1675, Plymouth Colony sprawled over 1,600 square miles and included 7,500 people — tensions grew. In 1675 war broke out. The Wampanoags, led by Massasoit's son, Metacom (the English called him King Phillip), were all but exterminated. Metacom was beheaded and his skull put on display for the next 25 years, not far from where his father had feasted with the Pilgrims.

About the only survivors were the so-called praying Indians, who retreated to coastal communities like Mashpee, a reservation of sorts 20 miles from Plymouth. But a century later, their young male descendants were all but wiped out fighting on the American side in the Revolutionary War.

Mashpee became a town in 1870 and was Wampanoag-run until the whites started moving in during the late 1960s. Now there are 4,000 people — 14,000 in summer, but only 400 are Wampanoags — and they are generally at the bottom of Mashpee's economic ladder.

A tribal survey found that more than half of Wampanoag adults in Mashpee make less than $6,000 a year, and about 40% don't have a high-school diploma. A Massachusetts study says the town suffers serious childhood malnutrition; Wampanoags themselves say alcoholism and teenage pregnancy are major problems.

Source: Stephen P. Morin, "Time Hasn't Blessed Indians Who Shared 'First Thanksgiving.'" *Wall Street Journal*, November 23, 1983.

RACE AND ETHNIC STRATIFICATION ● 389

Americans and Europeans. If for no other reason, there was accommodation because Europeans did not yet claim much Native American land, and the military power of European settlers was inferior to that of Native Americans.

By the late 1700s, however, warfare between Native Americans and white settlers emerged. The primary cause of warfare was the beginning of expropriation of Indian lands by whites. Prior to 1784 white settlers had taken land along the east coast and down through the Gulf Coast. By 1850, however, almost all territory east of the Mississippi River had been taken, and by 1890 whites had taken most of the remaining lands. It was also during 1890 that the last major battle occurred, which was actually a massacre of 300 Sioux at Wounded Knee, North Dakota (Brown, 1970).

In the process of taking Native American lands, white settlers in most cases simply told American Indians to leave and herded them into reservations, which were in effect concentration camps. Many Native Americans, however, were simply killed. Although never as systematic as the German attempt to exterminate the Jews in World War II, there was an unofficial and sometimes semiofficial policy by the U. S. Army to kill as many Native Americans as possible. The most common method of killing them was slaughter by gunfire when whole villages were destroyed (Brown, 1970). But there were other methods such as distributing clothing known to be infested with smallpox to reservation Indians (Wax, 1971, pp. 17–18). When Europeans first came to North America, there were an estimated 850,000 Native Americans living in what is now the United States. By 1860 the number had already been reduced to 250,000 (Hraba, 1979, p. 212).

Today, Native Americans live in conditions worse than those of any other group in the United States. About half of all American Indians live in rural areas and on reservations or former reservation lands, and most are unemployed (Sorkin, 1978; Stanley and Thomas, 1978). There has been some improvement in the economic and educational position of Native Americans who have migrated to cities, but overall, they still have the highest poverty rate of any group in the United States.

Blacks in America. While land was being taken from Native Americans, black slaves were being transported to America to work the land for white settlers. Slave trading companies sent boats to Africa, where blacks were captured, sometimes with assistance of rival tribes, then shipped to the new lands in the Americas to be sold. In total, about 340,000 slaves were sold in the Americas during the 1600s, 6 million during the 1700s, and about 2 million during the 1800s (Curtin, 1969). Only about 400,000 of these slaves were sold in the United States, but through reproduction the number of slaves in this country totaled about 4 million by 1860 (Genovese, 1974, p. 5).

In most respects, black slavery in the Americas was the most brutal in human history. In contrast to slavery elsewhere, these people were torn from their families when captured, then torn from new families again and again as they were resold in the Americas. It is estimated that perhaps *9 million* slaves died on ships coming to the Americas, compared with 6 million Jews murdered by the Nazis (Clark, 1969, p. 323).

Slavery has existed from the beginning of agricultural societies, when it first became profitable to own another human for labor. But in previous history, for example, in ancient Greece and the Roman Empire, slaves were more likely to be respected as humans, with rights and usually the chance of eventual freedom. In the Americas, however, slaves were seen as subhuman property. Soon after slavery became extensive in the United States, a racist belief system was developed to justify the holding of slaves by claiming they were subhumans (Turner and Singleton, 1978).

It has been argued that slaves in the United States were taken care of adequately in a physical sense. Like farm animals that must be kept healthy to serve an economic function, slaves were usually well fed and sheltered (Fogel and Engerman, 1974). This assumption is borne out by the natural increase in slaves' numbers through reproduction from 400,000 to 4 million by 1860. The United States, in fact, was one of the few places where black slaves reproduced in large numbers, though this is primarily due to the practice of importing women and not just men. But though the basic physical needs of slaves were usually taken care of, psychological and social deprivation was immense. As noted above, families were frequently broken apart, there was no hope of freedom, labor was extremely hard, and slaves were subject to a dehumanizing racist ideology.

In contrast to common assumptions, blacks did not accept their condition in a passive childlike manner. Whenever they had the chance, they were likely to revolt, to fight back, and to flee (Aptheker, 1969). From time to time there were revolts in which white slave owners were killed, and because slaves outnumbered whites in many places in the Southern United States, whites lived in almost constant fear.

Any show of independence or "disrespect" was treated harshly, and slave revolts were put down with brutal force. In their desperate attempt to control slaves, whites invoked the Christian religion. After reading the sermon approved for slaves in Box 14.2, one gets the impression that slave owners agreed with Marx on the function of religion to control the lower classes.

After the American Civil War, slaves were legally freed, though total freedom was hardly the lot of former slaves. Although slavery had been an issue in the Civil War (the Civil War was precipitated by congressional legislation to allow no more slave states), it was not necessarily the primary issue. The Civil War was a conflict between elites in the North

---

BOX 14.2 *A Christian Religion to Control Slaves*	One of the most efficient ways of controlling people is to get some of them to accept domination. Because it can provide a powerful means for guiding behavior, religion has often been used to control people throughout history, or at least since organized religion emerged with advanced horticultural societies.

What follows is part of a sermon from the early 1800s authorized for slaves by the Alabama Baptist Association (quoted from Aptheker, 1969, p. 57). Sermons in the South during slavery often required prior authorization because the Christian religion can be used to support equality and liberation as well.

There is only one circumstance which may appear grievous that I shall now take notice of; and this is CORRECTION. Now, when *correction* is given you, you either deserve it, or you do not deserve it. But whether you deserve it or not, it is your duty, and Almighty God requires, that you bear it patiently. You may, perhaps, think that this is a hard doctrine; but if you consider it rightly, you must needs think otherwise of it. Suppose, then, that you deserve correction; you cannot but say that it is just and right you should meet with it. Suppose you do not, or at least you do not deserve so much or so severe a correction for the fault you have committed; you perhaps have escaped a great many more, and are at last paid for all. Or suppose you are quite innocent of what is laid to your charge, and suffer wrongfully in that particular thing; is it not possible you may have done some other bad which was never discovered, and that Almighty God, who saw you doing it, would not let you escape without punishment one time or another? And ought you not in such a case to give glory to Him, and be thankful that He would rather punish you in this life for your wickedness, than destroy your souls for it in the next life? But suppose that even this was not the case — a case hardly to be imagined — and that you have by no means, known or unknown, deserved the correction you suffered; there is this great comfort in it, that if you bear it patiently, and leave your cause in the hands of God, He will reward you for it in heaven, and the punishment you suffer unjustly here shall turn to your exceeding great glory hereafter.

who were pushing for political policies supporting their industrial economy and elites in the South who were trying to protect their agrarian-based economy.

With the end of the Civil War there was also much hope that oppression of blacks would end. Some blacks, in fact, were elected to political office in the South soon after the Civil War. Also, there were federal government plans to give all freed slaves "forty acres and a mule." But such plans did not materialize. Instead political bargains were struck in Washington that allowed Southern states to deal with blacks in their own way in exchange for the support of Southern politicians on other issues.

In response to black freedom, Southern states rapidly enacted "Jim Crow" legislation, which eliminated the right to vote for most blacks, curtailed their access to courts, and segregated them in schools and other public places. In many respects, conditions for blacks became worse after the Civil War. Life expectancy declined by 10 percent, wages slowly went down compared to whites' wages, and blacks became more and more concentrated in farm occupations (Hraba, 1979, p. 268). There was also increased effort to control and suppress a legally free black population through extralegal means. It was at this time that the Ku Klux Klan emerged as a quasi-secret terrorist organization to frighten blacks with violence. But not all the violence was organized by groups like the Klan; lynchings were often collective acts by white citizens in response to some perceived infraction of informal behavior codes by blacks.

Just as slaves revolted in the face of oppression, so did the formally free blacks. The National Association for the Advancement of Colored People (NAACP) was founded in 1910. Protest movements in the early 1900s with capable black leaders like W. E. B. DuBois were in many ways similar to the Civil Rights Movement of the 1950s and 1960s.

Blacks had to wait for other changes in America before these protest movements had any success. The most important of these changes emerged slowly in the early 1900s but then came in a flood after World War II. In 1910 almost 90 percent of black Americans lived in the South and in rural areas (Broom and Glenn, 1965). By 1940, 77 percent of blacks still lived in the South, but by 1970 only about half lived there. Even more important, by 1970 over half of all blacks in the United States lived in major cities, compared with only 28 percent of whites.

This migration of blacks was due in part to a "pull"; jobs for blacks were opening in urban areas outside the South. But primarily it was a "push"; farm mechanization eliminated most jobs held by blacks. They were forced into urban areas if they did not want to starve. This economic change caused one of the biggest internal migrations of a population in history, and any understanding of the situation of blacks in America today must not neglect it. In many ways, blacks today are like the new immigrants who arrived poor and uneducated from Europe in the late 1800s and early 1900s in the United States (Sowell, 1981). These early immigrants had many of the same problems found among poor blacks in urban areas today such as family disruption and crime. But for blacks there has been the added burden of racism, which makes overcoming conditions like poverty more difficult.

With the massive internal migration of blacks came the black urban ghettos. There were, of course, some black urban areas like Harlem in New York City before World War II, but by the 1960s every major city in the United States had a black ghetto of significant size. And as noted above, because of the condition of the people who crowded into these black ghettos, there was poverty, crime, and many other social problems, just as there were with poor white immigrants before them.

It was in this context that the Civil Rights Movement began in the 1950s. With conditions in these black ghettos in mind, many people assume that the black protest movement and riots in the 1960s were born of frustration and desperation. But whereas frustration and desperation were certainly present for urban blacks in the 1950s and 1960s, their desperation was clearly extensive (perhaps even more so) before this period. As we will see in Chapter 16, social movements are born not just of deprivation but also of new resources that give the deprived the ability to organize and challenge their opponents (McCarthy and Zald, 1977). For urban blacks in the 1950s and 1960s, what helped provide this ability were large numbers living close together, large black churches, some civil rights protection when away from small Southern towns, and national political elites who needed black votes (Morris, 1981; Piven and Cloward, 1977).

There have been some successes from the Civil Rights Movement, but the outcome is mixed. Some blacks have benefited from more educational and occupational opportunities, but many blacks live in conditions worse than those of the 1960s.

White Ethnics. After Native Americans, the original European settlers, and blacks, the next important wave of immigrants to the United States came again from Europe. Except for Native Americans (who were not yet incorporated into the society) and blacks (who were almost all slaves), the U.S. population was rather homogeneous until 1860. Of the 5 million immigrants who came to the United States between 1820 and 1860, 90 percent were from England, Ireland, and Germany. These immigrants were basically white Anglo-Saxon Protestants (WASPs) and blended easily with the original white settlers.

After the Civil War, as shown in Table 14.2, this changed rapidly. Between 1860 and 1920 there was a flood of 30 million immigrants from central and eastern Europe. The immigrants from places like Italy, Poland, and Russia were less similar to the earlier white immigrants in culture and religion, and blending was, therefore, more difficult. The earlier immigrants discriminated against these new white ethnics. Even the newer Jewish immigrants from places like Poland were often denied equal status in the already established Jewish communities of America (Howe, 1976).

These eastern and central European immigrants poured into the big cities, creating ghettos later taken over by blacks and Puerto Ricans. They began at the bottom of the stratification system, with the lowest pay and lowliest jobs, that is, when jobs could be found. But as the American ideology goes, at least to some extent, the second and third generation of white ethnics were able to "move up the ladder of success." And although most of the later generation blended with the overall white population and culture, there are still pockets of white ethnics in

TABLE 14.2. *European sources of immigration to the United States, distribution by percentages and decades, 1820–1920*

Decade	Total European immigration	Northern and Western European (percent)*	Southern and Eastern European (percent)*
1821–1830	98,817	98	2
1831–1840	495,688	82	1
1841–1850	1,597,501	93	.3
1851–1860	2,452,660	94	.8
1861–1870	2,065,270	88	2
1871–1880	2,272,262	74	7
1881–1890	4,737,046	72	18
1891–1900	3,558,978	45	52
1901–1910	8,136,016	22	71
1911–1920	4,376,564	17	59

* Percentages may not total to 100 because of rounding and European immigration from other countries.
SOURCE: Hraba (1979, p. 10).

America, especially in some large cities, where Italian, Polish, and other ethnic traditions are maintained.

Asian Americans. Although fewer than European immigrants, as can be seen in Table 14.3, Asians made up a significant part of the overall immigration to the United States between 1850 and 1920, especially on the West Coast. They came at first almost exclusively from China, but by the 1890s Japanese immigrants became more numerous.

By the second half of the 1800s, China was an extremely poor and dependent periphery nation where Western powers had carved up Chinese territory for their individual exploitation. With such extensive poverty owing to China's economic decline, and with Western contact, many of the very poor Chinese found their way to America, especially California. On the West Coast of the United States these Chinese filled an important need for low-skilled, low-wage labor to build the railroads and other structures needed in the expanding West. These Chinese often met extreme racism and discrimina-

TABLE 14.3. *Asian sources of immigration to the United States, distribution by percentages and decades, 1850–1920*

Decade	Total Asian immigration	From China (percent)*	From Japan (percent)*
1851–1860	41,455	100	0
1861–1870	64,630	99	0
1871–1880	123,823	99	0
1881–1890	68,382	90	3
1891–1900	71,236	21	36
1901–1910	243,567	8	53
1911–1920	192,559	11	44

* Percentages may not total to 100 because of rounding and Asian immigration from other countries: India and Turkey.
SOURCE: Hraba (1979, p. 10).

tion, much like that of blacks in the rural South before World War II.

The Japanese came later primarily because Japan had much less contact with the West until the later 1800s. In fact, Japan was basically a closed country until forced open by the United States in the 1860s. When Japan opened up and began to industrialize with Western contact, many Japanese saw opportunities in the United States because of the higher level of industrialization here. Thus, many Japanese came, but they brought more economic assets with them than did the earlier Chinese immigrants and were more likely to purchase land or begin commercial establishments, especially in California.

The Japanese immigrants, though originally better off than the Chinese, experienced the same level of discrimination and racism in the American West. From time to time legislation restricted their right to own land and become U.S. citizens. By the 1920s, laws were passed by Congress that basically eliminated Japanese and other Asian immigration. The most drastic action against the Japanese was their internment during World War II. Soon after the beginning of the war with Japan, President Roosevelt signed the order to remove about 90 percent of the 126,000 Japanese-Americans from their homes to what were in reality concentration camps (Kitano, 1969). Over two-thirds of these Japanese-Ameri-

cans were actually U. S. citizens, but they were nonetheless taken from their homes and sent to concentration camps in the deserts of the American Southwest. There was little physical mistreatment of these people, but most lost everything they had while in the camps. It is clear that racism was, in part, involved in this internment of Japanese. There was almost no support for Japan's war effort among Japanese-Americans, no acts of sabotage, and in fact, many of the Japanese-Americans volunteered for military service. It is significant that German and Italian ethnic communities in the United States were not mistreated during World War II.

Finally, the most recent Asian immigrants to this country have come from Southeast Asia (primarily Vietnam, Cambodia, and Laos). Currently there are approximately 650,000 of these immigrants living in the United States (Caplan, 1985). The first wave came during the middle 1970s, when the Vietnam War was drawing to a close and it was clear who would win. These first Southeast Asian immigrants were usually middle class, with some possessions, education, and job skills. They have met with some discrimination in many parts of the United States, especially when their economic activities have brought them into conflict with local citizens. (An important example of this conflict occurred on the Gulf Coast when their commercial fishing brought them into conflict with established fishermen). For the most part, however, these new Asian immigrants have adjusted and become successful in their new business activities.

The second wave of Southeast Asian immigrants in the late 1970s and early 1980s came under different circumstances. These people were often poor farmers or from fishing villages, and they had no money or education. These were the lower classes who could not leave Southeast Asia at first, and came to be known as "boat people." They have had extreme difficulty finding new homes, and even entrance into nations like the United States. Often they were met with protest by local citizens in the United States because of fear over competition for jobs. And though this second wave of immigrants has been in the United States only a short time, there are already at least some remarkable success stories. By considering the reasons for such success

---

BOX 14.3

Southeast Asian "Boat People": Factors Influencing Their Success in America

They were known as "the Boat People" — a second, post-1975 wave of refugees who left Southeast Asia a few years after the withdrawal of U. S. forces from Vietnam. Their subsequent plight as homeless refugees, literally adrift at sea, became an international issue.

The Boat People had been farmers, fishers, craftspeople, students, and laborers in Southeast Asia. Arriving with little or no savings or other resources, little or no command of English, and few transferable labor market skills, those who reached the United States also faced a severely depressed national economy. The obstacles to their achieving self-sufficient lives in this country seemed insurmountable.

"And yet," says ISR (Institute for Social Research) researcher Nathan Caplan, "considering their hardships and all the odds against them, this group of immigrants has in fact demonstrated remarkable progress."

Caplan, in association with John K. Whitmore and with the assistance of Quang Bui and Marcella Trautmann, directed a three-year study of Southeast Asian refugees now living in the United States.

Nearly nine out of ten of the sample households reported that at least one household member was employed, and, for individuals, unemployment ranged from a high 86 percent during the first four months in the U. S. to a low of 19 percent by the 44th month. More than three-quarters of the employed refugees held full-time jobs (35 or more hours per week) at the time of interviewing.

In a separate series of analyses from this study, Caplan and his colleagues investigated the academic achievement of approximately 350 school-aged children from the sample of refugee families. All of the children had arrived in the U. S. after October 1978; most of them spoke *no* English upon arrival here. Yet, after an average of just three years in this country, these children were doing extremely well in school.

On national standardized tests of academic achievement, 27 percent of the refugee children scored in the 90th percentile on math achievement — almost three times better than the national average. And although they scored somewhat lower than the national average in English language proficiency, they outperformed their school-aged peers on general grade-point average, with 27 percent earning A or A-minus.

A multivariate analysis of attitude and background characteristics revealed the factors that were significantly linked to scholastic success. The highest-achieving children were from families that embodied what are traditional Confucian cultural values, emphasizing the family as a cohesive unit working to achieve shared goals, and encouraging a strong respect for education and for the family's cultural traditions and history.

Achievement was also highest among children from families in which parents read to their children — and it made no difference whether they read in English or in their native language. Higher achievement was also associated with greater equality between the two parents in family influence and decision making.

Source: "Working Toward Self-Sufficiency." Reprinted with permission from *ISR Newsletter*, Institute for Social Research, University of Michigan, (Vol. 16, No. 1 Spring/Summer 1985), Ann Arbor, MI, pp. 4–7.

we can also understand why other race and ethnic groups have sometimes had less success (see Box 14.3).

Hispanic Americans. As indicated in Table 14.1, Hispanic Americans are the second-largest ethnic/racial minority group in the United States, just behind blacks. But even more important, because of immigration Hispanics are the most rapidly growing minority group in the United States. At the current rate of increase, Hispanics can be expected to overtake blacks as the largest ethnic/racial minority group in a few decades. And in some states, especially California, Hispanics may soon come to outnumber whites.

The term "Hispanic" refers to people with ethnic backgrounds in the old Spanish colonies of Latin America. In 1980, Mexican-Americans made up the largest group of Hispanics in this country, with Puerto Ricans a distant second. Hispanics are an ethnic group of diverse racial composition. Mexico, for example, may have a greater biological mixture (amalgamation) of races than any other large nation (van den Berghe, 1978). Most Mexicans are "mestizo," a mixture of Native American and European characteristics. Puerto Ricans, however, represent an even greater mixture, which is a combination of European, Native American, and African.

Mexican-Americans first became a part of the American population through conquest and annexation. Much of the southwestern United States was taken from Mexico following the Mexican War in 1848. Most Mexican-Americans, however, have come to this country as immigrants from Mexico, both legally and illegally. During the 1970s Mexican-Americans accounted for 15 percent of all legal immigrants to the United States, and a much greater percentage of illegal immigrants.

Puerto Ricans also first became an American minority group through conquest. Puerto Rico became U.S. territory after it was taken from Spain during the Spanish-American War of 1898; in 1917 all Puerto Ricans became American citizens. Thus, Puerto Ricans are free to move about the United States, although most are concentrated in New York City, there is a circular pattern of migration back and forth, resulting in ethnic neighborhoods where many of the people never learn English (Lewis, 1965).

More recently immigration from Latin America has increased, presenting controversial political decisions. Many Latin Americans are fleeing dictatorships and oppression in Central America and Cuba, but because Central American dictators are friendly to the U.S. government (with the exception of Nicaragua), these immigrants are sent back to the political violence. From time to time, however, the United States has accepted Cuban immigrants.

Eighty percent of the largest group of Hispanic-Americans, Mexican-Americans, live in just two states—California and Texas. Most of the remaining 20 percent are located in Arizona, New Mexico, and Colorado. Because of the importance of agriculture in these states, and because of the political attention directed toward illegal immigrants working in agriculture, it is assumed by many that most Mexican-Americans work in agriculture. This assumption is highly inaccurate, however, because less than 5 percent are in agricultural occupations, though a greater than average number are in blue-collar occupations.

One of the most difficult political questions concerning Mexican-Americans is that of illegal immigration. The political conflict over this issue represents a classic case of class conflict. Most wealthy individuals in states with a large agricultural industry are in favor of ignoring the issue or allowing even more Mexicans into the country legally, because the abundant supply of cheap labor keeps profits high. Most middle-class Americans also benefit from illegal aliens because food costs are kept low with competition for jobs in agriculture. Agricultural workers and other workers in low-skilled occupations, however, oppose illegal immigration because it takes their jobs and reduces their wages.

Continued WASP Dominance. As we have already seen, with the exception of slaves and Native Americans the vast majority of the early U.S. population were primarily of British origin, combined with a few other western Europeans. It was the "old stock" Americans who therefore established the dominant

Stricter immigration laws and enforcement have made illegal immigration across the Mexican border much more difficult. Nevertheless, the "American dream" of working for economic mobility continues to motivate Mexicans to come to the United States. Once here, however, they often do the kinds of service jobs that native-born Americans don't want to do. They are, in other words, a source of cheap labor. (© Alex Webb/Magnum)

political and economic institutions and the dominant cultural values. Although each new wave of immigrants has made an impression on these institutions and values, WASPs still dominate.

This dominance can be seen most clearly in the upper class and economic elites. Studies of the backgrounds of corporate elites have found a large majority are WASP, and the same is found with graduates of elite universities, which supply the greatest proportion of these elites (Alba and Moore, 1982). Studies of particular industries have found today's economic elites are very likely to have ancestors among the earliest British immigrants (Ingham, 1978).

Although other sectors of America, especially politics, are also dominated by WASPs, the dominance is not quite as great (Alba and Moore, 1982).

The president's cabinet, however, has been especially dominated by upper-class WASPs (Mintz, 1975). In addition to showing the exclusion of all other racial and ethnic groups in general, these studies show the inaccuracy of the widespread belief that Jews hold extensive political and economic power in the United States. In their study of institutional elites in America, Alba and Moore (1982) found only media elites to have significant Jewish backgrounds, but even there the figure was only 25 percent.

RACE AND ETHNIC RELATIONS

The simple presence of various racial and ethnic groups in a society tells us very little. We need to know the relations among the groups and the form or group structure in the society. As we have already seen, the form and characteristics of group networks have a big impact on many aspects of the society. Thus, societies can differ drastically even though the racial and ethnic mixture of their populations are similar.

Switzerland, for example, is an ethnically diverse country with four main languages and two primary religions. Switzerland, however, has not had any significant ethnic group conflict in many years. India, in contrast, has seen bloody religious and ethnic group conflict for many years, and especially since independence in 1947. In one striking example of this conflict, during 1984 men from a minority religious-ethnic group (Sikh) killed Prime Minister Indira Gandhi. Many attacks by Hindus against Sikhs followed, and hundreds on both sides were killed. During 1985 in the Indian city of Ahmadabad dozens were killed when Hindus attacked Muslims over a government-sponsored program to improve educational opportunities for Muslims. During a similar conflict in that state in 1969, 800 Hindus and Muslims were killed.

Patterns of Race and Ethnic Relations

Irrespective of the particular race or ethnic group involved, specific patterns of race and ethnic relations can be identified. Two general patterns are called "assimilation" and "pluralism," but within these two patterns are degrees of racial or ethnic assimilation, as well as varying degrees of conflict within a pluralist society.

Assimilation. **Assimilation** is a process of boundary reduction between two groups, wherein one group is absorbed into the other (Yinger, 1981). There are various theories about how the assimilation process occurs, all of which use ideas from the functional theory of society. Before examining these theories, however, we should consider the four types of assimilation.

Cultural assimilation refers to a situation in which one group comes to adopt the values and culture of another group. Cultural assimilation would mean that an ethnic group in the United States has

come to speak English and adopt the primary values of the country, along with the life-style and other dominant cultural characteristics. For example, a high degree of cultural assimilation can be found among most third- and fourth-generation Asian-American students on college campuses throughout the United States.

Structural assimilation refers to increased social interaction among two groups. By structural we mean group properties — have the networks of group interactions *within* the two groups been extended to networks *across* the two groups? When the social interactions within the group are as strong and numerous as the interactions across the two groups, then structural assimilation has occurred. Cultural assimilation and structural assimilation do not necessarily occur together. For example, although most blacks in the United States have been assimilated culturally, there continues to be less structural assimilation.

Biological assimilation or **amalgamation** refers to intermarriage and thus the biological blending of two groups. Amalgamation occurs in a very high stage of overall assimilation. Again, amalgamation does not necessarily follow cultural and structural assimilation because one or both groups involved may have strong preferences for marriage within the racial group.

Finally, **psychological assimilation** refers to self-identity. Even though a particular individual accepts much of the culture of another group and interacts with members of the other group, the person can continue to identify with his or her own racial or ethnic group. And as we have seen, self-identity is a social product. If a self-identity placing the person in one group or another is to develop, significant others must also come to identify that person as a member of the group.

Racial and ethnic groups within a society must be considered with respect to all four of these aspects of assimilation because the four aspects do not always go together. And racial and ethnic groups certainly vary with their ranking on each of the four.

Theories of Assimilation. Within American sociology Robert Park (1950) developed the first respected theory of assimilation. Park considered assimilation as an evolutionary process occurring in stages when a new group is brought into a society. The first stage involves initial *contact* through migration or annexation. Once the contact has occurred, there develops *competition* wherein the two groups are in conflict over valued resources, status, and influence. In time there is *accommodation,* where the two groups come to work together, and finally *assimilation,* when the two groups merge.

Park's view of the process of assimilation describes the historical pattern of various European immigrants (e.g., Irish, Italians) in the United States somewhat accurately. But other groups do not fit this pattern, most notably blacks, Native Americans, and to some extent Jews. Some groups simply remain stuck in one stage, and the process doesn't necessarily occur in these stages. Blacks in the United States, for example, have varied between "competition" and "accommodation" over the years.

More recently, Milton Gordon (1964) developed a more complex theory of the assimilation process. Like Park, Gordon views the process as occurring in stages, but he recognizes there is no simple line of progression and that a group can become stuck in one stage without moving to eventual assimilation. As can be seen in Table 14.4, the first four stages outlined by Gordon correspond to the four types of assimilation described above. The remaining three stages primarily refer to the response of the dominant society. In the fifth stage there is reduced prejudice toward the racial or ethnic group, or even the elimination of prejudice. Next there is reduced discrimination; in other words, there is less treating people differently because of race or ethnic background. Finally, Gordon describes civic assimilation where conflict over resources and power has been eliminated.

Gordon's theory is more useful than Park's in helping us understand the complex history of race and ethnic relations in a country like the United States, but both theories suffer from a general functional theoretical assumption — conflict is assumed to be somehow unnatural. From the social order perspective, assimilation is considered natural because it eliminates group conflicts. As we will see, however, elites or others may have a strong self-in-

TABLE 14.4. *Gordon's stages of assimilation*

Stage	Characteristics
Cultural or behavioral assimilation (acculturation)	Change of cultural patterns to those of host society
Structural assimilation	Large-scale entrance into cliques, clubs, and institutions of host society, on primary group level
Marital assimilation (amalgamation)	Large-scale intermarriage
Identificational assimilation	Development of sense of peoplehood based exclusively on host society
Attitude receptional assimilation	Absence of prejudice
Behavior receptional assimilation	Absence of discrimination
Civic assimilation	Absence of value and power conflict

SOURCE: Milton M. Gordon, *Assimilation in American Life: The Role of Race Religion, and National Origins* (New York: Oxford University Press, 1964), p. 71.

terest in keeping conflict alive and/or maintaining the boundaries of race and ethnic groups for the purpose of exploitation.

Factors Supporting Assimilation. Gordon's theory of assimilation, despite the criticism above, is useful in understanding how some ethnic groups have or have not reached assimilation in a society, especially when considered with the following factors that can enhance or impede the process of assimilation (Marger, 1985, pp. 76–78).

First, we must consider the *manner of entrance;* that is, how the ethnic or racial group was brought into the dominant society. If the entrance was due to voluntary immigration, then assimilation is more likely. However, if the immigration is involuntary or due to conquest, eventual assimilation is less likely. Slavery is one source of involuntary immigration and, of course, occurred originally for blacks in the United States.

The length of *time* since immigration or conquest is another important factor in assimilation. Assimilation takes time, and if the entrance occurred through forced immigration or conquest, it takes time for anger to subside. In most cases, when voluntary immigration has occurred, the process of assimilation takes at least one generation, and quite often three or four. With cases of conquest the assimilation may never occur, or at least not totally, and there is continuing threat of a resurgence of old ethnic nationalism. The Basque movement and terrorism against Spain is a good example of resurgent ethnic nationalism.

Demographic factors such as population size and rate of immigration can effect assimilation. For example, if large numbers of new immigrants come in a very short period, the new immigrants will be more visible and likely perceived as a threat to the host population, thus producing more conflict and resistance to assimilation. Also, within the immigrant population there will be more people to share and maintain the old culture, again reducing assimilation. After changes in U.S. and Cuban policies allowed extensive immigration from Cuba to Florida in the late 1970s, conflicts and a much larger Cuban population were created, which will no doubt make assimilation more difficult. Many groups are similar in cultural traits and such *cultural similarity* can increase the chances of assimilation. A person from France, for example, will be more easily assimilated in the United States than a person from Cambodia.

Visible physical differences have often affected assimilation. The differences can set people apart, remind both the majority and the minority of their unique history and traditions, and create prejudice, all of which may impede assimilation. The physical differences themselves are not important (biologically, that is); rather the beliefs about these physical differences are the critical factors. Both blacks in the United States and Caucasians in Japan have found assimilation more difficult for this reason.

Pluralism. The older theories of assimilation assumed that modern societies, with easy geographical mobility and a mass media, would have strong tendencies toward assimilation of all groups. These theories have underestimated the degree to which race and ethnic divisions can be maintained in modern societies. Today it is recognized that race and ethnic divisions can certainly persist and in many ways provide a useful service for individuals in modern societies.

Pluralism refers to a society in which ethnic and/or racial divisions have been maintained. In a sense, pluralism is the opposite of assimilation, and like assimilation, has several dimensions. Two are useful to describe — *cultural pluralism* and *structural pluralism*. The former refers to maintaining dissimilarities in culture, and the latter refers to group barriers to social interaction.

When two or more race or ethnic groups remain rather distinct, the potential for conflict is quite high, indeed, almost certain over time. But as we have seen, group conflict can be tame, even beneficial, or conflict may become destructive. Two types of pluralism are related to these extremes of conflict — equalitarian pluralism and inequalitarian pluralism.

Equalitarian pluralism refers to a situation in which the balance of power among groups is roughly equal and there is some consensus over rules of "fair" competition in the society. The distribution of valued resources will not be extremely unbalanced if the balance of power and consensus over rules is maintained. Switzerland, as already noted, is an ethnically diverse nation that has maintained social order through laws that maintain the balance of power among ethnic groups. Lebanon, however, has disintegrated into civil war because the political system and consensus over "rules of the game" were disrupted by the influx of Palestinians in the early 1970s and again by Israeli invasion in the early 1980s.

If equalitarian pluralism can be maintained, there may be positive outcomes in contrast to complete assimilation. For example, ethnic diversity may provide a stronger sense of group identity in the face of a large, impersonal society. Also, new ideas, creativity, and an interesting sense of cultural diversity may counter what some people criticize as a tendency toward drab uniformity created by a nationwide mass media.

Inequalitarian pluralism, in contrast, refers to a society in which one racial or ethnic group holds extensive power over others and where there is a high degree of inequality based on race or ethnic divisions. The range of power and material inequalities can differ extensively among societies classified as inequalitarian pluralist societies. The most extreme form is found in slave societies, as in the American South before the Civil War. In this case, the power of one group over another is almost complete, though there have been more extensive rights and protection granted to slaves in most other slave societies throughout history. In South Africa today there is very extensive power held by one racial group (whites) over another, though it is short of total slavery. In what is called the system of **apartheid** in South Africa there is extensive separation of the races by law. Blacks cannot hold political office or vote, though recently, people of mixed race and other races besides black Africans (all called "colored" to separate them from blacks) can vote for a limited number of political offices. These coloreds, however, continue to be extremely powerless. There are also many laws restricting the freedoms and movement of all nonwhites, such as laws prohibiting nonwhites from entering certain areas of cities without permission.

In modern industrial societies, the extensive, almost total dominance held by one race or ethnic group over others is less likely because of the slow growth of democratic ideas and institutions described in Chapter 11. (van den Berghe, 1978). Another reason is the need for more open, flexible societies if industrial economies are to remain healthy. It becomes very inefficient to waste talent and resources attempting to maintain a system of apartheid or total dominance, as South Africa is discovering.

None of this is to say that inequalitarian pluralism does not exist in modern industrial societies. It exists in degrees, with slavery and apartheid at one extreme and the lower level of race and ethnic inequalities found in an industrial society such as France at the other extreme. The United States has a high degree of race and ethnic inequalities compared with most other industrial societies. To a large extent the race and ethnic inequalities in industrial societies have come to overlap with the class system. This interrelation between class and race or ethnicity in industrial societies like the United States is a very important topic and must be covered in some detail. Before that, however, we must consider the causes of racism and discrimination in light of the information we have covered thus far.

Causes of Racism and Discrimination

Over the years, social scientists have developed many theories about the causes of racism, some of which are more useful than others. In this section we examine some of these theories, then consider the relationship between racism and discrimination.

Social Psychological Theories. Because racism is an attitude and an aspect of personality, many people began looking for the causes of racism in the psychology of individuals. Of these social psychological theories, two have received the most attention — frustration-aggression theory and authoritarian personality theory.

Frustration-aggression theory claims that racism and prejudice are the result of frustrations projected upon others who are weak in the society (Dollard et al., 1939; Allport, 1958). The true source of frustration experienced by individuals may be unknown or the individuals are unable to strike out at the true source of their frustrations. However, frustration is believed to produce a need for aggressive behavior that can reduce the psychological stress of frustration. Thus, if the aggression cannot be directed toward the true source of frustration, frustrated individuals will direct their aggression toward another convenient group in the society; that is, a group considered an out-group and powerless.

There is plenty of evidence supporting the general theory of frustration-aggression. To cite some historical examples, there is reason to believe that frustration-aggression was behind the attack upon Jews in Germany prior to World War II. After defeat in World War I, Germany experienced many humiliations and severe economic problems. In this context, anti-Semitism became extreme, with beliefs that Jews were somehow responsible for Germany's problems. Once, when asked what would have happened had Jews not been a convenient target of attack for mobilizing people in Germany, Hitler replied that another group would have been found (Hoffer, 1966). In another striking case, Koreans were attacked in Japan after that country's most severe earthquake in 1923. About 100,000 Japanese were killed by the earthquake and fires that followed, primarily in Tokyo. In the context of fear and frustration, rumors of Koreans taking advantage of Japanese spread, resulting in attacks that killed about 5,000 Koreans (Mitchell, 1967).

Throughout history there have been many cases of attack on weak out-groups when frustration hits the more powerful group. These attacks, or scapegoating, are far more common in history than is racism. Thus, whereas the frustration-aggression pattern may sometimes be related to racism, we cannot say it is a cause of the major cases of racism.

One of the most respected theories of racism views an **authoritarian personality** as a major cause (Adorno, 1950). Developed soon after World War II, this theory had as one goal to explain the existence of anti-Semitism in Germany. As the name

implies, this theory suggests that a certain personality type can be developed that makes one more prone to racism. Basic characteristics of this personality type include respect for force, submission toward superiors, rigidity of outlook, intolerance of ambiguity, antiscientific attitudes, and gullibility.

Some studies have shown a relationship between this authoritarian personality type and racism, though the theory has been heavily criticized on several counts (Simpson and Yinger, 1965, pp. 65–74). For example, some research indicates the authoritarian personality is more simply a reflection of low intelligence than any deeply rooted personality type.

In general, social psychological theories of racism and discrimination can help explain why some individuals are more prone to racism. But as we have seen, the major cases of racism have developed in only a few societies in history. Thus, to best explain racism we must consider something of the nature of these societies and the historical events giving rise to racism.

Conflict Theories. At the heart of major cases of racism and discrimination is conflict between two or more groups. Thus, we must begin with the nature of this conflict to understand the development of racism.

As we have seen in an earlier chapter, in-group and out-group conflict is a natural result of social organization and group boundaries. To maintain in-group unity a perceived threat from an out-group is often useful. Also, to help define what is acceptable behavior and which norms are the most important, deviants or an out-group with negative characteristics are identified or even created. But again, out-groups and deviants have seldom been associated with race throughout history. To understand the major cases of racism in places like South Africa and the United States, we must look elsewhere.

One of the best comparative and historical works on racism was done by van den Berghe (1967). Through examination of the major cases of racism in modern history, he concludes that economic conflict during the development of colonialism is primarily responsible for widespread racism. Not all colonial societies were equally likely to develop racism, how-

Which theories regarding racism and discrimination would you use to explain this Ku Klux Klan rally in Greensboro, North Carolina in 1987? It was the first rally the Klan had held since 1979, and five people died in the associated violence. Do you think the causes of racism are psychological, sociological, or both? (© Bill Briggart/Impact Visuals, Inc.)

ever, and thus additional factors must be involved. Van den Berghe believes three factors were the most critical.

1. Racism developed with economic exploitation as industrial societies began to emerge and dominate colonies. "There is no question that the desire to rationalize exploitation of non-European peoples fostered the elaboration of a complex ideology of paternalism and racism . . ." (van den Berghe, 1967, pp. 16–17). Economic conflict has existed throughout history, and some colonial nations were more prone to racism, thus, there must be additional factors.

2. Racism in European nations and their colonies emerged in the context of Darwin's theory of evolution. Though scientifically Darwin's theory did not suggest the racial superiority of any one group, which Darwin himself even stressed was not the case, it was easy for some people to draw such a conclusion. If humans evolved from other animals, then it might be argued that some humans had evolved further and were thus "superior."

3. A third primary factor, ironically, was the new liberal and egalitarian value system developing with new industrial democracies. "Faced with the blatant contradiction between the treatment of slaves and colonial peoples and the official rhetoric of freedom and equality, Europeans and white North Americans began to dichotomize humanity between men and submen (or the 'civilized' and the 'savages')" (van den Berghe, 1967, pp. 17–18). In so doing, their exploitation of people could be justified, and the contradiction with liberal values ignored, if these people were not really human.

With these three conditions, therefore, the development of racism directed toward American Indians and black slaves can be understood. Particular individuals may be racist; however, if a systematic belief system of racism becomes a dominant aspect of the society, we must look beyond individual personalities. Once the system of racism becomes tradition in a society it can be taught and passed on to individuals with no characteristics of an authoritarian personality and who have no particular need to exploit the minority group for economic gain.

We do find that racism is not always randomly distributed in a society, and the same can be said for simple prejudice and hatred toward ethnic groups. The common pattern is to find more racism or prejudice among people most directly in economic competition or potential competition with the racial or ethnic group. The corporate executive may not be prejudiced, but the working-class family whose jobs are threatened if minorities are given equal treatment is more likely to be prejudiced.

There is another important aspect of the relation between economic conflict and racism or prejudice. It can be asked, who benefits from the prejudice that keeps the minority out of better-paying jobs? One obvious answer is that the person holding the better-paying job is gaining the most. Some evidence supports this by showing that wages are higher for majority workers because job competition is reduced through excluding minorities. However, research also shows that *both* majority and minority workers are harmed by the occupational discrimination, to the benefit of the wealthy through higher profits. In essence, this is a divide-and-conquer effect. The findings are therefore mixed, and no doubt other factors are involved (such as type of industry and region of the country) that help produce one outcome at one time versus the other (Szymanski, 1976; Villemez, 1978).

Another economic cause of ethnic prejudice can be found in what is called the **split labor market.** Because of successive waves of immigrants to this country from different parts of the world, new immigrants often produced new competition for the previous immigrants who are still toward the bottom of the occupational ladder. The competition has often resulted in ethnic hostilities that divide the working class to the advantage of the wealthy (Aronowitz, 1974). A divided working class will find it more difficult to press management for higher wages; thus again, we find a divide-and-conquer effect. The tactic of dividing workers in this manner has been consciously used by corporations, especially in times when unions had less legal protection. For example, during a strike against United States Steel in 1919, loyal employees were asked "to stir up as much bad feeling as you possibly can between the Serbians and the Italians. . . . Call up every question you can in reference to racial hatred between these two nationalities" (Goldman, 1953, p. 305).

The Cycle of Racism and Discrimination. Once a belief system of racism becomes accepted in a society, it often spreads to groups that are not in economic conflict with the minority. It must also be noted that once a racist or prejudiced belief system becomes widespread, it can be maintained even if the need to exploit the minority is eliminated. The reasons for this can be found in the way a cycle of racism and discrimination, once developed, can perpetuate itself.

As indicated in Figure 14.1, the racism or prejudice originally produced by economic conflict often leads to systematic discrimination. This discrimination keeps the minority in low-paying jobs or unemployed, prevents educational achievement, and often results in psychological harm in the form of low self-esteem. There are usually many other important outcomes of discrimination, such as involvement in crime, family disruption, run-down housing, among others. These effects come to reinforce the racist or prejudiced belief as shown in the dashed line in Figure 14.1. The racist rationalizes, "See what those people are like, that shows they are inferior." Thus, there is continued discrimination, and racist beliefs continue to be maintained.

FIGURE 14.1. A cycle of racism and discrimination.

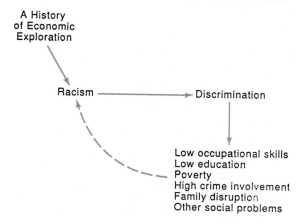

If such a cycle is to be broken, it must be attacked at various points. Attempts to change attitudes could be made, perhaps through the mass media. The actual discrimination can be attacked through laws against discrimination and strong enforcement of these laws. But in addition to this, there must be programs to reduce the effects of past discrimination, such as low education, poor housing, family problems, and poverty. As we will discuss later in this chapter, attempts have been made at all points in this cycle to reduce prejudice and discrimination in the United States, however weak the attempts have sometimes been.

Institutional Discrimination. Even if by some miracle or mysterious force all racism and attitudes of prejudice could be eliminated, there would continue to be race and ethnic inequality in a society with a past history of racism if nothing else is done. Even if negative beliefs are eliminated, there will still be institutional discrimination.

Institutional discrimination refers to the way in which primary institutions in the society (e. g., economy, schools, political system) produce discrimination through their normal operations when race and ethnic inequalities are high because of past overt discrimination and racism. For example, occupational and income inequality between races may exist because the minority race has low educational achievement. In a traditional manner for an industrial society, the best jobs and income go to those who achieve a certain level of education. Higher education may not be as likely among the minority group for several reasons; the need to work before high school is completed, lack of money to attend college, and poor academic achievement in high school. Poor achievement in high school may also be related to several factors: parents with low education who cannot help children learn, attending lower quality schools in poor areas of the city where poor minorities must live, and family problems related to poverty that lead to poor psychological development for children. Good jobs and higher income are related to educational achievement, but the lingering effects of past discrimination make the achievement more difficult for minority groups. Even with no intent of doing so, the dominant institutions in the society perpetuate discrimination.

RACE AND CLASS

One very important implication of institutional discrimination is that it suggests racial and ethnic inequalities have become tied to class inequalities. If people are born into poverty in the United States their chances of moving up the stratification system are less compared with people born higher in the stratification system. Therefore, if minorities are born at the bottom of the stratification system, their chances of social mobility will be at least as limited as those of poor whites. This means that when minorities are concentrated toward the bottom of the stratification system, their life chances and rewards become a matter of their class position as well as their race or ethnic status.

William Wilson (1978) has in fact argued that race is declining in significance today and that class position is more important in affecting the life chances of blacks. Blacks are low in income, occupation, and education from one generation to the next because of their class position, which of course was determined by past racism and discrimination. Wilson certainly does *not* argue that racism and racial discrimination have been eliminated. But his thesis is controversial because sociologists disagree over the extent to which racism and racial discrimination remain important.

Race and Inequality

If minorities and whites were equally distributed throughout the stratification system, and if valued resources such as income were not distributed unequally by race or ethnic status but only by class position, then minority status would have no relation to the class system. As we will see, however, race and ethnic status are certainly related to class position.

Table 14.5 shows the median income figures for major racial and ethnic groups in the United States. As can be seen, the distribution of income is cer-

TABLE 14.5. *Median family income by race and ethnic status, 1970–1984*

Race/Ethnic Group	Median family income (in 1984 dollars)			
	1970	1975	1980	1984
Whites	$10,236	14,268	21,904	27,686
Blacks	6,279	8,779	12,674	15,432
Spanish Origin	NA	9,551	14,716	18,833

SOURCE: U.S. Bureau of the Census, Current Population Reports (1985).

tainly related to race and ethnic status. The highest median income is held by Jewish-Americans, and the lowest is held by Puerto Ricans. The median income for whites is close to the top. Mexican-Americans, blacks, and American Indians all have incomes well below whites. These figures do not tell us that race or ethnic status per se produces these income differences, for it may be something else that causes the income inequality such as class position, and thus race or ethnicity may be only secondary factors. This is Wilson's (1978) thesis in his book *The Declining Significance of Race*.

As would be expected from the other information, the rates of unemployment for blacks, Mexican-Americans, and Native Americans are higher than that of whites. Table 14.6 shows the black unemployment rate is about 200 percent higher than that of whites. Table 14.7 shows that the level of education among adults is substantially lower for blacks, Mexican-Americans, and Native Americans compared with that of whites. Also, we have already seen in Chapter 12 that these minorities have a much higher rate of poverty than whites. In some cases, such as for blacks, the poverty rate is 300 percent higher than for whites.

Occupation, Authority, and Property. So far we have seen that material rewards, jobs, and education are unequally distributed, but we cannot yet say clearly that class position is involved in the unequal distri-

TABLE 14.6. *Black and white unemployment rates, 1972–1983 (%)*

	1972	1975	1977	1978	1979	1980	1981	1982	1983
All Workers	5.6	8.5	7.1	6.1	5.8	7.1	7.6	9.7	9.6
White	5.1	7.8	6.2	5.2	5.1	6.3	6.7	8.6	8.4
Male	4.5	7.2	5.5	4.6	4.5	6.1	6.5	9.9	8.8
Female	5.9	8.6	7.3	6.2	5.9	6.5	6.9	9.4	7.9
Black	10.4	14.8	14.0	12.8	12.3	14.3	15.6	18.9	19.5
Male	9.3	14.8	13.3	11.6	11.4	14.5	15.7	20.1	20.3
Female	11.8	14.8	14.9	13.8	13.3	14.0	15.6	17.6	18.6

SOURCE: U.S. Bureau of Census, *Statistical Abstract of the United States, 1985* (1986), p. 406.

bution. You will remember from the stratification chapters that class can be measured in more than one way. A standard measure of class position, though not necessarily the best measure, is occupational position. As shown in Table 14.8, occupational skill level is certainly related to race and ethnic status. There is a greater concentration of blacks and Mexican-Americans in working-class positions and a higher concentration of whites in white-collar and especially professional and managerial positions.

Class position in industrial societies is related to bureaucratic authority position and property control, as well as occupational skill level. Research has indicated that blacks are significantly lower in authority and property, and we presume the situation is similar for Mexican-Americans and Native Americans, though recent research on these groups is

lacking (Robinson and Kelly, 1979). Table 14.9 presents the findings on the authority and property position of black and white men from a study by Wright and Perrone (1977). The employer category indicates substantial ownership and the employment of workers, and the manager position indicates little property but a high position in an economic bureaucracy. The petite bourgeoisie (such as shopowners and small contractors) own only a little property and hire no or few workers, and workers own little or no property and must work for others in a low-authority position. As Table 14.9 indicates, black men are concentrated in worker positions, with fewer in manager and employer positions compared with white men.

This means that blacks, Mexican-Americans, and Native Americans tend to be low in the major factors

TABLE 14.7. *Educational attainment for whites, blacks, and spanish origin, 1984*

	Percent Distribution					
	Elementary		High School		College	
	5 years or less	5 to 8 years	1 to 3 years	4 years	1 to 3 years	4 years or more
Whites	.8	5.2	12.4	40.9	19.1	21.6
Blacks	1.7	8.3	18.4	41.5	18.5	11.6
Spanish origin	7.4	19.2	18.2	31.8	15.1	8.3

SOURCE: U.S. Department of Labor (1985), pp. 165–168.

TABLE 14.8. *Occupational status of whites, blacks, and Spanish origin, 1983 (%)*

	Whites	Blacks	Spanish origin
Middle class			
Managerial and professional	24.3	14.1	11.8
Technical, sales, and clerical	31.7	25.4	25.3
Working class			
Craft and skilled labor	12.6	9.0	14.4
Operators and laborers	15.1	24.1	25.0
Service occupations	12.5	24.5	17.7
Farming, fishing, forestry	3.8	3.0	5.8
	100	100	100

SOURCE: U.S. Department of Labor (1985), p. 48.

behind the stratification system in the United States. Because most black ancestors came here as slaves and then remained in rural areas as low-skilled farm workers after the Civil War, their occupational skill level remained low. And for most blacks today, or at least their parents, even this low skill became useless with farm mechanization. Because of their current low job skills and recent immigrant status, blacks continue to be in low-authority positions and have very little capital or property to make their own living without working for others. Mexican-Americans have been farm workers in the past, and they are also often recent immigrants. Thus, the Mexican-American position on occupational skill level, authority, and property is similar to that of blacks.

Native Americans were forced to agricultural areas with the worst land, though about 50 percent have migrated to cities rather recently. Like blacks, Native Americans tend to be low in occupation and authority. However, they have had some interesting gains in median income since the 1970s. Though Native Americans still have the highest rate of poverty, their median income has moved above that of blacks and Mexican-Americans only recently (U.S. Commission on Civil Rights, 1978). In part, Native Americans have been moving to cities where employment prospects are better, and extensive government grants and tribal money have been used to obtain better educational opportunities (Kerbo, 1981b; Havinghurst, 1978; Sorkin, 1978; Tax, 1978). However, much of the improved economic situation for some Native Americans is related to property ownership and control of this property. Although most land was taken from Native Americans long ago, some tribes were able to hold on to some land, and a few tribes have recently won legal battles to reclaim land illegally taken.

Most important, many Native American tribes have learned to maintain control of this land and its mineral rights for the collective benefit of tribal members (*Newsweek,* March 20, 1978). For example, rather than allowing mineral rights to be taken at a very low price (as the early Oklahoma Cherokee

TABLE 14.9. *Wright and Perrone's class divisions (authority and ownership) by race and sex*

Class	White males, %	Black males, %	White females, %	Black females, %
Employers	10.9	6.6	3.0	0.0
Managers	42.9	36.8	27.7	22.9
Workers	41.5	55.3	66.6	77.1
Petite bourgeoisie	4.6	1.3	2.7	0.0
Total	100	100	100	100

SOURCE: Wright and Perrone (1977, p. 49).

had done with their oil land [Wax, 1971]), many tribes now have their own lawyers and business advisers to ensure that a fair price is obtained.

Still, Native Americans remain poor on reservation lands. Thus, their poverty rate is still the highest of all groups. However, many have had an advantage that blacks and Mexican-Americans are less likely to have. The favorable position in the property structure has now helped many tribes improve their class position.

Programs and Prospects for Reduced Inequality

Overall there has been another change in the class position for many minorities in the United States. Authority position, remember, is influenced by both position in the occupational authority structure and the political authority structures. The political position of minorities in the United States has improved somewhat in recent decades and this improvement has helped the life chances of some.

Minority Political Gains. We have seen how the position of the working class (mostly whites) was improved through increased political influence. Through union organization, and because the Democratic Party began seeking working-class votes to prevent Democratic losses, the working class was able to achieve at least some economic protection from the state (Piven and Cloward, 1977, 1982). In a similar fashion, minorities have made some political gains in recent years. First, a black Civil Rights Movement was able to grow and achieve some gains since the 1950s. But also important was the need by the Democratic Party to gain new voters since the 1950s. Thus, many civil rights laws and aid programs came into being in the 1960s and 1970s to attract and keep minority votes (Piven and Cloward, 1982). Research has shown the Democratic Party has helped Mexican-American farm workers in a similar manner (Jenkins and Perrow, 1977).

The demographics of minority migration have produced some political gains, especially for blacks. Isolated and scattered in the rural South, blacks could not vote in a unified fashion, if they were even allowed to vote. Today, however, with urban concentrations of blacks, more visibility, and some civil rights protection in big cities, blacks can maintain significant political influence at all levels of government. The significant influence of Jesse Jackson as a presidential candidate in 1984 and, especially, 1988 is another indicator of the increasing importance of blacks in politics.

Table 14.10 shows the magnitude and speed of these political changes between 1970 and 1981. There has been a substantial increase in black elected officials, especially at the state and local levels of government.

Some Gains and Losses. The improved political position of minorities along with demographic factors like relocation to areas with better jobs and schools and economic growth since World War II have produced some gains for minorities. The results have been very mixed, however, as we will see. First, let's consider some gains.

As Table 14.11 shows, there have been some gains in occupational position in private industry for blacks in recent years. And in line with our discussion above of political influence, the gains in high occupational positions (managerial, professional) have been greater in government agencies. In Table 14.12 we find significant improvement in black educational attainment.

Some of the most important gains, however, are shown in Table 14.13. Presented here is a standard "outflow" mobility table as described in the stratification chapter, but in this case it is for black men only. Reading down the left margin of the table we find the father's occupational position — that is, the class position where sons grew up. Across the top is the position of sons in adult years. Thus, we can compare where sons "flow" after leaving home. With such a table we can judge the open or closed nature of the stratification system.

Beginning with the 1962 data we find that the stratification system did not work well for blacks. Most striking is that most black sons ended up in the lowest jobs *no matter where they were born.* If you can remember the white patterns presented in an earlier chapter, this is even more striking. In the

TABLE 14.10. *Change in number of black elected officials by category of office, 1970–81*

Year	Total black elected officials N*	% change	Federal N	% Change	State N	% Change	County N	% Change	Municipal N	% Change
1970	1,469	—	10	—	169	—	92	—	623	—
1971	1,860	26.6	14	40.0	202	19.5	120	30.4	785	26.0
1972	2,264	21.7	14	0.0	210	3.9	176	46.6	932	18.3
1973	2,621	15.7	16	14.3	240	14.3	211	19.8	1,053	12.9
1974	2,991	14.2	17	6.3	239	−0.4	242	14.7	1,360	29.2
1975	3,503	17.1	18	5.9	281	17.6	305	20.6	1,573	15.7
1976	3,979	13.6	18	0.0	281	0.0	355	16.4	1,889	20.1
1977	4,311	8.3	17	−5.6	299	6.4	381	7.3	2,083	10.3
1978	4,503	4.5	17	0.0	299	0.0	410	7.6	2,159	3.6
1979	4,607	2.3	17	0.0	313	4.7	398	−3.0	2,224	3.0
1980	4,912	6.6	17	0.0	323	3.2	451	13.3	2,356	5.9
1981	5,038	2.6	18	5.9	341	5.6	449	−0.4	2,384	1.9

* Total includes some local law enforcement and education officials elected to office not given in local government totals.
SOURCE: Joint Center for Political Studies, National Roster of Black Elected Officials (Vol. 11), Washington, DC, 1984.

top, upper-middle-class jobs, about 60 percent of white sons born there were able to keep upper-middle-class jobs when they grew up. But in 1962, the figure for blacks was only 13.3 percent! And 63 percent of the sons of black doctors, lawyers, and so on ended up in the lowest jobs. This shows that even if a few blacks could make it to top occupational positions, in contrast to whites, few could help their sons stay there. Black sons born at the bottom were more likely to stay there—71 percent of blacks born to lower-working-class fathers stayed, in contrast to about 40 percent for whites. The sons of

TABLE 14.11. *Occupational status in private industry for blacks, 1970–1981 (%)*

Occupational position	1970	1981
Officials/managers	1.7	4.3
Professionals	2.1	3.6
Technicians	2.7	4.3
Sales workers	3.7	5.8
Clerical workers	12.2	16.5
Craft workers	7.5	8.9
Operatives	32.7	26.9
Laborers	19.5	12.3
Service workers	18.1	17.4
	100	100

SOURCE: U.S. Equal Employment Opportunity Commission, 1970, 1981.

TABLE 14.12. *Black and white educational attainment, 1959–1984*

	Median school years completed	% High school graduates	% Finishing 4 years of college or more
Whites			
1959	12.1	52.6	10.3
1984	12.8	81.6	21.6
Blacks			
1959	8.6	25.5	4.1
1984	12.5	71.6	<E11.6

SOURCE: U.S. Department of Labor (1985), pp. 165–6

Blacks			
1959	8.6	25.5	4.1
1984	12.5	71.6	<E11.6

SOURCE: U.S. Department of Labor (1985), pp. 165–END OF DIRECTORY

TABLE 14.13. *Outflow mobility changes for black men, 1962 and 1973 (%)*

Father's occupation	Son's current occupation					
	Upper middle class	Lower middle class	Upper blue collar	Lower blue collar	Farm	Total
1962						
Upper middle class	13.3	10.0	13.7	63.0	0.0	100
Lower middle class	8.3	14.0	14.0	63.7	0.0	100
Upper blue collar	8.2	10.9	10.9	67.0	3.0	100
Lower blue collar	6.7	9.1	11.1	71.0	2.1	100
Farm	1.2	5.4	7.1	66.3	19.9	100
Total	4.5	7.7	9.4	67.9	10.5	100
1973						
Upper middle class	43.9	11.8	8.3	36.0	0.0	100
Lower middle class	19.5	20.8	13.4	45.5	0.8	100
Upper blue collar	16.3	13.9	15.8	53.7	0.2	100
Lower blue collar	12.1	12.2	13.7	61.0	1.0	100
Farm	5.1	6.8	16.5	63.2	8.4	100
Total	11.6	10.8	14.7	59.4	3.5	100

SOURCE: Featherman and Hauser (1978, p. 326). The samples include American men in the experienced civilian labor force aged twenty-one to sixty-four.

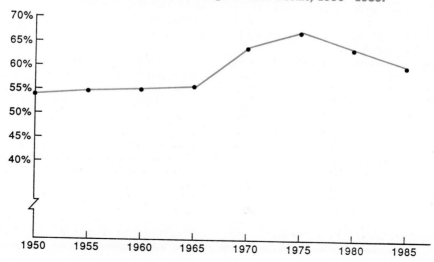

FIGURE 14.2. Black percentage of white income, 1950–1985.

black doctors, lawyers, and so on found educational barriers and job discrimination about as much as did the sons of black lower-skilled workers.

The 1973 data for blacks show significant improvements in some positions. At the top, now almost 44 percent of black sons born there are able to stay. That is still below the white figure of about 60 percent, though still significant improvement. And now only 36 percent of blacks born at the top fall to the bottom, though the figure for whites is only 7 percent. At the bottom there are smaller gains for blacks in the 1973 data. Now 61 percent born in the lower-working-class occupations must remain there, compared with 71 percent in 1962, and about 40 percent for whites.

As these figures show, there have been gains, but mostly for blacks already advantaged in some way. Other figures suggest the same pattern. As we have already seen, the poverty rate for blacks, Mexican-Americans, and Native Americans remains much higher than the rate for whites. In major cities like New York, Chicago, and Los Angeles the rate of poverty among minorities is higher than it was 20 years ago. Figure 14.2 shows that the income gap between blacks and whites was reduced somewhat up to the 1970s, then began to increase again. Among blacks, the rate of family separation has increased to the point where over half of all black children are living in a home without a father present.

BOX 14.4

Continuing Racial Discrimination in Housing

A quarter of a century after the state Civil Rights Act went into effect, and 20 years after the federal statute was enacted, housing discrimination is still a significant problem in California and nationwide, housing experts say.

"You could say housing discrimination has gone underground in its approach . . . but it's still there in significant numbers," said John J. Knapp, general counsel for the U. S. Department of Housing and Urban Development (HUD) in Washington.

A HUD report concludes that "racial discrimination is pervasive in American housing markets and is difficult to combat," Knapp said.

The HUD report noted that:

—A national study conducted in 40 metropolitan areas in 1977 concluded that blacks could expect to encounter discrimination 72 percent of the time if they visited four rental apartments, and 48 percent of the time if they visited four real estate agents.

—A 1979 study in Dallas found that dark-skinned Mexican-Americans encountered discrimination in 42 percent of the cases, and light-skinned ones in 16 percent of the audits.

—A 1982 study of Houston, Dallas, and Denver found that blacks and Hispanics tended to receive less information about available housing than whites in both the rental and sales markets.

—The greater number of visits a minority makes in search of a home or rental property, the greater number of chances he or she will be discriminated against, the report concluded.

In California, the state Department of Fair Employment and Housing conducted a statewide audit earlier this year using minority and white checkers to apply for apartments.

Preliminary figures indicate that the minority apartment seekers are discriminated

Antidiscrimination Programs. Federal government action to reduce discrimination actually began during World War II with attempts to reduce discrimination in the military and in government employment. The most noted action against discrimination, however, began in the federal courts during the 1950s. A series of court cases outlawed discrimination in education, the most famous of which was the 1954 Supreme Court decision *Brown* vs. *Board of Education of Topeka.* In this case the court ruled that the "separate but equal" doctrine that allowed for segregated schools created by the *Plessy* vs. *Ferguson* decision in 1896 was invalid. The desegregation of all schools was ordered "with all deliberate speed," and when it was found that housing segregation was responsible for sending blacks to all-black schools, the courts began to order the busing of school children across school district lines to integrate schools during the 1970s (Schaefer, 1979, pp. 228–234). Although busing has created extensive controversy in the United States, and there may be other ways of reducing segregation in the schools, recent data indicate that black children who have attended racially integrated schools have significantly more educational achievement by the time they are adults.

The next important stage of antidiscrimination activity came with congressional legislation. Most important, the Civil Rights acts of 1964 and 1968 and the Voting Rights Act of 1965 outlawed many forms of discrimination in employment, education,

against an average of 60 percent of the time, said Celia Zager, housing program manager.

In Los Angeles County, the number of complaints received by the four fair housing councils has risen 20 percent yearly for the past three years, according to the Fair Housing Congress of Southern California.

Housing officials and civil rights groups blame a weak federal statute, which has "virtually no enforcement teeth," a tight housing market, laxity of the Reagan administration to enforce the laws, and a lessening of Civil Rights interest as factors that have caused a lack of progress against housing discrimination.

The alarming aspect of today's discriminatory practices, local and national housing officials said, is that now many minorities don't realize when they are discriminated against because the practices have taken on a more insidious nature.

Landlords no longer blatantly tell minorities that "Your type isn't wanted here." Instead they use more complex tactics: they say that the apartment has just been rented, they quote rent and deposit fees which will discourage the apartment seeker, show them only inferior apartments; they fail to give them rental applications, federal and state housing officials said.

Federal auditors also found that housing agents were more likely to introduce themselves to whites, hold longer interviews with them, and present them with business cards more often than they did black customers, according to one HUD study.

It's difficult for a typical renter or buyer to detect such tactics, officials said. Even the agencies which investigate discrimination must rely on an elaborate auditing system in which they send several minority and Caucasian "checkers" to the apartments to determine if unequal treatment is meted out.

Source: Carol McGraw, "Housing Market Bias Still Rampant in State." *Los Angeles Times,* May 3, 1984.

housing, and voting. No longer could public places restrict access because of race or ethnic background. Voting must be carried out in a fair manner, and a government agency was created to oversee voting activities in all elections. No longer could landlords legally discriminate, nor could contracts prohibit homeowners from selling their property to minority group members. Significant changes have been achieved because of these acts, though in some cases such as fair housing, the laws are difficult to enforce (see Box 14.4).

Finally, the concept of **affirmative action** must be discussed. Affirmative action is government policies to promote and require fair treatment of minorities throughout the society. No single law created affirmative action; rather, the concept evolved from some early wording used by President John Kennedy in policies to promote fair employment (Schaefer, 1979, p. 97). As the policies evolved, the federal government used its power to make sure private companies and state agencies such as universities did not discriminate. The power that the federal government used was primarily financial. Private companies could not receive government business if they were found to discriminate, and other government agencies could not receive federal grants.

CHAPTER SUMMARY

Key Terms

race, 383
ethnic group, 383
minority group, 383
racism, 384
genocide, 384
assimilation, 397
cultural assimilation, 397
structural assimilation, 397
amalgamation, 397
psychological assimilation, 397

pluralism, 399
equalitarian pluralism, 399
inequalitarian pluralism, 399
apartheid, 400
authoritarian personality, 401
split labor market, 402
institutional discrimination, 403
affirmative action, 412

Content

Widespread, systematic racist belief systems are actually rather rare and recent in human societies. The major cases of racism developed during the later stages of colonialism in European nations and some colonies established by them—especially Australia, South Africa, and the United States.

When settlers first came to North America there was accommodation with Native Americans. However, by the later 1700s warfare developed as white settlers began taking native lands. By the late 1800s most native land had been taken and Native Americans were forced onto reservations.

Blacks were the next important racial group in America, with the original 400,000 slaves increasing to 4 million in the United States by 1860. During the late 1800s, however, many other race and ethnic groups were migrating to the United States. White ethnics from eastern and central Europe were the biggest group at the time, but also Chinese, then Japanese came in large numbers. Hispanic-Americans first became a part of the U.S. population through United States conquest of Mexican territory, but more recently Mexicans have been the largest group migrating to the U.S.

It was once assumed that industrial societies would assimilate all racial and ethnic groups. Some sociologists have identified typical stages in the process of assimilation. However, it is now recognized that assimilation will not necessarily occur in industrial societies. Ethnic and racial pluralism is likely to remain in the United States and may have advantages. Equalitarian pluralism operates to assure fair competition among race and ethnic groups, and inequalitarian pluralism results in domination, as in South Africa.

Social psychological theories of racism have identified a process of frustration and aggression that can lead to racial conflict and racism. Also, an authoritarian personality type is said to make some people more prone to racism. However, group conflict seems to be responsible for the most extensive cases of racism. The major cases of racism came *after* Europeans began dominating colonial peoples.

Once racism develops, a cycle can operate to maintain racism and discrimination over extensive periods of time. Also, institutional practices can maintain discrimination even if racism is eliminated.

Some sociologists argue that class position is growing more important in shaping the life chances of minorities in the United States than is racism. We do find that the class system, like institutional dis-crimination, maintains race and ethnic inequalities today, though racism has not been eliminated.

The Civil Rights Movement and the need for new voters by the Democratic Party have given minorities more political influence in recent years. With this political influence, civil rights laws have been passed and programs to reduce discrimination developed. Many of these programs have been successful, though middle-class minorities have achieved the most gains, creating a gap between middle-class and poor minorities.

Personality and Social Structure: A Photo Essay in Sociology

Throughout this text, we have tried to demonstrate the influence of different elements of social structure upon the ways in which people in society carry on their daily lives. We have maintained that the material structure of people's existence shapes many of their ideas, attitudes, and life opportunities. Thus, the character of every society's economy becomes a strong determining factor for each individual. At the same time, there are universal human events and experiences that occur across cultures and societies. How similar are we? How different?

As you study these photographs, use the sociological perspective to compare and contrast the experiences depicted. Consider not only the other's life, but your own.

This Indonesian newborn lies on the dirt floor, umbilical cord still uncut, surrounded by his relatives.

© C. Rentmeester/Time-Life Picture Agency

The American baby lies in her crib, a colorful mobile over her head to stimulate and entertain her. What are the material aspects of each scene?

© Erika Stone

What are the social aspects? What can you infer about the communities into which these children have been born?

The Navajo baby is swaddled, a custom practiced in a number of societies in the world. Swaddled babies are often, though not necessarily, strapped on one of their parents' backs to be carried around throughout their workday.

© John Running

The Russian infant is rocked by his grandfather in a small cradle. In many societies with extended family patterns, old relatives tend to infants while their parents do other work.

© John Launois/Black Star

Compare all four photos. What kinds of assumptions might these different societies hold about the nature of childhood and the needs of children? What might you infer about the relationships between adults and children in these four societies?

In the postindustrial society of Japan, as in the United States, children play and learn in age-graded peer groups in settings called schools and child care centers.

The Guatemalan child, who is only three or four years old, learns to weave using the same technique that all female adults in her community use. Her toy represents her working life.

© Eugene Gordon

In Thailand, as in many other countries, child care is just that, the responsibility of children for their younger siblings. The older child learns many of the skills of parenting at an early age.

© Barbara Gundle/Archive Pictures Inc.

What do these various children learn about their societies and their place in it from these experiences? What do they learn about their relationship to their peers? Are peers defined similarly in each of these societies? Are these children being equally prepared to deal with the requirements of adult life in their society? How do you think each of these different children conceptualizes his or her future?

> *Every society is concerned about the gender identity of its members, although societies differ with respect to the range of options they give their members. Formal and informal social rituals and behaviors govern the processes of becoming a man or woman.*

© Christian Zuber/Photo Researchers, Inc.

What kinds of things are these young women in Kenya and Bulgaria learning? What effect does the similarity in costume and makeup produce?

© Daily Telegraph by Adam Woolfitt/Woodfin Camp and Associates

© Marc and Evelyne Bernheim/Woodfin Camp and Associates

These Touareg men in Africa fence for pleasure and display. The Kamayara of the Amazon pursue another activity for the same purpose. But are there other things happening here?

© Loren McIntyre/Woodfin Camp and Associates

Do you think these processes are more similar than different across cultures?

Does the primping and posturing shown in these photographs have any function for the society as a whole?

Why are the members of a society concerned about the gender identity of the young? What does gender identity have to do with sexual reproduction? How does the sexual reproduction of its members affect a society?

Dancing is universal. It is almost always an occasion of celebration and it usually has sexual elements to it. Sometimes each sex dances separately for the other. And at still other times in different societies, the sexes dance in seclusion, their rituals an affirmation of a particular gender indentity. But in many societies the sexes dance together as shown here on Cook Island in the South Pacific, at a school for Flamenco dancing in Spain, disco dancing in Miami, and at a Ukranian festival in Canada.

© Kal Muller/Woodfin Camp and Associates

© Joe Viesti

© Jose Fernandez/Woodfin Camp and Associates

Where the sexes dance together the movements may be heavily ritualized or spontaneous. Does that necessarily make a difference to the meaning of the dance? Study the photographs closely.

© Kul Bhatia/Photo Researchers, Inc.

What kinds of messages are being communicated? Are men and women very different in their communications? Which seem to be greater: the cross-cultural similarities or the differences?

Work is the activity that occupies most people's time. How do we finally arrive at a job or career? Does it always maintain and provide for us?

What choices might this Guatemalan coffin maker have had?

How did these men come to be working in an office with computers? Did these women actively choose their occupation in the factory? What might you infer about each society from the work and the work setting?

What work will you pursue? How different would your choice be if you lived in Thailand or Nigeria or Norway? How much of your choice was framed by the socioeconomic status of your family and the technological characteristics of your society?

The marketplace—whether the open market of the Ivory Coast, the Moscow department store, GUM, a shopping mall in Sydney, Australia, or the New York Stock Exchange— is the site of one of the most fundamental transactions of society, economic exchange.

© J. Messerschmidt/The Stock Market

Almost every member of society participates in this exchange, and every type of society has some form of it.

© David Ball/The Stock Market

How are these marketplaces similar and how different? With which are you familiar?

How do these places structure the social behavior that goes on within them? How does this economic exchange affect our lives? Is there any continuity between the character of our birth and childhood and the character of the economic exchange in our society?

CHAPTER 15

Gender, Age, and Inequality

415

What in unenlightened societies, colour, race, religion or, in the case of a conquered country, nationality, are to some men, sex is to all women; a peremptory exclusion from almost all honorable occupations, but either such as cannot be fulfilled by others, or such as those others do not think worthy of their acceptance.
— John Stuart Mill, "The Subjection of Women"

Throughout history the status and position of women has varied greatly. At times, at least some women have held high status and were given extensive freedom. There were goddesses in Greek mythology but there was also a status of women in ancient Greek society who were somewhat like the Japanese geisha. These Greek women, called *hetaira,* developed outstanding cultural skills and were honored for their intelligence and charm. The status held by hetaira, however, was in striking contrast to that of most other women in Greek society who had very little freedom and few rights. In the majority of human societies throughout history the position of women has been more like that of the average Greek woman, if not much worse.

In India, until quite recently, women were almost totally dominated by men — first by fathers and then by husbands. Women had few legal rights and could actually be burned alive if found unfaithful to their husband. (From time to time there continues to be reports of such deaths.) Among the elite in India, a wife was expected to accept cremation (alive) on her husband's death. Women have perhaps held a very low status for the longest period of time in Middle Eastern societies. Their status was, and in some places still is, not much better than slaves. Girls were often given as brides at a young age (that is, traded for considerable wealth). Sometimes the trade occurred when a girl was only 13 years old because her virginity was more assured. In another method to increase the certainty of a virgin daughter on her wedding night, the clitoris was sometimes cut out at an early age. In any case, on her wedding night the groom was required to display a bloodstained cloth proving to close relatives that the bride had in fact been a virgin. If the bride was found not to be a virgin, she would be returned to her father (who then had to return the payment for her). At this point the father or brothers could kill the girl to maintain the family's honor.

While in the possession of either the father or husband, Muslim women were required to stay in seclusion (called purdah) most of the time, and when going out they were required to wear veils. The women of poorer peasants, however, were "allowed" outside to work in the fields. These Muslim women were in an especially low position and even considered unclean during menstruation, at which time they could not cook or even touch their husband, and at times were required to be isolated in a special menstruation hut. By Muslim law, a man could have up to four wives, though multiple wives were uncommon because the purchase price for that many wives was usually prohibitive. A husband, however, could divorce his wife at any time and for any reason, and simply marry another.

As in most preindustrial societies, there was much happiness at the birth of a son, but depression at the birth of a daughter. In Arab society, the first person to tell the father of the birth of his son was given a valuable gift, after which there was a celebration. The news of a daughter's birth was met with silence. In other societies girls are sometimes killed at birth, as continues to be the case at times in rural China because families restricted to one child by the state want a boy.

Examples of the low position of women could go on and on, and we will consider other examples when tracing the changing status of women through history. The point has been made, however, but with one addition. The honored hetairas of Greece and the peasant women in the Middle East shared a common characteristic; both remained dependent on men. Though the position of one was high and the other low, both were given their positions by men, and men could revoke the position if they were not served well.

In this chapter we first consider the position of women in some detail. We consider the history of women's roles and theories that attempt to explain the status of women in society. After doing so we examine the current level of male-female inequality in industrial societies and the causes of this inequality. Finally, we explore the status of the elderly in a similar manner.

GENDER INEQUALITY

Before we consider the position of women throughout history, there are a few basic facts and definitions to consider. This is especially the case with the subject of gender inequality, which, like racial inequality, is heavily influenced by various ideologies.

Gender Role Socialization. Interesting studies have been conducted with children who have required sex changes at a very early age, with one case even involving two identical boy twins, one of whom had to be changed to a girl when its penis was severed (Money and Ehrhardt, 1972). In these cases the children were successfully taught to be a "proper" girl in the socialization process. The point, of course, is that we must be taught to be either a boy or a girl.

The term **gender roles** describes the socially acquired and socially defined sex-linked behavior expectations. By themselves, these gender roles reflect only gender differences — that is, how men and women are taught to be different and assigned different tasks. However, **sex stratification,** as we will see, is developed when the gender roles lead to material, social, and political inequalities between men and women.

A History of Women in Human Societies

Throughout history we find at least some division of labor between men and women in all societies. There has been a strong tendency for men to provide food and protection from outside threats to the family, while women do the "domestic" work of cooking and caring for children. There is much variation in this division of labor between men and women throughout history, however, and this division of labor is strongly influenced by culture and the level of technology in a society. It can be argued that the strict division of labor of the past is no longer useful or necessary in advanced industrial societies.

Women in Preindustrial Societies. Before industrial societies, the relative position of women was probably the most favorable in early hunting and gathering societies. There was always some division of labor between men and women, with men doing the hunting and women taking care of infants and gathering food that could more easily be collected around the home base. A simple division of labor, as already noted, does not necessarily mean that social inequality and social stratification must result. But this is often the case when one role or occupation is seen as much more important or provides resources that can be used to dominate others. In hunting and gathering societies, for example, providing food was critical. Care for children was also important for group survival, as has always been the case, but the effects of successful child-rearing are seen only after many years. With the exception of breast feeding in the earliest months of childhood, men can also care for children. Women could not always perform the man's role of food gathering, however, especially hunting. And food gathering was obviously a critical need, which therefore gave men higher status.

The step from hunting and gathering societies to simple horticultural societies began about 10,000 years ago, and it was at this time that the level of male-female inequality became much greater. Some anthropologists believe women were in fact responsible for this step because of their focus on gathering plants rather than hunting. But if this is true, it is a step women might look back on with some regret.

The relative loss of status by women can be viewed in many ways. For example, more work in the fields could be done by women who must stay close to home with children. Men were therefore freed of much of this hard work. A recent United Nations study has estimated that today, worldwide, women do two-thirds of the work (*Los Angeles Times,* July 7, 1985). In primarily agricultural areas like Africa, women today do three-quarters of the work producing food. We can imagine this figure was worldwide before industrial nations appeared. Another factor in the increased work for women in most preindustrial societies was related to organized politics and warfare. Men did the talking and fighting among themselves, while women provided labor for food and human care.

The power men attained from political organization and warfare in preindustrial societies often gave them a more dominant position in the family and led to cultural views and traditions of extensive dominance. Women were prohibited (by men's laws) from owning property and participating in most occupations, and they were required to obey their husband or father without question. Women were therefore given few options; they had nowhere to turn for support except to the dominant males.

Women in Industrial Societies. With early industrialization the position of women generally became even worse. Here is meant most women; there had been queens and other highly respected women among the elites before and after industrial societies. For the average woman, however, there was usually no improvement in standard of living or status and authority compared with men. Early industrialization often forced families to leave small towns and rural areas for big cities, where conditions were worse for them. Families were commonly torn apart, with women sometimes left to begging, prostitution, or exploitation in factory jobs.

During this early period of industrialization women and children from the working class were preferred workers because they were docile, easily controlled, and therefore less likely to strike over low wages and poor working conditions. Irving Howe's (1976) descriptions of working conditions for immigrant women in the New York City garment industry are also typical. Women and children were forced to work in very crowded, dangerous little workshops for many hours, day after day. They had few breaks from work, and there was seldom clean air to breathe or sanitary restrooms. Many injuries and deaths resulted from these unsafe conditions, as during the Triangle Shirt Factory fire in 1911, which killed 146 young women in New York City.

Women from more affluent families did not have to work in the factories, but they faced many forms of discrimination. Women could not vote, were seldom allowed into most occupations, were less likely to be educated, had no control over family property, and so on.

In advanced industrial societies, however, we find the status of women changing. There are still many forms of inequality between men and women, but in no major society since horticultural societies emerged about 10,000 years ago have sex inequalities been lower. To cite only a few examples, women are entitled to vote and hold political office in all advanced industrial societies. Labor laws have benefited women in the workplace, and many unions represent workers in jobs dominated by women. Women can now get credit from financial institutions and have more rights in divorce cases and in the legal system more generally. Women are not as restricted to certain jobs, though they are certainly underrepresented in many jobs. But because jobs have been opened up to them, and jobs traditionally held by women have increased, women currently make up almost 45 percent of the U.S. labor force.

Other improvements in the status of women include the right to hold property. In the past, all property held by a family was totally controlled by the male head of the family. If there was a divorce, women were often left with no property and in many cases could not even gain custody of their children. This has changed only recently in Japan, where men still obtain custody of children in about 50 percent of the divorces (Fukutake, 1981). Many improvements for women in advanced industrial societies have come because of civil rights laws like those passed in the 1960s in the United States and soon after World War II in Japan. In the United States the civil rights laws and feminist movements have created such rapid change that young women today take for granted new opportunities their mother's helped produce only 20 years ago.

Forces Producing Change. Much of the improved position of women is related to a shift in attitudes. For example, as late as 1938, only about 20 percent of the population approved of married women working, compared with almost 80 percent today (Public Opinion, 1980). But other changes are behind the changes in attitudes today. As we have found in

Why do we traditionally think of typists and switchboard operators as women? Do you think jobs should be allocated on the basis of gender traits? Do you think there will be any status changes for telephone operators if there are more men in the job? (Top: © *Bettman Archive;* bottom: © *AT&T Co. Graphics Center*)

other cases where a minority group has experienced socioeconomic gains, we must recognize that the improved position of women is related to underlying changes in the basic nature of society. Improvements do *not* come simply because the dominant group suddenly has a change of heart. The improved status of women is related to economic and political changes brought by industrialization, as well as the push given by women's movements.

The economic changes that have helped the position of women are in some cases obvious. With industrialization many new jobs and occupations have been created that women may now occupy. Women may sometimes be unable to compete with men in jobs requiring heavy physical labor, though even here the abilities of women have been extremely underestimated in the past. With the majority of jobs no longer requiring heavy physical labor, women are clearly qualified for the vast majority of jobs in industrial societies. Equally important, women are not unqualified for the highest status jobs. Women were at a disadvantage compared with men for the higher-status jobs such as hunter or warlord in earlier societies, but this is not true today, with positions such as corporate executive, professionals, and political leaders.

Many less obvious changes also occur when economic opportunities for women are improved. One of the most important is related to the general dependency of women. In the past, for example, women were heavily dependent on men for economic security. With the ability to enter the labor force on their own, however, women gained an important freedom or option. If necessary and desired, women can now survive independently of men. The importance of this change for many aspects of the status of women must be recognized in understanding the position of women today.

Another technological change underlies all the above—reproductive control. In previous ages, women usually had dependent children until late in life and gave birth to many more children than in industrial societies today. Although most of these children died before reaching adulthood, their existence still meant that women were less free to enter the labor force even when jobs existed for them. The advent of birth control, in other words, has meant more than increased sexual activity without fear of unwanted pregnancy. Birth control has meant the freedom to control the number of children so that women can become more active in other areas like the pursuit of a career.

Political changes have also been important to the status of women. There has been increasing democracy in advanced industrial societies, and, as we have already seen, the increasing democracy has helped many minority and lower-class groups, including women. In the United States the important step was granting women the right to vote in 1920. As can be seen in Table 15.1, the right to vote was achieved by women in most industrial societies and many developing societies around the same time. Switzerland provides an interesting contrast. Though it is one of the oldest democracies, women did not achieve the right to vote there until 1971. Given the relatively favorable position of women in Switzerland compared with many other nations, we must therefore recognize that the right to vote is not always of primary importance to women.

TABLE 15.1. *Women's right to vote—an international comparison*

Country	Year women first allowed to vote in national elections
New Zealand	1893
Finland	1906
Norway	1913
Denmark	1915
Netherlands	1917
Soviet Union	1917
Austria	1918
Czechoslovakia	1918
Poland	1918
Sweden	1918
Germany	1919
United States	1920
Great Britain	1928
South Africa	1930
Spain	1931

SOURCE: Britannica (1985, vol. 27, pp. 321–322).

How women in the United States have used their right to vote is of critical importance. In general, women vote in numbers equal to men, and the voting patterns of women are often not significantly different from those of men. This means that the same candidates, with the same policies, would usually be elected even if women could not vote. In recent elections, though, there have been some growing gender divisions on candidates and policies. For example, women have been less likely to support President Reagan's military expansion, welfare cuts, and foreign policies. And in recent elections, the "gender gap" with respect to some political issues has made politicians cautious in their congressional voting records and campaign rhetoric.

The improved position of women in general can be overestimated in the face of the many continuing inequalities in such things as income and authority in the workplace. But also, the improved position of women can be underestimated without an eye to the past. In the past ten years the gains may seem few and slow, but viewed over centuries, the gains of women are striking.

Women's Movements. There is a final, very important factor in the changed position of women. Political, economic, and technological changes may have made the improved status of women possible, but a push from organized women's movements was also necessary.

Women have been active in reform movements on the local level since the early days of the United States. But a very large, active coalition of women emerged for the first time during the 1830s with the primary purpose of abolishing slavery. Naturally, the attention of these women would come to focus on rights for women as well. In 1848 the first national convention devoted to women's rights was held in Seneca Falls, New York, and in many ways this convention can be seen as a first step toward an effective American women's movement (Giele, 1977, p. 309).

In the second half of the 1800s the women's suffrage movement became stronger. Supported by such crusaders as Susan B. Anthony and Elizabeth Cady Stanton, the women's suffrage amendment to the Constitution was put before Congress every year, beginning in 1878, until it was passed in 1920. During this time, women were also involved in other reform efforts, from better living conditions for immigrants in urban slums to better pay and a more healthy work environment in the new industries employing women (Howe, 1976). One large organization, the Women's Christian Temperance Union (WCTU), was also involved in the prohibition of alcohol as well as the suffrage movement. During the 1880s the WTCU had a membership of perhaps several hundred thousand women.

During the nineteenth century most of the success of women's movements was concentrated in achieving rights in the home (Giele, 1977). For example, during this time women achieved the right to own property, make contracts, and serve as legal guardians of children. But during the later 1800s and early 1900s, especially during the Progressive period of the early 1900s, successful reforms were passed that had wider community implications. Laws protecting industrial workers, health-related government programs, and the right to vote are major examples.

After the 1920s, there was little significant activity by a women's movement until the 1960s. During a period in many ways like the Progressive era, the 1960s brought political activity by women on many issues. And as the early women's movement was stimulated by the Abolitionist Movement in the 1830s, the most recent stage of the women's movement was stimulated by the Civil Rights Movement. Major organizations like the National Organization of Women (NOW) have been successful in the courts and in Congress in securing laws further increasing opportunities for women. During this time it became illegal to discriminate on the basis of sex, and affirmative action policies have been used to promote women's educational and occupational opportunities in many ways. For example, just as the affirmative action policies have been applied to help racial minorities, if discrimination is shown against women by a business or government agency, that business or agency can lose all federal government contracts and aid.

A Comparative View of the Status of Women

Although there have been historical gains for women in the United States, gains have also been made by women in other industrial nations. Industrial nations do vary with respect to the status of women, however, and it is thus important to consider this variation. With a cross-cultural comparison we note some remarkably similar limits to equality for women in some respects.

Table 15.2 presents comparative information on some indicators of the political and economic status of women in several developing and developed nations. In one respect, this table indicates what our historical analysis has already described; there is a significant difference in the status of women in industrial versus preindustrial societies (developing countries). The developing nations have few women in either the labor force or political office.

But there continues to be significant variance among the industrial nations themselves. With respect to political office, the United States is behind most industrial nations in the percent of positions held by women in the legislature. In particular, the Scandinavian countries (Norway, Sweden, Denmark, and Finland) are considerably ahead of the United States with respect to political offices held by women, as are the three socialist nations shown in Table 15.2. There is somewhat less variance in the percent of the total labor force held by women

TABLE 15.2. *International comparison of women in political office and in the labor force*

	Parliament (% women)	Percentage of total labor force
Developing Countries		
Egypt	0.0 (1970)	7.5 (1966)
Philippines	2.4 (1970)	31.9 (1970)
Pakistan	3.8 (1970)	8.8 (1961)
Mexico	4.8 (1968)	19.2 (1970)
Bangladesh	5.0 (1970)	15.1 (1961)
India	7.0 (1963)	17.4 (1971)
Ghana	13.6 (1966)	38.3 (1960)
Developed, Capitalist Nations		
Canada	1.6 (1968)	33.9 (1973)
France	1.6 (1969)	34.5 (1968)
United States	2.3 (1974)	37.4 (1972)
Japan	2.9 (1970)	39.1 (1970)
United Kingdom	4.1 (1970)	35.7 (1966)
Austria	8.2 (1970)	38.9 (1972)
West Germany	8.8 (1963)	36.0 (1971)
Norway	9.3 (1968)	37.1 (1972)
Sweden	10.4 (1968)	37.1 (1972)
Denmark	11.2 (1970)	40.1 (1972)
Finland	21.5 (1970)	42.1 (1970)
Eastern European, Socialist		
Poland	12.4 (1968)	46.0 (1970)
Czechoslovakia	17.6 (1967)	44.7 (1970)
USSR	28.0 (1968)	50.4 (1970)

SOURCE: Giele (1977, p. 17).

among these industrial nations, but the ranking from lowest to highest generally follows the political participation ranking.

Another way to consider the economic position of women is through comparison of their access to top occupational positions. Table 15.3 provides comparative data on the percent of women who are physicians, lawyers, and engineers in eight industrial nations. The position of women in the United States is quite low and the position of women in the Soviet Union quite remarkable. Women make up 76 percent of Soviet physicians compared with 6 percent in the United States by the late 1960s. As we will see below, there have been gains for women in these occupations since the 1960s, but the gap between the United States and these other nations remains substantial.

With respect to economic returns in the workplace, Table 15.4 indicates that women earn substantially less than men in all the industrial nations listed. The income ratio between men and women (i.e., the average income of women compared with that of men) is around 60 to 70 percent for most of these nations. The United States is among the lowest, with women receiving 61 percent of the income of men in 1976 (Table 15.4). By 1987, however, the income position of women in the United States had improved, with the income ratio approaching the 70 percent range.

TABLE 15.3. *International comparison of percentage of women in three professions**

	Medical	Barristers	Engineers
USSR	76.0	38.0	37.0
Great Britain	25.0	4.0	0.06
France	22.0	19.0	3.7
West Germany	20.0	5.0	1.0
Austria	18.0	7.0	nd
Sweden	13.0	6.7	nd
Denmark	nd	10.0	nd
USA	6.0	3.0	0.07

* nd = no data.
SOURCE: Adapted from Evelyne Sullerot. *Woman, Society and Change* (New York/Toronto: McGraw-Hill, World University Library, 1971), pp. 151–152.

Sweden versus Japan. All these comparisons show gains for women in industrial societies, but there are still national differences. Some of these differences are not clearly shown in the rough statistics. Contrasts in the status of women can be seen most clearly by comparing Sweden and Japan.

Women in Sweden experience many of the same problems related to sexism that are found in other industrial nations. Compared with men in Sweden, women get less pay and are more often in low-status jobs — those labeled "women's jobs." But there are career opportunities, and many government laws and programs have been established to help working women in Sweden (Hutter, 1981, pp. 257–258). For example, women must be offered maternity leave by their employer and this leave must not affect career opportunities. Also, maternity leave can be taken by either the mother or father, which means a woman can return to her job soon after childbirth if she chooses (Kahn and Kamerman, 1978). Also, to help working women there are government-assisted day-care centers, many of which are operated by employers.

With some basic statistics, and in legal status, the position of women in Japan looks favorable compared with other industrial societies. Soon after World War II, the new Japanese constitution included a law similar to the Equal Rights Amendment, which has *not* become law in the United States (Reischauer, 1977). Universities and schools were opened to women after World War II, and many women entered the labor force. There are almost as many women in the labor force in Japan as in the United States, although this comparison does not hold for married women in the labor force in Japan. Finally, the wages of women in Japan compared with men are similar to the male-female income ratios of other industrial nations. But some of these figures are misleading by making the status of women look better than is actually the case, and the overall status of women in Japan is probably lower than in any other industrial nation.

To begin with, about one-third of the women counted in the labor force in Japan are unpaid workers on the small family farms or small family-owned shops found in abundance in Japan. Another large portion of these working women are young

TABLE 15.4. *Male-female income ratio: international comparison*

	Women's earnings as a percentage of men's	Notes*
Belgium	73	Average hourly earnings of adult workers in industry; October 1975
France	69	Average annual earnings of full-time labor in private and semiprivate industry; 1973
Great Britain	71	Median gross hourly earnings of full-time adult manual workers; 1976
	62	The same, for nonmanual employees
The Netherlands	78	Average gross hourly earnings of adult industrial workers; 1975
Sweden	69	Average monthly salaries of adult white-collar employees in mining and manufacturing; 1976
	87	Average hourly earnings of labor in mining and manufacturing; 1976
Switzerland	66	Gross hourly earnings of skilled workers in industry and trade; 1976
	70	The same, for semiskilled and unskilled workers
	65	Gross monthly earnings of white-collar employees in all sectors; 1976
United States	61**	Median earnings of full-time wage and salary workers over 25; May 1976
West Germany	74	Gross hourly earnings of skilled workers in industry; 1976
	77	The same, for semiskilled workers
	83	The same, for unskilled workers
	67	Gross monthly earnings of technical employees in industry, trade, and financial institutions; 1976

* The terms *worker* and *labor* exclude white-collar employees.
** When allowance is made for the longer hours that full-time men work, this figure jumps to 66 percent, judging from previous analyses (Fuchs, 1971).
SOURCE: Swafford (1978, p. 670).

girls waiting marriage. Women in Japan are not expected to marry in college or soon after, but wait until about 24 or 25 years of age (which is average in Japan). Thus, women leave high school or college to work for a few years, then get married. The new couple usually meet while working in the same company in Japan, not in college as in the United States. It is the policy of most Japanese employers to pressure women to quit their job after marriage (and well over 90 percent of young women do marry in Japan). In fact, because young women workers are fully expected to marry soon and stop working, they are not offered career entry jobs. Only 6 percent of management jobs in Japan are held by women, and with few exceptions, it is the job of these women to run for tea (or other small tasks), in addition to regular duties, when male workers request it.

Women in Japan have been entering the labor force in greater numbers in recent years. Most of these women are the young girls described above, but there are also older women whose children have grown. These older women, however, tend to have the same low-status jobs as the younger women and are even more likely to have only part-time jobs. The severe lack of day-care facilities prevents most mothers from working (Pharr, 1977 p. 236), which is also one reason many grandparents are appreciated when they live with their adult children (Morgan and Hiroshima, 1983).

Japan is praised for having the lowest divorce rate of any industrial society. Although this low divorce rate is seen by most people as commendable, it has its negative side. Women are less likely to become divorced in Japan because they have few options beyond marriage. Women in Japan can seldom find jobs that will support them, employers have very unfavorable views of divorced women, and there is much less welfare aid for women (Christopher, 1983).

The status of women in Japan is changing. The change, however, will be slow and full of conflict. This can be seen in the rapid change in the attitudes of the women themselves. As late as 1970, 80 percent of Japanese women believed a wife should not be employed (Christopher, 1983, p. 115). By 1976, however, only 49 percent of Japanese women held this belief, and only 36 percent in 1979. In citing these figures, Christopher writes, "Curiously, not too many Japanese men, so far as I can detect, fully comprehend what is happening to them," or, I would add, what is in store for them.

Theories of Gender Inequality

Before we turn to more information on gender inequalities in the United States, a brief look at theories of gender inequality will be helpful. In light of our historical and comparative examination of gender roles we can now better evaluate these theories. There have been two primary types of theories used by sociologists to explain gender inequality — functional and conflict theories.

Functional Theory. A basic functionalist assumption is that if social arrangements have existed for an extended period of time, they must have been somehow functional or necessary for the society. In other words, they must help (or at least did help) the society effectively accomplish necessary tasks. From this perspective, therefore, functionalists argue that in modern societies a division or labor by sex must be serving positive functions. Specifically, the familly must obtain basic material necessities, provide protection for its members, and care for and socialize children. Because of biology, males tend to provide basic economic necessities and protection, and females are primarily oriented toward caring for children. The male usually assumes an **instrumental role** and the female an **expressive role** — that is, the female provides emotional support and sustains family members (Parsons and Bales, 1953). This theory further assumes that it is functional for the

male to be dominant and the female to be in a subservient position. When this dominant-subservient role division exists, there is less tension and conflict, as well as more efficient decision making.

In modern societies, this division of labor in the family based on gender results in the lower status of women in general. Because of the need for women to remain within the family and perform the role of mother and caretaker, the chance to achieve status outside the family is limited. Parsons (1953, p. 117) writes, "Obviously the whole situation . . . produces another fundamental limitation on full 'equality of opportunity' in that women, regardless of their performance capacities, tend to be relegated to a narrower range of functions than men, and excluded, at least relatively, from some of the highest prestige statuses."

As is often the case, the functionalist view tends to make what already exists seem right and proper and for this reason has very conservative implications. What do we find in the way of historical, comparative, and empirical information that can support this theory?

We have seen a strong tendency through history for a division of labor in the family based on sex. Since hunting and gathering societies, men have more likely done the hunting and provided the physical protection against outside threats. Women have tended to stay closer to home and care for children. The evidence shows most preindustrial societies have similar sex role divisions (Murdock, 1935). There are some exceptions, however, so this division must be considered only a tendency in preindustrial societies.

The main critique of the functional theory of sex inequality and sex roles begins with the question, because something was once functional for a society will it always remain functional? And if it is no longer functional, then will the social arrangement be altered as functional theory suggests? These questions, of course, are directed to modern industrial societies. Is the old division of labor between men and women still necessary and functional?

From the evidence of change in industrial societies considered earlier, it appears that the old sex roles and male dominance are not only no longer functional but can even be dysfunctional. First, they can be dysfunctional because the talents of many women are not being used for the full benefit of the society. Second, it is creating stress and psychological problems for women. Especially when their children leave home, many women feel their life no longer has meaning.

Conflict Theory. The basic assumptions of conflict theory are that people and groups usually have conflicting interests (along with common interests) and there are variations in the balance of power among groups and individuals. With these simple assumptions we can trace the history of sex role divisions.

In hunting and gathering societies men were favored in the balance of power, especially in hunting societies. Men tend to be larger and stronger so they are better able to provide food in these societies. Also, women are more restricted owing to the burden of child care. And we should not neglect the simple fact that men are usually able to physically overpower women. In the final analysis, physical force is often a key resource (Collins, 1975, pp. 230–233). Among primates males are dominant only in the primate species that have greater size differences between the sexes.

In agrarian and horticultural societies, the physical differences continue to give men dominance. Women can work in the fields, but child care still restricts their activities. Now the added importance of warfare gives men the edge.

With industrial societies the situation has changed. Women are no longer unqualified for the highest-ranked and highest-paid jobs (professionals, executives, etc.); furthermore, reproductive control, labor-saving devices in the home, and child care facilities leave women less restricted. Thus, there is strong potential for much greater equality between the sexes and more flexible sex roles.

As we have already seen, and will see in more detail, there continues to be a high degree of inequality between men and women in all industrial societies. How do conflict theorists explain this? First, they point to the strength of old traditions and ideologies proclaiming the necessity and legitimacy of sex role divisions and inequalities. The socialization

process, as we have seen, can strongly influence self-images and therefore keep old traditions alive. Second, men continued their dominance from the previous type of societies and are in positions of power in the society. They are the "gate keepers" to top positions in the society and women are usually excluded.

We have also seen less inequality between the sexes in industrial societies and the potential for even more change. Again, we consider this change with respect to conflict assumptions. The most simple advantage men have held throughout the ages is physical size and brute force. However, in modern societies the state has come to hold the final element of brute force. In individual interactions between men and women, if men attempt to employ brute force, women can usually find at least some protection from the police and a court order.

When there is some competition in the society by business and other organizations, it becomes very difficult to keep a "gentleman's agreement" not to hire women or use the talents of women when this will help the business or organization. Gradually, therefore, because women have fewer restrictions, they will start to take these new opportunities.

All of this has a powerful impact on male-female relationships within families. There is more equality of decision making between husband and wife today. One reason for this is that the options of women have increased. Women need no longer simply accept male dominance. Unlike in the past, when women could not obtain basic necessities without a male provider, women can now say, "I feel competent to do it on my own" and leave. This option is a great equalizing force.

None of this is to say total male-female equality will appear soon. To achieve total equality, women must have total economic independence (Etheridge, 1978). Women are still somewhat restricted by the biology of bearing and caring for children. A strong desire and ideology calling for equality could work to overcome or extensively reduce this barrier, however. For example, as is done in Sweden, either the mother or father could be given maternity leave, and more extensive child care facilities could be provided. In time, many programs such as these can reduce further the level of inequality between women and men.

Gender Stratification

As we have found with race and ethnic inequalities, many of the inequalities between men and women are due to class position and occupational opportunities. In the past it was assumed by sociologists that the class position of women was determined by their husband's or father's class position, and there was little study of the socioeconomic position of women themselves. Industrial societies are changing very rapidly in this respect, with many women now the head of their household and with most married women in the labor force. Thus, an analysis of the class position of women becomes very important. We will look at the income and occupational position of women, then attempt to explain the male-female inequalities in this country.

Gender Inequalities. A recent United Nations report states that worldwide, women do two-thirds of the work but receive only 10 percent of the income, and only 1 percent of the wealth compared with men (*Los Angeles Times,* July 17, 1985). Within industrial nations like the United States, these gender inequalities are less, but certainly in evidence.

We begin by considering income inequality between men and women in the United States in recent years. Table 15.5 indicates that the ratio of male-female income was remarkably stable between 1955 and 1982. In 1955 women in the labor force received 60 percent of the average male income, and in 1982, 62 percent. Income inequality grew in the late 1950s and early 1960s, and reached the 1955 level of around 60 percent only recently. Since 1982, however, this income ratio has improved, reaching 70 percent in 1987. We also see in Table 15.5 that the gender income inequality by age remained similar between 1955 and 1982. Young women (20–24 years) start in jobs earning about 80 percent or more of the average male income for that age group. But as we move up the age categories this inequality increases rapidly. We examine some of the reasons for this below, but one obvious factor is that compared with men, women are not advancing as rapidly in their careers over the years.

In Table 15.6 we find another indicator of what produces this income inequality. In every type of occupation except nurse, the 1982 weekly earnings of men are substantially higher. The inequalities are generally greater for jobs more likely in private industry, such as sales workers, and less for jobs most likely in government, such as postal clerks. It is in governmental agencies that civil rights laws have had the most effect, as we saw with racial and ethnic minorities.

It may come to mind that women are paid less because they have less experience and less education compared with men. The effect of less experience is questioned by the data in Table 15.5, showing inequality by age categories. However, women may be out of the work force for a while; thus age does not always equal job experience. We examine job experience and gender inequalities in more

TABLE 15.5. *U.S. male-female income ratio, by year and age (%)*

Age	1955	1960	1965	1970	1975	1980	1982
Total	60	55	54	57	56	59	61
20–24	84	81	79	74	78	78	87
25–35	66	65	62	65	66	69	72
35–44	63	58	57	54	55	56	60
45–54	62	58	58	56	54	54	56
55–64	65	65	62	60	58	57	58

SOURCE: U.S. Bureau of Labor Statistics (1985).

TABLE 15.6. *Male-female income differences within occupations, 1982*

Occupation	Average weekly male income ($)	Average weekly female income ($)
Accountants	468	325
Assemblers	319	220
Bank officers and financial managers	574	336
Bartenders	224	177
Bus, taxi, and truck drivers	328	237
Clerical workers	347	236
Computer specialists	529	401
Craft and kindred workers	384	247
Editors and reporters	451	325
Engineers	592	479
Farm workers	192	174
Firefighters and police officers	338	254
Lawyers and judges	660	502
Mechanics and repairers	346	318
Nurses (registered)	363	366
Personnel and labor relations workers	530	354
Physicians, dentists (and related practitioners)	530	421
Postal clerks	427	403
Sales managers and department heads (retail)	386	227
Sales workers	383	212
Service workers	246	180
Social workers	382	307
Teachers (college and university)	528	415
Teachers (except college and university)	413	338
Textile operatives	232	198
Waiters	229	149
Writers, artists, and entertainers	444	314

SOURCE: U.S. Bureau of Labor Statistics (1985).

detail later. However, we can say that educational differences may be partly related to income differences between men and women by looking at Table 15.7. Women are more likely to finish high school than are men, but men have a higher rate of college completion.

Even though we found that women receive less income even in the same occupations, part of the gender income inequality is due to differing occupational positions between men and women. In the past, women were often restricted to certain jobs by law. For example, in Victorian England, laws required women clerks in the civil service to work in a room that was always locked to men. There was also debate in Parliament over the suitability of women to file mail because, it was argued, these women might read dirty language in some of the mail. And when the typewriter was first invented it was believed that women were too weak physically to ever be typists.

In contrast to the past, with a few exceptions such as combat positions in the military, no U.S. laws restrict women to particular occupations. There are women police officers and fire fighters, and in some states like California, there are women guards in all-male prisons. But despite these examples, and despite the lack of legal barriers, women continue to be concentrated in certain places in the occupational structure. Table 15.8 indicates that overall, women are more likely to be in white-collar jobs than are men. However, Table 15.8 also shows that women are much more likely to be found in the lowest-ranking and lowest-paying white-collar jobs, such as clerical workers. That is one reason these jobs are sometimes called "pink-collar" jobs. And in blue-collar jobs, again women are more likely to be found in the lower-paying service jobs, such as maid and waitress.

You may remember that class position is made up of occupational position, as well as authority and control of property. In the previous chapter we found that both minorities and women are lower in authority and property control compared with white men. Wright and Perrone (1977) have estimated that whereas 42.9 percent of white males are in managerial-type positions giving them control over the work of others, only 27.7 percent of white fe-

TABLE 15.7. *Educational attainment by sex, 1982*

	Males 25 years or older (%)	Females 25 years or older (%)
Not high school graduate	28.2	29.7
High school graduate	33.1	41.3
Some college	15.7	14.8
College graduate	21.9	14.0
Total	100.0	100.0

SOURCE: U.S. Bureau of Census (1985).

males are in such positions. Also, although 10.9 percent of white males are employers (own property and hire workers), only 3 percent of white women are employers. In short, compared with men, women are low in occupation, authority, and property control in the United States.

Social Mobility for Women. As we have seen, social mobility is the movement up or down the stratification system. In the case of blacks social mobility patterns were significantly different from those of whites. A primary barrier to black economic achievement was therefore revealed in social mobility restrictions. It will be useful to make the same assessment for females compared with males.

We begin with a comparison between men and women in the labor force. Tyree and Treas (1974) found that daughters of professional fathers were more likely to be in lower white-collar occupations than sons of professional fathers. Also, daughters of farm workers were more likely to be in lower white-collar occupations and less likely to be in blue-collar occupations than sons of farm workers. Further, Hauser and Featherman (1977, p. 204) found that, overall, working women are less likely to be in an occupational status close to their father's when compared with men.

As might be expected when comparing the different occupational distributions of men and women in Table 15.8, most of the difference in mobility pat-

TABLE 15.8. *Occupational distribution by sex, 1985*

Occupation	White (%)			Nonwhite (%)	
	All	Males	Females	Males	Females
Professional	15.1	15.6	16.4	10.5	14.2
Managers	10.5	14.9	6.8	6.9	3.4
Sales workers	6.3	6.4	7.4	2.5	3.1
Clerical workers	18.1	6.0	35.9	7.6	29.0
Total white-collar	50.0	42.9	66.5	27.5	49.7
Craft	13.2	22.0	1.9	16.6	1.2
Operatives	15.4	16.8	11.0	23.9	15.3
Laborers	5.1	6.7	1.3	12.7	1.6
Service	13.5	7.7	18.1	15.8	31.4
Farming	2.7	4.0	1.3	3.5	0.8
Total blue-collar	49.9	57.2	33.6	72.5	50.3

SOURCE: U.S. Bureau of Labor Statistics (1986).

terns between men and women is due to this differ-ing occupational distribution (Hauser and Featherman, 1977, p. 203). Following the previous statement that working women are less likely to keep their fathers' occupational status than men, this is because women are both more down-wardly *and* more upwardly mobile (compared with their father's positions) than men are.

Women are more concentrated in lower nonman-ual or lower white-collar occupations such as clerical workers. Thus, no matter whether their fathers are higher or lower in occupational rank, women are frequently pushed up to, or down to, the lower white-collar positions. There is a sex as well as a race bias in the occupational structure. Black men, it will be remembered, are often pushed down to lower manual positions no matter what the occupational position of their fathers.

There are, however, two mobility patterns among women. As noted above, the status of women in the stratification system has traditionally been assumed to follow that of their husbands. With more than 50 percent of married women now in the labor force, this assumption must increasingly be ques-tioned. This also means, however, that only slightly less than 50 percent of married women are not in the labor force. To the extent that the occupational structure shapes life chances and the distribution of rewards in the society, the occupational structure more clearly affects this second group of women through the occupational attainment of their hus-bands. In this case we can consider the intergenera-tional mobility patterns of women with reference to the occupational position of fathers vis-à-vis that of their husbands.

Such a mobility analysis of married women not in the labor force has been conducted by Chase (1975), Tyree and Treas (1974), and Glenn, Ross, and Tully (1974). In these studies, the intergenerational mo-bility patterns of women were found to be much closer to those of men, in contrast to the other stud-ies described above. In other words, women tend to marry men who hold occupational positions close to those of their brothers (even when women are em-ployed). Put another way, father-son mobility pat-terns are closer to father-son-in-law mobility patterns than to father-daughter mobility patterns

as measured by the employment position of women. (Hauser and Featherman, 1977, p. 197). Thus, for a significant number of women the marriage market more closely reproduces the intergenerational mo-bility patterns of men.

The Causes of Gender Inequality. It is time to consider more closely the cause of gender inequality in indus-trial societies like the United States. There are many possible causes; it may be simple sexism lead-ing employers to hire women less often and pay them less when they are hired. But many other things could produce gender inequality, such as less education for women, less skill, less experience, tak-ing time off for children, holding one job for only a brief period, and the lack of freedom (compared with men) to move to geographical areas with better jobs. It is important to know which of these factors is the most important if anything is to be done to effec-tively reduce gender inequality and so that time and money are not wasted on ineffective programs. Be-fore considering empirical studies we should con-sider some possible causes of gender inequality not yet discussed.

As is true of racism, women do face sexism in hiring and pay. But if the cause of gender inequality is primarily sexism, we must show that the attitudes of people lead them to treat women differently. One problem often discussed is the reservations some people have about having a woman as their boss; and this attitude is not restricted to men. If this attitude has an effect, it means that women are not placed in higher positions of authority over others, and there-fore get less pay.

In this country, people often get better jobs, with more pay, by moving from one job to another. Women, however, may be restricted from these moves up the job rankings for two reasons: First, they may be less involved in the information net-work ("old boy network") where one can hear about better jobs (Lin, Ensel, and Vaughn, 1981). Second, even when women hear of better jobs, their mobility may be restricted. Married women are less likely to move to a better job in another location, taking along their husband, than are men. And there is the other side of this effect; men are more likely to move when a better job is found, taking the wife away from her job even if a suitable job in the new area is unlikely. Though over half of married women work today, still the assumption is often that the man's career is the more important.

Also, we must consider the types of jobs women are likely to have. We have already seen that women are concentrated in low-paying white-collar jobs and low-paying service jobs. But even in professional occupations that require college and even graduate degrees, women and men are separated. In professions, men are more likely to be doctors, lawyers, or accountants, for example, and women are more likely to be social workers, public school teachers, nurses, and so forth. These "women's jobs," even with the same education and skill requirements, often pay less to women than men.

Several empirical studies have shown that all the factors above are important in explaining some of the male-female income inequality. For example, in a study that examined education level, time away from careers due to child birth, job tenure, and lack of geographical mobility, Wolf and Fligstein (1979) found all these factors had at least some importance in explaining why women are in jobs giving them less authority, and therefore less income. But when it comes to attaining jobs with authority, Wolf and Fligstein (1979) found the attitudes of employers were more important; the idea described above where people are sometimes reluctant to have a woman boss does exclude some women from top jobs.

In another study, McLaughlin (1978) asked a sample of people to judge whether or not a job could be described as typically male or typically female. After the judgments were made, it was found that the jobs labeled "female" received less pay regardless of the education required.

Other studies have shown the effects of the dual economy on gender inequality. You will remember that the dual economy concept refers to a split between large monopoly-type industries and industries with smaller firms having more competition. The core firms (monopoly sector) have more job ranks, union workers, profits, among other things that lead to higher wages, compared with periphery firms. Females and minorities are more often found in periphery firms, compared with white men, and

This woman is Hannah Holborn Gray, President of the University of Chicago. Do you think of the job of college president as typically male or female, black or white, or hispanic or Asian? (© *University of Chicago*)

therefore have lower wages, authority, and career job mobility (Tolbert, Horan, and Beck, 1980; Beck, Horan, and Tolbert, 1978).

There are some signs that gender inequality will be further reduced in the future. As we have already seen, just between 1982 and 1987, the male-female income ratio improved significantly. Affirmative action and civil rights laws are showing some effects, as well as changed attitudes on the part of both men and women. Some of the indicators showing no improvement in recent years can be misleading. For example, we saw very little improvement in the male-female income ratio between 1955 and 1982. Part of this lack of improvement is due to more women from working-class families entering the job market, thus increasing the percentage of women in lower-ranking jobs. Thus, even if women in professional jobs have better pay in recent years, on the average women's pay did not improve, owing to more women in lower-ranked, lower-paying jobs.

Other signs of change are found in the big increase in women holding jobs traditionally seen as men's jobs. And perhaps more significant, there have been very important changes in the fields of study chosen by college women. No longer do we find women studying only for degrees in education, home economics, recreation, or social work. Many women now study law, medicine, engineering, accounting, and other majors traditionally seen as male-dominated. For example, in 1970 women accounted for only 8 percent of the M.D. degrees conferred that year. By 1980, however, the percentage of M.D.'s going to women had increased to 23 percent. The increase in law degrees going to women in this ten-year period was from 5 percent to 30 percent, and Ph.D.'s from 13 percent to 30 percent (Taeuber and Valdisera, 1986, p. 15). As these young women begin moving up in their careers, many indicators of gender inequality should diminish.

AGING AND INEQUALITY

We conclude this chapter with a look at another group, which has experienced *increased* discrimination and reduced status in industrial societies. To understand that the role of "elderly" is a social product more than a biological product, we will see how this social role has changed through history and remains different around the world today. We must begin with this historical and comparative view to better understand (1) our own social role for the elderly and (2) how this social role is related to changing social structure.

The Aged in History

Beauvoir (1973) has noted that nature has seldom been kind to the aged. All animals have a tendency to care for their young, for if this were not the case the species would not survive into the next generation. But this is not the case with the elderly, who can no longer care for themselves. In hunting and gathering societies the aged are usually treated with respect and are able to hold positions of influence as long as they can take care of themselves. This honor and influence is related to the special wisdom the elderly have gained and can pass on to others. When failing

health sets in, however, the treatment of the elderly in hunting and gathering societies depends on the level of resources held by that society (Crandall, 1980, pp. 60–64). If the hunting and gathering society cannot obtain a food surplus, and if their food sources require the tribe to be mobile, the weak elderly simply cannot be cared for. The elderly have received the best treatment in "primitive" societies that have adequate food, permanent residence, a religion that honors ancestors, and where the special knowledge or skills of the aged are most useful to the society.

In general, before industrialization, the aged were treated favorably and given high respect in agricultural societies. The aged remained the head of household, continued to control any property held by the family, and were seen as a resource of wisdom and information to be passed on to the young. From written records we can estimate the extent of respect for the aged beginning around the period 2000 B.C. The Hebrews, for example, "associated wisdom with a gray beard. It was widely believed that the young men were not as experienced as their elders and were more likely to act hastily and to formulate poor decisions" (Crandall, 1980, p. 68). In ancient Greece there was a dual view of the aged; people dreaded the physical limitations old age would bring, but they also admired the aged for their wisdom and experience. These views can especially be seen in Homer's *Iliad* and Plato's *The Republic*.

As we approach the era of industrial societies, however, views of the aged and their role begins to change. Until about 1790 it appears that the aged were still highly respected in the United States. The early Puritans, for example, believed the elderly had been favored by God because of their long life. But also, the elderly continued to control financial assets as a means of holding continued influence.

Fischer (1977) has studied the status of the aged in American history and found their position declining around 1790. For example, he found records showing that the elderly were given prestigious seats at town meetings before this time. But after the late 1700s, various indicators of status for the elderly changed. Their special privileges were reduced, mandatory retirement laws emerged, and terms such as "old fogey," "codger," and "geezer"

These elderly Solomon Islanders are participating in a ceremonial war dance. The elderly woman is sitting on a park bench in a large American city. What is the difference in the quality of their lives? Why do you think the elderly are treated as marginal persons in our society? (Top: © Eugene Gordon; bottom: © Stephen Shames/ Woodfin Camp)

first appeared. As all of this suggests, the aged did not always have the honored and respected position in their families they once held. They came to be seen more as a burden to be tolerated than anything else.

Because people began to live longer in industrial societies, there has been a slow increase in the percent of the population over 65. And because of widespread mandatory retirement laws, there was an increasing problem of elderly people with no means of support. In the United States, by 1910 about 23 percent of the elderly were dependent on others for their basic necessities. By 1922 the number had reached 33 percent, then 40 percent by 1930, and 66 percent by 1940 (Crandall, 1980, p. 76). During this period the plight of the aged came to be seen as a social problem.

Also during this period, however, the aged slowly emerged as a political force. The elderly were hit especially hard by the Great Depression of the 1930s, and out of this depression came one of the first organized political groups of the aged to pressure government for their economic interests. Through the Townsend Movement, or "Ham and Egg" movement as it was sometimes called, the elderly pressured the Roosevelt administration and Congress to enact old-age insurance, as was being done in most other industrial societies. It was in large part because of this pressure that the Social Security system came into being in 1935.

Today the elderly are a major political force still, with voter participation higher than in any other age group. They are a continuing force behind the steady increase of the Social Security system, as any politician learns after threatening to reduce Social Security benefits. Many other government aid programs are also helping the elderly, such as Medicare. Recently, the federal and local governments have tried to improve the status of the elderly through laws against forced retirement at age 65 and against other forms of discrimination directed toward the elderly.

Yet the United States is still a nation that worships youth. Though there is recently some change, TV commercials, TV programs, and movies continue to stress positive images of being young and negative images of the elderly (Hess, 1974; Francher, 1973). The most important change, though, has come with the actual conditions for the elderly. We consider these conditions in more detail below, but one figure we have seen earlier is very significant. In striking contrast to previous decades, the elderly today have a lower rate of poverty than any other minority group.

The Aged in Japan. The status of the aged has been shaped by the level of technology in the society. But many other factors such as cultural images and family systems produce varied conditions for the aged even in industrial societies. Recently, there has been considerable interest in the status of the aged in Japan because in many ways it appears that the status of the aged in that country is better than in any other industrial nation. Like many other images Americans have of Japan, however, this one is only somewhat accurate.

In contrast to other industrial nations, the elderly are highly respected in Japan. The Japanese continue to have a ranking system based on age, with social status increasing as a person becomes older. In contrast to the "Pepsi generation" image in the United States, for example, gray hair is a sign of higher social status and people with gray hair are given more respect. Because fewer Japanese have gray hair at an early age, gray hair can provide a strong symbol of position in the age-ranked system (a situation that can be used to the advantage of a Caucasian who happens to have gray hair at an early age).

As would be expected in this age-ranked society, the elderly have an honored position in the family. The Japanese even have a special word (*gimu*) that describes the obligations and respect adults must maintain toward their parents and others with authority over them (Benedict, 1946; Doi, 1973). The elderly in the Japanese family are often consulted by younger family members before any major decision is made, and the advice is usually taken seriously (Palmore, 1975). One indicator of the status of the elderly in the Japanese family is the number of aged parents living with their adult offspring. As shown in Table 15.9, the percentage of people over 65 years of age living with their offspring is in striking contrast between Japan and the United States. In the 1970s, almost 80 percent of the elderly in Japan were living in the same household with one of their children (Vogel, 1979, p. 196), and the decline in this percentage in recent years has reversed (Morgan and Hiroshima, 1983). Opinion polls continue to show that these living arrangements are accepted and even favored by the Japanese (*Japan Times,* Sept. 15, 1985). One reason that these living arrangements are accepted by adult children in Japan is that the child care and other benefits provided by

TABLE 15.9. *International comparison of aged living with adult children (%)*

Composition	Japan		Great Britain		USA		Denmark	
	M	F	M	F	M	F	M	F
Couples								
Alone	16	15	67	68	77	82	80	84
With child	79	79	29	28	18	15	17	14
With relatives	4	5	3	5	3	2	1	—
With nonrelatives	1	1	1	2	2	1	2	2
	100	100	100	100	100	100	100	100
Single								
Alone	10	8	37	45	52	46	58	63
With child	82	84	41	37	38	37	20	21
With relatives	6	6	14	13	11	22	6	7
With nonrelatives	2	2	8	5	8	5	10	9
	100	100	100	100	100	100	100	100

SOURCE: Palmore (1975).

the elderly are valued (Morgan and Hiroshima, 1983).

A related indicator of the integration of the elderly within the family in Japan is the number of homes for the aged. The Japanese often react in disbelief when told about the extent of homes for the aged in the United States. In all Japan in 1963 there was only one home for the aged (Fukutake, 1981, p. 113). By 1978 there were still only 790 homes for the aged, a significant increase, but still *much* less than in other industrial nations. More popular in Japan are "day care centers" for the aged. If the adult children must work, and their elderly parents cannot care for themselves, these elderly parents may be taken to day care facilities so they can continue to live in their children's home.

Because the elderly are not excluded from extensive interaction with other family members, because they also continue as members of other social groups, and because of the continued respect they received in Japan's age-ranking system, life satisfaction does not decline with age as it sometimes does in the United States (Vogel, 1979). However, as other works on Japan point out, the life satisfaction of the aged in Japan is much lower than it once was (see Box 15.1), and in some respects the attainment of elderly status is more harsh in Japan than in the United States (Taylor, 1983). This difficulty for the elderly in Japan has developed especially since World War II and is related to economic well-being and employment.

Table 15.10 indicates another striking difference between Japan and other industrial nations. A high percentage of the population over 65 years old in Japan remain in the labor force. This in part reflects a strong work ethic, for over 90 percent of those over 65 who are working say they want to continue working. But there is a negative side to these employment figures. With retirement pensions less adequate than those of other industrial nations, and without a Social Security system as extensive as that of the United States, most of the elderly in Japan work because of economic necessity. A very high percentage of the elderly want to continue working because they do not want a severe drop in their standard of living.

As we will see below, most social scientists agree that it is usually better for the elderly to remain employed as long as their health is good. In this respect, therefore, the elderly may be better off in Japan. However, the primary problem for the elderly who must work in Japan is the type of job they

Japan's "Life Time" Employment, Which Really Isn't

Japan's celebrated lifetime employment system, when examined closely, shows some unsightly flaws. Contrary to myth, Japanese employment guarantees extend only into late middle age, after which workers are left to fend for themselves. . . .

Japanese corporations do hire graduates just out of high school and keep them on the company payroll until they reach retirement. But most companies mandate retirement at 55, and some at ages up to 58. Meanwhile eligibility for welfare pensions doesn't begin until age 60. To support themselves in the interim, most retired workers find themselves taking a substantial cut in pay to work in small and medium-sized companies.

Moreover, pensions are so low that work doesn't stop at 60. According to the 1980 national census, 81.6% of Japanese men between the ages of 60 and 64, and 45.4% of those 65 and over, are still in the labor force. These figures are *by far the highest in the industrialized world.* A 1980 survey by the Labor Ministry indicated that nearly half of those 65 and over work in order to maintain the standard of living they are used to.

Japanese employment is structured around young workers, whereas in the West, the emphasis is placed on safeguarding the livelihoods of older employees. American and European workers are protected by seniority rights won for them by their unions. Laying off employees with long years of service is unheard of, and statistics show that the percentage of older employees who have worked for the same company is higher in Western countries than in Japan.

Japan has experienced several recessions since the oil crisis of 1973. But even in these hard times, new university graduates have been in a seller's market. By contrast, workers 55 and over have found 10 applicants waiting in line for every job. It is onto this buyer's market that retiring employees between 56 and 60 are being unceremoniously dumped.

Even in companies in which the retirement age is moved past 55, it is not uncommon for workers over 55 to be excluded from pay raises agreed on between management and labor. Older workers opting to stay on may also be forced to accept a humiliating cut in pay. This is the reality of lifetime employment, Japanese-style.

Source: Mitsuo Tajima, "Japan's Cold Indifference Toward Old People," *Los Angeles Times,* Nov. 8, 1982.

---

must hold. Most of the elderly in Japan must retire from their jobs at age 55 to 60 and are forced to seek new employment at a lower status and lower-paying position. Behind this forced retirement is the strict age stratification in Japan.

When young workers join major corporations soon after college graduation in Japan, they form a new age cohort that stays together until retirement. They will always be junior to workers hired before them and senior to workers hired after them (Vogel, 1979). All these workers in core industries are promoted together over the years, and in the majority of cases, without regard to merit. As already pointed out, very few workers leave the corporation, either through voluntarily changing jobs or through layoffs. The problem comes at about age 55, however, when the corporate hierarchy narrows; there are fewer jobs for the age cohort that has moved up the corporate ladder together since college graduation. It is not considered acceptable to have a boss

TABLE 15.10. *Percent of population 65 and older employed full time, international comparisons, 1984*

Nation	% 65 and older population in the labor force		
	Both sexes	Men	Women
United States	10.5	15.7	7.0
Canada	8.1	12.6	4.7
France	3.6	5.5	2.4
West Germany	4.2	6.3	3.0
Italy	10.7	18.1	4.8
Japan	24.8	37.6	15.9
Sweden	7.2	11.1	3.8
United Kingdom	5.3	7.8	3.8

SOURCE: U.S. Bureau of Census (1986, p. 848).

who is the same age as oneself (and certainly not younger), nor a boss who was once one's equal in rank. Thus, when the few in the 55-year-old age cohort are selected for promotion to higher corporate positions, those not promoted must retire. This practice continues on up the age scale until the top corporate executive is chosen from the vice-presidents, who finally retire as well.

There is considerable anguish as workers reach the age of 55 because it is usually known who will stay and who will be forced to go (Taylor, 1983, p. 167). If the job is with a major corporation, the company can help the retired worker find employment in a smaller company that subcontracts work from the major corporation. But these jobs will offer less status and less pay. Those who have worked for smaller companies all their lives face even more difficult job prospects.

The status of the elderly in Japan involves conflict and change. On the one hand, the aged are more respected and integrated into the society than in any other industrial nation. On the other hand, however, the elderly are treated rather harshly in the economic organizations. These economic organizations and their practices are new to Japan; in fact, many of the corporate practices such as forced retirement at 55 and "lifetime" employment before 55 became well established only since World War II. Thus, it is

too early to tell if the status of the elderly in Japan will continue to erode.

A Conflict Perspective on Aging

Our comparative and historical analysis of the elderly and their social status has raised a number of questions. For example, in contrast to the status of women in industrial societies, we find that the status of the elderly has been generally reduced. Why have the elderly been able to hold a better position in modern Japan compared with other industrial nations, though the position of the elderly has been reduced in Japan's economic organizations?

As can be done with other groups in a society, many sociologists use a form of conflict theory to explain the position of the elderly (Collins, 1975; Dowd, 1975). Conflict theory suggests that the status of a group is related to its power and resources in relation to those of others in the society. If, for example, a group has a valued occupational skill or influence in the state, this group is likely to be of higher status than a group with lower skills and less influence. The first group has more resources to demand and hold its higher status.

In contrast to the position of women, which has been improving as industrial societies advance, the position of the elderly has deteriorated in industrial societies. The position of women has been enhanced, in part, by reproductive control and a changing occupational structure. Now women are not so dependent on men for economic support but can enter the labor force and even hold top corporate positions. The economic changes in industrial societies have reduced the position of the elderly, however. In hunting and gathering societies the aged are respected for their wisdom and survival skills that the young have yet to master. In agrarian societies the elderly still control the most important resource —land. But in industrial societies, whereas the elderly who have had great wealth in their younger years face fewer problems, the skills of most elderly people are no longer so highly valued. With rapid technological and social change, the more recently trained may in fact have more skills than those who completed their education many years ago.

Aging: Problems and Myths

There are obviously many negative consequences associated with becoming an old person, but they have often been misunderstood in our society. There are, in fact, many positive sides to becoming an old person that many people do not realize. In this section we first examine some of the problems of aging, then consider some of the myths about aging.

Problems of Aging. One of the first negative consequences of aging that comes to mind are health problems. Aging is, of course, a biological as well as a social process, which means that the body becomes more susceptible to illness. Although the elderly make up only around 11 percent of the population they account for about one-third of all hospital patients at any one time. And as can be seen in Table 15.11, limitations in normal activity caused by some health condition increases with age.

Most of the aged today are not confined to beds, wheelchairs, or nursing homes. Only about 5 percent of the population over 65 are in nursing homes, though some 26 percent of the elderly will be in a nursing home some time in their lives. Of the approximately 1 million nursing home patients in the United States, 75 percent are women, 50 percent are without a close living relative, and their average age is 82 (Harris and Cole, 1980, pp. 350–351). Conditions for these elderly are often quite depressing. In addition to the 50 percent with no close relative, about 60 percent receive no visitors *at all,* and only 20 percent can ever expect to leave the nursing home.

TABLE 15.11. *Health limitations by age*

	No limitation on activity		Some limitation		Limitation on major activity	
	1970	1980	1970	1980	1970	1980
Under 45 years	94.7	93.2	5.3	6.8	3.3	4.2
45 to 64 years	80.5	76.1	19.5	23.9	15.7	18.8
Over 64 years	57.7	54.8	42.3	45.2	37.0	39.0

SOURCE: U.S. Bureau of Census, 1982.

Another problem related to the health of the aged has been increasingly recognized with the rapid advances in medical technology. A person in pain and anguish or in a coma can be kept alive for years with new medical technology. Thus, a legal and ethical question is, "At what point do we allow a person to die?" The elderly (and others as well) who are in pain and facing certain death often ask to be left alone to die. Equally tragic, elderly people are often faced with watching their spouse die in this manner. They would often prefer to let their spouse die in peace but are prevented from doing so. There are increasing reports of double suicides by the elderly facing this situation. Similarly, one spouse may kill the other spouse who is being kept alive with medical technology, then commits suicide. The legal and moral questions involved in these cases are far from being solved in our society.

Another negative consequence of aging is the loss of social relationships, and thus, loneliness and isolation. The loss of these social relations is less than most people believe, but there is certainly a loss. The death of a spouse or close friend reduces social relations, as does retirement for those who have been employed most of their lives. When asked if they have daily interaction with many people, 72 percent of those aged 50 to 55 say yes, but the percentage responding yes drops to 45 percent for those aged 65 to 69, and only 15 percent for those 75 and older (Schwartz, Snyder, and Peterson, 1984, p. 128).

There is disagreement over the exact extent to which reduced social interaction is forced or voluntary among the aged, but it is clear that reduced social relationships can cause stress. Evaluations of the extent of stress and readjustment following various life events have found the death of a spouse to be the most serious (Holmes and Rahe, 1967). With death of a spouse given a value of 100 for a comparison of stress and readjustment levels, the death of a close family member rates 63, personal injury or illness rates 53, retirement 45, and death of a close friend 37. These ratings are not the same for each individual, of course, but a primary point is that the aged may face many of these stressful life events. Despite this stress, however, the rate of suicide actually goes down as people get older. The exception

TABLE 15.12. *Public opinion on the problems of the aged and personal experiences, 1981*

Rank as actual very serious problem for 65 and over		Personal experience	Public expectation	
		"Very serious" problems felt personally by public 65 and over (%)	"Very Serious" problems attributed to most people over 65 (%)	
			By public 18–64	By public 65 and over
4	Not having enough money to live on	17	68	50
3	Poor health	21	47	40
6	Loneliness	13	65	45
10	Poor housing	5	43	30
2	Fear of crime	25	74	58
8	Not enough education	6	21	17
8	Not enough job opportunities	6	51	24
7	Not enough medical care	9	45	34
1	High cost of energy, such as heating oil, gas, and electricity	42	81	72
5	Getting transportation to stores, to doctors, to places of recreation, and so forth	14	58	43

SOURCE: National Council on Aging.

to this decrease is found only among white men, though in all categories of aged, many social scientists are questioning the accuracy of these suicide figures. Older adults often use methods of suicide that are more difficult to detect, such as starving themselves, refusing medication, or delaying medical treatment (Perlmutter and Hall, 1985, p. 166).

Myths About Aging. People in our society tend to have a rather harsh view of conditions for the elderly. Much of this negative image is due to the way the elderly are presented in the media (Hess, 1974). No doubt some of the misinformation about conditions for the elderly is due to recent changes; in many respects some conditions for the elderly (such as a reduction of poverty) have improved so rapidly that most people don't yet realize the change.

Table 15.12 presents some interesting questions from a national opinion poll about aging in 1981. When compared with what the elderly say about their own personal experience, both the general public and the elderly themselves think conditions for the elderly in general are worse than the reality, though the views of the elderly are somewhat more accurate. In their personal lives the aged were concerned about high energy costs, but so were many other people with the rapid increase in the cost of energy during the late 1970s and early 1980s. The elderly's second greatest concern for themselves

personally was crime, but again, this concern is high across all age groups of adults. Poor health is the third major concern, but only 21 percent see poor health as a very serious problem in their own life. "Not having enough money to live on" is seen as a very serious personal problem by only 17 percent of the elderly, and 68 percent of those less than 65 years old believe it is a serious problem for the elderly.

It is in the realm of economic well-being that conditions for the elderly have improved the most in recent years. As noted in an earlier chapter, poverty among the elderly has gone down considerably since the 1960s. In fact, poverty has been reduced more for the elderly than for any other group in the United States. And although the rate of poverty has again increased substantially during the 1980s, for only one category of people has the poverty rate gone down before 1985 — the elderly.

It is clear that in large measure the improved economic standing of the elderly is the result of government pensions and aid programs. It has been estimated that, on the average, these government programs have increased the income of the elderly by 50 percent (Uhr and Evanson, 1983). Table 15.13 provides striking figures in this respect. By 1978, over 95 percent of all aged households received at least some type of government transfer payment (primarily Social Security). In Part B of this table we find that it was because of the government

TABLE 15.13. *Cash transfers by age categories*

	Nonaged male head	Nonaged female head	Aged male or female head
A. Percentage of all households receiving any cash transfer.			
1965	23.2	36.6	87.6
1978	25.8	38.4	95.9
B. Probability of pretransfer poor households being removed from poverty by cash transfers.			
1965	.15	.18	.50
1978	.33	.21	.72
C. Percentage of households with income less than the official poverty line after the receipt of cash transfers.			
1965	9.7	34.1	32.3
1978	6.9	29.1	17.2

SOURCE: Danziger and Plotnick (1981).

transfers that most of the elderly were above the poverty line.

Finally, we should consider simply "life satisfaction" or happiness among the aged. A common stereotype is of the lonely, cranky old person who is often depressed, with few friends, and nothing to do. There are, of course, elderly people who are very unhappy; but so too are many nonelderly. In one study, Cameron (1975) interviewed 6,000 people from 4 years old to 99 years old. He found that happiness and life satisfaction was at similar levels for the young, middle-aged, and old. Life satisfaction was more influenced by things like class position and immediate conditions for the individual, not age per se. Larson (1978) found much the same thing in similar research; more important are conditions like income and health in determining life satisfaction. The elderly, of course, do have more problems with conditions such as health, but it seems that "as people age, their expectations may change, and these changing expectations may well offset negative life experiences" (Perlmutter and Hall, 1985, p. 280).

CHAPTER SUMMARY

Key Terms

gender roles, 418   instrumental role, 426
sex stratification, 418   expressive role, 426

Content

Biological differences between men and women affect behavior and social roles, but the importance of these differences are much less than most people realize, especially in industrial societies. Most of the differences between men and women are created in the socialization process.

Gender roles specify the accepted behavior, activities, and other individual characteristics for men and women in a society. These gender roles are a part of social traditions and because they are social products, they are subject to change.

The status of women has changed broadly throughout history. In hunting and gathering societies we find a tendency toward equality between the sexes, though there is a division of labor. With the development of agricultural societies, however, the status of women began to decline significantly. Women were dominated by men in all segments of the society. With industrial societies the status of women began to improve, at least in the advanced stages of industrial societies.

Functional theories suggest that a division of labor by sex, with men in authority over women, serves positive functions for the society. Conflict theories, in contrast, argue that the roles of men and women are related to the balance of resources and power between the sexes. Characteristics of a society, such as the level of technology, strongly influence this balance of power. In industrial societies, for example, women are required to care for children less often and almost all occupations can be performed equally well by either men or women. These factors give women more options in life and reduce their dependence on men.

The continued level of inequality between men and women is related to many factors. Sexual discrimination and the need to drop out of the labor force for child care are among many causes of such things as income inequality. But the trend has been toward less inequality as the social institutions (religion, political system, etc.) that were shaped in an agricultural age when women had fewer options are themselves changing.

Like gender roles, there are roles for different age groups in a society. And like gender roles, these roles for the aged are more social than biological products.

In contrast to the status of women, the status of the elderly has generally declined in industrial societies. From a conflict perspective, this decline can be understood as a result of the declining influence of the elderly. With rapidly changing technology the skills of the elderly often become outdated, and with nuclear families more important, the elderly lose much of their influence in the family system.

There are many myths about the problems of the aged in the United States. The elderly do face problems related to declining health and a decline in social relationships. But for the most part they do not face despair and a struggle to live. With respect to economic conditions, there has been marked improvement in recent decades. This has primarily been the result of government transfer programs, especially Social Security. The improved economic well-being of the aged is very much the result of their political influence coming from increasing numbers and a high voter participation rate.

National liberation, national renaissance, the restoration of nationhood to the people, commonwealth: whatever may be the headings used or the new formulas introduced, decolonization is always a violent phenomenon.

—*Franz Fanon,* The Wretched of the Earth

By the midcentury it was already evident that the twentieth would be the bloodiest century in over 2,000 years, perhaps the bloodiest in human history (Sorokin, 1941). Even since World War II there have been another 80 major military conflicts around the world, 40 of which were still raging in the mid-1980s. (When the lesser military conflicts are included, one estimate places the number at about 300 since World War II.) More than 20 million people have been killed in these wars and revolutions since 1945, about twice as many civilians as military personnel. The percentage of civilian casualties has, in fact, been increasing. During World War I about 17 percent of the casualties were civilians, but by the time of World War II the percentage of civilian casualties had increased to 45 percent, then to 70 percent in the Korean and Vietnam wars (Geyer, 1985). The nature of warfare has clearly changed.

A primary reason for the change in the nature of warfare is that most major armed conflicts since World War II can be classified as civil wars or revolutions, rather than conventional international wars such as the Spanish-American War, World War I, and World War II. Civil wars and revolutions are principally internal conflicts between two or more groups within a society over the issue of major social change. Of the 13 most deadly conflicts in the past 150 years, 10 have been civil wars or revolutions. Included in the ten are the American Civil War and the Chinese and Russian revolutions. Most cases of internal armed conflicts (we can call them political violence), however, have been less grand, though their total effects are no less important. One study found the existence of at least some political violence in 114 of 121 nations examined between 1961 and 1969 (Gurr, 1969).

Although these deadly conflicts have primarily been internal affairs in origin, outside actors have often become involved. This outside involvement has increased the bloodshed considerably, as it did in Vietnam. About half of the wars and revolutions around the world since World War II can be classified as "proxy battles," wars waged between local armed forces and/or revolutionaries but supported and encouraged by rival superpowers. In contrast to the cases of guerrilla war 20 years ago, about half today are anticommunist and supported by the Western powers — primarily the United States. As a reflection of these conflicts, military spending in Third World nations has increased more than 500 percent since 1960. Superpower military involvement is often more direct, however, with 778,000 Soviet troops stationed in 22 foreign nations during 1985, and 479,000 U.S. troops based in 40 countries.

To understand the nature of these bloody conflicts (and others not so bloody) we must examine the internal social structures of the societies involved, as well as the influence of the world system on these societies. It is for this reason that the present chapter has been placed at the end of Part III, The Structural Bases of Inequality and Conflict. A stratification system helps determine "who gets what, and why," and operates to provide legitimacy for the unequal distribution of valued resources and positions. But from time to time the unequal distribution of resources is questioned by people receiving less, and there are organized attempts to change the distribution of resources, and indeed, the stratification system itself. A recent comparative study of 51 nations has found a significant statistical relationship between high-income inequality and political violence (Muller, 1985). This seems to indicate that when inequality is high, there is a tendency for political violence to result from the attempts by some people to increase the distribution of rewards going to their group. However, inequality in a society does not always produce social movements, riots, guerrilla wars, or revolutions. As already noted one of the most unequal societies in world history was India, where we find very little evidence of political violence before the 1800s. Thus, a major task of this chapter is to explain why inequality only sometimes produces social movement challenges.

Before proceeding it is time for a few brief definitions. The term *social movement* refers to relatively organized attempts to produce change in the society that is resisted by other groups. We must specify the nature of social movements in more detail later, and we must distinguish between different types of social movements such as reform movements and revolutionary movements. For now, however, the distinction between social movements and social change is most important. **Social change** is the process through which major characteristics of a society are transformed in the absence of any specifically organized attempts to produce the change. Social change is normally a gradual process that is unrecognized without a comparison of distant historical reference points. The industrial revolution is a good example of social change (though the term "revolution" in this context is inaccurately used). No particular group sat down together to plan the industrial revolution and the multiple consequences it had for modern societies. The industrial revolution was the result of thousands of human actors seeking individual profits with the new technology that became available.

THE NATURE OF SOCIAL MOVEMENTS AND REVOLUTIONS

During 1911 China began what was to be one of the most dramatic and tragic events of the twentieth century. Though it is often difficult to pinpoint the precise beginning of a revolution, it was in October 1911 that the old imperial government in China fell, soon after the Boxer Rebellion raged. The Boxer Rebellion itself was a comparatively minor uprising against foreign domination, but it was the event that demonstrated that the old political system could no longer govern China's masses.

Between 1911 and 1949 there was almost constant revolutionary struggle in China. Many millions died, not only from the direct fighting, but also because of economic collapse and the resulting famine. With Mao's Communist Party finally in power by 1949, radical changes in China's agriculture and in-

dustry began. Although there were many mistakes and setbacks, the economy was revived and few people were hungry in China by the 1960s. The revolution, however, was not yet over. Disputes over how the development of China's revolution should proceed led to the bloody Cultural Revolution in 1965, which lasted until the middle 1970s. Because much of China was closed to the outside world during the Cultural Revolution, we are only now learning of the thousands killed and injured during this phase of the Chinese Revolution.

The bloody events such as the revolution in China are in many ways related to the general subject of social change. It is social change that often sets the stage for revolutionary conflict. In the case of China it was industrialization in other nations, which could then exploit China through the world economic system, that left China weak economically and politically. In this condition it took only a small push in 1911 for the imperial government to crumble (Skocpol, 1979). But revolution involves a very particular kind of social change; it involves human struggle with the specific intent to produce basic change. Similar to Mao, Lenin, for example, planned the Russian Revolution of 1917, though it did not occur when and how he expected.

We have many questions to ask about the causes of revolutions, as well as the less dramatic forms of social movements and political violence. For example, when it is realized that one's life expectancy can be severely reduced by joining a revolutionary army we must ask why do people do that? What made it possible for Mao to mobilize millions of peasants in the name of revolution? And why are there revolutions raging in Central America and many other places around the world today?

There are many definitions of social movements and revolutions, but they all have some common points. **Social movements** are organized, purposeful attempts by individuals to produce social change. These attempts are usually resisted by powerful people who profit from the status quo, and it is often difficult for social movement participants to use the accepted and legal means of producing social change (such as the courts and political institutions). Thus, social movement participants often find disruptive street tactics their only means of action. The antiwar movement in the 1960s, the Civil Rights Movement that emerged strongly in the 1950s, and the antiabortion movement of the 1980s are all examples of social movements in America that have involved both legal and illegal activities to achieve their goals. In fairness to social movement participants, however, their powerful opponents are just as likely to use illegal activities and violence to stop the social movement (Marx, 1974; Gamson, 1975; Stohl, 1976).

Although there are disagreements over the definition of revolution (Skocpol, 1979), there is a standard view that revolutions are successful social movements on a much grander scale, that is, involving more people and much more social change. Although social movements like the U.S. Civil Rights Movement may be working to enact some law or produce some reform in the society, **revolutions** like the Chinese Revolution are aimed at major social change. The goals of revolutionaries are commonly the overthrow of a government, basic change in the political and economic system, and more generally a basic change in the stratification system in the country. Because of the extent of change sought, revolutions are always accompanied by extensive violence. The stakes are so high that opponents will kill to prevent the revolution, and revolutionaries must be ready to kill to achieve their goals. This is not to say all revolutions are equally bloody. The American Revolution, for several reasons, was less bloody than the other grand revolutions such as the French Revolution of 1789 and the Russian Revolution of 1917. But compared with revolutions everywhere, almost all social movements have much less violence. Still, most social movements are also associated with at least some minimal violence. Marches get out of hand and some people are attacked; a few individuals will usually be willing to use some planned violence (e.g., sending letter bombs, attacking opponents) that may be condemned by most movement members. This is one reason the term **political violence** is often used to describe most varieties of social movements and attempts at revolution (Gurr, 1970). The other reason the term political violence is often used is that most attempts at change are directed toward the political system.

With the modern, expanded state, all goals that social movement members may seek can be influenced, if not achieved, through government action.

It is useful to specify several varieties of political violence at this point. We can distinguish three general types with reference to where opponents are located in a stratification system. As shown in Figure 16.1, a pure case of revolution involves attempts at basic change by groups relatively low in the stratification system, with those higher in the system opposing them. This is not to say that all revolutionaries are from the lower classes, because some factions within the higher classes often "throw in" with the revolutionaries, especially if they are seen as winning, and most revolutionary leaders have had higher-class origins. In the French Revolution of 1789, for example, the increasingly powerful merchants formed an alliance with workers and peasants to overthrow the old aristocracy and its state (Soboul, 1974).

In the case of **civil war** the split is down the middle of the stratification system. As in the American Civil War of 1861–1865, the elites and masses in the North were united against the elites and masses in the South. The primary issues in that war involved economic policies that favored the North

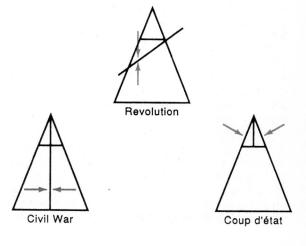

FIGURE 16.1. Types of political violence.

Revolution

Civil War

Coup d'état

over the South. The dispute in a civil war usually pertains to vital issues other than those directly related to the stratification system. This is also the case with a **coup d'état,** or simply a coup. A pure case of a coup involves one set of elites trying to displace another set, with the masses primarily uninvolved (and sometimes uninterested).

I have said that the above represent pure cases or ideal types to emphasize that actual cases often contain a mixture of more than one form of political violence. Major cases of political violence are com-

plex affairs with many groups and many issues involved. We can begin with further examples of **nationalist revolutions,** which are revolutions as well as attempts to free a country from colonial domination. As is often the case, the colonial power had a hand in shaping the stratification system and placing current elites in office. Thus, along with fighting for liberation from the colonial power, revolution in the dependent nation is directed toward changing the political/economic/stratification systems (the three are tied together). A good example is the Vietnam-

In the eighteenth century American war of independence, George Washington was a nationalist revolutionary leader. In the twentieth century, Ho Chi Minh was a nationalist revolutionary leader of the North Vietnamese in their war against the United States. Each man became a symbol of hope and strength for his own countrymen. What kind of symbol were they to those outside their own country? (Left: Painting by Gilbert Stuart/© The Bettman Archive Inc.; right: © The Bettman Archive Inc.)

ese Revolution, which began before World War II but gained enough strength to eliminate French rule in half of the country by 1954. With the French moving out in 1954, however, the United States moved in to support the South Vietnamese government until the United States was also forced out at the end of the Vietnam War in 1975. The American Revolution of 1776 was in one way similar to the Vietnamese Revolution in throwing out a colonial power, in this case the British. However, in America's nationalist revolution, the emphasis on revolution was less because domestic elites (Washington, Jefferson, etc.) were generally accepted by the population, along with the basic stratification system already in existence. There were some minor rebellions against the American stratification system soon after the American Revolution (Ash-Garner, 1977), but the basic goal of most Americans was to push out the British.

It is also common for one form of political violence to follow another. A nationalist revolution may later set the stage for a civil war, as it eventually did in the United States. In the Soviet Union, the Revolution of 1917 stimulated a relatively small civil war because some regions in Russia did not support Lenin's rule or policies.

Finally, coups often involve more than just a new leadership, and thus other forms of political violence may be mixed with the coup (Hagopian, 1974). We can refer to a "revolutionary coup" when the new elites in power plan revolutionary changes and are supported by the general population. A good example of this is the military coup in Portugal in the mid-1970s. The military leaders taking power in this coup changed the government from a fascist dictatorship to a socialist democracy, and eliminated Portugal's remaining colonial ties in Africa. A more common occurrence is the "counterrevolutionary coup." In this case a group of elites (most often from the military) take power from a relatively new revolutionary or reform government. The new military elites are supported by the upper class that have been losing wealth because of the revolutionary or reform government. Also, outside support for the military counterrevolutionary coup may come from powerful nations that have an interest in reversing the reforms. As we saw earlier, an example of a

counterrevolutionary coup is the 1973 military coup in Chile.

Among many other similar cases is the 1981 military coup in Poland, supported by the Soviet government. When the union called Solidarity was allowed to become very influential politically, martial law was imposed and a top military leader took power as prime minister.

The Causes of Social Movements

During 73 B.C. the Roman Empire faced extensive revolts by slaves, and particularly a strong revolt led by the gladiator Spartacus. In Europe during the fourteenth and fifteenth centuries there were many revolts in which peasants organized attacks on landowners. Beginning in the mid-1950s, black Americans began a massive Civil Rights Movement by marching in the streets, sitting at lunch counters reserved for whites only, and boycotting buses that required blacks to sit at the back. During these events and the thousands like them throughout history the question asked by most people is "why?" What caused these rebellions aimed at social change?

A common "answer" is that the group involved became angry and would not bear the oppression any longer. When asked why the Civil Rights Movement occurred, many Americans today say that blacks simply became "fed up" with their position in this country. But when we consider this answer in some detail, it is clearly inadequate. Why did the Civil Rights Movement occur in the 1950s and not before? Were conditions worse for blacks in the 1950s, and thus did they create more anger? The answer to the last question is no, and in fact, some important conditions were actually improved by the 1950s. So why was there no extensive black civil rights movement before the 1950s when conditions were worse?

Figure 16.2 also indicates that a source of deprivation is not always sufficient to spark social movement activity. During the 1930s there was massive protest by the unemployed and poor in the United States. There was, of course, massive unemployment during the 1930s, reaching a high point of

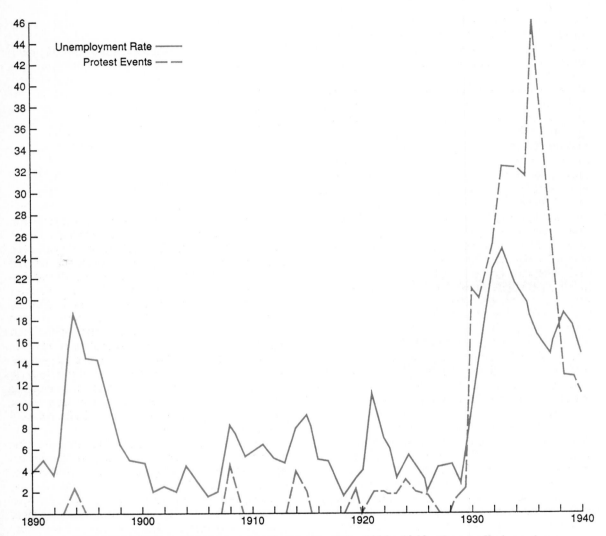

FIGURE 16.2. Unemployment and protest in the U.S., 1890–1940. *(Source: Kerbo and Shaffer, 1986.)*

almost 25 percent in 1933. But as Figure 16.2 shows, there were other periods of very high unemployment between 1890 and 1940 with almost no protest. And if you look closely at Figure 16.2 you will notice that the massive protest began in 1930, when unemployment was only around 8 percent and no one knew it would reach 25 percent within three years. The deprivation produced by unemployment does not always stimulate protest, just as the degradation of discrimination does not always stimulate a civil rights movement.

Social scientists have developed two basic theories to explain the causes of social movements and political violence. In one, **relative deprivation**

theory, the focus is on social conditions producing a sense of anger that leads to social movement activity. In the other, **resource mobilization theory,** the focus is on social conditions that allow a group to obtain the various material and power resources needed to organize a social movement. We examine both these theories, then later consider the causes of major revolutions that require additions to them.

Relative Deprivation Theory. Relative deprivation theory is primarily a social psychological theory of social movements asking how the angry state of mind leading people to revolt is created. As the term "relative" implies, all types of deprivation are not assumed to produce this anger. What must be considered are the relative expectations of individuals; how do conditions people experience now compare with what they expect these conditions to be? If conditions are bad, but people have come to expect no better, then revolt is unlikely. People get angry and are more prone to join revolts, the theory says, when conditions are much worse than people expect them to be.

In the 1840s French social scientist Alexis de Tocqueville (1955) was one of the first to notice a pattern fitting relative deprivation behind social movements. As protest increased before the French Revolution of 1789, de Tocqueville recognized the ironic situation in which protest seemed to increase when bad economic conditions were actually improving. From this observation came the idea that when conditions are improving, people's expectations for improvements race ahead of the actual improving conditions, producing the anger.

James Davies (1962) refined this relative deprivation theory in the 1960s and called the historical pattern that seemed to produce rebellion a "J-curve." Figure 16.3 represents this J-curve pattern with a solid line indicating actual conditions in the society and the dashed line indicating people's expectations (also see Gurr, 1970). In Davies's view, the point of high relative deprivation leading to anger and social movement activity is when the gap between the two lines is the greatest. When conditions have been bad for a long time, people lower their expectations and the two lines in Figure 16.3 are close together. But when conditions improve, so

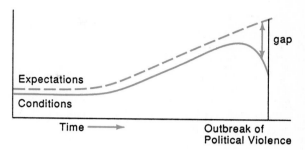

FIGURE 16.3. The "J-curve" of rising expectations producing relative Deprivation. *(Source: Davies, 1962.)*

do people's expectations. As shown in Figure 16.3, however, conditions are seldom able to improve in a steady, upward line. When conditions actually stop improving and are temporarily reversed, the gap between actual conditions and expectations produces rebellion. Davies uses several historical cases of social movements to support his theory. In the black Civil Rights Movement, for example, he notes that political and economic conditions for blacks in the United States were improving after World War II. By the later 1950s, however, there were some reversals to the improvements related to economic recession and increasing resistance by Southern whites to further improvements for blacks. It was during this time, Davies argues, that the Civil Rights Movement grew rapidly.

Relative deprivation theory became popular among social scientists attempting to explain the urban riots of the 1960s. At first some studies supported the idea that relative deprivation was the primary factor behind such things as riot participation (Miller, Bolce, and Halligan, 1977), joining working-class movements opposed to the Civil Rights Movement (Ransford, 1972), and differences in the level of political violence among nations (Gurr, 1968). After some initial research support for the relative deprivation concept, however, more and more negative research began to appear.

In a massive study of France covering a period of more than one hundred years, Snyder and Tilly (1972) found no significant relationship between their measures of relative deprivation and political violence. In a similar manner, in Figure 16.2 we saw that high unemployment does not always produce extensive protest by the unemployed. Data from other nations have shown much the same thing (Tilly, Tilly, and Tilly, 1975).

Some social scientists have responded to these findings by suggesting that discontent is not an important factor behind the development of protest (McCarthy and Zald, 1977). Most social scientists, however, agree that anger and discontent produced by something like relative deprivation may be an important factor making social movements and political violence likely. But an underlying discontent alone is not enough to produce social movement involvement or political violence. Generally, before a social movement can grow the people must have various kinds of resources that will allow them to do things such as organize, recruit members, and protect themselves from attacks by opponents. The new theory of social movements to counter relative deprivation theory has come to be known as resource mobilization theory.

Resource Mobilization Theory. Resources that may help promote the growth of social movements include such things as free time, money, numerous people, communication and recruitment networks, many forms of political support, and even talented leaders. Resource mobilization theory, therefore, focuses on the "balance of power" between social movement organizers and their opponents. "Bal-

In recent years, South Korea's student movement has grown in size and fervor. Even with South Korea's rapid economic development and expanded educational opportunity, students are demanding reforms that push the state towards democratization. How would you use the theory of relative deprivation to explain this? (© Bettmann Newsphotos.)

ance of power" means the relative balance of resources between social movement organizers and the people who would like to stop or prevent the social movement. Seen in this manner, resource mobilization theory is a form of conflict theory that recognizes that changing conditions in a society can change the balance of resources. It is the change in the resources held by one or both groups in conflict that can start a social movement, or increase or decrease the strength of a social movement. The main critique of relative deprivation theory from this perspective is that without sufficient resources for social movement activity no amount of anger, discontent, or deprivation can produce a social movement. Likewise, with abundant resources, even a low level of anger, discontent, or deprivation can produce a social movement (Kerbo, 1982). This is one reason nations sometimes experience waves of social movements of many kinds in certain periods, such as the early 1900s, 1930s, and 1960s in the United States. Changes in these periods gave more resources to social movements and/or weakened the forces supporting the status quo.

It is useful to examine recent research on a few social movements to show the value of resource mobilization theory. The black Civil Rights Movement, we have already seen, cannot be explained by worsening conditions producing more anger among blacks in the 1950s and 1960s. To understand how new resources helped spark the Civil Rights Movement it is necessary to consider how a lack of resources prevented such a movement before the 1950s. During the early 1900s and before, about 90 percent of blacks lived in small towns and rural areas, primarily in the South. Several factors related to where blacks lived reduced the potential for social movement activity. First, because population density was very low it was difficult to get a large number of blacks together to organize a social movement. Second, the local forces of control were strong. If blacks tried to go against white authorities, they were jailed, killed, or lost their jobs. Third, because of poverty and the need to work many hours in the fields, there was often little time or energy for social movement activities.

After the rapid migration of blacks from rural areas because of farm mechanization in the mid-1900s, this relative lack of resources began changing. With many blacks crowded into urban areas, their ability to organize was increased. Related to this, research has found that the early stages of the Civil Rights Movement were centered around the large black churches that emerged in these urban areas. These churches could work through their membership to reach out for social movement participants and collect funds for necessary activities such as transporting people to the scene of protest, bailing people out of jail, and printing literature to advertise movement goals and activities. Also important was the ability of the large black churches to financially support full-time leaders like Martin Luther King, Jr. Like everyone else, social movement leaders must feed their families. Without the secure paycheck from a black church, the social movement leader would most likely have to depend on whites for a job that could be lost in retaliation for social movement activity.

Equally important was the reduced social control over blacks in urban areas, which itself was related to several factors. One, with so many blacks in one area, forces of social control like the police have a more difficult job maintaining social order. Second, increased public attention can reduce arbitrary police action in an urban area. Hidden away in small towns, the police can more easily enforce unconstitutional white rules.

Finally, political factors were very important. Blacks in the 1950s came to represent potential voting blocks, especially at a time when the Democratic Party needed new votes. For example, John Kennedy once had his brother, the future attorney general of the United States, apply pressure on a Southern police chief to release Martin Luther King, Jr., from jail. Through the process of party politics, black issues like poverty and discrimination were brought to wider attention and made legitimate; at the same time, hope for social change was provided. The new nationwide attention and hope that social change was in fact possible was another resource that stimulated the participation of many blacks in the Civil Rights Movement.

Research on other social movements has also shown the importance of resources in expanding social movement activity. In their study of farm worker movements in the United States, Jenkins and Perrow (1977) found that a changed "political environment" was responsible for the growth and success of these movements in the late 1960s in contrast to previous years. Specifically, in this changed political environment Jenkins and Perrow found more political speeches in support of farm workers, as well as other concrete resources like outside support by famous people to aid in fund raising.

In a similar manner, Kerbo and Shaffer (1986b) found a changed political environment important in the rise of protest by the unemployed in the 1930s. As shown by Figure 16.2, we found that the high unemployment before the Great Depression of the 1930s did not bring massive protest movements; however, in 1930, even before people realized that unemployment would be higher than in any other period by 1933, there was massive protest. Our task was to find out why. As one measure of "political environment" we recorded all speeches made by important people about unemployment reported in the *New York Times* between 1890 and 1940. Our data showed an interesting pattern; before the 1920s there was almost nothing said about unemployment in the major newspapers. But suddenly, in 1921 and during several other years of the 1920s there was extensive public discussion about unemployment, even when it was relatively low. Then, when it did go up rapidly in 1930, the protest exploded.

Our interpretation of the data is similar to that of Jenkins and Perrow. There was a changed political environment, in part, because the Democratic Party needed working-class votes after the Democrats' Progressive coalition fell apart after World War I. Thus, the working-class issue of unemployment was politicized and workers came to feel the government could do something about high unemployment. When President Hoover did not respond to the increasing unemployment by 1930, the protest began. There was now one group of political elites willing to support the working class in their demands and prevent others from blocking organized protest.

Finally, a very impressive study of peasant revolts in Third World nations should be described. In a massive research project with data from 70 na-

tions, Paige (1975) found that the best predictor of political violence in these nations was the resources of the peasants or farm workers versus the resources of landowners for preventing rebellion. For example, if peasants could receive outside support and organize more freely because they worked in large groups, then protest movements were more likely. Paige even found a correlation between the type of crop produced in an area and the likelihood of political violence there. This correlation seems puzzling until we recognize that farm work is organized differently, depending on the type of crop produced. Differences in work organization can make it more or less easy for farm workers to organize themselves for rebellion. Thus, peasants tending rice fields are more likely to be drawn into protest movements than peasants tending coffee plantations or rubber plantations.

To summarize the main points of the resource mobilization theory, we must begin with the place of discontent. Most social scientists agree that it is discontent, anger, and feelings of injustice that fuel social movements (Moore, 1978). However, there is much of what many people see as injustice in this world. Most societies, including our own, have extensive inequalities and advantages for the few. A major question becomes, why do these people who experience injustice not rebel more often? In the previous chapters on social stratification and inequality we have seen some of the ways in which inequalities are maintained and those people with less are encouraged to accept their place in society. At times, however, these people no longer accept "their place" and because of social change obtain some resources to organize protest against their low position. This, then, is a primary point of resource mobilization theory. The key for social movement activity is not so much discontent; there is plenty of that around the world. Rather, the key is the balance of resources between those unhappy with the status quo and those who find the status quo to their advantage.

The Causes of Revolution

As we have already seen, social movements, political violence, and revolution are certainly related phenomena. They all involve conflict over attempts to produce social change, and they all can be understood, at least in part, through theories like those described above. However, some social scientists argue that revolutions are not simply social movements on a grand scale. Revolutions develop from major problems in the structure of society that lead to breakdown and the inability of a society's basic institutions such as the state and the economy to maintain social order and sustain life. In this sense, therefore, revolutions require more than simply a group of people trying to push for change. And organized push by a social movement may produce reforms and some social change, but without major structural problems weakening a society and the hold on power by elites, revolution will not occur. As one writer on this subject puts it, "revolutions are not made, they come" (Skocpol, 1979, p. 17). It is when breakdown occurs that revolutionaries can try to pick up the pieces and shape a new social order according to their interests and values.

Consider the case of the Russian Revolution of 1917. By 1917, Lenin and most other Russian revolutionaries were either hiding in some other country or exiled to Siberia. In fact, shortly before the 1917 Revolution, Lenin was making speeches saying, "I will never see the revolution in my lifetime." On a February day during 1917, however, while living in Zurich, Switzerland, Lenin picked up a newspaper with the headline "Revolution in Russia." He responded, "they can't have a revolution without me," and hurried off to lead a revolution that he finally came to control (Salisbury, 1977).

The revolution that came to Russia was actually sparked by a minor labor strike, but a strike in the context of growing hunger and the breakdown of social institutions during World War I. Suddenly, on February 25, 1917, it became apparent to people that support for the old government was gone. People poured into the streets and broke into government stocks of food (Salisbury, 1977). Police were ordered to stop the crowds, but when a few police tried to follow this order they were shot by soldiers now supporting the people. At the Czar's Winter Palace crowds confronted cossacks on horseback guarding the front gate. One brave member of the crowd slipped under a cossack's horse and at-

tempted to enter the Winter Palace. The guards did not interfere and the crowd surged forward, realizing the forces of control no longer supported the Czar. The revolution had begun, but by the second day the crowds were still in the streets in search of leaders.

At the time of revolution in 1917, there was a weak Parliament in Russia, called the Duma, which was mostly ignored by the Czar. In February 1917, however, the Duma took over the functions of government under the leadership of Alexander Kerensky, politically a social democrat. But Kerensky lacked solid popular backing, and political power was still up for grabs, with every type of revolutionary attempting to grab that power. Lenin's Bolshevists were better organized and, giving the people what they most wanted to hear in the slogan "Bread and Peace," they gained more and more popular support. In October 1917, Lenin's group staged a revolutionary coup, and power went to the Communist Party, which has ruled Russia since that time.

Our brief sketch of the Russian Revolution has been designed to raise several pertinent questions. Why did the Revolution "just come"? What was responsible for social breakdown that finally made Lenin's revolutionary work pay off? We can also ask, why did the Russian Revolution go through the stages it did, and are these stages common to other revolutions? Finally, what are the possible outcomes of revolution?

Class Conflict and Revolution. Revolutions may appear to come suddenly, but the underlying conditions that make them possible develop over a long period of time. In the case of the Russian Revolution the process began in the middle 1800s, if not earlier than 1825 when the first attempted revolution occurred in Russia (Crankshaw, 1976). The long process that leads to revolution involves many changes and conflicts, but of key importance are class conflicts and the place of the state in these conflicts.

As we have already seen, classes have differing interests that can bring them into conflict. During stable times, one class or a coalition of classes are strong and able to assure that their interests are served at the expense of other classes. And as we also have seen, the dominant class often uses the state to make sure the interests of this class are maintained. In the drift toward revolution, however, the power of the dominant class weakens relative to other classes and/or the state weakens, no longer able to maintain social order and the dominance of one class over others.

Although Marx may have been incorrect in predicting some of the future trends of capitalism and communism, he did provide a useful model for analyzing revolutions. As we have seen, Marx considered societies to have a substructure and superstructure. The substructure shapes the basic features of the society through its influence on the superstructure (which includes the state, family, religion, ideologies, etc.). Within the substructure are the means of production and relations of production. It is especially change in the means of production, according to Marx, that leads to revolution.

The means of production are the technology of producing valued goods in the society. In an agrarian society land is the most important factor and the class that owns and controls it is dominant. In industrial societies the most important means of production is factories and thus, the owners of industrial capital are dominant. The relations of production refer to these ownership patterns, as well as the type of work organization and distribution of profits (Anderson, 1974).

Most revolutions in major nations of the past two hundred years or so have been related to change from an agrarian means of production to industrial production. The agrarian, feudal societies were ruled by the landed aristocracy—the class that owned and controlled the land. This aristocracy also controlled the state, at least at first, and used this state to maintain control. Research has shown that the state in agrarian societies grew most when needed to suppress conflict arising from the challenge of other classes (Hechter and Brustein, 1980). As industrialization began, however, there was a new class of merchants growing in wealth. In many ways the interests of the merchant class and old aristocracy came into conflict. For example, the merchant class often found state taxes and trade policies harmful to their interests. The old aristocracy, however, needed the taxes for state functions protecting them and the trade barriers to prevent the merchants from becoming too wealthy. As the conflicts between the two classes grew, and as the merchant influence grew while that of the aristocracy weakened, the state was pressured by both groups in contradictory ways. The state itself often became weak and no longer able to function. In the end, it was the inability of the state to maintain social order and assure basic necessities that led to a decline in support of the state by the masses. Only a final crisis was needed to activate the revolution and bring a new class coalition to power.

This was the basic process behind the French Revolution of 1789 (Soboul, 1974), the English revolutions during the 1600s, and the Dutch revolution in the 1560s. This was also the basic process behind the Russian Revolution of 1917, though neither the merchant class nor the aristocracy was strong enough to take power, which was finally taken by Lenin's Communist Party (Moore, 1966).

Following the pattern of history outlined above, in the mid-1800s it appeared to Marx that the next round of revolutions would come in the advanced stages of capitalist societies. The substructural change that brought the merchants or capitalists to power would go through further change to bring workers to power in a communist state. The "contradictions of capitalism" described earlier were predicted to weaken capitalists and the state, which maintains the power of capitalists. At the same time, the relations of production were changing in ways favoring workers. For example, in monopoly capitalism there would be more and more workers laboring together in large factories. This would make working-class unity for political power a greater possibility, thus enhancing the chances of a revolutionary force in the working class.

History, of course, has yet to follow Marx's predictions from the mid-1800s. The major nations that have emerged from revolution to proclaim themselves communist have not followed the line of progression outlined by Marx. China and Russia were not advanced capitalist industrial nations with a working class large enough or strong enough to have much influence on the new state. Many now argue that it was for this reason that the new communist states developed with policies far removed from the interests of the workers in these societies.

International Conflict and Revolution. In her study of major revolutions (principally the French, Russian, and Chinese), Skocpol (1979) observed that revolution often comes because of international competition. The nation that drops far behind in international economic competition becomes weak, and impending crises can bring revolution. Military conflict often produces the internal crisis that brings on the revolution.

Skocpol recognizes the class conflicts behind the inability of a nation to compete internationally, as I have described above. In the cases of Russia before the 1900s, France in the 1600s–1700s, and China before the 1900s, the old aristocracy was powerful enough to prevent the rise of a merchant class and new forms of production when other countries were advancing. The result was an inability to compete with other nations. Economic conflicts grew, the state was weakened trying to manage increasing crisis, and revolution finally broke out. In the case of France, Russia, and now possibly China, from the destruction of revolution a new state and social order eventually developed that allowed these countries to compete much more successfully in the world economy.

The World System and Third World Revolutions. Revolutions in major nations like France, Russia, and China are not the only ones influenced by international competition. In fact, as briefly mentioned in the world system chapter, changes in the modern world system are currently responsible for many revolutions and potential revolutions in periphery and semiperiphery nations around the world. These revolutions in faraway places like Vietnam, Cambodia, Angola, and Iran, as well as places not so far away like Cuba and Nicaragua, have many similar causes related to their position in the world system. It is equally important to recognize that the potential for revolution in many periphery and semiperiphery nations is increasing, and that there are active revolutionary armies in most of these nations around the world. Because of the effects these revolutions will have in the world, and because of the American tendency to get involved in these events, it is important that we have a better understanding of them.

During 1979 there were two revolutions that were similar in many respects, though they occurred in very different nations. In Central America, the Sandinista revolutionaries finally overthrew the Samoza dictatorship in Nicaragua. The Samoza family had owned much of the land and industry in Nicaragua for many generations, and, in typical fashion, controlled the government. A major reason that the Nicaraguan revolution succeeded in 1979 was the United States refusal to continue supporting the Samoza government, which had so obviously lost the support of almost all groups within Nicaragua. As it had done in many other Central American and South American nations, the United States had strongly backed the ruling families and their governments for decades, at times even rescuing them from revolutionaries and democratic elections by sending in the U.S. military to restore the power of these elites. In nearby Guatemala, for example, the CIA overthrew the government in 1954 when newly elected officials threatened to nationalize the United Fruit property there. The U.S. secretary of state at the time was formerly a partner in a corporate law firm representing United Fruit, and his brother, CIA Director Allen Dulles, happened to be a major stockholder in the company (Mosley, 1978).

After the Samoza government was overthrown, a coalition government of religious leaders, business leaders, and Sandinista revolutionaries headed the new government. There were the usual conflicts in policy goals after the revolution, and some of the moderate leaders left the government. With a new conservative government in the United States in 1980, U.S. policy toward Nicaragua changed, leading to renewed threats to the Sandinista government. The threats soon turned to reality when the CIA began actively funding the counterrevolutionary army, known as the Contras, trying to regain power. In a common pattern, the new Sandinista government pushed out the remaining moderate members of the coalition and went more actively to the Cubans (and the Soviet Union) for help in fighting the CIA-sponsored counterrevolutionaries.

The United States had also been actively involved in the government of Iran before their revolution in 1979. Especially after World War II with the decline of British power in the Middle East, the United States became heavily involved in Iran. After

World War II, however, there was growing anger against Western involvement in Iran, especially directed toward American and British oil companies. In 1951 a bill passed the Iranian Parliament that would have reduced the power of these oil companies and forced them to sell some of their property to the Iranian government. Before this action could be completed, however, in 1953 the CIA organized a military coup that overthrew the Iranian government and placed a shah more firmly in power who favored U.S. interests. (The book written by the CIA operative in charge of this coup, who happens to be a relative of President Franklin Roosevelt, provides interesting details on this coup [Roosevelt, 1979].) By 1979, however, the social disruption caused by massive protest led by the religious leader Ayatollah Khomeini produced another crisis in Iran. Though the United States tried, no significant support for the shah's government could be found to stop the coming revolution even among the Iranian military (Kiddie, 1981). The Iranian revolution of 1979 reestablished a centuries-old tradition of a religious state in Iran, with Ayatollah Khomeini at the top.

To understand why these two revolutions and others like them occurred and will continue to occur, we must return to some of the basic characteristics of the modern world system. The modern world system, you will remember, is similar to an international stratification system. The powerful core nations are able to influence the periphery nations so as to receive many benefits from these weaker nations. As we saw in the world system chapter, the people in these periphery nations are harmed in many ways by the involvement of core nations in the economies of periphery nations. For example, economic growth is severely reduced, and there is disruption with rapid urbanization and agricultural changes. The misery and discontent resulting from these factors, however, are not enough to create a successful revolution. As we have already discussed, a revolutionary movement needs resources to be effective and a crisis rendering the old government weak.

Several changes in the world system have helped provide these resources and crisis in periphery nations around the world (Chirot, 1986). First, commercialization of agriculture has pushed peasants into cities where they are usually unemployed and more easily organized for a revolutionary movement. Second, capable revolutionary leaders have been inadvertently supplied by the old colonial powers. It was common practice of the British and French, for example, to sponsor some of the native people in their colonies for education in major universities in core nations. Once educated, these people would return to the colonies to help administer the colonial government for the core nation. Yet many of these educated people soon became leaders of revolutionary movements. They were able to understand the impact of core involvement in their nation and how a new government could be organized after a successful revolution.

A third, very important factor is related to core competition in the world system in recent years. A successful revolution requires guns, artillery, and many other military supplies. In earlier years a revolutionary movement in Nicaragua, for example, was more easily stopped by the Nicaraguan government or the United States because the revolutionary movement was unlikely to have obtained significant military resources. With superpower conflict between the capitalist core nations and the Soviet-bloc nations, however, the military resources are likely to be forthcoming for any serious revolutionary movement. Because one side in the core conflict would like to take periphery nations from the other side, that side is willing to supply the arms. The Soviets and Cubans were supplying arms to the Sandinista revolutionaries and continue to do so. But because Nicaragua is now in the Soviet camp, the United States is supplying arms to the counterrevolutionaries in Nicaragua, as is also the case in other pro-Soviet nations like Angola and Afghanistan. In one respect today the dominant core nations are fighting among themselves as did the British and French in the 1700s. The superpowers, however, are not so willing to directly confront each other with the threat of nuclear war today, so they fight for periphery and semiperiphery dominance through proxy wars in places like Nicaragua.

The factors producing revolutionary movements just described are consistent with the resource mobilization theory of social movements. The disrup-

tions in many Third World nations caused by core exploitation have caused tremendous suffering among the people. But this suffering alone will not produce significant revolutionary threats. For a strong revolutionary movement, there must be new resources for the rebels and/or a growing weakness in the state that is given the task of repressing them.

THE OUTCOMES OF SOCIAL MOVEMENTS AND REVOLUTIONS

What happens after a social movement has gained sufficient strength to produce at least some social change? What happens after a revolution has toppled a government? Do the social movement activists and revolutionaries frequently achieve the goals that motivated them and their followers? As we will see, these questions have complex answers that differ with respect to each revolution or social movement. Some general tendencies, however, can be described.

The Stages of Revolution

Major revolutions have produced some similar patterns of change, from the fall of the old order to the rise and consolidation of a new social order. The pattern of change, or the stages in the process, are not exactly reproduced in every case, and at times whole stages are missed. Many factors influence the pattern of change; one of the most important is the nature of the society that preceded the revolution. Despite the variation, however, a general common pattern of stages can be detected. Understanding the pattern and its variations can be quite useful in understanding the nature of revolutions currently in progress as well as those yet to occur.

With the fall of the old order because of institutional weakness described above, there is typically an attempt, only briefly successful, to form a "moderate" government with "moderate" leaders in power. Moderate here means a government and leaders who are neither pushing for extremely radical changes nor using extreme means for achieving change. During the Russian Revolution, for example, the moderate government and leader were represented in Kerensky's short-lived liberal democracy. In the case of the revolution in Iran of 1979 moderate leaders (Bazargan and Bani Sadr) attempted to establish a Western-style democratic government soon after the shah's government fell (Keddie, 1981).

With the fall of an old government, however, the stage is often set for complex, many-sided conflicts. As the old social order is sliding to its doom, many revolutionary groups will emerge with differing ideas about what should follow it. Soon various groups are mobilized for conflict against one another.

During this stage of *radical rule* there is commonly extensive change and a *reign of terror*. The group in power is implementing extreme goals, and the angry masses are often seeking revenge against people favored by the old order. But equally important is the reign of terror needed to hold power and achieve the change. Many groups, with many goals, are fighting for power. The current group holding power must often use extreme means such as mass arrests and executions to keep that power. This is the case in Iran in the 1980s and was the case during the bloody Cultural Revolution in China. Revolution, as Mao once said, "is not a dinner party."

Finally, all revolutions must cool and reach their "Thermidor," if for no other reason because people become tired of the upheaval. ("Thermidor" refers to the time this occurred after the French Revolution according to the French revolutionary calendar.) After many years (the time varies) of radical leaders pushing for ever more extensive change, asking for sacrifices, and violent conflict among revolutionary factions, the appeal of revolutionary ideals diminishes. The population often becomes ready to follow a different kind of leader — one who is more "practical" and brings promise of social order. After the French Revolution this person was Napoleon Bonaparte. In the Soviet Union this person was Stalin. And in China it seems as if Deng Xiaoping will fill this role, whereas in Iran this stage is yet to come. This final stage of revolution does not always bring new leadership, for a highly perceptive leader may understand that more social stability is needed, and thus shift directions with the mood of the people.

Figure 16.4 provides a rough picture of the stages of revolution described above. Brinton's (1965) study of major revolutions found only a tendency for them to progress in this manner, for some revolutions have skipped entire stages, whereas others remain in particular stages longer. But it is useful to analyze revolutions with the tendency toward the stages in mind. For example, for many reasons—perhaps business profits or military alliance—Iran is unlikely to enter its "Thermidor" until the Ayatollah Khomeini dies. But at that point there is also the more immediate chance of growing crisis with revolutionary factions in conflict over who takes over leadership.

Outcomes of Revolution. Revolutionaries never achieve all their goals, nor do most even get close. Once a revolution is set in motion there are many unexpected turns and outcomes. As Marx (1963, p. 15) once put it, "men make their own history, but they do not make it just as they please; they do not make it under circumstances chosen by themselves, but under circumstances directly encountered, given and transmitted from the past." We have seen that during the first stage of revolution—the fall of the old order—revolutionaries are seldom in control of events. So it goes, throughout the whole process of revolution because there are simply too many factors influencing the direction of a revolution, or setting limits on what it can achieve.

One way to approach the subject is to ask, are the people in general "better off" after the revolution? There are many difficulties with this question, however, because "better off" means different things to different people, and because we must also ask "who" and "when." But we can give a few general answers to these questions.

In most of the great revolutions, the country was not able to advance and compete with other nations until an outdated state structure and class structure could be eliminated and a new state and class structure was stabilized (Skocpol, 1979). After the French Revolution, France was able to modernize, though the people living in the immediate aftermath of the revolution were certainly worse off because of the disruption and bloodshed of the reign of terror (Soboul, 1974). Certainly the old aristocratic families and wealthy clergy were not better off after the French Revolution because their wealth and influence were severely reduced.

A general tendency is reduced inequality soon after the revolution, but a new growth in inequalities a few decades after revolution (Kelley and Klein, 1977). This trend must be viewed with caution and applies to revolutions primarily in agrarian societies that have been able to achieve some economic

FIGURE 16.4. The stages of revolution.

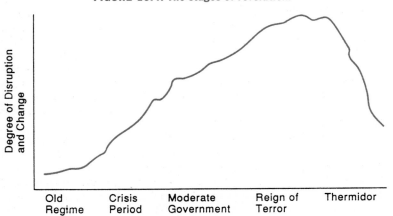

growth after social order is restored. The logic of this trend, however, is rather simple. With revolution the old upper classes lose their wealth and power as they did in France, Russia, China, Iran, and the other major revolutions. Also, people lose their top positions in many institutions before the revolution, which creates opportunities for upward mobility in the society. In China, for example, there was extensive upward social mobility soon after Mao came to power in 1949. By 1958 the number of college students from peasant families had increased to around 67 percent, whereas there had been almost none before. And the overall illiteracy rate in China had been reduced about 90 percent by the 1960s (Snow, 1970, 1971).

The second part of the trend may occur some years after the revolution when social order has been regained. If the revolution has cleared away obstacles to expansion in the society, then the expansion can create many new opportunities for talented people. This is also to say, many people will be upwardly mobile, leaving others behind. Thus, we again find the growth of inequality due to economic expansion, and as the expansion progresses into the next generation, social mobility tends to diminish. Those who have made it to higher positions after the revolution will find ways to assure their children need not fall below the level they have achieved.

None of this necessarily means a return to the prerevolutionary conditions in the society. The level of inequality reached years after the revolution is likely to be lower than in the prerevolutionary years, and the overall standard of living may be much higher. Thus, though inequality may increase, the standard of living for those on the bottom and in the middle may be higher than in prerevolutionary years. It is also quite possible that nonmaterial conditions like political and other personal freedoms will have improved.

China again provides a good example. Mao was clearly aware of the historical trend of more inequality a few years after a revolution, and he tried to prevent it. Following his idea of "continuous revolution," he sponsored many movements that redirected China's progress, often replacing people in top positions (Eckstein, 1977). The Cultural Revolu-

tion of the mid-1960s to the mid-1970s was the last and most tumultuous of the changes. Again, with the Cultural Revolution there were more college students from peasant backgrounds, and people in advantaged positions in China's cities were sent to the rural areas to work on farms for a few years.

In the end, however, it appears that Mao's idea of continuous revolution could not last. The disruption of the Cultural Revolution severely harmed China's economy, educational institutions, and many other aspects of China's society. Upon Mao's death, new "practical" leaders stepped in to power and China now seems to be following a more typical postrevolutionary pattern. In the 1980s, inequalities between lower-skilled workers and higher-skilled workers are increasing, as are inequalities between rural and urban people. But it does appear that prospects for growth in China are good. Things may not progress as Mao had hoped, though it seems clear that the standard of living for most Chinese will improve extensively.

We should note that people in the United States who stress the value of "freedom" will argue that the people of a nation *must* be worse off after a communist revolution. There will certainly be a loss of political freedoms, though few people had these freedoms in most of the governments that preceded the communist revolution. But the stress on freedom must not blind Americans to the fact that many people, in many ways, are sometimes better off after communist revolutions. For example, Russia changed from a country with a backward economy and political crisis in 1917 to a country with the world's third-largest (or, by some measures, second-largest) economy today. The Soviet standard of living is currently below that of most Americans, and many people were killed in Stalin's purges along the way (Ulam, 1973), but most Soviet citizens look back with pride on their country's accomplishments since 1917.

Cuba is another case that many Americans do not understand. In spite of all the anti-Castro rhetoric in this country, in vast contrast to Cuba's prerevolutionary years, Cubans now have the best statistics on such measures as health, nutrition, housing, and education of all Latin America. With respect to eco-

Since the Cuban revolution, Cuba has made considerable gains in providing services and material necessities to its population as a whole, but with costs to individual freedoms. Some sociologists would like to know how successful Cuba would have been without almost three decades of a U.S. blockade and Soviet aid. (© Fred Baldwin/Woodfin Camp & Associates.)

nomic modernization, however, the Cuban revolution seems to have had no great impact (Lewis-Beck, 1979), no doubt because of the continuing U.S. economic boycott and aid from the Soviet Union.

In contrast to the "success" stories in the Soviet Union and China, of course, it must also be noted that many communist revolutions in Third World nations have not produced better conditions for the population (Lenski, 1978). The upper classes are clearly worse off after a communist revolution, but when hungry people see that virtually no one is

starving in China today in contrast to the millions before, a communist revolution can look appealing.

Outcomes of Social Movements. It is time to move from the grand affairs of revolution to consider outcomes of social movements and other forms of political violence. We begin with a brief look at possible outcomes of rioting by the lower classes. Because of the extensive urban riots that hit major U.S. cities in the period between 1964 and 1968, we now have extensive research on the subject. A general conclusion

from this research is that the more than 300 major riots in this period seem to have produced *no* improvements for blacks in the rate of poverty, occupational status, unemployment, or the black/white income ratio (Kelly and Snyder, 1980). In fact, these material conditions have gotten steadily worse since the riots. Other research, however, has shown these riots did result in welfare expansion (Piven and Cloward, 1977; Isaac and Kelly, 1981). We can interpret these findings by noting that jobs, higher pay, and other material values are more difficult to provide. When jobs are scarce, for example, if an angry lower class is to make gains, the gains will be at someone else's expense. Welfare, however, can be provided with less conflict because the costs in higher taxes or government deficits can be spread more widely.

For social movements in general, the outcomes are considerably varied and depend on many factors like the goals sought, characteristics of the society at the time, as well as characteristics and tactics used by the social movement. Gamson (1975) has examined 53 social movements from a larger group of 500 found to exist in the United States between 1800 and 1945. Surprisingly, he concluded that more than one-half achieved at least some of their goals, but many factors influenced which ones did or did not achieve goals. Very important were the goals themselves; as we might expect, if the goals involved only small reforms, they were more likely to be attained. But in addition to those movements seeking bigger changes, the movements seeking to replace important elites tended to be unsuccessful.

A reexamination of this study suggests that social movements are also more likely to achieve some success during times of crisis in the society, when authorities are weak (Goldstone, 1980). And it should be noted that violence does affect social movements' success. Although violence does not always bring success, and there are degrees of violence, no matter how much we may deplore violence, it sometimes works. One of Gamson's most striking findings is that social movements that have violence directed toward them but do not use violence themselves are the most likely to fail. Those social movements that use some violence are some-

what more likely to succeed, though violence may work only in some situations, and most violence in U.S. history has been used *against* social movements rather than by them (Stohl, 1976; Gamson, 1975). The violence has come most often from government authorities and guards employed by corporations trying to stop the social movement.

Terrorism. We conclude this chapter with a brief consideration of the important issue of terrorism. **Terrorism** is the selective use of violence to produce maximum fear and disruption in order to achieve political goals. Defined in this manner, it must be recognized that state authorities around the world use terrorism *much* more often than do groups opposing the authorities and trying to produce social change. In Latin American countries, for example, thousands of people have been killed and tortured by government authorities to further their political goals. In El Salvador alone the government-backed "death squads" have been charged with killing thousands of people. Authorities in Latin America are certainly not alone in the use of terrorism, nor are either communist or capitalist dictatorships.

As terrorism has been defined, it can be found in many places around the world and throughout recorded history. The term "assassin" can be traced to an Arab group 900 years ago called the Society of Assassins (the name was related to their fondness for hashish), which used various terrorist tactics like assassination to achieve political goals (Dobson, 1974). But terrorism has certainly not been limited to the Middle East. There were terrorist groups during the French Revolution and terrorists in the 1800s in Russia as that country moved toward revolution. Terrorism can often be found where there is a group highly dedicated to achieving social change but lacking other resources to produce that change. This is to say that terrorism is a cheap resource that relatively small, relatively powerless groups turn toward. This is especially true in an age when mass media coverage can spread information on the existence of the revolutionary group and its grievances.

Killing innocent people in an airport, killing Olympic athletes, and blowing up buildings filled with shoppers seem like irrational acts of violence when reported on our TV screens. The cold logic behind these acts must be recognized if the problem is to be dealt with effectively. Although there are questions about the effectiveness of terrorism as a tool of revolutionary groups, some goals of terrorism can be identified.

Terrorism is often used to attract mass media attention that can show the group exists and can strike out at people representing the enemy. The hope of terrorists in this case is to attract recruits among other angry people. In a related manner, a goal of terrorism is to trick the authorities into overreacting by striking back in areas believed supportive of the revolutionaries. For example, if the authorities randomly beat and arrest people in response to acts of terrorism (i.e., use extensive counterterrorism), it may increase antigovernment feelings and spread support for the revolutionaries.

Terrorism can also gain bargaining power over an enemy. In the typical process of bargaining one party gives something the other party wants in return for something the first party wants. But if the group lacks any positive benefits to exchange, terrorist acts can sometimes be used as a negative benefit. Thus, a terrorist group says, "I will stop doing something you dislike if you will meet our demands."

Finally, there is debate among revolutionaries and social scientists over the possibility of *protracted revolution* versus *natural revolution* (Oppenheimer, 1969). The idea of natural revolution suggests that revolution will occur *only* when basic conditions in the society make the revolution possible. Many of these conditions have already been discussed in this chapter. From this point of view, no amount of action like terrorism or other activity by a revolutionary group will make a revolution until these conditions exist. The idea of protracted revolution, however, is that a relatively small group of revolutionaries can actually make conditions ripe for revolution if they can cause enough disruption in the society through their terrorist activities. The evidence, in contrast, suggests that attempts at protracted revolution most likely result in political repression and no social change, if they have any effect at all (Oppenheimer, 1969).

CHAPTER SUMMARY

Key Terms

social change, etc. 448
social movements, 448
revolution, 449
political violence, 449
civil war, 449
coup d'état, 450
nationalist revolution, 450
relative deprivation theory, 452
resource mobilization theory, 453
terrorism, 465

Content

In contrast to social change, social movements and revolutions refer to conscious, organized attempts to produce social change. Social movements vary in the type and extent of change the group is seeking, whereas revolutions involve action to produce extensive and rapid change in many aspects of society.

Two major theories attempt to explain the causes of social movements. Relative deprivation theory focuses on conditions that produce feelings of discontent and anger that motivate people to become active in social movements. The concept of relative deprivation refers to the gap between what people believe they deserve in contrast to what they believe they can attain.

Resource mobilization theory views the changing level of resources between groups with opposing interests as the primary cause of social movements. This theory assumes that many people are discontented in a society, and thus social movements stem not necessarily from new anger but from a new ability to organize for change.

Revolutions must be understood with reference to social changes producing crisis and a weakened state. Underlying class conflicts are then brought into the open with attempts to drastically alter the nature of society. Most major revolutions have been related to international competition producing crisis, and revolutions in the Third World today are related to disruptions produced by ties to the world system and core nations.

Revolutions have a tendency to progress through a set of stages, beginning with a moderate government that falls to more radical leaders. After much change, disruption, and violent conflict, however, revolutions tend to finally cool, with what is called the Thermidor reaction.

Revolutions can have many varied outcomes, but there are some general tendencies. Soon after a revolution there is usually a reduction in inequality and more social mobility because the old upper classes have lost their positions and wealth. As the society again stabilizes and new growth occurs, inequality tends to increase, but does not necessarily revert to prerevolutionary levels.

Terrorism refers to the use of violence to instill fear as a means of achieving political goals. Governments are responsible for far more acts of terrorism than any other groups. However, most attention in recent years has been given to small groups of revolutionaries who use highly dramatic acts of terrorism in attempts to achieve political goals.

Supporting Institutions

The Family

The family serves the social order even in the dissolution of its authority. It teaches the child his first lessons in the corruption of authority and thereby exposes him, at an impressionable age, to prevailing modes of social control.
— Christopher Lasch, Haven in a Heartless World

The family is one of the most important social institutions in all human societies. It can also be said that the family was the first social institution in history. Like all other institutions, however, the family has historical variations and periods of transition within these historical periods. What can be called the modern family system in the United States is certainly different from the traditional family system in seventeenth-century Europe and in some places still today. As for the transitions, we will consider the Japanese family in some detail for what we can learn about the transition in progress in that country today. Finally, different cultural, economic, religious, and even geographical factors influence the historical variations in the family system. This variety and change in the family is examined extensively in this chapter after we consider some basic definitions and theoretical perspectives on the family.

SOCIOLOGICAL PERSPECTIVES ON THE FAMILY

A **family** consists of at least two generations of people living together and sharing economic resources, who are related by marriage, birth, or adoption. With today's increase in people living together and having children without marriage, this definition needs only slight amendment by including what can be called "common law marriages." An **extended family** includes three or more generations living in close geographical proximity whereas a **nuclear family** consists of only the married couple and their children (if any). Finally, when referring to **the family** we mean the family as an institution within the society — the cluster of norms and roles that guide reproduction, intimacy, and the care of family members.

It is quite clear that families, in some form, have always been found in human societies. Even in mod-

ern societies, with many opportunities for alternative life-styles, the family remains strong. Much has been written about the high divorce rate in the United States, and some writers suggest the American family is on the verge of extinction. Nothing could be further from the truth. The high American divorce rate is accompanied by the highest rate of remarriage in the world. The American family is not becoming extinct, it is only changing.

The importance of families can also be shown by specific attempts to reduce the family role in a society — attempts that have always ultimately failed. One of the most famous attempts to reduce the importance of nuclear families occurred in the early Israeli kibbutzim (collective farms). In the years before Israel became a state (before 1948), many Jews moved to the area and formed small collective farms. Many of these people came with ideologies stressing strict equality, and because male-female inequalities were believed to be rooted in the division of labor required in nuclear families, these families were to be eliminated. To accomplish this change children were placed in a communal nursery to be cared for day and night by members of the kibbutz who were assigned these jobs (Spiro, 1958; Gerson, 1972). A whole generation of kibbutz children were in fact raised in this manner, but the importance of the nuclear family was not eliminated. Through pressure from kibbutz citizens the natural parents were given at least an hour a day with their children. The hour came to be very important "quality" time between children and parents, thus maintaining the nuclear bonds even though nuclear family members slept in different locations. Children still strongly identified with their parents to the point of bragging about their parents' job in the kibbutz.

The kibbutz children who grew up with communal child-rearing turned out quite well (Tiger and Shepher, 1975). Emotionally and educationally they have done much better than other Israelis. But in addition to the failure to eliminate nuclear family bonds, communal child-rearing did not totally eliminate male-female inequalities or make child-rearing more "cost-efficient" in terms of the quality and number of hours needed to raise children. Men still held most of the top occupational and political positions in the kibbutzim. Class distinctions, however, have been extensively reduced in these kibbutzim, and especially the inheritance of class inequalities over the generations.

All of the above suggests that the family is one of the most important institutions in human societies. At one point in social evolution the family was the master institution. Though this is not the case in modern societies, we must still understand the nature of the family system to understand many other aspects of human societies.

Functional Views

There are many benefits for a society served by a healthy family system. The family is, of course, a unit of human reproduction and care. Newly born members of the society must have their material and emotional needs met, and with very few exceptions (such as some early Israeli kibbutzim), it is the family that serves this function. Also important, as we saw in an earlier chapter, the young need socialization so they can develop into functioning members of society. Especially in the earliest years of childhood, the family best serves this function of socialization.

Other family members will need care as well, and the family is the primary place where both young and old adults receive emotional and material care. In a sense the family is the first source of psychological, medical, and economic care. In emotional stress, people most often turn to other family members for help; in physical illness, people first turn to family members, and if the illness is serious the family provides crucial supplemental help for medical professionals caring for a family member.

Throughout history the family has been a very important economic unit. In our age of economic organizations and a greater separation between the family and the workplace, the economic function of the family can be overlooked. Before industrialization the family usually worked together to meet common economic needs — in the fields, in small craft shops, or in small stores or service establishments. Even today the family is an economic unit in that one or more family members bring in wages shared with other family members. There is a division of labor within the family unit; some members provide work for household maintenance, and others obtain outside, economic resources. Until recently in most industrial societies, women were more dependent than men because women could often receive economic support only by attaching themselves to adult men.

The family has also been the basic unit regulating sexual relations throughout history. All societies have had rules pertaining to sexual relations, because of the potential for extensive conflict over sexual relations noted above. But there is tremendous variation in the sexual rules among societies, though these rules usually center around the family system. Sexual relations between husband and wife are approved, whereas sexual relations among children and nonfamily members are usually disapproved, though there is some variation with rules pertaining to nonfamily members.

Throughout history the family has often served other functions not found in modern societies. As we will see, the extended family unit has sometimes served as a ministate, criminal justice system, school, military unit, and religious unit. But as societies become more complex these other functions have been taken over by other institutions.

Finally from the functionalist's perspective, a society's institutions are seen as interrelated, each serving special functions for the others. If one of the social institutions is no longer performing its functions as expected, other aspects of the society are adversely affected. For example, in the United States, many social problems like crime and poverty are considered as outcomes of family breakdown. There is some evidence to support this view, but as we will see later, a complex chain of problems also adversely affects the family system itself.

Conflict Views

The conflict perspective, you will remember, views a society as a setting for conflicts among various groups, each seeking valued, scarce resources. Because strong social bonds are usually formed in families, the family is therefore often a cooperating unit in conflicts with outsiders to protect the interests of family members. In preindustrial societies we commonly find conflict between clans (or extended family units) over land and other economic rights. Also, if a transgression was made against any family member, the clan had a duty to avenge the wrong by harming any member of the other clan. Throughout history, peasants have often been unable to unite in protecting their common interests against wealthy landowners because the peasants were divided by clan conflicts.

At other times several families or clans may recognize their common interests and the conflicts occur among opposing clans. These clan or family alliances can also be drawn along class lines. For example, lower-class families may come to recognize that their sons and daughters will likely remain in the lower class when they grow up because the educational system does not properly educate their children. However, the changes lower-class families seek in the educational system may harm the interests of middle-class families, if for no other reason because middle-class children will have more competition from lower-class children if educational reforms are made. Thus, families that are seeking to create advantages for their children can be brought into class conflicts of this type.

From a broader societal view, the conflict perspective can apply to conflicts between sectors or institutions in the society. In contrast to the functional view, which stresses how institutions provide functions for one another, the conflict view can help us see that one sector of the society (e.g., business) may be in conflict with another sector (e.g., the family). For example, it may be in the interest of the business sector to require more hours of work from fathers or mothers, which may conflict with the needs of a family. Some Japanese social problems like increasing crime among middle-class youth have been blamed on the common practice of requiring men in middle-class occupations to work 10- to 12-hour days, sometimes six days a week.

Finally, the family itself must be viewed as a power structure (Collins, 1975). Although family members usually have strong emotional bonds and many common interests, there are, as always, some conflicts of interest within the family. Who will do more housework? Who will decide where and when to take a trip? Who spends more money? All these questions can create conflicts in a family.

Because of traditional family roles and the distribution of resources among family members, some people will have more power than others, and therefore more rewards. For example, until recently (and still in reality) men had more legal rights than women in Japan. Moreover, a Japanese woman without a husband has a very low status. (The word for "widow" in Japan is *mibojin*—a not-yet-dead person—stressing the loss of status without a man. Widowers are not given such a name [Taylor, 1983, p. 200].) As we have already seen, a woman is usually unable to find employment paying a livable wage in Japan. For these and other reasons, therefore, Japanese women occupy an unfavorable position compared with their husbands. Wives are usually harmed much more by divorce than husbands; thus the wife is likely to obey her husband and tolerate his behavior. There is an interesting exception to this. Because the ancestral family line is so important in Japan, families without a male heir may officially adopt their daughter's husband, who then becomes heir to the family wealth. But this occurs only when the man stays married. Wives in this position are expected to be more "strong-willed," and any "strong-willed" wife will be suspected by others as being in this more powerful situation.

Family Forms and Rules

All societies have a rule called *incest taboo* prohibiting sexual relations among nuclear family members other than husband and wife. All other rules pertaining to the family organization and conduct vary widely around the world. Although we have already discussed nuclear and extended family systems, in this section we examine some important rules in the family and other differences in the form of family systems.

One important set of rules is related to dominance and the line of descent in families. **Patriarchal** family systems give more power to males, whereas **matriarchal** family systems give more power to females. **Egalitarian** families have more equal male/female relationships. In terms of the line of descent, or the family line seen as more important, **patrilineal** families trace the line of descent through the male's relatives, and **matrilineal** families trace the line of descent through the female's relatives. Again, **bilateral** descent gives equal importance to both sides of the nuclear family when tracing descent. Similar terms apply when describing where the newly married couple will live. In **patrilocal** societies the wife must move to the man's extended household and come under its dominance, whereas the reverse is the case in **matrilocal** societies. In **neolocal** societies the new couple is not required to enter the household of either side of the family. As you may expect, these family characteristics are interrelated.

In preindustrial societies the family system is most often patriarchal, patrilineal, and patrilocal. As we have already seen in Chapter 15 on male/female inequalities, males were more likely to be dominant in preindustrial societies, a situation reflected in the family system. As the resources of women improved in advanced industrial societies, we find more egalitarian families, bilateral descent, and neolocal residence. A typical practice in patrilineal societies, for example, requires the wife to take her husband's last name upon marriage. Industrial societies like the United States still generally follow this practice, though it is slowly changing with women combining both their family name and husband's last name (e.g., Jane van Lawick-Goodall). Thus, more egalitarian families in industrial societies are slowly producing a change in this practice, though we are yet to find many husbands including the wife's family name in his last name.

Societies also have important rules pertaining to the acceptable number of mates either the husband or wife is allowed. In our own society **monogamy** is strictly enforced; husband and wife can have only one mate. Many societies, however, have allowed **polygamy,** that is, multiple spouses. There are logically two types of polygamy: **polygyny,** which allows the husband multiple wives, and **polyandry,** which allows the wife multiple husbands.

Monogamy is the dominant family form in industrial societies, but not throughout the world. About 75 percent of the societies studied by Murdock (1967) actually approved of polygyny, though even in these societies monogamy was more common. In societies approving of polygyny only wealthy males are able to support more than one wife. Monogamy is therefore much more common around the world today and throughout history, whereas polyandry is quite rare.

THE FAMILY: EVOLUTIONARY AND COMPARATIVE PERSPECTIVES

Before the existence of agricultural societies, social organization was almost totally based on kinship relations. People interacted with outsiders as a representative of a particular family, and it was very important to trace the type of kinship relation one had with another upon first meeting (Lenski and Lenski, 1982, p. 114). There was no state, organized religion, or economic organizations; there was only the family. It was the family, or rather the extended family forming the kinship system, that provided all social functions. The kinship system was the ministate, it took care of protecting members from outsiders, and it was the economic unit, educational system, and welfare system. It is for this reason that the family is often referred to as the master institution. Before societies became more complex, it was the family that served all social functions and formed the primary unit of group conflict.

With the first step toward agriculture about 10,000 years ago, the simple horticultural societies in existence today suggest that the kinship system was no less important. In fact, with people living in settlements among more and more people, the need for social organization through the kinship system became even more important. Within a community there was usually a dominant clan whose male leader took the role of community leader. The continued importance of the kinship system is also seen in the large increase in ancestor worship found in horticultural societies. As shown in Figure 17.1, 71 percent of the simple horticultural societies and 82 percent

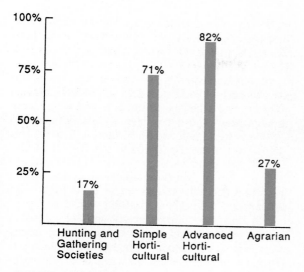

FIGURE 17.1. Extent of ancestor worship by type of society. (Source: Lenski and Lenski, 1982, p. 153.)

of advanced horticultural societies studied by Murdock (1949) practiced ancestor worship, compared with only 17 percent of hunting and gathering societies and 27 percent of the advanced agrarian societies. As we will see in Chapter 18, this importance of ancestor worship can be related to the high status of some leading family members, but also to the fact that with horticultural settlements the burial sites of ancestors are nearby and people continue to walk the land and village of their ancestors. With mobile hunting and gathering people, this was not the case.

With more technologically advanced agrarian societies we find some important changes in the family system (Lenski and Lenski, 1982, p. 208). Families are still very important to individuals, but for the overall society the kinship system is no longer the primary means of social organization because other social institutions have developed that supply functions once served by the family. A formal state has developed, and though top political positions may be inherited (e.g., king, queen), no one or a few families could supply all state positions. The same can be said for the military and religious institutions as well.

And although most children in agrarian societies are taught whatever skills they need at home, an educational system is starting to develop, primarily through religious organizations.

Until industrialization the family continued to be the main economic unit. People still worked together in the fields or small shops as families to provide economic necessities. And the welfare of family members was still the primary responsibility of the extended family, though religious organizations were now providing some welfare aid as well.

The Family in Industrial Societies

The past 200 to 300 years of industrialization have brought extensive changes in the family system. We must stress again that the family is still very important to most individuals in industrial societies, and families are still the basic units providing the care and nurturing humans require. But the family has changed in many ways, and other institutions have taken over more and more of the original family functions.

In his extensive study of families in industrial and preindustrial societies, Goode (1963) found several important changes, one of which was the decreased importance of the extended family. Aunts, uncles, cousins, and even grandparents are less important to members of a nuclear family; they are less likely to live close to these relatives and have extensive social interaction with them. These more distant relatives, in turn, feel less responsibility to help other relatives and have less influence on their lives in general. In large part the reduced importance of the extended family is a result of greater geographical mobility in industrial societies, but it is also a result of increased social mobility. With more movement up and down the class structure people are more likely to occupy different class positions and life-styles and to have different values from their relatives, which weakens the social bonds.

Another consistent pattern with industrialization is a decrease in the birthrate. As we saw in Chapter 6, industrialization reduces the economic incentives to have more children, and increased affluence and opportunities for leisure activities lead more and more families to limit the number of children to take advantage of these opportunities. Moreover, we cannot overlook the effect of new contraceptives in reducing family size.

All these changes are reflected in the figures shown in Table 17.1 indicating reduced household size during this century in the United States. Household size has been diminishing because families are having fewer children, but also because of the greater emphasis on nuclear families. Grandparents are today less likely to live in the household of their adult offspring.

Industrialization has also brought new technology into the home, changing traditional tasks for women, or at least changing the way these tasks are accomplished. In the 1870s gas stoves became available, along with refrigerators. The vacuum cleaner arrived in 1859, the washing machine in 1869, the electric iron in 1906, the dishwasher in 1946, and the garbage disposal in 1935 (Thomas, 1979, p. 384). Not many homes had this new household technology until after World War II, but these examples of changes in the home have in most respects reduced the amount of labor required to take care of a household.

With less time required for housework and with fewer children, women had more time for other activities. While this was occurring the occupational structure was changing, creating more job opportunities for women. Figure 17.2 shows the increase in women in the labor force in this century, which passed the 50 percent mark in the 1970s.

In part because of more options for women, but also because of more freedom to choose marriage partners and a decline in the patriarchal extended family system, there have been egalitarian trends in husband–wife family roles. Table 17.2 shows this change just since the 1960s in the United States. The biggest change is shown in the first item, where 32.5 percent of American women in 1962 said the important decisions should *not* be left to men, compared with 71.3 percent in 1980.

Yet there are important divisions in American society with respect to these egalitarian family roles. The more "modern" or egalitarian family is prevalent among the middle class and more educated, whereas male-dominated "traditional" families are more prevalent among the working class (Thornton, Alwin, and Camburn, 1983). But the trend in general in the United States is toward more egalitarian family roles.

The Japanese Family

As the only industrial society without Western cultural traditions, Japan again provides an interesting

TABLE 17.1. *U.S. household size since 1790*

Year	Number of households (1,000s)	Distribution of household sizes (percent)					Mean size
		1 Person	2 Persons	3 Persons	4 Persons	5+ Persons	
1790	558	3.7	7.8	11.7	13.8	62.9	5.79
1900	15,946	5.1	15.0	17.6	16.9	45.5	4.76
1940	34,946	7.1	24.8	22.4	18.1	27.6	3.67
1950	43,468	10.9	28.8	22.6	17.8	20.0	3.37
1960	52,610	13.1	27.8	18.9	17.6	22.6	3.33
1970	62,874	17.0	28.8	17.3	15.8	21.1	3.14
1975	71,120	19.6	30.6	17.4	15.6	16.8	2.94
1978	76,030	22.0	30.7	17.2	15.7	14.5	2.81

SOURCES: *Current Population Reports,* "Households and Families by Type: March 1978," series P–20, no. 340 (1979), Table B; U.S. Bureau of the Census, *Historical Statistics of the United States Colonial Times to 1970,* Part 1 (Washington, D.C.: GPO, 1975), pp. 41–42.

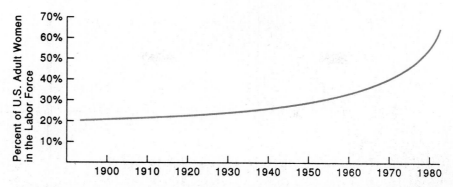

FIGURE 17.2. Rate of employment for U.S. women, 1900–1984, and international comparisons. *(Source: U.S. Bureau of Census, 1975, pp. 131–132; 1986, p. 848.)*

TABLE 17.2. *Changing attitudes in the traditional role of wives in the United States, 1962–1980*

Traditional beliefs	% of mothers disagreeing		
	1962	1977	1980
1. Most important decisions should be made by husbands.	32.5	67.4	71.3
2. It is not ok for mothers to be active outside the home.	44.1	59.1	64.8
3. There should be a separation between men's work and women's work.	56.4	77.0	66.6
4. A wife should not expect a husband to help around the house.	47.4	61.7	69.2
5. Women are happier if they do not work.	—	66.8	71.9
6. It is more important for a wife to help her husband's career than have her own.	—	49.2	54.4

SOURCE: Adapted from Thornton, Alwin, and Camburn (1983, p. 214).

test of the relative importance of industrialization versus culture in shaping institutions. Marriage and family roles in Japan clearly show that industrialization is very important but not the only factor shaping the family system.

The extended family is stronger in Japan than in the United States, though there has been a trend toward nuclear families. We have already seen that grandparents are more respected and given meaningful roles within extended families in Japan. Recent data, however, show that the percent of elderly parents living with their adult children has dropped in the past 20 years, though in recent years the percent has stabilized at a higher rate living with adult children compared with other industrial societies (Morgan and Hiroshima, 1983). In other ways there continues to be greater influence from the extended family (or household, which the Japanese call *ie*) on many decisions made by family members compared with other industrial nations (Fukutake, 1981, p. 34).

In most respects the more egalitarian family among middle-class Americans has not found favor in Japan — at least not among men. Only recently have changes given wives some legal rights once reserved for husbands. In other respects, however, wives are not powerless in Japan. Japanese husbands, as we have seen, work more hours away from home than men in any other industrial society; they usually leave for work early and come home after

Mealtime offers the family a chance to come together as a group and to reinforce its bonds of belonging. What social norms regarding family relationships can you infer from these photos of a typical American and a typical Japanese family? What is the difference in the organization of the eating and dining spaces? *(Top: © William U. Harris; bottom: © Robert A. Isaacs/Photo Researchers, Inc.)*

their children are in bed. Outside the home men dominate, but women control most domestic matters. Women have more influence on how household money will be spent, and men are often given an allowance (Vogel, 1971, p. 194). Women also have extensive influence on child-rearing and planning for the future of their children. And as the above would suggest, Japanese men are not expected to help with housework; in fact their help with housework is less than that of husbands in all other industrial nations (Morgan and Hiroshima, 1983, p. 277). (I was once surprised when asking Japanese college students if they had ever seen their fathers helping in the kitchen. Almost all the students raised their hand. However, I realized my mistake and asked how many had seen their fathers help in the kitchen more than once in several months—almost no hands went up. I was told there is a negative term for husbands who in fact invade the wife's kitchen too often—"cockroach husband.")

This extensive role separation between husband and wife leads to separate lives that would cause extensive conflict in most American marriages. The Japanese husband and wife seldom socialize together outside the home. The wife spends time with other women in the neighborhood, and husbands spend most of their time with co-workers. Sundays, however, are days for family activities. The trains in Tokyo are as crowded on Sunday as on week days, but they are crowded all day on Sunday with families going out together.

Another factor that is quite different in the Japanese family system is the manner in which marriage partners come together. Japan still has a tradition of arranged marriages called *omiai,* with about 40 percent of the young people today still finding marriage partners by this method. The *omiai,* however, is not as restrictive as the old arranged marriages in most preindustrial societies. With the Japanese *omiai* a family member, an employer, or some other respected person suggests to a man or woman that there is someone looking for a mate that he or she should meet. If both parties are willing, a meeting is arranged in which the two people can ask each other questions about themselves. After the meeting the two express their interest or lack of it to the matchmaker, who then informs the other person. If there

is mutual interest, the couple will date for a while to determine if they are compatible partners. There is a good deal of free choice in the matter of marriage, though there is much more family pressure to marry by a certain age (about 25 for women, 30 for men) and to marry an individual approved by parents in Japan than in Western industrial nations.

These differences in the marriage and family system in Japan should not be overstated. In many respects the Japanese are changing in the direction of the modern family patterns in other industrial nations. In other words, though there are cultural differences rooted in Japan's past that shape its family system, it seems these differences are being reduced by industrialization.

COURTSHIP AND MARRIAGE IN MODERN SOCIETIES

The process leading to marriage differs widely around the world, and as we will see is unique in industrial societies like the United States. The mate selection process is an important subject in itself, but it also tells us much about other general characteristics of a society.

The idealized form of mate selection in Western industrial societies, and especially the United States, involves what is called *romantic love*—the situation in which two people who believe they are ideal for each other meet and form a strong emotional bond that leads to marriage. We consider this idea of romantic love in more detail below, but the major point at present is how unique this process of mate selection is when considering the process in all other societies. Romantic love involves a freedom of mate selection that most preindustrial societies had to a much lesser degree than even Japan.

Marriages throughout history have primarily been arranged not by the marriage partners—usually by parents. Even today the extent of choice by a young couple such as we find in the United States is rather rare elsewhere. One comparative study of 39 societies found only 6 to have free choice by the young couple in mate selection (Bell, 1983, p. 55). In most places in history, marriage was made

---

BOX 17.1

Marriage in Egypt

The following description shows that the Western ideal of romantic love leading to marriage is far from a reality in a traditional society like Egypt. In fact, even Japan allows much more choice for women in choosing a marriage partner.

Hassan Rasmi was stopped near his home the other day by a young man with whom he had a nodding acquaintance.

"Excuse me," the man said, coming right to the point. "I have seen your sister, and I would like to marry her."

Rasmi's 18-year-old sister, Sahar, had never seen her suitor, 25-year-old Fuad Hakki, but that was not important. He was from a good family, he was pious, did not drink and, a college graduate, he earned a respectable salary, the equivalent of $200 a month. Rasmi quickly agreed to arrange an appointment with his sister.

Three days later Hakki knocked on the door of the Rasmi home. He wore a gray business suit. Coffee was served, and Rasmi's parents quizzed the suitor about his job, his salary, his personal habits. The suitor in turn quizzed Sahar about her friends, her interests, her attitude toward having children. He looked pleased when she said she would rather be a housewife than a career woman.

Finally Hakki said, "This is very good coffee," a code phrase meaning that the meeting had gone well and that, yes, he did want to marry Sahar. The young couple recited a verse from the Koran — a ritual known as *fatiah,* in which the woman promises to consider no other marriage proposal — and a wedding date was set for late next year.

During the year of courtship, Sahar and Hakki will meet only in the presence of family members. They will not go to movies or parties together. They will not hold hands or share any moments of intimacy. Should the two engage in any premarital sexual activity — a rare thing in Egypt — chances are that Hakki would promptly sever his relationship with Sahar, considering her immoral and unworthy of marriage.

"I remember holding hands with my fiance in Cairo in the '60's" Nayra Atiya, an American author who married an Egyptian, said, "and people would come up and say, 'You shouldn't do that. Remember where you are. This is Egypt.'"

Zenib Hosni, a university professor, said: "If you do slip off alone with a boy you care for, you feel tremendous guilt, because you know it is wrong, even if you are only talking. You live with the fear that you'll be caught. To fall in love in Egypt subjects you to a great deal of pressure."

---

for purely economic or political reasons. The male head of household would judge the economic value of a potential marriage, either in terms of the direct price offered to "buy" the young female or in terms of the economic fortunes that could be merged through the marriage. Or the choice of marriage partners was made in terms of family alliances that could be created, for whatever reason such alliances were needed.

For the most part, these marriage arrangements were accepted by the young, for they saw no alternative. Emotions were seen as barriers to rational decision making. This does not mean that love did not exist, but only that love and marriage were not seen as related. As one cultural historian put it when referring to medieval Europe, "Medieval marriages were entirely a matter of property, and, as everybody knows, marriage without love means love without marriage" (Clark, 1969, p. 64).

There is evidence that the idea of romantic love behind marriage first began during the days of the Roman Empire, but it was in the Middle Ages in Europe where it clearly took root (Thomas, 1979, pp. 232–233). This was the time of chivalry, ro-

Indeed, in a conservative, Islamic and sexually segregated society such as Egypt's, where the television series "Dallas" and "Love Boat" have recently been banned as immoral, there are few places where love can bloom and fewer places still where lovers can go. Love denied is the pain that many young Egyptians must silently suffer.

"In my village I've known women who have gotten married with tears in their eyes," a male Egyptian doctor said. "They are marrying one man and they love another, but they never had the possibility of making their feelings known to anyone other than themselves."

Increasingly, educated and economically secure urban Egyptians are breaking with tradition and choosing their own spouses, although most marriages are still arranged, often matching the children of brothers. In those cases the bride is only a bystander in the negotiations for her future.

Because the family is the central unit in Egyptian society, it is assumed that everyone will take a spouse soon after reaching marrying age — about 16 for a girl and 21 for a man. People who do not marry are viewed with suspicion, and unmarried adults often continue to live with their families. For a single man, living alone would be unusual; for a woman, unthinkable.

"My brother-in-law is 28, and he was getting very panicky to be still single," an Egyptian novelist said. "So he went to his mother the other day and said, 'I want to get married.' His mother got a photograph of an unmarried younger woman who lives nearby. A meeting was set up. He said he liked the coffee, and as soon as he can afford an apartment and the furnishings, they will be married."

Marriage is a civil contract here rather than a religious sacrament. Written into the contract are the precise size of the *mahr,* or bride payment — perhaps $2,000 for a man of average means — and how much the groom will pay in the event of divorce.

Popular television shows and novels promote the idea that love should precede marriage, as in the West, although the opposite usually happens here. Many Egyptians say that the love that takes root after marriage has a more solid foundation than the starry-eyed crushes that often lead to marriage in the United States and Europe.

"My friends who thought love came first usually ended up with failed marriages," the novelist said. "They tended to romanticize the virtues of their counterparts and think life together would be paradise, and we all know this just doesn't live up to the realities."

Source: David Lamb, "Love in Egypt Still Bound by Tradition," *Los Angeles Times,* Jan. 11, 1983.

---

mantic poetry, and novels — which is to say the printing press helped the spread of this ideal. And it was also at this time that we find the status of women in the upper classes slowly improving, which Collins (1975, p. 244) suggests was tied to the rise of romantic love. If women are to be courted and have a choice in deciding on a marriage partner, the influence of women is certainly enhanced. Along with this idea of romantic love emerged the ideal of mutual fidelity in marriage, restricting sexual relations to marriage. Again, women gain bargaining power they did not so often have before, when men had more freedom to seek sexual pleasure outside of marriage.

Mate Selection in the United States

With romantic love and free mate selection in modern societies, the next questions that occur are, who marries and who falls in love? The romantic idea that there are only two people in the world exactly right for each other is clearly a myth. There are factors that limit who may fall in love with whom, but the possible love matches are legion.

Sociologists have found several rather "unromantic" factors that tend to bring the "right" people together at the "right" time. One theory of role reciprocity and love (Orlinsky, 1972) suggests that people fall in love when they satisfy mutual needs of personal growth and development. People in this situation respond positively to an individual who fills these needs, and the person receiving the positive feedback returns more positive feedback, producing a greater level of attraction. However, there are many people who can fulfill each other's needs in this manner, so there must be other selective factors.

Several studies have shown three other factors to be important in mate selection (Jorgensen, 1986, pp. 286–289). A quite simple factor, but one no less important, is *residential location*. People are much more likely to marry someone who lives within one or two miles of their residence than someone farther away. Another factor involves *racial and religious similarities*. These factors are more important in some societies than others (e.g., blacks and whites are less likely to marry in South Africa, whereas Protestants and Catholics are less likely to marry in Northern Ireland). Racial and to some extent religious differences continue to restrict mate selection in the United States, but even without strong social pressure, people are more likely to be attracted to others of similar background. This is also the case with *social and cultural similarities*. People of similar social background and subcultures are more likely to be attracted, fall in love, and marry.

One question that is particularly important for a society is the extent of marriage **endogamy** and **exogamy**—the extent to which marriages tend to occur within the group or across groups. The group can refer to any important collective, such as class, religious, or racial groups. In most societies there are at least some pressures or rules encouraging endogamy, but even when there are few rules specifying endogamy, it tends to be extensive anyway. If you think about it this does not seem hard to understand. People are more likely to fall in love with someone who lives close by and is similar in race, religion, and social background. This also means there is usually extensive class endogamy in mar-

riage. The poor but pretty girl may marry a millionaire in the United States, but this is very rare.

Because class background cannot always be seen easily in a mass society like the United States, an open marriage market can often create fear for parents in the middle and upper classes. As one upper-class writer put it, "the democratic whims of romantic love often play havoc with class solidarity" (Baltzell, 1958, p. 26). The upper classes in the United States, however, have many ways of informally restricting the marriage market for their sons and daughters to other upper-class members. Among these are exclusive residential patterns, prep school attendance, debutante balls, and sending sons or daughters to the "right" universities (Domhoff, 1983). However, with more "commoners" going to Yale, Princeton, and Harvard, a serious problem remains for upper-class parents. This is one reason why upper-class parents support exclusive fraternities and sororities, which help regulate the marriage markets in large universities, thus reducing this upper-class concern somewhat.

MAJOR PROBLEMS AND ISSUES IN THE AMERICAN FAMILY

Because the family remains a very important institution in all societies, any major problem in this institution can have extensive repercussions throughout a society. It is for this reason that all societies have concerned themselves with the health of the family institution. In this section we examine the problems of divorce, illegitimacy, family violence, and what some see as the potential problem of mothers in the labor force.

Divorce

Figure 17.3 shows the United States to have the highest divorce rate of all major industrial societies, and Japan's rate is the lowest. The contrast between the United States and Japan leads us again to seek

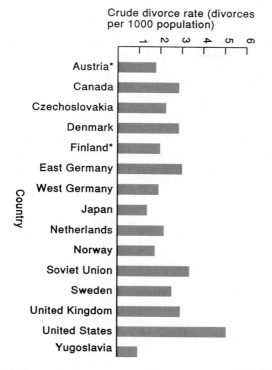

Crude divorce rate (divorces per 1000 population)

Country

- Austria*
- Canada
- Czechoslovakia
- Denmark
- Finland*
- East Germany
- West Germany
- Japan
- Netherlands
- Norway
- Soviet Union
- Sweden
- United Kingdom
- United States
- Yugoslavia

FIGURE 17.3. Divorce rates of major industrial societies. (Source: United Nations, 1983, pp. 517–519.)

answers by contrasting the characteristics of these two nations.

To begin with, the answers cannot be found with religion. In contrast to Roman Catholic nations like Ireland and Italy, divorce is not restricted on religious grounds in Japan. In fact, as we will discuss in more detail later, Japan is the least religious of all industrial societies, and the United States is in some ways the most religious.

Better explanations for the contrasting divorce rate between the United States and Japan have to do with the nuclear family, geography, women's options, and the contrasting ideals of marriage. Japan's extended family provides more relatives who are

likely to encourage the married couple to remain together, and these family members may even "lose face" if their relatives divorce. The higher rate of geographical mobility in the United States also reduces pressures from extended family members that can restrict divorce because relatives are simply further away.

Another important factor reducing divorce involves the greater options of women in the United States compared with women in Japan. The divorced woman in Japan is usually in a very difficult position. She will find it difficult to support herself economically, and divorce laws do not give her as many property rights, and often not even custody of her children (Vogel, 1971; Taylor, 1983). Options are even further limited because it is more difficult for divorced women to remarry in Japan. An assumption held by some Japanese men is that either the woman is still too devoted to her first husband to be a good wife again, or she was not devoted enough to her first husband, in which case she would not make a good wife now.

One of the most important factors influencing divorce rates, however, are the differing ideals of marriage between Americans and Japanese. Many writers have noticed that most Japanese do not have a very high expectation of happiness in marriage. The husband–wife relationship is not expected to be especially strong, nor do spouses spend much time together. Americans, however, have highly idealized views of marriage. Husband and wife are supposed always to remain much in love, have common interests, and enjoy doing everything together. Thus, when these high ideals are not met, American couples are more likely to seek a "better" marriage partner, in contrast to the Japanese, who never expected much companionship out of marriage anyway.

When considering the issue of divorce, we must also recognize that many problems occurring outside the family can create strain in a marriage, making divorce more likely. One of these outside problems is often economic. Married couples are more likely to argue over money matters than anything else, and figures show that divorce is more

BOX 17.2

Marriage, Divorce, and Affairs in Italy

A small band of veterans of the Italian marriage wars recently formed the Society for the Separated and Divorced, an organization with a dubious future.

The problem is the growth prospects; there are not many qualified candidates for membership.

A little less than a decade ago, when record numbers of Italians voted in a bitterly contested national referendum to uphold the country's first divorce law, anguished churchmen and conservative politicians were forecasting millions of legally broken marriages.

On the contrary, according to a survey just made public by the Italian Institute of Statistics, divorce Italian style is still pretty much what it was before it was legalized — rare enough to qualify Italy as one of the Western world's last bastions of enduring marriage.

Italy has 18.5 million married couples and an average of only about 11,000 divorces a year. The chances of an American couple getting divorced are 25 times what they are here. In Britain, the chances are 15 times as high and, in the Soviet Union, 17 times.

What accounts for the astonishing difference? Tradition and a historically shrewd sense of practicality, according to Italians, who have been boasting and joking about the new figures since the divorce study was published.

"The fact is that we Italians are influenced by a completely different mentality: that of the family as bulwark, of the family as primary foundation," said Leonarda Roveri Carannante, one of the two researchers who prepared the report.

One factor is the Roman Catholic Church, although the authors of the Institute of Statistics' study said it is not the major one. About 60% of the voters ignored the warnings of the Vatican, their bishops and parish priests to affirm the divorce law, and public opinion samples show that religion does not play a major role in the lives of most Italians.

According to a variety of Italian men and women who have toyed with the idea of

likely among people with low incomes (Jorgensen, 1986, p. 446). However, economic crisis does not always produce divorce. Liker and Elder (1983) found that economic crisis during the depression of the 1930s in the United States was as likely to strengthen marriages as to result in divorce. What is most important, therefore, is the overall strength of the marriage before the family experiences economic crisis.

Working Mothers

Over half of all married women are in the labor force today in the United States. Many of these women, of course, have young children. There is a problem when working mothers cannot afford child care and leave young children at home after school (called "latch key children"). Many women choose not to work because of the absence of day care facilities and thus remain poor, whereas other women take a chance with their "latch key children" in an attempt to work their way out of poverty.

There is another issue with the increase in working mothers that is not directly related to economic status. We must consider how children are affected when their mothers spend less time with them and their care. People who stress traditional family roles are afraid of the long-term negative effects of work-

divorce and rejected it, the real reasons — quite aside from religious considerations — are often a blend of financial fright on the part of the husbands and a deep fear of social blight on the part of the wives.

One woman whose husband wanted to divorce her said she nipped his plan in the bud by pointing out to him that under the divorce law's community property rule he would be forced by her lawyer to make full disclosure of his income and property holdings, which were substantial.

Like many other Italian couples (unofficial estimates even before the divorce law ranged as high as 2 million), the battling couple chose informal but permanent separation in order to keep the marriage, if not the relationship, going until death ends it.

In the man's case, that simply meant moving in with a mistress he had been keeping for years. In the woman's, it meant continued respectability as a married woman.

The institution of the mistress is so time-honored in Italy that even the church appears to turn a blind eye to it, and most Italians accept it as an ordinary way of life adopted by necessarily unknown numbers of their compatriots. That some countries frown upon it to the point of forcing politicians and ministers out of office when they are caught in extramarital liaisons is a subject of amusement here.

"If that happened in Italy, you would empty Parliament," said a close social observer of the national legislature.

A columnist in the nation's leading newspaper, *Corriere della Sera,* wryly noted the membership problems of the recently formed Society for the Separated and Divorced and proposed instead a League for Adulterous Lovers, because there are so many more of them. He suggested that it be called the Assn. for Marrieds Who Manage to Keep Going With Corrective, Extraconjugal Sentiments."

Source: Don A. Schanche, "Divorce: It's Still Not the Italian Style," *Los Angeles Times,* March 30, 1983.

ing mothers on these children, but recent research does not support these fears (Bell, 1983, p. 272). For example, the rate of delinquency among the children of working mothers is no higher, and, in fact, several studies have found no differences in many characteristics of the children studied.

Other problems have been suspected when traditional family roles are altered by working wives, but again, these possible negative outcomes have not been found in recent studies. For example, Booth et al. (1984) found there was no greater risk of marital instability among working wives. And in another interesting study, working wives were not found to have higher signs of mental stress or depression (Ross, Mirowsky, and Huber, 1983). In fact, working women are *less* likely to be depressed than women not in the labor force if their husbands approve of their employment and help with some of the housekeeping chores.

Illegitimacy and Family Breakdown Among the Poor

We have already seen that just because the divorce rate is very high in the United States we cannot conclude that the family is in crisis. Rather, there is simply a more "fluid" family system; a high rate of people who divorce remarry. But there is a serious

For "latch-key" children television may be the babysitter. The child of working parents lets himself or herself in and stays at home alone or with siblings until an adult returns. What are the alternatives? (© Maureen Fennelli/Photo Researchers, Inc.)

problem with respect to family breakdown among the poor, and especially poor blacks in the United States. Currently, over half of all black children have unmarried teenage mothers. Most of these young mothers will never marry or at least never form stable marriages. This problem was first recognized by Moynihan (1965), and at the time he received much criticism for his negative portrayal of the black family. But the situation has only worsened since Moynihan studied the problem.

There has been considerable discussion about the causes of illegitimate births in the United States in general, and the breakdown of the black family in particular. It is interesting to note that again the United States has the highest rate of teenage births among industrial societies, whereas Japan has the lowest rate (Table 17.3). Many people charge that the American welfare system contributes to teenage births by supporting young women when they have behaved irresponsibly. There is no doubt a problem with a welfare system that can *to some extent* encourage a social problem like this while helping to solve many other problems. It must be recognized, however, that the American welfare system is in fact more restricted than those of other industrial nations, but the United States has the highest rate of teenage births. Thus, the American welfare system cannot be the primary factor producing teenage illegitimacy.

It is also suggested that widespread pornography in the United States contributes to this problem. But again, the international comparison does not give much support to this view. Pornography is actually more widespread in Japan than in the United States, for example. On the streets of Tokyo are many coin-operated vending machines where anyone can buy

TABLE 17.3. *Percent of all births to teenage mothers, international comparisons*

Nation	Births to mothers 19 years old or younger as % of all births	Year
United States	16	1980
Canada	8	1981
Austria	12	1980
Belgium	7	1978
Czechoslovakia	11	1981
Denmark	5	1981
Finland	5	1981
France	5	1980
West Germany	6	1981
Japan	1	1981
Netherlands	3	1981
Norway	7	1981
Poland	6	1981
Soviet Union	9	1974
Sweden	4	1981
United Kingdom	9	1981

SOURCE: Constructed from United Nations (1982, pp. 280–290).

pornographic magazines. Yet Japanese teenagers are much less sexually active than their counterparts in the United States (Taylor, 1983, p. 190).

Two explanations for the high rate of illegitimacy among black girls seem the most plausible. First, slavery in the United States was in some respects more severe than in any other nation. In particular, family ties were not respected when slaves were bought and sold, which in time weakened the tradition of the family among American blacks. Second, to be poor in an affluent society creates a very negative self-image, no matter what race is involved. Where illegitimacy is not highly stigmatizing, a baby provides much personal gratification. There is someone to love and someone to return that love, as well as a valued possession when material ones are lacking. Thus, the matter of teenage pregnancy is not simply a matter of no birth control; it is often a matter of choice.

CHAPTER SUMMARY

Key Terms

family, 473	patrilocal, 476
extended family, 473	matrilocal, 476
nuclear family, 473	neolocal, 476
family institution, 473	monogamy, 476
patriarchal, 475	polygamy, 476
matriarchal, 476	polygyny, 476
egalitarian, 476	polyandry, 476
patrilineal, 476	endogamy, 484
matrilineal, 476	exogamy, 484
bilateral, 476	

Content

This chapter has been concerned with one of the important social institutions that was the first to appear in human societies. The family has often been called the "master institution" because it was the first to exist in human societies and continues to exist in some form in all societies.

As we have seen when considering other aspects of society, the functional perspective assumes that if a characteristic of society is widespread, it must serve some positive function for the society. In the case of the family, the main functions include reproduction, socialization, and emotional support for family members. From a conflict perspective we considered how the family unit or alliances of family units often provide a base for conflict over resources with out-groups. Also, we considered how the conflict perspective can help us understand relations within the family through an analysis of the differing resources and influence of particular family members or family roles.

Throughout history and around the world there have been many family forms. Families can vary with respect to which ancestors are more important (the male or female line, or both), how many spouses are acceptable, among many other characteristics. In industrial societies, however, we find a trend toward nuclear as opposed to extended families, and more egalitarian family roles, at least among the middle class. There are certainly differences in the family system among industrial societies, though, as we saw with the more male-dominated extended Japanese family.

In most societies, young people have not been free to select mates as they pleased. Most marriages were either arranged by parents or mate selection was severely restricted by other relatives. During the Middle Ages in Western societies, however, mate selection based on romantic love became the ideal. Mate selection is still influenced by race, religion, geography, and class position; with all these criteria, there is more endogamy than exogamy.

The American family is facing many problems, perhaps more so than in other industrial nations. A particularly serious problem is the American divorce rate, which is the highest in the world. This does not mean that the family is faced with extinction, though, because the rate of remarriage is equally very high. We also considered the phenomenon of mothers employed in the labor force but found much evidence to suggest this is not necessarily a problem. The high rate of teenage illegitimate births in this country, however, is clearly a very serious problem.

CHAPTER 18

Religion

Moral life has not been, and never will be, able to shed all the characteristics that it holds in common with religion.

— *Emile Durkheim, "Sociology and Philosophy"*

The family has been called the "master institution" because among the earliest human groups it was the institution serving all group needs. In all societies throughout history, the family has been found in some form or another, but the family is no longer the only major institution in modern societies. We have learned that as societies became more complex through social evolution, other institutions emerged to take over some of the tasks once performed within the family. The evidence from contemporary hunting and gathering tribes and the archaeological record suggest that the first new institution to emerge was religion. In most hunting and gathering societies today there are priests, shaman, or witch doctors. The earliest civilizations have also left records of a big increase in the importance of religion as they emerged around the world. About 4,000 years before the time of Christ we find religious monuments in the Egyptian Empire, and these are not the first in the archaeological record. In fact, wherever humans began to settle in the earliest civilizations, a temple or groups of temples dominated the city landscape.

The importance of the Christian religion in Europe, for example, can be seen in the dominance of the Roman Catholic Church, which emerged as an established religious organization in the latter part of the Roman Empire. Long after the fall of the empire many historians claim that it was the Catholic Church that brought Western civilization out of the Dark Ages with the Renaissance (Clark, 1969). At this time the pope was involved in political issues in countries throughout Europe, and the Vatican was also at center stage in cultural and technological advance. In the early 1500s Leonardo da Vinci, Raphael, Michelangelo, and many other talented artists were employed by the Vatican. The Vatican today still holds the record of that eminent power it once had over the centuries before industrialization.

The influence of religion around the world forces us to ask why we find religious institutions in all but the least complex societies and why religion and religious elites have gained so much influence. A preliminary answer can begin by noting human insecurity. Humans are the only animals to think in an abstract manner, at least in any extensive way, and indeed we are the only animal to understand that death must some day be our fate. This ability to think abstractly creates both insecurity and a need to explain the world in a manner that will reduce some of this insecurity. Religion can often provide some meaning to a threatening world and identify forces that seem to be in control. Through prescribed methods a religion may suggest how humans can somehow influence these forces, thereby reducing some of the mental insecurity that other animals do not experience.

We can add to the above some insights from conflict theory that help us understand how religious organizations and elites sometimes attain so much power and material wealth, as did the Catholic Church when it was first able to build and stock the massive monuments in the Vatican. We have again and again seen how elites, when able to control important resources, have achieved more and more resources and power through time. Religious elites have not been exempt from this pattern. When people believe that religious leaders alone can influence the world forces, these leaders have at times appealed to human insecurity to increase their power. As this view would suggest, the archaeological record indicates that the first rulers of early civilizations were religious elites (Pfeiffer, 1977).

I have not fully explained religion, nor described all its functions and characteristics, but I have given you a sample of a *sociological perspective on religion*. The task for sociology is not to consider if one religion is "correct" or to consider the existence of a god. Rather, sociologists want to ask the same types of questions about religion that we have asked about other aspects of society. We want to know why religion developed, why religion takes many forms, and the consequences of these different forms for human societies.

In this photo you can see the interior of one of the Vatican libraries in Rome. The Catholic Church's role as patron and preserver of the arts during the Renaissance provokes some interesting sociological questions about the relationship between religion and politics and between elites with both secular and religious power. In our society, is there a complete separation of church and state power? (© Leonard Von Matt/Photo Researchers Inc.)

THE NATURE OF RELIGION

Before proceeding we must agree on a definition of our subject matter. At first thought this may appear an easy task, but there are several difficulties in attempting a simple definition of religion. For example, is communism in the Soviet Union equivalent to a religion? There is collective ritual, the founders of communism and the Soviet Union (Marx and Lenin, respectively) are revered somewhat like saints, and there is extensive faith in a belief system that claims to explain much of the world. Also, what about the practice of magic, which requires a belief that supernatural forces are in control of natural events? Is magic equivalent to religion? In both these cases we conclude that there are some similarities to religion, but they do not involve religion per se.

Religion is a system of collectively held beliefs and practices that attempt to explain the universe (or cosmos) with reference to a sacred and supernatural realm. **Sacred** means things held in awe and reverence by society and set apart from the everyday world of the **profane.** Thus, although communism may create a feeling of awe when sponsored by a powerful state that can inspire its population through monuments and collective rituals, it does not claim a supernatural realm beyond the experience or empirical reality of mortals. And though a simple belief in magic may claim a supernatural realm, it falls short of a systematic set of beliefs attempting to explain the cosmos with reference to a sacred realm.

Another important component of religion is **ritual.** Most religions have specific practices that their members must precisely follow directed toward the supernatural and sacred. These rituals are a means of showing devotion to the supernatural as well as displaying to the faithful's continuing devotion. Large, collective rituals can have a powerful effect on maintaining faith and group solidarity. When many people simultaneously show emotional support for something, the thing becomes much more significant and perhaps "real."

A final comment on this definition of religion should be directed toward religious beliefs. A religion attempts to explain the world, or more generally the cosmos, in a manner that can give believers a sense of security by reducing the unknown. These religious beliefs commonly involve (1) a story of where the group (or humans in general) came from, (2) where they are going (the group in general and individuals in particular after their death), and (3) rules pertaining to personal conduct in the present.

The first component of these beliefs usually describes some act of creation. Hundreds of creation myths are contained in the vast number of religions that have existed throughout history. They do have some commonality, however, in that most creation myths claim that nothing existed before the creation, and then some deity created the universe in some manner similar to biological reproduction. Typical of beliefs about what existed before creation is that of the Aranda of central Australia, which is close to Christian, Islamic, and Jewish beliefs on this question. "In the very beginning everything was resting in perpetual darkness; night oppressed everything like an impenetrable thicket" (Sagan, 1980, p. 257).

As to where humans are headed, most religions do not have a concept of heaven and hell exactly like the Christian, Jewish, and Islamic religions, but most religions foresee some type of afterlife. There may be a vision of some kind of spirit world where ancestors are located, or as in the Hindu religion, reincarnation. And in most of the major religions, where a person spends the afterlife depends on how well that person follows the religious rules in this life.

A final characteristic of religion that we need to outline is the variation in its forms of social organization. Some religions are firmly established in society, with formal organizations, widely accepted beliefs, and considerable resources. Other religions are smaller in membership, more loosely organized, less accepted, and have fewer resources. The former religions are called **churches,** and the latter are called **sects.** There is a common pattern for new religious groups to become churches if they gain wide acceptance and more members in the future. The Christian religion is a good example. As a church becomes established, however, many of its original beliefs and practices are compromised to widen its acceptance in society. For example, perhaps members are no longer required to make extensive sacrifices and reject material comforts.

When these religious principles are compromised, some members who see themselves as more devoted to religion may reject the church and form a sect — that is, they break away from the church to form their own group. In time, the sect may also become more accepted, make its own compromises, and thus become another denomination of an established church (Niebuhr, 1929; Wallis, 1975). It is through this process of splintering and institutionalization that the many varieties of major religions arose around the world today.

THE RELIGIOUS BASE OF SOCIAL ORDER AND SOCIAL CONFLICT

Whenever a social institution, practice, or belief system exists in societies around the world throughout history, we must ask why. Functional theorists ask what function is served for overall societal survival by an institution, practice, or belief found in so many societies. But conflict theorists can also ask how some characteristic of the society is functional for only some groups in the society and is maintained because these groups are more powerful. In addition, we must examine how religion can also influence group conflict within a society, as well as conflicts between societies.

The Positive Functions of Religion

As we have already seen, the earliest sociologists like Durkheim (1954) have stressed how religion can help enforce social norms. In contrast to many other sociologists at the time, Durkheim believed that religion must be more than an outdated legacy from the primitive past. Through studying Australian aborigines Durkheim argued that religion, in fact, is a representation of the social group itself; when praising their religion, they are showing emotional support for their own group and its values. In this manner strong social bonds and support for group values are maintained by religion.

Also, we have noted that religion can give *meaning to life* — religion can give people a sense of having an important place in something much larger than themselves. And we have seen how religion can *make a threatening, confusing world seem more orderly and less threatening* by "explaining" the forces that operate in the world and how these forces may be influenced or controlled.

An interesting example of how religion can reduce anxiety was given by an early social anthropologist, Malinowski (1925). While studying a group of South Sea islanders, Malinowski realized that their religious beliefs allowed them to overcome the fear associated with the dangerous way they acquired their food. These people depended on fishing, but the seas were dangerous and many men were lost at sea. These fisherman had a tradition of religious rituals that reduced their anxiety over entering the rough sea and made them feel protected.

None of the above, however, means that religion has no dysfunctions. The status quo at a particular point in history may be in need of change. For example, two groups of people may be headed for deadly conflict that can be solved to everyone's benefit only through some form of compromise. However, religious principles may be involved that prevent such compromise. For another example, highly religious societies often believe that everything has been explained by their religious beliefs, and that these beliefs cannot be questioned. Consequently, the society is resistant to new ideas that may stimulate progress or change, and indeed, people with new ideas that can lead to such advance may be persecuted.

Religion and Group Conflict

Throughout world history we find many cases of differing religious groups in conflict. Muslims and Christians fought one another during the Crusades from A.D. 1095 until 1250. Hindus and Muslims have fought one another in India for centuries. Currently, Jews and Muslims are fighting one another in the Middle East, and Protestants and Catholics are fighting in Northern Ireland.

The list of religiously related conflicts could be greatly extended, but in many ways the nature of these conflicts can be misleading. At their heart we often find reasons for conflict not simply explained by contrasting beliefs. In the Middle East there is "holy war" between Jews and Muslims because in a 1948 revolution Jews took land from Arabs that Jews believe was historically theirs, a belief disputed by Arabs. The roots of Protestant-Catholic conflict in Northern Ireland do not go back as far as the Jewish-Muslim conflict in the Middle East, but the conflict is still an old one. During the 1650s the conflict between Ireland and England was intensified when Cromwell's army invaded Ireland. The British at this time were Protestant and the Irish were Catholic. British citizens were given the best land in Northern Ireland after Cromwell's army took con-

trol, and many Irish Catholics were left in poverty. Many of the more wealthy Protestants in Northern Ireland today are the descendents of those British invaders of the 1650s. Thus, a primary issue in the violence in Northern Ireland today pertains to class conflict that corresponds to religious divisions.

This is not to say that conflicts over religion per se are unimportant. It is often true that religion helps intensify the conflict and make both sides believe they are superior. Religion can promote a belief that the group will ultimately win the struggle because they have the support of their deity in a holy cause. In a similar manner a violent conflict can be maintained, as in the Iran–Iraq war, if people are willing to fight to the death because their religion provides them with an honored place in the "afterlife" owing to their "brave sacrifice."

We leave this subject by noting that religion can also provide support for a group seeking social change and the end to exploitation. The example of the black Civil Rights Movement in the 1950s and 1960s in the United States has already been considered, but there are other examples. In South Africa today the black struggle for freedom is in part organized by the Christian churches. One of the black leaders, Bishop Desmond Tutu, won the Nobel Peace Prize in 1985 for his work in South Africa, as did Martin Luther King, Jr., for his work with the American Civil Rights Movement about two decades earlier. In Latin America today the fight against the dominance of wealthy economic and political elites has been supported and even organized by local leaders of the Catholic Church.

Marx believed that religion always played the role of suppressing social change because elites used it to justify their privilege and help the lower classes cope with their misery. It was for this reason Marx called religion the "opiate of the masses." We have seen that religion can help people cope with anxiety and unhappiness, thus allowing them to live with a situation they might otherwise be more motivated to change. Evidence for Marx's view can be found throughout history, though the examples cited above show that religion does not always keep the lower classes passive and indeed can help support their fight for change.

Bishop Tutu of South Africa believes that apartheid is morally and religiously wrong. Do you think his position as a bishop adds credence and legitimacy to this view? Are there political implications when a church leader challenges a government? What types of authority are involved in that kind of encounter? (© Guy Tillim/Impact Visuals.)

DEVELOPMENT AND TYPES OF RELIGION

Before proceeding to the nature of religion in industrial societies, we examine the change in religious institutions throughout history and the many forms of religion found throughout the world. For most people in the past, religion was quite different from the major religions today because the nature of society was different — the two, religion and society, as we have already seen, are interrelated.

Simple Supernaturalism

Religions can be classified a number of ways: complexity of beliefs, number of deities recognized, and so on. In terms of complexity, the most elementary form of religion, **simple supernaturalism** (McGee, 1975), is found in most hunting and gathering societies. This form of religion maintains that there is some type of supernatural force operating in the world, but it does not recognize a particular god. A good example are tribal people who recognize no specific god or even identify the spirit force they believe operates in the world, but who believe there are forces of good and evil. They may believe that if a particular species of bird perches outside their cave early in the morning it is a sign from the friendly spirits that there could be danger that day.

Animism

In a somewhat more complex belief system, religions classified as **animism** recognize spirits that are believed to have motives and emotions much like humans. These spirits can be found in animate objects or normally inanimate objects such as the sun or mountains, which are assumed to have motives and emotions like those of the people who believe in them. A major characteristic of this type of religion is the use of magic to influence these animate spirits. At this point we find religion as a distinct institution within the society. With simple supernaturalism humans had fewer specific beliefs about how spirits influence the world, and no idea they might use magic to influence these spirits. With animistic religion, however, there is a need for religious specialists like shamans or "witch doctors," who attempt to influence these spirits. It must be stressed, though, that these spirits are not seen as gods to be worshiped — only influenced through magic.

BOX 18.1

Lord Bhairon, the Whiskey-Loving Hindu God

"Lord Bhairon loves whiskey," the head priest of the Hindu temple said, smiling.

That is why, he explained, every Sunday several thousand whiskey-bearing residents of the Indian capital flock to his small temple set against the wall of a crumbling ancient fort between the Jamuna River and the city zoo.

On round trays, the devotees present the image of the hard-drinking Hindu god Bhairon, a manifestation of the Hindu deity Shiva, with flowers and betel nut paste and bottles of Indian whiskeys with names such as Double Dog, Drum Beater, White Stag, Red Knight, Black Prince, Black Eagle, Black Stallion and Black Bird.

One favorite offering, distilled by Polychem Ltd., of Bombay, is White House whiskey. It features a picture of the famous Washington landmark and the slogan "Fit for a President."

Temple workers dutifully pour White House into the gaping mouth of one of several images of Bhairon in the temple. It dribbles from his chin and falls into a tray below.

Hinduism, the religion of more than 550 million Indians here as well as scattered millions more in Africa, Malaysia and the West Indies, is the most eclectic and, to a Westerner, confusing of all the great faiths.

It happily embraces those who believe in monotheism (one god), polytheism (several or many gods) and even atheism (no god). Its ranks include those whose strict nonviolence extends to all living things, and others who perform the ritual sacrifice of animals and occasionally even human beings, although this practice has been officially banned since the days of the British Empire.

Its large temples are a steamy chaos of worshiping men and women, some swathed in robes and beads, others in jeans or dresses; a cacophony of clanging bells, chanting priests and wailing children; a swirling cloud of incense and burning oils. Its diversity and free-form worship make it difficult to define in Western terms.

"Hinduism," wrote Edward Rice, a scholar of Eastern religions, "is noted as being the only one of the major beliefs that cannot be defined, for any definition is inadequate, contradictory and incomplete."

In Rajasthan state, near Bikaner in the Thar Desert in northwestern India, is a temple dedicated to rats, where the rodents are carefully fed and tended by the temple priests. In Tamil Nadu in southern India is another famous temple where devotees are asked to demonstrate their faith by "sacrificing" their hair to the temple, which then sells it for use in wigs and other products. And scattered around India, but particularly here in the north and Rajasthan, are temples to the angry, whiskey-drinking god Bhairon.

"There are at least 330 million gods. Bhairon is one of them," said the high priest of the main Bhairon temple here.

The priest's full name is Sri Mahant 108 Baba Dina Nath Ja Nashin, which literally means "Honored temple custodian who sits on the throne." The 108 number in the name comes from the belief by many Hindus that Shiva, who, along with Brahma and Vishnu, is one of the main trinity of Hindu gods, is manifested in 108 forms. However, in Hinduism's typically confusing and contradictory style, others believe that Shiva appears in 1,008 forms. Many priests in other Bhairon temples are called Sri Mahant 1008.

In Hindu temples he is usually represented as a broad, nearly featureless face embedded in a wall. However, modern renditions . . . show him as a black-skinned god with a sinister mustache, a snake draped around his neck. His four arms and hands hold the severed head of a demon, a bowl, a bottle of whiskey and a club.

Bhairon is worshiped according to the Tantric ritual or, more specifically, in "the left-hand way." Tantra, also known as *kundalini* yoga, stresses the darker, forbidden and erotic side of the human psyche.

Dr. Lokesh Chandra, a religious scholar and former member of Parliament, said: "In Hinduism the divine and the satanic are not distinguished. Everything, both good and evil, emanates from the supreme. Individuals have an element of both. Life goes on in the gray area between the two."

The Tantric ritual uses five offerings to please the gods — ritual sex, wine, meat, fish and certain finger gestures, all of which are forbidden in other forms of Hinduism.

In the case of Bhairon it is *madya* — wine or its more potent cousin, whiskey — that devotees think is the best way to win the god's grace.

"Bhairon is the ferocious aspect of the divine," said Chandra. "He is pleased only with things that are not normal — human blood, whiskey and so on. When in India you have a very serious problem, the solution lies outside the ordinary. So if your child is very ill you might go to Bhairon and say 'You have the experience of all the terrible calamities so take me out of mine.' It is a replacement for going to the psychiatrist. Nearly every politician goes to a Tantric ritual."

Chandra, who is also an expert on Chinese religious thought, said that the Tantric use of alcohol in ritual is not unique to Hinduism: "It is integral to practically every religious system. To me, Holy Communion is very much a Tantric rite."

Sri Mahant 108, meanwhile, would prefer that fewer devotees honor the god with whiskey and more with money or other traditional *prasads,* or offerings, such as flowers or coconut. For one thing, he said in a recent interview at the temple, he is suspicious of the motives of some of the worshipers.

"They offer a little to the gods and then they take the rest home to drink themselves. At home, people cannot object because it is a blessed offering."

The priest, 45, a gray-haired man with an enormous belly and betel-stained teeth, said one Indian man, now living in Sweden, visits the temple every year with 10 or 15 cases of whiskey.

Sri Mahant 108 said that he would rather have money.

"Only money pays the electric bill," he said.

Source: Los Angeles Times, Nov. 13, 1986, p. 28.

Theism

In contrast to these, **theism** is the belief in some god or gods that influence the world and must be worshiped. These gods are seen as very powerful and at least somewhat involved in human affairs.

This more complex form of religion first emerged with agricultural societies, and a sun god was often worshiped. The early Greeks built a temple to their sun god, and the Egyptians had similar beliefs and practices as early as 4000 B.C. (Thomas, 1979, p. 129). The first theistic religions were quite different from major Western religions today, however, because there were commonly many gods — thus, the name **polytheism.** In present-day Iraq, about 4000 B.C. there were goddesses of love and war, gods of vegetation, fish, moons, and water, among many others. Each god or goddess ruled its own province or domain of human life and at times was seen to be involved with human-type exploits like war or love. Egypt had an even greater number of gods; each of the 42 provinces of Egypt had a separate god, as did even the smallest city.

Monotheism and a universalistic view of religion developed much later. In this view, there is only one god, who is in control of all people, whether they realize it or not. The monotheistic view of religion developed about 1500 B.C. in the Middle East, with Jews among the first to adopt this outlook around 1200 B.C. But before this time there was a trend toward monotheism in the later stages of the Egyptian Empire when the pharoahs began ranking the gods so that one was dominant over all the others.

The three largest and most dominant monotheistic religions all developed in the Middle East and to some extent are related. Judaism was the first to emerge in the area, with Christianity then Islam emerging with many related ideas and even some common historical prophets like Moses (Judaism and Christianity) and Jesus (Christianity and Islam). Their view of god is also similar in that they project human characteristics onto their god.

A big boost to monotheism came in the fourth century A.D. when the Roman Empire accepted Christianity as the dominant religion, but as the Roman Empire declined, the void was filled by the Islamic Empire, which also continued the spread of a universalistic monotheistic religion. A key to the spread of all three of the major monotheistic religions is related to their views of universalistic religion. Because they saw their religion as the only true religion, they set out to convert the rest of the world to their view. It was the Islamic Empire that spread the Muslim religion around much of the world after the fall of the Roman Empire, then the Christian European nations spread Christianity around much of the world with the growth of the modern world system beginning in the 1400s.

In the East there were other universalistic religions. Most of these, however, did not develop with the concept of a deity having many human characteristics. The Eastern religions such as Buddhism, Hinduism in India, Confucianism in China, and Shintoism in Japan are more accurately described as religions based on **abstract ideals** that are guides to living.

Of these religions, Buddhism is most accurately described as universalistic. The founder of Buddhism, Gautama, was born in India between 600 and 500 B.C. into an upper-class family. The roots of Buddhist philosophy stem from his rejection of the extremely luxurious, hedonistic life-style he pursued until his middle age. A basic principle of Buddhism sees the root of human misery in selfishness, which only a simple life-style and self-discipline will overcome.

All other Eastern religions have had more limited export from their native lands. Buddhism has spread to much of Asia, however, and has been most popular in China and Japan rather than in India, where it first developed. Even those Asians who kept their native Confucianism or Shintoism incorporated many principles of Buddhism into the native religions. In Japan, for example, it is totally acceptable to follow both the Buddhist and Shinto religions, and these two religions have cooperated by dividing the religious tasks between themselves. Shinto priests are more often in charge of the important events in this life — ceremonies of thanks for a good harvest, blessings for good luck when starting a new business, and marriages. Buddhism, on the other hand, more often takes care of funerals and the souls of ancestors.

TABLE 18.1. *Estimated membership of principal religions of the world*

	Africa	East Asia	Europe	Latin America	Northern America	Oceania	South Asia	U.S.S.R.	World	%	Countries
Christians	271,035,700	78,100,000	413,920,700	395,554,500	232,048,400	21,287,100	129,076,700	103,373,400	1,644,396,500	32.9	254
Roman Catholics	102,522,200	9,204,000	257,155,000	371,863,600	91,209,800	7,434,000	81,694,100	5,111,900	926,194,600	18.5	242
Protestants	71,883,000	32,100,000	76,652,000	13,960,000	94,965,500	7,510,000	26,142,100	8,803,800	332,016,400	6.6	230
Orthodox	24,746,700	81,000	35,606,100	570,000	5,910,000	507,400	3,200,000	89,442,300	160,063,500	3.2	98
Anglicans	22,389,900	334,000	32,886,200	1,210,000	7,511,000	5,350,000	290,000	400	69,971,500	1.4	148
Other Christians	49,493,900	36,381,000	11,621,400	7,950,900	32,452,100	485,700	17,750,500	15,000	156,150,500	3.1	110
Muslims	245,110,500	23,795,000	8,901,500	645,000	2,682,600	96,000	547,350,500	31,807,200	860,388,300	17.2	172
Nonreligious	1,495,000	641,756,600	50,923,940	13,237,000	21,047,700	2,884,400	20,651,100	84,332,030	836,327,770	16.7	220
Hindus	1,410,000	10,100	590,000	660,000	810,000	295,000	651,918,900	1,200	655,695,200	13.1	88
Buddhists	12,800	154,796,300	216,000	490,000	190,000	16,000	153,585,000	320,000	309,626,100	6.2	86
Atheists	240,000	136,886,000	17,803,000	2,538,000	1,073,000	512,000	5,300,000	60,774,500	225,126,500	4.5	130
Chinese folk religionists	9,500	179,103,100	49,000	60,000	110,000	16,000	8,169,400	100	187,517,100	3.7	56
New-Religionists	13,000	42,217,200	34,000	370,000	1,075,600	6,100	66,990,000	200	110,706,100	2.2	25
Tribal religionists	68,219,450	730,000	100	1,160,000	60,000	81,000	24,508,200	0	94,758,750	1.9	98
Jews	257,000	1,800	1,483,600	990,000	8,084,000	86,000	4,050,000	3,123,000	18,075,400	0.4	125
Sikhs	26,000	1,000	215,000	6,000	9,500	6,600	16,340,000	50	16,604,150	0.3	20
Shamanists	1,000	12,500,000	400	400	200	200	10,000	250,000	12,762,200	0.2	10
Confucians	500	5,900,000	1,000	500	10,000	200	2,000	200	5,914,400	0.1	3
Baha'is	1,265,000	48,400	70,500	570,000	310,000	59,000	2,300,000	5,000	4,627,900	0.1	205
Jains	47,500	500	9,900	2,000	2,000	900	3,400,000	20	3,462,820	0.1	10
Shintoists	50	3,400,000	360	800	1,000	500	200	100	3,403,010	0.1	3
Other religionists	65,000	62,000	310,000		750,000	25,000	230,000	6,000	8,216,800	0.2	170
Total Population	589,208,000	1,279,308,000	494,529,000	423,053,000	268,264,000	25,372,000	1,633,882,000	283,993,000	4,997,609,000	100.0	254

NOTES:

Continents. UN demographic practice divides the world into eight continental areas as shown above (see United Nations, *World Population Prospects*, New York, 1986, with populations of all countries covering the period 1950–2025).

Countries. The last column enumerates sovereign and nonsovereign countries in which each religion has a significant following.

Rows. The list of religions is arranged by descending order of magnitude of global adherents in 1987 (last two columns but one).

Adherents. As defined and enumerated for each of the world's countries in *World Christian Encyclopedia* (1982), projected to mid-1987.

Christians. Followers of Jesus Christ affiliated to churches (church members, including children), plus persons professing in censuses or polls though not so affiliated.

Other Christians. Catholics (non-Roman), marginal Protestants, crypto-Christians, and adherents of African, Asian, Black, and Latin-American indigenous churches.

Muslims. 83% Sunnis, 16% Shi'ahs, 1% other schools.

Nonreligious. Persons professing no religion, nonbelievers, agnostics, freethinkers, dereligionized secularists indifferent to all religion.

Hindus. 70% Vaishnavites, 25% Shaivites, 2% neo-Hindus and reform Hindus.

Buddhists. 56% Mahayana, 38% Theravada, 6% Tantrism.

Atheists. Persons professing atheism, skepticism, disbelief, or irreligion, including antireligious (opposed to all religion).

Chinese folk religionists. Followers of traditional Chinese religion (local deities, ancestor veneration, Confucian ethics, Taoism, universism, divination, some Buddhist elements).

New-Religionists. Followers of Asiatic 20th-century New Religions, New Religious movements, radical new crisis religions, and non-Christian syncretistic mass religions, all founded since 1800 and mostly since 1945.

Jews. 84% Ashkenazim, 10% Orientals, 4% Sephardim.

Confucians. Non-Chinese followers of Confucius and Confucianism, mostly Koreans in Korea.

Other religionists. Including 50 minor world religions and a large number of spiritist religions, New Age religions, quasi religions, pseudoreligions, pararreligions, religious systems, mystic systems, religious and semireligious brotherhoods of numerous varieties.

Total Population. UN medium variant figures for mid-1987, as given *World Population Prospects* (1988, p. 303).

SOURCE: Britannica World Data (1986), pages 72–77.

(DAVID B. BARRETT)

Secularization in Industrial Societies

As we move to the period of industrialization we find that religion has lost some of the influence that it had in preindustrial societies. There must be many qualifications to that statement; the influence of religion varies among industrial societies, religion may still serve important needs, and there are many religious people in industrial societies.

In the past some social scientists believed that religion would become extinct as societies advanced. For example, Freud (1927) thought religion was a "childish illusion" and hoped that it would become obsolete. It now seems clear that Freud was incorrect and that religion will remain, though in altered form (Stark and Bainbridge, 1985).

By *secularization* we mean that many of the functions once performed by religious institutions are now performed by other institutions. For example, the church was a primary agency for social welfare in preindustrial societies, but we now find government welfare agencies in all industrial societies. The church was also a primary agency for education outside the home, but again we find government educational programs dominating in industrial societies. And the church has lost its function of explaining the world to more and more people in industrial societies. This is not to say that most people reject the moral teachings of a church; but questions concerning such things as how the world and humans came into existence, why people behave in a deviant manner, and how the solar system operates have been taken over by secular belief systems. This trend creates a potential conflict in society between groups who hold strictly to the traditional religious belief systems and groups who now accept secular explanations. But with the exception of the United States, these conflicts have been minimized in industrial nations. Most people have divided up the questions between those seen as religious and those seen as relevant for secular explanations. We will consider the particular situation of conflict between science and religion in the United States, but it is important to note that the conflict is not unique in preindustrial societies. Especially in societies trying to industrialize in the context of powerful traditional religious institutions, the conflict can be extensive.

This conflict was most extreme in Iran since World War II, and was a significant factor in the revolution in Iran in 1979.

Religion has not lost all its functions even in industrial societies. Science cannot explain the ultimate questions such as what is the "meaning of life." And even if we accept science's "big bang" theory of how the universe was formed, there are many unanswered questions, such as where did all the physical matter come from that was involved in the big bang. Thus, though religion is no longer consulted for some answers that have been given over to science, it continues to help answer questions for many people about the cosmos.

Religion also remains important for many people in industrial societies because of the moral guidance it gives. And religion is still important in providing a sense of community and personal belonging for many. Religious communities can in fact provide an important network of individuals willing to help others during a decline of the extended family system in most industrial societies.

It was noted above that the importance of religion varies in industrial societies. One of the standard measures of this is simply asking people about the importance of religion in their life and if they believe in a god. As shown in Tables 18.2 and 18.3 these

TABLE 18.2. *Comparative religious beliefs*

Nation	% of Population believe in life after death
Republic of Ireland	76
United States	71
Spain	55
Finland	49
Italy	47
Great Britain	45
Norway	44
Netherlands	42
West Germany	39
Belgium	37
France	35
Denmark	26

SOURCE: *The Gallup Report,* May 1985, p. 53.

TABLE 18.3. *Comparative views on a god*

Nation	Importance of god in life (average responses on 10-point scale; high = 10)
South Africa	8.55
United States	8.21
Republic of Ireland	8.02
Italy	6.96
Spain	6.39
Belgium	5.94
Great Britain	5.72
West Germany	5.67
Finland	5.35
Netherlands	5.33
France	4.72
Japan	4.49
Denmark	4.47
Sweden	3.99

SOURCE: *The Gallup Report*, May 1985, p. 52.

measures indicate that the United States is the most religious of all major industrial societies, and Japan is one of the least religious. This pattern is in some ways contrary to what we might expect, given the historical lack of official government support for religion in the United States, which is in contrast to the history of other industrial societies.

This international comparison of popular support for religion also conflicts with some standard assumptions about the necessity of religion for maintaining social order, controlling deviance, and preventing many social problems in a society. Though the United States is the most religious of major industrial nations, we have already seen that the United States also has the highest crime rate and the highest divorce rate among these societies. In contrast, although Japan is one of the least religious of industrial societies, it has the lowest crime rate and divorce rate, as well as the lowest rate of many other forms of social problems. This is not to say that religion does "no good" in the United States, but it does say that there are other means of reducing deviance and many social problems. As we have seen, however, Japan's homogeneous population, cultural unity, and collectivist value orientation can-

not be copied by the United States as a means of reducing its social problems.

RELIGION IN THE UNITED STATES

Because religion continues to be very important in the United States, we conclude with this major subject. We will examine what has been called civil religion in the United States, the religious orientation of particular groups of Americans, and the recent visibility of fundamentalist religions and cults.

Civil Religion

As we have already seen, the United States is the most religious of all industrial nations — this country has the highest rate of church attendance, belief in a god, and belief in life after death. But in some respects, this high rate of religiosity is misleading, and there are two other important though misleading characteristics of religion in America: the separation between church and state is taken very seriously, and there is extensive religious pluralism. Again, this is in contrast to the recent history and current situation of most other industrial nations. For example, although citizens of other industrial nations are no longer required to belong to a state religion, because this was done in the past most religious people in these countries today do belong to the same religious denominations. In England it was the Church of England, in Germany it was a Protestant religion, and in Spain and Italy it was Roman Catholicism. In the United States, however, whereas about 90 percent of the population is Christian, the largest denomination — Roman Catholicism — accounts for only 27 percent of the population. About 60 percent of Americans claim to be Protestants, but no particular Protestant denomination claims more than 10 percent of the population (Melton, 1979).

It is time to suggest why both the high rate of religiosity and the separation between church and state in the United States are misleading. In some respects, and with many people, religion and nationalism are interrelated. Religion often involves praise for the "American way of life" (Herberg, 1960).

This is an American family who converted to the Sikh religion. How do you think the American principle of religious freedom applies to members of religious groups like the Sikhs or the Amish who choose to follow religious beliefs and behaviors very different from those of the majority of the population? (© Arvind Garg/Photo Researchers Inc.)

Although there is religious freedom in the United States, there is also a strong assumption in the population that being non-Christian is somehow un-American. The Pledge of Allegiance says this is "one nation under God," and our coins have the saying "In God we trust." Almost every presidential inaugural address has made at least passing reference to the deity.

The main point is that religion and nationalism are more strongly tied together in the United States than in any other industrial nation. The term **civil religion** has been developed to describe this situation (Bellah, 1970). Not all Americans personally connect religion with patriotism, but the fact that many do helps us understand why only about 40 percent of Americans attend church services at least once a month though over 90 percent claim to have

religious beliefs—it would seem un-American to reject religion. This situation in the United States is compatible with Durkheim's thesis that religion can symbolize the group itself and worship can in part involve praise for one's own reference group.

Religion and Class

Americans are a diverse people, and we would expect them to differ with respect to religion as they differ in many other ways. For example, there are geographical differences in religious participation, though these differences are less than most people realize. When we examine rates of church membership and attendance (per month), we find similar patterns across the United States (about 600 members per 1,000 population, and about 60 to 70 percent attend church at least once a month), except for the West Coast, where both rates are about one-half that of other parts of the country (Stark and Bainbridge, 1985). In this respect there is no distinct "Bible belt" in the South, though there is what has been called an "irreligious belt" in the West. However, religion in the South also differs because the conservative fundamentalist churches like the Southern Baptist dominate more than in other parts of the country.

One important difference in religion across the United States is related to social class. There are class differences in rates of church membership and in the type of churches people attend. The higher the class position of a person, the greater the chance that she or he is a member of one or more voluntary organizations. This general statement can be extended to religious organizations (Vanfossen, 1979, p. 313). The upper middle class are most likely to be church members, and the working class are less likely to be church members. To some extent, however, this class difference is misleading. The upper middle class are not necessarily more religious; they are simply more likely to be involved in all sorts of community organizations. In contrast when the working class and poor are involved in religion they are usually more emotionally involved than are the upper middle class. An outcome of this is that styles of religious expression may differ. The working class are more attracted to church services that are emotional in content and often involve a good deal of singing, dancing, and participation by the congregation during the church service. The upper middle class, on the other hand, are more attracted to quiet, restrained church services that stress less emotional or even intellectual themes.

It is partly for this reason that we find significant differences in the class backgrounds of the members of different religious denominations. The class backgrounds of Episcopalians tend to be the highest, whereas Baptists and Catholics tend to have working-class backgrounds. An exception to this pattern is the South, where Baptists outnumber all other denominations. In the South we therefore find upper-middle-class Baptist churches, middle-class Baptist churches, and so on. The class backgrounds

of Catholics are also more varied than most other churches. On the average, more Catholics are from the lower classes because so many low-income Mexican-Americans are Catholic. The ranking of Protestant denominations in Table 18.4 follows roughly the description above. The churches with members from higher-class positions tend to rank lower in orthodox beliefs, as measured by a personal belief in a god, life after death, and the existence of Satan.

Fundamentalist Churches

Fundamentalist churches or religions are usually defined as those that stress that the Bible is literal truth. Fundamentalist churches are commonly very conservative in their political views as well, showing

TABLE 18.4. *Orthodox religious beliefs* by American denominations*

Protestant denomination	Percent scoring high on orthodox beliefs
Unitarian	0
Congregational**	28
United Presbyterian	38
Episcopal	41
Christian Church (Disciples of Christ)	46
Methodist	49
Presbyterian Church, U.S.A.	50
American Lutheran	50
Evangelical and Reformed	50
Lutheran Church—Missouri Synod	52
American Baptist	55
Other Baptist bodies	63
Southern Baptist	75
Other sects	76
All Protestants	55
Roman Catholics	54

* Beliefs measured include a belief in a personal god, a belief in life after death, and a belief in Satan.
** Now the United Church of Christ.
SOURCE: Stark and Glock (1968).

the relation between religious and political values discussed above as civil religion.

Fundamentalist churches have received extensive attention in the United States during the 1980s, in large part because of their support for Ronald Reagan when he first ran for the presidency during 1980. The organization Moral Majority especially received considerable media attention, but there have been other active associations related to fundamentalist churches. In addition to their sponsorship of political candidates, these fundamentalist groups have been working for various conservative causes such as antiabortion, antipornography, antigay rights, and the teaching of creationism in opposition to evolution. These fundamentalist groups have not achieved extensive success in their causes but they have achieved increased support. For example, studies show an increase in the membership of fundamentalist churches beginning in the 1970s and continuing in the 1980s (Stark and Bainbridge, 1985).

Despite popular assumptions about the unique nature of the current rise of fundamentalism in the United States, fundamentalist groups and "revivalism" have had a long tradition of rise and fall in this country (Ash-Garner, 1977; Kanter, 1972). Because of the nature of our civil religion, fundamentalist groups usually gain strength with a turn from liberalism to conservatism or in times of economic crisis for some people. There were revivalist movements in the early 1800s and again in the late 1800s, with revivalist groups calling for a return to traditional religious and American values to reverse some social changes they viewed as negative.

The pattern of rise and fall of revivalist or fundamentalist movements can in part be understood with what we have learned about social movements in Chapter 16. As the resource mobilization theory predicts, a social movement can be explained, at least in part, by an increase in resources for mobilization. Many people in this country felt threatened and were in some ways actually harmed by the many types of reform and changes in the 1960s. By the late 1970s and 1980s, the strength of liberal movements had eroded and a more conservative mood in the nation increased the amount of resources going to fundamentalist-type organizations. There were

also political leaders now using government influence to help fundamentalist groups. The result was a new revivalist movement trying to move America back to traditionalist values.

Cults

Another form of religion that has gained attention in recent years are cults. **Religious cults** are small, relatively less organized religious groups that follow beliefs and have practices viewed as deviant by the dominant society. In other words, the characteristics of cults are even further from established churches than are sects. Cults also often hold new religious beliefs, or at least religious beliefs new to a society. This means that most people in that society have negative attitudes toward cults and view cult members as strange. Yet all religions were once seen as strange when they were small and new — that is, still cults. This was the case with Christianity, for example, when Jesus and his group of disciples were trying to gain adherents. Jesus was killed as a threat to the Roman Empire, but when the popularity of Christianity became extensive in the later stages of the Roman Empire, Christianity gained the status of an established religion.

Many varieties of cults have emerged in the 1960s and 1970s, attracting primarily young adults. One of the most publicized cults was the People's Temple led by the Reverend Jim Jones. Their notoriety came in 1978 when over 900 members died (most committed suicide, others were killed) in Guyana on the orders of Jones (Coser and Coser, 1979). Of course, most cults are less extreme in their beliefs and behavior. For example, cults like the Children of God and followers of the Reverend Sun Myung Moon ("Moonies") follow Christian beliefs but take these beliefs and practices to extremes that are rejected by traditional churches. And there are cults like Hare Krishna and the Divine Light Mission that have imported various Eastern religions to America. In all these cults, members are asked to give extreme devotion to their religion, often to the point of rejecting almost all aspects of the traditional society. Members must often live in communes, wear special clothing, reject all outsiders or at least extensively reduce contact with them, turn over all property to the cult, and devote many hours a day to worship and other religious activities. Such total changes in life-style and beliefs have prompted many people (especially the parents of members) to claim cult members have been "brainwashed."

We can understand the spread of cults from two levels — a broader societal level and a social psychological level. When looking at the general society, we find that cults can become widespread when there is extensive alienation and discontent among people in a society but a worldly solution to their problems seems impossible. For example, the roots of the religious cults of the 1960s and 1970s in the United States may be located in the youth rebellion of the 1960s. Many of the people who turned to religious cults had first participated in social movements like the anti-Vietnam War movement, which tried to produce social change. But as they became frustrated in these worldly attempts to produce change, they often turned to religious cults (Mauss and Petersen, 1973). The same pattern can be found in Russia after 1905. There were many "worldly" social movements and even an attempted revolution in Russia in 1905. But after these "worldly" movements failed, many youth and intellectuals turned to mysticism and cults (Salisbury, 1977).

The pattern of turning to an otherworldly solution when all else has failed is also found with a religious cult among American Indians in the late 1800s known as the Ghost Dance movement. This cult spread among many Indian tribes at a time when they were facing clear defeat in wars with U.S. troops. The leaders of the Ghost Dance movement believed that if the proper dances were followed their members could not be killed by the white man's bullets and that their ancestors and land would be returned. Although there were many factors leading some tribes to accept the Ghost Dance while others did not, it is clear that the Ghost Dance was a movement of people who had lost hope of achieving their goals by any other means (Thornton, 1981).

To understand cults we also need to examine who and why particular people join them. One of the most useful explanations of this comes from a study of the followers of the Reverend Moon by Lofland and Stark (1965). The process of becoming a member of this cult showed that seven factors were involved.

1. *Tension.* In this stage Lofland and Stark found that potential members were experiencing some personal problems that made them unhappy with their present life. An unhappy marriage or failure in school or on the job are all examples of situations producing tension.

2. *Type of Problem-solving Perspective.* Our culture and upbringing give us perspectives from which to view the world and attempt solutions to our problems. In our culture three types of perspectives are common — religious, political, and psychological. A personal problem may be explained by any or a combination of these three. The "Moonie" recruits interviewed in the study were all found to have been given a religious perspective at some point in their lives, which made them more receptive to this particular new religious perspective.

3. *Seekership.* The previous means of solving problems had now been rejected as useless by these people, making them seekers; that is, they were now looking for other means to solve their personal problems.

4. *The Turning Point.* To make a significant change in life-style and outlook, people often need some event that will break their old routines and habits. Such an event can include moving to a new area, a divorce, losing a job, or finishing school. With events like these a change in other aspects of life is made easier, such as joining a religious cult.

5. *Cult-affective Bonds.* When the previous four factors had set the stage for a life change, the future "Moonies" came into contact with someone from the cult and formed friendship ties. In a later study of other cults, Stark and Bainbridge (1980) have also found a network of social ties among cult members very important in attracting new members. As with future "Moonies," this social network can catch potential members at critical stages in life when they need friendship.

6. *Extra-cult Affective Bonds Cut.* To be brought into a cult usually requires the gradual severing of ties with people not attracted to the cult. Because cults are usually seen as strange and deviant, strong friendship ties to noncult members will lead to pressure to reject the cult.

7. *Intensive Interaction.* Intensive interaction with cult members will likely produce more and more commitment to the cult and its beliefs.

This process can also work in reverse, leading people to reject their cult membership. I mentioned above that many people believe that conversion to a cult involves some mysterious process called "brainwashing." Actually, the process as described above is not so mysterious and has been used in reverse by "deprogrammers" who have been hired by the parents of cult members in attempts to bring their children back into the traditional society.

CHAPTER SUMMARY

Key Terms

religion, 494	animism, 497
sacred, 494	theism, 500
profane, 494	polytheism, 500
ritual, 494	monotheism, 500
church, 495	abstract ideals, 500
sect, 495	civil religion, 504
simple supernaturalism, 497	fundamentalist, 505
	religious cults, 506

Content

The institution that first emerged from the "master institution" (the family) was religion. The first simple religious beliefs and religious leaders were quite different from those in industrial societies, but all major types of societies have had religious institutions.

Religion can serve many positive functions in a society, such as providing a "meaning of life" and maintaining social order. But throughout history religion has also created bases for more extensive conflict. Religious conflicts, however, are often related to underlying class conflict in society.

Like the family system, there have been many forms of religion. There has been a rough trend toward more complex religious beliefs through the social evolutionary process, however. And with industrialization there has been an increase in secularization, though religion is still an important institution in industrial societies. When comparing industrial societies, we find that the United States is the most religious society, whereas in many ways Japan is the least religious, thus showing there is variance in the importance of religion in industrial societies.

The importance of religion in the United States is in part related to the overlap between religious values and nationalism, called civil religion. This form of religion makes revivalistic movements a recurring aspect of American history, with the fundamentalist movement the most recent.

CHAPTER 19

Education, Science, and Technology

We are born weak, we need strength: helpless, we need aid; foolish, we need reason. All that we lack at birth, all that we need when we come to man's estate, is the gift of education. This education comes to us from nature, from men, or from things. This inner growth of our organs and facilities is the education of nature, the use we learn to make of this growth is the education of men, what we gain by our experience of our surrounding is the education of things.

—Jean Jacques Rousseau, *Emile*

One of the basic characteristics of capitalism is the private ownership of the major means of production — capital. We have seen in earlier chapters how the ownership of significant amounts of capital can bring extensive profits, as well as economic and political power. Some recent theorists, however, have argued that our society has moved to a new stage of evolution that they call "postindustrial" society (Bell, 1976). One important change in a postindustrial society is that the ownership of significant amounts of capital is no longer the only or even the most important source of profits and influence; knowledge as well as material capital brings profits and influence.

There are many problems with the thesis above, not the least of which is that wealthy capitalists can buy the experts and knowledge they need to keep their profits and influence. But this does not deny the importance of knowledge in an advanced industrial society, as the emergence of some new industries indicates. For example, genetic engineering has created many new firms and has made a few university scientists very rich. And everyone knows how the development of new computer technology has made some other scientists quite rich. In line with criticism of the postindustrial society thesis, however, it must also be recognized that those already in control of huge amounts of capital (i.e., major corporations) soon stepped in to take most profits in these industries based on new knowledge.

Moving down from the level of wealth and power, we still find knowledge increasingly important. For example, we have seen how our occupational structure is being pulled apart at the middle. Many new high-tech jobs are being created at the upper-middle-class level, but even more new jobs are being created in the low-skill, low-paying service industries. Something like a caste line is emerging cen-

tered around knowledge. Individuals who fall too far behind in the pursuit of knowledge at a young age will find it almost impossible to catch up later, no matter how hard they try. Illiteracy in the English language has been a severe handicap for many years in the United States, but we are also moving to the point when computer illiteracy will handicap many more people and condemn them to a life of low-skill and low-paid labor.

Central to these changes are education and science. This final chapter takes a look at these two institutions that have become so important only in the past few centuries in human history. We consider how these institutions developed, how they compare across societies today, their position in the overall society, and the problems faced by them.

EDUCATION

To a far greater degree than any other animal, humans must be taught how to survive. In fact, in a sense humans must learn how to be human. In the earliest years of life, most children learn how to be human from their parents. But after the first years of life, in most societies today the task of socialization is no longer assumed by parents alone. From the "master institution" of the family came other institutions with responsibility for socializing the young. To some extent socialization has been carried out in religious institutions, but in most societies today *educational institutions* are in charge of socialization after the first years of life. This does not mean that educational institutions are independently responsible for all socialization, for we have already noted other agents of socialization. Educational institutions, however, have most responsibility for passing on technical information in language, math, science, and to an extensive degree socialization in moral values and "citizenship" as well. But as we will see, educational institutions do much more, such as provide an important means of social control.

Education in Evolutionary Perspective

In hunting and gathering societies the technical means of survival, myths, values, and norms of the tribe are passed on to children in the course of day-to-day activities. Because the socialization process is carried out in day-to-day activities, childhood is not an extended social status as it is in modern societies. There is no need for a special childhood status during which the young are exempt from adult responsibilities while they learn to be functional members of society.

Once societies become more complex, however, separate educational institutions became necessary to pass on the more extensive, complex culture that has developed. In early horticultural societies only a few people received an education other than what could be provided by relatives. But as more people were freed from daily work as peasants and the culture accumulated more information in science, art, and religion, more and more people received at least some formal education.

Some of the earliest educational institutions emerged around 3000 B.C. in Egypt and Mesopotamia. At this time (and until quite recently) educational institutions were not yet independent of religion (Good and Teller, 1969; Meyer, 1965). In Egypt, for example, priests were in charge of teaching science, math, geometry, and writing, as well as religion. There were two types of schools in Egypt, one for general education and one for priests, though both were only for the children of elites. Much like today, children entered these schools around the age of five and continued their schooling until age 16 or 17. At the age of 13 or 14, these Egyptian children also began course work designed as practical training for the positions they were expected to hold as adults.

In east Asia, educational systems were emerging at about the same time in stable agricultural societies. China, for example, had schools that were more secular than European schools, though they still devoted much teaching to moral values. By 1000 B.C. China also had schools for the common people as well as elites, with written records showing that some peasants were able to attend school in the evenings after their work. As the Mandarin civil service became important in running China's massive state bureaucracy, competitive exams were established to select students for university training. At about the time of Christ, China had a major national university with 30,000 students.

The Western tradition of university education, however, was most influenced by the Greeks. Around 400 B.C. in Greece there was a university system open to all citizens (who had the time and money) under the influence of Socrates. At this time in the Roman Empire, in contrast, education was still the primary responsibility of the family, and especially the mother. However, by the second century B.C. the Romans had also seen the value in Greek educational institutions and extensively copied them. For the educated Roman it was even preferable by this time to be fluent in Greek. It should be added that the Romans did make some unique contributions to Western educational institutions such as professional schools in law.

After the Roman Empire, the general decline in Western educational institutions continued until around 800 A.D., when some political unity and support for education again developed in Charlemagne's Europe. But there is an important new element in Western education; the reemergence of educational institutions in Europe was dominated by the Catholic Church. Thus, to a much greater extent than before, the orientation of education became religious. It was not until the late 1600s, especially in Germany, that universities in particular regained a view that teaching religion was not the only major function of higher education.

Education in Industrial Societies. Writing about education during the late Middle Ages in Europe, Wells (1971, p. 718) states, "Their idea of education was the idea of capturing young clever people for the service of their betters. Beyond that they were disposed to regard education as a mischievous thing." This conservative function of education was to

Education socializes by transmitting knowledge from one person to another and from one generation to another. Telling stories is one means of sharing information; working with a keyboard is another. Compare the four photos. What do they tell us about education as a process? *(top left: © Lee/Anthro-Photo File; top right: © Culver Pictures, Inc.; bottom left: © Charles Harbutt/Archive Pictures Inc.; bottom right: © Cindy Reiman/Impact Visuals.)*

change with industrialization, but only to some degree.

With industrialization, a mass of uneducated peasants would be a drag on the nation's economy. There was need for technicians of many kinds, engineers, and scientists, to name just a few occupations that emerged with modern societies. Thus, as can be seen from Table 19.1, all industrial nations, whether capitalist or communist, have a high rate of their population finishing high school as well as college.

The increase in the percent of the population receiving formal education has produced extensive change in educational institutions around the world. What was once only education for elites became "mass education." This was a radical shift in the historical position of education in societies. In all these industrial nations the state has taken major responsibility for funding and operating the school

system — from the elementary level to higher education.

Details do vary, however, among these industrial nations. For example, some nations have much more centralized school systems, such as France and Japan (Taylor, 1983). It is said that the Minister of Education in France can look at the calendar and his watch, then tell you exactly what all third-grade children in the nation are doing at the moment. In contrast to this, other nations, such as the United States, have more decentralized school systems. The federal government, through the Department of Education, helps fund some educational programs and provides some guidance on educational matters, but primary control of education and most funding is the responsibility of state and local governments. In most communities in the United States the most heated political issues often involve education be-

TABLE 19.1. *Comparative high school enrollment and college completion rates*

Country	% High school age population enrolled in high school	% of population over 25 with at least some college attendance
Australia	71	4.7
Austria	76	2.6
Belgium	84	2.6
Canada	94	8.8
East Germany	86	8.5
France	88	2.7
Italy	67	2.6
Japan	96	5.5
Netherlands	81	1.3
Norway	90	6.6
Poland	60	5.4
Portugal	80	1.1
Soviet Union	80	4.2
Spain	76	3.7
United Kingdom	76	1.6
United States	86	21.1*
West Germany	70	4.3

* The U.S. figure is inflated by the extensive junior college system in the United States.
SOURCE: Adapted from Kurian (1979, Tables 275, 277). Figures are for the mid-1970s.

TABLE 19.2. *Per capita spending on education, by U.S. states, 1985*

State	Per capita education spending	State	Per capita education spending
Alabama	$ 428	Montana	$ 760
Alaska	1,380	New England	519
Arizona	488	Nevada	510
Arkansas	435	New Hampshire	467
California	577	New Jersey	733
Colorado	591	New Mexico	732
Connecticut	676	New York	739
Delaware	613	North Carolina	442
District of Columbia	612	North Dakota	583
Florida	484	Ohio	545
Georgia	499	Oklahoma	612
Hawaii	556	Oregon	640
Idaho	499	Pennsylvania	589
Illinois	522	Rhode Island	527
Indiana	625	South Carolina	520
Iowa	573	South Dakota	518
Kansas	628	Tennessee	425
Kentucky	472	Texas	696
Louisiana	496	Utah	618
Maine	554	Vermont	628
Maryland	604	Virginia	538
Massachusetts	584	Washington	643
Michigan	667	West Virginia	541
Minnesota	594	Wisconsin	616
Mississippi	395	Wyoming	1,196
Missouri	452		

SOURCE: U.S. Bureau of Census, (1986, p. 142).

cause of the importance of educational issues to parents, and because parents do have at least some influence in these issues.

Even in the United States, however, there are strong pressures to standardize curriculums around the nation. An industrial society requires competency in some basic subjects, and because of extensive geographical mobility there is pressure to keep each school system competitive with others in the nation. As Table 19.2 indicates, though, there are differences among states on educational funding. We cannot say that the rate of funding per student is a simple indicator of educational quality, but there is some relationship between funding levels and quality (Griffin and Alexander, 1978).

Another common aspect of educational institutions in industrial societies is the concern with equality of educational opportunities. When the goal of education is to train the most qualified people to fill the complex jobs, there must be at least some regard for educational opportunities for the very bright who happen to come from lower-class families. In this regard it is interesting that while the United States was introducing new programs to increase equality of educational opportunities for the poor and minorities in the 1960s and 1970s, much the same was happening in the Soviet Union (Matthews, 1978; Yanowitch, 1977). The Soviets have been concerned that working-class and rural children do not have sufficient opportunities for a good education, as indicated by data showing that the rate of college attendance in the Soviet Union is much higher among the middle and upper classes.

Expansion of Education in the United States. Soon after this nation became independent of British rule, Thomas Jefferson mounted a campaign to insure every child (male, free white children, that is) an opportunity for at least a few years of elementary education. However, he was successful only in establishing the nation's first clearly secular and state-run university, the University of Virginia. Two major groups were working against Jefferson's ideal: on the one hand, there was opposition against allowing government to become involved in education at all; on the other hand, there was pressure from religious organizations to maintain their control over education so as to continue exposing children to their religion. But by 1837, Massachusetts had become the first state to sponsor basic public education, and most other New England states soon followed.

The second important period of educational expansion in the United States occurred with high schools from 1870 to the early 1900s. It is no coincidence that this was also the period of rapid industrial growth in the United States, for as already noted, education and industrialization are tied together because an industrial economy requires a more educated population. The next stages of educational expansion occurred after World War II and during the 1960s. After World War II there was an increased demand for higher education in large measure because of the GI Bill, which provided the first extensive aid for education at the federal level. During the 1960s, the greater demand for higher education was related to the "baby boom" generation, which reached college age at this time while the high rate of college attendance from the previous period was maintained.

Table 19.3 indicates these historical trends de-

TABLE 19.3. *School attendance rate in the United States, 1850–1957*

Year	Enrollment rate of 5 to 19 age group		
	Total	White	Nonwhite
1957	87.8	88.2	85.3
1950	78.7	79.3	74.8
1940	74.8	75.6	68.4
1930	69.9	71.2	60.3
1920	64.3	65.7	53.5
1910	59.2	61.3	44.8
1900	50.5	53.6	31.1
1890	54.3	57.9	32.9
1880	57.8	62.0	33.8
1870	48.4	54.4	9.9
1860	50.6	59.6	1.9
1850	57.2	56.2	1.8

SOURCE: U.S. Department of Commerce (1960, p. 213).

scribed above. In 1850, 47.2 percent of the population from 5 to 19 years old were enrolled in school. By 1920 the figure had increased to 64.3 percent, and to 87.8 percent in 1957, where it has remained somewhat stable. The female population has not substantially differed from males on these historical figures, though the figures for nonwhites were very different at first. In 1850 only 1.8 percent of nonwhites in the 5-to-19 age group were enrolled in school. This changed significantly after 1890, but a difference of less than 5 percent between whites and nonwhites did not occur until 1950.

Two other important developments in education in the United States deserve mention. The first was the major push by the federal government to improve educational quality, especially in science, soon after the Soviet Union put the first satellite in orbit in the late 1950s. Then again there was a new push to improve educational quality in the 1980s, when the competitive position of the American economy was clearly in relative decline, and it was realized that the educational attainment of American students was worse than that of students in almost all other industrial nations.

Theoretical Perspectives on Education

In the case of educational institutions many questions need answers that both functional and conflict theory have tried to supply. For example, why did educational institutions become so important in industrial societies? One obvious answer has already been considered; with a more complex economy and culture, a more specialized institution to supply technical training was required. But as we will see, this answer, though not inaccurate, is far from complete.

The Functional View. The most important point from the functional perspective is that educational institutions are needed to pass on culture to the next generation as that culture becomes more complex and the family alone can no longer serve this socialization function. Educational institutions expanded greatly as the level of technology became more complex. This also suggests that educational institutions have an important economic function in industrial societies.

Recent research has supported this view. Walters and Rubinson (1983) examined historical data on educational expansion and economic output in the United States between 1890 and 1969. After controlling for the influence of several other factors affecting economic output, these sociologists concluded that educational expansion has, in fact, positively influenced economic expansion.

It is important to stress that education is even more important in other respects, and even the value of education for providing technical information required of workers is rather limited. For example, research shows that most people learn primarily on the job, even highly technical jobs, not in school (Rawlines and Ulman, 1974).

We may now ask, why do employers place so much emphasis on education when considering job applicants? It seems clear that level of education indicates to potential employers much more than the amount of technical information an individual may have absorbed; educational achievement shows that a person has (1) learned to obey rules in bureaucratic organizations, and (2) can stick to goals like achieving an educational degree. Jencks et al. (1979) notes that if a college education was most important to an employer for the technical information it gives to workers, we should find a steady increase in income and occupational status as we move from workers with less education to workers with more education. Such steady, progressive increase, however, is not the case. Attaining a four-year college degree, for example, provides much more income than only three years of college credits. Three years of college, on the other hand, provides only a small increase in income compared with attaining one or two years of college.

Functional theorists also stress that educational institutions in an industrial society provide an important means of upward mobility for the most talented and motivated people in that society. This function is especially important in a society like the United States, which places much emphasis on the value of equality of opportunity. We have already seen that the process of status attainment and social mobility depends on educational achievement, but we have also seen that education alone is less important in social mobility than most people believe.

The Conflict View. As you can guess by now, conflict theorists stress that educational institutions have an important place in the nature of group conflict in a society. In contrast to a means of social mobility, for example, we can also say that educational institutions provide a class maintenance function as well. In other words, in the conflict between classes over what their offspring will receive in their adult lives, higher-class parents are better able to use educational institutions to enhance the future of their offspring. Because of the importance of this aspect of education, we consider the subject in more detail in the next section.

In addition to individual competition for educational attainment, the upper classes have used education in another way to maintain their class positions. In the past, when college degrees were much more limited and the middle class typically had only high school degrees, middle-class occupations required a high school degree. But as more of the middle class obtained college degrees and more of the working class obtained high school degrees, the requirements for middle-class occupations were typically upgraded so that a college degree was necessary for employment. Thus, the class boundaries of middle-class occupations were maintained through an upgrading of educational requirements.

Collins (1971) provides information showing that the same process has occurred with working-class, upper-middle-class, and elite occupations. As might be expected, this historical process of educational upgrading of occupations has produced a reduction in the relative occupational and income returns for each year of education (Featherman and Hauser, 1978, p. 223; Jencks et al., 1979, p. 228). Whereas a college degree once brought an elite occupational position with elite pay, it now brings only a middle-class position with middle-class pay. From this conflict perspective, therefore, education is more a *certification* of class membership than of technical skills.

Another latent function of education that benefits the upper classes is selective mobility. Educational success often certifies that people have learned to respect authority and accept the values, ideals, and system of inequality in the occupational structure. This means that elite privilege will less likely be challenged by individuals who move into higher positions through success in education (Bowles and Gintis, 1976). As Collins (1971, p. 1011) puts it, "Educational requirements for employment can serve both to select new members for elite positions who share the elite culture and, at a lower level of education, to hire lower and middle-class employees who have acquired a general respect for these elite values and styles."

Educational institutions can also serve the interests of the upper classes by leading the lower classes to believe their own low positions are due to their failure to achieve more education. People blaming *themselves* for a low position are less likely to challenge elite privilege. In his detailed interviews with working class men, Lane (1962) found a common theme, "If I had gone to college . . . I would be higher up in this world." But this attitude has a face-saving side as well; "At least it is only the fault of an irresponsible youth, not a grown man" (Lane 1962, p. 71). As we will see in more detail, it is important to note that these people do not realize that they have many educational handicaps simply because they were brought up in lower class families and communities. Thus, it is less a matter of "an irresponsible youth" than they believe, but this belief leads them to more likely accept their low position.

It may be added that the junior college system in the United States, which is much more extensive than in other industrial societies, can also help maintain this self-blaming attitude. A high rate of junior college students are from working class families, and a high rate of these students drop out of junior college when they are unable to maintain acceptable grades. The junior college system does provide a last chance to move out of working class jobs for a few, but it also puts a final cap on the hopes and self-esteem for many others.

One should not get the idea that educational institutions are relevant only to the conflicts among economic classes. Many racial, ethnic, and religious groups in this country have been critical of the educational system for presenting "inaccurate and negative" views of their group. Studies of the material presented in textbooks have shown many of these claims of negative stereotyping to be accurate (Kane, 1970; Bowker, 1972). In one famous case in the 1970s there was extensive violence in Kanawha County, Kentucky, over the issue of "nonreligious" and "anti-American" views claimed to be presented in school textbooks (Billings and Goldman, 1983; Page and Clelland, 1978). The belief of many parents in this rural area of Kentucky was that liberal and antireligious textbook writers and New York City publishing companies were trying to instill values in their children they found unacceptable.

We conclude this examination of the conflict perspective by stressing that in contrast to the functional view, which sees educational institutions as working for societal advance and unity, conflict theorists see educational institutions as often associated with group conflicts. Because of the wide influence of what is taught in schools, conflicting interest groups would like to assure their views and interests are protected by getting educational institutions to teach the "correct ways of thinking."

Education and Social Mobility: Myth versus Reality

In the classical tradition of education passed on to us from the ancient Greek civilization, education is respected in and of itself; the pursuit of knowledge needed no justification. In the Middle Ages in Europe, and still in European nations to a greater extent than in the United States, the scholar is accorded great respect. The same can be said for feudal Japan, where two life-styles of honor were combined that seem very foreign to Americans. The tough samurai warrior was also expected to pursue art and literature, and the combined roles of samurai and poet especially brought great honor. In the United States, however, the "practical" individual is more likely to be respected than the scholar. Many people around the world would find the attitude expressed in the saying "If you're so smart, why aren't you rich" a confusing combination of ideas.

Education and Economic Returns. In the mass education of modern America, the attitude described above means that education requires some justification to most people; there must be a "practical" outcome of education. You are not expected to go to college just to learn; a college education is usually justified in terms of the income and job prospects that are expected to be forthcoming with the attainment of a college degree. This attitude is combined with the American value on achievement to make education an important factor in the quest for upward mobility.

The belief that education is a practical investment for future monetary returns is supported by the data. As shown in Table 19.4, on the average, high school graduates will earn less than college graduates, and individuals with advanced college degrees will attain even more income. The return for education becomes much greater when considered over a lifetime. A college education not only brings more money soon after graduation, but this is much

TABLE 19.4. *Average income by years of education, 1983*

Years of education	Average income
Less than 8 years	$12,791
8 years	15,697
9–11 years	18,091
12 years	24,436
College, 1–3 years	28,813
4 years of college	37,772
5 years or more	43,839

SOURCE: U.S. Bureau of Census (1985, p. 33).

more the case after a person has had experience in an occupation. These figures refer to average incomes within educational categories. Some careers requiring a college degree, and this is also to say that some major fields of study, will bring a greater income than others.

The common complaint that a college degree no longer guarantees a good job or a higher income is in part correct. As noted earlier, perhaps one hundred years ago, a college education would bring an elite job and elite income. But in recent years, with mass education and most of the middle class sending their sons and daughters to college, a college education brings only a middle-class job and a middle-class income. It must also be noted that a high school education alone no longer brings a middle-class job and income. Thus, although a college education may bring less relative economic returns than in the past, so does a high school education.

Limits in Equality of Educational Opportunities. Chapter 12 briefly considered education as a means of social mobility in industrial societies. At present we should be more specific about the ways education does and does not promote social mobility. Before we turn to this subject, however, a few words of review and emphasis are in order.

We have seen that education is an important means of attaining higher occupational positions. Nevertheless, there are certainly limits to equality of opportunity in education. As shown in Table 19.5,

TABLE 19.5. *College attendance of Wisconsin high school students by measured intelligence and class background*

Class background	Intelligence (%)			
	High	*Middle*	*Low*	*Total*
High	91.1	78.9	58.0	84.2
Middle	64.9	43.3	24.0	46.8
Low	40.1	22.9	9.3	20.8

SOURCE: Sewell and Shah (1968, p. 199).

data from one state (which can be generalized to the overall United States) indicates that more affluent but not so intelligent young people go to college more often than low-income young people who score quite high on IQ tests. (This Table, of course, does not indicate all of the rich but less intelligent young people finish college, but at least they are given a chance to make it in college.) We have seen earlier that about 50 percent of what influences educational achievement is related to family background — that is, ascriptive factors that are contrary to equality of opportunity (Jencks et al., 1979).

None of the above suggests that equality of educational opportunity cannot be increased, even though total equality of opportunity may be elusive. Some industrial societies do have more equality of opportunity in education than the United States. Japan's strict college entrance exams seem to promote more equal opportunities for a college education, and some programs to equalize educational opportunities have been successful in the United States. But before we consider these programs we must have a better understanding of the factors limiting equality of opportunity.

These limitations start with the early years of a child's life. Children from higher-class families are more likely to have a home environment that provides the intellectual skills they need to do well in school. Their toys and books give them an early advantage, and they are more likely to see their parents engaged in activities like reading and writing — thus, the image that these are valued skills. Because of all this, studies indicate, middle-class children are already ahead of lower-class children in intellectual ability before the first year of school. Intellectual capacity (as distinguished from educational achievement) is to some degree biologically inherited, but the best estimate is that only about 45 percent of IQ is biologically determined, and IQ is only weakly related to social class (Jencks et al., 1972, pp. 65, 81).

By the time children are in school the process of separating the "winners" from the "losers" in educational achievement becomes even clearer. An important factor in this process is teacher expectations; several studies have shown teachers expect more of children from higher-class backgrounds, and the differential treatment of children in terms of teacher expectations leads to better performance among these children (Rosenthal and Jacobson, 1968; Rist, 1970; Good and Brophy, 1973; Stein, 1971). There have been some negative reports on the importance of teacher expectations in children's performance (Claiborn, 1969), but the weight of evidence remains in favor of this argument.

Perhaps more important in separating the winners from the losers in the early years of schooling is the practice of **tracking.** It has been estimated that about 85 percent of the public schools place children in different tracks that prepare some for college and others for vocational skills that do not lead to college (Jencks et al., 1972, p. 33).

There have been numerous studies on both the factors that influence track placement and the outcomes of track placement. As for the factors that help determine track placement, it was commonly believed that track placement is directly influenced by the class background of children. But such a direct influence of class must be rejected as overly simple. Measured intellectual skills have been found to be most responsible for track placement (Heyns, 1974), although class background is also involved to some extent (Alexander, Cook and McDill, 1978, p. 65). But the effect of track placement, because cognitive skills and academic performance are influenced by class background, is the same; tracking tends to separate children by class background and race (McPortland, 1968).

Many outcomes of track placement have been

found; some studies indicate that children in the college preparatory, or higher, track improve in academic achievement over the years, whereas those in the lower track perform at lower levels (Rosenbaum, 1975; Persell, 1977). But children in the higher track are also less likely to drop out of school (Schafer and Olexa, 1971), have higher educational aspirations, and are more likely to attend college (Alexander, Cook, and McDill, 1978). In conclusion we can say that tracking reinforces class differences and has an independent effect on further differentiating children in terms of family background.

In large part, because of the advantages noted above, students from higher-class backgrounds are more likely to go to college. But this outcome is not simply because of greater educational success in precollege years. We saw in Chapter 12 that higher aspirations and more self-confidence help produce a higher rate of college attendance among students from higher-class backgrounds. Money, of course, is also important; even where tuition is low, however, there are many other living expenses required for college attendance, not to mention free time that is not taken up by the necessity to work full-time to obtain basic necessities.

A final question on the topic of equality of educational opportunities pertains to college completion. A good indicator of completing a four-year college is a student's college grade point average (GPA) (Stanfiel, 1973; Barger and Hall, 1965). Several studies, however, have found class background to be a very weak predictor of college GPA (Barger and Hall, 1965; Labovitz, 1975; Bayer, 1968). In fact, these studies have found high school GPA and college entrance exam scores to be about the only, though weak, predictors of college GPA, even when a number of psychological scales are included in the research (Hemelstein, 1965).

In contrast to its importance in earlier years, the reduced importance of class background in predicting college GPA and ultimate college completion is due to the rather homogeneous class background of college students (most are middle class). Whatever factors do produce higher college GPAs and college completion, the low effect of class background at this level seems to indicate that achievement is more important than ascription on the college level. And it

is perhaps at this higher level of education that class ascription is prevented from being higher than it otherwise would be.

Educational Opportunities in the Soviet Union. As in any industrial society, the educational system in the Soviet Union provides a link to both occupational mobility and inheritance (Jones, 1978, p. 522). But given ideological differences between the United States and the Soviet Union, we may be surprised to find that the process of educational attainment is quite similar in both nations. The evidence we have, however, indicates that this is precisely the case. There is much competition for higher education in the Soviet Union, but people from families higher in the class system have a strong advantage.

In the early school years we find some interesting similarities between the United States and the Soviet Union (Yanowitch, 1977, pp. 61–65). Almost all Soviet children receive an education to the eighth-grade level (about 90 percent), but then one of four directions is taken. Students can (1) continue high school in a (highest) college track, (2) move to the higher technical track (for four years of technical training), (3) move to a lower technical training track, or (4) leave school for employment.

As in the United States, track placement of Soviet children is influenced by family class background. The influence of family background is shown by several studies in different cities and regions of the Soviet Union. The general findings are that about 70 percent of children with higher-class origin are placed in the college track, whereas only 40 to 50 percent of the children with working-class origins are placed in the college track, and about 90 percent of the children in the lower-level technical track are from working-class origins (Yanowitch, 1977, p. 69). Track placement is influenced to some extent by grades, but the studies have found that higher-class students with low grades are more likely to get into a college track than lower-class children with high grades.

College track placement in high school does not ensure college attendance in the Soviet Union. College entrance depends on passing strict exams. As would be expected, those in the college track have the edge in these exams, no matter what their class background. But children from higher-class families have other advantages. They often attend better high schools and their parents can pay for extra tutoring (an extensive practice) so they can pass the college entrance exam.

Behind this educational attainment process is another factor found important in similar American studies — higher-class children in the Soviet Union have higher educational aspirations. Thus, as in the United States, there is a self-selection process leading higher-class students to strive for more education and to have greater confidence in their abilities to achieve higher education (Yanowitch, 1977, pp. 81–82). The result is that higher-class children in the Soviet Union are more likely to pass college entrance exams and go to college (Jones, 1978; Geiger, 1969; Matthews, 1972, pp. 284–297).

Although a higher proportion of working-class children go to college than in capitalist nations, almost all Soviet universities have only a minority of working-class students. Considered another way, although families with working-class or farm-labor status account for about 75 percent of the Soviet population, they account for only 30 percent of the college students.

This state of affairs is contrary to Soviet ideology, given its praise of the working class and the value of egalitarianism. And it is not a situation that has been ignored. Debate over the lack of educational opportunity and criticism of such things as tracking in the Soviet Union is strikingly similar to the same debates in the United States.

Under Nikita Khrushchev in the early 1960s, new educational reforms were instituted in an attempt to increase college attendance by working-class children, reforms that are again strikingly similar to many in the United States in recent years. These reforms included easing the entrance exam requirements for college attendance, requiring students to work for a time before entering college, and the development of special programs for working-class children to increase their academic abilities (Anweiler, 1972; Matthews, 1978). There is some evidence that many of these reforms were effective, but the charge that they were producing lower-quality education (Jones, 1978) resulted in their reduc-

tion when the liberal political climate shifted after Khrushchev's fall from power.

Programs to Improve Educational Opportunities in the United States. The Civil Rights Movement and efforts to reduce poverty in the United States in the 1960s brought efforts to increase educational opportunities as well. It was clear that poverty and racial inequality were associated with the lack of educational opportunities.

The controversial practice of *busing* discussed in Chapter 14 was one of the first programs aimed at increasing educational opportunities for minorities. In the mid-1960s important research indicated that integrated schools would raise the level of educational achievement among minority children (Coleman et al., 1966). However, some later research of the actual effects of busing indicated that the benefits to minority children were less than expected, and busing seemed to create another problem called "white flight" from the public schools (Coleman, 1975). A review of many other studies of the effects of busing, however, does show more positive results in educational achievement for minorities in integrated schools (Mahard and Crain, 1983), but social scientists continue to see negative effects of busing such as "white flight" and community conflict. The positive effects of integrated schools seem clear, but a way of increasing integrated schools that does not produce many negative side effects is difficult to find.

One of the more successful programs to promote equal educational opportunities is *Headstart.* Instituted in the late 1960s as part of President Johnson's War on Poverty, the Headstart program is designed to reduce the one-year gap in educational ability between poor children and middle-class children that exists before they even begin the first grade. Headstart is essentially a preschool program for poor children that provides many educational experiences these children would not otherwise have. Studies have shown that the Headstart program does in fact reduce the one-year gap in educational ability, but until recently it was believed that the gains made by Headstart children would be eliminated as they move to the higher grade levels (Etzioni, 1982). More recent research, however, has shown that people from poor families who attended Headstart programs as children, compared with people from poor families who did not attend, are less likely to be on welfare or in prison, and more likely to have achieved higher education and good jobs.

Other programs have been aimed at helping students from poor and minority families attend college. Many types of student loans have made it possible for poor students to attend college, and affirmative action programs have induced colleges to recruit more minority students. As mentioned above, however, one of the important problems keeping many poor and minority students away from college has involved self-image and few contacts with anyone who has ever attended college. To counter this barrier, programs like Upward Bound were established. In the Upward Bound program, high school students from poor families are given the opportunity to spend a few weeks on a college campus in the summer before they graduate from high school. The hope is that they will find college a less threatening place and increase their motivation to attend one.

Although all the programs described above have not been equally successful, minorities have made significant educational gains in the United States. The gap in SAT scores between blacks and whites has been reduced since the middle 1970s, and as shown in Table 19.6 the percentage of minorities

TABLE 19.6. *Percent of college students who are minorities, 1968–1982*

Year	% Blacks	% Other minorities
1968	6.0	3.5
1970	6.9	3.7
1972	8.3	4.0
1974	9.0	4.5
1976	10.5	5.8
1978	10.6	6.1
1980	10.4	6.6
1982	10.0	7.1

SOURCE: U.S. Bureau of Census (1986, p. 153).

attending college has increased substantially. Other figures for minorities, however, have not shown improvement, and in some cases have gotten worse. For example, the high school dropout rate has increased, as has the rate of illiteracy. With respect to education, the figures for blacks in particular correspond to the poor figures for income, occupational status, unemployment, and poverty seen in Chapter 14. There have been many improvements for middle-class blacks, whereas conditions have worsened for poor blacks.

Problems in the American Educational System

Although not all American Public schools are experiencing extensive problems and American universities are among the best in the world, it is clear that the American educational system as a whole has many problems. We can divide these problems into those that are primarily academic (even though they may have other causes) and those that are brought into the public schools from the wider society. In many ways this separation is artificial because the two types of problems are sometimes interrelated, as we will see. This creates many problems for teachers who try to provide a learning environment as well as for the students who are trying to learn. These problems, of course, are not randomly distributed among all public schools but rather are concentrated in the urban and especially inner-city schools, which contain the children who desperately need educational achievement to escape the problems they inherited at birth.

There is increasing awareness of the problems of academic achievement in American public schools, and some of these problems can be blamed on the school systems. However, with the problems confronting these schools by the larger society, it is surprising our schools are not in worse condition. Reforms of American schools can help reverse the decline in academic achievement, but substantial improvement will also require solutions to the social problems, prevalent in the wider society.

Declining Academic Achievement. Since 1984 considerable public attention has been focused on the decline in academic achievement in American schools. The concern was stimulated by a report issued by the National Commission on Excellence in Education (1983), which called this country a "nation at risk" because of the rising "tide of mediocrity" in educational achievement. Figures indicating this decline have been around for some time, but were brought to the attention of most people only with this well-publicized report.

Table 19.7 shows part of the problem indicated by declining SAT scores from exams taken by high school students seeking to enter college. There has been a steady decline in both math and verbal scores since the late 1960s, which have improved only slightly in the past couple of years.

The problem of low academic achievement can also be seen with international comparisons. Table 19.8 shows that among students from 18 nations, on a comprehensive math exam, American eighth-grade students scored below average (set at 50 percent), and they scored better than students from only four other nations (three of which are Third World countries). Perhaps even worse, in a comparison of the *top* 5 percent of 12th-grade students on math scores in each of 12 industrial nations, American students scored *last*.

The causes of low educational achievement in the United States are complex, yet there is much agree-

TABLE 19.8. *International comparison of math achievement test scores for eighth-grade students (%)*

Rank	Country	National average score, 1982*
1	Japan	62
2	Netherlands	57
3	Hungary	56
4	Belgium (Flemish)	53
5	France	53
6	Canada (British Columbia)	52
7	Hong Kong	50
8	Canada (Ontario)	49
9	Scotland	48
10	England and Wales	47
11	Finland	47
12	New Zealand	46
13	Israel	45
14	United States	45
15	Sweden	44
16	Thailand	42
17	Nigeria	34
18	Swaziland	31

* The average score for all students was set at 50 percent.
SOURCE: U.S. Dept. of Education (1986).

ment on the main causes. But several possible causes have received considerable attention.

The declining SAT scores since the 1960s have corresponded to the increase in poor and minority students attending colleges because of programs promoting equality of educational opportunity described above. This means that more students taking the SAT exams required to enter college are from backgrounds associated with lower educational achievement, thus, contributing to a decline in average SAT scores (Bruner, 1982). When we look at international comparisons, however, even the top achievers in the United States are below students in other industrial nations. Though the decline in overall test scores may be related in part to the slight increase in educational opportunities in America, this has not affected the students scoring highest, who are still behind other nations.

With the tax revolts raging against local govern-

TABLE 19.7. *Declining SAT scores, 1967–1984*

	Scholastic aptitude test	
	Verbal	**Math**
1967	466	492
1970	460	488
1975	434	472
1977	429	470
1978	429	468
1979	427	467
1980	424	466
1981	424	466
1982	426	467
1983	425	468
1984	426	471

SOURCE: U.S. Bureau of Census (1986, p. 147).

ments in the late 1970s, many people associated these tax revolts (like California's Proposition 13) with educational decline. But this argument must contend with data showing that spending on education in the United States per student is among the highest in the world, and substantially above what Japan pays for education. What must be considered is how this money is spent. Japan's teachers are by law among the highest paid professionals in the country, and Japanese schools attract some of the most talented college graduates as teachers (Vogel, 1979, p. 177). Japanese school systems save money by spending less on sports, buildings, and extra school personnel (students do much of the work janitors would have to do). In terms of actual academic quality, American schools seem to get much less for their money.

One of the most popular explanations for the decline in educational achievement, and the explanation with the best evidence, cites a decline in demands made on students by schools. In the 1960s and 1970s students were not required to take as many difficult courses, were required to do less homework, and were sometimes passed from grade to grade even when they could not fulfill course requirements (Dollar, 1983). The study of 17 nations described above found that even though American eighth-grade students took an average of 115 hours of math instruction a year and Japanese students took only 101 hours, the Japanese students took much more difficult math courses (Savage, 1986).

Because of findings like these, and as the National Commission on Excellence in Education recommended, the United States is experiencing a "back to basics" movement in the public schools. Schools are beginning to demand that students take more difficult courses, there are now more strict graduation requirements, there is more homework, and teachers are required to pass exams in basic subjects to keep their jobs. In this context, Japan is becoming an interesting model for education, not only because the Japanese usually score highest on international test comparisons, but also because they already do many of the things suggested by the back to basics movement. The Japanese educational system, therefore, is worth examining in some detail.

The Japanese Educational System: A Comparison. There was a new major political issue a few years ago in Japan that will surprise most Americans; in the summer of 1985 Japanese newspapers were filled with stories about a Japanese government report that described extensive problems in the traditional Japanese educational system. These problems involve such things as a lack of creativity among students and extreme pressure on children that was believed responsible for suicides and a problem they call "bullying." Many scholars have long recognized that Japan's universities are substandard, as we will see later, but this new report refers to a crisis in primary and secondary education. Moreover, there were recommendations that the Japanese study the positive aspects of the educational system in the United States!

The Japanese are aware of their high ranking on international test score comparisons, but they are also aware that the United States dominates the Nobel prizes, whereas Japan has won very few (see Figure 19.1). As one Japanese educator put it, "The Americans produce a lot of idiots, but also a large number of geniuses; the Japanese produce very few of either." Much of this problem is related to Japan's system of higher education, but it has roots in the earlier school years, and perhaps even the larger culture.

The Japanese school system is very good at teaching basic facts. Some people note this may be partially related to the Japanese need to learn two alphabets and about 3,000 Chinese *(kanji)* characters by high school if they are to read at grade level. They go to school long hours (they have very few holidays, no long summer vacation, and also attend school Saturday mornings) and they are given a lot of homework. Mothers, often called "education Moms," push their children very hard, commonly beginning in preschool. And all Japanese children in public schools are treated the same way; there are almost no special classes for slow or bright students, each child must wear the school uniform every day, and students are passed together from year to year, meaning very few students are sent back a grade (Taylor, 1983; Vogel, 1979). By the time these Japanese students finish the 12th grade they have learned an impressive amount of facts to prepare

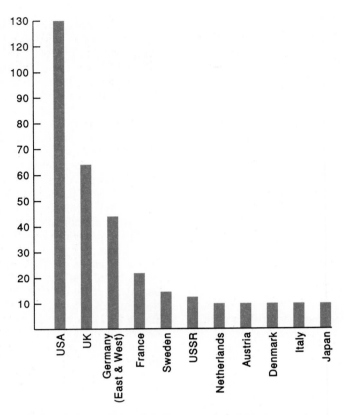

FIGURE 19.1. Number of Nobel Prize recipients in science by country, 1901–1983. *(Source: U.S. Bureau of Census, 1985.)*

them for one of the most important events in their life — the college entrance exams. Most important, though, they are seldom required to do much creative thinking up to that point, and if they are accepted by a university, they are required to do very little there as well.

We close this discussion with a brief description of Japanese universities. As noted above, Japanese students spend years cramming for the college entrance exams, and if they do not pass these exams the first year (the exams are given only once a year), many students almost drop out of the world for a year (sometimes two and three years) to study for these exams. By the time Japanese students get into college they have accumulated almost as much knowledge as American college graduates. Once in college, however, Japanese students are required to do very little compared with American students. They must pass exams for some basic college courses, eventually. Attendance at lectures is very low — much lower than on American college campuses. And the most important activities center around many clubs.

Japanese universities are also not stimulating places for research and expanding knowledge. Like the students, university faculty are led to conformity rather than independence and creativity. Young faculty members are careful not to criticize the ideas and work of senior professors, and most research and writing is supervised by senior professors (Nakane, 1970). Because of this environment, Japan's poor showing on Nobel prizes is no longer as surprising.

SCIENCE AND TECHNOLOGY

Despite the recent emergence of science, by the twentieth century it is clear that science and the new technology that science helped create are major forces in modern societies. Technology and changes in technology have, as already shown, shaped societies for thousands of years. In previous periods of history, however, the process of change stimulated by new technology was very gradual. The difference today is that with science an important institution in society, the process of change is more rapid and extensive because of the systematic effort at producing new technology that science makes possible.

So important is advanced technology, and the science that makes it possible, that international conflicts are often carried out in research laboratories. The United States is in competition with Japan to see which nation can build better consumer goods for export, because the nation that does so can have economic dominance. The same situation is found in military conflicts. It is no longer a simple matter of counting troops and guns on either side of a military conflict; it is now a question of comparative military technology as well. Battles among the advanced industrial nations can be fought by soldiers hundreds of miles apart, each pushing buttons to fire missiles or to counter the accuracy of the incoming enemy missile's guidance systems. In a recent book that describes what World War III might be like (*The Third World War,* by Sir John Hackett, 1978), the United States is assumed to defeat the Soviet Union because of superior military technology, even though American troops and arms are far outnumbered by the Soviets.

The dangers of science and technology, however, are not limited to nuclear war. During the early months of 1986 the dangers of new technology were shown most clearly, first with the dramatic and tragic explosion of the space shuttle Challenger, and then history's worst nuclear power plant accident at Chernobyl in the Soviet Union. A world population that had already become concerned about the future dangers of science and technology has become even more concerned.

The Nature of Science

Science, as we have seen in Chapter 2 is a method of discovery rather than a specific body of knowledge. And though technology is often uttered in the same breath with the word science, the two terms refer to different things. **Technology** is the application of knowledge, whether this involves tools and other material things or the application of knowledge alone in achieving some end. Science is now a major institution in modern societies because the role of scientist and the specific norms of science are now important aspects of the society.

Four primary norms underlie the foundation of modern science (Merton, 1942). The first is *universalism,* which means that scientific research and the findings from this research must always be evaluated in the same manner, using the same criteria. In other words, research findings should not be accepted or rejected because we dislike the person doing the research but should be accepted or rejected on the basis of objective, universal criteria.

A second major norm of science is *communalism,* which means that scientific knowledge is not the personal property of a particular person, even the person who created the knowledge. Einstein's theory of relativity was published and used by anyone in the scientific community to further advance knowledge of the universe. This norm often creates conflict among science, business, and what may be seen as national interests, because businesses would prefer to withhold scientific knowledge that they can turn into profits, and governments would like to control scientific knowledge related to defense. In the case of business-related technology, states have provided patents, or legal title, to profits resulting from the application of scientific knowledge, which means that under certain conditions the technology resulting from scientific knowledge can become private property.

Large research projects, like the one necessary to build the supercollider shown here, involve both the sharing of intellectual resources and intense competition, as countries vie to produce "bigger and better" versions. Do you think scientific research efforts require a different balance between cooperation and competition than other kinds of work? (© *Peter Menzel/ Stock, Boston.*)

The third norm involves *disinterestedness,* which means that scientists should put aside personal prejudices and personal interests in their role as seekers of knowledge. Put another way, scientists should not use research simply to advance themselves personally. If, for example, a scientist's research should prove that his or her theory is inaccurate, then the research should be so reported and not withheld.

Finally, the fourth norm involves *skepticism.* Scientists must always question facts and theories; they must keep an open mind toward their subject. It is most clearly at this point that political ideology and religion differ from science. The bumper sticker that reads "God said it, I believe it, so that settles it" provides an excellent counterpoint between unquestioned religious faith and this ideal of science.

The four norms guiding science just described are only ideals. They are often broken or interpreted broadly, and when strong egos are involved it is difficult for people to be completely objective when considering their own work or that of their friends (or enemies, for that matter). But the norms of science are at least to some extent internalized in the professional training of scientists, and scientific disciplines have formal procedures to provide checks on the objectivity and accuracy of research findings (such as anonymous reviews of research articles before publication).

Science, Technology, and Class Conflict

Science and advances in technology benefit humans in many ways. However, and this is a big however, some groups in society benefit more than others, and many groups are actually harmed by advances in science and technology.

The Dangers of New Technology. During 1984 more than 2,000 people were killed by a chemical leak at a Union Carbide plant in Bhopal, India. A year and a half later one of the worst fears of nuclear energy opponents came true for people in the town of Chernobyl, Soviet Union, when at least a partial meltdown of a nuclear reactor core filled the air with nuclear radiation. Several people died soon after this nuclear accident and thousands more Soviet citizens will likely experience early deaths owing to radiation exposure in the years ahead. As the result of another accident during research in a laboratory in a South American nation, "killer bees" are finding their way into the southern United States. Killer bees were

The partial meltdown at Chernoybl was a powerful reminder that nuclear energy is not risk-free. What effect, if any, do you think such disasters have on you? (© Gamma-Liaison.)

BOX 19.1

*Nuclear Power
Accidents: A History*

On April 26, 1986, what was most likely the worst nuclear power plant accident in history occurred at Chernobyl in the Soviet Union. (I say this was most likely the worst accident because there is evidence of another major accident in the Soviet Union in 1957 which we know very little about.) There were at first hysterical reports in American newspapers of as many as 2000 deaths on the first day of the accident in Chernobyl, with thousands more to follow. No one, it seems, believed the Soviet reports of only two deaths on the first day. It turns out that the Soviet reports were accurate, but there were over 20 more deaths by one month after the accident, and thousands of Soviet citizens were exposed to high levels of radioactive material which will cause many cancer deaths in the years to come. Millions of Europeans were also exposed to low levels of radiation as a cloud of radioactive material drifted over Northern Europe. Some of this radiation even showed up in the United States about one week later, though at levels which were not dangerous.

Nuclear power is in many ways symbolic of the dangerous new technology developed in advanced industrial societies. Nuclear power can be used to generate almost unlimited amounts of electrical energy, but the risk of a disastrous accident is always in the background. Because of the fear of a nuclear disaster in the United States, protest has all but stopped plans for building any new nuclear power plants, especially after the near disaster with a partial meltdown at the Three Mile Island plant at Middletown, Pennsylvania, in 1979.

By 1985 many nations have become dependent on nuclear power for a significant percentage of their electricity. The United States gets about 15 percent of its electricity from nuclear power, which is less than in many other nations. France gets about 65 percent of its electricity from nuclear power, while Belgium gets about 60 percent, Sweden 42 percent, Switzerland 40 percent, Finland 38 percent, West Germany 31 percent, Japan 25 percent, and England about 20 percent. With all of these nuclear power plants in operation there have been relatively few accidents. But critics note that only one accident could cause hundreds or thousands of deaths. While the Chernobyl accident has caused less than a hundred deaths so far, the number of deaths from this accident will go much higher in months after the accident, and it came close to being a far worse disaster.

In what follows is a partial list of other nuclear accidents around the world:

Dec. 2, 1952: At Chalk River near Ottawa, Canada, an employee error leads to 1 million gallons of radioactive water leaking inside an experimental nuclear reactor. It took six months to clean it up.

Oct. 7–10, 1957: At Windscale Pile, a plutonium production reactor north of

created during cross-breeding experiments in an attempt to produce a bee that could make more honey. But scientists instead produced a very aggressive type of bee that escaped the laboratory and began producing at a fast rate in the wild. There will likely be more deaths from these bees in this country then there have been in South America as these bees migrate northward.

The cases above represent only a few of the dangers and negative consequences of science and

Liverpool, England, a fire leads to the largest known accidental release of radioactive material. Government later attributes 39 cancer deaths to mishap.

1957: A nuclear accident, probably at a weapons facility, occurs in the Ural Mountains in the Soviet Union. Little information exists, but it is believed that hundreds of square miles had to be evacuated.

May 23, 1958: A second accident at Chalk River sparked by an overheated fuel rod leads to another long cleanup.

Jan. 3, 1961: A steam explosion at a military experimental reactor near Idaho Falls, Idaho, kills three servicemen.

Oct. 5, 1966: At the Enrico Fermi plant, an experimental breeder reactor near Detroit, part of fuel core melts. No injuries, but radiation levels are high inside the plant. Plant was closed in 1972.

Oct. 17, 1969: At a reactor in Saint-Laurent, France, fuel loading error leads to partial meltdown. No injuries and only small amount of radioactive material escapes.

Nov. 19, 1971: Over 50,000 gallons of radioactive waste water spills into the Mississippi River when the waste storage space at the Northern States Power Co.'s reactor in Monticello, Minn., overflows.

March 22, 1975: A worker using a candle to check for air leaks at the Brown's Ferry reactor in Decatur, Ala., causes a $150 million fire, which lowers cooling water to dangerous levels. No injuries or release of radioactivity.

March 28, 1979: Three Mile Island in Middletown, Pa., has a partial meltdown and some radioactivity is released into the atmosphere in what many consider the worst U.S. commercial nuclear accident. Reactor is still being decontaminated.

Aug. 7, 1979: The accidental release of enriched uranium at a top secret fuel plant near Erwin, Tenn., exposes about 1,000 people to above-normal doses of radiation.

Feb. 11, 1981: At least eight workers are exposed to radiation at Sequoyah I, a Tennessee Valley Authority power plant, when more than 100,000 gallons of radioactive coolant leaks into the containment building.

April 25, 1981: Workers are exposed to radioactive material at a nuclear plant in Tsuruga, Japan, during repairs.

Jan. 25, 1982: At the Ginna plant near Rochester, N.Y., a tube ruptures and a small amount of radioactive steam escapes into the atmosphere.

April 19, 1984: Sequoyah I has a second accident when superheated radioactive water erupts during maintenance procedure. No injuries.

June 9, 1985: Davis-Besse plant near Oak Harbor, Ohio, loses cooling water supplies due to human and equipment error. Problem is caught in time to prevent meltdown.

Source: Los Angeles Times, April 30, 1986.

new technology, and because there are many more cases, people are becoming quite cautious and worried. There is increasing pressure from citizen organizations, consumer groups, and local governments to require strict regulation of scientific research and the introduction of new technology. Especially worrisome to many is the potential danger from organisms created through genetic engineering that may escape into the environment.

The dangers and dysfunctions of science and

technology, however, are not new. With the rapid advance of technology there may be more dangers around, and vocal groups are drawing attention to the dangers, but the working class have long experienced such dangers. Exact estimates are usually hard to obtain, but in 1972 the secretary of health, education and welfare estimated that occupational diseases kill as many as 100,000 workers annually and newly disable at least 390,000. At about the same time, the secretary of labor in the United States estimated that accidents in the workplace annually account for about 14,200 deaths and 2.2 million temporarily or permanently disabling injuries (Mintz and Cohen, 1976, pp. 422–423). In 1985, 11,600 workers died from job-related illnesses or injuries, and another 2 million workers suffered disabling injuries (U.S. Bureau of Census, 1987, p. 410). The main threats are machines, haz-ardous chemicals, and unsafe environments in the workplace. Asbestos poisoning constitutes another danger.

Class conflict is partially behind the above examples of dangerous technology because it is workers and consumers who are more likely to suffer injury, and it will often require a loss in profits if changes are made to make the products and working environment less dangerous. The classic example of this emerged in a court case in which Ford Motor Company was sued by relatives of individuals killed when the fuel tank of a Ford Pinto exploded in a collision. During the trial, documents were presented showing that Ford had estimated it would lose more money by redesigning the car than from lawsuits claiming injuries, so the dangerous design was not altered (Coleman, 1985, p. 41). The conflict over injuries from products and an unsafe workplace are

Science, technology, and social progress create landscapes like this where the timelessness of agriculture occupies the same space as a very contemporary satellite dish. Understanding the changes that accompany these types of social activity is the ongoing goal of sociology. (© Ulrike Welsch/Photo Researchers Inc.)

focused on government where citizen groups try to pressure for more protection while corporations try to counter these pressures to preserve their profits and freedom to operate as they please.

Loss of Jobs. Class conflict can result from research and new technology that threatens jobs. A long history of this conflict extends back to the earliest days of industrialization. Some of the first workers threatened were English weavers in the textile industry when new weaving machines were introduced. The response from many of these workers was organized destruction of the new machines and the birth of this practice of destruction now commonly called "Luddism" (Rudé, 1964).

The threat to jobs from new technology has proceeded more rapidly than ever in recent decades. Computers are replacing office workers, automated bank tellers are replacing bank workers, farm machinery is replacing farm workers, robots are replacing auto workers, and the list goes on. The state has often entered the conflict on the side of corporations because the extensive research behind this new technology has often been financed by the federal government. In general, research funding comes primarily from foundations (such as the Rockefeller Foundation and Ford Foundation), corporations, and the federal government. In the case of funding from upper-class foundations and corporations, it is not difficult to understand that the research will more likely be directed to helping corporate profits at the expense of jobs. But in the third source of funding, from what we have seen in previous chapters, the best bet is that research funded by the federal government to develop new technology will also help corporate interests at the expense of workers because of the greater political influence of the upper classes.

We end, then, with a theme we have found throughout the history of human societies. People within a society have common interests and typically work together achieving these common interests. Social norms and institutions are among the means by which these common interests are maintained. But there is another side to humans and human societies that can be ignored only at the expense of creating a fantasy; behind human societies are group conflicts that, while sometimes hidden, are no less real.

CHAPTER SUMMARY

Key Terms

tracking, 520   technology, 527
science, 527

Content

In modern societies, education has become a distinct institution responsible for passing on an increasingly complex culture. Although educational institutions developed with early empires about 5,000 years ago (3000 B.C.), few people received a formal education until the emergence of industrial societies, when it then became necessary to have a more educated population. Before this time most people were simply taught at home what they needed to learn.

Educational programs grew slowly in the United States until the late 1800s, when secondary schools were established in an increasing number of states during the time of rapid economic growth. After World War II the G.I. Bill greatly expanded the university system in response to returning war veterans. The system expanded again in the 1960s when the "baby boom" generation reached college age.

The functional perspective regards education as a basic institution that provides socialization and technical training in modern societies. The conflict perspective, however, points out that education has an important part to play in the nature of group conflict in modern societies. For example, education is a means of social control because the dominant values of a society are learned and supported through education, thus supporting the status quo. Education also certifies to employers that a person can follow rules and accept the inequalities that will be found in the workplace.

Although the relative economic return from a college education has been reduced in recent decades, a college degree continues to bring more economic return than a high school diploma, especially throughout the working life of an individual. There has been an upgrading of the educational requirements for most jobs in this century, not so much because of increased technical requirements of the jobs, but because of educational expansion and class certification. When many of the working class began completing high school, the middle class jobs that once required only a high school degree began requiring a college degree.

Whereas there is more equality of educational opportunities in the United States than in preindustrial societies, there are still very significant limits to educational opportunities. We have reviewed a number of the factors working to reduce educational opportunities related to early childhood experiences, teacher expectations, tracking, and lower self-confidence among the lower classes. What may seem surprising to some people is that many of these same barriers to equal educational opportunities are found in the Soviet Union. Several programs in the United States have been designed to promote educational opportunities, such as Headstart, busing, and Upward Bound.

The educational system in the United States, because of the universal requirement to attend school, is a dumping ground for almost all the other social problems in the society, such as crime, violence, and racism. One problem receiving extensive attention is the declining achievement scores for American students, especially compared with the scores of other industrial nations.

Japanese students attain the highest scores on most tests that can be compared internationally, but surprisingly the Japanese are unhappy with their schools. Secondary education in Japan creates extensive pressures on students, which sometimes produces side effects like suicides but also leads to a focus on memorizing facts at the expense of critical thinking and creativity.

With industrial societies, science and technology have become a foundation for economic well-being. Science has developed as an institution with a unique set of norms that work toward objectivity and the free exchange of new ideas. But despite the ideals of science, we find group conflicts within science just as we find them in other areas of human societies.

In addition to the conflicting groups within the scientific community, science and technology are related to the wider group conflicts in society. Conflicts are especially centered around profits and the safety of new technology. Also, science and technology become involved in class conflicts when profitable new technology creates a less safe work environment and science is used to produce new technology that reduces jobs and workers' wages.

Bibliography

Abegglen, James C., and George Stalk, Jr. 1985. *Kaisha: The Japanese Corporation*. New York: Basic Books.

Abrahamson, Mark. 1973. "Functionalism and the Functional Theory of Stratification: An Empirical Assessment." *American Journal of Sociology* 78:1236–1246.

———. 1979. "A Functional Theory of Organizational Stratification." *Social Forces* 58:128–145.

Adorno, T. W., E. Frenkel-Brunswik, D. J. Levinson, and R. N. Sanford. 1950. *The Authoritarian Personality*. New York: Harper & Row.

Alba, Richard, and Gwen Moore. 1982. "Ethnicity in the American Elite." *American Sociological Review* 47:373–383.

Alexander, Karl, Martha Cook, and Edward McDill. 1978. "Curriculum Tracking and Educational Stratification: Some Further Evidence." *American Sociological Review* 43:47–66.

Allen, Michael. 1977. "Economic Interest Groups and the Corporate Elite Structure." *Social Science Quarterly* 58:597–615.

———. 1981. "Power and Privilege in the Large Corporation: Corporate Control and Managerial Compensation." *American Journal of Sociology* 86:1112–1123.

Allport, Gordon W. 1958. *The Nature of Prejudice*. New York: Doubleday.

Alves, Wayne, and Peter Rossi. 1978. "Who Should Get What?: Fairness Judgments of Distribution of Earnings." *American Journal of Sociology* 84:541–564.

Amory, Cleveland. 1960. *Who Killed Society?* New York: Harper & Row.

Anderson, Charles. 1974. *The Political Economy of Social Class*. Englewood Cliffs, N.J.: Prentice-Hall.

Andrews, Frank, and Stephen Withey. 1976. *Social Indicators of Well-Being*. New York: Plenum.

Antonio, Robert. 1979. "The Contradiction of Domination and Production in Bureaucracy: The Contribution of Organizational Efficiency to the Decline of the Roman Empire." *American Sociological Review* 44:895–912.

Anweiler, Oskar. 1972. "Educational Policy and Social Structure in the Soviet Union." Pp. 173–210 in Boris Meissner (ed.), *Social Change in the Soviet Union*. Notre Dame, Ind.: University of Notre Dame Press.

Appelbaum, Richard. 1978. "Marx's Theory of the Falling Rate of Profit: Towards a Dialectical Analysis of Structural Social Change." *American Sociological Review* 43:67–80.

Aptheker, Herbert. 1963. *American Negro Slave Revolts*. New York: International Publishers.

Ardrey, Robert. 1976. *The Hunting Hypothesis*. New York: Atheneum.

Aronowitz, Stanley. 1974. *False Promises: The Shaping of American Working Class Consciousness*. New York: McGraw-Hill.

Asch, Solomon E. 1952. *Social Psychology*. Englewood Cliffs, N.J.: Prentice-Hall.

Ash-Garner, Roberta. 1977. *Social Movements in America*. Chicago: Rand McNally.

Auletta, Ken. 1983. *The Under Class*. New York: Vintage.

Baker, Wayne E. 1984. "The Social Structure of a National Securities Market." *American Journal of Sociology* 89:775–811.

Baltzell, E. Digby. 1958. *Philadelphia Gentlemen: The Making of a National Upper Class*. New York: Free Press.

———. 1964. *The Protestant Establishment: Aristocracy and Caste in America*. New York: Random House.

Barger, Ben, and Everett Hall. 1965. "The Interaction of Ability Levels and Socioeconomic Variables in Prediction of College Dropouts and Grade Achievement." *Educational and Psychological Measurement* 25:501–508.

Barnes, Harry Elmer. 1948. *An Introduction to the History of Sociology*. Chicago: University of Chicago Press.

Barnet, Richard, and Ronald Muller. 1980. "The Global Shopping Center." Pp. 381–398 in Mark Green and Robert Massie (eds.), *The Big Business Reader: Essays in Corporate America*. New York: The Pilgrim Press.

Baron, James, and William Bielby. 1980. "Bringing the

Firms Back In: Stratification, Segmentation, and the Organization of Work." *American Sociological Review* 45:737–766.

Barrett, Richard, and Martin King Whyte. 1982. "Dependency Theory and Taiwan: Analysis of a Deviant Case." *American Journal of Sociology* 87:1064–1089.

Bayer, Alan. 1968. "The College Dropout: Factors Affecting Senior College Completion." *Sociology of Education* 41:305–316.

Beauvoir, Simone de. 1973. *The Coming of Age.* New York: Warner Communications.

Beck, E. M., Patrick Horan, and Charles Tolbert. 1978. "Stratification in a Dual Economy: A Structural Model of Earnings Determination." *American Sociological Review* 43:704–720.

Bell, Daniel. 1976. *The Coming of Post-Industrial Society.* New York: Basic Books.

Bell, Robert R. 1983. *Marriage and Family Interaction.* Homewood, Ill.: Dorsey Press.

Bell, Wendell, and Robert Robinson. 1980. "Cognitive Maps of Class and Racial Inequalities in England and the United States." *American Journal of Sociology* 86:320–349.

Bellah, Robert. 1970. *Beyond Belief.* New York: Harper & Row.

Beliaev, Edward, and Paul Butorin. 1982. "The Institutionalization of Soviet Sociology: Its Social and Political Context." *Social Forces* 61:418–435.

Bendix, Reinhard. 1960. *Max Weber: An Intellectual Portrait.* New York: Doubleday.

————. 1978. *Kings or People: Power and the Mandate to Rule.* Berkeley: University of California Press.

Benedict, Ruth. 1946. *The Chrysanthemum and the Sword.* Boston: Houghton Mifflin.

Berger, Peter, and Thomas Luckmann. 1966. *The Social Construction of Reality.* New York: Doubleday.

Berk, Richard. 1974. "A Gaming Approach to Crowd Behavior." *American Sociological Review* 39:355–373.

————, K. J. Lenihan, and Peter Rossi. 1980. "Crime and Poverty: Some Experimental Evidence from Ex-Offenders." *American Sociological Review* 45:766–786.

Berlant, S. L. 1975. *Profession and Monopoly.* Berkeley: University of California Press.

Berle, Adolf, and Gardiner Means. 1932. *The Modern Corporation and Private Property.* New York: Macmillan.

Berlin, Isaiah. 1963. *Karl Marx: His Life and Environment.* New York: Oxford University Press.

Beteille, Andre (ed.). 1969. *Social Inequality.* Baltimore: Penguin Books.

Betz, Michael. 1974. "Riots and Welfare: Are They Related?" *Social Problems* 21:345–355.

Billings, Dwight B., and Robert Goldman. 1983. "Religion and Class Consciousness in the Kanawha County School Textbook Controversy." Pp. 68–87 in Allen Batteau (ed.), *Appalachia and America.* Lexington: University of Kentucky Press.

Blair, John. 1976. *The Control of Oil.* New York: Vintage Books.

Blau, Judith, and Peter Blau. 1982. "The Cost of Inequality: Metropolitan Structure and Violent Crime." *American Sociological Review* 47:114–129.

Blau, Peter. 1964. *Exchange and Power in Social Life.* New York: Wiley.

————. 1977. "A Macrosociological Theory of Social Structure." *American Sociological Review* 83:26–54.

————, Carolyn Beeker, and Kevin M. Fitzpatrick. 1984. "Intersecting Social Affiliations and Intermarriage." *Social Forces* 62:585–606.

Blau, Peter, and Otis Dudley Duncan. 1967. *The American Occupational Structure.* New York: Wiley.

Bloch, Mark. 1961. *Feudal Society.* London: Routledge & Kegan Paul.

Bloom, Benjamin. 1985. *Developing Talent in Young People.* New York: Basic Books.

Bluestone, Barry, and Bennett Harrison. 1982. *The Deindustrialization of America.* New York: Basic Books.

Blumberg, Paul. 1980. *Inequality in an Age of Decline.* New York: Oxford University Press.

Blumer, Herbert. 1939. "Collective Behavior." Pp. 221–279 in Robert Park (ed.), *Principles of Sociology.* New York: Barnes and Noble.

Bolin, Robert, and Susan Bolton Bolin. 1980. "Sociobiology and Paradigms in Evolutionary Theory." *American Sociological Review* 45:154–159.

Booth, Alan, and John Edwards. 1976. "Crowding and Family Relations." *American Sociological Review* 41:308–321.

————, David Johnson, Lynn White. 1984. "Women, Outside Employment, and Marital Instability." *American Journal of Sociology* 90:567–583.

Bollen, Kenneth, and Scott Jones. 1982. "Political Instability and Foreign Direct Investment: The Motor Vehicle Industry, 1948–1965." *Social Forces* 60:1070–1088.

Bornschier, Volker, and Thank-Huyen Ballmer-Cao. 1979. "Income Inequality: A Cross-National Study of the Relationships Between MNC-Penetration, Dimensions of the Power Structure and Income Distribution." *American Sociological Review* 44:487–506.

Bornschier, Volker, Christopher Chase-Dunn, and Richard Rubinson. 1978. "Cross-National Evidence of the Effects of Foreign Investment and Aid on Economic Growth and Inequality: A Survey of Findings and a Reanalysis." *American Journal of Sociology* 84:651–683.

Bottomore, Thomas B. (ed.). 1973. *Karl Marx*. Englewood Cliffs, N.J.: Prentice-Hall.

Bouvier, Leon F., Henry Shryock, and Harry Henderson. 1977. "International Migration: Yesterday, Today, and Tomorrow." *Population Bulletin* 30:3–24.

Bowker, Lee. 1972. "Red and Black in Contemporary American History Texts: A Content Analysis." Pp. 101–109 in Howard Bahr, Bruce Chadwick, and Robert Day (eds.), *Native Americans Today: Sociological Perspectives*. New York: Harper & Row.

Bowles, Samuel. 1983. *Beyond the Wasteland: A Democratic Alternative to Economic Decline*. New York: Anchor.

———, and H. Gintis. 1976. *Schooling in Capitalist America: Educational Reform and the Contradictions of Economic Life*. New York: Basic Books.

Bradburn, N. M., and David Caplovitz. 1965. *Reports on Happiness*. Chicago: Aldine.

Brinton, Crane. 1965. *The Anatomy of Revolution*. New York: Random House.

Britannica World Data. 1985. Chicago: Encyclopedia Britannica.

Bronfenbrenner, Urie. 1970. *Two Worlds of Childhood*. New York: Russell Sage Foundation.

Broom, Leonard. 1965. *The Transformation of the American Negro*. New York: Harper & Row.

———, and Robert Cushing. 1977. "A Modest Test of an Immodest Theory: The Functional Theory of Stratification." *American Sociological Review* 42:157–169.

Brown, Dee. 1970. *Bury My Heart at Wounded Knee: An Indian History of the American West*. New York: Holt, Rinehart & Winston.

Brownstein, Ronald, and Nina Easton. 1983. *Reagan's Ruling Class*. New York: Pantheon.

Bruner, Jerome. 1982. "Schooling Children in a Nasty Climate." *Psychology Today* (Jan.):57–63.

Brunt, P. A. 1971. *Social Conflicts in the Roman Republic*. London: Chatto and Windus.

Bryant, Clifton D., and C. Eddie Palmer. 1975. "Massage Parlors and 'Hand Whores': Some Sociological Observations." *The Journal of Sex Research* 11:227–241.

Burch, Philip. 1980. *Elites in American History. Vol. III: The New Deal to the Carter Administration*. New York: Holmes and Meier.

Burgess, Ernest W. 1925. "The Growth of the City." Pp. 47–62 in Robert E. Park and Ernest W. Burgess (eds.), *The City*. Chicago: University of Chicago Press.

Burnham, James. 1941. *The Managerial Revolution*. New York: Day.

Burrage, Michael, and David Corry. 1981. "At Sixes and Sevens: Occupational Status in the City of London From the Fourteenth to the Seventeenth Century." *American Sociological Review* 46:375–393.

Cameron, P. 1975. "Mood as an Indicant of Happiness: Age, Sex, Social Class, and Situational Differences." *Journal of Gerontology* 30:216–224.

Caplan, Nathan. 1985. "Southeast Asian Refugees: Achieving Independence in America." *Institute for Social Research Newsletter* (Spring/Summer):4–7.

Carcopino, Jerome. 1973. *Daily Life in Ancient Rome*. New Haven: Yale University Press.

Carnahan, Douglas, Walter Grove, and Omer Galle. 1974. "Urbanization, Population Density, and Overcrowding." *Social Forces* 53:62–72.

Chagnon, N. A. 1983. *Yanomamo: The Fierce People*. New York: Holt, Rinehart & Winston.

Chase, Ivan. 1975. "A Comparison of Men's and Women's Intergenerational Mobility in the United States." *American Sociological Review* 40:483–505.

Chase-Dunn, Christopher. 1975. "The Effects of International Economic Dependence on Development and Inequality: A Cross-National Study." *American Sociological Review* 40:720–738.

Childe, V. Gordon. 1936. *What Happened in History*. Baltimore: Penguin.

———. 1951. "The Urban Revolution." *Town Planning Review* 21:3–17.

———. 1952. *New Light on the Most Ancient East*. London: Routledge & Kegan Paul.

Chirot, Daniel. 1977. *Social Change in the Twentieth Century*. New York: Harcourt Brace Jovanovich.

———. 1986. *Social Change in the Modern Era*. New York: Harcourt Brace Jovanovich.

Choldin, Harvey M. 1978. "Urban Neighborhoods and Environment." *American Journal of Sociology* 84:457–563.

———. 1985. *Cities and Suburbs: An Introduction to Urban Sociology*. New York: McGraw-Hill.

Christopher, Robert C. 1983. *The Japanese Mind: The Goliath Explained*. New York: Simon & Schuster.

Claiborn, W. L. 1969. "Expectancy Effects in the Classroom: A Failure to Replicate." *Journal of Educational Psychology* 60:377–383.

Clark, Kenneth. 1969. *Civilization*. New York: Harper & Row.

Clark, Ronald. 1971. *Einstein: The Life and Times*. New York: Times Mirror World Publishing.

Clubb, Oliver. 1985. *KAL Flight 007: The Hidden Story.* New York: Permanent.

Coe, Richard. 1978. "Dependency and Poverty in the Short and Long Run." In G. J. Duncan and J. N. Morgan (eds.), *Five Thousand American Families— Patterns of Economic Progress.* Ann Arbor: Institute for Social Research.

Cohen, Jere. 1980. "Rational Capitalism in Renaissance Italy." *American Journal of Sociology* 85:1340–1355.

———, Lawrence Hazelrigg, and Whitney Pope. 1975. "De-Parsonizing Weber." *American Sociological Review* 40:229–241.

Cohen, Mark. 1977. *The Food Crisis in Prehistory: Overpopulation and the Origins of Agriculture.* New Haven: Yale University Press.

Cole, Robert. 1979. *Work, Mobility, and Participation: A Comparative Study of American and Japanese Industry.* Berkeley: University of California Press.

Coleman, James W. 1985. *The Criminal Elite: The Sociology of White-Collar Crime.* New York: St. Martin's Press.

Coleman, James S., Ernest Q. Campbell, Carol J. Hobson, James McPartland, Alexander M. Mood, Frederic D. Weinfeld, and Robert L. York. 1966. *Equality of Educational Opportunity.* Washington, D.C.: U.S. Government Printing Office.

Coleman, James S., Sara D. Kelly, and John A. Moore. 1975. *Trends in School Segregation, 1968–73.* Washington: The Urban Institute.

Collins, Randall. 1971. "Functional and Conflict Theories of Educational Stratification." *American Journal of Sociology* 85:1337–1339.

———. 1979. *The Credential Society.* New York: Academic Press.

———. 1981. "On the Microfoundations of Macrosociology." *American Journal of Sociology* 86:984–1015.

Collins, Robert. 1977. "Positive Business Responses to the New Deal: the Roots of the Committee for Economic Development, 1933–1942." *Business History Review* 22:103–119.

Colvin, Mark, and John Pauly. 1983. "A Critique of Criminology: Toward an Integrated Structural-Marxist Theory of Delinquency Production." *American Journal of Sociology* 89:513–551.

Comstock, George, Steven Chaffee, Natan Katzman, Maxwell McCombs, and Donald Roberts. 1978. *Television and Human Behavior.* New York: Columbia University Press.

Condry, John, and Sandra Condry. 1976. "Sex Differences: A Study of the Eye of the Beholder." *Child Development* 47:812–819.

Cooley, Charles Horton. 1902/1922. *Human Nature and the Social Order.* New York: Scribner's.

Coser, Lewis. 1956. *The Functions of Social Conflict.* New York: Free Press.

———. 1967. *Continuities in the Study of Social Conflict.* New York: Free Press.

Coser, Rose Laub, and Lewis Coser. 1979. "Jonestown as a Perverse Utopia." *Dissent* 158–163.

Couch, Carl J. 1968. "Collective Behavior: An Examination of Some Stereotypes." *Social Problems* 15:310–322.

Crandall, Richard. 1980. *Gerontology: A Behavioral Science Approach.* Reading, Mass.: Addison-Wesley.

Crankshaw, Edward. 1976. *The Shadow of the Winter Palace: Russia's Drift to Revolution, 1825–1917.* New York: Viking Press.

Cummings, Scott, and Del Taebel. 1978. "The Economic Socialization of Children: A Neo-Marxist Analysis." *Social Problems* 26:198–210.

Curtin, Philip D. 1969. *The Atlantic Slave Trade: A Census.* Madison, Wis.: University of Wisconsin Press.

Curtiss, Susan. 1977. *Genie.* New York: Academic Press.

Dahl, Robert. 1961. *Who Governs?* New Haven: Yale University Press.

———. 1982. *Dilemmas of Pluralist Democracy: Autonomy vs. Control.* New Haven, Conn.: Yale University Press.

Dahrendorf, Ralf. 1959. *Class and Conflict in Industrial Society.* Stanford, Calif.: Stanford University Press.

———. 1969. *Essays in the Theory of Society.* Stanford, Calif.: Stanford University Press.

Dallin, Alexander. 1985. *Black Box: KAL 007 and the Superpowers.* Berkeley: University of California Press.

Davies, James. 1962. "Toward a Theory of Revolution." *American Sociological Review* 34:248–249.

Davis, Kingsley. 1949. *Human Society.* New York: Macmillan.

———, and Wilbert Moore. 1945. "Some Principles of Stratification." *American Sociological Review* 10:242–249.

deGramont, Sanche. 1969. *The French: Portrait of a People.* New York: Putnam.

Della Fave, L. Richard. 1974a. "The Culture of Poverty Revisited: A Strategy for Research." *Social Problems* 21:609–621.

———. 1974b. "Success Values: Are They Universal or Class-Differentiated?" *American Journal of Sociology* 80:153–169.

———. 1980. "The Meek Shall Not Inherit the Earth: Self-Evaluation and the Legitimacy of Stratification." *American Sociological Review* 59:62–84.

———, and George Hillery. 1980. "Status Inequality in a Religious Community: The Case of a Trappist Monastery." *Social Forces* 59:62–84.

Denzin, Norman K. 1975. *Childhood Socialization.* San Francisco: Jossey-Bass.

de Tocqueville, Alexis. 1955. *The Old Regime and the French Revolution.* New York: Doubleday.

———. 1969. *Democracy in America.* New York: Doubleday.

Devine, Joel. 1985. "State and State Expenditure: Determinants of Social Investment and Social Consumption Spending in the Post War United States." *American Sociological Review* 50:150–165.

DiMaggio, Paul. 1982. "Cultural Capital and School Success: The Impact of Status Culture Participation on Grades of U.S. High School Students." *American Sociological Review* 47:189–201.

Dobson, Christopher. 1974. *Black September: Its Short, Violent History.* New York: Macmillan.

Doi, Takeo. 1981. *The Anatomy of Dependence.* Tokyo: Kodansha International.

Dollar, Bruce. 1983. "What is Really Going on in Schools." *Social Policy* 14:7–19.

Dollard, John, et al. 1939. *Frustration and Aggression.* New Haven: Yale University Press.

Domhoff, G. William. 1970. *The Higher Circles.* New York: Random House.

———. 1974. *The Bohemian Grove and Other Retreats.* New York: Harper.

———. 1978. *Who Really Rules? New Haven and Community Power Reexamined.* Santa Monica, Calif.: Goodyear.

———. 1979. *The Powers That Be.* New York: Vintage Press.

———. 1983. *Who Rules America Now?* Englewood Cliffs, N.J.: Prentice-Hall.

Dowd, James J. 1975. "Aging as Exchange: A Preface to Theory." *The Journal of Gerontology* 30:103–121.

Drucker, Peter. 1984. "Why America's Got So Many Jobs." *Wall Street Journal* (Jan. 24):32.

Dumont, Louis. 1970. *Homo Hierarchieus: The Caste System and Its Implications.* Chicago: University of Chicago Press.

Duncan-Jones, Richard. 1974. *The Economy of the Roman Empire.* Cambridge, Mass.: Cambridge University Press.

Durkheim, Emile. 1951. *Suicide.* New York: Free Press.

———. (1915.) *The Elementary Forms of the Religious Life.* Glencoe, Ill.: Free Press, 1954.

———. (1897.) *Suicide.* New York: Free Press, 1966.

Dye, Thomas R. 1978. "Oligarchic Tendencies in National Policy-Making: The Role of the Private Policy-Planning Organizations." *Journal of Politics* 40:309–331.

———. 1979. *Who's Running America?* Englewood Cliffs, N.J.: Prentice-Hall.

———. 1983. *Who's Running America? The Reagan Years.* Englewood Cliffs, N.J.: Prentice-Hall.

Eckstein, Alexander. 1977. *China's Economic Revolution.* London: Cambridge University Press.

Edwards, I. E. S. 1976. *Treasures of Tutankhamun.* New York: Ballantine.

Edwards, Richard. 1979. *Contested Terrain: The Transformation of the Workplace in the Twentieth Century.* New York: Basic Books.

Elkin, Frederick, and Gerald Handel. 1978. *The Child and Society: The Process of Socialization,* 3d ed. New York: Random House.

Ellis, Dean. 1967. "Speech and Social Status in America." *Social Forces* 45:431–437.

Ellis, Godfrey, Gary Lee, and Larry Peterson. 1978. "Supervision and Conformity: A Cross-Cultural Analysis of Parental Socialization Values." *American Journal of Sociology* 84:386–403.

Epstein, Samuel. 1980. "The Asbestos 'Pentagon Papers.'" Pp. 154–166 in Mark Green and Robert Massie (eds.), *The Big Business Reader: Essays on Corporate America.* New York: The Pilgrim Press.

Erikson, Kai T. 1976. *Everything in Its Path.* New York: Simon & Schuster.

———. 1966. *Wayward Puritans: A Study in the Sociology of Deviance.* New York: Wiley.

Etheridge, Carolyn F. 1978. "Equality in the Family: Comparative Analysis and Theoretical Model." *International Journal of Women's Studies* 1:50–63.

Etzioni, Amitai. 1982. "Education for Mutuality and Civility." *Futurist* 16:4–7.

———. 1984. *An Immodest Agenda: Rebuilding America Before the 21st Century.* New York: McGraw-Hill.

Evans, Peter B. and Michael Timberlake. 1980. "Dependence, Inequality, and the Growth of the Tertiary: A Comparative Analysis of Less Developed Countries." *American Sociological Review* 45:531–552.

Evanson, Elizabeth. 1981. "The Dynamics of Poverty." *Focus* 5:9–11, 19–20.

Farnsworth, Elizabeth, Richard Feinberg, and Eric Leenson. 1976. "The Invisible Blockade: The United States Reacts." Pp. 338–373 in Arturo Valenzuela and J. Samuel Valenzuela (eds.), *Chile: Politics and Society.* New Brunswick, N.J.: Transaction Books.

Feagin, Joe R. 1975. *Subordinating the Poor.* Englewood Cliffs, N.J.: Prentice-Hall.

Featherman, David, and Robert Hauser. 1978. *Opportunity and Change.* New York: Academic Press.

Fendrich, James. 1977. "Keeping the Faith or Pursuing the Good Life: A Study of the Consequences of Participation in the Civil Rights Movement." *American Sociological Review* 42:144–157.

Festinger, Leon, H. W. Riecken, and S. Schachter. 1956. *When Prophecy Fails.* Minneapolis: University of Minnesota Press.

Fila, Robert. 1983. "Inequality and the Service Sector in Less Developed Countries: A Reanalysis and Respecification." *American Sociological Review* 48:421–428.

Fischer, Claude S. 1976. *The Urban Experience.* New York: Harcourt Brace Jovanovich.

Fischer, David H. 1977. *Growing Old in America.* New York: Oxford University Press.

Flacks, Richard. 1971. *Youth and Social Change.* Chicago: Rand McNally.

Focus. 1984. "Poverty in the United States: Where Do We Stand Now?" 7:1–13, University of Wisconsin, Institute for Research on Poverty.

Fogel, Robert William, and Stanley L. Engerman. 1974. *Time on the Cross: The Economics of American Negro Slavery.* Boston: Little, Brown.

Footnotes. 1980. "Sociology in China: Its Restoration and Future Role." 8 (Oct.):4.

Foreign Press Center/Japan. 1985. *Facts and Figures of Japan.* Tokyo: Foreign Press Center.

Fox, Thomas, and S. M. Miller. 1965. "Economic, Political, and Social Determinants of Mobility: An International Cross-Sectional Analysis." *Acta Sociologica* 9:73–91.

Francher, Scott J. 1973. "It's the Pepsi Generation: Accelerated Aging and the Television Commercial." *International Journal of Aging and Human Development* 4:134–143.

Fraser, Ann. 1974.

Freeman, Derek. 1983. *Margaret Mead and Samoa: The Making and Unmaking of an Anthropological Myth.* Cambridge: Harvard University Press.

Freitag, Peter. 1975. "The Cabinet and Big Business: A Study of Interlocks." *Social Problems* 23:137–152.

———. 1983. "The Myth of Corporate Capture: Regulatory Commissions in the United States." *Social Problems* 30:480–491.

Freud, Sigmund. 1927. *The Future of an Illusion.* Garden City, N.Y.: Doubleday.

———. 1930. *Civilization and Its Discontents,* trans. James Strachey. New York: W. W. Norton.

Fried, Morton. 1973. "On the Evolution of Social Stratification and the State." Pp. 15–25 in John C. Leggett (ed.), *Taking State Power: The Sources and Consequences of Political Challenge.* New York: Harper & Row.

Friedman, Milton, and Rose Friedman. 1980. *Free to Choose.* New York: Avon Books.

Fukutake, Tadashi. 1981. *Japanese Society Today.* Tokyo: University of Tokyo Press.

Galbraith, John Kenneth. 1969. *The New Industrial State.* New York: Signet.

———. 1977. *The Age of Uncertainty.* Boston: Houghton-Mifflin.

Gamson, William. 1975. *The Strategy of Social Protest.* Homewood, Ill.: Dorsey Press.

Gans, Herbert J. (ed.). 1968. *People and Plans: Essays on Urban Problems and Solutions.* New York: Basic Books.

Gardner, R. Allen, and Beatrice Gardner. 1969. "Teaching Sign Language to a Chimpanzee." *Science* 165:664–672.

Garfinkel, Harold. 1956. "Conditions of Successful Degradation Ceremonies." *American Journal of Sociology* 61:420–424.

Garraty, John. 1978. *Unemployment in History: Economic Thought and Public Policy.* New York: Harper & Row.

Geiger, H. Kent. 1969. "Social Class Differences in Family Life in the USSR." Pp. 284–295 in Celia S. Heller (ed.), *Structured Social Inequality.* New York: Macmillan.

Genovese, Eugene D. 1974. *Roll, Jordan, Roll: The World the Slaves Made.* New York: Pantheon Books.

George, Vic, and Roger Lawson (eds.). 1980. *Poverty and Inequality in Common Market Countries.* London: Routledge & Kegan Paul.

Gerson, Menachem. 1978. *Family, Women, and Socialization in the Kibbutz.* Lexington, Mass.: D. C. Heath.

Gerth, Hans, and C. Wright Mills. 1946. *From Max Weber: Essays in Sociology.* New York: Oxford University Press.

Geyer, Georgie Anne. 1985. "Our Disintegrating World: The Menace of Global Anarchy." Pp. 10–27 in *Britannica Book of the Year.* Chicago: Encyclopedia Britannica.

Gibbs, Jack, and Maynard Erickson. 1976. "Crime Rates of American Cities in an Ecological Context." *American Journal of Sociology* 82:605–620.

Giddens, Anthony. 1973. *The Class Structure of the Advanced Societies.* New York: Harper.

————. 1978. *Emile Durkheim*. New York: Penguin Books.

Giele, Janet Zollinger. 1977. "Introduction: Comparative Perspectives on Women." Pp. 1–33 in Janet Zollinger Giele and Audrey Chapman Smock (eds.), *Women: Roles and Status in Eight Countries*. New York: Wiley.

Gilder, George. 1981. *Wealth and Poverty*. New York: Basic Books.

Gillis, A. R. 1974. "Population Density and Social Pathology: The Case of Building Type, Social Allowance and Juvenile Delinquency." *Social Forces* 53:306–314.

Gitlin, Todd. 1979. "Prime Time Ideology: The Hegemonic Process in Television Entertainment." *Social Problems* 26:251–268.

Glenn, Norval, Andreain Ross, and Judy Corder Tully. 1974. "Patterns of Intergenerational Mobility of Females Through Marriage." *American Sociological Review* 39:683–699.

Goffman, Erving. 1959. *The Presentation of Self in Everyday Life*. Garden City, N.Y.: Doubleday.

————. 1961. *Asylums*. Garden City, N.Y.: Doubleday.

————. 1963a. *Behavior in Public Places*. New York: Free Press.

————. 1963b. *Stigma: Notes on the Management of Spoiled Identity*. Englewood Cliffs, N.J.: Prentice-Hall.

————. 1967. *Interaction Ritual: Essays on Face-to-Face Behavior*. Garden City, N.Y.: Doubleday.

————. 1971. *Relations in Public*. New York: Basic Books.

Goldberg, P. 1975. "The Politics of the Allende Overthrow in Chile." *Political Science Quarterly* 90:93–116.

Goldman, Eric F. 1953. *Rendezvous with Destiny*. New York: Alfred Knopf.

Goldscheider, Calvin. 1971. *Population, Modernization, and Social Structure*. Boston: Little, Brown.

Goldstone, Jack. 1980. "The Weakness of Organization: A New Look at Gamson's 'The Strategy of Social Protest.'" *American Journal of Sociology* 85:1017–1042.

Good, Harry G., and James D. Teller. 1969. *A History of Western Education*. New York: Oxford University Press.

Good T., and J. Brophy. 1973. *Looking in Class-Rooms*. New York: Harper & Row.

Goodall, Jane van Lawick. 1971. *In the Shadow of Man*. Boston: Houghton Mifflin.

Goode, William J. 1963. *The Family*. Englewood Cliffs, N.J.: Prentice-Hall.

Gordon, Milton. 1947. "The Concept of the Sub-Culture and Its Application." *Social Forces* 26:38–49.

————. 1964. *Assimilation in American Life*. New York: Oxford University Press.

Gouldner, Alvin. 1973. *For Sociology: Renewal and Critique in Sociology Today*. New York: Basic Books.

————, and Richard A. Peterson, 1962. *Notes on Technology and the Moral Order*. Indianapolis: Bobbs-Merrill.

Gove, Walter R., Michael Hughes, and Omer R. Galle. 1979. "Overcrowding in the Home: An Empirical Investigation of Its Possible Consequences." *American Sociological Review* 44:59–80.

Griffin, Larry, and Karl Alexander. 1978. "Schooling and Socioeconomic Attainments: High School and College Influences." *American Journal of Sociology* 84:319–347.

Grusky, David. 1983. "Industrialization and the Status Attainment Process: The Thesis of Industrialism Reconsidered." *American Sociological Review* 48:494–506.

————, and Robert Hauser. 1984. "Comparative Social Mobility Revisited: Models of Convergence and Divergence in 16 Countries." *American Sociological Review* 49:19–38.

Guppy, Neil, and John C. Goyder. 1984. "Consensus on Occupational Prestige: A Reassessment of the Evidence." *Social Forces* 62:709–726.

Gurr, Ted. 1968. "Psychological Factors in Civil Strife." *World Politics* 20:245–278.

————. 1969. "A Comparative Study of Civil Strife." Pp. 204–235 in H. Graham and Ted Gurr (eds.), *Violence in America*. New York: Signet Books.

————. 1970. *Why Men Rebel*. Princeton: Princeton University Press.

Hagan, John and Patricia Parker. 1985. "White Collar Crime and Punishment." *American Sociological Review* 50:302–316.

Hagopian, Mark. 1974. *The Phenomenon of Revolution*. New York: Dodd-Mead.

Hall, Edward T. 1959. *The Silent Language*. New York: Doubleday.

Halliday, John. 1975. *A Political History of Japanese Capitalism*. New York: Monthly Review Press.

Hamblin, Dora Jane. 1973. *The First Cities*. New York: Time-Life Books.

Harms, L. S. 1961. "Listener Judgments of Status Cues in Speech." *Quarterly Journal of Speech* 47:164–168.

Harrington, Michael. 1976. *The Twilight of Capitalism*. New York: Simon & Schuster.

———. 1977. *The Vast Majority: A Journey to the World's Poor.* New York: Touchstone Book.

Harris, Chauncey D., and Edward L. Ullman. 1945. "The Nature of Cities." *The Annals of the American Academy of Political and Social Science* 242:7–17.

Harris, David. 1977. "Alternative Pathways Toward Agriculture." Pp. 231–248 in Charles Reed (ed.), *Origins of Agriculture.* The Hague, Netherlands: Mouton.

Harris, Diana K., and William E. Cole. 1980. *Sociology of Aging.* Boston: Houghton Mifflin.

Harris, Marvin. 1980. *Cultural Materialism: The Struggle for a Science of Culture.* New York: Random House.

Hartjen, Clayton. 1974. *Crime and Criminalization.* New York: Praeger.

Haskell, Martin, and Lewis Yablonsky. 1974. *Criminology: Crime and Criminality.* Chicago: Rand McNally.

Havinghurst, Robert. 1978. "Indian Education Since 1960." *The Annals* 436:13–26.

Hawley, Amos H. 1981. *Urban Society.* New York: Wiley.

Hazelrigg, Lawrence, and Maurice Garnier. 1976. "Occupational Mobility in Industrial Societies: A Comparative Analysis of Differential Access to Occupational Ranks in Seventeen Countries." *American Sociological Review* 41:498–510.

Hechter, Michael, and William Brustein. 1980. "Regional Modes of Production and Patterns of State Formation in Western Europe." *American Journal of Sociology* 85:1061–1094.

Heise, David Gerhard Lenski, and John Wardwell. 1976. "Further Notes on Technology and the Moral Order." *Social Forces* 55:316–337.

Heller, Celia (ed.). 1969. *Structured Social Inequality.* New York: Macmillan.

Heller, Robert, and Norris Willatt. 1975. *The European Revenge.* New York: Charles Scribner's.

Hertzberg, Daniel. 1984. "Citicorp Leads Field in its Size and Power—And in its Arrogance." *Wall Street Journal.*

Hess, Beth B. 1980. "Stereotypes of the Aged." Pp. 126–133 in Jill S. Quadagno (ed.), *Aging, the Individual and Society.* New York: St. Martin's.

Hewitt, Christopher. 1977. "The Effect of Political Democracy and Social Democracy on Equality in Industrial Societies: A Cross-National Comparison." *American Sociological Review* 42:450–463.

Hewitt, John P., and Peter M. Hall. 1973. "Social Problems, Problematic Solutions, and Quasi-Theories." *American Sociological Review* 38:367–374.

Heyns, B. 1974. "Social Selection and Stratification Within Schools." *American Journal of Sociology* 79:1434–1451.

Higgins, Paul C., and Richard R. Butler. 1982. *Understanding Deviance.* New York: McGraw-Hill.

Hill, Martha. 1981. "Some Dynamic Aspects of Poverty." In M. Hill, D. Hill and J. N. Morgan (eds.), *Five Thousand American Families—Patterns of Economic Progress,* vol. 9. Ann Arbor: Institute for Social Research.

Himelstein, Philip. 1965. "Validities and Intercorrelations of MMPI Subscales Predictive of College Achievement." *Educational and Psychological Measurement* 25:1125–1128.

Hirschi, Travis. 1969. *Causes of Delinquency.* Berkeley: University of California Press.

Hobbs, Charles D. 1978. *The Welfare Industry.* Washington, D.C.: The Heritage Foundation.

Hodge, Robert, Paul Siegel, and Peter Rossi. 1964. "Occupational Prestige in the United States." *American Journal of Sociology* 70:286–302.

Hodge, Robert, Paul Siegel, and Peter Rossi. 1966. "Occupational Prestige in the United States, 1925–1963." Pp. 322–334 in R. Bendix and S. M. Lipset (eds.), *Class, Status, and Power.* New York: Free Press.

Hodge, Robert, Donald Treiman, and Peter Rossi. 1966. "A Comparative Study of Occupational Prestige." Pp. 309–321 in R. Bendix and S. M. Lipset (eds.), *Class, Status, and Power.* New York: Free Press.

Hoffer, Eric. 1966. *The True Believer.* New York: Harper & Row.

Hofstader, Richard. 1955. *The Age of Reform: From Bryan to FDR.* New York: Knopf.

Holmes, T. H., and R. H. Rahe. 1967. "The Social Readjustment Rating Scale." *Journal of Psychosomatic Research* 11:213–218.

Homans, George C. 1950. *The Human Group.* New York: Harcourt Brace Jovanovich.

Hong, L. K. 1978. "Risky Shift and Cautious Shift: Some Direct Evidence on the Culture-Value Theory." *Social Psychology Quarterly* 41:342–346.

Hope, Keith. 1982. "Vertical and Nonvertical Mobility in Three Countries." *American Sociological Review* 47:99–113.

Horan, Patrick. 1978. "Is Status Attainment Research Atheoretical?" *American Sociological Review* 43:534–541.

Horowitz, Irving Louis. 1967. *The Rise and Fall of Project Camelot.* Cambridge, Mass.: MIT Press.

Howe, Irving. 1976. *World of Fathers: The Journey of the East European Jews to America and the Life They Found and Made.* New York: Harcourt Brace Jovanovich.

Hoyt, Homer. 1939. *The Structure of Residential Neigh-*

borhoods in American Cities. Washington, D.C.: Federal Housing Administration.

Hraba, Joseph. 1979. *American Ethnicity.* Itasca, Ill.: Peacock.

Huber, Bettina J. 1984. "Career Possibilities for Sociology Graduates." *ASA Footnotes* (Dec.):6–7.

Hughes, Everett C. 1962. "Good People and Dirty Work." *Social Problems* 10:3–11.

Hunter, Floyd. 1953. *Community Power Structure: A Study of Decision Makers.* Chapel Hill: University of North Carolina.

Hurst, John. 1983. "High Prison Rate Doesn't Curb Crime, Study Finds." *Los Angeles Times* (Dec. 26):3.

Hutter, Mark. 1981. *The Changing Family: Comparative Perspectives.* New York: Wiley.

Huttman, Elizabeth. 1979. *Introduction to Social Policy.* New York: McGraw-Hill.

Ingham, John. 1978. *The Iron Barons.* Chicago: University of Chicago Press.

Inverarity, James. 1976. "Populism and Lynching in Louisiana, 1889–1896." *American Sociological Review* 41:262–280.

Isaac, Larry, and William Kelly. 1981. "Racial Insurgency, the State, and Welfare Expansion: Local and National Level Evidence from the Postwar United States." *American Journal of Sociology* 86:1348–1386.

Isaak, Robert. 1980. *European Politics: Political Economy and Policy Making in Western Democracies.* New York: St. Martins.

Jackman, Robert. 1974. "Political Democracy and Social Equality: A Comparative Analysis." *American Sociological Review* 39:29–45.

Jacobs, David. 1979. "Inequality and Police Strength: Conflict Theory and Coercive Control in Metropolitan Areas." *American Sociological Review* 44:913–924.

Jacobs, Jerry. 1983. "Industrial Sector and Career Mobility Reconsidered." *American Sociological Review* 48:415–421.

Jameson, Sam. 1984. "Mid-Career Joblessness New Japanese Concern." *Los Angeles Times* (Oct. 22):1.

Janis, Irving L. 1972. *Victims of Groupthink.* Boston: Houghton Mifflin.

Jencks, Christopher, et al. 1972. *Inequality: A Reassessment of the Effect of Family and Schooling in America.* New York: Harper.

———. 1979. *Who Gets Ahead? The Determinants of Economic Success in America.* New York: Basic Books.

Jenkins, J. Craig. 1981. "On the Neofunctionalist Theory of Inequality: A Comment on Cullen and Novick." *American Journal of Sociology* 87:177–180.

———, and Charles Perrow. 1977. "Insurgency of the Powerless: Farm Worker Movements." *American Sociological Review* 42:249–268.

Jennings, Edward T. 1983. "Racial Insurgency, the State, and Welfare Expansion: A Critical Comment and Reanalysis." *American Journal of Sociology* 88:1220–1236.

Jensen, Gary. 1972. "Parents, Peers, and Delinquency Action: A Test of the Different Association Perspective." *American Journal of Sociology* 78:562–575.

Jerison, H. J. 1973. *Evolution of the Brain and Intelligence.* New York: Academic Press.

Jewell, 1952.

Jones, T. Anthony. 1978. "Modernization and Education in the USSR." *Social Forces* 57:522–548.

Jorgensen, Stephen R. 1986. *Marriage and the Family: Development and Change.* New York: Macmillan.

Kahn, Alfred, and Sheila Kamerman. 1978. *Not for the Poor Alone: European Social Services.* New York: Harper Colophon.

Kalleberg, Arne, and Larry Griffin. 1980. "Class, Occupation, and Inequality in Job Rewards." *American Journal of Sociology* 85:731–768.

Kane, Michael. 1970. *Minorities in Textbooks.* Chicago: Quadrangle.

Kanter, Rosabeth Moss. 1972. *Commitment and Community.* Cambridge, Mass.: Harvard University Press.

Kasarda, John D., and Morris Janowitz. 1974. "Community Attachment in Mass Society." *American Sociological Review* 39:328–339.

Keddie, Nikki R. 1981. *Roots of Revolution: An Interpretive History of Modern Iran.* New Haven: Yale University Press.

Keller, Suanne, and M. Zavalloni. 1964. "Ambition and Social Class: A Respecification." *Social Forces* 43:58–70.

Kelly, Jonathan, and Harbert S. Klein. 1977. "Revolution and the Rebirth of Inequality: A Theory of Stratification in Postrevolutionary Society." *American Journal of Sociology* 83:78–99.

Kelly, William, and David Snyder. 1980. "Racial Violence and Socioeconomic Changes Among Blacks in the United States." *Social Forces* 58:739–760.

Kentor, Jeffrey. 1981. "Structural Determinants of Peripheral Urbanization: The Effects of International Dependence." *American Sociological Review* 46:201–211.

Kerbo, Harold R. 1978. "Foreign Involvement in the Pre-conditions for Political Violence: The World System and the Case of Chile." *Journal of Conflict Resolution* 22:363–392.

———. 1981. "College Achievement Among Native Americans: A Research Note." *Social Forces* 59:1275–1280.

———. 1982. "Movements of 'Crisis' and Movements of 'Affluence': A Critique of Deprivation and Resource Mobilization Theories." *Journal of Conflict Resolution* 26:645–663.

———. 1983. *Social Stratification and Inequality: Class and Class Conflict in the United States.* New York: McGraw-Hill.

———, and L. Richard Della Fave. 1983. "Corporate Linkage and Control of the Corporate Economy: New Evidence and a Reinterpretation." *Sociological Quarterly* 24:201–218.

———, and L. Richard Della Fave. 1984. "Further Notes on the Evolution of Corporate Control and Institutional Investors: A Response to Niemonen." *Sociological Quarterly* 25:279–283.

———, and Richard A. Shaffer. 1984. "Political Environment and Protest: The Response of the U.S. Unemployed, 1890–1940." Paper presented at the Annual Meeting of the American Sociological Association, Detroit (Aug.).

———, and Richard A. Shaffer. 1986. "Unemployment and Protest in the United States, 1890–1940: A Methodological Critique and Research Note." *Social Forces* 64:1046–1056.

Kerckhoff, Alan. 1976. "The Status Attainment Process: Socialization or Allocation?" *Social Forces* 55:368–381.

———, and Kurt W. Back. 1968. *The June Bug: A Study of Hysterical Contagion.* New York: Appleton-Century-Crofts.

Kitano, Harry. 1976. *Japanese Americans.* Englewood Cliffs, N.J.: Prentice-Hall.

Kluegel, James, Royce Singleton, and Charles Starnes. 1977. "Subjective Class Identification: A Multiple Indicator Approach." *American Sociological Review* 42:599–611.

Knoke, David. 1981. "Commitment and Detachment in Voluntary Associations." *American Sociological Review* 46:141–158.

———, and Michael Hout. 1974. "Social and Demographic Factors in American Political Party Affiliations." *American Sociological Review* 39:700–713.

Kohlberg, Lawrence. 1980. *The Philosophy of Moral Development: Moral Stages and the Idea of Justice.* San Francisco: Harper & Row.

Kohn, Melvin. 1969. *Class and Conformity.* Homewood, Ill.: Dorsey Press.

———. 1976. "Occupational Structure and Alienation." *American Journal of Sociology* 82:111–130.

Krohn, Marvin D., and James L. Massey. 1980. "Social Control and Delinquent Behavior: An Examination of the Social Bond." *Sociological Quarterly* 21:529–543.

Kurian, George Thomas. 1979. *The Book of World Rankings.* New York: Plume/Times Mirror.

Labovitz, Eugene. 1975. "Race, SES Contexts and Fulfillment of College Aspirations." *Sociological Quarterly* 16:241–249.

Laffer, Arthur, and Jan P. Seymour. 1979. *The Economics of the Tax Revolt.* New York: Harcourt Brace Jovanovich.

Lane, Robert. 1962. *Political Ideology.* New York: Free Press.

Larson, M. S. 1977. *The Rise of Professionalism.* Berkeley: University of California Press.

Larson, R. 1978. "Thirty Years of Research on the Subjective Well-Being of Older Americans." *Journal of Gerontology* 33:109–125.

Larve, Gerald A. 1975. *Ancient Myth and Modern Man.* Englewood Cliffs, N.J.: Prentice-Hall.

Lasson, 1971.

Leakey, Richard, and Roger Lewin. 1977. *Origins.* New York: Dutton.

———. 1978. *The People of the Lake.* New York: Doubleday.

Leavitt, Gregory. 1977. "The Frequency of Warfare: An Evolutionary Perspective." *Sociological Inquiry* 14:251–265.

Leavy, Marvin. 1974. "Commentary." *American Journal of Sociology* 80:723–727.

LeBon, Gustave. 1960. *The Crowd: A Study of the Popular Mind,* 2d ed. Dunwoody, Ga.: Norman S. Berg (1897).

Leggett, John C., Deborah Vidi DeJames, Joe Somma, and Tom Menendez. 1978. *Allende, His Exit, and Our 'Times.'* New Brunswick, N.J.: New Brunswick Cooperative Press.

Le Masters, E. E. 1975. *Blue-Collar Aristocrats: Life-Styles at a Working-Class Tavern.* Madison, Wisc.: University of Wisconsin Press.

Lemert, Edwin M. 1972. *Human Deviance, Social Problems, and Social Control.* Englewood Cliffs, N.J.: Prentice-Hall.

Lenski, Gerhard. 1966. *Power and Privilege.* New York: McGraw-Hill.

———. 1976. "History, and Social Change." *American Journal of Sociology* 82:549–564.

————. 1978. "Marxist Experiments in Destratification: An Appraisal." *Social Forces* 57:364–383.

————, and Jean Lenski. 1982. *Human Societies,* 4th ed. New York: McGraw-Hill.

Le Roy Ladurie, Emmanuel. 1978. *Montaillou: The Promised Land of Error.* New York: George Braziller.

Letelier, Isabel, and Michael Moffitt. 1980. "How American Banks Keep the Chilean Junta Going." Pp. 399–412 in Mark Green and Robert Massie (eds.), *The Big Business Reader: Essays on Corporate America.* New York: The Pilgrim Press.

Lewis, Oscar. 1959. *Five Families: Mexican Case Studies in the Culture of Poverty.* New York: Basic Books.

————. 1966. *La Vida: A Puerto Rican Family in the Culture of Poverty.* New York: Random House.

Lewis-Beck, Michael. 1979. "Some Economic Effects of Revolution: Models, Measurement, and Cuban Evidence." *American Journal of Sociology* 84:1127–1149.

Liker, Jeffrey, and Glenn Elder. 1983. "Economic Hardship and Marital Relations in the 1930's." *American Sociological Review* 48:343–359.

Lin, Nan, Walter M. Ensel, and John C. Vaughn. 1981. "Social Resources and Strength of Ties: Structural Factors in Occupational Status Attainment." *American Sociological Review* 46:393–405.

Linton, Ralph. 1936. *The Study of Man.* New York: Appleton-Century.

Lipset, Seymour Martin, and William Schneider. 1983. *The Confidence Gap: Business, Labor, and Government in the Public Mind.* New York: Free Press.

Lipsky, Michael. 1980. *Street-Level Bureaucracy: Dilemmas of the Individual in Public Services.* New York: Russell Sage.

Lofland, Lyn. 1973. *A World of Strangers: Order and Action in Urban Public Space.* New York: Basic Books.

Lofland, John, and Rodney Stark. 1965. "Becoming a World-Saver: A Theory of Conversion to a Deviant Perspective." *American Sociological Review* 30:865–875.

Logan, John. 1976. "Industrialization and the Stratification of Cities in Suburban Regions." *American Journal of Sociology* 82:333–348.

————. 1978. "Growth, Politics, and the Stratification of Places." *American Journal of Sociology* 84:404–416.

Lombroso, Cesare. 1968. *Crime: Its Causes and Remedies,* trans. Henry P. Horton. Montclair, N.J.: Patterson Smith (1911).

Lord, George, and William Falk. 1980. "An Exploratory Analysis of Individualist Versus Structuralist Explanations of Income." *Social Forces* 59:376–391.

Lukes, Steven. 1973. *Emile Durkheim: His Life and Work: A Historical and Critical Study.* New York: Penguin Books.

MacDougall, A. Kent. 1984. "Progress Is Harbinger of Inequality." *Los Angeles Times* (Nov. 15):1.

————. 1984. "Rich-Poor Gap in U.S. Widens During Decade." *Los Angeles Times* (Oct. 25):1.

MacMullen, Ramsay. 1974. *Roman Social Relations.* New Haven: Yale University Press.

McAdam, Doug. 1983. "Tactical Innovation and the Pace of Insurgency." *American Sociological Review* 48:735–754.

McCarthy, John D., and Mayer N. Zald. 1977. "Resource Mobilization and Social Movements: A Partial Theory." *American Journal of Sociology* 82:1212–1241.

McGee, Reece. 1975. *Points of Departure.* Hinsdale, Ill.: Dryden Press.

McLaughlin, Steven. 1978. "Occupational Sex Identification and the Assessment of Male and Female Earnings Inequality." *American Sociological Review* 43:909–921.

McLellan, David. 1973. *Karl Marx: His Life and Thought.* New York: Harper & Row.

McPortland, J. 1968. *The Segregated Students in Desegregated Schools: Sources of Influence on Negro Secondary Students.* Baltimore, Md.: Johns Hopkins University Press.

McQuillan, Kevin. 1984. "Modes of Production and Demographic Patterns in Nineteenth Century France." *American Journal of Sociology* 89:1324–1346.

Mahard, Rita E., and Robert L. Crain. 1983. "Research on Minority Achievement in Desegregated Schools." Pp. 132–161 in Christine H. Rossell and Willis D. Hawley (eds.), *The Consequences of School Desegregation.* Philadelphia: Temple University Press.

Malinowski, Bronislaw. (1922.) *Argonauts of the Western Pacific.* New York: E. P. Dutton (1961).

————. 1925. *Magic, Science and Religion.* New York: Free Press.

Mann, David. 1981. "Age and Differential Predictability of Delinquent Behavior." *Social Forces* 60:97–113.

Marcuse, Herbert. 1971. "Industrialization and Capitalism." Pp. 133–150 in Otto Stammer (ed.), *Max Weber and Sociology Today.* New York: Free Press.

Mare, Robert. 1981. "Change and Stability in Educational Stratification." *American Sociological Review* 46:72–87.

Marger, Martin N. 1985. *Race and Ethnic Relations: American and Global Perspectives.* Belmont, Calif.: Wadsworth.

Mariolis, Peter. 1975. "Interlocking Directorates and the Control of Corporations: The Theory of Bank Control." *Social Science Quarterly* 56:425–439.

Marwell, Gerald, and Ruth Ames. 1979. "Experiments on the Provision of Public Goods: Resources, Interest, Group Size, and the Free-Rider Problem." *American Journal of Sociology* 84:1335–1361.

Marx, Gary T. 1974. "Thoughts on a Neglected Category of Social Movement Participant: The Agent Provocateur and the Informant." *American Journal of Sociology* 80:402–442.

Marx, Karl. 1906. *Capital: A Critique of Political Economy*. New York: Random House.

———. 1964. *Karl Marx: Early Writings,* ed. T. B. Bottomore. New York: McGraw-Hill.

———. 1971. *The Grundrisse,* ed. David McLellan. New York: Harper Torchbooks.

———, and Friedrich Engels. 1965. *The German Ideology*. New York: International Publishers.

Matthews, Mervyn. 1978. *Privilege in the Soviet Union: A Study of Elite Life-Styles Under Communism*. London: George Allen & Unwin.

Matras, Judah. 1984. *Social Inequality, Stratification, and Mobility*. Englewood Cliffs, N.J.: Prentice-Hall.

Matza, David. 1969. *Becoming Deviant*. Englewood Cliffs, N.J.: Prentice-Hall.

Mauss, Armand L., and Donald W. Petersen. 1973. "The Cross and the Commune: An Interpretation of the Jesus People." Pp. 150–170 in Robert Evans (ed.), *Social Movements: A Reader and Source Book*. Chicago: Rand McNally.

Mayer, A. J., and T. F. Hoult. 1955. "Social Stratification and Combat Survival." *Social Forces* 34:155–159.

Mayhew, Bruce. 1980. "Structuralism Versus Individualism: Part II, Ideological and Other Obfuscations." *Social Forces* 59:627–648.

Maxim, Paul S. 1985. "Cohort Size and Juvenile Delinquency: A Test of the Easterlin Hypothesis." *Social Forces* 65:661–681.

Mead, George Herbert. 1935. *Mind, Self and Society*. Chicago: University of Chicago Press.

Mead, Margaret. 1928. *Coming of Age in Samoa*. New York: William Morrow.

Meddin, Jay. 1979. "Chimpanzees, Symbols, and the Reflective Self." *Social Psychology Quarterly* 42:99–109.

Melton, J. Gordon. 1979. *Encyclopedia of American Religions*. Wilmington, N.C.: McGrath.

Merton, Robert K. 1957. *Social Theory and Social Structure*. New York: Free Press.

———. 1968. *Social Theory and Social Structure,* enlarged ed. New York: Free Press.

Meyer, Adolph E. 1965. *An Educational History of the Western World*. New York: Wiley.

Milgram, Stanley. 1970. "The Small-World Problem." Pp. 29–36 in James McConnel, *Readings in Social Psychology Today*. Del Mar, Calif.: CRM Books.

———. 1973. *Obedience to Authority: An Experimental View*. New York: Harper & Row.

———. 1974. *Obedience to Authority*. New York: Harper Colophon.

Miliband, Ralph. 1969. *The State in Capitalist Society*. New York: Basic Books.

Miller, Abraham, Louis Bolce, and Mark Halligan. 1977. "The J-Curve Theory and the Black Urban Riots: An Empirical Test of Progressive Relative Deprivation Theory." *American Political Science Review* 71:964–982.

Miller, David L. 1985. *Introduction to Collective Behavior*. Belmont, Calif.: Wadsworth.

Miller, Dorothy. 1977. "Evolution of the Primate Chromosomes." *Science* 198:1116–1124.

Miller, S. M. 1960. "Comparative Social Mobility." *Current Sociology* 9:81–89.

———, and Donald Tomaskovic-Devey. 1983. *Recapitalizing America: Alternatives to the Corporate Distortion of National Policy*. London: Routledge & Kegan Paul.

Miller, Walter B. 1958. "Lower Class Culture as a Generating Milieu of Gang Delinquency." *Journal of Social Issues* 14:5–19.

———. 1971. "Is the Income Gap Closed—No!" Pp. 61–66 in Louis Ferman, Joyce Kornbluh, and Alan Harber (eds.), *Poverty in America*. Ann Arbor: University of Michigan Press.

Mills, 1967.

Mills, C. Wright. 1953. *White Collar*. New York: Oxford University Press.

———. 1956. *The Power Elite*. New York: Oxford University Press.

Mintz, Beth. 1975. "The President's Cabinet, 1897–1972: A Contribution to the Power Structure Debate." *Insurgent Sociologist* 5:131–148.

———, and Michael Schwartz. 1981. "Interlocking Directorates and Interest Group Formation." *American Sociological Review* 46:851–869.

———, and Michael Schwartz. 1985. *The Power Structure of American Business*. Chicago: University of Chicago Press.

Mintz, Morton, and Jerry Cohen. 1971. *America, Inc.: Who Owns and Operates the United States*. New York: Dell.

Mitchell, Richard. 1967. *The Korean Minority in Japan*. Berkeley: University of California Press.

Mitzman, Arthur. 1969. *The Iron Cage.* New York: Grosset & Dunlap.

Modelski, G. 1972. "Multinational Business: A Global Perspective." *International Studies Quarterly* 16:5–30.

Molotch, Harvey. 1976. "The City as a Growth Machine: Toward a Political Economy of Place." *American Journal of Sociology* 82:309–332.

Molotch, Harvey, and M. Lester. 1975. "Accidental News: The Great Oil Spill as a Local Occurrence and National Event." *American Journal of Sociology* 81:235–260.

Money, John, and Anke Ehrhardt. 1972. *Man and Woman, Boy and Girl.* Baltimore, Md.: Johns Hopkins University Press.

Moore, 1982.

Moore, Barrington. 1966. *Social Origins of Dictatorship and Democracy: Lord and Peasant in the Making of the Modern World.* Boston: Beacon.

———. 1978. *Injustice: The Social Bases of Obedience and Revolt.* White Plains, N.Y.: M. E. Sharpe.

Morgan, S. Philip, and Kiyosi Hiroshima. 1983. "The Persistence of Extended Family Residence in Japan: Anachronism or Alternative Strategy." *American Sociological Review* 48:269–281.

Morris, Aldon. 1981. "Black Southern Student Sit-In Movement: An Analysis of Internal Structure." *American Sociological Review* 46:744–767.

Moska, Gaetano. 1939. *The Ruling Class.* New York: McGraw-Hill.

Mosley, Leonard. 1969. *On Borrowed Time: How World War II Began.* New York: Random House.

Mosley, Leonard. 1978. *Dulles.* New York: The Dial Press.

Moynihan, Daniel Patrick. 1965. *The Negro Family: The Case for National Action.* Washington, D.C.: U.S. Department of Labor.

———. 1973. *The Politics of a Guaranteed Income.* New York: Vintage.

Muller, Edward. 1985. "Income Inequality, Regime Repressiveness, and Political Violence." *American Sociological Review* 50:47–61.

Mullins, Nicholas. 1973. *Theories and Theory Groups in Contemporary American Sociology.* New York: Harper & Row.

Mumford, Lewis. 1961. *The City in History.* New York: Harcourt Brace Jovanovich.

Murdock, George P. 1935. "Comparative Data on the Division of Labor by Sex." *Social Forces* 15:551–553.

———. 1949. *Social Structure.* New York: Macmillan.

———. 1957. "World Ethnographic Sample." *American Anthropologist* 54:664–687.

Myrdal, Gunnar. 1970. *The Challenge of World Poverty.* New York: Pantheon.

Nakane, Chie. 1970. *Japanese Society.* Berkeley: University of California Press.

Nam, Charles B. 1982. "Sociology and Demography: Perspectives on Population." *Social Forces* 61:359–373.

National Commission on Excellence in Education. 1983. *A Nation at Risk.* Washington, D.C.: U.S. Government Printing Office.

Neal, 1983.

Newman, Oscar. 1972. *Defensible Space.* New York: Macmillan.

Niebuhr, H. Richard. (1929). *The Social Sources of Denominationalism.* New York: Meridan (1957).

Niemonen, Jack E. 1984. "Response to Harold R. Kerbo and L. Richard Della Fave's 'Corporate Linkage and Control of the Corporate Economy: New Evidence and a Reinterpretation.'" *Sociological Quarterly* 25:273–278.

Nolan, Patrick D. 1983. "Status in the World System, Income Inequality, and Economic Growth." *American Journal of Sociology* 89:410–419.

North, C. C., and P. K. Hatt. 1947. "Jobs and Occupations: A Popular Evaluation." *Opinion News* 9:3–13.

Oberschall, Anthony. 1973. *Social Conflict and Social Movements.* Englewood Cliffs, N.J.: Prentice-Hall.

O'Connor, James. 1973. *The Fiscal Crisis of the State.* New York: St. Martin's.

Ogburn, William F. 1937. *Social Change.* New York: Viking Press.

———. 1964. *On Culture and Social Change: Selected Papers,* ed. and with an intro. by Otis Dudley Duncan. Chicago: University of Chicago Press.

Oliver, Pamela. 1980. "Rewards and Punishments as Selective Incentives for Collective Action: Theoretical Investigations." *American Journal of Sociology* 85:1356–1375.

Olsen, Nancy. 1973. "Family Structure and Independence Training in a Taiwanese Village." *Journal of Marriage and Family* 35:512–519.

Olson, Mancur, Jr. 1965. *The Logic of Collective Action: Public Goods and the Theory of Groups.* Cambridge: Harvard University Press.

Oppenheimer, Martin. 1969. *The Urban Guerrilla.* Chicago: Quadrangle Books.

Orlinsky, D. F. 1972. "Love Relationships in the Life Cycle: A Developmental Interpersonal Perspective." Pp. 135–150 in Otto, H. A. (ed.), *Love Today.* New York: Association Press.

Orum, Anthony M. 1978. *Introduction to Political Sociology: The Anatomy of the Body Politic.* Englewood Cliffs, N.J.: Prentice-Hall.

Owen, D. R. 1972. "The 47 XYY Male: A Review." *Psychological Bulletin* 78:209–233.

Page, Ann L., and Donald Clelland. 1978. "The Kanawha County Textbook Controversy: A Study of Politics of Lifestyle Concerns." *Social Forces* 57(1):32–56.

Paige, Jeffrey. 1975. *Agrarian Revolution.* New York: Free Press.

Palen, J. John. 1981. *The Urban World.* New York: McGraw-Hill.

Palmer, C. Eddie. 1974. "Traversing the Subterranean: An Examination of the Deviant Function of the Private Investigator." *Sociological Symposium* 11:43–60.

Palmore, Erdman. 1975. *The Honorable Elders.* Durham, N.C.: Duke University Press.

———. 1975. "What the U.S.A. Can Learn from Japan About Aging." *Gerontologist* 15:64–67.

Parcel, Toby. 1979. "Race, Regional Labor Markets and Earnings." *American Sociological Review* 44:262–279.

Pareto, Vilfredo. 1935. *Mind and Society.* New York: Harcourt Brace Jovanovitch.

Park, Robert E. 1950. *Race and Culture.* New York: Free Press.

Parsons, Talcott. 1951. *The Social System.* New York: Free Press.

———. 1964. *Essays in Sociological Theory.* New York: Free Press.

———. 1970. "Equality and Inequality in Modern Society, or Social Stratification Revisited." Pp. 13–72 in Edward O. Laumann (ed.), *Social Stratification.* New York: Bobbs-Merrill.

———, and Robert F. Bales. 1953. *Family, Socialization and Interaction Process.* Glencoe, Ill.: Free Press.

Patterson, M. L., et al. 1971. "Compensatory Reactions to Spatial Intrusion." *Sociometry* 34:114–121.

Payne, Robert. 1964. *The Life and Death of Lenin.* New York: Simon & Schuster.

Pearlin, Leonard I. 1971. *Class Context and Family Relations: A Cross-National Study.* Boston: Little, Brown.

Perlmutter, Marion, and Elizabeth Hall. 1985. *Adult Development and Aging.* New York: Wiley.

Perrin, Robert. 1976. "Herbert Spencer's Four Theories of Social Evolution." *American Journal of Sociology* 81:1339–1359.

Persell, C. H. 1977. *Education and Inequality: A Theoretical and Empirical Synthesis.* New York: Free Press.

Peterson, William. 1975. *Population.* New York: Macmillan.

Petras, James, and Morris Morley. 1975. *The United States and Chile.* New York: Monthly Review Press.

Pfeffer, Richard. 1979. *Working for Capitalism.* New York: Columbia University Press.

Pfeiffer, John E. 1972. *The Emergence of Man.* New York: Harper & Row.

———. 1977. *The Emergence of Society: A Prehistory of the Establishment.* New York: McGraw-Hill.

Pharr, Susan J. 1977. "Japan: Historical and Contemporary Perspectives." Pp. 217–256 in Janet Zollinger Giele and Audrey Chapman Smock (eds.), *Women: Roles and Status in Eight Countries.* New York: Wiley.

Philips, Kevin P., and Paul H. Blackman. 1975. *Electoral Reform and Voter Participation.* Washington, D.C.: American Enterprise Institute for Public Policy Research.

Phillips, A. W. 1958. "The Relation Between Unemployment and the Rate of Change of Money Wage Rates in the United Kingdom, 1861–1957." *Economica* 25:283–299.

Phillips, David P. 1982. "The Behavioral Impact of Violence in the Mass Media: A Review of the Evidence from Laboratory and Nonlaboratory investigations." *Sociology and Social Research* 66:387–398.

Piaget, Jean. 1970. *The Construction of Reality in the Child.* New York: Basic Books.

Piven, Frances Fox, and Richard Cloward. 1982. *The New Class War: Reagan's Attack on the Welfare State and Its Consequences.* New York: Pantheon.

Piven, Frances Fox, and Richard Cloward. 1971. *Poor People's Movements: Why They Succeed, Why They Fail.* New York: Pantheon Books.

Plaut, 1983.

Polsby, Nelson W. 1980. *Community Power and Political Theory,* 2d ed. New Haven, Conn.: Yale University Press.

Population Reference Bureau. 1980. *Intercom* 8 (Feb.). Washington, D.C.: U.S. Government Printing Office.

———. 1976. *World Population Data Sheet, 1976.* Washington, D.C.: U.S. Government Printing Office.

Putnam, Robert. 1976. *The Comparative Study of Elites.* Englewood Cliffs, N.J.: Prentice-Hall.

Quarantelli, Enrico L., and James Weller. 1974. "The Structural Problem of a Sociology Specialty: Collective Behavior's Lack of Critical Mass." *American Sociologist* 9:59–68.

Quinney, Richard. 1977. *Criminology: Analysis and Critique of Crime in America.* Boston: Little, Brown.

Ragin, Charles, and David Zaret. 1983. "Theory and Method in Comparative Research: Two Strategies." *Social Forces* 61:731–754.

Ransford, Edward H. 1972. "Blue Collar Anger: Reactions to Student and Black Protest." *American Sociological Review* 37:333–346.

Ratcliff, Richard, Mary Elizabeth Gallagher, Kathryn Strother Ratcliff. 1979. "The Civic Involvement of Bankers: An Analysis of the Influence of Economic Power and Social Prominence in the Command of Civic Policy Positions." *Social Problems* 26:298–313.

Rawlins, V. L., and L. Ulman. 1974. "The Utilization of College Trained Manpower in the United States." Pp. 78–107 in M. S. Gordon (ed.), *Higher Education and the Labor Market*. New York: McGraw-Hill.

Redman, Charles. 1978. *The Rise of Civilization: From Early Farmers to Urban Society in the Ancient Near East*. San Francisco: Freeman.

Reischauer, Edwin O. 1977. *The Japanese*. Cambridge: Harvard University Press.

Riegel, Donald. 1982. "The Psychological and Social Effects of Unemployment." *American Psychologist* 45:187–209.

Riegel, Klaus F. 1979. *Foundations of Dialectical Psychology*. New York: Academic Press.

Rist, R. C. 1970. "Student Social Class and Teachers' Expectations: The Self-fulfilling Prophecy in Ghetto Education." *Harvard Educational Review* 40:411–450.

Robinson, Robert, and Jonathan Kelley. 1979. "Class as Conceived by Marx and Dahrendorf: Effects on Income Inequality, Class Consciousness, and Class Conflict in the United States, and Great Britain." *American Sociological Review* 44:38–58.

Rodman, Hyman. 1963. "The Lower Class Value Stretch." *Social Forces* 42:205–215.

Rogoff, Natalie. 1953. *Recent Trends in Occupational Mobility*. New York: Free Press.

Roosevelt, Kermit. 1979. *Counter Coup: The Struggle for the Control of Iran*. New York: McGraw-Hill.

Rosenbaum, J. E. 1975. "The Stratification of the Socialization Processes." *American Sociological Review* 40:48–54.

Rosenfeld, Eva. 1951. "Social Stratification in a 'Classless' Society." *American Sociological Review* 16:766–774.

Rosenthal, Elizabeth Clark. 1970. "'Culture' and the American Indian Community." Pp. 82–92 in Stuart Levine and Nancy O. Lurie, *The American Indian Today*. Baltimore: Penguin Books.

Rosenthal, R., and L. Jacobson. 1968. *Pygmalion in the Classroom*. New York: Holt, Rinehart & Winston.

Ross, C. E., J. Mirowsky, and Joan Huber. 1983. "Dividing Work, Sharing Work, and in Between: Marriage Patterns and Depression." *American Sociological Review* 48:809–823.

Rossi, Peter, and Katharine Lyall. 1976. *Reforming Public Welfare*. New York: Russel Sage.

Rubinson, Richard. 1976. "The World Economy and the Distribution of Income Within States: A Cross-National Study." *American Sociological Review* 41:638–659.

———, and Dan Quinlan. 1977. "Democracy and Social Inequality: A Reanalysis." *American Sociological Review* 42:611–623.

Rude, George. 1964. *The Crowd in History, 1730–1848*. New York: Wiley.

Sagan, Carl. 1977. *The Dragons of Eden: Speculations on the Evolution of Human Intelligence*. New York: Ballantine Books.

———. 1980. *Cosmos*. New York: Little, Brown.

Sahlins, Marshall. 1972. *Stone Age Economics*. Chicago: Aldine.

———, and Elman Service. 1960. *Evolution and Culture*. Ann Arbor: University of Michigan Press.

Salert, Barbara, and John Sprague. 1980. *The Dynamics of Riots*. Ann Arbor, Mich.: Inter-University Consortium for Political and Social Research.

Salisbury, Harrison. 1977. *Black Night, White Snow: Russia's Revolutions, 1905–1917*. New York: Doubleday.

Sallach, David. 1974. "Class Domination and Ideological Hegemony." *Sociological Quarterly* 15:38–50.

Sampson, Anthony. 1975. *The Seven Sisters*. New York: Viking.

Sanford, Rojas. 1976. *The Murder of Allende: The End of the Chilean Way to Socialism*. New York: Harper & Row.

Sapir, Edward. 1929. "The Status of Linguistics as a Science." *Language* 5:207–214.

Sawyer, Jack. 1967. "Dimensions of Nations: Size, Wealth, and Politics." *American Journal of Sociology* 73:145–172.

Savage, David G. 1986. "U.S. Students Top Only Third World in Math." *Los Angeles Times* (Apr. 1):1.

Schaefer, Richard T. 1979. *Racial and Ethnic Groups*. Boston: Little, Brown.

Schafer, W. E., and C. Olexa. 1971. *Tracking and Opportunity: The Locking-Out Process and Beyond*. Scranton, Pa.: Chandler.

Schattschneider, E. E. 1960. *The Semi-Sovereign People: A Realist's View of Democracy in America*. New York: Holt, Rinehart & Winston.

Schlesinger, Arthur M. 1957. *The Age of Roosevelt: The*

Crisis of the Old Order, 1919–1933. New York: Houghton Mifflin.

———. 1959. *The Age of Roosevelt: The Coming of the New Deal*. New York: Houghton Mifflin.

———. 1960. *The Age of Roosevelt: The Politics of Upheaval*. New York: Houghton Mifflin.

Schram, Sanford F., and Patrick Turbett. 1983. "Civil Disorder and the Welfare Explosion: A Two Step Process." *American Sociological Review* 48:408–414.

Schwab, William A. 1982. *Urban Sociology: A Human Ecological Perspective*. Reading, Mass.: Addison-Wesley.

Schwartz, Arthur N., Cherie L. Snyder, and James A. Peterson. 1984. *Aging and Life: An Introduction to Gerontology*. New York: Holt, Rinehart & Winston.

Sennett, Richard, and Jonathan Cobb. 1973. *The Hidden Injuries of Class*. New York: Vintage.

Sewell, William, A. O. Haller, and G. W. Ohlendorf. 1970. "The Educational and Early Occupational Status Process." *American Sociological Review* 35:1014–1027.

Sewell, William, and Robert Hauser. 1975. *Education, Occupation, and Earnings: Achievement in the Early Career*. New York: Academic Press.

Sewell, William, and Vimal Shah. 1968. "Parents' Education and Children's Education Aspirations and Achievements." *American Sociological Review* 33:191–209.

Shaffer, Richard, and Harold Kerbo. 1987. "Welfare Development in the United States: An Empirical Test of Competing Theories." Paper presented at a meeting of the Research Committee on Social Stratification of the International Sociological Association, Berkeley (Aug.).

Sherif, Muzafer. 1966. *In Common Predicament: Social Psychology of Intergroup Conflict and Cooperation*. Boston: Houghton Mifflin.

Shoup, Laurence. 1975. "Shaping the Postwar World: The Council of Foreign Relations and U.S. War Aims During WW II." *Insurgent Sociologist* 5:9–52.

Simmel, Georg. 1905/1955. *Conflict and the Web of Group Affiliations*, ed. Kurt H. Wolff and Reinhard Bendix. New York: Free Press.

Simonton, Dean. 1976. "The Sociopolitical Context of Philosophical Beliefs: A Transhistorical Causal Analysis." *Social Forces* 54:513–523.

Simpson, George E., and J. Milton Yinger. 1965. *Racial and Cultural Minorities: An Analysis of Prejudice and Discrimination*. New York: Harper & Row.

Sjoberg, Gideon. 1965. *The Preindustrial City: Past and Present*. New York: Free Press.

Skocpol, Theda. 1979. *States and Social Revolutions: A Comparative Analysis of France, Russia, and China*. New York: Cambridge University Press.

Smelser, Neil J. 1962. *Theory of Collective Behavior*. New York: Free Press.

———. 1976. *Comparative Methods in the Social Sciences*. Englewood Cliffs, N.J.: Prentice-Hall.

Smith, Adam. 1950. *The Wealth of Nations*. London: Dent.

Smith, David. 1974. *Who Rules the Universities?* New York: Monthly Review Press.

Snow, Edgar. 1970. *Red China Today*. New York: Random House.

———. 1971. *The Long Revolution*. New York: Random House.

Snyder, David. 1975. "Structural Position in the World System and Economic Growth, 1955–1970." *American Sociological Review* 40:259–278.

———, and Charles Tilly. 1972. "Hardship and Collective Violence in France." *American Sociological Review* 37:520–532.

———, and Edward Kick. 1979. "Structural Position in the World System and Economic Growth, 1955–1970: A Multiple Analysis of Transnational Interactions." *American Journal of Sociology* 84:1096–1128.

Soboul, Albert. 1974. *The French Revolution, 1787–1799: From the Storming of the Bastille to Napoleon*. New York: Random House.

Sonquist, John, and Thomas Koening. 1975. "Interlocking Directorates in the Top U.S. Corporations: A Graph Theory Approach." *Insurgent Sociologist* 5:196–229.

Sorokin, Pitirim A. 1941. *The Crisis of Our Age*. New York: E. P. Dutton.

Sorkin, Alan. 1978. "The Economic Base of Indian Life." *The Annals* 436:1–12.

Sowell, Thomas. 1978., *Essays and Data on American Ethnic Groups*. Washington, D.C.: The Urban Institute.

———. 1981. *Ethnic America: A History*. New York: Basic Books.

Spengler, Oswald. 1932. *The Decline and Fall of the West*. New York: Knopf.

Spenner, Kenneth. 1979. "Temporal Changes in Work Content." *Americal Sociological Review* 44:968–974.

Spiro, Melford. 1958. *Children of the Kibbutz*. Cambridge: Harvard University Press.

———. 1970. *Kibbutz: Venture in Utopia*. New York: Schocken Books.

Stack, Steven. 1978. "The Effect of Direct Government Involvement in the Economy on the Degree of Income Inequality: A Cross-National Study." *American Sociological Review* 43:880–888.

Stanfiel, James. 1973. "Socioeconomic Status as Related

to Aptitude, Attrition, and Achievement of College Students." *Sociology of Education* 46:480–488.

Stanley, Sam, and Robert Thomas. 1978. "Current Demographic and Social Trends Among North American Indians." *The Annals* 436:111–120.

Stanworth, Philip, and Anthony Giddens. 1975. "The Modern Corporate Economy: Interlocking Directorships in Britain, 1906–1970." *Sociological Review* 23:5–28.

Stark, Rodney, and William Sims Bainbridge. 1980. "Networks of Faith: Interpersonal Bonds and Recruitment to Cults and Sects." *American Journal of Sociology* 85:1376–1395.

Stark, Rodney, and Charles Y. Glock. 1968. *American Piety: The Nature of Religious Commitment.* Berkeley: University of California Press.

Steiber, Steven. 1979. "The World System and World Trade: An Empirical Exploration of Conceptual Conflicts." *Sociological Quarterly* 20:23–36.

Stein, A. 1971. "Strategies for Failure." *Harvard Educational Review* 41:158–204.

Steward, Julian, and Louis Faron. 1959. *Native Peoples of South America.* New York: McGraw-Hill.

Stohl, Michael. 1976. *War and Domestic Political Violence.* Beverly Hills, Calif.: Sage Publications.

Stokes, Randall, and David Jaffee. 1983. "Another Look at the Export of Raw Materials and Economic Growth." *American Sociological Review* 47:402–407.

Stolzenberg, Ross. 1978. "Bringing the Boss Back In: Employer Size, Employee Schooling, and Socioeconomic Achievement." *American Sociological Review* 43:813–828.

Strasser, Hermann. 1976. *The Normative Structure of Sociology: Conservative and Emancipatory Themes in Social Thought.* London: Routledge & Kegan Paul.

Suleman, Ezra. 1978. *Elites in French Society: The Politics of Survival.* Princeton, N.J.: Princeton University Press.

Sumner, William Graham. *Folkways.* Boston: Ginn (1906/1940).

Sutherland, Edwin H. 1961. *White Collar Crime.* New York: Holt, Rinehart & Winston.

Suttles, Gerald D. 1972. *The Social Construction of Communities.* Chicago: University of Chicago Press.

Szymanski, Albert. 1973. "Military Spending and Economic Stagnation." *American Journal of Sociology* 79:1–14.

———. 1976. "Racial Discrimination and White Gain." *American Sociological Review* 41:403–414.

———. 1978. *The Capitalist State and the Politics of Class.* New York: Academic Press.

Taeuber, Cynthia, and Victor Valdisera. 1986. "Women in the American Economy." *Current Population Reports: Special Studies.* Washington, D.C.: U.S. Government Printing Office.

Taylor, Jared. 1983. *Shadows of the Rising Sun: A Critical View of the "Japanese Miracle."* Tokyo: Charles Tuttle.

Terell, Ross. 1982. *Mao.* New York: Harper & Row.

Terkel, Studs. 1972. *Working.* New York: Pantheon.

Thapar, Romila. 1966. *A History of India.* London: Routledge & Kegan Paul.

Thernstrom, Stephen. 1970. "Immigrants and Wasps: Ethnic Differences in Occupational Mobility in Boston, 1890–1940." Pp. 125–164 in Stephen Thernstrom and Richard Sennett (eds.), *Nineteenth Century Cities.* New Haven: Yale University Press.

Thomas, Hugh. 1979. *A History of the World.* New York: Harper & Row.

Thornberry, Terence P., and Margaret Farnworth. 1982. "Social Correlates of Criminal Involvement: Further Evidence on the Relationship Between Social Status and Criminal Behavior." *American Sociological Review* 47:505–518.

Thornton, Arland, Duane F. Alwin, and Donald Camburn. 1983. "Causes and Consequences of Sex-Role Attitudes and Attitude Change." *American Sociological Review* 48:211–227.

Thornton, Russell. 1981. "Demographic Antecedents of a Revitalization Movement: Population Change, Population Size, and the 1890 Ghost Dance." *American Sociological Review* 46:88–96.

Thurow, Lester. 1980. *The Zero-Sum Society.* New York: Basic Books.

Tiger, Lionel, and Joseph Shepher. 1975. *Women in the Kibbutz.* New York: Harcourt Brace Jovanovich.

Tilly, Charles. 1978. *From Mobilization to Revolution.* Reading, Mass.: Addison, Wesley.

———. 1981. *As Sociology Meets History.* New York: Academic Press.

———, L. Tilly, and R. Tilly. 1975. *The Rebellious Century: 1830–1930.* Cambridge, Mass.: Harvard University Press.

Timberlake, Michael, and Kirk R. Williams. 1984. "Dependence, Political Exclusion, and Government Repression: Some Cross-National Evidence." *American Sociological Review* 49:141–146.

Toffler, Alvin. 1970. *Future Shock.* New York: Random House.

Tolbert, Charles M., II. 1977. "Industrial Segmentation and Men's Career Mobility." *American Sociological Review* 47:457–477.

———. 1983. "Industrial Segmentation and Men's Intergenerational Mobility." *Social Forces* 61:1119–1138.

———, Patrick Horan, and E. M. Beck. 1980. "The Structure of Economic Segmentation: A Dual Economy Approach." *American Journal of Sociology* 85:1095–1116.

Tonnies, Ferdinand. 1887/1957. *Community and Society*. New York: Harper Torchbooks.

Toynbee, Arnold J. 1946. *A Study of History*. Oxford, England: Oxford University Press.

Treas, Judith. 1983. "Trickle Down or Transfers? Postwar Determinants of Family Income Inequality." *American Sociological Review* 48:546–559.

Treiman, Donald J. 1977. *Occupational Prestige in Comparative Perspective*. New York: Academic Press.

Tufte, Edward. 1978. *Political Control of the Economy*. Princeton: Princeton University Press.

Tully, J. C., E. F. Jackson, and R. F. Curtis. 1970. "Trends in Occupational Mobility in Indianapolis." *Social Forces* 49:186–200.

Turner, Jonathan. 1970. "Entrepreneurial Environments and the Emergence of Achievement Motivation in Adolescent Males." *Sociometry* 33:147–166.

Turner, Jonathan, and Royce Singleton, Jr. 1978. "A Theory of Ethnic Oppression: Toward a Reintegration of Cultural and Structural Concepts in Ethnic Relations Theory." *Social Forces* 56:1001–1018.

Turner, Jonathan, and Charles Starnes. 1976. *Inequality: Privilege and Poverty in America*. Santa Monica, Calif.: Goodyear.

Turner, Ralph N., and Lewis Killian. 1972. *Collective Behavior*. Englewood Cliffs, N.J.: Prentice-Hall.

Tyree, Andrea, and Judith Treas. 1974. "The Occupational and Marital Mobility of Women." *American Sociological Review* 39:293–302.

Tyree, Andrea, Moshe Semyonov, and Robert Hodge. 1979. "Gaps and Glissandes: Inequality, Economic Development, and Social Mobility in 24 Countries." *American Sociological Review* 44:410–424.

Uhr, E., and Elizabeth Evanson. 1983. "The Relative Economic Status of the Aged." *Focus* 6:1–8.

Ulam, Adam. 1973. *Stalin: The Man and His Era*. New York: Viking Press.

United Nations. 1973. *The Determinants and Consequences of Population Change* vol. 1. New York: United Nations.

———. 1974. "International Migration Trends, 1950–1970." Conference Background Papers. New York: United Nations.

———. 1976. *Demographic Yearbook — 1975*. New York: United Nations.

———. 1977. *Demographic Yearbook — 1976*. New York: United Nations.

———. 1982. *Demographic Yearbook — 1982*. New York: United Nations.

———. 1983. *Demographic Yearbook — 1983*. New York: United Nations.

U.S. Bureau of the Census. 1975. *Historical Statistics of the United States, Colonial Times to 1970*. Bicentennial ed., part 2. Washington, D.C.: U.S. Government Printing Office.

———. 1977. "Projections of the Population of the United States: 1977 to 2050." *Current Population Reports*. Washington, D.C.: U.S. Government Printing Office.

———. 1980. *Social Indicators III: Selected Data on Social Conditions and Trends in the United States*. Washington, D.C.: U.S. Government Printing Office.

———. 1980. *Statistical Abstracts of the United States*. Washington, D.C.: U.S. Government Printing Office.

———. 1982. *Statistical Abstract of the United States: 1982*. Washington, D.C.: U.S. Government Printing Office.

———. 1985. *Statistical Abstract of the United States: 1985*. Washington, D.C.: U.S. Government Printing Office.

———. 1986. *Statistical Abstract of the United States: 1986*. Washington, D.C.: U.S. Government Printing Office.

———. 1987. *Statistical Abstracts of the United States*. Washington, D.C.: U.S. Government Printing Office.

U.S. Central Intelligence Agency. 1986. *Handbook of Economic Statistics, 1986*. Washington, D.C.: U.S. Government Printing Office.

U.S. Commission on Civil Rights. 1978. *Social Indicators of Equality for Minorities and Women*. Washington, D.C.: U.S. Government Printing Office.

U.S. Commission on Population Growth and the American Future. 1972. *Population and the American Future*. Washington, D.C.: U.S. Government Printing Office.

U.S. Department of Commerce. 1960. *Historical Statistics of the United States*. Washington, D.C.: U.S. Government Printing Office.

———. 1974. *Statistical Abstracts of the United States*. Washington, D.C.: U.S. Government Printing Office.

U.S. Department of Education. 1986. *Math Scores of 12th Grade and 8th Grade Students: International Comparisons*. Washington, D.C.: U.S. Government Printing Office.

U.S. Department of Justice. 1983. *Uniform Crime Re-

ports: Crime in the United States, 1980. Washington, D.C.: U.S. Government Printing Office.

———. 1985. *Uniform Crime Reports: Crime in the United States.* Washington, D.C.: U.S. Government Printing Office.

———. 1987. *Uniform Crime Reports: Crime in the United States.* Washington, D.C.: U.S. Government Printing Office.

U.S. Department of Labor. 1981. *Handbook of Labor Statistics.* Washington, D.C.: U.S. Government Printing Office.

———. 1985. *Handbook of Labor Statistics.* Washington, D.C.: U.S. Government Printing Office.

———. 1986. *Handbook of Labor Statistics.* Washington, D.C.: U.S. Government Printing Office.

U.S. Equal Employment Opportunity Commission. 1970. *Job Patterns for Minorities and Women in Private Industry.* Washington, D.C.: U.S. Government Printing Office.

———. 1981. *Job Patterns for Minorities and Women in Private Industry.* Washington, D.C.: U.S. Government Printing Office.

U.S. Senate Committee on Government Affairs. 1978a. *Voting Rights in Major Corporations.* Washington, D.C.: U.S. Government Printing Office.

———. 1978b. *Interlocking Directorates Among the Major U.S. Corporations.* Washington, D.C.: U.S. Government Printing Office.

———. 1980. *Structure of Corporate Concentration,* 2 vols. Washington, D.C.: U.S. Government Printing Office.

U.S. Senate Select Committee to Study Governmental Operations with Respect to Intelligence Activities. 1975a. *Alleged Assassination Plots Involving Foreign Leaders.* Washington, D.C.: U.S. Government Printing Office.

———. 1975b. *Covert Action in Chile, 1963–1973.* Washington, D.C.: U.S. Government Printing Office.

Useem, Michael. 1978. "The Inner Group of the American Capitalist Class." *Social Problems* 25:225–240.

———. 1979. "The Social Organization of the American Business Elite." *American Sociological Review* 44:553–571.

———. 1984. *The Inner Circle.* New York: Oxford University Press.

van den Berghe, Pierre. 1967. *Race and Racism: A Comparative Perspective.* New York: Wiley.

———. 1974. "Bringing Beasts Back In: Toward a Biosocial Theory of Aggression. *American Sociological Review* 39:777–788.

———. 1978. *Man in Society: A Biosocial View.* New York: Elsevier.

Vanfossen, Beth E. 1979. *The Structure of Social Inequality.* Boston: Little, Brown.

———, and R. I. Rhodes. 1974. "Commentary." *American Journal of Sociology* 80:727–732.

Vanneman, Reeve. 1980. "U.S. and British Perceptions of Class." *American Journal of Sociology* 85:769–790.

———, and Fred Pampel. 1977. "The American Perception of Class and Status." *American Sociological Review* 42:422–437.

Veblen, Thorstein. 1939. *Imperial Germany and the Industrial Revolution.* New York: Viking Press.

Vidmar, Neil, and Milton Rokeach. 1974. "Archie Bunker's Bigotry: A Study in Selective Perception and Exposure." *Journal of Communication* 38:36–47.

Villemez, Wayne. 1978. "Black Subordination and White Economic Well-Being." *American Sociological Review* 43:772–776.

Vogel, Ezra F. 1971. *Japan's New Middle Class.* Berkeley: University of California Press.

———. 1979. *Japan as Number One: Lessons for America.* Cambridge, Mass.: Harvard University Press.

von Hagen, Victor. 1961. *The Ancient Sun: Kingdoms of the Americas.* Cleveland: World.

Wallerstein, Immanual. 1974. *The Modern World-System.* New York: Academic Press.

———. 1978. *The Capitalist World-Economy: Essays.* Cambridge, England: Cambridge University Press.

———. 1980. *The Modern World-System II: Mercantilism and the Consolidation of the European World-Economy, 1600–1750.* New York: Academic Press.

Wallis, Roy. 1975. *Sectarianism.* New York: Wiley.

Walsh, Edward J., and Rex H. Warland. 1983. "Social Movement Involvement in the Wake of a Nuclear Accident: Activists and Free Riders in the TMI Area." *American Sociological Review* 48:764–780.

Walters, Pamela Barnhouse, and Richard Rubinson. 1983. "Educational Expansion and Economic Output in the United States, 1890–1969: A Production Function Analysis." *American Sociological Review* 48:480–493.

Walton, John. 1976. "Community Power and the Retreat from Politics: Full Circle After Twenty Years." *Social Problems* 23:292–303.

Washburn, Sherwood L. 1978. "The Evolution of Man." *Scientific American* 239:194–211.

Wax, Murray. 1971. *Indian Americans.* Englewood Cliffs, N.J.: Prentice-Hall.

Weber, Marianne. 1975. *Max Weber: A Biography,* trans. Harry Zohn. New York: Wiley.

Weber, Max. 1946. *From Max Weber: Essays in Sociology,* ed. and trans. Hans Gerth and C. Wright Mills. New York: Oxford University Press.

———. 1947. *The Theory of Social and Economic Organization,* ed. Talcott Parsons. New York: Free Press.

———. 1958. *The Protestant Ethic and the Spirit of Capitalism,* trans. Talcott Parsons. New York: Charles Scribner.

Weede, Erich. 1980. "Beyond Misspecification in Sociological Analysis of Income Inequality." *American Sociological Review* 45:497–501.

Weller, James, and Enrico L. Quarantelli. 1973. "Neglected Characteristics of Collective Behavior." *American Journal of Sociology* 79:665–685.

Weller, Robert H., and Leon F. Bouvier. 1981. *Population: Demography and Policy.* New York: St. Martins.

Wells, H. G. 1971. *The Outline of History.* New York: Doubleday.

Wenke, Robert. 1980. *Patterns in Prehistory: Mankind's First Three Million Years.* New York: Oxford University Press.

Whitt, J. Allen. 1979. "Toward a Class-Dialectical Model of Power: An Empirical Assessment of Three Competing Models of Political Power." *American Sociological Review* 44:81–99.

Wilson, Edmond O. 1975. *Sociobiology: The New Synthesis.* Cambridge, Mass.: Harvard University Press.

Wilson, William Julius. 1978. *The Declining Significance of Race.* Chicago: University of Chicago Press.

Wittfogel, Karl A. 1957. *Oriental Despotism.* New Haven: Yale University Press.

Wolf, Wendy, and Neil Fligstein. 1979. "Sex and Authority in the Work Place: The Causes of Sexual Inequality." *American Sociological Review* 44:235–252.

Wolff, Kurt H. 1950. *The Sociology of Georg Simmel.* Glencoe, Ill.: The Free Press.

Wooden, Kenneth. 1981. *The Children of Jonestown.* New York: McGraw-Hill.

The World Almanac. 1984. New York: Newspaper Enterprise Association.

Wright, Erik Olin. 1978a. *Class, Crisis and the State.* New York: Schocken.

———. 1979. *Class Structure and Income Determination.* New York: Academic Press.

———, and Luca Perrone. 1977. "Marxist Class Categories and Income Inequality." *American Sociological Review* 42:32–55.

Wright, James D., and Sonia Wright. 1976. "Social Class and Parental Values for Children: A Partial Replication and Extension of the Kohn Thesis." *American Sociological Review* 41:527–537.

Wrong, Dennis H. 1961. "The Oversocialized Conception of Man in Modern Sociology." *American Sociological Review* 26:183–193.

———. 1980. *Power: Its Forms, Bases and Uses.* New York: Harper & Row.

Yanowitch, Murray. 1977. *Social and Economic Inequality in the Soviet Union.* White Plains, N.Y.: Sharpe.

Yinger, Roy. 1975. *Sectarianism.* New York: Wiley.

Zeitlin, Maurice. 1974. "Corporate Ownership and Control: The Large Corporation and the Capitalist Class." *American Journal of Sociology* 79:1073–1119.

———, L. Ewen, and Richard Ratcliff. 1974. "New Princes for Old? The Large Corporation and the Capitalist Class in Chile." *American Journal of Sociology* 80:87–123.

Zeitlin, Maurice, Kenneth Lutterman, and James Russel. 1973. "Death in Vietnam: Class, Poverty, and the Risks of War." *Politics and Society* 3:313–328.

Zimbardo, Philip G. 1972. "Pathology of Imprisonment." *Society* 9:4–8.

Zucker, Lynn, and Carolyn Rosenstein. 1981. "Taxonomies of Institutional Structure: Dual Economy Reconsidered." *American Sociological Review* 46:869–884.

Name Index

Subject Index

A

Abstract ideals, in religion, 500
Achievement, social stratification and, 229
Affirmative action, 412
Age distribution, 138, 140
Aging/aged
 conflict theory and, 438
 historical view, 433–435
 in Japan, 435–438
 myths related to, 441–442
 problems, 439–441
Agrarian societies, 67, 71–75
 aged, 433
 cities and, 74–75
 elite groups, 72–74
 inequality, 73–74
 kinship system, 476–477
 military/warfare, 73–74
 plow, importance of, 71–72
 politics, 72
 religion, 72
 standard of living, 72–73
 women 419–420, 427
Agriculture and Third World
 agricultural disruption, 370
 agricultural reform, 377–378
Allocation process, social mobility, 343–344
Amalgamation, 397
American Indians. *See* Native Americans
American society
 individualism, 94, 96
 social speedup problem, 78–79

American society *(cont.)*
 See also United States
Animism, 497
Anomie, deviance and, 213
Anorexia nervosa, 18–19
Anticipatory socialization, 174
Antidiscrimination programs, 411–412
 affirmative action, 412
Applied research, 41
Ascription, social stratification and, 229, 232
Asian Americans in America, 392–394
 Chinese, 392
 historical view, 392
 Japanese, 393
 Southeast Asians, 393–394
Asian mode of production, 76
Asian system, social stratification, 236–237
Assimilation, 397–399
 biological, 397
 cultural, 397
 enhancing/impeding factors, 398–399
 evolutionary theory, 397–398
 Gordon's theory, 398
 psychological, 397
 stages, 398
 structural, 397
Assyria, 154
Attila the Hun, 386
Authoritarian personality type, racism/discrimination and, 401
Authority (state), 300–302

Authority (state) *(cont.)*
 charismatic authority, 301–302
 ideal types, 302
 legal-rational authority, 301
 traditional authority, 301
Autocracy, 303

B

Baby boom, 38
 echo, 147, 149
 effects, 138, 147, 149
Babylon, 74, 154
Banks, as institutional investors, 280–281
Baptists, 505
Belief systems, 98–99
 ideologies, 98, 99
 mythologies, 98–99
Bilateral descent, 476
Biological assimilation, 397
Biological theories
 cautions about, 11
 nature versus nurture, 12
Birth order, effects, 175
Birth rate
 crude, 143, 144
 population and, 143–144
Blacks in America, 389–392
 Civil Rights Movement, 391–392
 illegitimate births and, 488–489
 migration to urban areas, 391
 outflow mobility table, black men, 407–410
 political participation, 407

Binou

Logone

Chan

Miltou

Aoukadebbe

Kouka

Ngaundere

Bahar el-Abiad

Oasia

Bahar Koutt

Kouting

Bahar el Arbe

Doka

Limite du bassin

Lac Nghiri

Bangala

Mobeka

Boukonn

Loulembou

Makomeli

Ikelemba

Irebou

Equateur Station

Oubangi

Lac Matoamba

Agande

Franceville

Bembo

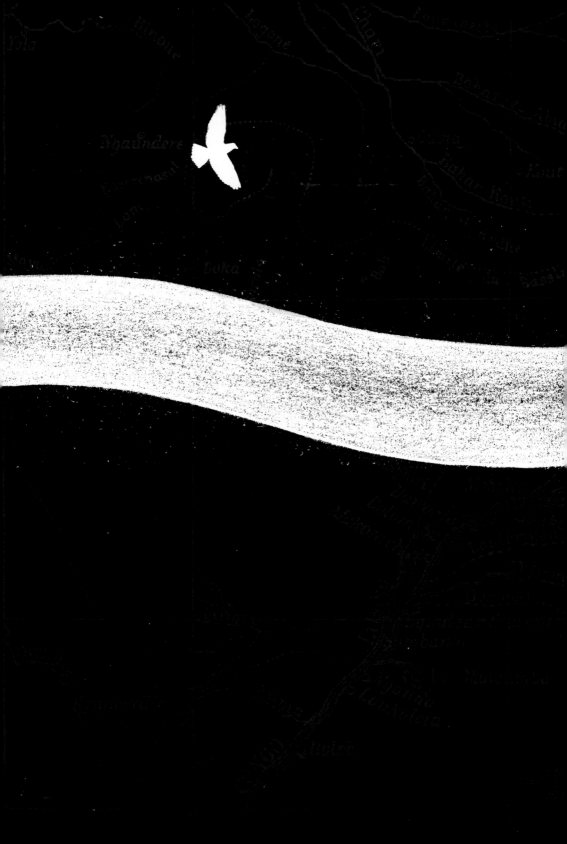

Joseph Conrad's

HEART

of

DARKNESS

Binou

Logone

Chari

Aoukadebbe

Ngaündere

Bahar -el-Abiad

Ousia

Koutı

Bahar Kouti

Masrenasal

Lom

Bahar el Ardhe

Limite du Bassin

Bali

Lac Nghiri

Mbeka

Bangala

Boukoi

Bolombo

Mokomeha

Loulembou

Ikelemi

Ourouki

Licona

Equateur Station

Oubangi

Lac Matoumba

Franceville

Alima

Ngondo

Loukolela

CONGO

Bolobo

50   100

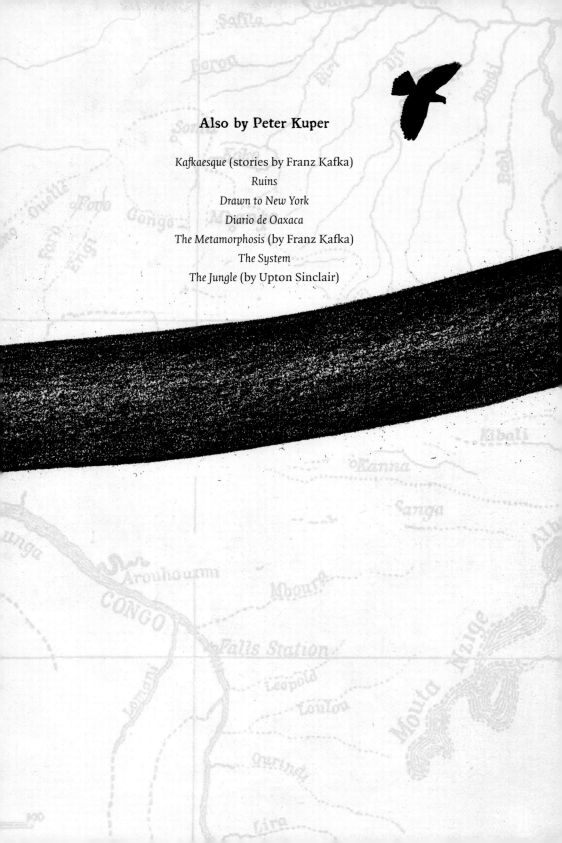

Also by Peter Kuper

Kafkaesque (stories by Franz Kafka)
Ruins
Drawn to New York
Diario de Oaxaca
The Metamorphosis (by Franz Kafka)
The System
The Jungle (by Upton Sinclair)

For information about permission to reproduce selections from this book, write to
Permissions, W. W. Norton & Company, Inc., 500 Fifth Avenue, New York, NY 10110

For information about special discounts for bulk purchases, please contact
W. W. Norton Special Sales at specialsales@wwnorton.com or 800-233-4830

Manufacturing by Versa Press
Book design by Daniel Lagin Design
Production manager: Julia Druskin

ISBN 978-0-393-63564-5

W. W. Norton & Company, Inc., 500 Fifth Avenue, New York, N.Y. 10110
www.wwnorton.com

W. W. Norton & Company Ltd., 15 Carlisle Street, London W1D 3BS

1 2 3 4 5 6 7 8 9 0

Dedicated to my first mate and captain,
Betty Russell

FOREWORD

by Maya Jasanoff

The thirty-two-year-old Polish sailor Józef Teodor Konrad Korzeni-owski arrived in the Congo Free State in June 1890 with a sense of anticipation. Though not officially a European colony, the Congo Free State was administered by Belgium's King Leopold II, who held it up as an exemplar of Europe's mission to "civilize" sub-Saharan Africa. Korzeniowski had come on a three-year contract to captain a Congo River steamboat for a Belgian trading company. "I like this prospect very much," he wrote to a cousin. "The only thing that makes me rather uneasy is the information that 60 per cent. of our Company's employees return to Europe before they have completed even six months' service. Fever and dysentery!"*

It didn't take long for Korzeniowski to discover the ugly reality of European intervention in Congo. The other white men he met were hard-bitten, small-minded, mean-spirited careerists. "Prominent characteristic of the social life here: people speaking ill of each other," he grumbled into his diary. Making his way overland from the coast to Léopoldville

---

* Joseph Conrad to Karol Zagorski, May 22, 1890, in Frederick Karl and Laurence Davies, eds., *The Collected Letters of Joseph Conrad*, vol. 1 (Cambridge, UK: Cambridge University Press, 1983), pp. 52–53.

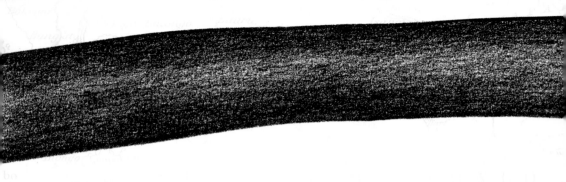

(Kinshasa), he encountered gruesome signs of the regime's violence: the corpses of dead laborers, "a skeleton tied up to a post" and a "youth about 13 suffering from a gunshot wound in the head."[*] From there, he boarded a boxy steamboat, the *Roi des Belges*, and chugged one thousand miles upriver to Stanley Falls (Kisangani), the hub of the ivory trade, where European merchants cut deals with a middleman notorious for his involvement in the slave trade. Korzeniowski fell ill with "fever and dysentery"; one of his traveling companions died on the downriver journey. By the time he returned to Léopoldville, he had had enough. "Everything here is repellent to me. Men and things, but men above all," he wrote.[†] He quit his contract after less than six months and returned to Europe, racked by profound depression and despair.

The trip to Congo was something of a turning point in the life of Konrad Korzeniowski, who soon stopped sailing and became the full-time writer we know as Joseph Conrad. Eight years later, it also inspired the plot of what has become his most widely read book, *Heart of Darkness*.

Remarkably, many of the details in *Heart of Darkness* can be traced to real-life sources, starting with its opening scene. The *Nellie* was the name of a yawl kept by one of Conrad's good friends, a former

---

[*] Joseph Conrad, *Congo Diary and Other Uncollected Pieces* (Garden City, NY: Doubleday, 1978), pp. 13, 15.

[†] Joseph Conrad to Marguerite Poradowska, September 26, 1890, in Karl and Davies, eds., pp. 61–63.

sailor turned "Director of Companies" (as Conrad phrased it in *Heart of Darkness*), with whom he sailed on the Thames. Several of the novel's images, characters and episodes resemble Conrad's recorded experience; Marlow's tone of voice in places echoes Conrad's journal and letters from 1890. And though Conrad gives Marlow's journey in *Heart of Darkness* an animating objective that his own trip did not have—to retrieve the rogue agent Mr. Kurtz—even this character, as Adam Hochschild has pointed out, may have been based on a historical figure.

These time- and place-specific details sit in tension with *Heart of Darkness*'s overtly universalizing quality as a meditation on the capacity for evil—humanity's heart of darkness. Notably, Conrad never names the river, the country or even the continent in which Marlow's journey is set. It's because *Heart of Darkness* in so many ways transcends its specific setting that Francis Ford Coppola could so successfully transpose the plot to Vietnam in *Apocalypse Now* (1979). Conrad packs the text with enough metaphors of darkness and light to keep generations of students busy analyzing them, even as he defies straightforward interpretation by ringing the story in layers of narration: Marlow's journey, Marlow describing his journey, somebody listening to Marlow describing his journey. All this can make interpreting *Heart of Darkness*, as Marlow's listener says of his yarn, a rather "inconclusive experienc[e]."[*]

But it was also Conrad's effort to draw a universal lesson from a specific history that prompted Chinua Achebe in 1975 to condemn

[*] *Youth/Heart of Darkness/The End of the Tether* (London: Penguin, 1995), p. 52.

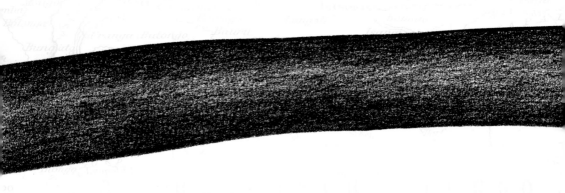

Conrad as a "bloody racist" and *Heart of Darkness* as "an offensive and totally deplorable book." By reducing Africa to a "setting and backdrop which eliminates the African as a human factor," he argued, *Heart of Darkness* was complicit with the West's persistent dehumanizing of Africa.[*] And for all that *Heart of Darkness* is a ferocious assault on European imperial hypocrisy, Conrad (like Marlow) didn't have much of a problem with what he believed was the kinder, gentler British form of imperialism. When European abuses in the Congo Free State became an international scandal in the early 1900s, earning opprobrium from writers including Mark Twain and Arthur Conan Doyle, Conrad pointedly refused to add his voice to the protest.

Achebe's critique has left later generations wondering whether *Heart of Darkness* deserves to be read at all. Barack Obama recalled being asked by his college friends why he was reading "this racist tract." "Because the book teaches me things," he explained. "See, the book's not really about Africa. Or black people. It's about . . . a particular way of looking at the world."[†]

Perhaps a better question is *how* it should be read. Peter Kuper's adaptation represents not only a triumph of graphic art but a compelling work of literary interpretation. He has designed a masterful synthesis

---

[*] Chinua Achebe, "An Image of Africa," *Massachusetts Review* 18, no. 4 (Winter 1977): 788, 790. This article is the published version of a lecture delivered in 1975.

[†] Barack Obama, *Dreams from My Father*, rev. ed. (New York: Three Rivers Press, 2004), pp. 102–3.

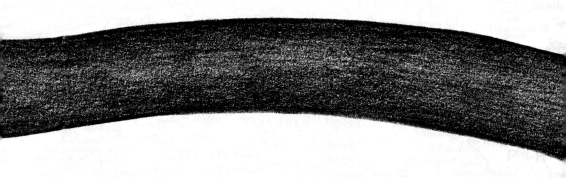

that retains Conrad's language while pressing beyond the limits of Conrad's vision. In an implicit response to Achebe, Kuper portrays Africans as seers, not merely parts of the scene.

What follows will leave anyone already familiar with *Heart of Darkness* with a startling new appreciation of the book. For anyone who is not, a powerful journey awaits into a *Heart of Darkness* that resonates today.

MAYA JASANOFF is the Coolidge Professor of History at Harvard University and the author of *The Dawn Watch: Joseph Conrad in a Global World*.

Art of Darkness

Doing a graphic novel interpretation of *Heart of Darkness* has been an odyssey. The novel is a cultural touchstone, but as I contemplated this nineteenth-century text through my twenty-first-century lens, I wrestled with its archaic vision. In 1975 the Nigerian author, Chinua Achebe, declared it a racist work and argued that it should be discredited as a classic. To adapt it meant addressing the confounding and repellent aspects of the book without undermining what has placed it in the canon of great literature.

Reading the book triggered memories of my own past travels, trudging through the rainforest jungles of Ecuador, Guatemala, Sumatra and Irian Jaya. Though I never visited the Congo, I brushed against its border in 1989 while hitchhiking from Tanzania to Rwanda. On deck with Marlow as he ventured into the unknown and grappled with its trials, I relived the experience of moving to Oaxaca, Mexico, with my wife and daughter from 2006 to 2008, a journey that presented parallel, albeit far different, challenges of adapting to a new culture and language. During this period a new looseness seeped into in my drawing style, the result of keeping a visual diary. Conrad referred to his own Congo diary to develop *Heart of Darkness*; my Oaxaca diary informed the drawing style for Marlow's tale.

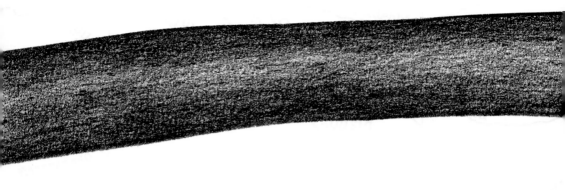

Engaging with Conrad's narrative, I also reflected on current events: corruption in our highest offices, rampant xenophobia, racism at home and abroad, all disturbingly similar to the transgressions committed in the name of colonialism portrayed in *Heart of Darkness*. Joseph Conrad's book, though a product of its age, has much to offer modern readers. Beyond his distinctive literary achievements, Conrad also produced a work that, in its day, raised public consciousness of the atrocities committed in the Congo and emboldened the reform movement. The more I read, the closer I felt to the subject and the more I thought a graphic interpretation would have relevancy.

I knew, tackling this project, that immersion would be the best way to imbue the art with a dimension beyond lines on paper. Like the book's characters I wanted to feel displaced from my familiar environment. My home, New York City, is certainly a jungle of sorts, but it wouldn't put me in Marlow's shoes. Oaxaca isn't the Congo, but it held out the promise of an immersive atmosphere, and I plotted a return lasting several months.

In Mexico, I dove in, transported, as I'd hoped, by the surround-sound barks from hundreds of dogs and braying donkeys; the smell of simmering menudo mixed with burning wood and plastic; buzzing, flitting insects including a wasp that dropped on my head stinger-first. Immersion was completed when I was stricken with a vicious bout of the flu.

During weeks of semi-feverish recovery, I lay in bed (at times feeling more like Kurtz than Marlow), digging into research. Norton's

Critical Edition of *Heart of Darkness*, edited by Paul B. Armstrong, became an indispensable resource and trusted companion. Among other insights into Conrad and his times, it provided an unflinching depiction of Belgian King Leopold II's reign of terror in the Congo from 1885 to 1908. Maya Jasanoff's biography, *The Dawn Watch: Joseph Conrad in a Global World*, arrived in perfect time, published just as I was beginning my exploration of Conrad and his time in the Congo. That Maya subsequently agreed to write the foreword to this adaptation is a genuine honor.

I watched online lectures, reviews and the film adaptations I could find: CBS's *Playhouse 90* from 1958 (laughable), Nicolas Roeg's 1993 made-for-TV version (dreadful). Fortunately, there was also *Apocalypse Now*, Francis Ford Coppola's brilliant reimagining of *Heart of Darkness*, set during the Vietnam War, a classic in its own right.

I gathered reference material, sometimes happily—stumbling upon images of old England's Thames river painted by John Atkinson Grimshaw—sometimes miserably, as when confronted by horrific photos by Alice Seeley Harris, a missionary who documented the brutalizing of Congolese men, women and children at the behest of King Leopold. At times the weight of history felt unbearable.

Finally, I was ready to put pencil to paper, using an approach I've formulated and refined over several previous graphic novels. One of the primary challenges when adapting a work of prose into comics is determining where art can convey events and where text is imperative.

Fig. 1   Fig. 2

I began homing in on key passages, determining what should be kept and what I might jettison without betraying the story's foundation. Simultaneously, I began roughing out sketches of various characters based on Conrad's descriptions, which is where another aspect of history reared its head.

Confronting the book's racist elements forced me to likewise address the fraught history of cartoon stereotypes. Subtle and not-so-subtle racism is embedded in the history of cartooning and caricature, which rely on visual shorthands to represent emotions, body language and ethnicity. Using substantial photo references taken in the Congo in the late 1800s and early 1900s, I was able to determine traditional dress, facial features and the environment. From these, I tried to identify the the simplifications that serve the art, excise those that reinforced racial stereotypes, yet maintain accurate portrayals. Where there was the opportunity, I also took Conrad's exterior view of Africa and flipped the perspective. By choosing a different point of view to illustrate, otherwise faceless and undefined characters were brought to the fore without altering Conrad's text.

Next, I paced out the story in "thumbnails" (Fig.1) summing up in words what might happen on each two-page spread. Still working in thumbnails, I indicated possible visuals and identified what dialogue would land on each page (Fig. 2). Working in miniature lets me track how the reader's eyes might travel across the page and where a page

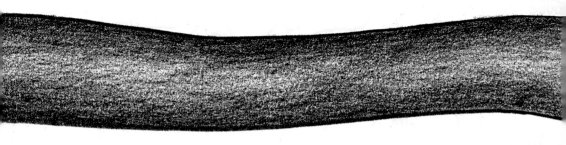

turn might conceal or reveal a dramatic event. I then created booklets one-third the size of the printed book (Fig. 3), which gave me space to introduce more detail and determine where the text would fit. The booklets also approximated the reading experience of the final book. The booklets were scanned, and the text was placed using a font based on my hand-lettering. This allowed me to easily edit the text (Fig. 4). At this step I shared the material with my editor and a variety

Fig. 3   Fig. 4

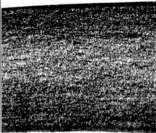
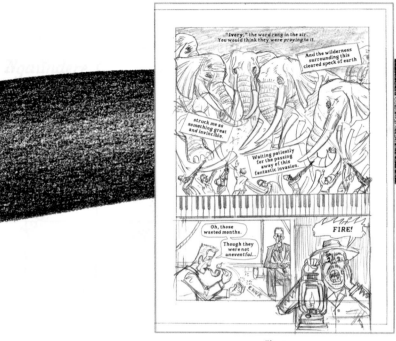

Fig. 5

of readers, among them eminent scholars. Based on their feedback I began tighter drawings done at print size (Fig. 5) and gathered yet more photo references. Again the art was scanned and text placed. These pages were then enlarged 125 percent and drawn directly onto a smooth watercolor paper with the aid of a light box. To convey the "present" where Marlow regales his boatmates, I used pen and ink. For the yarn he's spinning about the past, the panel borders change from ruled lines to shakier hand-drawn strokes in black pencil and ink wash (Fig. 6). In the final stage, I refined all the word balloons and digitally added gray tones to the "present" sections to further distinguish them from the narrated story (Fig. 7)

I hope the path my adaptation has taken does justice to the story,

Fig. 6

Fig. 7

its range of characters and the very real history it mines. More than ever, we need art that engages with the social discourse. Having the opportunity to wade into these waters gave me the chance to not only confront the novel's darkness but also attempt to illuminate its heart.

—Peter Kuper
New York City
2019

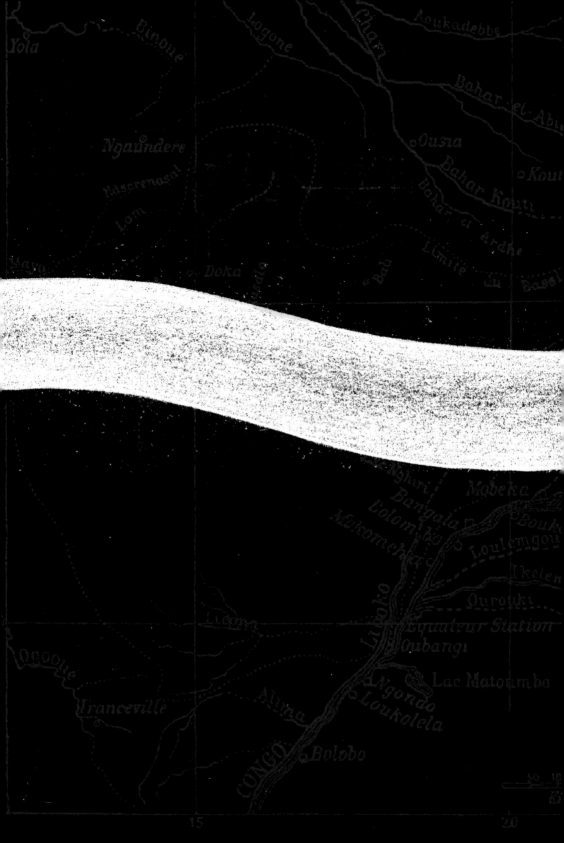

HEART

of

DARKNESS

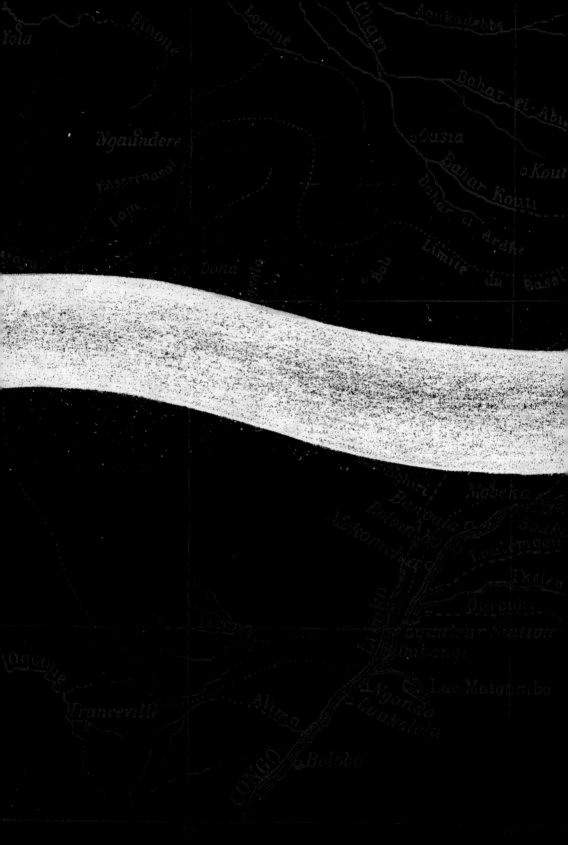

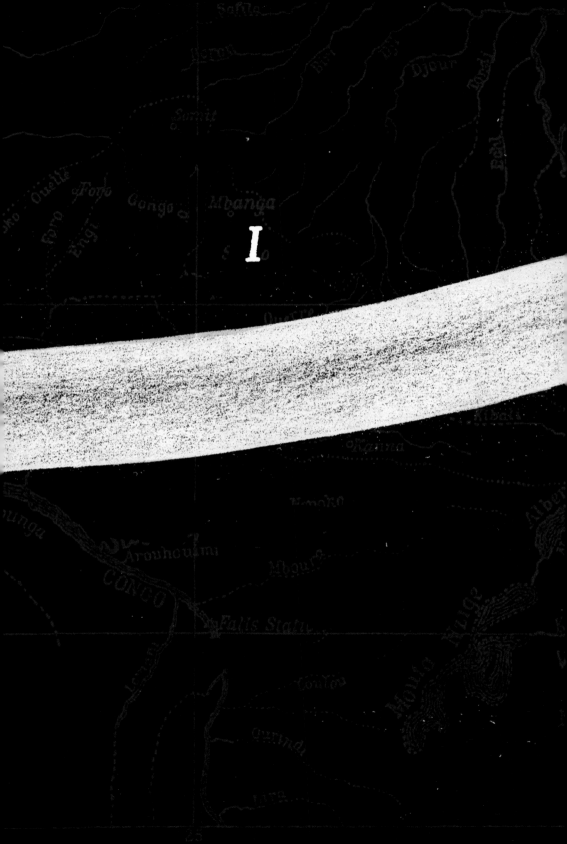

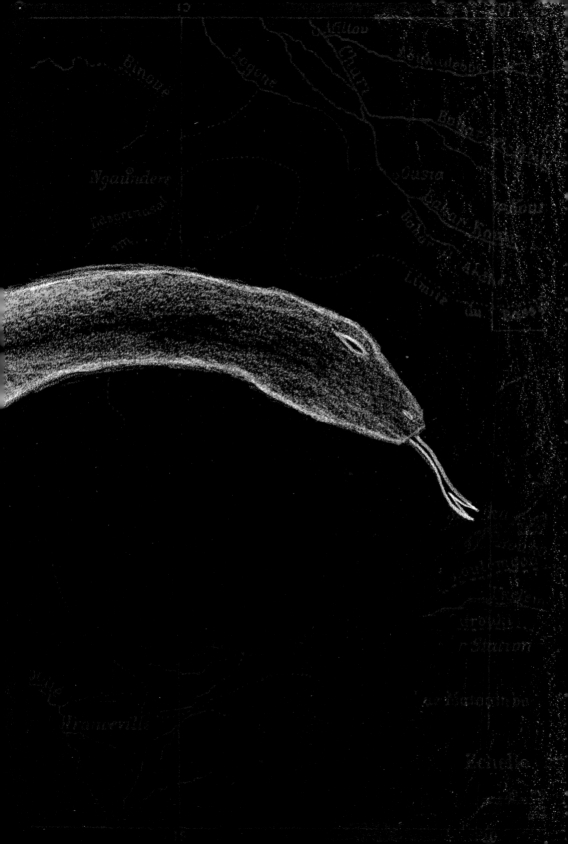

1899, THAMES RIVER,
UNITED KINGDOM

NELLIE

The sea-reach stretched
before us as we waited
for the turning of the tide.

Our cruising vessel swung to her anchor

and was at rest.

The group of us had the bond of the sea even through our long periods of separation.

Among us was a lawyer...

The biggest, blankest place, so to speak, drew me the most.

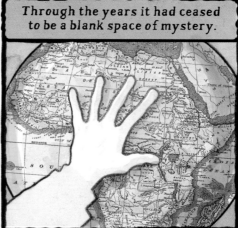
Through the years it had ceased to be a blank space of mystery.

It had become a place of darkness.

But there was in it one river,

a mighty big river,

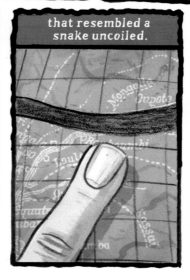
that resembled a snake uncoiled.

And it had charmed me!

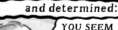

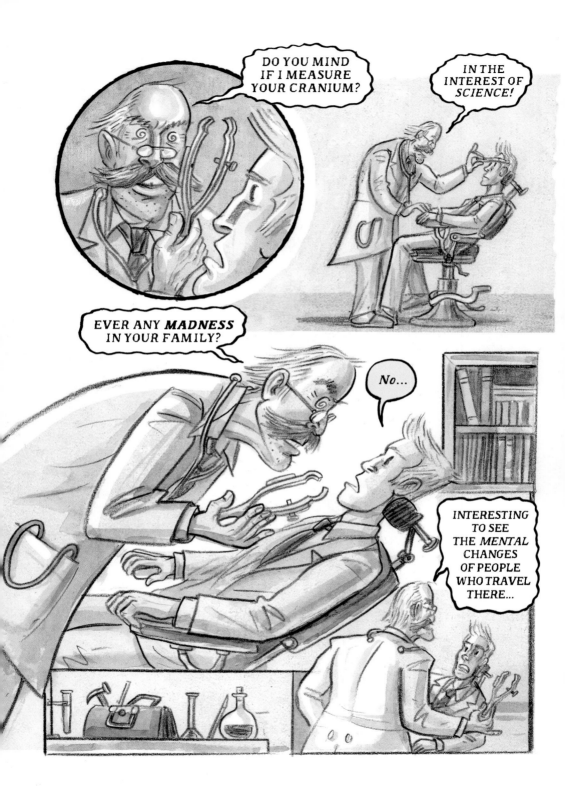

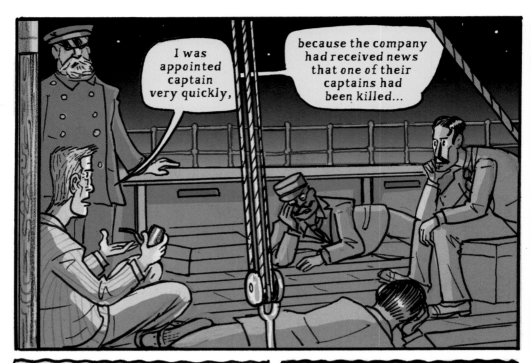

I was appointed captain very quickly,

because the company had received news that one of their captains had been killed...

He was a Dane named Fresleven. I was told he was the gentlest, quietest soul to ever walk on two legs.

Yet a quarrel with the natives arose from a misunderstanding about two hens —

Yes, he *died* quarreling over hens!

I set off for Africa, aboard a French steamer,
though I felt instead of going to the center of the continent,
I was heading for the center of the earth.

We stopped in every blamed port and
every day the coast looked the same.
The edge of a colossal jungle.

Now and then a boat from shore
gave one a momentary contact
with reality.

For a time I'd feel like I belonged to a world of straightforward facts.

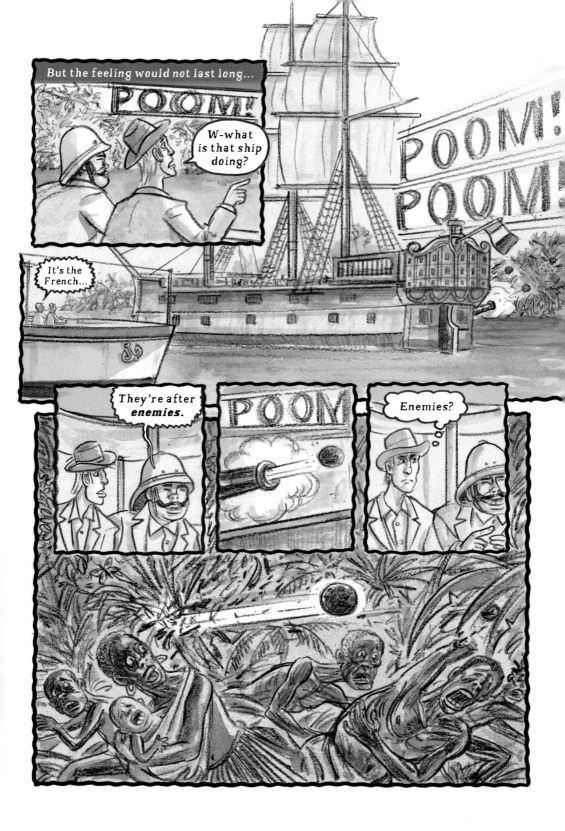

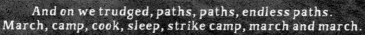

And *on* we trudged, paths, paths, endless paths.
March, camp, cook, sleep, strike camp, march and march.

At last, on the fifteenth day,
we hobbled up to the central station.

Ooh

There were no rivets.

What did arrive was a sordid band, calling itself "The Eldorado Exploring Expedition." They were a greedy bunch of buccaneers with no more morals than burglars breaking into a safe...

Their leader was the station manager's uncle.

HEEYA!

T*H*W*A*K

...IVORY

HAH!

HA!

IVORY...

I finally gave up worrying about the rivets.

And wondered if I'd ever meet Mr. Kurtz.

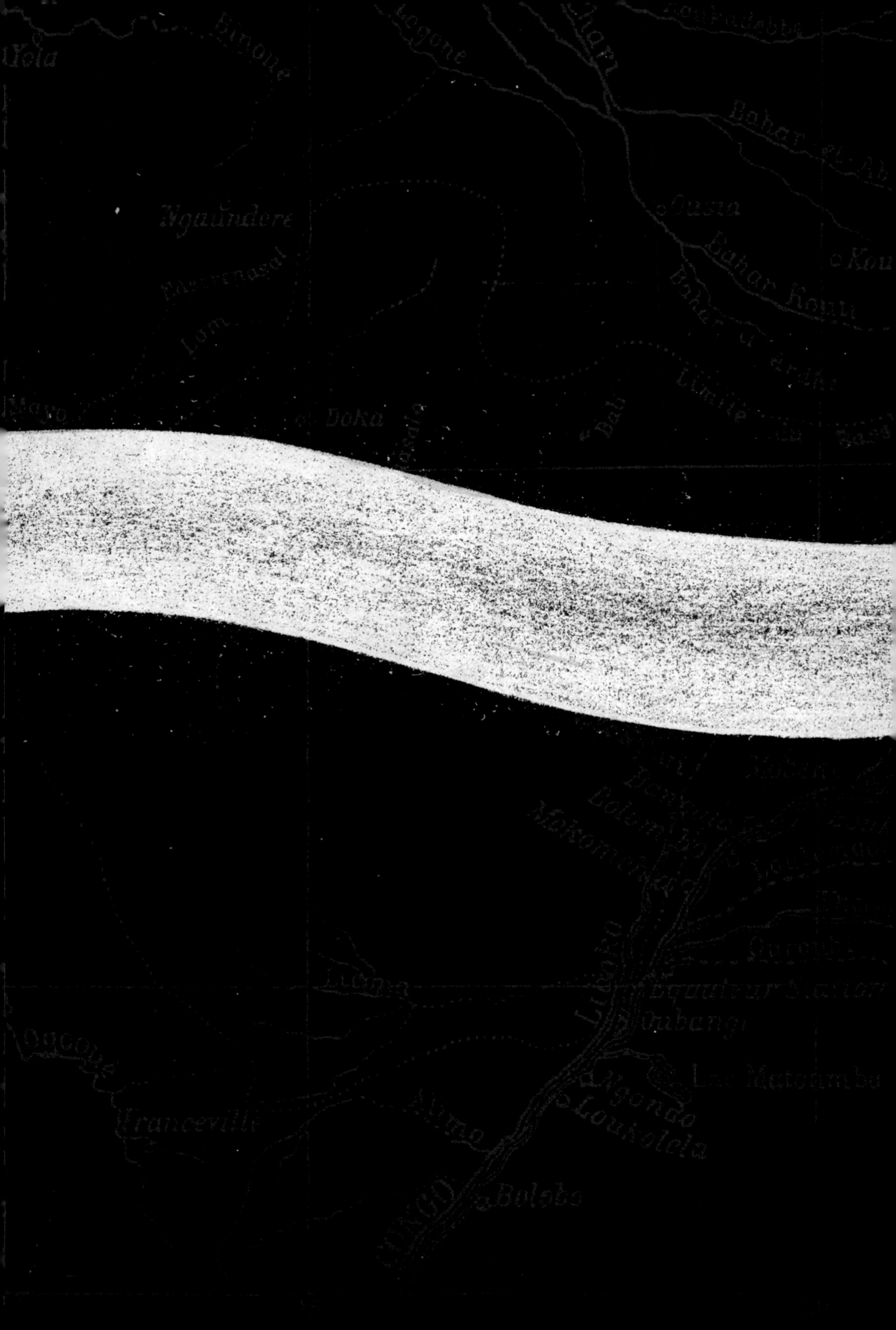

Yola

birone

Logone

Ngaündere

Bahar el A...

Gasia

Bahar Kou...

Bokar

Limite

Mayo

el Doka

Bai

Bang

Bolem...

Moïom...

Donville

Ouoma

équateur ...

Oubang...

Ougoué

Ngondo

Les Matamb...

Loukolo...

Franceville

Aïma

Bolobo

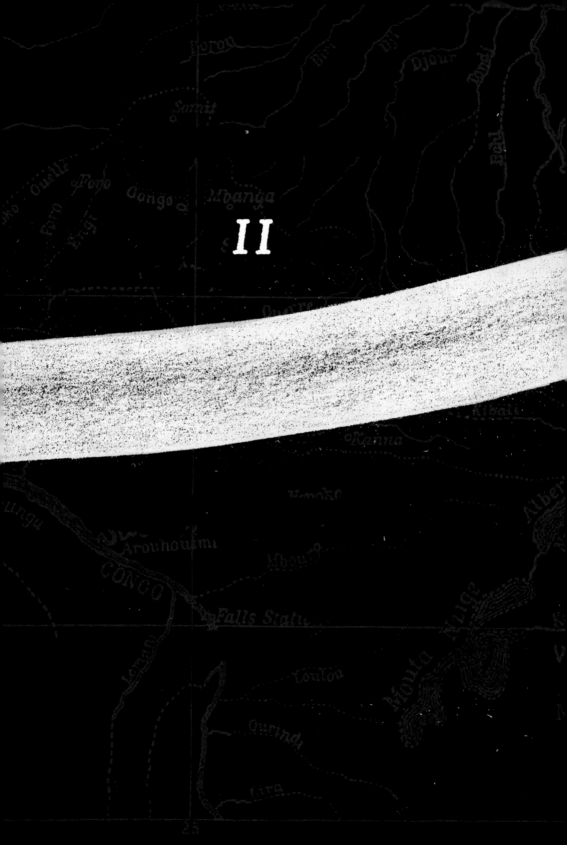

II

I don't pretend it was smooth sailing from there.

More than once I had to enlist the crew to push the boat through shallows.

These chaps were fine fellows—men you could work with and I was grateful for them.

They were cannibals. Why in the name of gnawing hunger didn't they go for us? Instead they ate rotten hippo meat.

Phoo! I can still smell it!

Their restraint still amazes me. It's easier to face perdition of one's soul than prolonged hunger.

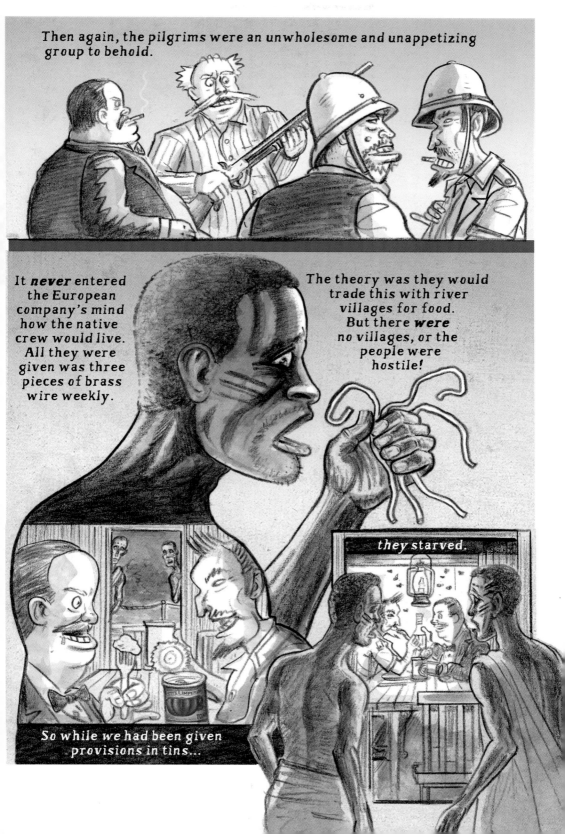

On we crawled
towards Kurtz,
like a sluggish beetle,
feeling very small as
we penetrated deeper
and deeper into the
heart of darkness.

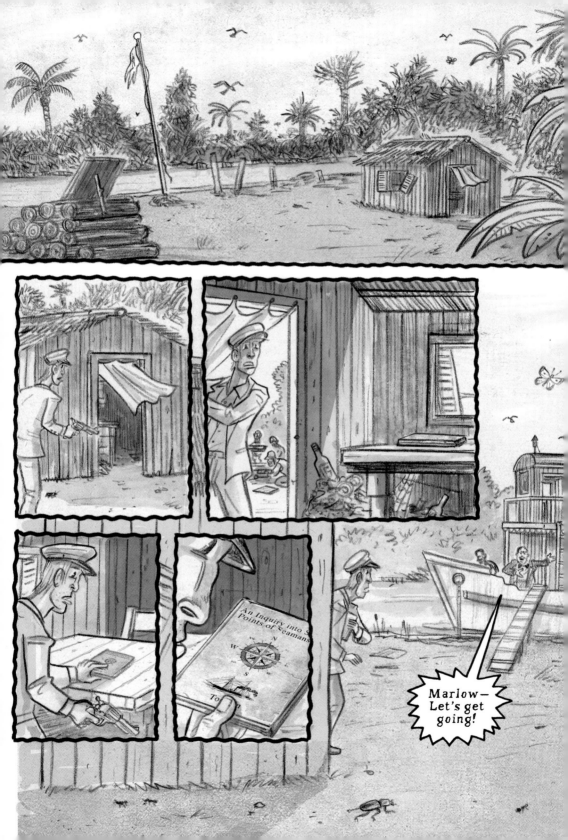

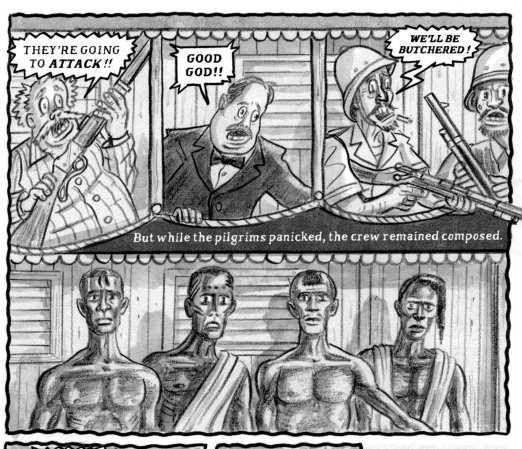

But while the pilgrims panicked, the crew remained composed.

As the mist departed, we hoisted the anchor urgently.

Then, like a white shutter, the fog came down again!

Oh—

Drop anchor!

AAAAAAAAAAHH!

THEY'RE OVER **HERE**!

NO!

THEY'RE OVER **THERE**!

WE'VE GOT TO LEAVE **NOW**!

I didn't even bother to answer.
In this fog, we both knew, that was impossible.

But I didn't fear they would attack...

Their cries sounded like sorrow. Like unrestrained grief—

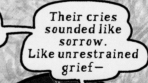

cough Could you pass me a bit more tobacco?

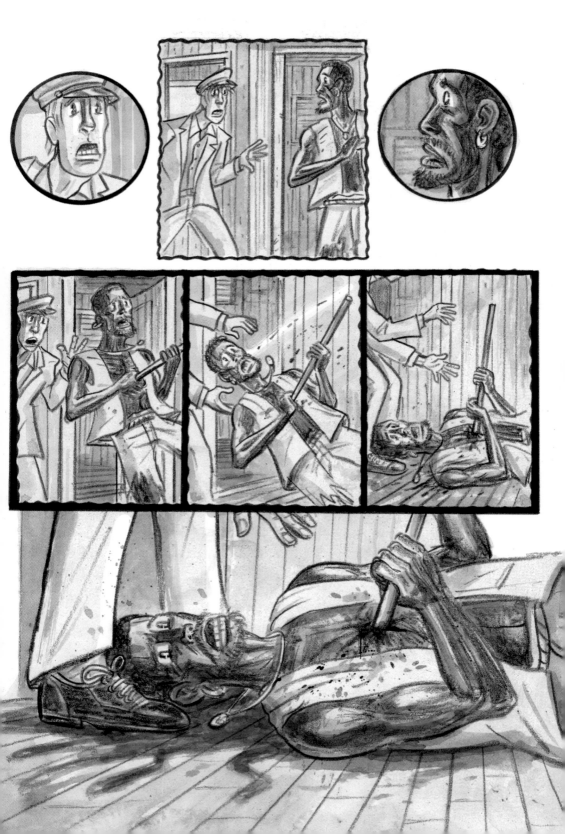

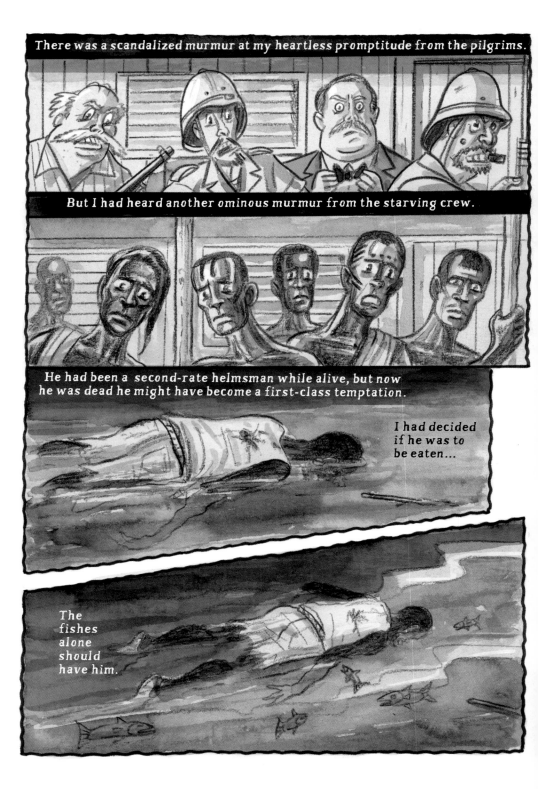

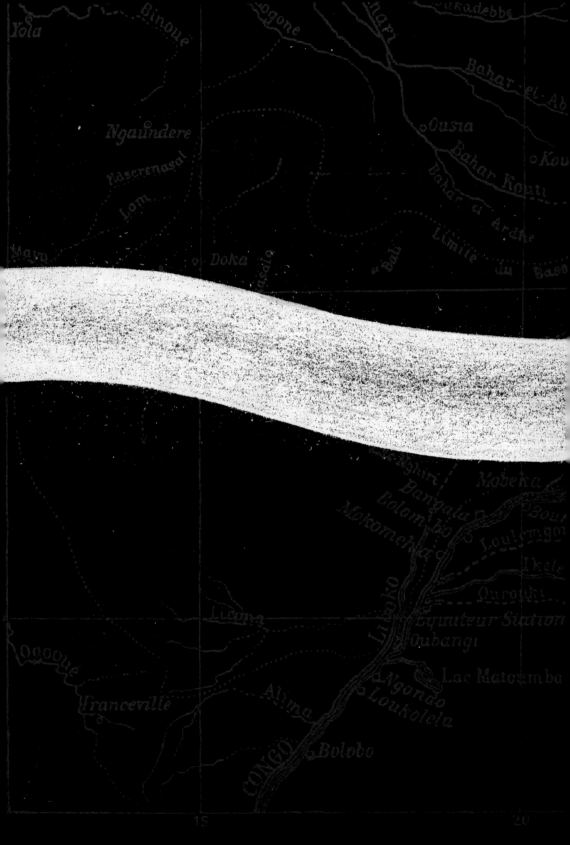

III

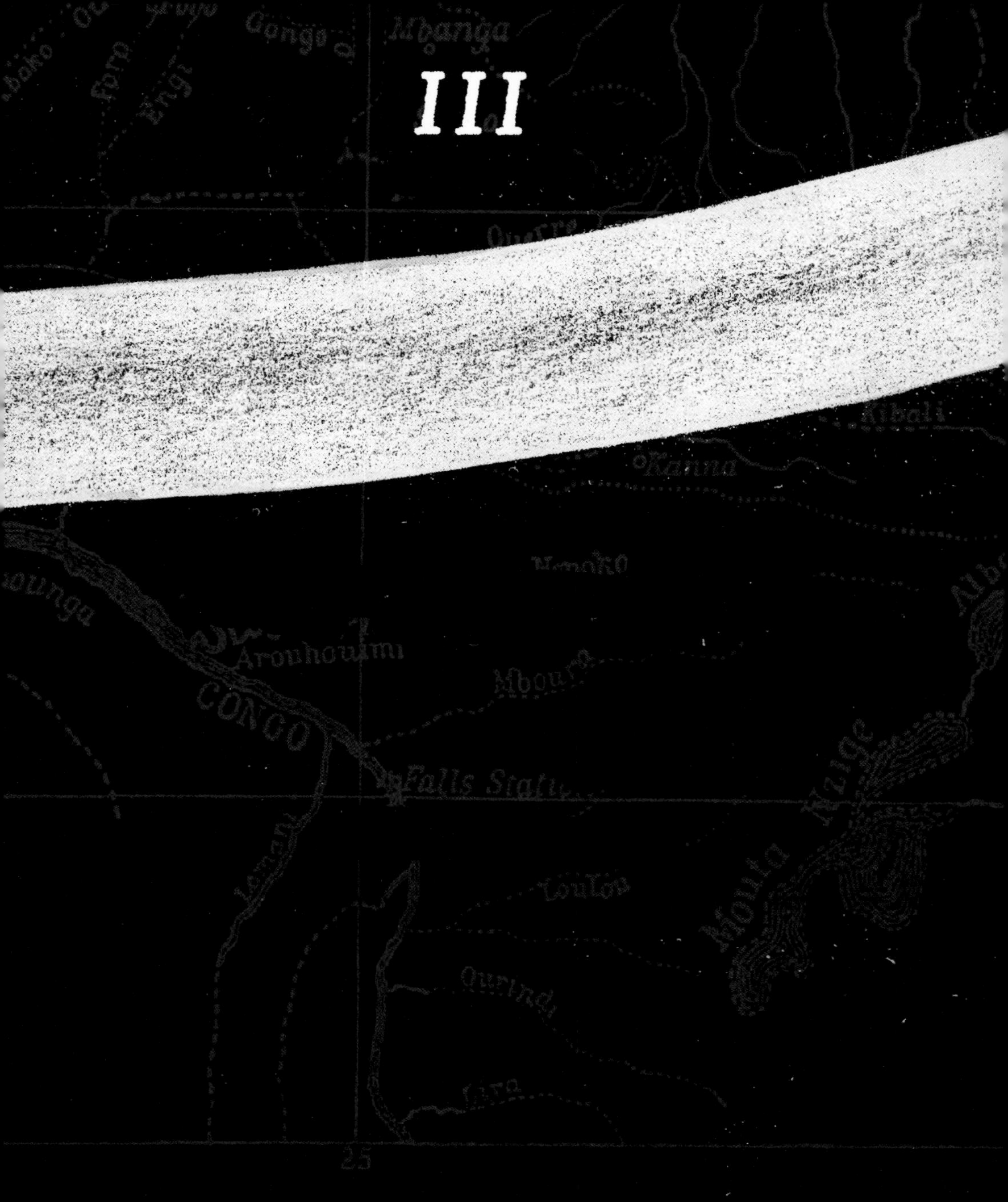

Gongo Mbanga

Fort

Engi

Ouarra

Kibali

oRanna

Menako

ounga

Arouhouimi

Mboura

Albe

CONGO

Falls Station

Nzige

Loulou

Lemani

Mouta

Ourindi

Lira

The International Society for the Suppression of Savage Customs had entrusted him with the making of a report, for its future guidance.

"Not alone, surely!"

"He got the tribe to help?"

"Y-yes—"

"They **adored** him."

"And what can you expect?"

"He came to them with thunder and lightning."

"He was frightening. Nothing on earth could prevent him from killing whomever he pleased."

"He wanted to shoot **me**, too, over ivory..."

"But I don't judge him."

"SHOOT YOU??"

"He's mad!"

"No—"

"You can't judge him as you would an **ordinary** man."

"If you only heard him **talk**, you'd understand."

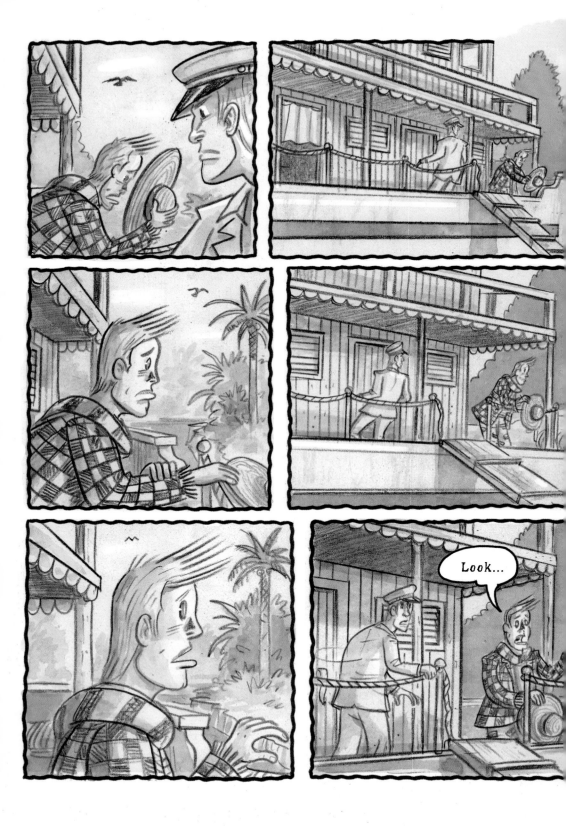

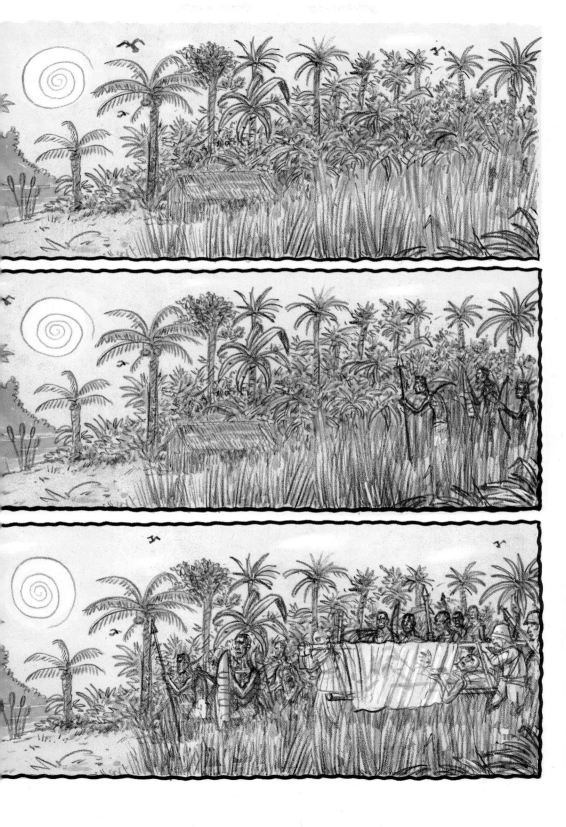

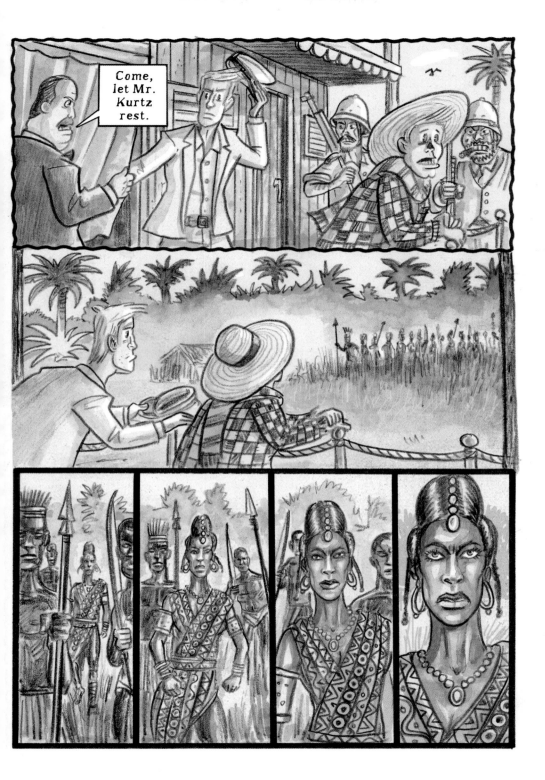

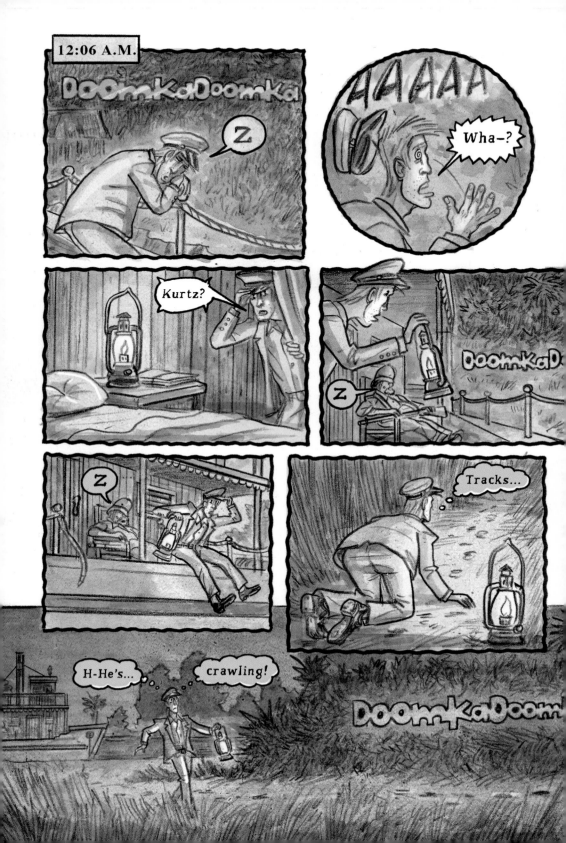

Kurtz!
GO AWAY-
HIDE YOURSELF!
Do you know what you are doing?
PERFECTLY.
mPadoomkado

doomKadoomKa
You will be lost!
I HAD IMMENSE PLANS...
I WAS ON THE THRESHOLD OF GREAT THINGS!
I-
You have to come with me...
Y-your success in Europe is **assured.**
omKadoomKad

The pilgrims looked upon me as numbered with the dead, my unforeseen partnership with Kurtz forced upon me by these greedy phantoms.

M-Mr. Kurtz?

COME HERE— YOU MUST GUARD THESE...

LETTERS FROM MY INTENDED WIFE.

I DON'T WANT THOSE NOXIOUS FOOLS TO GET THEM.

NOW CLOSE THE CURTAIN—

I CAN'T BEAR TO LOOK AT THE JUNGLE ANYMORE.

LIVE RIGHTLY

DIE, DIE...

COUGH

Downriver the *old boat* experienced engine trouble...

TAP TAP

With the help of the crew, I set about to repair the steamer while the pilgrims looked on idly.

One evening I paid Mr. Kurtz a visit...

I looked at him as you peer at a man lying at the bottom of a precipice where the sun never shines.

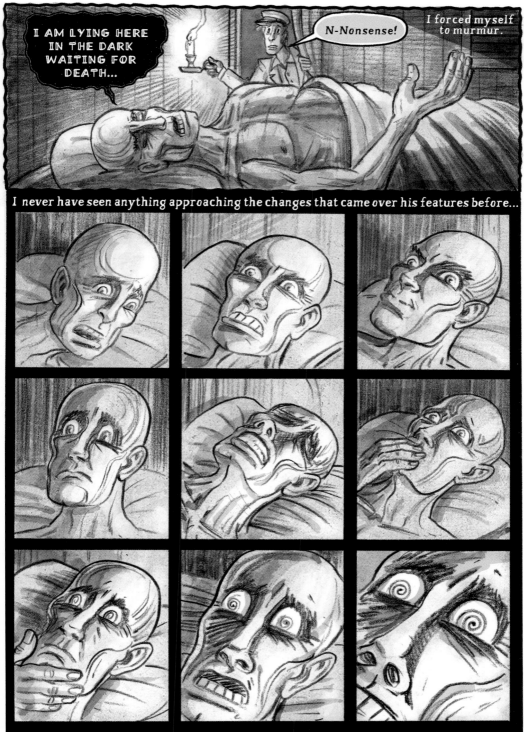

The voice...

The voice...

was gone.

What else had been there?

I found myself back in the sepulchral city.

I resented the sight of people hurrying through the streets, dreaming their insignificant silly dreams.

Filching money from each other.

Devouring food and gulping beer.

I daresay I was not very well at the time...

Into the heart

of an immense darkness.

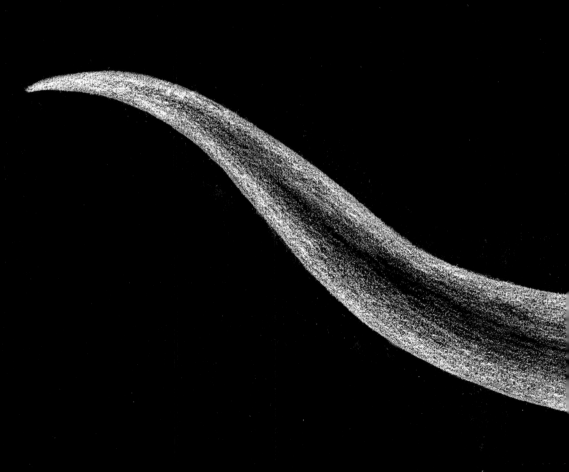

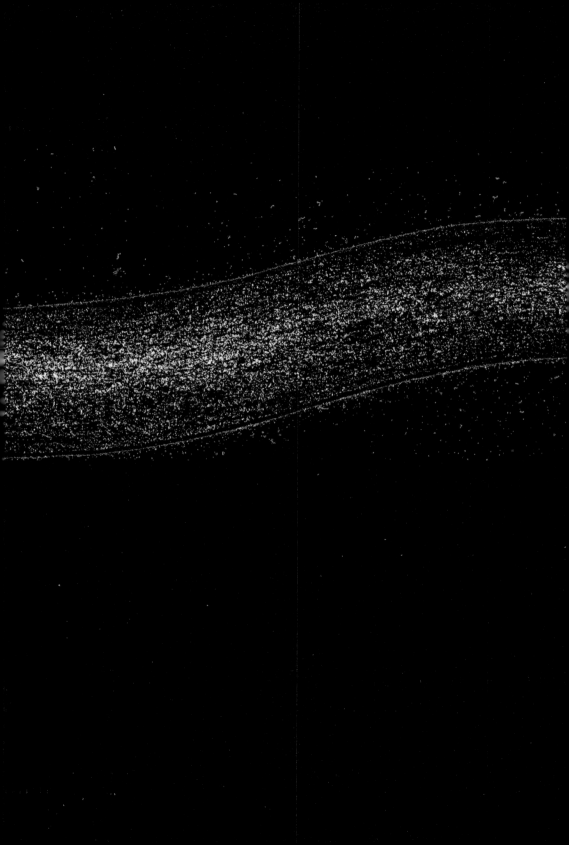

ACKNOWLEDGMENTS

My deepest gratitude to all the people who helped steer this project or acted as anchors:

Tom Mayer, Nneoma Amadi-obi, Judy Hansen, Emily Russell, Jeremy Dauber, Betty Russell, Paul B. Armstrong, Maya Jasanoff, Simon Gikandi, Amy King, Jonathan Grey, Calvin Reid, Emily Kuper, John Thomas, Angela Huang, Minah Kim, Hilary Allison, Anthony Stonier, Seth Tobocman, Steve Ross, Deirdre Barrett, Ruth Lingford, Sarahmay Wilkinson, Joe Lops, Julia Druskin, Will Scarlet, Don Rifkin, Molly Bernstein, Philip Dolin, Scott and Elena Cunningham, Terisa Turner, Leigh Brownhill and, of course, Joseph Conrad.

Joseph Conrad was born Józef Teodor Konrad Korzeniowski in Ukraine in 1857. Between the French and British merchant marines he served for nineteen years earning the rank of captain while traveling the world. When he settled in England to pursue a literary career, he drew upon his time at sea to create many of his novels including *An Outcast of the Islands*, *Lord Jim*, *Typhoon*, *Nostromo*, *The Mirror of the Sea* and *Victory*. In 1899, he wrote the modernist classic *Heart of Darkness*, inspired by a six-month commission piloting the steamer *Roi des Belges* (King of the Belgians) upriver in the Congo in 1890. It was first serialized in *Blackwood's Magazine*, then published as a novella in 1902. Though Conrad is regarded as one of the greatest novelists in the English language, it was his third language after Polish and French, and he only learned to speak it fluently in his twenties. Conrad died in 1924, the same year as Franz Kafka's death.

Peter Kuper's illustrations and comics have appeared in publications around the world including *The New Yorker* and *Mad* magazine, where he has written and illustrated "Spy vs Spy" every issue since 1997. He is the cofounder of *World War 3 Illustrated*, a political comics magazine, and has remained on its editorial board since 1979. He has produced over two dozen books including *The System*, *Diario de Oaxaca*, *Drawn to New York* and *Ruins*, which won the 2016 Eisner Award for best graphic novel. Peter previously adapted Upton Sinclair's *The Jungle* as well as Franz Kafka's *The Metamorphosis* and *Kafkaesque*, a collection of fourteen short stories. He has taught at The School of Visual Arts in New York City since 1987 and taught Harvard University's first dedicated course on graphic novels. More of his work can be found at peterkuper.com.